COMPARATIVE ADMINISTRATIVE LAW

COMPARATIVE ADMINISTRATIVE LAW

Administrative Law of the European Union, Its Member States and the United States

René Seerden
(ed.)

Fourth edition

intersentia
Cambridge – Antwerp – Portland

Intersentia Ltd
Sheraton House | Castle Park
Cambridge | CB3 0AX | United Kingdom
Tel.: +44 1223 370 170 | Fax: +44 1223 370 169
Email: mail@intersentia.co.uk
www.intersentia.com | www.intersentia.co.uk

Distribution for the UK and Ireland:
NBN International
Airport Business Centre, 10 Thornbury Road
Plymouth, PL6 7 PP
United Kingdom
Tel.: +44 1752 202 301 | Fax: +44 1752 202 331
Email: orders@nbninternational.com

Distribution for Europe and all other countries:
Intersentia Publishing nv
Groenstraat 31
2640 Mortsel
Belgium
Tel.: +32 3 680 15 50 | Fax: +32 3 658 71 21
Email: mail@intersentia.be

Distribution for the USA and Canada:
International Specialized Book Services
920 NE 58th Ave. Suite 300
Portland, OR 97213
USA
Tel.: +1 800 944 6190 (toll free) | Fax: +1 503 280 8832
Email: info@isbs.com

Comparative Administrative Law. Administrative Law of the European Union, Its Member States and the United States

ISBN 978-1-78068-630-1
D/2018/7849/25
NUR 823

British Library Cataloguing in Publication Data. A catalogue record for this book is available from the British Library.

CONTENTS

Administrative Law in the United States

PREFACE TO THE FOURTH EDITION

At the end of 2016 the list of (new) authors was completed by me and I could start with the fourth edition of this book. It was decided with the publisher not to enlarge the number of States addressed in the third edition. A special welcome to the new authors: Lamprini Xenou (France), Hermann Pünder and Anika Klafki (Germany) and Jeff Lubbers (United Stated of America).

Some authors really well followed my instructions to update or (re)write the contribution of the previous edition. For various reasons I did not succeed to get this fourth edition ready before September 2017, so around the beginning (at some universities at least) of the new academic year. Around that time (most of) the draft-contributions were handed in. After that also the editing proceedings took some extra time. I expect that the book will be for sale in the bookstores in the beginning of 2018.

I want to thank the authors who are not participating anymore in this fourth edition: Meinhard Schröder (Germany), Brian Jones (United Kingdom) and Philip Harter (United States of America).

As you can see, the fourth edition is not published anymore in the previous Intersentia/Metro Series. This also means that Marjo Mullers, who was involved in the production (camera-ready copy) of the previous editions, did not participate. A special thank for her as well. Of course I thank the other authors for their (renewed) participation. Without them this book could not have been realized. Again in this fourth edition some did better than others.

The aim of the fourth edition is the same as for the first three editions: the book is to give introductory insight into administrative law in various States and will provide the reader with a concise synopsis of the state of administrative law at the level of the European Union, in the various EU Member States and the United States of America. Hopefully it helps students at especially universities to get this introductory insight into (the developments of) administrative law.

René Seerden
Maastricht, November 2017

PREFACE TO THE THIRD EDITION

In the beginning of the summer of 2011 the publisher and I talked about a third edition of this book. We agreed not to enlarge the number of States since the number of pages is more or less restricted and adding a 'new' state would mean skipping an 'old' one.

In January 2012 the co-authors of the second edition let me know that they were willing to participate again and would send in their updates/changes around the beginning of May 2012, so that there was time for possible editorial comments. The intention was to get this third edition ready before September, so around the beginning (at some universities at least) of the new academic year.

The proceedings for the third edition lasted somewhat longer than expected because a few co-authors needed some extra time for the updates/changes of their contribution. I expect that the book will be for sale in the bookstores around October 2012.

More problematic is that the author for Belgium after she agreed to come with an update around half July 2012 broke this promise. A last e-mail from my side to give her time until 1 August remained unanswered. Unfortunately this means that Belgium is not in the third edition anymore and no time was left to deal with a new country. That is something for a next edition.

Now I am very happy that Marjo Mullers started the production of the camera-ready copy. A special thank for her again. I also want to express my gratitude to Daniëlle Wenders, who succeeded Frits Stroink as co-author for the Dutch contribution. Last but not least I thank the other authors for their (renewed) participation. Without them this book could not have been realized. Of course some did better than others in the sense that the first did not confine themselves to a simple update (in time) of the previous contribution but came with a more substantial change regarding proposed items by me, such as the exact contents of the court proceedings (remedies, test), the fees for and costs of these proceedings, the possibility of claiming financial compensation and the (growing) European dimension.

The aim of the third edition is the same as for the first and second one: the book is to give introductory insight into administrative law in various States and will provide the reader with a concise synopsis of the state of administrative law at the level of the European Union, in the various EU Member States and the United States of America. Hopefully the third edition will like the first two editions help especially students at Maastricht University but also at other universities to get this introductory insight into administrative law.

René Seerden
Maastricht, August 2012

PREFACE TO THE SECOND EDITION

In the spring of 2006 I started with the proceedings of the second edition of this introductory book about comparative administrative law, because the first edition proved to be very worthwhile for especially students in the European Law School at Maastricht University (but also at other universities).

The intention was to get this second edition in the bookstores in the beginning of 2007. Due to email delivery problems my message to the authors to get started did not receive many of them. In the late fall of 2006 this became clear and I had to wait somewhat longer before all the draft contributions – here and there a new co-author joined – received me.

Now in the fall of 2007 – the text for this book was concluded in the spring of 2007 – I am very happy to introduce the second edition. Although it was the second edition various emails were necessary to get all the contributions timely and (as much as possible) within the set format. Apart from an update a few important new elements are addressed by the authors, especially enforcement by and liability of the administration. I decided for the second edition not to enlarge the number of States. One of the reasons is that the book is of an introductory nature and the number of pages is more or less restricted. An enlargement of the number of states is maybe something for a next edition.

In closing the short foreword to this book, I thank all the authors for their (renewed) participation. Of course, without them this book could not have been realized. I also want to express my gratitude to Frits Stroink, who acted as my co-editor in the first edition and during the completion of this second edition got other responsibilities. A special thank you goes to Marjo Mullers, for the production of the camera-ready copy. Although it was the second edition it was not an easy job to 'synchronize' the various contributions. Naturally, the final responsibility for its completion lies with me. I hope that the second edition like the first edition of this book will provide the reader with a concise synopsis of the state of administrative law at the level of the European Union, in the various EU Member States and the United States of America.

René Seerden
Maastricht, October 2007

PREFACE TO THE FIRST EDITION

About two years ago René Seerden and Frits Stroink started working out the idea of writing an introductory book about comparative administrative law in Europe. One reason for this idea was the necessity of providing the students in the European Law School at Maastricht University with some materials about administrative law, particularly in (several of) the Member States of the European Union. We believed that a suitable and up-to-date comparative introductory description of administrative law of at least five EU countries was missing and would be very worthwhile to realise.

Now in the fall of 2002 – the text for this book was concluded on 1 July 2002 – we are happy to introduce this book. After several e-mails we managed to find native authors who wanted, within a certain framework and within a set period of time, to write about the administrative law in Belgium, Germany, France, the Netherlands, Sweden and the United Kingdom. Unfortunately the author for Sweden withdrew, but we managed to find authors who wanted to write about administrative law at the level of the European Union and in the United States of America. This means that this book deals with seven systems of administrative law. We hope that it is possible in the future (in subsequent editions) to extent this book with at least three other European countries.

In closing the short foreword to this book, we thank all the authors for their participation. Of course, without them this book could not have been realised. We also want to express our gratitude to Chris Fretwell for the English editing of most of the chapters and especially to Marjo Mullers, for the production of the camera-ready copy for this book. Naturally, the final responsibility for its completion lies with the editors. We hope that this book will provide the reader with a concise synopsis of the state of administrative law at the level of the European Union, in the various EU Member States and the United States of America.

René Seerden and Frits Stroink
Maastricht, August 2002

INTRODUCTORY REMARKS

René SEERDEN

As pointed out in the foreword to this fourth edition, this book is intended to contribute to the insight into (the developments of) *administrative law* within some of the EU Member States, at the level of the European Union and the United States of America. But what is 'administrative law'?

Administrative law can be described as the law that concerns relations between the administration (governments) and private individuals. It traditionally forms a part of public law (in addition to the other parts of public law: international, European, constitutional and penal law). Nowadays there is at least some merger between all these parts, but they still have their own features. Administrative law is partly formal and partly substantial. The latter deals with competencies based on sectoral statutes (environmental law, social security law, asylum law, tax law, public service law, etc.). The former is more general and of a procedural nature and deals with how the various competencies in the various specific fields of administrative law are executed by the administration (rules and principles) and what individuals can do against actions and decisions of the administration (access to justice/judicial review). But of course general (formal) and specific (substantial) administrative law influence one another. In this book the focus is still on the general dimensions of administrative law, but more than in the third edition reference is made to areas of substantive law.

The issuing of decisions (based on sectoral statutes) is probably the most important instrument of the administration to achieve public goals or put more abstractly 'to serve the general interest'. But it follows from practice that the administration in this perspective also acts in a factual way or makes use of (traditional) private law instruments, like the conclusion of contracts, the use of public property rights and the initiating of actions under (general) tort law. This may lead to different competent courts and also to different methods of review.

Administrative law in some of the EU Member States, the European Union and the United States of America is presented in separate chapters for each EU Member State, the European Union itself and the United States of America. In order to encourage compatible contributions and a basis for some comparative notes, a framework of leading items and themes was given to each author – for this fourth edition there are a few new authors – as a structuring device for their contributions. Thus certain uniformity in presentation has – hopefully – been attained, whilst at the same time the framework allows for the description of the unique features and merits of each system of administrative law. I think that the reader also (again) in the fourth edition will still see that the various contributions show differences in style, the topics addressed, the depth of description, etc. As far as I am concerned these differences contribute to more engaging and lively reading.

The main parts of the framework are:

1. *What is Administrative Law?*

Definitions, general administrative law versus specific areas of administrative law, general administrative law in the context of constitutional law (*trias politica*, federal-unitary state aspects), basic principles and the practice/evolution of administrative law etc. How is national administrative law influenced by international and European law?

2. *Who is Administrating?*

An outline of the administration (organs, agencies, individual persons etc.) in the framework of the territorial and functional organization of the State (with some illustrations of the competent public bodies/organs in specific areas of administrative law).

3. *Which Instruments are Available to the Administration?*

An overview of the available public law instruments and the possibility to use private law instruments.

4. *Which (Formal) Rules/Principles (Written or Unwritten) Govern Administrative Actions?*

An elaboration on decision-making procedures (public participation etc.) under general administrative law and specific areas of administrative law as well as more substantive rules/principles for administrative actions/decisions: 'due process in administrative matters'.

5. *Access to (Administrative) Courts against Administrative Actions/Decisions*

Who can go to which courts (constitutional, administrative or ordinary, appeal courts) and are prior out-of-court proceedings necessary? How intensive or marginal is the test (of discretionary administrative powers) by the courts and what are the possible rulings of the court (based on a remedy-system for the plaintiff or on more general powers for the courts)? Are courts easily accessible (time limits, fees, costs). Is interim relief possible and what are the dispute-settlement powers of the administrative courts? How active can the judge be?

6. *Enforcement by the Administration*

Which enforcement instruments of an administrative law nature are available for the administration and what is the relation, if any, between enforcement under administrative law and civil/criminal law enforcement?

7. *Financial Liability of the Administration for (Un)lawful Actions*

When can administrative authorities be held liable for administrative actions and non-performance? Is there apart from liability for unlawful actions also room for compensation in case of lawful actions of the administration? Which courts are competent to deal with claims in this perspective and which rules/ principles are applicable?

8. *Recent and Future Developments and Summary and Conclusions*

How (fast) is administrative law developing?

Within this framework the contributions from each EU Member State will be presented in the following chapters in alphabetical order. After that the administrative law of the European Union and the United States of America will be addressed. In the final chapter of this book, the editor makes a comparative analysis.

As already pointed out, the main purpose of this book is to give an introduction to the most important aspects of administrative law in a number of EU Member States, the European Union itself and the United States of America. Although it is mainly an introduction I think that it can be of great importance for education, research and also for practice. It could play a major role in the development of (comparative) administrative law in the various EU Member States and in that respect in the research of the *Ius Commune* of European countries. In addition it is interesting to identify differences and similarities in the administrative law of the United States and at the level of the European Union: 'maybe not everything should everywhere be the same'.

I also hope that this book will lead to closer contacts between the various authors and other interested readers.

ADMINISTRATIVE LAW IN FRANCE*

Jean-Bernard AUBY,
Lucie CLUZEL-METAYER,
Lamprini XENOU

1. DEFINITION AND SCOPE OF ADMINISTRATIVE LAW

1.1. HISTORICAL BACKGROUND

There is no unanimity as to when in history the origins of French administrative law can be situated. Some authors assert that it has its roots in various medieval institutions. However, it is commonly accepted that, in fact, administrative law's birth derived from the creation of what is still the French supreme administrative court: the *Conseil d'Etat.*

The *Conseil d'Etat* was created in 1799, at the very beginning of the Napoleonic period: under the constitutional regime of the *Consulat*, which immediately preceded the Napoleonic Empire, but during which Napoleon had already taken over. What will be extremely important for the future of administrative law is the fact that the *Conseil d'Etat*'s position was not only that of a judge. The *Conseil d'Etat* was, and still is, simultaneously a judge and the central government's advisory body on legal matters. It has been suspected that this dual function would not be compatible with Article 6 § 1 of the European Convention on Human Rights. For this reason, a regulation made in 2008 neatly separated contentious and advisory functions of the *Conseil d'Etat*. The European Court of Human Rights seems to find this evolution satisfactory in relation to Article 6 § 1.[1] Since a constitutional amendment of 2008, the *Conseil d'Etat* has become also advisor to the Parliament (Article 39 of the Constitution).

Further evolution proceeded in two directions. Even if it stayed in the intermediate position that has just been mentioned, the *Conseil d'Etat* achieved

* In the previous editions this chapter was *co-authored by Jean-Bernard Auby*. This chapter is a revision and update of the previous chapters by the other authors.

1 ECHR 30 juin 2009 Union fédérale des consommateurs de la Côte d'Or c. France.

a growing independence in its adjudicating function: an important step in that direction was a statute adopted in 1872.

Leaning on that growing independence, the *Conseil d'Etat* evolved, especially at the end of the 19th century, and at the beginning of the 20th, a large set of judicial review techniques, noticeably the ones which still constitute the *recours pour excès de pouvoir*, the main action through which an administrative decision can be reviewed by administrative courts.

In 1873, the *Tribunal des Conflits* (which had been instituted in 1872, with function of deciding in cases of uncertainty whether ordinary courts or the *Conseil d'Etat* had jurisdiction) issued what is its most famous decision, in the case of *Blanco*.[2] The case was about a young girl who had been knocked down by a carriage in a public tobacco plant, and wounded. The *Tribunal des Conflits* made two quite important statements.

The first was that, in order to decide whether a case fell under the jurisdiction of the *Conseil d'Etat* – and not within that of the ordinary courts, one had to refer especially to whether it was related to a public service (*service public*).

The second was that administrative liability was not subject to private law rules, but to special rules, adapted to the *service public* necessities. The latter aspect was especially important in so far as it consisted in the acceptance of a very large scope for administrative law, as we will now see.

1.2. SCOPE OF ADMINISTRATIVE LAW. MATTERS SUBMITTED TO ADMINISTRATIVE LAW

One of the prominent features of French administrative law is the fact that, compared with what occurs in most of its foreign counterparts, the scope of legal issues it covers is particularly wide. We must explain what that statement means, before outlining the reasons why this situation exists.

If it is possible to assert that the range of issues falling under the rules of administrative law is especially wide, it is for two reasons.

The first is related to the types of special proceedings administrative law includes i.e. the types of special actions through which administrative judges can be led to review administrative authorities. What has to be underlined here, is the fact that these proceedings, these actions, are not only of judicial review in the sense of procedures leading to the review by judges of the legality of administrative decisions: some of them are related to public contracts, others are related to extra-contractual liability of public bodies. Contrary to many other legal systems, the French one does not consider that public liability and public contracts are matters for private law, for ordinary law. In French law, both issues are, not totally, but for their main part, subject to special rules of

2 Tribunal des Conflits, 8 février 1873, Blanco, Rec., 1° supplt. 61, conclusions David.

public law, and therefore to special judicial actions submitted to administrative courts.

This point already refers to the second reason why the scope of administrative law is particularly wide. It derives from the fact that, in reality, French law considers that there are a number of special administrative law rules relating to each and every kind of administrative action and entity. There is an administrative law for civil servants (*droit de la fonction publique*), for public contracts (*droit des contrats administratifs*), for administrative properties (*droit du domaine public*), for administrative works (*droit des travaux publics*), and so on. Not that all administrative acts and entities would always be submitted to public law. Not that all public officers, all public contracts, all administrative properties, all administrative works would be subject to public law. But they often are, and above all, they always can be if they meet certain criteria. There is no field of administrative activity which is not susceptible to belong in part to public law.

Why does this situation exist? The main cause rests in the way French law conceives the public-private law divide. Belonging to the romanistic legal systems, the French system places a strong emphasis on that division, which is considered as fundamental in the analysis of how law and the legal system work. Administrative law is firmly grounded on the division: it is mainly made up of special public law rules, corresponding to the special needs of administrative activities.

What particular attributes do administrative activities have which warrant such particular rules? The traditional answer of a French lawyer will be twofold: their function is generally to provide public services (*théorie du service public*) and the fact that the legal means through which they operate are special, as a result of public power (*théorie de la puissance publique*).[3]

The point is that these ingredients of *service public* and *puissance publique* can be found in all fields of administrative activities, even those which look quite similar to private activities. Even economic public activities – water distribution, power distribution, etc. – enshrine a part of public services, and a part of special powers (compulsory purchase, fiscal decisions…). Here lies the reason why, in the French view, there is no administrative activity which is not partly subject to Public Law and therefore partly subject to the special norms of administrative law.

As will be explained later, this conception has a strong relationship with the existence of a separate set of administrative courts and with the way in which their jurisdiction is delimited.

---

3 In fact, since the expression of these two theories (late XIXth century, early XXth), the question has constantly been discussed whether the service public, or the puissance publique element was predominant. See: R. Chapus, *Droit administratif général*, 15th ed., Paris, Montchrestien, p. 3.

2. LEGAL DESIGN OF THE ADMINISTRATION

2.1. PUBLIC LEGAL PERSONS AND PUBLIC ORGANS

In structural terms, the administration is considered as made up of specific legal persons, who are called public persons (*personnes publiques*), or public law legal persons (*personnes morales de droit public*). These entities are the ones which are in charge of public functions, even if it happens that some private legal persons or individuals, are entrusted with public tasks under appointment and responsibility of a public person. This situation can be found especially in case of a concession, or public service delegation (*delegation de service public)*, as will be indicated below.

Even if it is admitted by case law that this classification leaves room for other particular types, most public legal persons fit into three categories. The first one consists entirely of the State. The second is that of local entities (*collectivités locales*, or *collectivités territoriales*). The third, quite varied one, is that of 'public establishments' (*établissements publics*), which are entities in charge of public functions alongside the State or the local public persons.

Public persons are represented in legal activities by organs, which are entitled to issue legal acts on their behalf, and belong to two categories. Some are individual: a minister, a mayor, the director of an *établissement public*, etc. Others are assemblies: in local entities, for example, the most important decisions are taken by councils, elected by the population.

There is normally no uncertainty as to the fact that a particular legal person is public or private, this being stated in its founding acts. However, that kind of uncertainty sometimes arises. Judges solve it by using various criteria, concerning who created the entity, what its functions are, and the like.[4]

2.2. LEGAL ARRANGEMENT OF THE STATE

Within the State, most of the administrative powers are held by the government (Prime Minister and ministers) and the President. The distribution of these powers between the Government and the President is rather complex, but its main aspects are in the fact that some prominent decisions (main regulatory acts, appointment of top civil servants) have to be agreed on by the two parties.

Following, albeit slightly reluctantly at first, the same path as in other developed countries, large administrative powers have now been entrusted to quangos (*autorités administratives indépendantes*). Some of them have rather

---

4 For an example: Tribunal des Conflits, 14 février 2000, Groupement d'intérêt public 'Habitat et interventions sociales pour les mal logés et les sans abris', *Actualité Juridique Droit Administratif*, 2000, p. 465.

broad competences: the *Défenseur des Droits*, which is a kind of ombudsman, the *Commission Nationale de l'Informatique et des Libertés*, whose role is to protect citizens' private lives against intrusions linked with the development of databases, the *Autorité de la Concurrence*, which is the main implementing body in competition law, etc. Others are in charge of special economic or social fields: bank monitoring (*Commission bancaire*), stock exchange monitoring (*Autorité des marchés financiers*), broadcasting (*Conseil supérieur de l'audiovisuel*), postal services and electronic communications (*Autorité de regulation des communications électroniques et des postes*), energy (*Commission de regulation de l'énergie*), etc.

A relatively important feature of the State's legal pattern is the fact that it includes quite important organs and organizations which are local and not central, which means both that they are locally established, and that their competences are restricted to the administrative area where they are established (this concept is called *déconcentration*, as opposed to decentralization, which, as we will see below, is akin to local government). The main local State organs are the prefects (*préfets*). Established in regions and departments (*préfets de region* and *préfets de département*), appointed by the Government (in fact, by a joint decision of the government and the President, as was mentioned), placed under its hierarchical control, they represent it in local administrative life, and possess very extensive powers.

Figure 1. State organization

Executive national authorities President (Président de la République) Government + Autorités administratives indépendantes (quangos) + supervised by the government, the *établissements publics* (specialized national public bodies, with legal personality)	**Parliament** Two houses: *Assemblée Nationale* (directly elected by the citizens), and *Sénat* (elected by local authorities and the members of the *Assemblée Nationale*)
Local State authorities (*autorités déconcentrées*): Mainly at levels of *régions* and *departments* Prefects (*préfets*) and local branches of the various ministries	

2.3. LOCAL GOVERNMENT

France has a tradition of being a centralized country, where the State (be it through its central bodies or through its local branches) is in charge of most public interests and most public decisions. Nevertheless, this centralized feature has eventually been reduced, local democratic entities have been progressively developed and entrusted with real powers and financial means.

The decentralization process started in France in the 1980s and is still in progress. It could be presented in three steps (which are called *les trois actes de la décentralisation*). The first important step (*Acte I*) was made in the 1980s, with the 1982–1983 *Defferre* statutes, when a large decentralization reform was adopted. The French administrative system remains one of the least decentralized in Europe, but it has, in that period, started to move towards what can be found in neighbouring countries in terms of local government and regionalization. The second step (*Acte II*) was in 2003, when a constitutional reform has amplified its degree of decentralization. This reform has introduced a special mention in the 1st Article of the Constitution, asserting the decentralized organization of the French Republic ("*la France est une République indivisible… Son organisation est décentralisée*"). Thus, the principle of decentralization acquired a constitutional basis. The third step (*Acte III*) started in 2010 with a legislative reform the goal of which was to simplify the existing structure of the local administration. This reform was extended by a 2015 legislative Act which gave to the decentralized administration a new architecture by merging a number of local entities.

The main legal bases of decentralization derive from the following elements. Firstly, local entities are considered as legal persons. As mentioned earlier, they form one of the three categories of public legal persons: the *collectivités locales* (or *collectivités territoriales*). Secondly, a certain degree of autonomy is assured to *collectivités locales* by constitutional rules: the Constitution, in section 72, provides that *les collectivités territoriales… s'administrent librement par des conseils élus* (local entities are administered in a free way by elected assemblies). From that constitutional provision, the Constitutional Court has derived several consequences concerning protection of local entities' competences, about protection of their financial autonomy, etc. Since the 2003 reform, a rule of subsidiarity is mentionned in section 72: "*les collectivités locales ont vocation à prendre les décisions pour l'ensemble des compétences qui peuvent le mieux être mises en œuvre à leur échelon*" (local entities are entitled to decide on issues that are better implemented at the local level).

The architecture of local decentralized administration is designed as follows.

The basic structure has three layers. At the top, there are 13 regions (*régions*). In the middle, there are 96 departments (*départements*). At the bottom, there are about 35,756 municipalities (*communes*).

The very high number of *communes* sometimes makes it difficult for them to manage efficiently the problems they have to deal with: in spite of their often small size, *communes* are in charge of quite important tasks: public services such as power distribution, water distribution, waste management, primary schools, and so on are within their jurisdiction. This situation has made it necessary to develop various cooperating organizations between *communes*. In the recent past, the number and size of these cooperation organizations have strongly increased: most urban agglomerations are now covered with groupings: *communautés d'agglomération, communautés urbaines* or *métropoles* which are in charge of the agglomeration's urban and economic development instead of the *communes*. It has been decided to complete the regrouping process in 2014.[5]

Finally, it is also worth mentioning that overseas regions have a specific administrative structure, in which a fundamental distinction is made between overseas departments and regions (*départements et régions d'outre-mer*, Article 73 of the Constitution), and the overseas entities (Article 74), with a special statute for New Caledonia.

In a system which is only moderately decentralized, the State has kept a large range of methods for intervening in local issues: for instance, many decisions concerning infrastructures need a concurring decision to be taken by its authorities, or need its financial support (which is not very different). Generally speaking, this State contribution to local policies is wielded by its local authorities, in particular by the prefects (*préfets*).

The second type of relationship between *collectivités locales* and the State arises from the fact that *collectivités locales* are monitored by State organs – actually, by the *préfets* once again – who are supposed to check the legality of their decisions, and challenge them where they seem illegal and their authors refuse to modify or revoke them. Until the decentralizing reforms of the 1980s, the State – via the *préfets* – was entitled to exercise a much stronger control on local entities: in some cases, they were even empowered to quash their decisions, or to block them by a kind of veto. Nowadays, its monitoring has only the nature of a legality review (it is thus called *contrôle de légalité*), and in case of a persisting problem, it will be the administrative tribunal which will decide whether the decision is to be quashed.[6]

Figure 2. Local government structure (European part of the territory; overseas entities have special organizational schemes)

13 regions (*régions*), ruled by a *Conseil regional* (assembly, directly elected by the citizens) and a *president du conseil regional* (elected by the *Conseil regional*)
96 departments (*départements*), ruled by a *conseil general* (assembly, directly elected by the citizens) and a *president du conseil general* (elected by the *conseil général*).
35,756 municipalities (*communes*), ruled by a *conseil municipal* (assembly, directly elected by the citizens), and a *maire* (elected by the *conseil municipal*).

5 Loi n° 2010-1563 du 16 décembre 2010 de réforme des collectivités territoriales, ELI: www.legifrance.gouv.fr/eli/loi/2010/12/16/IOCX0922788L/jo/texte.

6 Corresponding rules are provided by the Code général des collectivités territoriales (General Local Government Code), Articles L. 2131-6 et seq.

3. SUBSTANCE OF ADMINISTRATIVE POWERS. ADMINISTRATIVE ACTS

3.1. PUBLIC POWERS

It is in the essence of the State, and more widely of the administration, that they are vested with specific legal competences, which individuals and private organizations do no not possess (or possess only occasionally, when they are associated with public duties). In French law, these specific legal competences are called public power prerogatives (*prérogatives de puissance publique*).

Of these specific competences, by far the most important is the ability to take unilateral decisions, imposing obligations upon their addressees without any consent from them to be required. In a case decided in 1982[7], the *Conseil d'Etat* expressed the view that the most fundamental public law rule was the one which allows administrative organs to take unilateral decisions imposing obligations upon citizens: in other terms, the power to make changes in the legal order by acts which can be issued without the consent of their addressees.

The scope of unilateral decisions that each administrative authority is entitled to issue is quite varied. For each administrative organ, aptitude to issue such decisions can be deduced from the statutes and regulations which define it and its competences. With one qualification, however: it is admitted that all heads of administrative bodies can issue unilateral decisions in order to establish the organization of the bodies they rule and arrange its functioning, and that the decisions they take accordingly can sometimes impose obligations upon citizens (for example, because they will determine the data that persons applying for authorization, financial support etc... must communicate to the administration).

Some details must be provided about the procedural requirements surrounding the issuing of administrative decisions, about revocation of administrative decisions, and about the specific characteristics of those administrative decisions which have a regulatory nature.

Until recently, procedural requirements concerning administrative decisions did not stem from a unique source, a general Code or a general statute concerning non-contentious administrative procedure, as it is the case in many other legal systems. They stemmed either from particular legal provisions (which includes particularly those of the Act of 11 July 1979, of a Decree of 28 November 1983, and of the Act of 12 April 2000)[8], or from general principles set out in case law.

This situation changed in 2015 when a new Code, called "Relations between the Public and Administration Code" (*Code des relations entre le public et*

---

7 Conseil d'Etat, 2 juillet 1982, Huglo, Rec., p. 257.

8 Loi du 11 juillet 1979 relative à la motivation des actes administratifs; Décret du 28 novembre 1983 relatif aux relations entre l'administration et les usagers; Loi du 12 avril 2000 relative aux droits des citoyens dans leurs relations avec les administrations.

l'administration) was issued in order to codify all the previous Acts (mentioned just above). This Code entered into force on 1 January 2016. It governs the relations between the administration (State, local entities, public establishments and, in general, public and private bodies in charge with a civil service mission) and citizens. In principle, the Code also applies to relations between administrations and their agents. The relations between administrations are, however, not concerned. It is a Code that clarifies procedural requirements concerning unilateral administrative decisions. The Code pattern is structured around the different steps of the administrative dialogue: it deals first with communication with administrations (how to make an administrative application; how an application is processed?...); then, it concerns unilateral administrative acts, access to administrative documents and open data, administrative dispute resolution and, finally, Overseas dispositions.

It is the first time that all these rules can be found in one Code. The most important are the following.

According to the Article L. 121–1 of the Relations between the Public and Administration Code, some decisions (mainly the negative decisions: those which impose duties, refuse permissions, forbid activities) must be preceded by a fair hearing in principle, with some exceptions: for example, in case of emergency or particular circumstances (Article L. 121–2); where the decision follows an application, a request from the person it is addressed to. Where a fair hearing is required, the decision will be illegal if the person to whom it is addressed did not receive notice of why the administration was considering the decision, or did not receive notice sufficiently in advance to be able to prepare his/her arguments, or was not put in a position to argue with the administration.

Some decisions must be reasoned, which means that the author must express in them, or in an attached document, the reasons why he took it. The spectrum of decisions which have to be reasoned is mainly established by the 11 July 1979 Act mentioned above, now codified in Articles L. 211–1 to L. 211–8 of the Relations between the Public and Administration Code: it is analogous to the requirement of a fair hearing scope, and concerns mainly negative decisions (mainly those which impose sanctions or restrictions on the exercise of public freedoms or fundamental rights).[9] When reasons are required, the decision will be illegal if no reason was given in the decision or in an attached document (and, normally, this illegality cannot be amended afterwards, by giving reasons *a posteriori*), as well as if reasons were given too vaguely, in a pure formal way (for example, by purely reproducing what a statute provides, without any reference to the particular situation).

There are countless situations in which administrative authorities are required to consult with other authorities before issuing their decisions, and even sometimes to get the assent of these authorities. Equally, legislation has, in the recent past, constantly increased the number of situations in which an inquiry,

[9] Article L. 211–2 of the Relations between the Public and Administration Code.

a public debate or an environmental assessment is required. Several articles of the Relations between the Public and Administration Code are related to this issue (L. 131–1 to L. 135–2 CRPA). The Code devotes a whole title called "Public participation in decision-making by the administration" (*L'association du public aux decisions prises par l'administration*).[10] It provides for different procedures, i.e. an open public consultation, a consultation with an advisory committee, an inquiry, in order to consult with other authorities or to seek the views of citizens before taking an administrative decision. Corresponding decisions will be illegal when the consultation has not been made, or not properly made, when the inquiry was not in conformity with the (very precise) rules concerning the conduct of such proceedings, etc. Today, the emphasis is on procedures that run through the internet. For example, electronic consultations, set up in France, were enshrined in the Act of 17 May 2011; this text makes it possible to replace the mandatory referral of an advisory committee with an open electronic consultation: any interested person can now participate to the drafting of the regulation.

Other requirements must be mentioned. Such as the one providing that the silence of the administration is worth rejection of the application was reversed by the Act of 12 November 2013: henceforth the rule is that the silence of the administration during 2 months is worth acceptance (L. 231–1 – D. 231–3 CRPA). However, it can be seen that there are very many exceptions provided by decrees, which partially deprives the rule of its generality (L. 231–4 – L. 231–6 CRPA).

Since 2015, the right to free re-use of public data has been widespread (L. 321–1 – L. 327–1) and since November 2016, most administrative services can be seized electronically (L. 112–8 – L. 112–15 CRPA).

The rules concerning revocation (or modification) of administrative decisions can be summed up in the following way (L. 240–1 – L. 243–4 CRPA).

In order to describe the extent to which revocation (or modification) of administrative decisions is possible, one has to refer to four essential dichotomies.

The first is the divide between individual (or particular: see below) and regulatory decisions: the latter can be much more easily revoked or modified.

The second opposes revocation from the outset (which is called *retrait*) and revocation for the future (which is called *abrogation*): the former is subject to stricter conditions.

The third separates lawful decisions from unlawful decisions: revocation (or modification) is, of course, more easily admitted for the latter.

The fourth is between decisions conferring rights (*actes créateurs de droits*) and decisions that do not confer rights (*actes non créateurs de droits*).[11] This divide is essential: it is much more difficult to revoke or modify decisions conferring rights

10 Title III of the Relations between the Public and Administration Code.

11 Here one must understand which decisions confer, or do not confer rights in the relationship with the administration: some decisions which administrative law considers as not conferring rights may create rights for some private person(s).

than decisions which do not have that effect. How is it determined that a decision confers rights or not? There are two guidelines in this matter. Firstly, regulations, regulatory acts never confer rights. Secondly, while, usually, individual (or particular: see below) decisions, confer rights, this is not the case for certain kinds of such decisions. Pure recognitive decisions, decisions which mechanically recognize a situation, are not considered as conferring rights: this concerns many pecuniary decisions, as far as there was no room for any flexibility in them (for example, the payment of a civil servant's salary). Also devoid of rights-creating effects are decisions obtained by fraud (for example, a planning permission obtained by giving false information about the characteristics of the project).

Based upon these four divisions, the main rules governing revocation or modification can be outlined by opposing two situations which are in practice the most significant ones.

The first arises where the decision which the administration intends to revoke (or modify) is a regulatory one. Then three principles come into play. Principle one: according to the Article L. 243–3 of the Relations between the Public and Administration Code, a regulation must not be revoked from the outset (*retirée*) unless it is unlawful and the revocation occurs within four months, running from the date when the regulation was issued. Principle two: a regulation can always be revoked for the future (in French *abrogée*), and citizens can never claim that this would harm their rights. This principle has been attenuated, however, by a jurisprudence, now codified in the Relations between the Public and Administration Code, admitting that legal certainty imposes on administration not to modify its regulation too suddenly.[12] Principle three: a regulatory decision must be abrogated by its author where it is unlawful, and the author has been asked to abrogate it.[13]

The second arises where the decision which the administration intends to revoke (or modify) is an individual (or particular) decision which has conferred rights. Then two principles come into play. Principle one: if the decision is lawful, it only can be revoked or modified if the statute on the ground of which it has been taken allows it (for example, authorizations granted for developing hazardous activities – *installations classées* – can be modified, and even revoked when a new risk appears, which has not been taken in account in the initial authorization). Principle two: if the decision is illegal, it can be revoked (or modified in order make it legally correct) within four months[14], running from the date when the decision was issued.[15]

12 Conseil d'Etat, Assemblée, 24 mars 2006, KPMG, ECLI:FR:CESSR:2006:283479.20060630. Today, this rule is codified in article L. 243–1 of the Relations between the Public and Administration Code.

13 Article L. 243–2 of the Relations between the Public and Administration Code.

14 4 months is the standard time-limit for revocation. Some special ones are provided for by special legislation: e.g. 3 months in the case of planning permissions.

15 Article L. 242–1 of the Relations between the Public and Administration Code.

Further details ought to be given about regulatory decisions, and about the regulatory power of administrative organs.

Contrary to other legal systems, French administrative law accepts that acts through which administrative organs issue regulations have substantially the same nature as individual decisions. Both types belong to the same species, that of administrative decisions, submitted to a series of common rules concerning the way they are issued (for example, rules on consultations, on the way they are made public…), the conditions of their legality, and the contentious techniques under which they can be challenged before a judge. However, apart from these common rules, there are also specific rules which are particular to regulatory decisions, or to individual decisions: for example, the latter are only (sometimes) subject to a fair hearing, while, as we have just explained, the former never confer rights and thus can be freely revoked (at least for the future) or modified, etc.

The criterion by which the two categories of decisions can be distinguished is rather simple. Where a decision addresses precise people, it is said to be individual (*décision individuelle*) if it has one addressee, and particular (*décision particulière*) if it has several. Where a decision has no precise addressee, where it is 'anonymous', in the sense that it lays a norm which will apply to any people who will find themselves in a certain situation, then it is said to be regulatory (*décision réglementaire*).[16]

How is the power of issuing regulatory decisions (*pouvoir réglementaire*) distributed within the administration? The main holder of that power is the Prime Minister: with the qualification already mentioned, that many of the main regulatory decisions he/she takes (*décrets* in French) also have to be signed by the President (who is then their co-author, and can object to them). Most of the regulations issued by the Prime Minister are taken in order to implement statutes adopted in Parliament (they correspond to what French Law calls *pouvoir réglementaire d'application des lois*). But the current Constitution (dating 1958) also bestows upon the Prime Minister the power of issuing, on some matters, regulations which do not implement statutory rules (they correspond to what is called *pouvoir réglementaire autonome*: autonomous regulatory power). This derives from the fact that Articles 34 and 37 of the Constitution delimits the spectrum of issues upon which the Parliament is entitled to issue statutes: regulations taken in that spectrum (which, actually, enshrines all the most prominent issues) will be to implement statutes, whilst outside this scope autonomous regulations can be issued.

Although the Prime Minister is the main holder of regulatory competences, he/she is not the only one. Even if it is not very frequent, it sometimes happens that ministers are entrusted with such competences on some particular issues.

16 In fact, a third and intermediate category – actes non règlementaires – has been identified, but there are only a few examples of it in case law: one is the decision under which a piece of land is classified as a natural site to be protected.

This is the case for local authorities. In municipalities, for example, mayors can issue local regulations concerning car traffic, parking and many other similar issues, while local assemblies have jurisdiction on local plans.

Moreover, it has been admitted in case law that all heads of administrative bodies are entitled to make regulations in order to establish the organization of the body they rule and arrange its functioning. We mentioned before that such regulations can sometimes impose obligations upon citizens.

Although the ability to take unilateral decisions is certainly the main special prerogative with which the administration is vested, it is not the only one. There are many other special powers (*prérogatives de puissance publique*) that the administration has in its possession. For example, the power of compulsorily purchasing assets where it is required in the public interest (*expropriation pour cause d'utilité publique*). Or, as we will see later, the power of the administration to modify the contracts in which it has entered where such modification can be justified by a public interest. Or, also, the power of imposing subjections (such as a temporary trespass on their land) where necessary for the achievement of public works.

This does not mean that administrative action is constantly based upon rules which confer legal superiority on the administration. Firstly, it is often the case that none of the special rights which have just been mentioned is used in a particular course of action: only because the use of these special rights is not necessary. Secondly, even the power of deciding unilaterally is sometimes yielded and replaced with contracting, as we will explain below. Thirdly, one must understand that the administration is also in many aspects of its functioning subject to special restraints, unknown in the private law world: obligation to select civil servants through special competition procedures, obligation to give the public access to information, obligation to make inquiries before taking certain decisions, etc. Alongside public law special powers, there are public law special constraints.

3.2. ENFORCEMENT

According to the presumption of their legality, administrative decisions automatically produce effects in the legal order. It derives from it that they are directly enforceable.[17] Citizens must conform to them and the complaint they can address to the administration or the judge doesn't have any suspensive effect. If one refuses to abide by an administrative decision, the administration can have recourse to three main kinds of measures: penal proceedings, administrative sanctions, and forced execution ("*exécution forcée*").

[17] Conseil d'Etat, 2 juillet 1982, Huglo.

Criminal law (Article R. 610–5 du Code pénal) allows proceedings in a case of acting contrary to a police act, in order to impose a fine or a prison sentence. This is a general provision but a lot of special ones organize penal enforcement by criminal court in case of a breach of certain decisions. The most famous special text is the Highway Code ("*Le Code de la route*") but one can mention the 1905 Consumer Protection Act, which holds that merchants must respect its implementation decrees on pain of penal sanctions. Where asked to do so, criminal courts must decide whether the administrative decision is lawful or not before inflicting sanctions. According to the Article 111–5 of the Criminal Code, and contrary to normal distribution of powers between administrative and ordinary courts, criminal judges are allowed to review the administrative acts' legality, provided that it is relevant to the issue they have to decide on. Where the administrative decision is found unlawful by them, penal sanctions are excluded.

Instead of criminal sanctions, administrative sanctions can sometimes be inflicted by the administration itself. Exceptional in the past, this kind of sanction has appeared in a growing number of contexts, particularly since independent authorities (*Autorités administratives indépendantes*) started to be created at the end of the seventies. Several administrative authorities are nowadays invested with powers of observation, recommendation, formal notification, injunction but also with powers of sanction, such as reprimand and, much more radically, banning of activity or financial sanctions. For example, the "*Autorité de la Concurrence*", can inflict financial sanctions in case of a breach of competition law. Most of the independent regulatory agencies, such as the *Conseil supérieur de l'audiovisuel* (broadcasting), the *Commission de régulation de l'énergie* (energy) or the *Autorité des marchés financiers* (stock exchange monitoring) have these kinds of powers. Some ministers can also impose fines called "administrative fines" – for instance the Minister for Ecology, as far as problems concerning the storage of waste are concerned.

These administrative sanctions are lawful only if they fulfil some requirements. In the first place, they must be justified and pronounced after due hearing of the parties. Then, the principle of impartiality – as a general principle of law – must be respected, since Article 6–1 of the European Convention on Human Rights is applicable to administrative sanctions.[18] Lastly, to be legal, administrative sanctions must be likely to be referred to courts – judiciary courts in some cases, administrative ones in most cases. Most of the time, appeals submitted to them will be a "*recours de plein contentieux*", which entitles the judge to change the sanction, for example the amount of the fine, if he deems it out of proportion. While recognizing the constitutionality, in principle, of administrative sanctions[19], the Conseil Constitutionnel has imposed guarantees,

---

18 Conseil d'Etat, 3 décembre 1999, Didier.

19 Conseil Constitutionnel, 17 janvier 1989, Conseil supérieur de l'audiovisuel.

inspired by criminal procedure, such as the principle of legality of sentences (*principe de la légalité des peines*), the principle of non-retroactivity of a more repressive law, the principle of proportionality between sanctions and facts, and the right to appeal to courts.

Last mean possessed by the administration in order to enforce its decisions, forced execution ("*exécution forcée*" or "*exécution d'office*"), remains exceptional. Theoretically, resorting to the police force is forbidden unless the judge ratifies the intervention, in order to avoid abuses. This principle is accompanied by three exceptions, exposed by the "*Commissaire du Gouvernement*" Romieu in a famous case in 1902 concerning the expulsion of nuns.[20] Firstly, forced execution is allowed when no other judicial way is opened (for example, housing requisitioning can be enforced by specific performance, as penal sanction is not provided for). Then, in certain cases, forced execution is allowed by the law itself. For instance, the mayor can order demolition or repairs of imperilled buildings (*Loi de 1898 sur les immeubles menaçant ruine*). Lastly, forced execution can be used in case of emergency, which is a fluctuating notion appraised by the judge.[21]

In these cases, forced execution is allowed. Nevertheless, administration intervention must fulfil several conditions: the administrative decision has to be legal, the person that is concerned must be really recalcitrant and the measure has to be proportional. The administration can be judged liable for the enforcement of an unlawful decision or for the illegal enforcement itself. When the unlawfulness is really serious and concerns personal freedom or property, it could become what is called a "*voie de fait*": a situation in which judiciary courts become competent, with enlarged powers.

3.3. ADMINISTRATIVE CONTRACTS

In order to describe how the problem of administrative contracts is grasped in French administrative law, one has to touch upon the scope open to contracts in administrative legal functioning, then to consider the main aspects of the legal status of administrative contracts.

Administrative bodies are not permitted to conclude contracts on any possible matter. They are not permitted to contract upon certain of their competences. Following case law, where an administrative body is entrusted by a statute with the power of taking unilateral decisions on a particular issue, it may not make contracts instead of unilateral decisions, and it must not fetter its decision-making power for the future by contractual provisions. This prohibition is made particularly strict in the field of what French administrative law calls

20 Tribunal des Conflits, 2 décembre 1902, Société immobilière Saint-Just.

21 For example, TC, 8 avril 1935, Action française, and TC 19 mai 1954 Office publicitaire de France.

administrative police (*police administrative*), which includes all situations in which administrative powers aim at protecting the public order in a wide sense. For example, planning permission, or an environmental authorization cannot be granted contractually.

In spite of these restrictions, the actual scope of administrative contracts is rather wide, and is constantly becoming wider. The most important categories of administrative contracts, of a constantly growing economic and legal importance, are those of public procurement contracts (*marchés publics*), and of public concessions or public-private partnerships (*délégations de service public, contrats de partenariat*). Equally expanding, especially in local administrative life, are contracts between public legal persons: contracts setting out their cooperation, framing the distribution of funds, concluded either between the State and local entities, or between local entities.

What must be strongly underlined is that, in French administrative law, administrative contracts (or, at least, most of them) are normally subject to special rules (and corresponding litigation is normally placed under the jurisdiction of administrative courts), and not to ordinary civil or commercial law. This is not the case for all administrative contracts, but for most of them since the criteria under which an administrative contract is deemed to be subject to public law (and then qualified as *contrat administratif*, or *contrat de droit public* as opposed to a *contrat de droit privé de l'administration*) are quite open (they refer to the fact that the contract includes provisions which would be unusual in private contracts, or entrust the contractor with a public service duty).[22]

Administrative contracts which are considered to be subject to public law (which, once again, are a large majority) are subject to some general common rules (and, as just mentioned, placed under the supervision of administrative courts). Some of these rules are quite different from private law rules on the same issues. The most strikingly specific of them is the one which allows the administration to unilaterally alter the contracts to which it is party, where public interest is deemed to so require (and subject to compensation for the contractor). But there are several others, concerning for instance what occurs when the contractual balance is undone by unpredictable events: in that kind of situation, the contractors must proceed with implementing the contract, but they can get compensation for (at least part of) the extra costs they have to bear.

Apart from these common rules, each of the various categories of administrative contracts possesses its own status, derived from legislation and case law. The main (i.e. most theoretically prominent, and practically most frequent) categories are the following four. Firstly, there are procurement contracts (*marchés publics*), whose regulation is provided for by a Code (*Code*

[22] Moreover, written legislation has stated that all pure procurement contracts – "marchés publics" – had a public law nature, whatever their content.

des marchés publics), reorganized and rewritten in 2006: this Code conveys the transposition of European directives, mixed with the national rules. Then, there are the concessions and other similar contracts corresponding to the idea of public-private partnerships. These contracts are of two kinds: those belonging to the first one, called public service delegations (*délégations de service public*) are governed by a 29 January 1993 Act[23] (called *Loi Sapin*, after the then finance minister); those belonging to the second one, called partnership contracts (*contrats de partenariat*) have been introduced in France by a 17 June 2004 Act ("*Ordonnance sur les contrats de partenariat*"), recently reformed by a 23 July 2015 Ordinance ("*marchés de partenariat*"). The third category is made up of contracts by which public assets are placed at the disposal of private parties (*contrats d'occupation domaniale*): most of the rules applicable to that particular category come from case law. Lastly, one finds the employment contracts. A large majority of administrative staff are civil servants, who are not in a contractual link with the administration, but there are also (even significantly numerous in local entities) public employees who are in a contractual position: their contracts are subject to a regulation which is partly common to all of them, and partly specific to the three parts in which public employment legislation is divided (depending whether the employer is a State body, a local one, or a public hospital).

4. ADMINISTRATIVE NORMS. ADMINISTRATIVE LEGALITY

4.1. HIERARCHY OF NORMS

The issue we will now consider is how French administrative law understands the submission of the administration to law. That includes two concerns: where do the rules the administration is supposed to conform with derive from, and how are they related to one another? What does abiding by the law mean for the administration, and what room does it leave for discretion?

French law traditionally has a hierarchical view of the way it is structured, a view akin to the one which underlies the *Kelsenian* pyramid. This characteristic applies to administrative law, where the rules with which the administration must conform to are considered as forming a hierarchical structure, called the legality bloc (*bloc de la légalité*). We will describe the general arrangement of this *bloc de la légalité*, and then focus on two of its most interesting aspects, the position of constitutional rules and international rules within it.

[23] Loi du 29 janvier 1993 relative à la prévention de la corruption et à la transparence de la vie publique et des procédures publiques.

The hierarchical structure of the *bloc de la légalité* is arranged as follows. At the top, according to national case law (we will turn back to that issue later), is the Constitution. Then, international rules. Then, parliamentary law (*lois*).[24] Article 55 of the current Constitution (dating 1958) explicitly provides that international treaties or agreements "prevail over Acts of Parliament".

The *Conseil d'Etat* in the case of *Sarran et Levacher* in 1998, ruled that the supremacy conferred by Article 55 on international treaties or agreements "does not apply, in the internal order, to provisions of a constitutional value".[25] In other words, according to the national case law, the French Constitution prevails over EU law. However, in a famous case of *Arcelor* in 2007, the *Conseil d'Etat* considered that the general principle of equality of EU law guarantees the effectiveness of compliance with the principle of equality as enshrined in the French Constitution. In the same way, the French administrative judge has recently recognised that the principle of precaution, provided in Article 191 of the Treaty of the Functioning of the EU (TFEU), ensures the effectiveness of the observance of the constitutional principle of precaution, enshrined in Article 5 of the Charter of the Environment.[26] The above examples illustrate how the French judge appropriates the doctrine of "equivalent protection" as it derives from the *Bosphorus* judgement of 2005 of the European Court of Human Rights. Furthermore, while not contesting the primacy of the French Constitution, they demonstrate a certain evolution of the hierarchical view that the French judge traditionally has on the way national et international rules are structured.

Just below the Constitution, the international rules and the parliamentary law, are the general principles of law (*principes généraux du droit*). These are unwritten principles recognised by the administrative judge to control the action of the administration (we will come back to that issue later).

At the bottom of the hierarchy, are regulatory rules. Where these rules are situated in the *bloc de la légalité* depends upon the following solutions. Regulations issued by national authorities prevail over regulations issued by local authorities. Within the same public legal person (whether the State, or any other), regulations made by a particular organ are subordinate to regulations made by another organ placed in a hierarchically superior position. These two principles frequently mean that a particular organ must conform to regulations issued by another administrative organ: that is the reason why regulations are considered as forming part of the administrative *bloc de la légalité*.

---

24 Even if it has the same Latin root as the English word Law, the word 'loi', in French, refers only to that layer of the legal structure, the French translation of Law being 'droit'.

25 Conseil d'Etat, 30 octobre 1998, Sarran et Levacher, ECLI:FR:CEASS:1998:200286.19981030.

26 In France, the Charter of the Environment has a constitutional value.

Figure 3. Hierarchy of norms according to the Conseil d'Etat

Constitutional rules, i.e.: Constitution 4 October 1958 + references made by it: 'declaration des droits de l'homme et du citoyen' 26 August 1789, Preamble to the 1946 Constitution, and '*principes fondamentaux reconnus par les lois de la République*' (identified by case law, mainly that of the *Conseil Constitutionnel*)
International rules Notably European Union and the European Convention on Human Rights Treaties are superior to parliamentary law (Constitution, Art. 55)
Parliamentary law (*lois*)
General principles of Law (*principes généraux du droit*), deriving from case law (essentially *Conseil d'Etat*)
Administrative Regulations (*Règlements administratifs*) issued by the Government and various other administrative authorities

4.2. CONSTITUTIONAL RULES

What are the constitutional rules that have impact on administrative law?

Before listing the main rules, one must specify where they can be found. The fact is that the constitutional bundle is a rather complex structure, made up of five component parts. The first one is the current Constitution, dating from 4 October 1958. The second, third and fourth, to which the current Constitution refers, are the Declaration on the Rights of Man and of the Citizen adopted during the French Revolution (*declaration des droits de l'homme et du citoyen*: 26 August 1789), the Preamble to the previous Constitution (27 October 1946) and the Environmental Charter (1 March 2005). The fifth part consists of the fundamental principles recognized by the laws of the Republic (*principes fondamentaux reconnus par les lois de la République*), which are mentioned in the 1946 Constitution.

In this set of texts and principles, there are actually a lot of principles which impact on administrative law. One way of listing the most important is to say they belong to four categories. Some (although few) are related to the existence of administrative law, to the scope of public intervention, and the field of administrative law: that is the case for the Freedom of Trade and Industry, and the Freedom of Undertaking. Some deal more precisely with the existence of judicial review and its scope: thus, the Constitutional Court (*Conseil Constitutionnel*) stated that there exists a constitutional rule which protects the independence of administrative courts (22 *juillet* 1980)[27], and a principle

[27] Conseil Constitutionnel, 22 juillet 1980, Indépendance de la juridiction administrative, Rec., p. 46.

under which cases aiming at the annulment (or modification) of administrative decisions, at least those which use public power prerogatives (*prerogatives de puissance publique*) must fall under the jurisdiction of administrative courts and tribunals (23 *janvier* 1987).[28] Then, there are rules concerning the protection of fundamental rights against the administration: equality (as we mentioned, it was traditionally referred to by the *Conseil d'Etat* as a general principle of law: but it is also a constitutional rule, according to Constitutional Court case law), *audi alteram partem*, freedom of education, etc. Lastly, there are a few principles concerning other aspects of administrative functioning, such as that of public services continuity (which has consequences on rules concerning strikes in public services).

4.3. INTERNATIONAL RULES

Like other similar countries, France is party to a growing number of treaties which have consequences for administrative law issues (concerning the status of foreigners, the environment, cooperation between administrative bodies, etc.).

In a recent case of 2012, the *Conseil d'Etat* set out the criteria determining whether a stipulation of a treaty or an agreement has direct effect: in other words, in which cases it can be directly invoked before a court as a ground for reviewing an administrative decision.[29] There are two criteria: a stipulation must be recognised as having a direct effect by the administrative judge when, firstly, it has not as its exclusive purpose to govern the relations between States; secondly, it does not require the introduction of any supplementary act to produce its effects in respect of individuals.

In practice, two sources of international rules have a prominent role in the field of administrative law: European Union Law, and the European Convention on Human Rights. They have acquired such a role mainly for the reason that both have direct effect in French law.[30] Besides, according to recent *Conseil d'Etat*'s case law departing from previous jurisprudence[31], directives can be directly invoked against a particular decision.[32]

---

28 Conseil Constitutionnel, 23 janvier 1987, Conseil de la concurrence, Rec., p. 8.

29 Conseil d'Etat, Assemblée, 11 avril 2012, *Gisti*, ECLI:FR:CEASS:2012:322326.20120411.

30 In the case of Gisti (mentioned just above) the Conseil d'Etat ruled that the Court of Justice of the European Union has exclusive competence to determine whether a treaty of the European Union has a direct effect. In any case, European Union Law and the European Convention of Human Rights, due to the precise character of their provisions and to their purpose to confer rights to citizens, produce a direct effect in French Law.

31 Conseil d'Etat, Assemblée, 22 décembre 1978, Ministre de l'Intérieur c. Cohn-Bendit, Rec., p. 524.

32 Conseil d'Etat, Assemblée, 30 octobre 2009, Mme Perreux, concl. Guyomar.

International rules (European, or otherwise) now have an extensive impact on administrative law and judicial review, since, almost thirty years ago, the *Conseil d'Etat* ruled that treaties were always superior to national laws. Until 1989 (case of *Nicolo*: 20 October 1989)[33], the *Conseil d'Etat* had held that, in case of a conflict between a treaty and a statute, the most recent prevailed. In *Nicolo*, they accepted that the treaty would always prevail, even over a more recent statute. Since then, the administrative judge controls the conformity of a statute with a treaty. In case of incompatibility with the latter, the administrative judge does not apply the statute. The *Nicolo* case has since then been perceived as a very important evolution of French administrative law.

4.4. GENERAL PRINCIPLES OF LAW

The administration is submitted not only to constitutional and international rules but also to unwritten rules as identified by the administrative judge: the general principles of law (*principes généraux du droit*). These principles are forming part of the legality bloc. Without being permitted to do so by the statutes by which it is ruled, the *Conseil d'Etat* started, in the middle of the XX° century, to detect the existence of general principles. Even if the *Conseil d'Etat* pretends not to create them, but only to deduce them from the general legal context, their uncovering is a real creative work, since the *Conseil d'Etat* never feels obliged to connect them to a precise source, either constitutional or statutory. In the case of *Aramu* in 1945 the *Conseil d'Etat* recognised the first general principle of law – the principle of fair hearing – and employed an expression that will later become common to these category of principles: "*principes généraux du droit applicables même en l'absence de texte*" (general principles of law applicable even in the absence of a text).[34]

Most of general principles of law which have been identified so far, are related to the protection of citizens' rights against harm by the administration: principle of equality (in taxation, in the use of public services, in the use of public assets), principle of non-retroactivity, principle of fair hearing etc. In the beginning, general principles were perceived as one of the most original pieces of administrative law, in particular of case law, and also as a significant example of the normative power of the administrative judge.

From 1945 to about 1990, the administrative judge has identified most of the general principles. After this period, the role of the general principles in references from administrative courts and in judicial review of administrative acts has been decreasing: it has decreased essentially because of the growing

[33] Conseil d'Etat, Assemblée, 20 octobre 1989, Nicolo, Rec., p. 190, concl. Frydman.

[34] Conseil d'Etat, Assemblée, 26 octobre 1945, Aramu, Rec., p. 213.

importance of constitutional and international rules which often have the same content.

However, in the case of *KPMG* in 2006 the *Conseil d'Etat* identified a new general principle which was, until that date, absent in the national legal order: the principle of legal certainty. According to this case law, regulatory authority has to adopt, "for reasons of legal certainty, the transitional measures which, if relevant, imply a new regulation".[35] Apart from the obligation to adopt transitional measures, the *Conseil d'Etat* gradually recognised, for reasons of legal certainty, different rules related, in particular, to the administrative contentious procedure.[36] Today, legal certainty is considered as a value of administrative law.

The principle of legal certainty, as enshrined in the case law of the European Court of Justice, is an example illustrating the influence of EU law on French administrative law. The principle of legal certainty of EU law was a source of inspiration for the *Conseil d'Etat* in creating a new general principle of French law. At this point, it must be mentioned that the administrative judge has not yet recognised, as principle of French law, the principle of legitimate expectations (*confiance légitime*), a corollary of the principle of legal certainty in EU law. This would be because the subjective nature of this principle is not compatible with the objective dimension of French administrative law. For the moment, the principle of legitimate expectations is applied by the French judge only within the scope of EU law, in line with the requirements of the European Court of Justice.

4.5. LEGALITY / DISCRETION

It is the very essence of the *Rechtsstaat*[37] that the administration is supposed to respect Law, to conform to the whole set of rules which are superior to it: that is what can be called the principle of legality (*principe de légalité*).

As we will see below, the enforcement of that principle is, in French administrative law, carried out in at least two ways. One is judicial review. The other is administrative liability: it is important to note already that any illegality, any unlawful decision is considered as constituting a fault, susceptible to lead to public liability if it is linked by causation with damage.

How is the problem of discretion – in all systems, an admitted limit to the rule of law – approached in French administrative law? Discretion is deemed to exist when the administration has power to make choices between two or several courses of action, or where, even though the end is specified, a choice

35 Conseil d'Etat, Assemblée, 24 mars 2006, KPMG, ECLI:FR:CESSR:2006:283479.20060630.

36 Conseil d'Etat, Assemblée, 13 juillet 2016, *Czabaj*, ECLI:FR:CEASS:2016:387763.20160713.

37 In French: 'Etat de Droit'.

exists as how that end should be reached. Of course, discretion does not include the possibility of opting for a lawful solution or an unlawful one: but of opting between two or more lawful alternatives.

In French administrative law, discretion is conceived as a matter of assessment of the situation in which the administration takes its decision, and a matter of relationship between administrative decisions and their factual grounds (*motifs de fait*). The basic question is always: in light of certain facts, what decision is the administration allowed or obliged to take? If the answer is that a particular decision must be taken, the administration will be said to possess a bound competence (*competence liée*). If the administration has a certain freedom of decision, according to the way it understands and assesses the situation, then there will be discretion (*pouvoir discrétionnaire*).

It is important to stress the fact that, in the eyes of French administrative law, the existence of discretion, or bound competence, is never black or white. There are no entirely discretionary decisions (case law departed from that concept at the end of the 19th century). In a particular decision, there is always a part of discretion, and a part of bound competence. For example: a planning permission must be refused where certain facts exist (building's height is more than what the local plan permits), but it only may be refused if, having assessed the situation, the local authority considers that the planned building will not be in harmony with the surrounding architecture.

Where the administration is entrusted with a discretionary competence, it can elaborate on the way it will use it (in other words, make 'policy rules') in directives.[38] The legal status of these directives was specified in the case of *Crédit Foncier de France*, in 1970.[39] Directives are binding on the administration, unless the latter is able to demonstrate that the situation it had to deal with was different from the one the directive had in mind.

Review of discretion by the administrative courts does not always have the same level of intensity. In most cases, the test they will use will be that of manifest error of appreciation[40]: the decision will be deemed illegal if it appears that it was based upon a manifest error in the assessment of the facts (for example: a sanction upon a civil servant was clearly excessive considering the kind of disciplinary fault that he/she had committed).

There are cases in which judges exercise no review at all on decisions enshrining a large amount of discretion: for example, where the decision is about the choice between direct operation and contracting out for the provision of public services.

In some cases, however, administrative courts review proportionality. Proportionality, as such, is not a general principle in French administrative

38 Same word in French.
39 Conseil d'Etat, Sect., 11 décembre 1970, Crédit Foncier de France, Rec., p. 750.
40 In French: erreur manifeste d'appréciation.

law, but it is the implicit rationale in a set of situations in which the question the judge will examine is: did the administrative authority balance correctly the advantages of its decision with its disadvantages?

This kind of review is traditionally operated in the field of 'police' (see above).[41] In the last decades it has been extended to several other fields such as compulsory purchase: in 1971[42], the *Conseil d'Etat* held that the judge could check the 'balance-sheet' of advantages and disadvantages of the project if asked to make sure that the compulsory purchase decision was really taken in the public interest.

5. ADMINISTRATIVE LITIGATION. PROTECTION OF THE CITIZENS AGAINST THE ADMINISTRATION

5.1. THE ORGANIZATION OF THE COURTS

Turning now to contentious administrative law[43], we will consider three kinds of issues in turn. The first question we will address is: what courts and tribunals are in charge of administrative litigation? Then we will describe the judicial action which is by far the most important in that field: the *recours pour excès de pouvoir*, which is a variety of judicial review. Finally, we will give an overview of the law governing administrative tortious liability.

The organization of the judiciary in administrative matters can be presented by means of four statements.

Concerning the management of administrative litigation, the French legal system belongs to the 'dualist' tradition, in which there is a special set of courts in charge of that litigation (or at least of most of it).

As was mentioned above, this characteristic has historical roots. Leaders of the French Revolution were generally not happy with the courts which had had quite a reactionary attitude at the end of the previous period. They wished to prevent the courts from interfering with political affairs, even when decided upon by the executive power. This led to the creation, in 1799, of the *Conseil d'Etat*, the first administrative court, separated from the ordinary courts (which are called the judiciary in French: *juridictions judiciaires*, as opposed to *juridictions administratives*).

As we will see below, other administrative courts were created later. The choice for a separate set of administrative judges was never reversed.

41 Conseil d'Etat, 19 mai 1933, Benjamin, Rec., p. 541.
42 Conseil d'Etat, Ass., 28 mai 1971, Ville Nouvelle Est, Rec., p. 409.
43 Most of the legal rules governing these matters (though, not all) are bundled in a Code: the 'Administrative Justice Code.

Nowadays, the administrative courts system is organized in the following way.

The core of the system consists of non-specialized courts (in charge of all cases falling under the jurisdiction of administrative courts, and not attributed to a specialized administrative court), and has three layers. At the top, is the *Conseil d'Etat*. In the middle, 8 administrative courts of appeal (*cours administrative d'appel*). At the bottom, 42 administrative tribunals (*tribunaux administratifs*).

The rules concerning the organization and the function of administrative courts are provided in a specific code, the Administrative Justice Code (*Code de justice administrative).* This code was established by an Act in 2000 and applies to the non-specialized courts namely the *Conseil d'Etat*, the administrative courts of appeal and the administrative tribunals. The rules of procedure concerning the specialised courts are established in other specific texts. The Administrative Justice Code is divided in two parts: the legislative and the regulatory. Different legal rules are bundled in this Code such as the rules concerning the recruitment procedures of the members of each administrative court[44], the material and territorial competence of administrative courts, the judicial remedies that can be exercised against the decisions of administrative courts or the enforcement of the judicial decisions. The Code has been recently amended by two Decrees of 2 November 2016. The first[45], called "Administrative Justice of Tomorrow" (*justice administrative de demain),* aims to adapt the organization and the functioning of the administrative courts to today's challenges. The second Decree[46] provides the possibility to file an application by electronic means in order to accelerate the judicial proceedings before the administrative courts.

Judgements issued by administrative tribunals can be challenged before administrative courts of appeal, which are entitled to re-adjudicate completely on the cases submitted to them. That means that the administrative courts of appeal re-examine the questions of fact and of law. Thus, they are entitled not only to check if the administrative tribunal has correctly interpreted the law but also if the latter has correctly considered the facts.

Judgements issued by administrative courts can be challenged before the *Conseil d'Etat* by the means of special proceedings (called *pourvoi en cassation*) which only entitles the *Conseil d'Etat* to check if the administrative court of appeal respected the procedural rules, and correctly interpreted the law. In this case, the *Conseil d'Etat* is not entitled to look into the facts but has only the power to re-examine the legal aspects of the case.

---

44 *For instance the 300 members of the Conseil d'Etat are recruited by competitive examination or by external appointment.*

45 N° 2016–1480.

46 N° 2016–1481.

Normally, cases are firstly submitted to administrative tribunals, and then, possibly to administrative courts of appeal, and possibly to the *Conseil d'Etat*. However, there are some cases which have to be submitted directly to the *Conseil d'Etat*, and which will be definitively disposed of by the latter: mainly cases concerning actions against some prominent regulatory decisions and some important decisions taken by the Government.[47]

There are also several categories of specialized administrative courts, dealing with litigation arising in areas such as social welfare, discipline of judges and teachers, public accounts monitoring, etc. Judgements issued by these courts can be challenged before the *Conseil d'Etat*.

Figure 4. Court organization

<table>
<tr><td colspan="2">Conseil Constitutionnel
(not a supreme court: in charge only of reviewing the constitutionality of parliamentary legislation:
- under direct challenge issued, before the statute enters into force by the President, the Government or Members of Parliament:
- or preliminary reference by Conseil d'Etat or Cour de Cassation where the issue of constitutionality has been raised by a plaintiff – "question prioritaire de constitutionnalité" – and they have found it sufficiently serious)</td></tr>
<tr><td colspan="2">Tribunal des Conflits
(only in charge of dispatching cases between administrative and judiciary courts when jurisdiction is debated)</td></tr>
<tr><td>Administrative Courts
(juridictions administratives)</td><td>Judiciary courts
(juridictions judiciaires)</td></tr>
<tr><td>Conseil d'Etat
Cours administratives d'appel
Tribunaux administratifs</td><td>Cour de Cassation
Cours d'appel
Tribunaux de grande instance et tribunaux d'instance (civil courts), tribunaux de commerce (commercial courts), conseils de prud'hommes (labour Law courts) ...</td></tr>
</table>

5.2. JURISDICTION OF ADMINISTRATIVE COURTS

Describing in a few sentences how the jurisdiction of administrative courts as a whole is delimited is a rather difficult task, since that delimitation is extremely complex. The main aspects are the following.

Firstly, emphasis must be put on the fact that the jurisdiction of administrative courts does not extend to all administrative cases. In accordance with the vision, noted below, that the administration is only partly subjected to special rules and to public law, only part of the contentious issues involving

[47] Décret-loi du 30 septembre 1953 portant réforme du contentieux administratif, Article 2.

administrative bodies is placed under the jurisdiction of administrative courts. Other cases are simply placed under the jurisdiction of the ordinary courts (*juridictions judiciaires*), either criminal, civil, or commercial.

Secondly, if delimitation of what belongs to the administrative courts' own domain is not easy to describe, it is because it is built upon several criteria. Sometimes, it is simply a statutory provision which vests either ordinary courts or administrative courts with the power of adjudicating on certain cases: for example, because of a 1987 statute, decisions of the body dealing with competition regulation (*Autorité de la Concurrence*) must be challenged before the ordinary courts although this body is an administrative one, whose decisions should normally fall under the jurisdiction of administrative courts. Sometimes, cases are, in a similar way, attributed to administrative courts, or to ordinary courts, not by statutory provisions, but by special unwritten principles, evolved by case law: for example, where a public body has caused harm to the fundamental rights of a citizen with a decision, or through its behaviour, which is seriously unlawful (this kind of situation is called a *voie de fait*), then the aggrieved citizen can head for the ordinary courts, even if, normally, the administrative courts would be competent.

Where there is no applicable statutory provision or special case law principle, the decision as to whether a case falls under the jurisdiction of administrative courts, or that of ordinary courts, requires the use of general concepts which delimit the field of public law in the administration's legal functioning:

- whether the activity which gave rise to the case is a public service, and, if it is, what kind of public service it is: French administrative law draws a division between so-called administrative public services (*services publics administratifs*), normally subject to public law, and industrial and commercial public services (*services publics industriels et commerciaux*), normally subject to private law;
- whether the contract in question is a public law contract;
- if the case is linked with a public asset placed under public law (*domaine public* as opposed to *domaine privé*, the part of public properties which is subject to private law).

Thirdly, there is a court of which the only function is to arbitrate where there is a disagreement as to whether a case falls under the jurisdiction of administrative courts or under the jurisdiction of ordinary courts. Called the *Tribunal des Conflits*, and created in 1872[48], it comprises half judges belonging to the *Conseil d'Etat*, and half judges belonging to the *Cour de Cassation*, which is the supreme ordinary court.

Only judges and some State authorities can act before the *Tribunal des Conflits*, not individuals.

48 Loi du 24 mai 1872 sur l'organisation du Conseil d'Etat.

5.3. ALTERNATIVE DISPUTE RESOLUTION

If one seeks to understand how conflicts occurring between citizens and the administration are solved, one has to consider that submitting them to courts is not the only solution.

As in all administrative law systems, other proceedings and bodies sometimes play an important role.

Where a citizen has a disagreement with a public body, he/she can always refer it to the administration itself (either the organ who took the contested decision, or a superior authority, or an organ with monitoring powers). Sometimes, because of statutory provisions, it is an obligation to make that first step (which is called a *recours administratif*: administrative recourse), before referring to the administrative tribunal. In either case, if the administration does not answer the administrative recourse after two months, it is supposed to reject it and the rejection can be challenged before the administrative tribunal (this is an exception to the general rule under which silence of the administration during two months is equivalent to an acceptation). If the challenge takes place within two months after the publication of the decision, it does not affect the time limit during which judicial review before a tribunal is possible.

Is is equally worth mentioning that citizens who are complaining about maladministration can appeal to a special mediator called *Défenseur des droits*. The *Défenseur des droits* is a kind of ombudsman, with a range of powers: gathering of information, conciliation, in some cases, injunction. However he/she cannot interfere when the case has been submitted to a court, but he can make observations during trial. He/she is appointed by the Government: however, the institution enjoys real independence thanks to its consecration in 2008 as a constitutional authority by Article 71-1 of the Constitution..

But, we must stress on the fact that, because the administration can't compromise with general interest and with legality, *Alternative Dispute Resolution* isn't usually used in French public law. Thus, arbitration is generally prohibited for public authorities (Civil Code, Article 2060).

For instance, mediation is not very widespread. The Justice for the XXIst Century Act 2016 should generalise it. It will facilitate the use of mediation by administrative judges. This Act encourages mediation in every field of administrative law (Article L. 231-1 et seq. of the Administrative Justice Code).

Mediation can be contractual or judicial. Parties can organise a mediation out of any judicial proceeding. In that case, the mediator is appointed by the parties themselves or by the President of the administrative tribunal. But mediation can also be decided by the judge after the approval of the parties.

5.4. FIELDS OF CONTENTIOUS PROCEDURES

Administrative law contentious procedures are traditionally divided into two species. Those belonging to the *contentieux de la légalité*, in which the judge is only in charge of deciding on a matter of objective legality, and will only annul the contested decision, or declare it to be illegal (the *recours pour excès de pouvoir* belongs to that species). And those belonging to the *contentieux de pleine juridiction* or *plein contentieux*, in which courts will pronounce on individuals' rights, and will be entitled not only to annul decisions – or declare decisions illegal – but also to allocate compensation – actions concerning public contracts and public tortious liability are the main parts of this *contentieux de pleine juridiction* or *plein contentieux*. In some specific fields of *contentieux de pleine jurisdiction*, the courts have the power to modify the challenged decision: it is the case in electoral litigation (the judge can rectify the election results) or in tax litigation (the judge can modify the tax amount).

We will now detail the judicial action that is by far the most frequent before administrative tribunals and courts: the *recours pour excès de pouvoir*. Akin to what English law calls judicial review, it is a proceeding which has two main features. Firstly, it only challenges the legality of the decision it criticizes: it claims that the decision does not respect one or several of the various rules to which the administration must conform. Secondly, if it succeeds, the court will quash the decision, and might order an injunction: but it could not grant compensation neither replace the decision of the administration, as it is not a *contentieux de pleine juridiction*. Normally, the quashing has a retroactive effect, and all consequences which the quashed decision has produced must be considered, but, recently, it has been admitted in case law that administrative courts could modulate the effects of an annulation in time, as an exception to the principle of retroactivity.[49]

We will consider four aspects of the *recours pour excès de pouvoir* in turn: the acts susceptible to review, the rules concerning standing, time limits, and the grounds of review.

It would not be far from the truth to state that any administrative act can be challenged by a *recours pour excès de pouvoir*. However, it would not be totally true, since only decisions can be challenged, and a few kinds of decisions are not susceptible to review.

Judicial review (*recours pour excès de pouvoir*) can only apply to administrative acts which have the nature of decisions. That condition precludes actions against certain acts which are not considered as decisions including:

- contracts, with the qualification that it is possible to challenge the decisions surrounding contracts, and even, the act by which the competent authority decided to enter into a contract;

49 Conseil d'Etat, 11 mai 2004, Association AC! et autres; CE 27 octobre 2006, Société Techna et autres.

- circulars, directives, guidelines and the like, since they are considered as having a purely interpretive nature, and not capable of creating norms. However, they are susceptible to review where, by exception, they create rules, and also where they have a mandatory character, in the sense that administrative services to which they are addressed have an obligation to implement them;
- opinions, recommendations, warnings and stances adopted by the regulatory authorities cannot, in principle, be challenged. However, there are two exceptions. Firstly, these acts of "soft law" are susceptible to review when, by exception, they are in the nature of general and imperative provisions. In other words, when they have a mandatory character. Secondly, when they will have significant, in particular economic, effects or have as purpose to significantly influence the behaviour of the persons to whom they are directed[50];
- consultations, proposals etc. Where, in the course of an administrative procedure, an authority, a committee etc. has to be consulted, the opinion or proposal issued is not in itself susceptible to review: it can only be contested within an action against the decisions taken at the end of the procedure;
- information: acts whose content is only to provide information cannot be challenged;
- declaratory acts: acts whose purpose is only to pronounce a certain fact (for example: acts concerning civil servants whose content is only made of facts about the number of years during which they have worked with the administration, the positions they had…). However, the courts are very cautious in wielding that exclusion because this type of act sometimes has real legal effects and it is important that they can be challenged in themselves (for example, the delimitation of the boundary between private properties and public properties can be reviewed, even if, in theory, it is a pure declaratory act).

If only decisions can be challenged, normally all decisions can be challenged, whether particular or regulatory. However, there are a few categories of acts which, although they have the nature of decisions, cannot be reviewed. Two kinds deserve to be mentioned.

Traditionally, judicial review has been excluded for certain decisions taken by the authorities in state schools, in the armed forces and in prisons, because they were considered as concerning matters of pure internal organization. This category has eventually shrunk, and the *Conseil d'Etat* has even dramatically reduced it in recent years. But there remain some examples:

---

50 Conseil d'Etat, Assemblée, 21 mars 2016, Fairvesta, ECLI:FR:CEASS:2016:368082.20160321.

- in schools: for instance, the decision of placing a student in one group of students rather than another. On the contrary, many decisions taken by school authorities can be reviewed: of course, exclusions, but also the decision which denies the possibility of attending a certain course of lessons;
- in the armed forces: for example, the decision forbidding an officer to get in touch with the media. Up to 1995[51] also some of the sanctions applied in the army could not be reviewed;
- in prisons: for example, decisions to transfer an inmate from one prison to another. This exception does not cover all internal decisions taken in prisons, though: in 1995 the *Conseil d'Etat* admitted that the placement of an inmate in solitary confinement for 8 days could be challenged.[52]

The second kind of acts that cannot be reviewed is what are called governmental acts (*actes de gouvernement*). The theory of *actes de gouvernement* is an old one, which considers that some decisions taken by the Government, or the President, cannot be reviewed because they are not really of an administrative nature (they are 'governmental'), or because they are taken within the relationship between the Government and institutions over which administrative courts have no jurisdiction (Parliament, foreign states).

In fact, the rationale which supports the theory is disputed. But there is, based upon case law, a rather established list of the decisions it covers. That list has been heavily reduced since its origins in the 19th century and nowadays includes two categories:

- decisions taken by the Government (or the President) in its relationship with the Parliament: whether to issue a bill, various interventions in parliamentary procedure (declaration of urgency), promulgation of statutes, decision to refer a statute to the Constitutional Court, etc.
- decisions taken by the Government (or the President) in relations with foreign states or international organizations: decisions concerning the negotiation of an international agreement, ratification of a treaty, etc. For example, a few years ago, the *Conseil d'Etat* declined to review the decision by the President to resume nuclear testing in French Polynesia.[53]

5.5. STANDING

In order to explain the rules on *locus standi*[54], three issues must be considered: in the abstract, who are the possible plaintiffs before administrative courts? In

[51] Conseil d'Etat, Ass., 17 février 1995, Hardouin, Rec., p. 82.
[52] Conseil d'Etat, Ass., 17 février 1995, Marie, Rec., p. 85.
[53] Conseil d'Etat, Ass., 29 septembre 1995, Association Greenpeace France, Rec., p. 348.
[54] Most of these rules come from case law. Some of them are written rules, many of which are included in the Administrative Justice Code.

relation to a particular decision, who has standing (in French: *intérêt pour agir*)? And a complementary question: who can act on behalf of such plaintiffs?

As regards the types of possible plaintiffs, three simple statements can be made. Firstly, legal persons can act as well as individuals. Provided that, normally, a legal person can only act when it has acquired legal personality. But there is an important exception to that requirement: associations can exercise a *recours pour excès de pouvoir* as soon as they have been created, even if they have not yet achieved the proceedings which confer the legal personality on them.

Secondly, public legal persons can act as well as private persons.

Thirdly, the plaintiffs can be foreign people or foreign legal persons. For example, the *Conseil d'Etat* has accepted that neighbouring local governments can challenge projects located near the frontier: nuclear plants[55], projects likely to impact on the level of pollution of a common river etc..

The crucial issue in determining who has standing is interest (*intérêt pour agir*). Before entering into more details, it must be said that case law has constantly enlarged the spectrum of *intérêt pour agir*, and that, nowadays, it is really very wide.

The essential details can be given on the basis of two questions.

Firstly: what does interest (*intérêt pour agir*) mean in the eyes of the administrative courts? It does not necessarily correspond to a material or economic interest: it can be a moral or an ideological interest (in the case of associations defending environment, natural sites, regional languages, etc.). It can be an individual interest, but it can also be a collective one, such as those which trade unions defend: with a qualification, however, since case law rules that, where the contested act is a negative decision taken against one of their members, they cannot act if that person does not act first.

It is rare that the interest (*intérêt pour agir*) only lies with one person. Generally speaking, there is a 'circle of interests'. The question is, then, to decide whose material or moral situation or expectations within that 'circle', are likely to be affected by the decision. Depending on the situation, case law is more or less generous. Sometimes, it is very generous: for example local taxpayers can challenge any local decision with financial consequences[56], and users of public services can challenge any decision concerning the arrangement of these services. Sometimes, it is stricter: for example, only neighbours can ask for planning permission to be quashed, not anybody living in the same town.

Secondly: how is the existence of the interest (*intérêt pour agir*) determined in a particular situation? There are some general rules[57] in this respect. Whether there is interest is determined at the date when the action is taken, not

---

[55] For example: Conseil d'Etat, 27 mai 1991, Ville de Genève, Rec., p. 205: action taken by Geneva local authorities against a decision concerning a nuclear plant located in a nearby part of France.

[56] Conseil d'Etat, 29 mars 1901, Casanova, Rec., p. 333.

[57] Still provided by case law.

the one when the challenged decision was taken: so, for example, people who settle in the neighbourhood just after planning permission has been granted can challenge it (if the time-limit is not reached, of course).[58] The existence of interest is determined according to what the plaintiff asks for, not according to the arguments he invokes, nor according to his motives (even if the purpose is racketeering somebody who has a stake in the decision).

For instance, if the plaintiff chooses the *recours pour excès de pouvoir*, the most frequent judicial action before administrative courts, he/she can only ask for the annulment of the contested decision. In this case the judge can quash the administrative decision if it is illegal. It is the interest in the annulment or the maintenance of the contested decision that will define the interest in bringing this action (*intérêt pour agir*). If the plaintiff chooses the *recours de plein contentieux*, in that case, as we already saw before, he/she can ask for the reformation of the administrative decision. Thus, the administrative judge can not only quash but also modify the contested decision. By consequence, the existence of the interest (*intérêt pour agir*) depends on the modification that the plaintiff has asked and especially on the consequences that this modification will have on the situation of the plaintiff.

As to the way the courts determine, in a particular situation, that the plaintiff belongs to a 'circle of interests' affected by the decision, it is very much a matter of circumstances. However, there seem to be two guidelines, two questions the courts ask themselves: will the interest invoked by the plaintiff be affected by the decision in a sufficiently direct way? Will it be affected in a sufficiently certain way?

Finally, there is the problem of representation, the issue of deciding who can act on behalf of such plaintiffs. That problem raises two main issues.

Where the action is taken by a legal person, who is entitled to make the application on behalf of that person, and to represent it in the procedure? Sometimes, that question is a source of hesitation. For example, when it comes to actions made by associations: it is only by looking in their statutes that one determines if the actions can be decided by their governing bodies, or if there is a need for a general meeting of their members.

Is the assistance of a lawyer required? The answer is negative in general. In the field of judicial review (*recours pour excès de pouvoir*), there is no such an obligation, whoever the plaintiff is, at least before lower courts (*tribunaux administratifs*).

Judicial review is normally subject to a two-month time limit.[59] However, there are some exceptions. Sometimes, the time limit is different, because of special statutory provisions: for examples, permission for polluting activities

58 Although recent legislation excluded this advantageous solution in the cases of applications made by associations: they must have been created before the planning permission was issued.

59 Décret du 11 janvier 1965 relatif aux délais de recours contentieux en matière administrative.

(*installations classes*) can be challenged within four years. In a small number of cases, there is no time-limit at all: that is the case, noticeably, for actions against decisions which are very seriously illegal and impinge upon fundamental rights (it corresponds to the *voie de fait*, which has been mentioned above), as well as for decisions which have been reached by fraud (for example, a planning permission granted on the ground of false information provided by the applicant).

When the time limit has run out, the decision is no longer vulnerable to a direct action in annulment. But two important points must be mentioned.

Firstly, if the decision is regulatory in nature (*acte réglementaire*), it remains vulnerable to an indirect challenge (*exception d'illégalité*) within an action directed against an implementing decision. Moreover, in 1989 (case of *Compagnie Alitalia*)[60], the *Conseil d'Etat* ruled that, where a regulatory act is illegal, citizens can, at any time, ask for its abrogation, and, in case of a refusal, proceed before administrative courts.

Secondly, the fact that the time-limit for a *recours pour excès de pouvoir* has run out is not an obstacle to an action in tortious liability, based upon the illegality of the decision (be the decision of a particular or regulatory nature): the decision will not be annulled, but the plaintiff will get compensation if they demonstrate that they suffered damage deriving from the decision's illegality.

How does the two-month limit operate? It begins to run when the decision is published or notified (normally, regulatory decisions are published in an official journal, individual decisions are notified to the addressees). Then, the time limit is concretely applied in the following manner. Its starting point is the day after the publication or notification. It ends on the day which, two months after, bears the same number. For a decision notified on the 4th of April, the end of the time-limit is the 5th of June, at midnight: the action in judicial review must have been registered in the administrative tribunal before that time.

A very important specification in practice derives from the fact that the time limit can be extended by challenging the decision before the administration itself (by a *recours administratif*: see above). If one does so within the two-month limit, then one keeps the possibility of an action before the courts when an answer has been given or after two months of silence on the part of the administration: then, the time-limit for going to the court is again two months.[61]

5.6. GROUNDS OF REVIEW

We now turn to the grounds of review in judicial review. The best way of getting into that issue is to say that the spectrum of grounds for review is based upon

60 Conseil d'Etat, Ass., 3 février 1989, Compagnie Alitalia, Rec., p. 44.

61 These rules apply both if there was an obligation to go to the administration before going to court, and if there was no such obligation.

a theoretical analysis of what an administrative decision consists of, i.e. a theoretical itemization of the administrative decision's component parts.

Any administrative decision:

- has an author: the person or collective body who took it;
- has a certain form and has been taken through a certain procedure;
- has a content: what it provides, what it 'says';
- has certain motives, certain reasons: it has been taken in light of certain facts, and with regard to certain legal grounds;
- has an aim, a purpose (or several): it is aimed at achieving a particular outcome (or several outcomes).

In the French pattern of judicial review, each of these elements corresponds to one of the grounds of review. So the spectrum of the latter is:

- incompetence (*incompetence*): the decision was not taken by the person, or the body, who was empowered to issue it;
- procedural irregularity (*vice de forme ou de procedure*): the decision is tainted in its form or the correct procedure was not followed in its adoption;
- violation of the law (*violation de la loi*): the decision's content is contrary to one (or several) of the rules with which the administration is supposed to conform[62];
- motivational illegalities (*vices des motifs*), of which three kinds exist: error of fact (*erreur de fait*), error of law (*erreur de droit*), inappropriate qualification or incorrect qualification of the facts (which also enshrines several types of illegalities: *erreur dans la qualification juridique des faits*, *erreur manifeste d'appréciation*, etc.);
- illegality in the purpose of the decision (*détournement de pouvoir*): the decision's aim was not a public interest one or, while being a public interest aim, it was not the one in which, according to statutes, the decision should have been taken.

Normally, it is for the plaintiff to state the grounds under which the court will review the decision. However, there are grounds that can be examined *ex officio*[63]: the main one being incompetence.

5.7. ADMINISTRATIVE LIABILITY

As regards administrative tortious, non-contractual liability, three kinds of issues have to be considered: the extent to which it is subject to special rules, the

62 That includes international rules and constitutional rules as well as the other parts of the administrative legality: see above, 4.

63 They are called "moyens d'ordre public".

situations in which the administration is liable for fault, and the situations in which it is liable without fault.

In most of the cases, public tortious liability falls under the jurisdiction of administrative courts, in conformity with the criteria delimiting that jurisdiction, which have been described above.

Furthermore, when adjudicating upon liability issues, administrative courts do not apply the ordinary tort law, the private law on torts. In the famous case of *Blanco*[64], the *Tribunal des Conflits* rules that liability in public services

> 'cannot be governed by the principles which are laid down in the Civil Code for relations between one individual and another;...this liability is neither general nor absolute;...it has its own special rules which vary according to the needs of the service and the necessity of reconciling the rights of the State with private rights'.

Effectively, from *Blanco* onwards, the *Conseil d'Etat* and the other administrative courts have evolved a separate set of rules on public liability. This set of rules is, in some aspects, less generous than its private law counterpart (for example, administrative courts are more reluctant to compensate pure economic damages than ordinary courts), but it is more generous in others (noticeably the large scope of liability without fault).

It must also be specified that, where they have to dispose of public liability cases, ordinary courts sometimes, also apply special rules. For example, when they have to adjudicate on damages caused by the police when searching for criminals or trying to arrest them (that activity is called in French *police judiciaire*), they will apply public law liability rules instead of private tortious liability law. This importation of public law rules will occur where ordinary courts are, because of special legal provisions, led to adjudicate on the liability of administrative bodies managing typical public power activities: it will not occur where their jurisdiction derives from the fact that the involved administrative activity is similar to private activities (in the case of *services publics industriels et commerciaux*: see above).

Normally, public liability is a liability for fault, i.e. it is subject to the condition that the administration has committed a fault. This statement requires three provisos.

The first is that French administrative law has quite a wide conception of what constitutes an administrative fault.

This is mainly shown by the fact that any illegality, in any administrative decision, is considered in and by itself as a fault.[65] It is considered so even if it is purely formal or procedural. However, that principle has a noteworthy limit:

---

64 *Supra* note 2.

65 This implies that a person who complains about an administrative decision can either ask for its annulment, or ask for compensation, or ask for both. The same courts (normally administrative tribunals at the first level) have jurisdiction in the three cases.

illegality will not be able to lead to liability where it appears that the decision procedurally vitiated was justified in fact and in substance.

The national case law has already admitted that the application of an administrative act or of a statute, which violates international law, is likely to involve State's liability. Thus, the *Conseil d'Etat* recognized explicitly the principle of liability, for the breach of international or EU law, arising from an administrative[66] or a legislative measure.[67]

Apart from illegality, there are various other types of faults. These range from negligence and omission, to excessive slowness. They also include promises not kept, all the more in case of unlawful promises.[68] Once the promise is clear and assured, the administration must keep its word, otherwise it will incur liability for fault.

Two aspects must be underlined. The first is that administrative courts do not use a standard method to figure out if administrative behaviour was faulty: in particular, it is not necessarily by construing the statutes under which the administration was acting that they will delimit the fault in a particular context.

The second provision is that, normally, the burden of proving that a fault was committed falls upon the plaintiff. However, French administrative contentious procedure being inquisitorial, the plaintiff can expect that the judge will help. Besides, in some situations, jurisprudence accepts a presumption of fault, reversing the onus of proof, for example, where a minor medical act made in a public hospital has had serious consequences, where a user of public installations suffers damage or where the complaint is about discrimination.

Thirdly, there are cases in which administrative liability is subject to a condition of gross fault (*faute lourde*). This is due to case law, not to statutory provisions: the *Conseil d'Etat* has long held that a special condition of gross fault would apply to the liability of administrative activities which are particularly difficult to perform.

The list of these activities has progressively shrunk, and nowadays, it only includes: police activities[69], at least where they do not consist of legal decision-taking, but rather of physical activities, tax services, but only where those services can meet special difficulties in the assessment of taxpayers situations, and activities consisting of control of local government and the various public or private institutions (such as banks) that State authorities are entitled to monitor.

Of course, for an administrative fault to bring about liability and compensation, some other conditions must be met. They are mainly related to damage and causation.

---

66 Conseil d'Etat, Assemblée, 28 février 1992, Société Arizona Tobacco Products et Philip Morris, ECLI:FR:CEASS:1992:87753.19920228.

67 Conseil d'Etat, Assemblée, 8 février 2007, Gardedieu.

68 Conseil d'Etat, 12 février 1990, Ministre de l'Industrie et PTT c/ Clouet.

69 Conseil d'Etat, 10 février 1905, Tomaso Grecco, Rec., p. 139.

As to damage, two rules are worth mentioning. The damage is not necessarily physical, or pecuniary and not necessarily material: it can be only a disturbance, psychological or moral damage, or mental pain. The damage can be already suffered, or yet to be suffered, but it must be certain. The condition of certainty frequently acts as an obstacle to the compensation of future economic losses.

As to causation, two rules are worth mentioning too. The first one is that it is for the plaintiff to prove that the administrative fault he alleges was effectively the cause of the damage he alleges: in a few cases, however (concerning mainly liability of public hospitals), there is an exemption of that proof, jurisprudence accepting the idea of loss of a chance (*perte d'une chance*). The second is that the administration will be able to escape liability (totally or partly) if it proves that the damage was (totally or partly) caused by something else than its fault: that 'something else' can be a fault of the plaintiffs themselves (*faute de la victime*), or the act of a third person, or a situation of *force majeure* (an event, particularly a natural one, altogether external to the parties, unpredictable and irresistible).

Since the end of the 19th century, French administrative law has considered that, in certain circumstances, the administration might find itself liable without fault.

Such an open liability corresponds to two rationales. In some cases, the theoretical background is a 'risk theory', which can be expressed in the following way. Sometimes, administrative activities, by their nature or their scope, create special risks (i.e. they are particularly susceptible to causing damage), even where they are operated lawfully, without any fault: and it would not be fair to leave the people who randomly suffer damage from these activities without compensation. The other cases are linked with an 'equality theory'. Sometimes, administrative activities, without any fault being committed, come to cause such special and serious damage for some people that not granting them compensation would be a breach of equality: these people will get compensation because they have suffered an abnormal and special damage (*dommage anormal et special*).

Liability without fault deriving from the idea of risk can arise in four kinds of situations, all of which have in common that they concern damages that are event-based and not permanent.

In the first, liability without fault will be the consequence of the fact that the administrative activity was in essence dangerous. The 'classic' example is that of the injuring of a bystander through the use of arms by the police (cases[70] of *Lecomte et Daramy*, 1949). But the solution has also been applied to damages caused by dangerous products, such as tainted blood (when used in public hospitals for transfusions).

The second is related to people who occasionally assist the administration, without being public employees (*collaborateurs bénévoles, ou occasionnels, du service public*). They are entitled to compensation where they suffer a damage,

70 Conseil d'Etat, Ass., 24 juin 1949, Lecomte et Daramy, Rec., p. 307.

even if there has been no fault on the part of the latter. This applies even to people who, for example, are injured or die while rescuing people in danger of being drowned in the sea or a river.

The third concerns damages caused by public works to people other than the users: for example, where a chemical product, spread on a road that is being repaired, pollutes an neighbouring agricultural property.

The fourth concerns damages caused by demonstrators. Damages inflicted by demonstrators to bystanders or shops located on the route of the demonstration, must be compensated by the State, even if there was no fault on the part of public authorities, under the only condition that demonstrators' behaviour can be qualified as a criminal offence.

There are three kinds of situations in which case law accepts administrative liability without fault on the basis of the idea of a breach of equality. What they have in common is that they suppose, as already mentioned, that special and abnormal damage was suffered.

Firstly where continuous (i.e. not accidental, not event-based) damages are caused by public works and public equipment: for example, where rebuilding a road makes the access to a shop or a hotel impossible for a certain time.

The second concerns (abnormal and special) damage caused by lawful administrative decisions. Because of the condition for the damage, this kind of liability is relatively rare. Its main example is where the administration refuses the assistance of the police for the enforcement of a judicial decision because of a threat to public order (case of *Couitéas*: 1923).[71]

The third is related to damages (also special and abnormal) caused by statutes or by international treaties. The *Conseil d'Etat* has admitted a possible State liability without fault, because of statutes in 1938 (case of *Compagnie La Fleurette*)[72], because of treaties in 1966 (case of *Compagnie d'énergie radio-électrique*).[73] In fact, this liability has been applied in only a very small number of cases. What makes this kind of liability quite exceptional is not only the condition on the damage, but also the fact that, according to jurisprudence, the State cannot be held liable where the statute or treaty, either expressly precludes liability, or is serving major public interests.

5.8. COSTS

In the past someone who started an administrative court procedure against an administrative authority had to pay a very small fee. At present there are no court

71 Conseil d'Etat, 30 novembre 1923, Couitéas, Rec., p. 789.

72 Conseil d'Etat, Ass., 14 janvier 1938, Société anonyme des produits laitiers La Fleurette, Rec., p. 25.

73 Conseil d'Etat, Ass., 30 mars 1966, Compagnie d'énergie radio-électrique, Rec., p. 257.

fees. Article L.761–1 of the *Code de Justice Administrative* holds the competence for the judge to deal with the costs of the procedure. In general the losing party has to pay for what in France is called *dépens*, mainly costs for investigations (experts) that the judge ordered. Since a reform in the 1980s the judge can order the payment of other costs to the winning party. So the claimant may ask the judge to reimburse from the losing party (the administrative authority) the costs that are not the *dépens*, for instance, the costs of the attorney (if there is one since legal representation is not obligatory). In practice the judge often will award only a part of the costs to the winning party. That may also be the administrative authority. There is a lot of discretion for the judge in this respect.

5.9. LEGAL REPRESENTATION

The rules concerning legal representation differ according to the judicial action brought by the plaintiff and to the level of jurisdiction. Before the administrative tribunals, recourse to a lawyer is not compulsory, especially for the *recours pour excès de pouvoir*, the most frequent judicial action. However, there is an exception regarding the pecuniary and contractual litigation (Article R. 431–2 of the Administrative Justice Code). Before the administrative courts of appeal, legal representation is necessary since the Decree n° 2003–543 of 24 June 2003 with some exceptions such as the disputes between civil servants and the State or the requests related to the enforcement of a judicial decision (see Article 10 of the Decree n° 2003–543). Before the *Conseil d'Etat*, lawyers must represent parties when it hears cases at the first instance. There are however some exceptions to this rule. The most significant one is the absence of legal representation for the *recours pour excès de pouvoir* that is brought, before the *Conseil d'Etat* (as first and last instance judge)[74] against administrative decisions (Article R. 432–2 of the Administrative Justice Code). Furthermore, while legal representation is not compulsory when the *Conseil d'Etat* hears cases on appeal, it is always compulsory when the latter reviews judgements and decisions rendered at the last instance by the administrative tribunals and courts. In other words, when the *Conseil d'Etat* rules as a court of cassation, legal representation is obligatory.

Because of the financial costs of lawyer's services, legal aid can be requested according to the Act of 10 July 1991. In this case, financial assistance is provided by the State in order to cover, either completely or partially, court costs and lawyer fees. People who benefit from this aid can choose the lawyer that they wish. If there is no lawyer that agrees to represent them, the President of the Bar association will appoint a lawyer.

---

[74] This is possible for matters of high importance such as governmental decrees and ministerial decisions.

5.10. EXPERTS

According to the Administrative Justice Code, judges may have recourse to experts either on their own initiative or at the request of the parties (Article R. 621–1). The investigating judge may order an expert report in environmental issues, expropriation procedures, urban planning matters, contractual litigation and hospital liability issues. An increasing use of experts has been observed in recent years. In the case of *Vincent Lambert*[75] of 2014, concerning the rights of sick people and the end-of-life care, the administrative judge ordered a committee of three doctors to carry out an expert appraisal in order to determine the medical situation of the patient. The expert report was useful to the judge in order for him to apply correctly the Public Health Code (*Code de la santé publique*). From 1 January 2017 the expert can not only give an opinion on a technical matter but also undertake a mediation mission (Article R. 621–1 of the Administrative Justice Code). Furthermore, the administrative judge in France has the possibility to invite any person, which has particular knowledge in an area examined by the court, to submit written observations of a general nature in order to give useful guidance to it on the comprehension and application of technical concepts (see Article R. 625–3 of the Administrative Justice Code).

6. CONCLUSION

French administrative law has undergone significant transformations in the recent past, notably the following.

Contentious administrative law has been transformed by the creation of the administrative courts of appeal (in 1987), and by various reforms tending to extend the powers possessed by administrative judges (especially in terms of injunctions). A very important reform was introduced in 2001: the administrative judge can order urgent and provisional measures before the case is settled. The most important interim measures that can be granted are the following: firstly, the urgent applications judge can suspend the application of the contested administrative act if the latter is legally doubtful and there are circumstances giving rise to urgency[76]; secondly, the urgent applications judge,

[75] Conseil d'Etat, 24 juin 2014, Vincent Lambert, ECLI:FR:CEASS:2014:375081.20140624.

[76] See Article L. 521–1 of the Administrative Justice Code: “"When an application is made to annul or reverse an administrative decision, even one of dismissal, the urgent applications judge, presented with such an application, may order the suspension of the execution of this decision, or of some of its effects, when its urgency so demands and when there are grounds to consider creating, in the current state of the proceedings, a serious doubt as to the legality of the decision. /When the suspension is ordered, a ruling on the application for annulment or reversal of the decision is made promptly. The suspension ends at the latest when a ruling on the application for annulment or reversal of the decision has been made”.

to whom an application justified by urgency is made, may order all necessary measures to safeguard a fundamental freedom which an administrative authority has seriously and clearly illegally infringed.[77]

The efficiency of administrative justice has been really improved by these reforms.

The adjustment of some of the most traditional concepts with the evolution of EU law remains difficult. It is especially the case for the concept of *service public*, which retains a scope and implication which goes further than those of the EU 'economic services in the general interest', even if the differences between the two concepts were reduced by EU law evolution – especially the *Commune d'Almelo* case.[78]

In the near future, various issues will have to be addressed, including stronger decentralizing reforms that should be made, in order to give regions more powers and financial means. France will probably narrow its administrative structure in relation to its main European counterparts. That will be a deep change in an administrative system which, in spite of the recent reforms, remains one of the most centralized in Europe.

BIBLIOGRAPHY

BOOKS

Chapus, R., *Droit administratif general*, Montchrestien, 15th ed., 2001.

de Laubadère, A., J.C. Venezia and Y. Gaudemet, *Traité de droit administratif, Librairie Générale de Droit et de Jurisprudence*, 16th ed., 2001.

Frier, P.L. and J. Petit, *Droit administratif*, Montchrestien, 10th ed., 2015.

Melleray, F., P. Gonod and P. Yolka (eds), *Traité de droit administratif*, Dalloz, 2011

Rivero, J. and J. Waline, *Droit administratif*, Dalloz, 26th ed., 2016.

Truchet, D., *Droit administratif*, Presses Universitaires de France, 6th ed., 2015.

Vedel, G. and P. Delvolvé, *Droit administratif*, Presses Universitaires de France, 12th ed., 1992.

PERIODICALS

Revue française de droit administratif (bimonthly – publisher: Dalloz).

Actualité Juridique Droit Administratif (monthly – publisher: Dalloz).

Droit Administratif (monthly – publisher: Lexis Nexis).

---

77 See Article 521-2 of the Administrative Justice Code.

78 European Court of Justice, 24 April 1994, ECLI:EU:C:1994:171.

PERMANENTLY UPDATED ENCYCLOPAEDIAS

Juris-Classeur Administratif (publisher: Lexis Nexis).
Répertoire Dalloz de Contentieux administratif – Répertoire Dalloz de responsabilité de la puissance publique (publisher: Dalloz).

WEBSITES

www.legifrance.gouv.fr
www.conseil-etat.fr
www.conseil-constitutionnel.fr
www.mediateur-de-la-republique.fr
www.premier-ministre.gouv.fr
www.service-public.fr
www.ena.fr
http://english.conseil-etat.fr/judging

ADMINISTRATIVE LAW IN GERMANY

Hermann PÜNDER and Anika KLAFKI

1. THE CONCEPT OF ADMINISTRATIVE LAW[1]

Administrative law may be described as the cornerstone of German public law. It forms its own scholarly discipline within the field of public law, equally respected as constitutional law. The German state has even been described as an administrative state, due to the dominant influence of the bureaucracy throughout the system.[2] Furthermore, the administrative courts play a significant role in the protection of fundamental rights (see 1.3.1.). The value of administrative law within German legal studies is also evident in the requirement of every law student to have profound knowledge, not only of the field of general administrative law (see 4.1.), but also of various fields of special administrative law (see 4.2.) in order to pass the state examinations (*Staatsexamen*) and enter a legal profession.

1.1. THE CONCEPT OF PUBLIC ADMINISTRATION AND ADMINISTRATIVE LAW

Administrative law is the epitome of written and unwritten legal norms which specifically apply to the administration – namely administrative functions, administrative procedure and administrative organization.[3]

1.1.1. Public Administration

It is the concept of administration, rather than administrative law, which is difficult to define. Therefore, German administrative law textbooks start with a

---

1 The following text is partly based on H. PÜNDER, 'German administrative law', in: F. J. HEIDINGER/ A. HUBALEK, *Angloamerikanische Rechtssprache/Anglo-American Legal Language 3*, LexisNexis/BDÜ Fachverlag, Vienna, 2016, p. 79–92 (translated by A. HUBALEK).

2 W. DODENHOFF, *Ist oder wird die Bundesrepublik Deutschland ein Verwaltungsstaat?* (1984) 75 Verwaltungsarchiv 1 ff.

3 H. MAURER and C. WALDHOFF, *Allgemeines Verwaltungsrecht*, 19th ed., C.H. Beck, Munich 2017, p. 40. See also D. EHLERS, 'Verwaltung und Verwaltungsrecht' in: D. EHLERS and H. PÜNDER (eds.), *Allgemeines Verwaltungsrecht* (eds.), 15th ed., de Gruyter, Berlin 2015, pp. 7, 138 f.

description of the term administration instead of a definition of administrative law.[4] Even today, there is no all-encompassing definition of public administration. The public administration fulfils public duties and in doing so protects and supports the common good. However, this description of public administration is insufficient to distinguish the administration from other state powers as the legislature and the judiciary. Therefore, the concept of public administration has traditionally been defined negatively as every fulfilment of public duties that is neither legislation nor jurisdiction.[5] The characteristics of public administration are that it shapes public society, that the administration must be oriented towards the public good and that it undertakes concrete actions which form future society.[6]

1.1.2. Distinction between General and Special Administrative Law

German jurisprudence as well as German legal doctrine distinguish between "general administrative law" (*allgemeines Verwaltungsrecht*) and "special administrative law" (*besonderes Verwaltungsrecht*).[7] General administrative law consists of law applicable to all spheres of administrative law and encompasses administrative organization law, administrative procedure law (including administrative planning), public property law, administrative action law, administrative enforcement law and public liability law.[8] Even though general administrative law falls within the competence of the states (*Länder*), it is quite uniform throughout Germany as all states adopted Administrative Procedure Acts which resemble the Federal Administrative Procedure Act (see below 1.4.).

Special administrative law sets rules for specific administrative activities such as police law, environmental law, water law, education law or building law. It consists of a multitude of different statutes, regulations, administrative principles and unwritten norms (see below at 4.2.).

1.2. HISTORICAL BACKGROUND

In order to understand the German idea of administrative law a brief description of the historical development of administrative law is important. It particularly explains why German administrative law is, comparatively, strongly influenced by constitutional law. ≠ US?

4 See H. J. Wolff, O. Bachof, R. Stober and W. Kluth, *Verwaltungsrecht*, Volume 1, 12th ed., C.H. Beck, Munich 2007, pp. 28 ff.

5 O. Mayer, *Deutsches Verwaltungsrecht*, Volume 1, 3rd ed., Duncker & Humblot, Leipzig 1924, p. 9, 13.

6 H. Maurer and C. Waldhoff, *Allgemeines Verwaltungsrecht*, 19th ed., C.H. Beck, Munich 2017, p. 6 ff.

7 See also M. Nierhaus, 'administrative law' in: M. Reimann and J. Zekoll (eds.), *Introduction to German Law*, C.H. Beck, Munich 2005, p. 91.

8 D. Ehlers, 'Verwaltung und Verwaltungsrecht' in: D. Ehlers and H. Pünder (eds.), *Allgemeines Verwaltungsrecht* (eds.), 15th ed., de Gruyter, Berlin 2015, pp. 7, 139.

1.2.1. Administrative Law under Absolutist Rule

German administrative law dates back to the 17th century, when the regional sovereigns managed to free themselves from the ties of the out-dated law of the "estates" (*Stände*). This development was based on the so-called *ius eminem*, which gave the ruler the right to interfere with the duly acquired rights (*iura quaesita*) of his subjects.[9] The rulers in the age of absolutism made frequent use of this right and required an effective administration to do so. As they believed they were responsible for the "felicity" (*Glückseligkeit*) and "welfare" (*Wohlfahrt*) of their subjects and for "good policy" (*gute policey*) in the realm, they interfered in all areas of social and economic life based on the *ius politiae* ("welfare state" or "police state").[10]

There was no independent judicial authority. Judgeship was a part (often the most important part) of regional sovereignty; the duty was discharged by the ruler himself, or delegated by him to dependent jurists (*Kameraljustiz*).[11] The administration was thus controlled to a certain extent but there was no legal protection against the ruler himself ("the king can do no wrong").[12] However, jurists developed the so-called fiscal theory (*Fiskustheorie*), according to which the subjects had to tolerate the ruler's interference but were compensated for it. For this purpose, following the ancient Roman *fiscus Caesaris*, the treasury or exchequer, the legal concept of a "fisc" was developed. This created a private law legal entity that was legally positioned beside the ruler. The maxim "tolerate and liquidate" (*dulde und liquidiere*) applied. In the Prussian General Land Law of 1794 (*Allgemeines Preußisches Landrecht*) liability claims were codified. This law still plays an important role in the current state liability system in German (see 7.2.).[13] It was said that "the fisc is the scapegoat of the nation".

---

9 For an in depth analysis of the concept of sovereignty in the 17th century see M. Stolleis, *Geschichte des Öffentlichen Rechts in Deutschland, Erster Band: Reichspublizistik und Policeywissenschaft 1600–1800*, C.H. Beck, Munich 1988, pp. 170–186.

10 Cf. M. Stürmer, "Staat und Gesellschaft – § 1 Die Suche nach dem Glück: Staatsvernunft und Utopie" in: K. G. A. Jeserich, H. Pohl and G.-C. von Unruh, *Deutsche Verwaltungsgeschichte, Band 2: Vom Reichsdeputationshauptschluss bis zur Auflösung des Deutschen Bundes*, Deutsche Verlags-Anstalt, Stuttgart 1983, pp. 1–19.

11 For a short overview of the historical developments of German administrative law in English, see M. P. Singh, *German Administrative Law in Common Law Perspective*, Springer, Berlin 2001, pp. 20–26.

12 See W. Rüfner, "Die Entwicklung der Verwaltungsgerichtsbarkeit" in: K. G. A. Jeserich, H. Pohl and G.-C. von Unruh, *Deutsche Verwaltungsgeschichte, Band 3: Das Deutsche Reich bis zum Ende der Monarchie*, Deutsche Verlags-Anstalt, Stuttgart 1984, pp. 909 ff. For a brief overview see W. Frotscher and B. Pieroth, *Verfassungsgeschichte*, 15th ed., C.H. Beck, Munich 2015, p. 66.

13 The relevant sections read as follows: § 74 EinlALR: "The furthering of the common good takes precedence over individual rights and privileges of the members of the state if a genuine conflict (collision) exists between these two positions." § 75 EinlALR: "The state is, however, bound to compensate anybody who is forced to sacrifice his particular rights and privileges for the common good." Translation by W. Rüfner, 'Basic Elements of German Law on State

1.2.2. *Influence of Early Constitutions*

Administrative law in the modern sense developed when constitutions came into force in the 19th century. Interference with liberty and property was only possible if it was based on a statute ("legal reservation"). The state was supposed to restrict itself to warding off dangers to "public safety and order" (*öffentliche Sicherheit und Ordnung*). Other than these responsibilities, society was left to itself and to the principle of unrestricted competition ("*laissez faire, laissez aller*"). Public law therefore guaranteed a liberal state in which civic freedoms were protected.

Moreover, a state based on the rule of law required separation of powers, including an independent judiciary. The structure of these powers was disputed. Many (for example, the legal scholar *Otto Bähr* in his book "*Der Rechtsstaat*", published in 1864) were of the opinion that the "ordinary" courts of law (*ordentliche Gerichte*) should not only settle legal disputes between citizens, but, like in Britain, should also control administrative actions.[14] In the end, the idea fought for, above all, by the jurist *Rudolf von Gneist*, prevailed that the ordinary courts of law should restrict themselves to dealing with private law disputes and that there would have to be separate administrative courts responsible for controlling state administration in support of the "common good".[15] This was in line with the credo of liberalism, according to which the state was to be distinguished from society. Gradually, administrative and higher administrative courts developed in the German states. A key institution was the Prussian Higher Administrative Court (*Preußisches Obververwaltungsgericht*), which enforced the restriction of police powers to the narrower area of just warding off of risks to public safety and order (the *Kreuzberg* judgement" of 1882)[16] and developed the principle of proportionality.[17]

However, court control was still considerably restricted. On the one hand, only certain "administrative acts" (*Verwaltungsakte*) were controlled by the courts; on the other hand, claimants had to prove conclusively that the administration had not only affected their interests detrimentally but had violated their "subjective public rights" (*subjektive öffentliche Rechte*). Furthermore, the administration's discretion was free from judicial control because it was "reserved to the executive". Finally, there was no judicial

Liability' in: J. Bell and A. Bradley (eds.), *Governmental Liability: A Comparative Study, United Kingdom National Committee of Comparative Law*, London 1991, p. 250.

14 O. Bähr, *Der Rechtsstaat: eine publicistische Skizze*, Wigand, Kassel 1864.

15 R. v. Gneist, *Der Rechtsstaat und die Verwaltungsgerichte in Deutschland*, 3rd ed., Darmstadt 1879. For a brief characterization of R v. Gneist's scholarly work, see M. Stolleis, *Geschichte des Öffentlichen Rechts in Deutschland, Zweiter Band: Staatsrechtslehre und Verwaltungswissenschaft 1800–1914*, C.H. Beck, Munich 1992, pp. 385–388.

16 PrOVGE 9, 353 ff.

17 PrOVGE 13, 426 ff.; 38, 421 ff.; 51, 284 ff.; O. Bühler, *Die subjektiven öffentlichen Rechte und ihr Schutz in der deutschen Verwaltungsrechtsprechung*, Kohlhammer, Berlin 1914, pp. 197 f.

protection for those citizens who, either voluntarily or by virtue of the law, were subject to a "special relationship of subordination" (*besonderes Gewaltverhältnis*) within the administration. Such a special relationship of subordination was assumed with regard to civil servants, soldiers, pupils and prison inmates.[18]

1.2.3. *Juristic Method (Juristische Methode)*

Towards the end of the 19th century, the "juristic method" (*juristische Methode*) developed in administrative law.[19] Whereas academics had previously only described the duties and activities of the different administrative branches and had not distinguished between law and politics (*staatswissenschaftliche Methode*, "political science method"), the task now was to develop, following the principles of civil law, "general concepts" and "general principles" i.e. the underlying doctrine of administrative law.

Otto Mayer's treatise, *Deutsches Verwaltungsrecht* (German Administrative Law), published in 1895, was pioneering.[20] As a law professor in Strasbourg (then part of Germany), the author had studied French administrative law and transferred his findings to Germany. *Mayer* wished to define interfering administration in terms of the rule of law and to restrict it. The concepts of "legal reservation" and "administrative acts" can be traced back to him.[21]

1.2.4. *Administrative Law under the Weimar Constitution*

It is remarkable that the overthrow of the monarchy at the end of World War I and the introduction of parliamentary democracy by the "Weimar Constitution" of 1919 hardly changed anything with respect to administrative law. *Otto Mayer's* sentence in the preface to the third edition of his textbook is characteristic of this trend: "*Verfassungsrecht vergeht, Verwaltungsrecht besteht.*" ("Constitutional law withers away, administrative law prevails") (1924).

1.2.5. *Hitler's Dictatorship*

Politically speaking, Germany did not come to rest. The obligations to pay exorbitant reparations to the victorious allies under the Treaty of Versailles

18 For a discussion of the concept of special relationships of subordination, which prevailed until the 20th century, see H. Krüger, 'Das besondere Gewaltverhältnis', (1957) 15 *VVDStRL (Veröffentlichungen der Vereinigung der Deutschen Staatsrechtslehrer)*, 109 ff.; C. H. Ule, 'Das besondere Gewaltverhältnis' (1957) 15 VVDStRL (*Veröffentlichungen der Vereinigung der Deutschen Staatsrechtslehrer*), 133 ff.

19 For a short overview, see H. Maurer and C. Waldhoff, *Allgemeines Verwaltungsrecht*, 19th ed., C.H. Beck, Munich 2017, p. 19.

20 O. Mayer, *Deutsches Verwaltungsrecht*, Duncker und Humblot, Berlin 1969 (reprint of the 3rd ed. of 1924).

21 For details, see M. Stolleis, *Geschichte des Öffentlichen Rechts in Deutschland, Zweiter Band: Staatsrechtslehre und Verwaltungswissenschaft 1800–1914*, C.H. Beck, Munich 1992, pp. 404 ff.

made economic recovery impossible. Radical parties, the Communists on the one side and the National Socialists on the other, gained more and more followers. The established republican parties, above all the Social Democrats and the Catholic Centre Party (*Zentrum*), lost their majority in the parliament of the German Reich (*Reichstag*). In the end the government was only able to govern on the basis of emergency regulations. Ultimately, *Adolf Hitler* was appointed as Chancellor (*Reichskanzler*) on 30 January 1933 by the president ot the German Reich (*Reichspräsident*) *von Hindenburg*. Shortly thereafter the *Reichstag* adopted the "Law to Remedy the Distress of People and Reich" (*Gesetz zur Behebung der Not von Volk und Reich*), which enabled the government to adopt laws and even to deviate from the constitution without the approval of the Reichstag. This so-called Enabling Act (*Ermächtigungsgesetz*) ended the separation of powers. It enabled *Hitler* to establish his inhumane dictatorship without restrictions.[22]

★ Why Admin Law is important!

1.2.6. Post-War Germany

Only after the "Third Reich" had been defeated in World War II were democratic structures governed by the rule of law able to develop once again. The 8 May 1945 became the "day of liberation" (as Federal President, *Richard von Weizsäcker*, described it in 1985). However, Germany remained divided into the occupation zones governed by the United States, Britain and France, on the one hand, and the Soviet Union on the other.

The "Parliamentary Council" (*Parlamentarischer Rat*) developed a constitution on behalf of the three Western occupying powers. The aim was to learn from the mistakes that had been made in the Weimar Constitution and to build a "defensive democracy" (*wehrhafte Demokratie*), i.e. one that was able to defend itself. To make clear that hope for a reunited single German state remained, the new legal regime was referred to not as a "constitution" but merely as the "Basic Law" (*Grundgesetz*). The Basic Law entered into force on 23 May 1949, after it had been approved by the military governors of the occupation zones and ratified by the federal states (*Bundesländer*). Thus, the Federal Republic of Germany (*Bundesrepublik Deutschland*) came into being.

In the territory of the Soviet occupation zone the "German Democratic Republic" (*Deutsche Demokratische Republik*) was born. Even though the constitution of the German Democratic Republic had an extensive catalogue of fundamental rights, they could hardly be enforced in political reality. The country was governed according to the principle of "democratic socialism" (*demokratischer Sozialismus*). Ultimately everything was decided by the

---

22 Cf. W. Frotscher and B. Pieroth, *Verfassungsgeschichte*, 15th ed., C.H. Beck, Munich 2015, pp. 275 ff.

"Socialist Unity Party of Germany" (*Sozialistische Einheitspartei Deutschlands*).[23] In 1989, a peaceful revolution led to the reunification of Germany. The accession of the German Democratic Republic to the Federal Republic of Germany took place on 3 October 1990. Since then, the Basic Law has applied also in the new states of Brandenburg, Mecklenburg-Western Pomerania, Saxony, Saxony-Anhalt and Thuringia. There was no referendum.

1.3. ADMINISTRATIVE LAW UNDER THE INFLUENCE OF THE BASIC LAW AND EUROPEAN UNION LAW

Figure 1. Hierarchy of norms

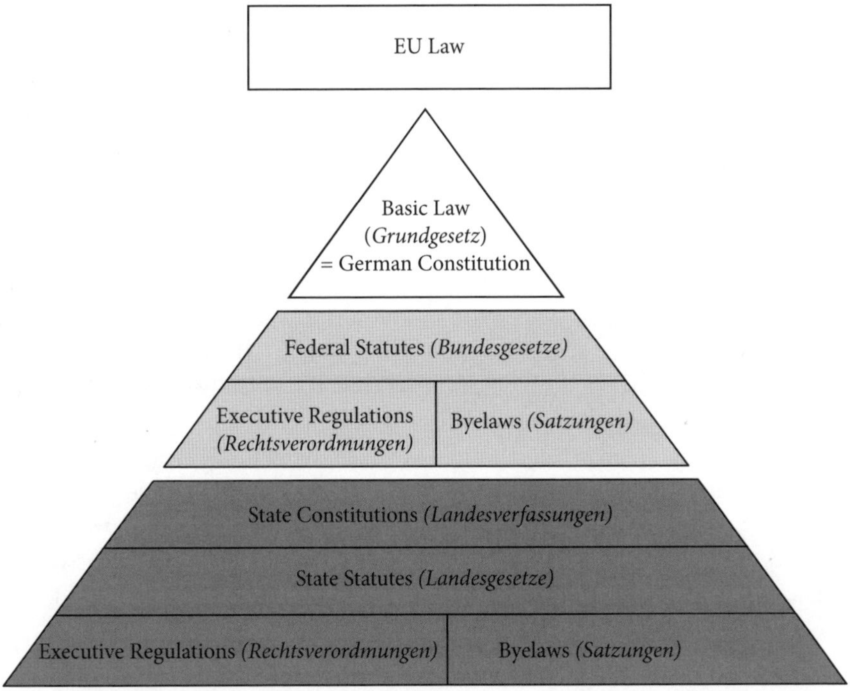

1.3.1. Administrative Law as "Specified Constitutional Law"

Compared to the Weimar Constitution, the new German constitution, the Basic Law (*Grundgesetz*), has much more influence on public law in general. Modern

23 For a brief overview, see W. Frotscher and B. Pieroth, *Verfassungsgeschichte*, 15th ed., C.H. Beck, Munich 2015, pp. 390 ff. For a more detailed analysis, see G. Brunner, 'Das Staatsrecht der Deutschen Demokratischen Republik' in: J. Isensee and P. Kirchhof, *Handbuch des Staatsrechts, Band 1: Historische Grundlagen*, 3rd ed., C. F. Müller Verlag, Heidelberg 2003, pp. 531 ff.

German administrative law was fully developed after the terrible experiences of the National Socialist dictatorship. From that time onwards, administrative law was regarded as "specified constitutional law" (*Verwaltungsrecht als konkretisiertes Verfassungsrecht*).[24]

Following the experience of the National Socialist dictatorship, the authors of the Basic Law wished above all to secure the rule of law principle (*Rechtsstaatsprinzip*).[25] Although the most frequent translation of *Rechtsstaat* into English is "rule of law", one should not overlook the fact that the purpose of the Basic Law is not only to formally guarantee a state that is governed by law, but also to ensure that the substantive contents of the Constitution are implemented.[26] Under the Weimar Constitution the only factor that mattered was the will of the majority. There were no limits as to the merits of its decisions. As *Otto Kirchheimer* wrote in 1929, four years before *Hitler* seized power, the Weimar Constitution was a "constitution without decision".[27] The Basic Law was constructed to change that. Today, the Basic Law is supreme in German law. It takes precedence over all other norms including statutes enacted by parliament.[28]

1.3.1.1. Fundamental Rights

Following the horrible inhumanity of the National Socialist dictatorship, the Basic Law intentionally begins with the words (Article 1 (I) Basic Law): "Human dignity shall be inviolable. To respect and protect it shall be the duty of all state authority." Additionally, at the beginning, in Article 1 (III) Basic Law it is made clear that fundamental rights bind the legislature, the executive and the judiciary together as "directly applicable law".[29] This is a deliberate renunciation of the legal regime under the Weimar Constitution, in which many fundamental rights were categorised as mere "programmatic rules" which were not enforceable in court.

Some fundamental rights are rights to which only German people are entitled (*Bürgerrechte*). This applies, above all, to the freedom of assembly (Article 8 Basic Law), the freedom of association (Article 9 Basic Law), the

---

24 F. Werner, *Verwaltungsrecht als konkretisiertes Verfassungsrecht*, (1959) 74 DVBl. 527.

25 E. Schmidt-Assmann, 'Der Rechtsstaat' in: J. Isensee and P. Kirchhof, *Handbuch des Staatsrechts, Band 2: Verfassungsstaat*, 3rd ed., C. F. Müller Verlag, Heidelberg 2004, p. 551. For a brief description of the genesis of the Basic Law see W. Frotscher and B. Pieroth, *Verfassungsgeschichte*, 15th ed., C.H. Beck, Munich 2015, pp. 369 ff.

26 E. Schmidt-Assmann, 'Der Rechtsstaat' in: J. Isensee and P. Kirchhof, *Handbuch des Staatsrechts, Band 2: Verfassungsstaat*, 3rd ed., C. F. Müller Verlag, Heidelberg 2004, pp. 554 ff.

27 O. Kirchheimer, 'Weimar – und was dann?' in: O. Kirchheimer, *Politik und Verfassung*, Suhrkamp, Frankfurt 1964, p. 52.

28 See also M. Nierhaus, 'administrative law' in: M. Reimann and J. Zekoll (eds.), *Introduction to German Law*, C. H. Beck, Munich 2005, p. 93.

29 For a brief overview of the constitutional implications of administrative law, see also M. Nierhaus, 'administrative law' in: M. Reimann and J. Zekoll (eds.), *Introduction to German Law*, C. H. Beck, Munich 2005, pp. 88 ff.

freedom of movement (Article 11 Basic Law) and the freedom to choose and practise one's occupation (Article 12 Basic Law). All other fundamental rights apply also to aliens (*Menschenrechte*). Where a fundamental right only applies to Germans, aliens are given a guarantee of a "general right to freedom of action" (Article 2 (I) Basic Law), which can, however, be more easily restricted. The freedom to act (*allgemeine Handlungsfreiheit*) in Article 2 (I) Basic Law acts a a "catchall fundamental right" (*Auffanggrundrecht*). From the right to free development of one's personality (Article 2 (I) Basic Law) and from the guarantee to protect human dignity (Article 1 (I) Basic Law), the Federal Constitutional Court deduced the "right to informational self-determination" (*Recht auf informationelle Selbstbestimmung*), above all in its ruling in the so-called Population Census case (*Volkszählungsurteil*) of 1983, thus creating the basis for German data protection law (see 4.2.1.).[30]

The fundamental rights of the Basic Law primariliy have the function to prevent individuals from interferences by state authorities. However, they also provide persons holding fundamental rights with a right to protection by the state (*Schutzrechte*) against encroachments upon protected legal interests by private third parties, non-German government agencies or force majeure. When it comes to deducing benefit rights (*Leistungsrechte*) from fundamental rights, the courts and academics are very restrictive.[31] The requirement of "interpretation in accordance with the constitution" (*verfassungskonforme Auslegung*) is especially important. Although only public authorities are bound by the fundamental rights, while citizens are not (Article 1 (III) Basic Law), these rights must be observed in the interpretation of private law regulations. This is known as an "indirect effect of the fundamental rights on third parties" (*mittelbare Drittwirkung*).[32]

1.3.1.2. Restrictions of Fundamental Rights

Except for "inviolable" human dignity (Article 1 (I) Basic Law), all fundamental rights may be restricted by statute or on the basis of a statute. In the case of some fundamental rights, e.g. with regard to the freedom of occupation or profession (Article 12 (I), 2nd sentence Basic Law), there is an expressed legal reservation (*Gesetzesvorbehalt*). Other fundamental rights, such as the freedom to profess a religious or philosophical belief (Article 4 (I), 1st sentence Basic Law) and

---

30 BVerfG 15.12.1983, BVerfGE 65, 1 – *Volkszählungsurteil*, ECLI:DE:BVerfG:1983:es19830216.2bve000183.

31 For the different functions of fundamental rights in constitutional reality, see K. Stern, 'Idee und Elemente eines Systems der Grundrechte' in: J. Isensee and P. Kirchhof, *Handbuch des Staatsrechts, Band 9: Allgemeine Grundrechtslehren*, 3rd ed., C. F. Müller Verlag, Heidelberg 2011, pp. 3, 80 ff.

32 K. Stern, 'Idee und Elemente eines Systems der Grundrechte' in: J. Isensee and P. Kirchhof, *Handbuch des Staatsrechts, Band 9: Allgemeine Grundrechtslehren*, 3rd ed., C. F. Müller Verlag, Heidelberg 2011, pp. 3, 90 f.

the freedom of the arts and sciences (Article 5 (III) Basic Law), are guaranteed "without reservation". However, this does not mean that those freedoms cannot be restricted. Such fundamental freedoms are subject to "barriers inherent in the constitution" (*verfassungsimmanente Schranken*).[33] If they conflict with other fundamental guarantees, they may, on a statutory basis, be restricted. The competing interests should be balanced so that any of the conflicting fundamental guarantees may be exercised as far as possible. This basic maxim to reach a reasonable balance between competing constitutional guarantees is known as "practical concordance" (*praktische Konkordanz*) in German constitutional law doctrine.[34]

If the legislature or, based on a statute, the administration restricts a fundamental right, the "principle of proportionality" (*Verhältnismäßigkeitsgrundsatz*) must be observed.[35] This principle stipulates that a measure must firstly pursue a legitimate aim. Secondly, the measure must be "suitable" (*geeignet*) in order to reach that aim. Thirdly, there must be no other means available that are equally suitable but easier for the person concerned; the measure must be "necessary" (*erforderlich*). Fourthly and finally, the measure must be "proportionate in *sensu stricto*" (*angemessen*), i.e. the disadvantages resulting from the interference with a fundamental right must be proportionate to the advantages obtained.

1.3.1.3. Judicial Review of Breaches of Fundamental Rights

In Germany, the administrative courts play an important role in the protection of fundamental rights and constitutional principles. As fundamental rights bind the entire state power (Article 1 (III) of the Basic Law), and as anybody whose rights are being breached by public authority may resort to the courts (Article 19 (IV) Basic Law), the courts must ensure that the public authorities observe the "supremacy of the law" (Article 20 (III) Basic Law). This is required by the principle of democracy and the rule of law. Any burdensome measure undertaken by the public administration constitutes a breach of fundamental rights. As mentioned above, the freedom to act (Article 2 (I) Basic Law) serves as a catchall clause in this respect (see 1.3.1.1.). Thus, the administrative courts must always examine whether interference with citizens' rights has been authorised

---

33 For details, see C. HILLGRUBER, 'Grundrechtsschranken' in: J. ISENSEE and P. KIRCHHOF, *Handbuch des Staatsrechts, Band 9: Allgemeine Grundrechtslehren*, 3rd ed., C. F. Müller Verlag, Heidelberg 2011, pp. 1033, 1039 ff.

34 The term 'praktische Konkordanz' was established by K. HESSE, *Grundzüge des Verfassungsrechts der Bundesrepublik Deutschland*, 20th ed., C. F. Müller, Heidelberg 1995, p. 28.

35 C. HILLGRUBER, 'Grundrechtsschranken' in: J. ISENSEE and P. KIRCHHOF, *Handbuch des Staatsrechts, Band 9: Allgemeine Grundrechtslehren*, 3rd ed., C. F. Müller Verlag, Heidelberg 2011, pp. 1033, 1053 ff.

by a statute as well as the proportionality of the administrative decision. The constitutional foundations of administrative law are thus particularly important in Germany.[36]

1.3.2. Administrative Law Overruled by European Union Requirements

Over the last few decades, administrative law has been increasingly overruled by the law of the European Union (EU), in particular by the fundamental freedoms (Article 30 et seq. TFEU), cartel law (Article 101 et seq. TFEU), the law governing state aids (Article 107 et seq. TFEU), and by EU regulations and directives (Article 288 TFEU). Normally, EU law is not executed by the European Commission (direct execution), but is administered on a decentralized basis by national authorities according to national administrative law (indirect execution). However, effective execution of European Union law must be ensured (*effet utile*). This has often led to a modification of national administrative law. Moreover, many administrative decisions with cross-border significance are nowadays made in co-operation with other member states ("horizontal composite administration"), or with the Commission ("vertical composite administration").

Europeanization sometimes conflicts with German administrative law principles.[37] This is particularly true with regard to judicial review of administrative action. The German judicial review system is focussed on the protection of individual rights. Thus, the admissibility of a court action always requires the allegation of the violation of an "individual public right" (*subjektives öffentliches Recht*), i.e. the right must be accorded to the individual by virtue of legislative choice or administrative decision (see 5.5.1.). Furthermore, the German administrative judicial review is characterised by the predominance of substantive law over procedural law. The administrative procedure has a more "supportive function" and is – in principle – only relevant when it influences the outcome of the substantial administrative decision (see also below 4.1.1.2).[38] These two characteristics of German administrative law are to some extent

---

36 F. Werner, *Verwaltungsrecht als konkretisiertes Verfassungsrecht*, (1959) 74 DVBl. 527; D. Ehlers, 'Verwaltung und Verwaltungsrecht im demokratischen und sozialen Rechtsstaat' in: D. Ehlers and H. Pünder (eds.), *Allgemeines Verwaltungsrecht* (eds.), 15th ed., de Gruyter, Berlin 2016, pp. 7, 239 ff. For a comprehensive overview of the constitutional foundations of administrative law in English, see M. P. Singh, *German Administrative Law in Common Law Perspective*, Berlin, 2001, p. 10 ff.

37 For an insightful analysis of the European influence on German administrative law, see F. C. Mayer, 'Die Europäisierung des Verwaltungsrechts' in: P. F. Bultmann et al (eds.), *Allgemeines Verwaltungsrecht. Festschrift für Ulrich Battis zum 70. Geburtstag*, C. H. Beck, Munich 2014, pp. 46 ff.

38 H. Pünder, 'Administrative Procedure – Mere Facilitator of Material Law versus Cooperative Realization of Common Welfare', in: H. Pünder and C. Waldhoff (eds.), *Debates in German Public Law*, Hart, Oxford 2014, pp. 239 ff.

incompatible with the European understanding of administrative procedure. Thus, especially in the field of environmental law, European law led to important alterations of the German system with regard to standing and the consequences of procedural errors.[39] However, no general change of the German principles can be seen. Instead, German law is changed punctually in specific fields where European law prevails.

1.4. LEGAL BASIS OF ADMINISTRATIVE LAW

1.4.1. Code of Administrative Court Procedure (Verwaltungsgerichtsordnung)

The codification of administrative law was not straightforward. Efforts to compile the results of liberal administrative law doctrine into a code during both the German Empire and the Weimar Republic were unsuccessful. Administrative law was inconsistent and was spread over special administrative laws of the Empire and the individual states. National Socialism stifled all endeavours to bring about reform. Under the Basic Law, codifying legislation was, first of all, concentrated on restructuring of the judicial system. In 1960, the Code of Administrative Court Procedure (*Verwaltungsgerichtsordnung* – VwGO) was enacted. Other than this measure, only the "general legal principles", as developed by court decisions, applied in administrative law. Whether practical needs could be met by way of a single codification was in doubt.[40]

1.4.2. Administrative Procedure Acts (Verwaltungsverfahrensgesetze)

It was not until 1977 that the federal Administrative Procedure Act (*Verwaltungsverfahrensgesetz* – VwVfG) entered into force, which the states followed by enacting regulations with practically the same wording. However, the Administrative Procedure Acts do not contain the entirety of general administrative law or even of administrative procedure law. Rather, the codes only regulate "the activities having an effect on third parties which aim at reviewing the requirements, preparing and issuing an administrative act and at concluding a public law contract" (§ 9 Administrative Procedure Act). Other instruments of the executive were not included. In this case, one still has to form conclusions by analogy or by referring to "general principles" of administrative law or to the constitution itself. Moreover, special regulations have priority for certain areas of the administration. This fragmentation of the law is condemned

[39] See ECJ, Case C-115/09, *Trianel* [2011] ECR I-3673, ECLI:EU:C:2011:289.

[40] For the development of the German Administrative Court Procedure Law, see F. Hufen, *Verwaltungsprozessrecht*, 10th ed., C.H. Beck, Munich 2016, pp. 24 ff.

by academics, as it has an adverse effect on the certainty and reliability of administrative law.[41]

1.5. SEPARATE ADMINISTRATIVE COURTS

It is derived from Article 92 and Article 95 Basic Law that the existence of an independent administrative judiciary as such is guaranteed. The organization of the administrative judiciary is governed by § 2 Code of Administrative Court Procedure which provides for a three-tiered system, including Administrative Courts (*Verwaltungsgerichte*), Higher Administrative Courts (*Oberverwaltungsgerichte*, which are named *Verwaltungsgerichtshöfe* in a number of states) and the Federal Administrative Court (*Bundesverwaltungsgericht*). The number of the lower administrative courts differs from state to state according to size and population.

1.5.1. Distinction between Private and Public Law

According to § 40 (I) Sentence 1 Code of Administrative Court Procedure, "recourse to the administrative courts shall be available in all public law disputes of a non-constitutional nature insofar as the disputes are not explicitly allocated to another court by a federal statute." Thus, public law disputes (*öffentlich-rechtliche Streitigkeiten*) have to be distinguished from private law disputes and criminal cases, which are dealt with by the "ordinary courts" (*ordentliche Gerichtsbarkeit*). While civil law is based on "private autonomy" and regulates conflicts of interest among private individuals, public law establishes and limits the powers of the state. Nonetheless, the line between public law and civil law is not easy to draw. According to the prevailing "subject theory" (*Subjektstheorie*) or the "special law theory" (*Sonderrechtstheorie*), a dispute is dealt with by the administrative judiciary if the law at hand exclusively authorises or obliges holders of sovereign authority.[42] Typical examples of public law disputes are disputes in the areas of police law, the law of assemblies, immigration law, spatial planning law or civil services law as opposed to commercial law disputes in which the administration conducts private transactions such as renting or purchasing buildings. However, today, due to the increasing economic activities of the state and the increasing transfer of public powers to private parties, the distinction of public and private law is starting to blur.

[41] Cf. D. Ehlers, 'Verwaltung und Verwaltungsrecht' in: D. Ehlers and H. Pünder (eds.), *Allgemeines Verwaltungsrecht*, 15th ed., de Gruyter, Berlin 2016, pp. 7, 139 f. For the development of the codification of German administrative law see H. Pünder, 'Verwaltungsverfahren' in: D. Ehlers and H. Pünder (eds.), *Allgemeines Verwaltungsrecht*, 15th ed., de Gruyter, Berlin 2016, pp. 407, 409–416.

[42] For a comprehensive overview, see F. Hufen, *Verwaltungsprozessrecht*, 10th ed., C.H. Beck, Munich 2016, pp. 152 f. For a brief English explanation, see N. G. Foster and S. Sule, *German Legal System & Laws*, 3rd ed., Oxford University Press, New York 2002, p. 249.

According to the German understanding, the state may also act under private law. Disputes arising out of such private transactions of the administration are assigned to the civil courts. This applies, in particular, where the state purchases the goods and services it needs to discharge its duties by way of "public procurement" (*Bedarfsdeckungsverwaltung*)[43], or where it engages in economic activities (*erwerbswirtschaftliche Betätigung*) by acting as a service provider in the market with the intention of making a profit.[44] In such cases, it is not the administrative courts that have jurisdiction, but the ordinary courts.

A different situation exists when the state fulfils its duties not only indirectly but also directly in the form of private law. In the administration of services (*Leistungsverwaltung*) the state is granted the freedom to choose between public law and private law action. This applies, for example, to the granting of subsidies. In order to ensure that the state does not "flee to private law", public law is, in this case, superimposed onto private law. Academics speak of "private administrative law" (*Verwaltungsprivatrecht*). In this context, the so-called "two-stage theory" (*Zweistufentheorie*) applies, according to which the question "whether" something is done, e.g. whether or not a subsidy is granted, is a matter of public law and is controlled by the administrative courts. In contrast, the question of "how" something is done, e.g. if the subsidy is granted in the form of a low interest rate contract or a surety, can be a matter of private law and can be controlled by the ordinary courts of law. The fact that the jurisdiction differs at each stage is disadvantageous, but generally accepted.[45]

1.5.2. Distinction between Administrative and Constitutional Law

Constitutional law disputes are excluded from the administrative jurisdiction according to § 40 (I) sentence 1 Code of Administrative Court Procedure. However, the exception only applies to disputes which satisfy the following two conditions. Firstly, parties to the dispute must be constitutional entities, such as the *Bundestag* (German Federal Parliament), the *Bundesrat* (legislative body representing the states), federal or state governments or political parties. Secondly, the substance of the dispute must concern constitutional law. Consequently, if a citizen claims that his fundamental rights under the Basic Law have been infringed by the administration, this would not constitute a constitutional law dispute according to § 40 (I) sentence 1 Code of Administrative Court Procedure and would thus fall into the jurisdiction of

43 H. Pünder and G. Buchholtz, *Einführung in das Vergaberecht* (2016) JURA (*Juristische Ausbildung*), 1246 ff., 1358 ff.

44 H. Pünder and R. Dittmar, *Die wirtschaftliche Betätigung der Gemeinden* (2005) JURA (*Juristische Ausbildung*), 760 ff.

45 For details, see E. Gurlit, 'Verwaltungsvertrag und andere verwaltungsrechtliche Sonderverbindungen' in: D. Ehlers and H. Pünder (eds.), *Allgemeines Verwaltungsrecht*, 15th ed., de Gruyter, Berlin 2015, pp. 405, 738 f.

the administrative courts.[46] Therefore, German administrative courts have an important function in the protection of fundamental rights.

Matters expressly excluded from the administrative jurisdiction are matters assigned to the social courts[47], matters assigned to the fiscal courts[48], and matters related to the administration of justice (*Justizverwaltungsakte*), which are assigned to the ordinary courts (civil and criminal courts).[49] Furthermore, state liability law is assigned to the ordinary courts according to § 40 (II) Code of Administrative Court Procedure.

2. ADMINISTRATIVE ORGANIZATION

2.1. AUTHORITIES OF THE STATES AND OF THE FEDERATION

Figure 2. State organization in Germany

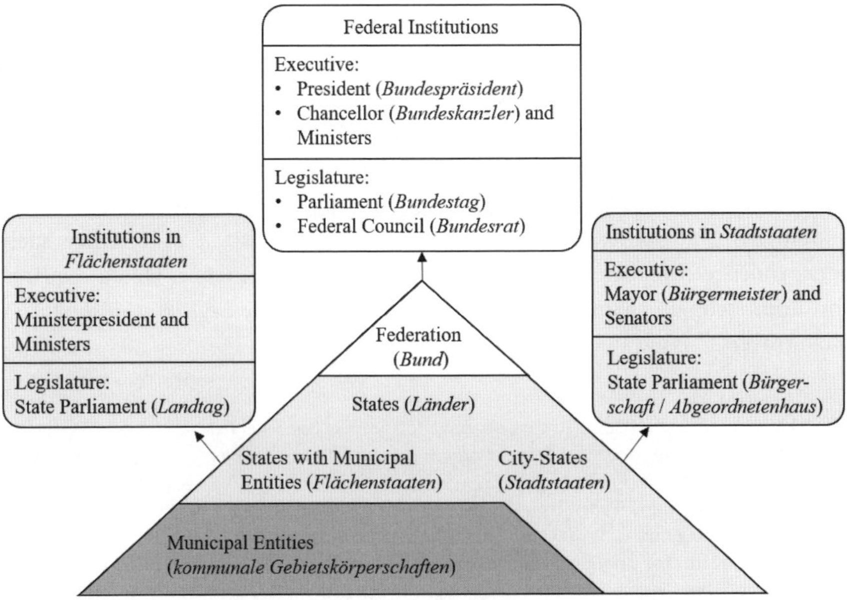

46 F. Hufen, *Verwaltungsprozessrecht*, 10th ed., C.H. Beck, Munich 2016, pp. 168 f.

47 § 51 Code of Procedure of the Social Courts (*Sozialgerichtsgesetz*). This also includes disputes concerning social and unemployment insurance payments as well as pension schemes for war victims.

48 § 32 Code of Procedure od the Fiscal Courts (*Finanzgerichtsordnung*). This includes disputes relating to federal and state taxes.

49 See § 23 of the Introduction Code to the Courts Constitution Act (*Einführungsgesetz zum Gerichtsverfassungsgesetz*, EGGVG).

In German federalism, there are mainly two levels of state power.[50] There are administrative authorities at the federal level and at the state level. Under the German constitutional system, the federal level is predominantly responsible for legislation, while the states are competent for the execution of the law.[51] The authorities of the states also usually execute federal laws (Article 83 Basic Law). Only in a few areas, the law of railways, for example, the federal level executes its laws through its own federal administrative bodies. Thus, in contrast to the system in the U.S., where the federal and the state level are more independent from each other, the federal system of Germany is characterised by a close interweaving of the federal and the state level.[52]

Within the states, the administration is more decentralized.[53] There are "lower administrative authorities", "higher administrative authorities" and "supreme administrative authorities". Furthermore, the municipalities have the right to local self-government (*kommunale Selbstverwaltung*, Article 28 (II) Basic Law) (see 2.2.2.). The administrative bodies are connected by a multi-level hierarchy. The right to the final decision is assigned to the respective state minister as the supreme administrative authority, who is also accountable to the state parliament. Thereby, the democratic legitimacy of the administration is ensured.[54]

However, there are some public authorities which are independent as required by European Union law. An example is the Federal Network Agency for Electricity, Gas, Telecommunications, Post and Railways (*Bundesnetzagentur*), whose tasks are to ensure competition between the providers in the areas of the economy which used to be state monopolies, and to secure the citizens' "basic supply" (*Grundversorgung*) of these services. The question of whether such independence complies with the German democratic principle, which requires an "uninterrupted chain of legitimacy" (*ununterbrochene Legitimationskette*), is a controversial issue among legal scholars.[55]

---

50 For an overview of administrative organization between the federal, state and municipal level in English, see M. P. SINGH, *German Administrative Law in Common Law Perspective*, Berlin, 2001, pp. 33 ff.

51 See C. WALDHOFF, 'Federalism – Cooperative Federalism versus Competitive Federalism', in H. PÜNDER and C. WALDHOFF (eds.), *Debates in German Public Law*, Hart, Oxford 2014, pp. 117, 121 ff. For a political science perspective, see F. W. SCHARPF, *The Joint Decision Trap: Lessons From German Federalism and European Integration*, (1988) 66 Public Administration, 239, 244 ff.

52 For a political science perspective see F. SCHNABEL, ‚Politik ohne Politiker' in: H. WOLLMANN (ed.), *Politik im Dickicht der Bürokratie*, Westdeutscher Verlag, Opladen 1980, pp. 49, 50, 52; H. ABROMEIT, *Der verkappte Einheitsstaat*, Leske & Budrich, Opladen 1992, p. 9.

53 For a brief overview see M. NIERHAUS, 'Administrative Law' in: M. REIMANN and J. ZEKOLL (eds.), *Introduction to German Law*, C. H. Beck, Munich 2005, pp. 93 f.

54 E.-W. BÖCKENFÖRDE, 'Demokratie als Verfassungsprinzip' in: ISENSEE and P. KIRCHHOF, *Handbuch des Staatsrechts, Band 2: Verfassungsstaat*, 3rd ed., C. F. Müller Verlag, Heidelberg 2004, pp. 429, 438 ff.

55 For a more sceptical view on independent administrative bodies, see E.-W. BÖCKENFÖRDE, 'Demokratie als Verfassungsprinzip' in: ISENSEE and P. KIRCHHOF, *Handbuch des*

2.2. ADMINISTRATIVE BODIES WITH THEIR OWN LEGAL PERSONALITY

2.2.1. *Indirect Public Administration of Legal Entities under Public Law*

Where the administrative authorities of the states – or exceptionally of the federal level – act, this is called "direct public administration" (*unmittelbare Staatsverwaltung*). The administrative authorities normally have no own legal personality but are rather seen as a part of the state or federation. However, some administrative bodies have their own legal personality. There are three types of "legal entities under public law" (*juristische Personen des öffentlichen Rechts*): public law corporations (*öffentlich-rechtliche Körperschaften*), public law institutions (*öffentlich-rechtliche Anstalten*) and public law foundations (*öffentlich-rechtliche Stiftungen*). When these administrative bodies act, this is known as "indirect public administration" (*mittelbare Staatsverwaltung*).[56] Such public law bodies with their own legal personality include universities, occupation-based chambers (chambers of commerce, chambers of crafts, bar associations, medical chambers, etc.) and the institutions of social security (health insurance, accident insurance, nursing care insurance, pension insurance and unemployment insurance).

2.2.2. *Local Self-Government*

In this context municipalities (*Gemeinden*) and counties (*Landkreise*) possess a special status. Their autonomy is guaranteed by Article 28 (II) Basic Law. They have extensive areas of responsibility, possess territorial sovereignty and may impose their own will, legitimised through directly elected bodies.[57] However, the elected municipal bodies are not seen as real parliaments in the sense of Article 20 (II) Basic Law but rather serve a self-governing purpose within the realm of the State (*kommunale Selbstverwaltung*). The municipalities have the right and the responsibility to regulate local affairs, within the limits prescribed by law. With regard to these tasks, the State only supervises the local administration with regard to legality (*Rechtsaufsicht*). Furthermore, the municipal administration also performs tasks on behalf of the state.

Staatsrechts, Band 2: Verfassungsstaat, 3rd ed., C. F. Müller Verlag, Heidelberg 2004, pp. 429, 444. For a more open approach, see E. Klein, *Die verfassungsrechtliche Problematik des ministerialfreien Raumes*, Duncker & Humblot, Berlin 1974, pp. 191 ff.

56 For details, see M. Burgi, 'Verwaltungsorganisationsrecht' in: D. Ehlers and H. Pünder (eds.), *Allgemeines Verwaltungsrecht* (eds.), 15th ed., de Gruyter, Berlin 2015, pp. 255, 279 ff.

57 For an overview in English, see M. P. Singh, *German Administrative Law in Common Law Perspective*, Springer, Berlin 2001, pp. 37 f.

With regard to these tasks, the respective state is also allowed to review the functional decisions of the local administration (*Fachaufsicht*).[58]

2.3. ADMINISTRATION BY PRIVATE ENTITIES

Lastly, the federal or state government may also authorise private law entities to discharge certain administrative tasks independently by means of public law. For this purpose, private bodies can be vested with public authority by statute (*Beleihung*).[59] An example is the collection of tolls for lorries using German motorways, which is carried out by the company *Toll Collect GmbH*, a joint venture of *Deutsche Telekom*, *Daimler* and the French *Vinci Group*. In the event of claims of individuals against the exercise of public power by those private entities, the administrative courts are competent.

The situation is different where the government establishes a private law limited liability company (*Gesellschaft mit beschränkter Haftung*) or a joint-stock corporation (*Aktiengesellschaft*) under a merely "formal privatization" procedure.[60] In this case, disputes are settled by the ordinary courts. This also applies to corporations with private entities under a public-private partnership, and cases where the state completely withdraws from an area of activity by way of "substantive privatization". In this case, the state no longer bears the "responsibility for performance" (*Erfüllungsverantwortung*), but only the "responsibility for warranty" (*Gewährleistungsverantwortung*), meaning that the state no longer fulfils the respective task by its own means but only monitors the performance of private bodies. The administrative courts will decide whether the state fulfils that task sufficiently. For example, public authorities have to control whether products, which have been given the CE mark by private certification companies, are indeed safe.[61] Otherwise, individuals may have a liability claim against public authorities (see 7.).

58 For details and an illustration of the difficulty in distinguishing between autonomous and delegated tasks, see H. Maurer and C. Waldhoff, *Allgemeines Verwaltungsrecht*, 19th ed., C.H. Beck, Munich 2017, pp. 643 ff.

59 For details, see M. Burgi, 'Verwaltungsorganisationsrecht' in: D. Ehlers and H. Pünder (eds.), *Allgemeines Verwaltungsrecht* (eds.), 15th ed., de Gruyter, Berlin 2015, pp. 255, 316 ff.

60 See J. Ziekow, *Öffentliches Wirtschaftsrecht*, 4th ed., C.H. Beck, Munich 2016, p. 152.

61 H. Pünder, 'Zertifizierung und Akkreditierung – private Qualitätskontrolle unter staatlicher Gewährleistungsverantwortung', (2006) 170 *ZHG* 567, 576.

3. ADMINISTRATIVE ACTS AND OTHER INSTRUMENTS OF THE ADMINISTRATION

Figure 3. Forms of administrative action

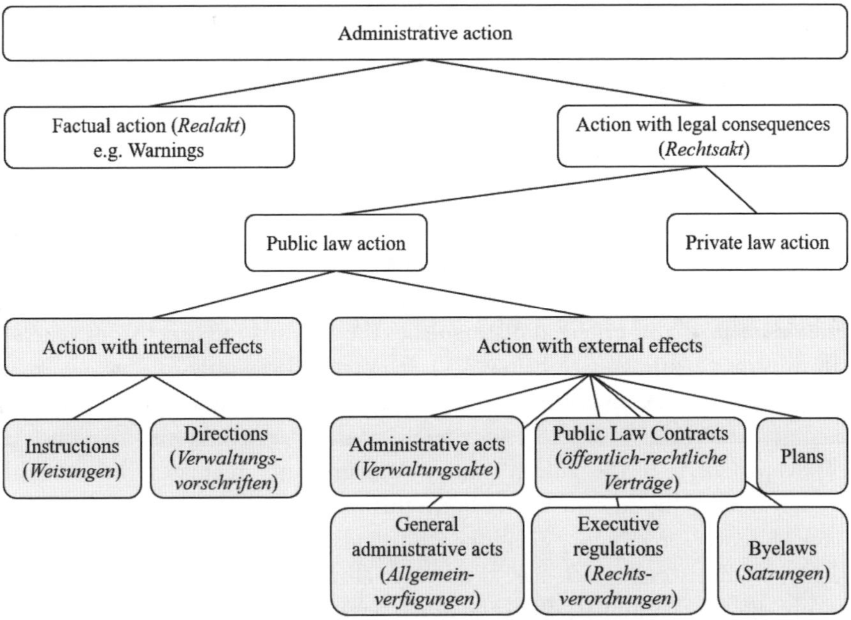

3.1. ADMINISTRATIVE ACTS (*VERWALTUNGSAKTE*)

Except where administrative authorities act through a private law entity, the administration usually acts by means of public law instruments. The most important of these is the so-called "administrative act" (*Verwaltungsakt*). It is defined in § 35 Sentence 1 of the Administrative Procedure Act as follows: "An administrative act shall be any order, decision or other sovereign measure taken by an authority to regulate an individual case in the sphere of public law and which is intended to have a direct external legal effect." This definition covers all kinds of administrative measures such as granting building permission, granting or withdrawing licences or implementing a certain safety measure to protect the public.

To qualify as an administrative act in the German sense, an administrative measure must fulfil all the criteria listed in § 35 Sentence 1 Administrative Procedure Act.[62] First, the administrative measure must regulate something.

---

62 For details, see M. Ruffert, 'Verwaltungsakt' in: D. Ehlers and H. Pünder (eds.), *Allgemeines Verwaltungsrecht*, 15th ed., de Gruyter, Berlin 2016, pp. 646, 653 ff.

This distinguishes the administrative act from factual action, where no legal effect is intended by the administration (see below 3.6.). Therefore, a warning cannot qualify as an administrative act, because it does not regulate anything but has a mere informational purpose. In contrast, the prohibition of a certain product is an administrative act, because it establishes an interdiction. Second, the measure must be taken by a public authority. According to § 1 Administrative Procedure Act, this term is to be understood in a broad sense. Every unit that fulfils tasks of the public administration constitutes a public authority. Furthermore, private bodies that carry out administrative tasks on behalf of a public authority autonomously (*Beliehene*) can be understood as public authority under § 35 Sentence 1 Administrative Procedure Act (see 2.3.). Third, the administrative measure must lie within the sphere of public law. Therefore, for example, the purchase of materials for the administration is not an administrative act. Fourth, the measure must be intended to regulate an individual case. This criterion distinguishes the administrative act from general administrative rulings (see below 3.3.). It must address only one person or a narrowly defined small group of people and only one concrete case. Finally, the measure must have an immediate external effect or external legal consequence (*Außenwirkung*). If the administrative measure only regulates the internal organization of the administrative body, this requirement is not met (see below 3.5.). Moreover, preparatory decisions are excluded by this requirement.[63]

An administrative act has three special characteristics which together ensure effective administration and legal certainty. Firstly, an administrative act becomes effective the moment it is communicated to the party concerned (§ 43 (I) Administrative Procedure Act) even if it suffers from legal errors (legal effectiveness independent of errors – *fehlerunabhängige Rechtswirksamkeit*). Only an administrative act that is obviously and severely illegal is "void" (*nichtig*) from the beginning (§ 44 Administrative Procedure Act). Secondly, an administrative act is characterised by the fact that its legal effectiveness becomes final and non-appealable (*bestandskräftig*), irrespective of potential unlawfulness, if there is no appeal against it within the statutory period (i.e. within one month; §§ 70 and 74 Administrative Procedure Act) or if an appeal against it has failed. The third characteristic of an administrative act is that the administration itself can enforce it (*verwaltungseigene Vollstreckung*). While citizens can enforce their demands only with the assistance of a judgement, a public authority is able to enforce the claims it has defined by an administrative

---

[63] For a more detailed explanation of the German concept of the administrative act in English, see M. P. Singh, *German Administrative Law in Common Law Perspective*, Springer, Berlin 2001, pp. 63 ff.; M. Nierhaus, 'Administrative Law' in: M. Reimann and J. Zekoll (eds.), *Introduction to German Law*, C. H. Beck, Munich 2005, pp. 97 ff. For some examples, see N. G. Foster and S. Sule, *German Legal System & Laws*, 3rd ed., Oxford University Press, New York 2002, p. 260.

act itself under public law. The enforcement of administrative law will be explained in more detail below (see 6.).

3.2. PUBLIC LAW CONTRACTS (*ÖFFENTLICH-RECHTLICHE VERTRÄGE*)

In practice, administrative acts are the most frequently used instrument. Nevertheless, a public authority may also choose to find a mutual public law agreement with a citizen, and may negotiate a "public law contract" (*öffentlich-rechtlicher Vertrag*) with him or her (§ 54 Administrative Procedure Act).[64] If the administration concludes a public law contract the general principles of civil law apply (§ 62 Administrative Procedure Act) but slight alterations in favour of the citizen are stipulated in §§ 54 et seq. Administrative Procedure Act. Other than under private law, where any non-compliance with the law leads to a voidance of the contract (§ 134 of the German Civil Code – BGB), under public law, contracts are only void when a severe "ground for voidance" (*Nichtigkeitsgrund*) exists (§ 59 Administrative Procedure Act). This restriction to special grounds for voidance is intended to ensure legal certainty and effective administration.

Public law contracts concern administrative law and thus any disputes relating to them fall under the jurisdiction of the administrative courts. Public law contracts are further classified into "co-ordinate contracts" and "subordinate contracts". Co-ordinate contracts are based on two declarations of intent of equal weight. For example, contracts between two municipalities to fulfil certain public duties can be classified as coordinate contracts. In opposition to that, subordinate contracts are concluded between parties which are in a relationship of superior and subordinate. They are executed in place of an individual administrative act (§ 54 sentence 2 Administrative Procedure Act). For example, the competent authority may conclude a public law contract with an individual in which the authority commits itself to issue a building permit for a multi-storey building if the citizen undertakes to build a playground. Due to the subordinate position of the citizen in subordinate contracts in §§ 55, 56, 59 (II) and 61 Administrative Procedure Act, particular rules apply which provide special protection to the citizen.[65]

---

64 For details, see E. Gurlit, 'Verwaltungsvertrag und andere verwaltungsrechtliche Sonderverbindungen' in: D. Ehlers and H. Pünder (eds.), *Allgemeines Verwaltungsrecht*, 15th ed., de Gruyter, Berlin 2015, pp. 405, 420 f.

65 For a more detailed explanation of administrative contracts in English see M. P. Singh, *German Administrative Law in Common Law Perspective*, Springer, Berlin 2001, pp. 94–102; M. Nierhaus, 'Administrative Law' in: M. Reimann and J. Zekoll (eds.), *Introduction to German Law*, C. H. Beck, Munich 2005, p. 100–102.

3.3. GENERAL ACTS: GENERAL ADMINISTRATIVE ACTS (*ALLGEMEINVERFÜGUNGEN*), EXECUTIVE REGULATIONS (*RECHTSVERORDNUNGEN*) AND BYLAWS (*SATZUNGEN*)

With regard to general acts, the German administrative law distinguishes between measures that address an indefinite number of people but have a concrete effect (general and concrete) and measures that address an indefinite number of people but set out an abstract ruling (general and abstract).[66]

The former measures are called "general administrative acts" (*Allgemeinverfügung*)[67] and are defined by § 35 Sentence 2 Administrative Procedure Act as "a general order directed at a group of people defined or definable on the basis of general characteristics or relating to the public law aspect of a matter, or its use by the public at large, shall be an administrative act." General administrative acts can be directed at a specific group of individuals in order to regulate a concrete factual situation. An example of such a general administrative act would be the obligation to keep dogs on a leash in certain public parks. General administrative acts can furthermore be issued to regulate the use of public property. For example, road signs are considered to be general administrative acts. Finally, general administrative acts can relate to the quality of public property. For example, the administration can decide to declare a street as open to the public by way of a general administrative act. To these general administrative acts the same judicial and administrative formal remedies apply as to individual administrative acts (see below 5.4.1).

With regard to general and abstract executive rulings, a distinction is made between executive regulations (*Rechtsverordnungen*)[68] and bylaws (*Satzungen*)[69] by autonomous administrative bodies. The administration may only enact statutory provisions with external legal effects if the legislator has specifically authorised it to do so (cf. Article 80 Basic Law). These are usually "*Rechtsverordnungen*" (executive regulations). If statutory provisions with external legal effects are issued by public law corporations like municipalities, universities, occupation-based chambers etc. they are called *Satzungen* (bylaws).

---

[66] For details, see H. Hill and M. Martini, 'Normsetzung und andere Formen exekutivischer Selbstprogrammierung' in: W. Hoffmann-Riem, E. Schmidt-Assmann and A. Vosskuhle (eds.), *Grundlagen des Verwaltungsrechts,* Volume 2, 2nd ed., C. H. Beck, Munich 2012, pp. 1025, 1041–1072.

[67] For details, see H. Maurer and C. Waldhoff, *Allgemeines Verwaltungsrecht*, 19th ed., C.H. Beck, Munich 2017, pp. 224 ff.

[68] See Article 80 Basic Law. H. Pünder, *Democratic Legitimation of Delegated Legislation – A Comparative View on the American, British and German Law* (2009) 58 ICLQ (*International and Comparative Law Quarterly*), 353 ff.

[69] For example, see Article 28 (II) Basic Law empowering the municipalities and associations of municipalities to issue bylaws. See also N. G. Foster and S. Sule, *German Legal System & Laws*, 3rd ed., Oxford University Press, New York 2002, pp. 251 f.

The external general legal instruments of executive regulations and bylaws cannot be challenged by means of an action to annul an administrative act. In some states there is a specific action to review bye-laws and regulations (§ 47 (I) No. 2 Administrative Procedure Act). In other states, abstract general executive ruling can only be reviewed by the courts in the course of another action brought against an individual administrative act which is based on the executive bylaw or regulation (*Inzidentkontrolle*).

3.4. PLANS

Another form of general action of the administration is planning.[70] By planning the administration often allocates scarce commodities. For example, municipal planning allocates the possible usages of municipal territory (see below 4.2.2). Special procedural provisions apply to planning, as third parties' interests have to be taken into consideration (§§ 72–78 Administrative Procedure Act). Plans can be adopted as executive regulations (*Rechtsverordnung*), bylaws (*Satzung*), as a form of autonomous legislation, or as general administrative acts (*Allgemeinverfügungen*). As the nature of a plan is halfway between legislative and executive activities, its classification is difficult. Administrative plans are common in the areas of budget law, building law and environmental law. The judicial remedies against administrative plans depend on their form of adoption. If the plan is adopted by means of a general administrative act, the action to annul an administrative act (*Anfechtungsklage*) is admissible (see below 5.4.1.). If it is adopted as an executive regulation or bylaw it can be challenged through the action for norm control (see below 5.4.4.). Generally, in judicial review proceedings of administrative action, the principal rule applies that non-compliance with the substantial law will render the statutory provision null and void. With regard to zoning plans, however, the legislator includes an exception to this so-called "nullity dogma" (*Nichtigkeitsdogma*). To strengthen legal certainty and administrative effectiveness, only particularly severe errors in law will lead to the annulment of the plan (§ 214 of the German Building Code – *Baugesetzbuch* – BauGB).

3.5. INSTRUCTIONS (*WEISUNGEN*) AND DIRECTIONS (*VERWALTUNGSVORSCHRIFTEN*) WITHIN THE ADMINISTRATION

Orders issued for internal application, which are of a concrete or individual nature, are known as "*Weisungen*" (instructions). Internal regulations

70 For details, see W. Köck, 'Pläne' in: W. Hoffmann-Riem, E. Schmidt-Assmann and A. Vosskuhle, *Grundlagen des Verwaltungsrechts, Band 2*, 2nd ed., C. H. Beck, Munich 2012, pp.1398 ff.

of an abstract or general nature are known as "*Verwaltungsvorschriften*" (administrative directions).[71] A distinction is made between administrative directions, which regulate the way the administration should exercise its discretion (*ermessenslenkende Verwaltungsvorschriften*), law-replacing administrative directions (*normersetzende Verwaltungsvorschriften*) and law-interpreting administrative directions (*norminterpretierende Verwaltungsvorschriften*), which refer to "non-defined legal terms" (*unbestimmte Rechtsbegriffe* see below 5.3.1.), and law-specifying administrative directions (*normkonkretisierende Verwaltungsvorschriften*), which concern non-defined legal terms with regard to which the authorities possess a "margin of interpretation" (*Beurteilungsspielraum*) and which, therefore, cannot be fully scrutinised by the courts (see below 5.3.1.). In principle, internal administrative directions have no legal effect on third parties. However, the fundamental right to equal treatment (Article 3 (I) Basic Law) requires that public authorities adhere to administrative practices created by administrative directions, unless there is a "sound reason" for digressing from them (*Selbstbindung der Verwaltung*). This is a legal position on which citizens may rely and which can be enforced by the administrative courts. If, for example, the administrative directions regulate how to grant a certain social benefit, individuals may have a right to that benefit based on the administrative direction in conjunction with the right to equal treatment.[72]

3.6. FACTUAL ACTION (*REALAKTE*): STATEMENTS OF KNOWLEDGE AND OTHER FACTUAL ACTS

Lastly, there is pure factual action (*Realakte*) under public law.[73] The term includes all measures taken in relation to citizens which are not intended to shape the law, but merely to achieve a factual result. In this context, a distinction must be drawn between "statements of knowledge" (*Wissenserklärungen*), such as information, warnings, etc., and "factual acts" (*tatsächliche Verrichtungen*), such as disbursements of money, rides on a government-owned vehicle, vaccinations, cleaning a street or road, etc. Also, informal cooperation of

[71] For details, see M. Möstl, 'Normative Handlungsformen' in: D. Ehlers and H. Pünder (eds.), *Allgemeines Verwaltungsrecht*, 15th ed., de Gruyter, Berlin 2016, pp. 595, 63–645.

[72] For an example, see Federal Administrative Court (BVerwG) 23.4.2003, NVwZ 2003, 1384, 1385. For a brief explanation of the concept of directions (*Verwaltungsvorschriften*) see N. G. Foster and S. Sule, *German Legal System & Laws*, 3rd ed., Oxford University Press, New York 2002, pp. 251 f.

[73] For details, see G. Hermes, 'Schlichtes Verwaltungshandeln' in: W. Hoffmann-Riem, E. Schmidt-Assmann and A. Vosskuhle (eds.), *Grundlagen des Verwaltungsrechts*, Volume 2, 2nd ed., C. H. Beck, Munich 2012, pp.1523 ff.; H. Maurer and C. Waldhoff, *Allgemeines Verwaltungsrecht*, 19th ed., C.H. Beck, Munich 2017, pp. 462 ff. For an English explanation of factual action, see M. P. Singh, *German Administrative Law in Common Law Perspective*, Springer, Berlin 2001, p. 107 f.

the administration with citizens constitutes factual action.[74] The question of whether factual action should be allocated to public law or private law is a difficult one. In these cases, court decisions consider the context. For example, if a minister warns against eating unhealthy food not as a private individual but in his or her capacity as a sovereign authority, then the persons affected must turn to the administrative courts. If the rights of a citizen are infringed by administrative factual action, judicial review can be obtained by means of an action to prohibit such factual acts for the future (general action for performance, see below 5.4.2.) or an action for a declaratory judgement (see 5.4.3.) that the factual act was unlawful.

4. RULES AND PRINCIPLES GOVERNING ADMINISTRATIVE ACTION

As seen above, German administrative law distinguishes between general administrative law, which is mainly, but not wholly, stipulated in the Administrative Procedure Acts, and special administrative law, which is governed by a multitude of statutes, executive regulations and administrative directives. The following section will first deal with general administrative law, focussing on the rules and principles governing administrative proceedings. Then, four fields of special administrative law will briefly be examined.

4.1. GENERAL ADMINISTRATIVE LAW

4.1.1. Administrative Proceedings

Administrative proceedings are important not only for the efficient and effective discharge of duties. They also serve the purpose of early protection of citizens' rights. The Federal Constitutional Court has stressed several times that the Basic Law requires the "protection of fundamental rights through procedure" (*Grundrechtsschutz durch Verfahren*).[75] In addition, a sound procedure may enhance the democratic legitimacy of administrative decisions (*Legitimation durch Verfahren*).[76]

74 For details on informal administrative action, see M. Fehling, 'Informelles Verwaltungshandeln' in: W. Hoffmann-Riem, E. Schmidt-Assmann and A. Vosskuhle (eds.), *Grundlagen des Verwaltungsrechts*, Volume 2, 2nd ed., C. H. Beck, Munich 2012, pp.1457 ff.

75 BVerfGE 53, 30, 65.

76 H. Pünder, 'Administrative Procedure – Mere Facilitator of Material Law versus Cooperative Realization of Common Welfare', in: H. Pünder and C. Waldhoff (eds.), *Debates in German Public Law*, Hart, Oxford 2014, pp. 239, 245–249.

4.1.1.1. Procedural Rights

The major procedural rights are embodied in the Administrative Procedure Acts (see 1.4.2.). The authority must investigate the facts of the case "ex officio" (§ 24 Administrative Procedure Act). The so-called principle of inquisition applies. If the authority issues an administrative act that interferes with the rights of a citizen, the affected party must be heard before the administrative act is rendered (§ 28 (I) Administrative Procedure Act). Citizens also have the right to inspect the files (§ 29 Administrative Procedure Act), which is, however, limited by the right to secrecy (§ 30 Administrative Procedure Act). In the proceedings, the parties may also be represented by an authorised person (§ 14 Administrative Procedure Act). An administrative act may be filed orally, electronically or in writing (§ 37 Administrative Procedure Act). No strict form requirement applies. However, if the administration decides to issue an administrative act electronically or in writing, it must state the grounds for the administrative decision (§ 39 Administrative Procedure Act). The authority must inform the citizen about all of these procedural rights (§ 25 Administrative Procedure Act).[77] Furthermore, in order to ensure procedural fairness, certain persons that may be biased are excluded from the administrative decision making process (§ 20 Administrative Procedure Act). Where grounds exist to justify fears of prejudice of certain public servants, persons who are involved in administrative proceedings may apply for their exclusion (§ 21 Administrative Procedure Act).

4.1.1.2. Treatment of Procedural and Formal Errors

Any administrative act that has been rendered in violation of competences, procedural or formal requirements is "unlawful in terms of competence, procedure or form" (*formell rechtswidrig*). The decision may, however, be "lawful in terms of substantive law" (*materiell rechtmäßig*) if it complies with the law with regards to its merits. Against this background, certain procedural or formal errors may be rectified, which can still be done during the legal proceedings (§ 45 Administrative Procedure Act). If, for example, an administrative authority has not heard the addressee before the issuing of a burdensome administrative act, it may amend the hearing retroactively and thereby cure the procedural error (*Heilung*).[78] Also, regarding discretionary decisions (see 5.4.2.)

[77] For details, see H. Pünder, 'Verwaltungsverfahren' in: D. Ehlers and H. Pünder (eds.), *Allgemeines Verwaltungsrecht*, 15th ed., de Gruyter, Berlin 2016, pp. 405, 454 ff.

[78] For details, see H. Pünder, 'Verwaltungsverfahren' in: D. Ehlers and H. Pünder (eds.), *Allgemeines Verwaltungsrecht*, 15th ed., de Gruyter, Berlin 2016, pp. 405, 488 ff. For a comparative perspective of the treatment of procedural and formal errors in administrative judicial review, see H. Pünder and A. Klafki, 'Grounds of Review and Standard of Review' in: C. Backes and M. Eliantonio (eds.), *Judicial Review of Administrative Action*,

the administrative authority may supplement its discretionary considerations as to the administrative act in the proceedings before the administrative courts (§ 114 Sentence 2 Code of Administrative Court Procedure). However, as the administrative judge must act neutrally, the competent authority will not explicitly be asked to cure procedural or formal errors. It is rather the administration's responsibility to cure procedural or formal errors to avoid an unfavourable judgement.

If the error cannot be remedied or is not cured by the competent authority, the citizen may, in principle, demand the court to annul the administrative act on grounds of unlawfulness in terms of formal or procedural law. However, if the decision is lawful in terms of substantive law and only procedural or formal rules have been violated, the courts cannot quash the administrative act provided that it is obvious that the violation of formalities or procedure has had no influence on the decision's merits (§ 46 Administrative Procedure Act). This is only assumed in cases where the administration has no discretion at hand. The possibility of remedying procedural errors (§ 45 Administrative Procedure Act), and the fact that mere formal or procedural errors may be ignored by the courts (§ 46 Administrative Procedure Act), express the traditional German view that formal and procedural law only has an "auxiliary function" (*dienende Funktion*) of enforcing substantive law. However, legal scholars are increasingly critical of this view since it marginalises procedural laws.[79] Furthermore, the German view of formal and procedural laws conflicts with European law, where procedural and formal rules are seen as important means to effectuate EU law. Therefore, the scope of § 46 Administrative Procedure Act is restricted to "relative procedural and formal flaws". "Absolute errors" (*absolute Verfahrensfehler*) may never be seen as irrelevant. Incompetence is especially considered to be an "absolute error". Furthermore, the omission of an environmental impact assessment or procedural flaws thereof constitute absolute errors, which can never be irrelevant in the sense of § 46 Administrative Procedure Act.[80] However, as seen above, some procedural flaws as for example the omission of a public hearing can be cured by performing the hearing retroactively (§ 45 No. 3 Administrative Procedure Act).

Hart, Oxford, forthcoming. For a brief explanation of the consequences of procedural errors in German administrative law, see H. Pünder, 'German administrative procedure in a comparative perspective: Observations on the path to a transnational ius commune proceduralis in administrative law' (2013) 11 *ICON* 940, 953 ff.

79 For a critique, see H. Pünder, 'Verwaltungsverfahren' in: D. Ehlers and H. Pünder (eds.), *Allgemeines Verwaltungsrecht*, 15th ed., de Gruyter, Berlin 2016, pp. 405, 493 ff.; M. Sachs, 'Verfahrensfehler im Verwaltungsverfahren' in: W. Hoffmann-Riem, E. Schmidt-Assmann and A. Vosskuhle, *Grundlagen des Verwaltungsrechts, Band 2*, 2nd ed., C. H. Beck, Munich 2012, pp.799, 844.

80 Cf. CJEU, Case C-72/12 (*Altrip*), ECLI:EU:C:2013:712. For details, see I. Appel, 'Staat und Bürger in Umweltverwaltungsverfahren' 2012 NVwZ (Neue Zeitschrift für Verwaltungsrecht) 1366 ff.

4.1.2. *Principles Governing Administrative Law*

Even though German administrative law is characterised by statutory law, general principles also play a significant role.[81] They are, for the most part, either derived from the constitution or incorporated in statutory law.[82] Amongst others, the proportionality principle, the equality principle, and the principle of legal certainty and legitimate expectations are of particular importance in German administrative law. Here, the importance of constitutional law for German administrative law becomes visible (see also above 1.3.1).

4.1.2.1. Proportionality Principle

Every administrative decision that interferes with the fundamental rights of the citizen is assessed on the basis of the proportionality principle (*Verhältnismäßigkeitsgrundsatz*), which is rooted in the rule of law principle (Article 20 (II) Basic Law). It can be described as a core principle of German public law.[83] The proportionality principle is firmly rooted in administrative law jurisdiction as well as in literature.[84] According to German doctrine, the proportionality assessment encompasses four steps: the measure must pursue a legitimate statutory aim (*legitimes Ziel*); the measure must be suitable to achieve or facilitate a legitimate interest of the state (*Geeignetheit*); the suitable measure must also be necessary in the sense that there is no less restrictive means available to achieve the legitimate interest (*Erforderlichkeit*); and, the measure must be proportionate in the strict sense (*Angemessenheit*). The measure serving the legitimate interest must not be excessive in relation to the effects on the affected citizen. Thus, the competing interests must be balanced.

4.1.2.2. Equality Principle

The principle of equality is firmly rooted in Article 3 Basic Law. With regard to judicial scrutiny in the application of the equality principle, there is some

---

81 For a comparative perspective on the role of principles in administrative judicial review, see H. Pünder and A. Klafki, 'Grounds of Review and Standard of Review' in: C. Backes and M. Eliantonio (eds.), *Judicial Review of Administrative Action*, Hart, Oxford, forthcoming.

82 J. Schwarze, *European Administrative Law*, revised 1st ed., Sweet and Maxwell, London 2006, p. 120.

83 Cf. E. Grabitz, 'Der Grundsatz der Verhältnismäßigkeit in der Rechtsprechung des Bundesverfassungsgerichts' (1973) 98 *AöR (Archiv des öffentlichen Rechts)* 568 ff. See also N. Marsch and V. Tünsmeyer, 'The principle of proportionality in German administrative law' in: S. Ranchordás and B. de Waard (eds.), *The Judge and the Proportionate Use of Discretion*, Routledge, New York 2015, pp. 19 ff.

84 For a comprehensive overview of the German concept, see J. Schwarze, *European Administrative Law*, revised 1st ed., Sweet and Maxwell, London 2006, pp. 685 ff.

unsteadiness in the case law of the Federal Constitutional Court concerning the applicable test.[85] The adjudication of the Federal Constitutional Court is of particular importance in administrative law as it also influences and shapes the application of constitutional principles by the administrative courts. From the outset, the Federal Constitutional Court only quashed arbitrary administrative decisions by applying a test which is somewhat comparable to the reasonableness test in English law.[86] Later, the Court introduced a "new formula" (*Neue Formel*) to test the conformity of administrative or legislative decisions which affect fundamental freedoms of the addressee. This new formula increased the level of scrutiny and allowed the courts to engage in the balancing process.[87] In some decisions, the court emphasises that the judicial test for reviewing decisions in light of the equality principle is closely linked to the proportionality test.[88] However, the level of scrutiny is dependent on the context of the case. In situations where unequal treatment is based on criteria of human conduct and behaviour, judicial scrutiny may be less strict than in cases where the criteria are not amenable to personal influence.

4.1.2.3. Principle of Legal Certainty and Legitimate Expectations

According to the German understanding, the principles of legal certainty and of the protection of legitimate expectations are vested in Articles 20 and 28 of the Basic Law, which enshrine the rule of law principle (*Rechtsstaatsprinzip*).[89] With regard to the withdrawal of administrative acts, those principles are implemented in § 48 and § 49 Administrative Procedure Act. The law differs between the withdrawal of lawful administrative acts (*Rücknahme)* and the revocation of unlawful administrative decisions (*Widerruf*). In order to protect legitimate expectations, strict limitations apply to the revocation or withdrawal of beneficial administrative acts. Under certain circumstances, compensation for the withdrawal or revocation is granted. However, according to EU law, the provisions protecting legitimate expectations are strictly limited when illegal European subsidies have been granted. According to the *Alcan* judgement

85 For a summary of the development of case law with regard to Article 3 (I) Basic Law, see U. Kischel, in: V. Epping and C. Hillgruber (eds.), *Beck'scher Onlinekommentar Grundgesetz*, 32 Ed. 2017, Article 3 para 28 ff.

86 BVerfGE 1, 14, 52: 'The principle of equality is infringed if a sound reason for legal differentiation or equal treatment, resulting from the nature of things or which is otherwise objectively plausible, cannot be found, in short, if the provision must be described as arbitrary.'

87 See e.g. BVerfGE 55, 72, 88 f.

88 BVerfGE 129, 49.

89 BVerfGE 8, 155, 172; E 30, 367, 386; E 30, 392, 401 ff.

of the Federal Administrative Court[90], which follows the Court of Justice of the European Union (CJEU) adjudication[91], in these cases, the legitimate expectations of the addressee generally weigh less than the public interest to ensure the effectiveness of the EU law.

4.2. SPECIAL ADMINISTRATIVE LAW

The fields of "special administrative law" are as many and varied as the duties of the administration. This chapter will only deal with those four areas in which German law students have mandatory courses.

4.2.1. Police and Public Order Law (Polizei- und Ordnungsrecht) and Law concerning Assemblies (Versammlungsrecht)

Police and public order law (*Polizei- und Ordnungsrecht*) regulates the conditions in which the police and other "public order authorities" (*Ordnungsbehörden*) may limit the fundamental rights of citizens in order to ward off "dangers to public safety or to public order" (*Gefahr für die öffentliche Sicherheit und Ordnung*). ~~As the federal government has no legislative power in this field of law~~ (Article 70 Basic Law), ~~the laws of the states are relevant.~~ The state police laws all have a general clause for preventive measures undertaken by the police[92] and special provisions for standard measures such as, for example, search and seizure. Measures which affect the fundamental rights of individuals to a great extent need a special legal basis. They may not be taken on the basis of the general clause. All measures taken must be proportionate.[93] An important issue in police law is which conditions have to be fulfilled in order for the authorities to be allowed to limit the constitutional "right to informational self-determination" (*Recht auf informationelle Selbstbestimmung*).[94] Many states have detailed statutes on data collection and processing by the police and

[90] BVerwGE 106, 328 ff.

[91] ECJ, Case C-24/95 (*Alcan*), ECR 1997 I-01591, ECLI:EU:C:1997:163. See also M. Ruffert, 'Verwaltungsakt' in: D. Ehlers and H. Pünder (eds.), *Allgemeines Verwaltungsrecht*, 15th ed., de Gruyter, Berlin 2016, pp. 646, 695 ff.

[92] For example, § 8 (I) of the Police Law of North Rhine-Westphalia: 'The police can take the necessary measures to ward off a concrete threat to public security or order (danger) that exists in a specific situation [...].'

[93] For details, see T. Würtenberger, 'Polizei- und Ordnungsrecht' in: D. Ehlers, M. Fehling and H. Pünder (eds.), *Besonderes Verwaltungsrecht*, Volume 3, 3rd ed., C. F. Müller, Heidelberg 2013, pp. 398 ff.

[94] The right to informational self-determination has been developed by the Federal Constitutional Court in BVerfG 15.12.1983, BVerfGE 65, 1 (*Volkszählungsurteil*).

the respective administrative authorities.[95] This is, for example, relevant with regard to surveillance measures in order to prevent terrorist attacks.

A separate law applies if the administration wants to impose limiting conditions on assemblies (*Versammlungsrecht*). The federation used to be competent for the law of assemblies but, after a constitutional reform in 2006 (*Föderalismusreform I*), the states attained the competency to regulate this subject matter. Until now, six states have introduced their own assembly laws.[96] In all the other states the federal law of assemblies remains in force. As freedom of assembly is especially protected by Article 8 Basic Law, the laws quite intensively restrict the administrative powers of intervention in demonstrations.[97] The Federal Constitutional Court has shaped the law of assemblies remarkably.[98] This case law is of utmost importance to the administrative courts when they decide on disputes over assembly law.

4.2.2. Building Law (Baurecht)

German building law consists of two areas. The first concerns the determination of the use of land.[99] The federal government holds legislative power regarding the regulation of "regional planning" (Article 74(1) No. 31 GG). The Building Code (*Baugesetzbuch* – BauGB) includes regulations governing citizens' involvement in municipal "zoning plans" (*Bebauungspläne*), and sets out the conditions that must be fulfilled in order to erect, alter or change the permitted use of buildings and other structures.[100]

The second area that building law deals with is the protection against danger to "public safety and order".[101] As with general police and public order law, the states have legislative power in this regard. The states' building codes (*Bauordnungen*) indicate, for example, that the building authorities may order

95 For details, see T. Würtenberger, 'Polizei- und Ordnungsrecht' in: D. Ehlers, M. Fehling and H. Pünder (eds.), *Besonderes Verwaltungsrecht*, Volume 3, 3rd ed., C. F. Müller, Heidelberg 2013, pp. 398, 497–515.

96 Namely Bavaria, Berlin, Lower Saxony, Saxony, Saxony-Anhalt and Schleswig-Holstein.

97 For details see C. Enders, 'Versammlungsrecht' in: D. Ehlers, M. Fehling and H. Pünder (eds.), *Besonderes Verwaltungsrecht*, Volume 3, 3rd ed., C. F. Müller, Heidelberg 2013, pp. 557 ff.

98 See, for example: Federal Constitutional Court (BVerfG), 14.05.1985, BVerfGE 69, 315 ff. (*Brockdorf*); Federal Constitutional Court (BVerfG), BVerfGE 128, 226 ff (*Fraport*) = ECLI:DE:BVerfG:2011:rs20110222.1bvr069906.

99 For details on spatial planning law see D. Dörr and R. Yamato, 'Raumordnung und Landesplanung' in: D. Ehlers, M. Fehling and H. Pünder (eds.), *Besonderes Verwaltungsrecht*, Volume 2, 3rd ed., C. F. Müller, Heidelberg 2013, pp. 1 ff.

100 For details, see M. Wickel, 'Bauplanung', in: D. Ehlers, M. Fehling and H. Pünder (eds.), *Besonderes Verwaltungsrecht*, Volume 2, 3rd ed., C. F. Müller, Heidelberg 2013, pp. 86 ff.

101 A.-B. Kaiser, 'Bauordnungsrecht' in: D. Ehlers, M. Fehling and H. Pünder (eds.), *Besonderes Verwaltungsrecht*, Volume 2, 3rd ed., C. F. Müller, Heidelberg 2013, pp. 208 ff.

demolition of buildings which were erected or altered in violation of public law regulations.

4.2.3. *Environmental Law (Umweltrecht)*

Environmental law is gaining increasing importance in Germany. In 1994, an explicit provision was included in the Basic Law stating that the government must protect "natural resources for future generations" (Article 20a Basic Law). The federal government has legislative power regarding the core areas of environmental law.[102] Legal academics have called for a comprehensive "environmental code" (*Umweltgesetzbuch*) for many years, but so far no such codification has been created.[103] Environmental law regulations are instead spread over various statutes. Legal education mainly covers the following statutes: the Federal Emission Control Act (*Bundesimmissionsschutzgesetz*), the Federal Preservation of Nature Act (*Bundesnaturschutzgesetz*) and the Water Management Act (*Wasserhaushaltsgesetz*).

4.2.4. *Administrative Business Law (Wirtschaftsverwaltungsrecht)*

Administrative business law (*Wirtschaftsverwaltungsrecht*) concerns the administration's influence on the economy, the limits of the administration's economic activities and public procurement.[104] The federal level is competent for the "law relating to economic matters".[105] Trade law (*Gewerberecht*) is above all concerned with the protection against "dangers to public safety and order" and has a long-standing tradition. The most important regulations are contained in the Trade Code (*Gewerbeordnung*), which dates back to a statute enacted in 1869 for the North German Confederation (*Norddeutscher Bund*). In addition to this code, there are a number of special laws: the Skilled Crafts Code (*Handwerksordnung*), the Foreign Trade Act (*Außenwirtschaftsgesetz*), the Telecommunications Act (*Telekommunikationsgesetz*), the Energy Industry Act (*Energiewirtschaftsgesetz*), the Passenger Transport Act (*Personenbeförderungsgesetz*), the General Railways Act (*Allgemeines Eisenbahngesetz*) and the Restaurant Act (*Gaststättengesetz*). The influence of European Union law, which has been discussed above, is particularly strong with respect to the law of administration of the economy.

---

102 Article 74 (I) Nos 29 and 32 Basic Law.

103 M. Kloepfer, 'Allgemeine Grundlagen des Umweltrechts' in: D. Ehlers, M. Fehling and H. Pünder (eds.), *Besonderes Verwaltungsrecht,* Volume 2, 3rd ed., C. F. Müller, Heidelberg 2013, pp. 354, 361.

104 For details, see D. Ehlers, M. Fehling and H. Pünder (eds.), *Besonderes Verwaltungsrecht,* Volume 1, 3rd ed., C. F. Müller, Heidelberg 2012.

105 Article 74 (I) No. 11 Basic Law.

5. REVIEW OF ADMINISTRATIVE ACTION

As seen above, the review of administrative action plays a vivid role in the protection of fundamental rights. First of all, it has to be understood, that the German system of legal remedies is focussed on the protection of individual rights (see 5.1). Review of administrative action takes place within the administration (see 5.2.) as well as in front of the administrative courts (5.3.). The scope of review will be analysed with regard to administrative decision-making freedoms such as discretion (*Ermessen*) and the margin of interpretation (*Beurteilungsspielraum*) (5.4.). For judicial review of administrative action, there are different legal remedies (*Klagearten*), depending on which type of administrative action the claimant is challenging and on the outcome (annulment or administrative action) he desires (5.5.). Finally, the citizen may seek speedy protection through interim relief (5.6.).

5.1. PROTECTION OF INDIVIDUAL PUBLIC RIGHTS (*SUBJEKTIV ÖFFENTLICHE RECHTE*)

The German judicial review system is focussed on the protection of individual rights.[106] In contrast to the system in France, where interested parties may demand objective control of the legality of administrative action, in Germany, the admissibility of a remedial action always requires the allegation of the violation of an "individual public right" (*subjektives öffentliches Recht*). Thus, only aggrieved parties have standing. A special "theory of protective norms" (*Schutznormtheorie*) has been developed in German administrative law to establish whether the alleged infringed law grants an actionable individual public right or solely protects a "general public interest".[107]

---

106 For an in-depth analysis of this characteristic of German judicial review of administrative action, see B. Wegener, 'Subjective Public Rights' in: H. Pünder and C. Waldhoff (eds.), *Debates in German Public Law*, Hart, Oxford 2014, pp. 219–237.

107 For a comparative analysis of this aspect of the German judicial review system, see T. Perroud, 'Grounds of Review and Standard of Review' in: C. Backes and M. Eliantonio (eds.), *Judicial Review of Administrative Action*, Hart, Oxford, forthcoming. See also B. Wegener, 'Subjective Public Rights' in: H. Pünder and C. Waldhoff (eds.), *Debates in German Public Law*, Hart, Oxford 2014, p. 220.

5.2. PROTECTION OF RIGHTS WITHIN THE ADMINISTRATION

5.2.1. *Informal Remedies*

Protection of rights within the administration includes so-called informal remedies. Citizens may ask the competent authority to reconsider its decision (remonstrance – *Gegenvorstellung*), or may resort to the supervisory authority requesting it to correct the decision of the initial authority (*Fachaufsichtsbeschwerde*). This process is based on the "right of petition", which is embodied in the constitution and stipulates that anybody has the right to address the competent authorities if they have a request or a complaint (Article 17 Basic Law). Citizens are not entitled to a specific decision, however, they have a right to an objective review of and response to their petition.

5.2.2. *Intra-administrative Objection Proceedings (Widerspruchsverfahren)*

In some cases an intra-administrative objection proceeding (*Widerspruchsverfahren*) is obligatory.[108] Before citizens can file an "action for annulment of an administrative act" (*Anfechtungsklage*) or an "action for issuing an administrative act" (*Verpflichtungsklage*) to the court (see below 5.4.), they must first lodge an intra-administrative objection (*Widerspruch*) against the challenged administrative act (§ 68 (I) Code of Administrative Court Procedure) or against the refusal to grant the administrative act (§ 68 (II) Code of Administrative Court Procedure).[109] The objection must be made in writing within one month after the administrative act has been announced to the aggrieved party (§ 70 Code of Administrative Court Procedure). Otherwise the administrative decision becomes non-appealable (*Bestandskraft*) and the court will dismiss any claim against it as inadmissible. However, the deadline period for the objection of one month is only initiated if the party concerned has been informed about the formalities and the deadline of the intra-administrative objection properly (§ 58 Code of Administrative Court Procedure).

In the intra-administrative objection procedure, the administration not only reviews the lawfulness of the administrative act (*Rechtmäßigkeit*), but

[108] For details, see F. Schoch, 'Widerspruchsverfahren' in: D. Ehlers and F. Schoch, *Rechtsschutz im Öffentlichen Recht*, De Gruyter, Berlin 2009, pp. 485 ff.

[109] For a comparative perspective on the necessary or facultative character of inter-administrative objection procedures throughout Europe, see M. Eliantio, 'Organisation of Judicial Review in Administrative Matters and Intra-Administrative Objection Procedure' in: C. Backes and M. Eliantonio (eds.), *Judicial Review of Administrative Action*, Hart, Oxford, forthcoming.

also its expediency (*Zweckmäßigkeit*, § 68 (I) Code of Administrative Court Procedure). If the initial authority does not "remedy" the objection (§ 72 Code of Administrative Court Procedure), the superior authority will issue a decision on the objection (*Widerspruchsbescheid*).[110] The initial authority which issued the original administrative act has no means to challenge the decision of the higher authority on the objection. The decision on the objection must be reasoned and inform about the judicial remedies available (§ 72 (III) Code of Administrative Court Procedure). It is disputed whether within the intra-administrative objection procedure the competent authority may also change its decision to the detriment of the complainant (*reformatio in peius*). The Federal Administrative Court (*Bundesverwaltungsgericht*) answered this question in the affirmative.[111]

If the objection is dismissed or if the aggrieved citizen is unsatisfied with the decision on the objection, he can file an action for annulment (*Anfechtungsklage*) or – in case of the refusal of a permit – an action for issuing an administrative act (*Verpflichtungsklage*, see 5.5.1.) within one month (§ 74 Code of Administrative Court Procedure). The subject matter of this action then is the original administrative act with the alterations which it has gained through the ruling on the objection (§ 79 (I) Code of Administrative Court Procedure). According to § 79 (II) Code of Administrative Court Procedure, the ruling on an objection can also be the sole subject-matter of the annulment action if and insofar as it contains an additional separate grievance *vis-à-vis* the original administrative act. For example, if a citizen objects against an administrative act which obliges him to cut three trees in his garden and the ruling on the objection states that he even has to cut ten trees, he can decide only to claim against the aggravation by the ruling on the objection and accept the original administrative act. If the aggrieved citizen fails to file the claim in due time, the administrative act becomes non-appealable (*bestandskräftig*).

110 § 73 Code of Administrative Court Procedure.
111 BVerwGE 51, 310, 314.

5.3. ADJUDICATION OF ADMINISTRATIVE COURTS

Figure 4. Court organization in Germany

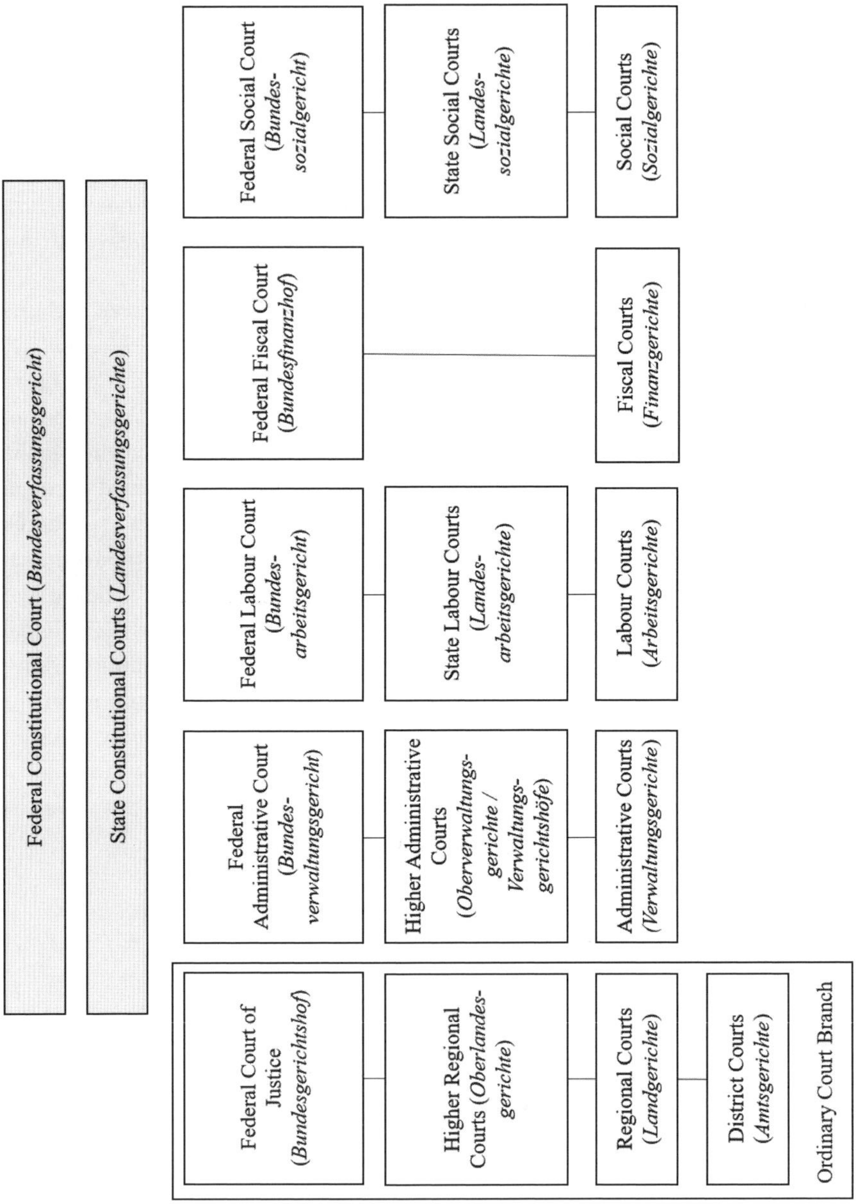

5.3.1. Administrative Court System

The administrative court system, as opposed to that of the "ordinary courts" (*ordentliche Gerichte*), has been dealt with above (see 1.5.). In this context it should be added, that there are also some "special administrative courts". Tax law disputes, for example, are settled by "finance courts" (*Finanzgerichte*) pursuant to the Finance Courts Code (*Finanzgerichtsordnung* – FGO) (§ 33 FGO). In social law matters the "social courts" (*Sozialgerichte*) have jurisdiction pursuant to the Social Courts Act (*Sozialgerichtsgesetz* – SGG) (§ 51 SGG). All other public law disputes of a non-constitutional nature can be brought before the general administrative courts according to § 40 Code of Administrative Court Procedure.

The structure of the German administrative courts system is described in § 2 Code of Administrative Court Procedure: "Courts of administrative jurisdiction in the states (*Länder*) shall be the Administrative Courts (*Verwaltungsgerichte*) and one Higher Administrative Court (*Oberverwaltungsgericht* or *Verwaltungsgerichtshof*) each, in the Federation they shall be the Federal Administrative Court (*Bundesverwaltungsgericht*), which shall have its seat in Leipzig." Thus, the courts of first instance are the Administrative Courts (§ 45 Code of Administrative Court Procedure). Their "chambers" (*Kammern*, i.e. panels) are made up of three professional judges and two lay assessors. Appeals on grounds of fact and law (*Berufungen*) are dealt with by "senates" at the Higher Administrative Courts (*Oberverwaltungsgerichte*), which consist of three professional judges (§ 46 Code of Administrative Court Procedure). Ultimately, the Federal Administrative Court (*Bundesverwaltungsgericht*) is the court in charge of appeals on points of law (*Revisionen*) (§ 49 Code of Administrative Court Procedure).

In principle, these are all stages of appeal.[112] However, citizens may still file an appeal known as a "constitutional complaint" (*Verfassungsbeschwerde*) with the Federal Constitutional Court after the exhaustion of all other legal administrative law remedies, if fundamental rights have been violated.[113]

5.3.2. Investigation Principle (Untersuchungsgrundsatz)

Administrative law judges investigate the relevant facts of the case *ex officio* (§ 86 (I) Code of Administrative Court Procedure). They are not bound by the parties' pleadings or motions to take evidence. This investigation principle (*Untersuchungsgrundsatz*), which also applies in criminal proceedings and proceedings before finance courts and social courts, is based on the idea that

---

[112] For details, see F. Hufen, *Verwaltungsprozessrecht*, 10th ed., C.H. Beck, Munich 2016, pp. 53 ff.

[113] Article 93 (I) No. 4a Basic Law.

the public interest in a correct decision requires an objectively correct and complete investigation of the facts and circumstances.[114] This is the material difference from civil proceedings before the ordinary courts of law, to which the Roman law rule "*da mihi factum, dabo tibi ius*" applies, i.e. the principle that the parties must present all relevant facts (§ 282 of the German Code of Civil Procedure, *Zivilprozessordnung* – ZPO). Administrative proceedings do not, however, strictly comply with the investigation principle. In the case of disputed issues, the involved parties must provide and prove those facts accountable to them. Accordingly, they bear the burden of proof (*Beweislast*).[115] Due to the investigation principle, the requirements for the reasoning of a claim are fairly low. Generally, the claimant only has to present facts in order to make plausible that his subjective public rights have been infringed.

5.3.3. *Costs of Court Proceedings*

In principle, for all types of administrative court proceedings process costs arise which have to be paid by the losing party (§ 154 (I) Code of Administrative Court Procedure). Nonetheless, there are particular fields of administrative law as e.g. asylum law and educational support law where no costs are levied. The court rules on the costs in the judgement (§ 161 Code of Administrative Court Procedure). Proceeding costs include the court costs (fees and expenses) and the expenditure of those concerned necessary to properly pursue or defend rights, including the costs of the intra-administrative objection proceedings (*Wiederspruchsverfahren*). However, in the first instance there is no obligation to be represented by a lawyer. This might reduce the costs, as the administration is usually represented by its own officers.

There are statutory court fees which depend on the economic value of the subject matter of the case (*Streitwert*). The value of the subject matter of the action is determined by the courts. If there are no concrete indications relating to the economic value of the subject matter of an action, the court will normally set it to 5.000 Euro pursuant to § 52 (II) of the Court Fees Act (*Auffangstreitwert*). The court fees for such a court action in front of a lower administrative court would then amount to 438 Euro if normal court proceedings took place.

According to § 166 (I) Code of Administrative Court Procedure, legal aid in administrative court proceedings is provided to the same extent as in civil law procedure. Pursuant to §§ 114 ff. Code of Civil Procedure (*Zivilprozessordnung*, ZPO), any parties who, due to their personal and economic circumstances, are unable to pay the costs of litigation, or are able to pay them only in part or only as instalments, will be granted assistance with the court costs upon filing

---

114 S. Rixen, in: H. Sodan and J. Ziekow (eds.), *Verwaltungsgerichtsordnung*, 4th ed., Nomos, Baden-Baden 2014, § 86 para. 7.

115 F. Hufen, *Verwaltungsprozessrecht*, 10th ed., C.H. Beck, Munich 2016, pp. 544 f.

a corresponding application, provided that the action they intend to bring or their defence against an action that has been brought against them has sufficient prospects of success and does not seem frivolous. The application for approval of assistance with court costs is to be submitted to the court hearing the case.[116] The application is to summarize the case and to cite the evidence. With the application, the party is to include a declaration describing his personal and economic circumstances (family circumstances, profession, assets, income and financial obligations), and is to attach the corresponding proof.

5.3.4. *Grounds for Review*

Unlike

Other than in the French or in the English legal system, there is no categorization of grounds for review.[117] German legal doctrine only differs between "formal illegality" (*formelle Rechtswidrigkeit*) – which encompasses errors of competence, procedure or form – and substantial illegality (*materielle Rechtswidrigkeit*). Formal illegality includes incompetence, procedural flaws and defects of form such as, for example, insufficient reasoning or the violation of a written form requirement.[118] As seen above (4.1.1.2.), procedural and formal errors often do not lead to the annulment of administrative acts, unless they also substantially affect the administrative decision.

Substantial illegality covers all sorts of flaws relating to the merits of the decision, such as the requirement of a legal basis for burdensome administrative action, law infringements, indeterminacy of the decision, discretionary errors (*Ermessensfehler*, see below 5.4.2.), proportionality (see 4.1.2.1.) and the legal or factual impossibility of execution. In principle, the administrative courts scrutinise the entire administrative action unless the law, by exception, grants the administration special freedoms such as discretion or a margin of interpretation (see below 5.4.1.).[119] Generally, the administrative courts always scrutinise the formal and material illegality of the challenged administrative action. Thus, in Germany, the last authoritative interpretation of administrative

---

116 It may be recorded with the registry for the files of the court (§ 117 (I) ZPO).

117 Therefore, the description by M. P. Singh, *German Administrative Law in Common Law Perspective*, Springer, Berlin 2001, pp. 136–149, where he categorises the German judicial review into different grounds of review, might be, to some extent, misleading. It is important to understand that the concept of grounds for review does not exist in the German administrative judicial review system. For a comparative perspective on the grounds for review in judicial review of administrative action, see H. Pünder and A. Klafki, 'Grounds for Review and Standards for Review' in: C. Backes and M. Eliantonio (eds.), *Judicial Review of Administrative Action*, Hart, Oxford, forthcoming.

118 See H. Pünder, 'German Administrative Law', in: F. J. Heidinger and A. Hubalek (eds.), *Anglo-American Legal Language* 3, BDÜ Fachverlag, Vienna 2016, pp. 79, 86 f.

119 See also E. Schmidt-Assmann and C. Möllers, 'The Scope and Accountability of Executive Power in Germany', in: P. P. Craig and A. Tomkins (eds.), *The Executive and Public Law*, Oxford University Press 2006, pp. 268, 286.

law generally rests with the administrative courts.[120] As mentioned above, the focus of judicial review in Germany lies on the protection of individual rights. Thus, flaws which do not infringe the subjective rights of the claimant will regularly not form a proper basis for judicial action. Exceptions to this rule can be found in environmental law due to the influence of European law.[121]

5.3.5. *Appellate Proceedings*

The German judicial appeal system differs between appeals on grounds of fact and law (§§ 124 ff. Code of Administrative Court Procedure, *Berufung*) and appeals only on grounds of law (§§ 132 ff. Code of Administrative Court Procedure, *Revision*).[122] In principle, an appeal on grounds of fact and law is the regular remedy against first instance court rulings, whereas an appeal on grounds of law is normally filed against second instance rulings. However, under certain conditions, an appeal on grounds of law can also be filed against a first instance ruling, thereby circumventing the second instance (*Sprungrevision*).

Both remedies, i.e. appeals on grounds of fact and law and appeals on grounds of law are only admissible after the judicial grant of leave. Only aggrieved participants of the preceding process may file an appeal. Third parties who participated in the first (and second) instance proceedings are only aggrieved where the challenged judgement directly affects their individual rights. In second and third instance proceedings § 67 Code of Administrative Court Procedure stipulates a duty to legal representation.

5.4. THE ADMINISTRATION'S FREEDOM OF MANOEUVRE AND INTENSITY OF JUDICIAL REVIEW

In all jurisdictions, the question arises as to what extent a freedom of manoeuvre of the administration can be recognised and to what extent the review by the courts should be limited. In Germany, administrative law norms are

[120] For an overview, see W. Kahl, 'Deutschland' in: A. von Bogdandy, S. Cassese and P. M. Huber, Handbuch Ius Publicum Europaeum, Volume 5, C. F. Müller, Heidelberg 2016, § 74 para 127 f.

[121] For details, see Article 2, 4 Environmental Appeals Act (*Umweltrechtsbehelfsgesetz*). An English translation is available under www.bmub.bund.de/fileadmin/bmu-import/files/english/pdf/application/pdf/umwelt_rechtsbehelfsgesetz_en_bf.pdf, assessed 30.04.2017. See also A. K. Mangold, 'The Persistance of National Peculiarities: Translating Representative Environmental Action from Transnational into German Law, (2014) 21 *Indiana Journal of Global Legal Studies*, 223 ff.

[122] For details, see F. Hufen, *Verwaltungsprozessrecht*, 10th ed., C.H. Beck, Munich 2016, pp. 605 ff. For a comparative perspective, see R. Widdershoven, 'Appellate Proceedings' in: C. Backes and M. Eliantonio (eds.), *Judicial Review of Administrative Action*, Hart, Oxford, forthcoming.

traditionally structured in a conditional way, with an "if-side" (*Tatbestand*), naming certain factual prerequisites, and a "then-side" (*Rechtsfolge*), defining which legal measures can be taken if the factual prerequisites are fulfilled.[123] With regard to administrative decision-making freedoms, a distinction must be drawn between a "margin of interpretation" (*Beurteilungsspielraum*), used to interpret "non-defined legal terms" (*unbestimmte Rechtsbegriffe*), on the "if-side", and "discretion" (*Ermessen*) in terms of the legal consequences on the "then-side" of the norm.[124]

5.4.1. *Margin of Interpretation (Beurteilungsspielraum)*

Due to the protection of rights granted by Article 19 (IV) Basic Law, the administration generally has no administrative freedoms with regard to the interpretation of non-defined legal notions. Examples of indefinite legal terms include legal concepts such as "public welfare", "public interest", "public need" and "public safety", which are commonly used in the statutes conferring powers on the administrative authorities. The interpretation of these terms is, as a general rule, fully reviewable by the courts.[125] Only in exceptional cases is an administrative "margin of interpretation" (*Beurteilungsspielraum*) recognised which entitles the administration to own factual assessments and is only controlled with limited scrutiny.[126] This is the case, for example, for examinations in schools or universities, for hiring and assessments of civil servants, and for the appraisal of decisions of a pluralist body of experts. Also, with regard to complex technical assessments (for example, the permission of nuclear power plants) a margin of interpretation is accepted by the courts. Here, it would be inappropriate if the courts replaced the administrative evaluation with their own assessments. In all these exceptional cases, the judiciary only examines whether procedural rules were observed, whether the facts and circumstances on which the decision was based were correct, whether consideration was given to irrelevant aspects, and whether "generally accepted evaluation standards" (*allgemein anerkannte Beurteilungsmaßstäbe*) were observed.[127]

---

[123] See also N. G. Foster and S. Sule, *German Legal System & Laws*, 3rd ed., Oxford University Press, New York 2002, p. 225.

[124] However, the distinction between margin of interpretation on the one hand and discretion on the other hand is contested in doctrinal writing. See O. Bachof, 'Beurteilungsspielraum, Ermessen und unbestimmter Rechtsbegriff im Verwaltungsrecht', 1955 JZ (*JuristenZeitung*), 97 ff.; M. Jestaedt, 'Maßstäbe des Verwaltungshandelns' in: D. Ehlers and H. Pünder (eds.), *Allgemeines Verwaltungsrecht*, 15th ed., de Gruyter, Berlin 2016, pp. 325, 332–371.

[125] For example, the Federal Administrative Court (BVerwG) held that the terms "serious reasons" (BVerwGE 15, 207, 208), "artistic value" (BVerwGE 23, 194, 200) and "suitability of a building as a monument" (BVerwGE 24, 60, 63 ff.) were fully reviewable.

[126] For a brief explanation see N. G. Foster and S. Sule, *German Legal System & Laws*, 3rd ed., Oxford University Press, New York 2002, pp. 256 f.

[127] For details, see H. Maurer and C. Waldhoff, *Allgemeines Verwaltungsrecht*, 19th ed., C.H. Beck, Munich 2017, pp. 157 ff.

5.4.2. *Discretionary Decisions (Ermessensentscheidungen)*

In terms of legal consequences, German doctrine distinguishes between "mandatory decisions" (*gebundene Entscheidungen*) and "discretionary decisions" (*Ermessensentscheidungen*). Discretion is implied in statutory provisions when, in the "then-part" of the norm, expressions such as "can", "may", or "is entitled to" are used.[128] The expressions "must" or "has to" indicate mandatory decisions. Where a statutory provision states that the administration "should" (*soll*) take a certain measure, the administration is generally bound to take that measure but has discretionary power in atypical factual circumstances.[129]

With regard to discretionary decisions, where the public authority can choose from different actions, the courts may only review the decision with regard to "discretionary errors" (*Ermessensfehler*) (§ 114 Code of Administrative Court Procedure).[130] If the authority did not realise that it had discretion in making its decision this constitutes a "failure to use discretion" (*Ermessensnichtgebrauch*). Incorrect use of discretion (*Ermessensfehlgebrauch*) arises when the administration has failed to investigate all relevant aspects or has considered irrelevant aspects. If a public authority fails to observe the statutory or constitutional limits of its authority, it has exceeded its discretion (*Ermessensüberschreitung*). This is especially true if a decision is deemed "disproportionate" (*unverhältnismäßig*), i.e. not suitable (*nicht geeignet*), not necessary (*nicht erforderlich*) or not proportionate *sensu stricto* (*nicht angemessen*) (see above 4.1.2.1.).

Moreover, German administrative law recognizes the category of the "reduction of discretion to zero" (*Ermessensreduzierung auf Null*). It means that, in spite of the theoretically existing choice given by the discretionary power to act one way or the other, in some specific cases only one course of action may be legal because all other options are disproportionate. In this case, the authority is obliged to only follow the legal and proportionate course of action.[131]

5.5. TYPES OF COURT ACTIONS AND SPECIAL PREREQUISITES FOR A JUDGEMENT ON THE MERITS

The German law distinguishes between several different kinds of court actions. This distinction is very important for judicial review of administrative action,

---

128 H. Maurer and C. Waldhoff, *Allgemeines Verwaltungsrecht*, 19th ed., C.H. Beck, Munich 2017, p. 145.

129 See BVerwGE 49, 16, 23; BVerwGE 318, 323; BVerwGE 90, 88, 93.

130 H. Maurer and C. Waldhoff, *Allgemeines Verwaltungsrecht*, 19th ed., C.H. Beck, Munich 2017, pp. 147 ff.

131 For example, the inspectors of buildings have full discretion as to whether or not they intervene if the owner of a building misuses his building. But where legally protected interests of neighbours are infringed or endangered by such misuse, the administration is under an obligation to intervene, BVerwGE 11, 95, 97; see also BVerwGE 47, 280, 283; BVerwGE 56, 63.

as the prerequisites for admissibility as well as the ruling of the court differ. Generally, before the administrative courts decide whether a claim is well-founded based on its merits, i.e. whether the administrative action was unlawful and a "subjective right" of the claimant was infringed, they will examine whether the claim is admissible (*zulässig*).[132] Admissibility depends on whether special prerequisites for rendering a judgement (*Sachentscheidungsvoraussetzungen*) are fulfilled which in turn depends on the type of action implemented. The question as to which types of action are admissible depends on the claim and the remedies sought (§ 88 Code of Administrative Court Procedure) and, crucially, on whether or not an "administrative act" (*Verwaltungsakt*, see above 3.1.) is involved. In all administrative court proceedings, the competing parties may at any time conclude a judicial settlement for the record of the court in order to end the court proceedings (§ 106 Code of Administrative Court Procedure).

5.5.1. *Action for Annulment of an Administrative Act (Anfechtungsklage) and Action for Issuing an Administrative Act (Verpflichtungsklage)*

If the claimant desires the annulment of a burdensome administrative act, such as a building-law demolition order (see 4.2.2.), an "action for annulment of an administrative act" (*Anfechtungsklage*) is the correct legal remedy (§ 42 (I) 1st alternative and § 113 (V) Code of Administrative Court Procedure).[133] If the claimant succeeds the administrative court will quash the challenged administrative act *ex tunc*. In order to be successful, the claimant must prove, that the challenged administrative act infringes an individual public right.

If the plaintiff wishes to obtain a beneficial administrative act, such as a building permit, an "action for issuing an administrative act" (*Verpflichtungs-klage*) (§ 42 (I) 2nd alternative and § 113 (V) Code of Administrative Court Procedure) must be filed[134], comparable to the "writ of mandamus" in English law.[135] As the issuing of administrative acts falls in the core competencies of the administration, the court cannot directly rule on the desired administrative act but will only compel the competent authority to issue the required administrative act in its judgement. The plaintiff must be entitled to the desired administrative act in order to be successful. He or she needs to have an "individual public

132 For a brief description of the prerequisites of admissibility such as competent court, competence to pursue action etc., see M. P. Singh, *German Administrative Law in Common Law Perspective*, Springer, Berlin 2001, pp. 213–222. For a brief explanation of the German concept of a subjective public right N. G. Foster and S. Sule, *German Legal System & Laws*, 3rd ed., Oxford University Press, New York 2002, p. 258.

133 For details, see D. Ehlers, 'Anfechtungsklage' in: D. Ehlers and F. Schoch, *Rechtsschutz im Öffentlichen Recht*, De Gruyter, Berlin 2009, pp. 603–640.

134 D. Ehlers, 'Verpflichtungsklage' in: D. Ehlers and F. Schoch, *Rechtsschutz im Öffentlichen Recht*, De Gruyter, Berlin 2009, pp. 641–658.

135 N. G. Foster and S. Sule, *German Legal System & Laws*, 3rd ed., Oxford University Press, New York 2002, p. 269.

right" to the sought administrative act. For example, in building law an individual public right to a building permit follows form the right to property (Article 14 Basic Law) in conjunction with the respective state building law, as long as the building project is compatible with building law. However, if the release of the sought administrative act constitutes a discretionary decision, the claimant can generally only file a suit for issuing an "administrative act free from discretionary errors" (*ermessensfehlerfreie Entscheidung*, § 113 (5) second sentence Code of Administrative Court Procedure). The court will then give an advisory judgement (*Bescheidungsurteil*) on the limits of discretion. Only if the "discretion is reduced to zero" (*Ermessensreduzierung auf Null*), the claimant can demand a judgement to compel the administration to issue the sought administrative act (§ 113 (V) sentence 1 Code of Administrative Court Procedure). This is the case when only one decision is free from discretionary errors.

As explained above (5.2.2.), both actions – the action for annulment of an administrative act (*Anfechtungsklage*) as well as the action for issuing an administrative act (*Verpflichtungsklage*) – require that the claimant initially completed the intra-administrative objection procedure (*Widerspruchsverfahren*) (§ 68 Code of Administrative Court Procedure) and observed the one-month deadline (§ 74 Code of Administrative Court Procedure). In addition, *locus standi* is only granted to the claimant if, according to his allegations, it seems possible that the administration infringed an "individual public right" (*subjektives öffentliches Recht*) of the claimant by issuing the challenged administrative act or by the refusal to grant an administrative act (§ 42 (II) Code of Administrative Court Procedure).

If an administrative act that has a positive effect on third parties is challenged, the courts will examine very closely whether the claimant has standing (*Klagebefugnis*).[136] This is in particular the case in building law, business law or the law of subsidies if a third party challenges an administrative act that favours someone else (such as a building permit) or wishes to obtain an administrative act that aggrieves someone else (such as a building law demolition order). Standing requires that the claimant is able to rely on an "individual public right".[137] For this purpose the "theory of protective norms" (*Schutznormtheorie*) applies.[138] According to this theory, a statutory provision (law or regulation) need not only impose an objective duty on the administration

---

136 For a comparative analysis of the requirement of standing in different European legal systems, see C. Backes, 'Access to Courts' in: C. Backes and M. Eliantonio (eds.), *Judicial Review of Administrative Action*, Hart, Oxford, forthcoming.

137 For an in-depth discussion of the German model of administrative legal redress with regard to European developments, see B. Wegener, 'Subjective Public Rights' in: H. Pünder and C. Waldhoff (eds.), *Debates in German Public Law*, Hart, Oxford 2014, pp. 219 ff.

138 B. Wegener, 'Subjective Public Rights' in: H. Pünder and C. Waldhoff (eds.), *Debates in German Public Law*, Hart, Oxford 2014, p. 220.

in the public interest that *de facto* favours the claimant, but must "at least also serve the purpose of protecting individual interests". The court must, by way of interpretation of the provision, discover whether the norm merely constitutes a "positive legal reflex" (*positiver Rechtsreflex*), which does not entitle the citizen to base a legal action on it, or whether it is a "protective statutory provision" (*Schutznorm*). In doing so, the court considers whether the statutory provision indicates a clearly defined group of entitled persons, i.e. a group which can be individualised and is not very large. For example, in building law, the interdiction to erect disfiguring buildings, installations or advertisements (*Verunstaltungsverbot*) is no such protective statutory provision (*Schutznorm*), as it protects only the general public. Thus, citizens cannot ask for a demolition order on that basis, because no subjective public right is infringed.

5.5.2. *General Action for Performance (allgemeine Leistungsklage)*

If a claimant wishes to appeal against factual action of public authorities or if he demands a certain factual action of the administration, he may invoke a "general action for performance" (*allgemeine Leistungsklage*).[139] By this action a claimant can seek an administrative performance or an omission. If the claimant is successful, the court will sentence the administration to perform the required action. In contrast to the action to annul an administrative act or to issue an administrative act, the general action for performance is aimed at factual action by the administration (see above 3.6.). For example, by means of a general action for performance, the claimant may require that a public construction site be better secured so that his customers do not hurt themselves. Furthermore, he can claim that the administration will no longer publish an official warning against eating certain foodstuffs, which he produces. For such an action to succeed, "standing" is also required (analogous to § 42 (II) Code of Administrative Court Procedure). Thus, the claimant must rely on a "subjective public right" (*subjektives öffentliches Recht*) to the desired action.

5.5.3. *Action for a Declaratory Judgement (Feststellungsklage)*

Another option is an "action for a declaratory judgement" (*Feststellungsklage*), which concerns a "declaration of the existence or non-existence of a legal relationship" or a "declaration of nullity of an administrative act" (§ 43 Code of Administrative Court Procedure).[140] According to the wording of § 43 Code of Administrative Court Procedure, the claimant must merely have a "legitimate

---

139 For details, see D. Ehlers, 'Allgemeine verwaltungsgerichtliche Leistungsklage' in: D. Ehlers and F. Schoch, *Rechtsschutz im Öffentlichen Recht*, De Gruyter, Berlin 2009, pp. 659–671.

140 For details, see D. Ehlers, 'Verwaltungsgerichtliche Feststellungsklage' in: D. Ehlers and F. Schoch, *Rechtsschutz im Öffentlichen Recht*, De Gruyter, Berlin 2009, pp. 673–699.

interest in a declaration in the near future" (*berechtigtes Interesse an der baldigen Feststellung*). Any legal, financial or non-material legitimate interest is sufficient. However, the Federal Administrative Court also requires locus standi according to § 42 (II) Code of Administrative Court Procedure. Thus, the claimant also needs to rely on a "subjective public right". An action for a declaratory judgement is "subsidiary". That means that an action for declaration is inadmissible if the claimant is or would have been able to pursue his rights by filing an action for the annulment or issuing of an administrative act or a general action for performance (*Leistungsklage*) (§ 43 (II) Code of Administrative Court Procedure).[141]

5.5.4. Norm Control (Normenkontrolle)

Finally, there is the "action to norm control" (*Normenkontrolle*) for the review of delegated legislation (§ 47 Code of Administrative Court Procedure).[142] Parliamentary statutes can only be reviewed by the Constitutional Courts (Art. 93 (I) no. 2a, Art. 100 Basic Law). Thus, by way the of "norm control" the validity of executive regulations (*Rechtsverordnungen*) and byelaws (*Satzungen*) of the states can be challenged. The competent courts for this procedure are the Higher Administrative Courts (*Oberverwaltungsgerichte*), which are – as seen above (5.3.) – courts of the states. Therefore, regulations of the federation may not be subject of a norm control action according to § 47 Code of Administrative Court Procedure.

If the court is convinced that the challenged regulation or bylaw is illegal, it will annul it. A judgement on this action has an *inter omnes* effect (§ 47 (I) Code of Administrative Court Procedure), whereas all the other actions described above only lead to judgements with *inter partes* effect. This type of action is particularly important in the context of municipal zoning plans.

5.6. INTERIM RELIEF

5.6.1. Suspensive Effect (Suspensiveffekt) of Intra-administrative Objections and Actions for Annulment of an Administrative Act

A very distinct feature of German administrative law is that, as a general rule, filing an intra-administrative objection (*Widerspruch*) or an action to

141 Also worth mentioning is the remedy of *Fortsetzungsfeststellungsklage*, which is relevant if an administrative act has been settled (*erledigt*) by withdrawal or otherwise before or after the court action was brought (§ 113(1) 4th sentence Code of Administrative Court Procedure). In these cases, the action for annulment or for the issuing of an administrative act can be converted to an action for declaration. For details, see D. Ehlers, 'Verwaltungsgerichtliche Fortsetzungsfeststellungsklage' in: D. Ehlers and F. Schoch, *Rechtsschutz im Öffentlichen Recht*, De Gruyter, Berlin 2009, pp. 659–671.

142 For details, see D. Ehlers, 'Verwaltungsgerichtliche Normenkontrolle' in: D. Ehlers and F. Schoch, *Rechtsschutz im Öffentlichen Recht*, De Gruyter, Berlin 2009, pp. 725–743.

annul an administrative act (*Anfechtungsklage*) suspends the enforcement of the challenged administrative act. These remedies thus have a "suspensive effect" (*Suspensiveffekt*, § 80 (I) Code of Administrative Court Procedure).[143] Consequently, the administrative act does not need to be complied with and the authority may not enforce it by means of coercion.

Of course, there are important exceptions to this rule in § 80 (II) Code of Administrative Court Procedure. In particular, the authority may order "immediate execution" (*sofortige Vollziehung*) of an administrative act if this is necessary "in the public interest or in the interest of the parties involved" (§ 80 (II) No. 4 Code of Administrative Court Procedure). The citizen may then turn to the administrative court and file a petition for the suspension of the administrative act by the courts (*einstweiliger Rechtsschutz*, § 80 (V) Code of Administrative Court Procedure). The petitioner is thereby granted provisional judicial relief. The admissibility of such a petition for suspension is also dependant on locus standi. Accordingly, the petitioner must claim that his individual rights are infringed by the challenged administrative act.

The suspension of an administrative act ends after the act becomes final and non-appealable (*bestandskräftig*). This can happen either if the citizen fails to file an action to annul the administrative act in due time after his intra-administrative objection has been rejected or if the time limit for legal remedies against a rejecting judgement by the administrative court has lapsed.

5.6.2. Interim Injunctions (einstweilige Anordnungen)

If the case does not concern an aggrieving administrative act but a beneficial one, or if it concerns mere factual action by administrative authorities, the administrative courts may issue an "interim injunction" (*einstweilige Anordnung*) regarding the matter in dispute if "there is a risk that by a change of the current situation the enforcement of a right of the petitioner could be rendered impossible or made much more difficult" (§ 123 (I) Sentence 1 Code of Administrative Court Procedure).[144] In addition, a situation may be regulated on a provisional basis if "such regulation, particularly in the case of permanent legal relationships, seems to be necessary in order to ward off material disadvantages or imminent danger or for other reasons" (§ 123 (I) Sentence 2 Code of Administrative Court Procedure).

---

143 For details, see F. Schoch, 'Aufschiebende Wirkung und verwaltungsgerichtliches Aussetzungsverfahren' in: D. Ehlers and F. Schoch, *Rechtsschutz im Öffentlichen Recht*, de Gruyter, Berlin 2009, pp. 785–850.

144 For details, see F. Schoch, 'Aufschiebende Wirkung und verwaltungsgerichtliches Aussetzungsverfahren' in: D. Ehlers and F. Schoch, *Rechtsschutz im Öffentlichen Recht*, de Gruyter, Berlin 2009, pp. 851–887.

6. ENFORCEMENT OF ADMINISTRATIVE ACTS BY THE ADMINISTRATION

Administrative acts may be executed by the administration. Unlike private parties no writ of execution issued by a court is needed.[145] The law of enforcement falls in the competency of the states. Only in rare cases, in which the federation executes its own laws (see above 2.1.), is the Federal Administrative Enforcement Act applicable. This makes the law of enforcement by the administration rather complex as all states have enacted their own Administrative Enforcement Acts (*Verwaltungsvollstreckungsgesetze*) which differ considerably. As the Enforcement Acts are classified as public law (see 1.5.1.), the administrative courts are competent for disputes arising thereof.

Nevertheless, there are some common features. Firstly, the enforcement of administrative acts is only possible if they have become final and non-appealable (*bestandskräftig*) or if they are exceptionally immediately executable, according to § 80 (II) Code of Administrative Court Procedure (see 5.6.2.). Furthermore, the administrative act must contain a warning and set a certain time period in which the citizen should comply with the administrative act to avoid means of coercion, unless an imminent danger requires immediate execution.

Finally, all Administrative Enforcement Acts contain the same four means of coercion to enforce administrative acts that impose a duty to act, to tolerate or to omit a certain action. Firstly, the administration can substitute the performance which is required from the citizen (*Ersatzvornahme*). For example, if an administrative act obliges the citizen to cut a tree on his property, the administration may cut the tree itself or order someone to do so at the expense of the citizen. Secondly, the administrative authorities may use direct force (*unmittelbarer Zwang*) to execute an administrative act. If, for example, the police has ordered a citizen to open the door and the citizen does not obey, the police is entitled to break the door in order to enter. Thirdly, the administration can impose a fine (*Zwangsgeld*) on a citizen if he does not obey the administrative order. Finally, as a means of last resort, the administration can order enforcement custody (*Erzwingungshaft*). The applied means of coercion must always be proportionate in order to be legal.

If the public authority remains inactive, even though the conditions of enforcement are fulfilled, third parties may file a general action for performance (*allgemeine Leistungsklage*) to have the administration sentenced to enforce an administrative act. The administration however still has discretion with regard to the means of coercion. More important is § 80a Code of Administrative Court Procedure, which allows the court to order the immediate execution of

[145] For a brief explanation of administrative enforcement, see also M. Nierhaus, 'Administrative Law' in: M. Reimann and J. Zekoll (eds.), *Introduction to German Law*, C. H. Beck, Munich 2005, pp. 105 f.

an administrative act which poses a burden on one party but favours another. This is particularly relevant in building law. For example, if the competent authority prohibits to use a private flat as a club because of noise nuisance and the addressee of the administrative act objects against it, the administrative act is generally unenforceable because of the suspensive effect of the addressee's remedy (§ 80 (I) Code of Administrative Court Procedure, see above 5.6.1.). However, the neighbour may then ask the competent authority and – in case of its rejection – the administrative court for immediate execution of the prohibition on the basis of § 80a Code of Administrative Court Procedure, because the prohibition serves his subjective public right to physical integrity with regard to noise pollution.

7. NON-CONTRACTUAL LIABILITY FOR ADMINISTRATIVE ACTION

The system of non-contractual liability for administrative action in Germany is rather complicated.[146] There are written and unwritten legal claims for public liability. The confusing complexity of the law of public liability can only be explained through "path dependency" of its historic development. In 1981, the federal parliament tried to introduce a federal Act on State Liability (*Staatshaftungsgesetz*) to regulate state liability in a more concise manner, however, the Federal Constitutional Court quashed it because it held that the federal level had no competency to regulate the matter.[147]

The German state liability law distinguishes between claims for damages (*Schadensersatz*) and claims for compensation (*Entschädigung*). Whereas a claim for damages aims at a full compensation of the suffered loss, including lost profit (*lucrum cessans*) and damages for pain and suffering, claims for compensation only cover a "just financial adjustment" which may fall short of the actual financial losses suffered.[148] Notably, damages for pain and suffering and damages for lost profit cannot be obtained by a claim for compensation.

The most important claim for damages against the state is the claim for office liability according to Article 34 Basic Law in conjunction with § 839 Civil Code (*Amtshaftungsanspruch*).[149] Furthermore, there is an autonomous claim for

---

146 For a detailed comparative analysis of state liability throughout Europe, see O. Dörr (ed.), *Staatshaftungsrecht in Europa*, de Gruyter, Berlin 2014. For a comparative analysis in English, see H. Pünder and A. Klafki, 'Liability' in: C. Backes and M. Eliantonio (eds.), *Judicial Review of Administrative Action*, Hart, Oxford, forthcoming.

147 BVerfGE 61, 149.

148 Cf B. Grzeszick, 'Staatshaftungsrecht' in: D. Ehlers and H. Pünder (eds.), *Allgemeines Verwaltungsrecht* (eds.), 15th ed., de Gruyter, Berlin 2015, p. 992. See also D. Ehlers, 'Verwaltung und Verwaltungsrecht' 7, pp. 923 f.

149 For an overview in English, see G. Robbers, *An Introduction to German Law*, 5th ed., Nomos, Baden-Baden 2012, p. 73.

damages resulting from breaches of EU law. The claims for compensation are based on fundamental rights and general administrative principles. According to § 40 (II) Code of Administrative Court Procedure, state liability issues are predominantly dealt with by the civil courts in Germany.

7.1. CLAIMS FOR DAMAGES (*SCHADENSERSATZ*)

7.1.1. Claim for Office Liability (Amtshaftungsanspruch)

According to Article 34 Basic Law in conjunction with § 839 of the German Civil Code (*Bürgerliches Gesetzbuch* – BGB), a citizen is entitled to damages if a civil servant deliberately or negligently breaches his official duties towards the citizen by exercising his or her public authority and thereby causing damages towards the citizen.[150] The claim for office liability does not only cover misconduct of civil servants in the strict sense but also any misconduct of persons exercising public power.

However, there are important limitations to the claim for office liability. Firstly, according to § 839 (III) Civil Code, a claim for damages is subsidiary to primary judicial actions against the violating act of the public authority (§ 839 (III) Civil Code).[151] Only where primary judicial protection could not have prevented the suffered damages, may the citizen claim damages according to § 839 BGB in conjunction with Article 34 Basic Law. Secondly, restrictions are made with regard to misconduct of judges. § 839 (II) Civil Code explicitly states that judiciary misconduct only entitles citizens to damages when the breach of the judicial duty constitutes a criminal offence. According to the German Criminal Code (*Strafgesetzbuch*), this is only the case in very serious matters, e.g. where a judge, in conducting or deciding on a legal matter perverts the course of justice for the benefit or to the detriment of one party (*Rechtsbeugung*, § 339 Criminal Code) or where the judge is accepting bribes (*Bestechlichkeit*, § 332 (II) Criminal Code). The rationale behind this restriction of state liability with respect to the judiciary is the protection of the legal validity of court decisions

150 The personal liability of civil servants is codified in § 839 (I) Civil Code which states "If an official wilfully or negligibly commits a breach of duty incumbent upon him towards a third party, he shall compensate the third party for any damage". This personal responsibility of civil servants is generally assumed by the state according to Article 34 of the Basic Law (*Amtshaftung*) which reads as follows: "If any person, in the exercise of a public office entrusted to him, violates his official obligations to a third party, liability shall rest in principle on the state or the public body which employs him." For details concerning the claim for office liability, see F. Ossenbühl and M. Cornils, *Staatshaftungsrecht*, 6th ed., C.H. Beck, Munich 2013, pp. 7 ff.

151 BGH 15.05.1986, *NJW* 1987, 491 (The plaintiff must attack the onerous administrative act itself before claiming damages resulting thereof.).

(res iudiata, Rechtskraft).[152] Accordingly, § 839 (II) Civil Code does not apply to judicial orders which do not terminate the dispute. Furthermore, § 839 (II) Civil Code only applies to judges in the restricted sense of Article 97 Basic Law and does not apply to any administrative authorities exercising judicial functions. Finally, liability for legislative wrongdoing is also very limited. According to settled case law, parliament generally exercises no official duties towards the citizen when issuing laws, but rather acts in the interest of the common welfare.[153] Thus, citizens are generally not entitled to damages for legislative wrongdoing.

7.1.2. State Liability for Breaches of EU Law (unionsrechtlicher Staatshaftungsanspruch)

The EU treaties are silent concerning the liability of the member states for any damage caused by their institutions or servants in breach of EU law. However, since the *Francovich* judgement of the ECJ it is well established that there is an EU law liability claim (*unionsrechtlicher Staatshaftungsanspruch*) in favour of the citizens against their Member State for the breach of EU law.[154] The basis of this EU law liability claim is highly disputed.[155] The prevailing opinion in Germany derives it from the *effet utile* principle in conjunction with the protection of individual rights.[156] The EU law liability claim requires (1) the violation of an EU law provision that confers rights to individuals[157], (2) that the breach is sufficiently serious[158], (3) a causal link between the violation of the individual right and (4) a certain damage suffered by the citizen resulting from the breach of EU law. Other than the national claim for office liability, the EU law liability claim does not depend on the fault of the Member Sate.

In German law, the Member States' liability for breaches of EU law compliments the liability actions available under national law, as national state liability claims are too limited to comply with EU requirements. Consequently, the EU law liability claim may still be successful even if German state liability

---

152 H. Maurer and C. Waldhoff, *Allgemeines Verwaltungsrecht*, 19th ed., C.H. Beck, Munich 2017, p. 727.

153 BGH, 29.03.1971, *BGHZ* 56, 40, 44.

154 See ECJ, Joined Cases C-6/90, C-9/90, *Francovich* [1991] ECR I-05357, ECLI:EU:C:1991:428; ECJ, Joined Cases C-178/94, C-179/94, C-188/94, C-189/94 and C-190/94, *Dillenkofer*, [1996] ECR I-4845, ECLI:EU:C:1996:375; ECJ, Joined Cases, C-46/93, C-48/93, *Brasserie du Pêcheur and Factortame* [1996] ECR, I-1029, ECLI:EU:C:1996:79_1; ECJ, Case C-224/01, *Köbler* [2003] ECR I-10239, ECLI:EU:C:2003:513.

155 For further details see F. Ossenbühl and M. Cornils, *Staatshaftungsrecht*, 6th ed., C.H. Beck, Munich 2013, pp. 595 ff.

156 B. Grzeszick, 'Staatshaftungsrecht' in: D. Ehlers and H. Pünder (eds.), *Allgemeines Verwaltungsrecht* (eds.), 15th ed., de Gruyter, Berlin 2015, pp. 962 ff.

157 BGH, 14.12.2000, *BGHZ* 146, 153, 158.

158 See ECJ, Case C-352/98, *Bergaderm und Goupil v. Kommission* [2000] ECR I-5291, ECLI:EU:C:2000:361.

claims are not[159], because, for example, the fault criterion of the German office liability claim (*Amtshaftungsanspruch*) is not met. Notably, the special claim for state liability for breaches of EU law also encompasses liability for legislative and judicial wrongdoing.[160]

7.2. CLAIMS FOR COMPENSATION (*ENTSCHÄDIGUNG*)

There are cases where the civil servant is not at fault or the infringement of the citizen's right is lawful but there is still a need to compensate the person affected. In these cases, a claim for compensation can be applicable. The rule of law (Article 20 (III) Basic Law), the right to recourse to the courts (Article 19 (IV) Basic Law) and the fundamental rights serve as a constitutional basis for these claims which are recognised by customary law. Furthermore, strangely enough, recourse is made to the Prussian General Land Law of 1794 *(EinlALR – Einleitung zum preußischen Allgemeinen Landrecht)*.[161]

On this basis, compensation is granted in the case of an "expropriatory infringement" of rights (*enteignender Eingriff, enteignungsgleicher Eingriff*). This is the case, where there is no formal expropriation but the administrative actions compel a citizen to sacrifice a special property right or privilege for the common good. In the case of infringements of non-pecuniary interests such as health or reputation, a similar action to compensation on the basis of devotion (*Aufopferungsanspruch aufopferungsgleicher Anspruch*) is admissible. This is relevant, for example, where the police, without acting negligently, hurts innocent bystanders while chasing a criminal.

The decisive factor for compensation is whether there has been a "special sacrifice" (*Sonderopfer*) of the citizen.[162] This is the case when infringements of rights and privileges of the citizen amount to a disproportionate burden. In the case of unlawful actions of the administration, the presence of a special sacrifice on the part of the citizen is assumed *prima facie*. When the administration acts lawfully, the disproportionate burden must be established by the claimant in order

159 BGH, 24.10.1996, *BGHZ* 134, 30, 43.

160 For legislative wrongdoing, see ECJ, Joined Cases, C-46/93, C-48/93, *Brasserie du Pêcheur and Factortame*, 1996 ECR, I-1029, ECLI:EU:C:1996:79_1. For judicial wrongdoing see ECJ, Case C-224/01, *Köbler* [2003] ECR I-10239, ECLI:EU:C:2003:513.

161 The two relevant sections read as follows: § 74 EinlALR: "The furthering of the common good takes precedence over individual rights and privileges of the members of the state if a genuine conflict (collision) exists between these two positions." § 75 EinlALR: "The state is, however, bound to compensate anybody who is forced to sacrifice his particular rights and privileges for the common good." Translation by W. Rüfner, 'Basic Elements of German Law on State Liability' in: J. Bell and A. Bradley (eds.), *Governmental Liability: A Comparative Study, United Kingdom National Committee of Comparative Law*, London 1991, p. 250.

162 For details, see F. Ossenbühl and M. Cornils, *Staatshaftungsrecht*, 6th ed., C.H. Beck, Munich 2013, pp. 124 ff., 259 ff.

to obtain compensation. An example would be the exposure of a citizen to unusual and considerable levels of noise because of street work conducted by the state.

8. RECENT AND FUTURE DEVELOPMENTS

8.1. EUROPEANIZATION AND THE INTERNATIONALIZATION OF ADMINISTRATIVE LAW

German administrative law is increasingly influenced by European law (see above 1.3.) as well as international law.[163] In several fields of administrative law, such as foreign commerce law (*Außenwirtschaftsrecht*), data protection or even environmental law, the national legislator only plays a subordinate rôle. Thus, citizens are increasingly subject to legal interventions which are no longer based merely on national legislation but mainly on supranational legal acts. As a result, the debate about the legitimacy of European and international regulation is becoming increasingly important.[164]

Furthermore, through ongoing Europeanization and internationalization, comparative administrative law gains in importance. Foreign legal concepts such as the interest based judicial review system, for example, are punctually introduced into German law through European legislation (especially in the field of environmental law, see above 5.3.3). The search for common administrative law principles throughout Europe[165] may pave the way for an ever more harmonised transnational *ius commune (proceduralis)* in administrative law.[166]

8.2. CONCEPT OF THE STATE IN TRANSITION

The German concept of the state is in transition. Whereas, in the past, the function of fundamental rights was limited to the protection of citizens from state interferences (*Abwehrrechte*), today, more and more entitlements to state services (*Leistungsrechte*) are deducted from the constitution. The

---

163 See A. Vosskuhle, 'The reform approach in the German Science of Administrative Law: The 'Neue Verwaltungsrechtswissenschaft'' in: M. Ruffert (ed.), *The Transformation of Administrative Law in Europe*, Sellier, Munich 2007, pp. 89, 109 ff.

164 See M. Kaufmann, 'The Legitimation of the European Union – Democracy versus Integration' in: H. Pünder and C. Waldhoff (eds.), *Debates in German Public Law*, Hart, Oxford 2014, pp. 263 ff.

165 See J. Schwarze, *European administrative law*, 1st revised Ed., Sweet and Maxwell, Luxembourg 2006.

166 H. Pünder, 'German administrative procedure in a comparative perspective: Observations on the path to a transnational ius commune proceduralis in administrative law' (2013) 11 *ICON* (*International Journal of Constitutional Law*), 940 ff.

concept of the liberal state is replaced by the concept of an "ensuring state" (*Gewährleistungsstaat*).[167] Recent German scholarly work has been inspired by the idea of the regulatory state.[168] The variety of new tasks for the state has led to a decrease of the "steering-force" (*Steuerungskraft*) of the state.[169] Instead of all public tasks being executed by state administration, market forces and private actors are increasingly included in the fulfilment of the common good. Important fields of administrative law are therefore characterised by guiding and controlling the public-private interplay in the realization of the public good.[170] Scholarly works adapt to this new public management approach. Furthermore, informal and cooperative administrative action gains further importance.[171] A new approach in the German science of administrative law has developed (*Neue Verwaltungsrechtswissenschaft*)[172]: Influential scholars now emphasise, that the law should be analysed from the perspective of "steering theory"[173] (*Steuerungstheorie*).[174] Thus, extra-legal measures should be considered in the design and analysis of administrative procedures in order to guarantee effective administrative decision making. Empirical analysis of the consequences of administrative actions is needed.[175]

New concepts of democratic legitimacy have arisen thereof. The classic input-focussed concept of democratic legitimacy is supplemented with output-oriented approaches.[176] This transition leads to frictions within the traditional

---

167 See M. Ruffert, 'Public law and the economy: A comparative view from the German perspective' (2013) 11 *ICON* 925, 932.

168 G. Majone, 'The Rise of the Regulatory State in Western Europe' (1994) 17 *West European Politics* 77; R. Ruge, *Die Gewährleistungsverantwortung des Staates und der Regulatory State*, Duncker & Humblot, Berlin 2004.

169 H. Ritter, 'Recht als Steuerungsmedium im kooperativen Staat' in: D. Grimm (ed.), *Wachsende Staatsaufgaben – sinkende Steuerungsfähigkeit des Rechts*, Baden-Baden 1990, pp. 69 ff., 82 f.

170 See M. Eifert, 'Conceptualizing Administrative Law – Legal Protection versus Regulatory Approach' in: H. Pünder and C. Waldhoff (eds.), *Debates in German Public Law*, Hart, Oxford 2014, pp. 203 ff.

171 M. Fehling, 'Informelles Verwaltungshandeln' in: W. Hoffmann-Riem, E. Schmidt-Assmann and A. Vosskuhle, *Grundlagen des Verwaltungsrechts*, Volume 2, 2nd ed., C. H. Beck, Munich 2012, pp.1457 ff.

172 A. Vosskuhle, 'The reform approach in the German Science of Administrative Law: The "Neue Verwaltungsrechtswissenschaft"' in: M. Ruffert (ed.), *The Transformation of Administrative Law in Europe*, Sellier, Munich 2007, pp. 89 ff.

173 The steering theory was developed by the social sciences. See R. Mayntz, 'Politische Steuerung und gesellschaftliche Steuerungsprobleme' in: R. Mayntz (ed.), *Soziale Dynamik und politische Steuerung*, Campus-Verlag, Frankfurt a. M. 1997, pp. 186 ff.

174 A. Vosskuhle, 'The reform approach in the German Science of Administrative Law: The "Neue Verwaltungsrechtswissenschaft"' in: M. Ruffert (ed.), *The Transformation of Administrative Law in Europe*, Sellier, Munich 2007, pp. 89, 115.

175 W. Hoffmann-Riem, 'The Potential Impact of Social Sciences on Administrative Law"' in: M. Ruffert (ed.), *The Transformation of Administrative Law in Europe*, Sellier, Munich 2007, pp. 203 ff.

176 For the concpet of output legitimacy, see F. W. Scharpf, *Demokratietheorie zwischen Utopie und Anpassung*, Univ.-Verlag, Konstanz 1970, pp. 21 ff.

understanding of the democratic legitimacy of administrative action. The traditional bureaucratic model of administrative law requires strict hierarchies and rule-based decision making[177], whereas the concept of a regulatory administration demands independency from political influences and decision making freedoms. Furthermore, European law is directed towards a more regulatory approach and has, for example, led to more independence of the Federal Agency for Electricity, Gas, Telecommunications, Postal Services, and Rail Transport (*Bundesnetzagentur*).[178]

Nevertheless, the privatization wave of the 1990s has also brought some disillusionment. Many tasks of basic public services, which were outsourced to the private sector at that time, are now renationalised.[179] In many cases, the expected increase of efficiency could not be realised. This development led to new challenges for German administrative law.[180]

8.3. DIGITALIZATION OF ADMINISTRATIVE LAW

An important subject of future legal research in the field of administrative law is the increasing digitalization of the administration.[181] The use of electronic documents and electronic communication allows an acceleration of administrative proceedings as well as court proceedings. According to § 55a Code of Administrative Court Procedure, the participants of administrative court proceedings may convey electronic documents. A qualified electronic signature is prescribed for documents which are equivalent to a document to be signed in writing. Furthermore, § 55b Code of Administrative Corut Procedure allows that procedural files may be kept in electronic form. However, both provisions only apply if electronic documents and files have been permitted by executive regulation by the federation for the federal courts and by the state authorities for the state courts. The federal government has permitted electronic documents and files for the federal courts. The states have implemented pilot projects for electronic legal proceedings (*elektronischer Rechtsverkehr*).[182]

---

177 E.-W. Böckenförde, 'Demokratie als Staats- und Regierungsform' in: J. Isensee and P. Kirchhof (eds.), *Handbuch des Staatsrechts,* Volume 2, 3rd ed., C.F. Müller Verlag, Heidelberg 2004, pp. 437 ff.

178 M. Ruffert, 'Public law and the economy: A comparative view from the German perspective' (2013) 11 *ICON* 925, 932. See also J.-P. Schneider, 'Regulation and Europeanisation as Key Patterns of Change in Administrative Law' in: M. Ruffert (ed.), *The Transformation of Administrative Law in Europe*, Sellier, Munich 2007, pp. 309 ff.

179 M. Ruffert, 'Public law and the economy: A comparative view from the German perspective' (2013) 11 *ICON* 925, 938.

180 See H. Bauer, C. Büchner and L. Hajasch (eds.), *Rekommunalisierung öffentlicher Daseinsvorsorge*, Univ.-Verlag, Potsdam 2012.

181 W. Hoffmann-Riem, *Innovation und Recht, Recht und Innovation: Recht im Ensemble seiner Kontexte*, Mohr Siebeck, Tübingen 2016, pp. 614 ff.

182 For an overview of the different projects see www.justiz.de/elektronischer_rechtsverkehr/index.php, assessed 20.06.2017.

Nonetheless, in practice, the digitalization of the German court system proceeds rather slow. To date, the written procedure is still predominant.

Furthermore, in order to support modern administration, an empowering basis for automated administrative decision making has been introduced to the Administrative Procedure Act. The newly introduced § 35a reads as follows: "An administrative act may be adopted entirely by automatic means, provided that this is authorised by law and that the administration has no discretion (*Ermessen*) or margin of interpretation (*Beurteilungsspielraum*) with regard to the issuing of the respective administrative act." Especially in tax law, the administration has made use of this possibility and issues automatic tax assessments in standard cases. This enables the administration to process tax declarations more efficiently and in a timely manner. This is only the first step of digitalization. With the "internet of things", new e-government concepts arise.[183] Smart City Strategies may influence a variety of administrative fields as traffic regulation, police work, waste disposal or resource planning.[184]

However, the issuing of automatic administrative acts poses new threats to the affected citizen. It is questionable, whether cases of hardship can be identified when administrative decisions are made by computers. While humans may identify atypical cases, which require a deviation from the normal rules to guarantee proportionality, algorithms can only decide on the basis of cases which have already been known or foreseen by the programmer.[185] Furthermore, algorithms are vulnerable to manipulation by hackers.[186] As programming is very complex, it is a realistic fear that such manipulations may remain undetected for a long time which would affect the fairness of administrative decision making.

8.4. PARTICIPATION BY THE PUBLIC IN ADMINISTRATIVE DECISION MAKING

Finally, public participation has become an important topic in administrative law. Throughout the western world, a crisis of representative democracy can

183 See M. Eifert, *Electronic Government – Das Recht der elektronischen Verwaltung*, Nomos, Baden-Baden 2006. For a more international point of view, see R. Weber and R. Weber, *Internet of Things: Legal Perspectives*, Springer, Berlin 2010.

184 C. Djeffal, 'Leitlinien der Verwaltungsinnovation und das Internet der Dinge' in: A. Klafki, F. Würkert and T. Winter (eds.), *Digitalisierung und Recht*, Bucerius Law School Press, Hamburg 2017, pp. 83 ff.

185 C. Ernst, 'Algorithmische Entscheidungsfindung und personenbezogene Daten' in: A. Klafki, F. Würkert and T. Winter (eds.), *Digitalisierung und Recht*, Bucerius Law School Press, Hamburg 2017, pp. 63 ff.; W. Hoffmann-Riem, 'Verhaltenssteuerung durch Algorithmen – Eine Herausforderung für das Recht', (2017) 142 *Archiv des öffentlichen Rechts* 1 ff.

186 For developments in the field of IT-security and e-government, see H. Strack, 'e-Government und IT-Sicherheit', F. Bieler and G. Schwarting (eds.), *e-Government*, Erich Schmidt Verlag, Berlin 2007, pp. 673 ff.

be observed.[187] Democracy suffers under the political lethargy of the citizenry. Discontent with political elites is growing. Trust in the political process has declined even though democracy as a form of government enjoys high levels of acceptance.[188] An important topic of administrative law, therefore, is the integration of the public in the administrative decision making procedure.

Originally, citizens' participation in the administrative procedure served mainly to make legal protection available to citizens. Today, participatory procedures are also expected to increase acceptance of administrative decisions.[189] Public participation is meant to calm and pacify conflicts of administrative actions. Especially in planning law, public participation is often attributed with conciliating functions.[190] Public participation is especially effective in regional contexts. However, for highly politicised federal issues, such as the storage of nuclear waste, the Federal Law for Selecting a Final Atomic Repository (*Standortauswahlgesetz)*[191] provides for a wide range of possibilities for public participation. Furthermore, public participation aims to overcome citizens' political disenchantment (*Politikverdrossenheit*) and engage the population.[192] However, there are sociological findings that show that the lower a person's level of education and income the less likely he or she is to participate. Therefore, critics argue that the expansion of participatory influence on administrative decisions is rather undemocratic as it, in fact, excludes vast contingent of the population.[193]

In environmental law, public participation also empowers the public to control the legality of administrative action. This function of public participation is rather foreign to the traditional concept of administrative law in Germany where judicial review is based on subjective public rights and where individuals are generally not allowed to challenge illegal administrative action which does not personally affect them. This is a further example of the pervasiveness of European influence.

---

187 See C. Pateman, Participation and Democratic Theory, University Press, Cambridge 1970; B. Barber, Strong Democracy: Participatory Politics for a New Age, 1984; C. Crouch, Post-Democracy, 2004; P. Norris, Democratic Deficit, 2011.

188 See also: H. Pünder, 'More Government with the People: The Crisis of Representative Democracy and Options for Reform in Germany' (2015) 16 *German Law Journal* 713.

189 See H. Pünder, 'Verwaltungsverfahren' in: D. Ehlers and H. Pünder (eds.), *Allgemeines Verwaltungsrecht* (eds.), 15th ed., de Gruyter, Berlin 2016, pp. 549 ff.

190 See J. Ziekow, *Gutachten D zum 69. Deutschen Juristentag: Neue Formen der Bürgerbeteiligung? Planung und Zulassung von Projekten in der parlamentarischen Demokratie*, C.H. Beck, Munich 2012.

191 Gesetz zur Suche und Auswahl eines Standortes für ein Endlager für Wärme entwicklende radioaktive Abfälle (Standortauswahlgesetz – StandAG), Federal Law Gazette 2013 I, p. 2553.

192 H. Rossen-Stadtfeld, 'Beteiligung, Partizipation und Öffentlichkeit' in: W. Hoffmann-Riem, E. Schmidt-Assmann and A. Vosskuhle (eds.), *Grundlagen des Verwaltungsrechts, Band 2*, 2nd ed., C.H. Beck, Munich 2012, pp. 663 ff.

193 See S. Verba, K. L. Scholzmann and H. Brady (eds.), *Voice and Equality*, Havard University Press, Cambridge (Mass.) 1995.

Additionally, new alternative forms of dispute resolution are being tested. In 2012, a Mediation Act was issued.[194] According to § 1 Mediation Act, mediation is a confidential and structured process in which the parties strive, on a voluntary basis and autonomously, to achieve an amicable resolution of their conflict with the assistance of one or more mediators. The law is also applicable to administrative law disputes. During the mass protests in Stuttgart in 2010 /2011 because of the construction of a new railway station (*Stuttgart 21*), the mediation procedure and a subsequent referendum pacified the heated conflict between citizens and the administration. Mediation could develop as an important means to mitigate conflicts in a timely and cost-effective manner in administrative law.[195] If a mediation of a public law dispute is successful any pending court proceedings will be mutually declared as settled, which significantly reduces court fees. However, there is no obligation of the parties to initiate mediation proceedings before going to court.

BIBLIOGRAPHY

Backes, C. & Eliantonio, M. (eds.), *Judicial Review of Administrative Action*, Oxford: Hart, forthcoming.

Bogdandy, A. von, S. Cassese and P. M. Huber (eds.), *Handbuch Ius Publicum Europaeum, Band V: Verwaltungsrecht in Europa*, Heidelberg: C. F. Müller, 2014.

Ehlers, D., Fehling, M. & Pünder, H. (eds.), *Besonderes Verwaltungsrecht*, Volumes 1–3, 3rd ed., Berlin: De Gruyter, 2012–2013.

Ehlers, D. & Pünder, H. (eds.), *Allgemeines Verwaltungsrecht*, 15th ed. Berlin: De Gruyter, 2016.

Ehlers, D. & Schoch, F. (eds.), *Rechtsschutz im Öffentlichen Recht*, Berlin: De Gruyter, 2009.

Foster, N. & Sule, S. (eds.), German Legal System and Laws, 3rd ed., New York: Oxford University Press, 2002

Hoffmann-Riem, W., Schmidt-Aßmann, E. & Voßkuhle, A. (eds.), *Grundlagen des Verwaltungsrechts*, Volumes 1–3, 2nd ed., Munich: C. H. Beck, 2012–2013.

Hufen, F., *Verwaltungsprozessrecht*, 10th ed., Munich: C. H. Beck, 2016.

Isensee, J. & Kirchhof, P. (eds.), *Handbuch des Staatsrechts*, Volumes 1–13, 3rd ed., Munich: C. H. Beck, 2003–2015.

Pünder, H., 'Democratic Legitimation of Delegated Legislation – A Comparative View on the American, British and German Law' (2009) 58 *ICLQ (International and Comparative Law Quarterly)*, 353–378.

Pünder, H., 'German administrative procedure in a comparative perspective: Observations on the path to a transnational ius commune proceduralis in

194 Meditationsgesetz, Federal Law Gazette 2012 I, p. 1577.

195 For details, see H. Pünder, 'Verwaltungsverfahren' in: D. Ehlers and H. Pünder (eds.), *Allgemeines Verwaltungsrecht* (eds.), 15th ed., de Gruyter, Berlin 2016, pp. 549 ff.

administrative law' (2013) 11, *ICON (International Journal of Constitutional Law)*, 940–961.
Pünder H. & Waldhoff, C. (eds.), *Debates in German Public Law*, Oregon: Hart, 2014.
Reimann, M. & Zekoll, J., *Introduction to German Law*, Munich: C. H. Beck, 2005.
Robbers, G., *An introduction to German law*, 5th ed., Baden-Baden: Nomos, 2012.
Singh, M. P., *German Administrative Law in Common Law Perspective*, 2nd ed., Berlin: Springer, 2001.
Maurer, H. & Waldhoff, C., *Allgemeines Verwaltungsrecht*, 19th ed., Munich: C.H. Beck, 2017.
Mayer, O., *Deutsches Verwaltungsrecht*, Volume 1, 3rd ed., Berlin: Duncker und Humblot, 1969 (reprint of 1924).
Ruffert, M. (ed.), *The Transformation of Administrative Law in Europe*, Munich: Sellier, 2007.
Stolleis, M., *Geschichte des Öffentlichen Rechts*, Volumes 1–4, Munich: C. H. Beck, 1988–2012.

WEBSITES

Legislation:

- www.gesetze-im-internet.de/vwvfg (Administrative Procedure Act, German)
- www.gesetze-im-internet.de/vwgo (Code of Administrative Court Procedure, German)
- www.bmi.bund.de/SharedDocs/Downloads/EN/Gesetzestexte/VwVfg_en.pdf?__blob=publicationFile (English Translation of the Administrative Procedure Act in the version of 2004)
- www.gesetze-im-internet.de/englisch_vwgo/ (English translation of the current status of the Code of Administrative Court Procedure)

Court Websites:

- www.bverwg.de/informationen/english/federal_administrative_court.php (Federal Administrative Court)
- www.bundesverfassungsgericht.de/EN/Homepage/home_node.html (Federal Constitutional Court)

ADMINISTRATIVE LAW IN THE NETHERLANDS[1]

René SEERDEN and DANIËLLE WENDERS

1. INTRODUCTION

1.1. WHAT IS ADMINISTRATIVE LAW?

Administrative law is closely linked with constitutional law. This makes it difficult to draw a line between the two. The literature offers different definitions, which regularly undergo changes. The distinction is made purely for didactical reasons and does not have any legal consequences. We will not bother with definitions, but rather provide a global picture of what is to be understood by constitutional law and what is to be understood by administrative law. Traditionally, constitutional law contains the following components: relation to international law; basic rights; legislation; parliamentary system; the organization of the judiciary and its powers; the relationship between the legislator, the executive power and the judiciary and decentralization. These aspects are dealt with in the Dutch Constitution (*Grondwet*) in Articles 93–94, Articles 1–23, Articles 50–111, Articles 112–122 and Articles 123–136 respectively.

The core of administrative law is the relationship between the (government of a) State and the citizen. The administration has the power to unilaterally affect the legal position of citizens and to direct and organize social relations in all possible policy areas. One of the major instruments available to the administration in this regard (paragraph 2) is the legal concept of *beschikking*, the juridical act (decision) governed by public law, which creates rights and/or duties for an individual in a concrete situation. Among other things, licenses, benefits, subsidies, tax assessments and enforcement orders fall within this concept (paragraph 3). A more formal part of administrative law forms the legal protection (possibilities of complaint, appeal and access to courts) against administrative acts (paragraphs 4 and 5).

1 For the purposes of this contribution on Dutch administrative law, we have used the (introductory) works as mentioned in the bibliography at the end of this contribution.

There is also a close relation between administrative law and criminal law. The administration itself disposes of a number of enforcement measures against acting without a license or in contravention of the license conditions, but often these actions constitute a criminal offence as well.[2] Traditionally these two parts of public law were separated because the guardian of criminal law in the Netherlands, the public prosecutor (*officier van justitie*), was not seen as a part of the administration. In more recent times however, for reasons of efficiency, it can be seen that the public prosecutor can act as an administrative organ and an administrative organ can issue sanctions which could be qualified as criminal charges (within the meaning of Article 6 European Convention on Human Rights (ECHR) or even act as a kind of prosecutor.[3] This mix of functions could give rise to problems when one is of the opinion that for criminal and administrative actions different rules and principles should apply and because of this merging that might be disregarded (paragraph 6).

Furthermore there is a relation with private law (mainly laid down in the Civil Code (*Burgerlijk Wetboek*). Administrative law determines the citizen's position under private law: it either restricts the citizen's freedom of contract or his freedom of ownership, for instance, as a result of a license, or enlarges these freedoms, through subsidies for example. Administrative acts therefore can determine a person's civil rights and obligations within the meaning of Article 6 ECHR. In addition the administrative organs (legal entities) can act in a private capacity as well, i.e. conclude contracts with individuals to buy iPads for its civil servants for instance, or even use private law instruments to realize policy goals, i.e. conclude a contract with a contractor to build a bridge or construct a road for public use under certain conditions (paragraph 6).

Administrative law is a large legal area consisting of very disparate components. These components are called the special parts of administrative law. They govern specific policy areas as opposed to the general administrative law rules and principles which apply to acts of the administration in general. Among these are environmental law, land-use (planning) law, social security law, the law governing public servants, education law, tax law, health law and asylum law.[4] The special parts have been developed by the legislator

---

2 Of primary importance in this respect is not the Penal Code (*Wetboek van Strafrecht*) but the Economic Offences Act (*Wet op de Economische Delicten*).

3 For instance, in the field of violation of traffic regulations the public prosecutor acts as an administrative organ and in the field of environmental enforcement an experiment is/has been pending to give the administrative organs the possibility to come to 'transactions' / decisions under criminal law.

4 It must be borne in mind that many of these legal areas, for instance, environmental law, are not purely administrative law, but also consist of criminal and private law elements. For a comparative description of (public) environmental law, see: Seerden, R., Heldeweg, M. & Deketelaere, K., *Public Environmental Law in the European Union and the United States. A Comparative Analysis*, Environmental Law and Policy Series, London-The Hague-Boston: Kluwer Law International, 2002.

over a period of time, after having been prepared by the different national ministries, and continue to be developed. The statutes and regulations relate to completely different social situations, and often show a different system and organization.[5]

The general part of administrative law is perceived as the body of rules and principles applying to all administrative law, and therefore, in principle, to all special parts as well unless the law in these fields explicitly deviates from it. In the Netherlands, the general part of administrative law was developed rather late. Until the beginning of the 1990s, the Netherlands lacked an administrative court with general jurisdiction (paragraph 5).

In many instances a special statute was enacted, the decision was open to appeal to the Crown or a special judicial body was installed, for instance, in the area of social security. Especially after the Second World War, all these appellate bodies have contributed towards the development of the general part of administrative law by developing unwritten general principles of proper administration (*algemene beginselen van behoorlijk bestuur*). These include the principle of due care: the administration must consider all relevant facts and interests before taking a decision; the reasoned-decisions principle: a decision must be properly reasoned and the (relevant legal) reasons must be accessible; and the principle of legitimate expectations: (in certain cases) raised expectations by the administration must be honoured (paragraph 4).

The general principles of proper administration developed by the appellate bodies and courts were for a large part codified in 1994 and laid down in the General Administrative Law Act (*Algemene wet bestuursrecht*). On the occasion of the amendment of the Dutch Constitution in 1983, it was established that there had to be created such a statute containing the general rules of administrative law. This has been laid down in Article 107, paragraph 2, Constitution. Since the beginning of the nineteenth century, the first paragraph of the Article already contained the duty to codify the substantive and procedural private law and the substantive and procedural criminal law.

The administrative law in the Netherlands seems to be under a permanent reconstruction. An important example in recent years has been the introduction of legislation dealing with the acceleration of procedures and the judicial dispute-settlement powers (paragraph 5). Also a further codification of the financial liability of the administration has seen the light (paragraph 5). It is the question whether or not all the changes are for the better (paragraph 7).

---

5 There are guidelines, issued in 1992 by the Prime Minister, to promote uniformity in (the drafting of) legislation, compiled by Borman, C., *Aanwijzingen voor de regelgeving*, Zwolle: W.E.J. Tjeenk Willink, 1993. From time to time they are adapted.

1.2. GENERAL ADMINISTRATIVE LAW ACT (*ALGEMENE WET BESTUURSRECHT*, AWB)[6]

The statute which has been created on the basis of Article 107, paragraph 2, Constitution is the General Administrative Law Act (GALA) or *Algemene wet bestuursrecht* (Awb). This act is one of the most important developments in (general) administrative law in the last two decades. At present it consists of 10 chapters.

The Awb not only contains codification (of case law) provisions, but also provisions with a view to achieve more clarity and simplicity in administrative law. All sorts of unnecessary differences in special legislation, such as in the procedures for objection and appeal, have been eliminated.

The Awb consists of a contentious and a non-contentious part. The first half of the Act comprises provisions governing the primary administrative decision-making process. The second half governs the objection procedure (*bezwaarprocedure*) against an administrative decision, appeal to a superior administrative body (*administratief beroep*) and judicial review to the administrative judge / the administrative court (*beroep bij de rechtbank*).

A second feature of the Awb is that it has been organized around the concept of administrative decision (*besluit*) in Article 1:3 Awb, meaning a juridical act governed by public law, which can comprise decisions in individual cases (*beschikkingen*), generally applicable regulations (*algemeen verbindende voorschriften*) and other decisions of general application (*besluiten van algemene strekking*). Important provisions in the Awb are also applicable to administrative actions, be it of a factual (non-legal) nature or those governed by private law (Article 3:1, paragraph 2, Awb).[7]

Another important feature of the Awb is its hierarchical organization, which means that there are a number of chapters containing provisions of a more general nature, followed by chapters with more specific provisions.[8] Chapter 3, for example, contains general provisions on administrative decisions (*besluiten*). These provisions apply therefore to all categories of the above-mentioned administrative decisions. Chapter 4(1) contains specific provisions for administrative decisions in individual cases (*beschikkingen*), whose provisions apply exclusively to these types of decisions. Consequently, in order to find out what provisions apply to a decision in individual cases, one must consult chapter 3 as well as title I of chapter 4.

---

6 Act of 4 June 1992 in force on 1 January 1994, *Staatsblad* (Official Journal) 1994, 1. Through its general application (albeit of a highly procedural nature) it can be compared with the position of the Civil Code and Penal Code and you could in that respect also speak of the Administrative Law Code. We use both terms: Act and Code and both abbreviations: Awb/GALA. See for key provisions: the Annex to this contribution.

7 Provisions as Article 3:1 Awb are called 'link provisions' (*schakelbepalingen*). This technique has been taken from the Dutch Civil Code.

8 Also taken from the Dutch Civil Code.

Further examples are chapters 6 and 8. Chapter 6 contains general provisions common to administrative objection, administrative appeal to a superior administrative body and judicial review by the administrative judge (*bestuursrechter*), in first instance mostly the District Court (*rechtbank*), whereas chapter 8 contains special provisions governing judicial review. If one wishes to learn about the proceedings before the District Court, one must consult both chapters 6 and 8 Awb.

Although, technically, the legal draftsmen did a fine drafting job with the Awb, its hierarchical organization does make it difficult for the layperson to consult the Awb. As a result of this hierarchy, a provision is likely to be overlooked.

Apart from having to consult the Awb in different places, a further complication is that the statutes containing the special rules for different policy areas must also be consulted. These special statutes have remained operative even after the Awb came into effect for the following reasons:

a. The principle of legality: the Awb does not grant powers, but provides guidelines on how powers must be used by the administration. The special statutes grant powers, which are limited powers by definition, only to be used for the purpose for which they have been granted;
b. Substantive administrative law is based on these special statutes. The Awb only contains rules on decision-making (procedural law). For example: the Awb sets out the decision-making *procedure* governing environmental licenses, but the special statute, for instance, the Environmental Management Act (*Wet milieubeheer*) and since the end of 2010 the Act on Environmental Licensing and General Provisions (*Wet algemene bepalingen omgevingsrecht*) and the rules derived from it determine the *substance* of these licenses, i.e. the rights and obligations of the licensee;
c. Finally, the special statute also needs to be consulted, because it is possible that the statute contains procedural provisions which depart from the provisions laid down in the Awb. Although the Awb provisions are intended to be generally applicable to the entire body of administrative law, it regularly occurs that a special statute contains derogations. Since a special statute has the same status as the Awb, namely a law enacted by the legislature in conformity with Article 81 Constitution (i.e. Act of Parliament/ formal legislator), (as a general rule) the *lex specialis* rule or *lex posterior* rule applies here: in the event of conflicting provisions, the special statute supersedes the general statute (or the later the former). These differences can occur in relation to aspects such as time limits for appeal, the range of persons that can appeal, the competent court, etc. For instance, in the field of residence permits and asylum law the time limit to file an appeal to the competent administrative court is 4 weeks or 1 week contrary to the rule in article 6:7 GALA that the time limit is 6 weeks (Article 69 Aliens Act) (*Vreemdelingenwet*).

Apart from its main contents, namely provisions on decision-making by the administration and judicial review by the administrative courts, it is also important to point out that the Awb holds a chapter on administrative enforcement (inspection and sanctions, chapter 5). Based on this chapter in combination with the more general provisions laid down in the Acts dealing with municipalities, provinces and waterboards and substantive legislation and regulations which apply to the specific policy area at hand, several inspection powers (*toezichtsbevoegdheden*) exist, such as powers to ask for information, to enter certain places and to search vehicles and goods, and also powers to sanction (*handhavingsbevoegdheden*) can be used, such as administrative orders under penalty (*dwangsom*), orders to end the illegal situation itself and to recover the costs from the offender (*bestuursdwang*) and provisions with regard to imposing administrative fines (on individuals (*bestuurlijke boete*).[9] The latter is introduced in 2009. This administrative fine is a punitive sanction, while the other two sanctions aim at restoring the illegal situation and are not seen as punitive. In 2009 also provisions were introduced that deal with financial decisions and failure to take a decision within the statutory time limit.

1.3. (THE USE OF) ADMINISTRATIVE POWERS

The principle of legality, which is based on the Constitution and unwritten law, is one of the most important principles of administrative law. For an administrative decision to be lawful, as a rule – there are exceptions – the powers of the administration must have originated in the Constitution or an Act of Parliament.

An essential feature of administrative power is that it is exercised unilaterally and has *erga omnes* effect. In this, administrative law differs essentially from private law, where two or more parties create obligations on the basis of consensus. Of course, this unilateral nature does not prevent citizens from being involved in the decision-making. On the contrary, in a modern developed State under the rule of law, the administration must take the rights and interests of its citizens to heart. In the end, however, it is the administration that bears the responsibility for the decision. Only the administration has the power to take binding decisions, or, in old-fashioned terms, exercise 'public authority', if necessary against the citizen's wishes, should public interest so require. As already mentioned, the administration also has the power to enforce its unilaterally taken decisions by administrative orders (see chapter 5 Awb).

---

9 Withdrawal of licenses is an administrative sanction that is not dealt with in the Awb (yet), but can be found in specific legislation. An example can be found in Article 5.19 Act on Environmental Licensing and General Provisions.

Sometimes recourse to civil law is necessary either because no administrative enforcement is possible or enforcement is based on property rights (see below) in order to execute *de facto* administrative enforcement measures.[10]

From a technical-legal perspective, the administrative organ can only be vested with powers in two ways: a) by *attribution* or b) by *delegation*. Attribution means granting original power by a legislative body; delegation means that the organ which has been granted the original power is authorized by law to transfer (delegate) all or some of its power to another organ.

The legislative draft for the fourth phase – it entered into force in 2009 – of the Awb contained several provisions on attribution.[11] Delegation implies the shift of power and responsibility. Therefore a legal basis is necessary (Article 10:15 Awb). For instance, on the basis of Article 107 of the Provinces Act (*Provinciewet*) it is possible for the provincial governments to delegate their powers to municipalities or water authorities 'when these powers are suited to be delegated in light of their scale and nature'. This is also the case for delegation within one body, for instance, from the municipal council to the board of Mayor and Aldermen.[12]

Attribution and delegation serve as tools, in particular for the judge, in establishing whether the organ is competent. Attribution and delegation must be sharply distinguished from *mandate*. An example of mandate is a public servant of a department taking decisions on behalf of the minister. Externally, it is the minister, as the organ, who decides and who is accountable for the decision. Mandate only relates to the internal division of labour. In case of mandate there is no shift of power and therefore no shift of responsibility. This is why as a general rule a legal basis is not required. Mandate is allowed unless a legal provision says otherwise or the nature of the power does not comply with it (Article 10:3, paragraph 1, Awb).[13]

In particular section 3.2 Awb contains a number of provisions that are of major importance and for the most part derived from the principle of legality:

- Article 3:2 Awb prescribes that in preparing a decision the necessary information about the relevant facts must be gathered and the interests

---

10 For *de facto* enforcement ('execution'), e.g. to collect penalties based on administrative orders, the ordinary private law ways have to be followed, although in 2009 also Awb-provisions dealing with financial *decisions* came into force.

11 Apart from incorporating new aspects, the present provisions of the General Administrative Law Code are evaluated from time to time by a specific evaluation commission (*Evaluatiecommissie Awb*). This may lead to adjustments.

12 For an example where this criterion was not met, see the Judicial Department of the Council of State (*Afdeling bestuursrechtspraak van de Raad van State*, ABRS) 28 December 2001, *Jurisprudentie Bestuursrecht* (JB), 2002/63.

13 For instance, the power of the provincial Board of Deputies to decide about a planning/ building decision is not suited for mandate by a provincial civil servant, see ABRS 1 May 2000, *JB* 2000/177.

involved must be weighed against each other (the principle of due care, *zorgvuldigheid*)[14];
- Article 3:3 Awb contains the principle of prohibition of *détournement de pouvoir*, which developed from the principle of legality: the power granted may not be used for a purpose other than that for which it was granted;
- Article 3:4, paragraph 1, Awb contains the principle of specificity (*specialiteitsbeginsel*), also developed from the principle of legality: in taking decisions, the administration may only consider and weigh those interests which the statute in question purports to protect;
- Article 3:4, paragraph 2, Awb finally, contains the principle of proportionality: the adverse effects of a decision on one or more interested parties must not be disproportionate to the aims to be served by the decision.[15]

2. WHO HAS ADMINISTRATIVE POWERS?

2.1. ORGANS AND LEGAL PERSONS

Administrative powers are used by 'organs' (*organen*), or in more modern terminology 'offices'. As natural and artificial persons have the power to create legal effects under private law, equally, under public law, administrative organs are empowered to create and enforce positive public law.

The State, Provinces and Municipalities are all legal persons (*rechtspersonen*) (Article 2:1, paragraph 1, Dutch Civil Code). In the literature, these bodies are sometimes referred to as public-law legal persons (*openbare lichamen*), the modifier 'public-law' indicating their internal organization. In their relations with other persons, they are legal persons, by definition governed by private law. Organs and public-law legal persons must be sharply distinguished. In the majority of cases, they are not two sides of the same coin. In Dutch administrative law the administrative organs can perform decisions, i.e. public law acts, whereas (public law) legal persons can only perform private law acts.

For the organization of the Dutch State in light of the Dutch Constitution see figure 1.

---

14 This is highly linked to the principle of reasoning (*motiveringsbeginsel*) in Article 3:46 Awb. See para 4.2.6.

15 The judge must exercise restraint in testing the discretion of the administration: see para. 5.3.3.3.

Figure 1. State organization of the Netherlands (decentralized Unitary State)*

Institutions	
Central Government	
Crown	Parliament
King and Cabinet of Ministers	1st and 2nd Chamber
Decentral government	
Provinces (12)	
Commissioner to the King and Board of Deputies	Provincial Council
Municipalities (388)**	
Mayor and Board of Mayor and Aldermen	Municipal Council
Water authorities (and other public bodies)	

* The Kingdom of the Netherlands consists of the Netherlands, Aruba, Curaçao and St. Maarten. Here we only deal with the Netherlands. A few islands (Bonaire, St. Eustatius and Saba) belong to the legal system of the Netherlands (see Statute of the Kingdom of the Netherlands, in its (changed) text since 10–10–2010).

** In the last decades, due to the merging of smaller municipalities, its number has decreased from more than 1000 to 388. Regional organizations of municipalities can be formed.

The organs at the municipal level are the Municipal Council, the Municipal Executive, consisting of the Mayor and the Aldermen, and the Mayor. The public body that is the municipality is the legal person. It is therefore not possible to enter into a contractual relation with the Executive or the Municipal Council, but one can do so with the Municipality as the public body. In cases governed by private law, the Executive (Article 160, paragraph 1 under e, Municipalities Act (*Gemeentewet*) will decide whereas the Mayor acts as the formal representative (Article 171 Municipalities Act). This distinction is relevant, among other things, for procedural law. In civil cases, the public body, the legal person, is the party; in administrative (judicial) review, the organ is the party. The same applies for the other authority levels (Provinces Act / Water Authorities Act (*Waterschapswet).*

For the purpose/application of the Awb an organ is defined in Article 1:1 Awb.[16] For this and other key provisions of the Awb, see the Annex to this contribution.

16 An interesting point in this respect is that for a body to constitute an organ for the purposes of the Awb, an explicit legal basis to perform a public law act is not always required. This is done to provide for legal protection but only in cases of conferring rights to individuals like benefits. Where duties are imposed by the administration the administrative judge sticks to the principle of legality. See also under para. 3.1.

Not only must the concepts of 'organ' ('office') and 'legal person' ('public body') be sharply distinguished; a distinction must also be made between the concepts of 'organ' ('office') and its representative, the 'officer'. Positive law does not make this distinction as clearly as it should. 'Office' and 'officer', for instance, are used interchangeably and are expressed by the same term, for instance, 'Mayor'.

Administrative powers are vested in the organ. If, for example, a Mayor issues a particular decision, for which the legal basis is a specific statute, this decision is issued by the office of the Mayor, not by the person holding the office at that particular moment, the officer. If after a period of time, another natural person holds the office, the decision continues to be valid, because the office is continuous.

From the above one could infer that the legal person that is the public body no longer plays a role. This is true from a strictly positive-law angle. Public bodies do not have the power to create positive law. This must not be taken to mean, however, that they are completely irrelevant from a public-law perspective. On the contrary, public bodies constitute a community which have their own place in the constitutional constellation. They are also strongly rooted in history. As a result of their communal nature, the organs of a single body are heavily involved with each other. The Municipal Executive of Mayor and Aldermen must account for its decisions to the Municipal Council.

The communal nature of public bodies may be deemed to have the following common traits:

- A certain common area or other common given. All persons residing in the area belong to the public body. It may also happen that a particular person possesses a certain capacity, for instance, that of landowner or practitioner of a particular profession, and belongs to the public body for that reason (functional delineation). Examples are such special corporate bodies as water authorities (*waterschappen*) and product corporations (*productschappen*). See Articles 133 and 134 Constitution in which it is stated that these authorities (and the abolishment of them) are regulated in Acts. The latter are abolished since 2015.
- (Direct) election of representatives on the highest organs of the public body. The members of the Municipal and Provincial Council for instance, are directly elected (Article 129 Constitution).
- The power of the highest organ to issue regulations. In the case of territorial decentralization, this power is rather undefined, rather open. Article 149 Municipalities Act provides that the Council issues those regulations (*verordeningen*), which it deems necessary in the interest of the municipality. This is sometimes called the autonomous power of the Municipal Council: it can establish rules of its own motion. The same applies to provinces (see Article 105 Provinces Act).

- Most regulations, however, are issued under what is called *medebewind*, under powers of implementation or delegated legislation. This means that a particular Act of Parliament prescribes that the Municipal Council (or the Provincial Council) at some point in time must issue an ordinance to implement the Act. In the case of *functional* (as opposed to *territorial*) decentralization the power is more defined, in the sense that the exercise of the power is only allowed in connection with the function the public body is expected to fulfil, for instance, a water authority only has the power to regulate water quantity where the Water Authorities Act has so provided. Depending on specific Acts competences are situated at the decentral level. Important decision-making powers for administrative organs in individual cases, such as the power to grant environmental licenses, water permits and social benefits etc. are also granted under this system. Of course in some areas such competences can also be at the central level, for instance related to ministers, for instance in the field of national infrastructure or in asylum cases. In the later a specific service is created that decides on behalf of the Minister of Justice (*Immigratie en Naturalisatie Dienst*).
- Its own rates area, from which expenditure, although often only partly, is defrayed, for instance, a municipal property tax.

2.2. DECENTRALIZATION VERSUS DECONCENTRATION AND INDEPENDENT ADMINISTRATIVE ORGANS

The concept of (territorial and functional) decentralization must be sharply distinguished from the concepts of 'deconcentration' and 'independent administrative organ' (*zelfstandige bestuursorganen*). Deconcentration refers to public servants, often working 'up country', who have their own original or derived powers. In spite of these powers, hierarchically, they are fully subject to the Minister, who may give them general instructions and is fully accountable for their actions. The legislature grants original powers to a deconcentrated office(r), since a large number of individual administrative decisions of an executive nature is usually involved, whose execution requires a specific expertise. A clear example is the tax inspector. Dutch (constitutional) law includes many other inspectorates, for instance, in the field of health care and labour conditions. Decentralization lacks this strict hierarchy.

Decentralized public bodies are, of course, not fully independent. The Netherlands is a decentralized unitary State. This implies that central government has specific supervisory powers with regard to lower authorities (see, for example, Article 132 Constitution).[17]

[17] Either before (preventative control) or after decision-making (repressive control) by their organs.

In some policy areas administrative organs are established to execute public tasks, but without a hierarchical relation between the minister and the organ (and the latter is not part of the decentralized authorities). These organs are called independent administrative organs or agencies (*zelfstandig bestuursorgaan,* ZBO). These organs are established by a special statute which grants them powers to take public law juridical acts. The Minister only has powers and the possibility to influence the execution of the public tasks by the organ which have been granted to him/her by the statute in question. Hence the word 'independent'. In the Netherlands, these independent organs have been allowed to proliferate wildly. There are hundreds of them now. Arguments in favour of establishing a ZBO are:

a. the involvement of the interested parties in the administration, for instance, representatives of both employers and employees are involved in the execution of social security laws;
b. the use of a specific expertise available in society (which may entail the granting of public powers to private individuals), for instance, in the case of car inspections; and
c. because the legislature thought it wise to have particular tasks executed at a certain distance from the traditional authorities.

The difference between ZBOs and decentralized powers is that ZBOs lack communality or only possess a rudimentary form of it, namely in the event that interested parties are involved.[18] A few (recently introduced) ZBOs (with important administrative powers) are operating in the field of competition law (*Autoriteit Consument en Markt*), financial law (*Autoriteit Financiële Markten*) and in the field of environmental emissions trading (*Emissieautoriteit*).

3. WHAT INSTRUMENTS ARE AVAILABLE TO THE ADMINISTRATION?

3.1. ACTIONS OF ADMINISTRATION (UNDER PUBLIC LAW)

The administration is made up of public bodies, who have legal personality (e.g. the state or the municipality) and their administrative organs (e.g. the Minister of Defence or the Mayor of Amsterdam). The public bodies can perform private law acts (e.g. buy and sell ground), whilst the administrative organs are the

18 A Bill governing independent administrative organs was sent to Parliament in 2001, *Kamerstukken II* (Parliamentary Documents) 2000–01, 27 426. At the eind of 2006 a Framework Act dealing with ZBO's was approved in Parliament (*Kaderwet zelfstandige bestuursorganen*).

'real users' of the administrative law powers. What an administrative organ (*bestuursorgaan*) is follows from Article 1:1 Awb.[19]

The most important legal instruments available to the administrative organs to defend public interests are the juridical decisions governed by public law (*publiekrechtelijke rechtshandelingen*). However, the administration can also take action in a (non-intended) factual (non legal) way (*feitelijke handelingen*). They include acts which could also be performed by private individuals and which are, in fact, increasingly performed by private individuals after being so commissioned by the administration. Examples are garbage collection, road maintenance and landscape maintenance. Liability under tort law of the legal person or entity can be at stake here.

The power to perform juridical acts under public law is founded, as a rule, in written law (principle of legality), although if a public body is sufficiently involved substantively and financially with the public task a private entity has to perform or if a general legal principle is the basis for an act, this can be sufficient to create public law decisions. In this respect the decision of the administration on the request of somebody to compensate the damage caused by the exercise of power by the administration is, although not based on a specific legal basis, in case law regarded as a public law decision and therefore a decision in the meaning of Article 1:3 Awb.[20] The possible range of (juridical) decisions under public law is outlined here as well as the possibility to appeal against these decisions. The extent to which the administration is allowed to (defend the public interest via the) use (of) private law, for instance, by concluding agreements or make use of property rights, is discussed in paragraph 3.3.[21]

3.2. ADMINISTRATIVE DECISIONS GOVERNED BY PUBLIC LAW (*BESLUITEN*)

The most important way for administrative organs to perform their public law tasks and competences is the administrative decision (*besluit*). The most important type of administrative decision is the decision in individual cases (*beschikking*). The generally applicable regulation (*algemeen verbindend voorschrift*, AVV) is also a part of administrative law. The concept of administrative decision (*besluit*) of Article 1:3, paragraph 1 Awb is defined very broadly so as to comprise all juridical acts governed by public law. However, Article 3:1, paragraph 1, Awb provides that section 3.2 is applicable only to

---

19 For the scope of the concept of administrative organ, see for instance, ABRS 17 september 2014, *ECLI:NL:RVS:2014:3379* (*Stichting bevordering kwaliteit leefomgeving*).

20 See key case of the ABRS 6 May 1997, *AB* 1997, 229 (*Van Vlodrop*) confirmed in later cases.

21 It is worthwhile mentioning here that there where private law is used this may not be contrary to written or unwritten public law, see Article 3:14 Civil Code. See also footnote 35 and accompanying text.

generally applicable regulations, where the nature of the decision so allows.[22] Within the range of the generally applicable regulations and administrative decisions for individual cases all kinds of concepts have developed which are neither AVVs nor individual decisions: certain plans, policy rules and the so called 'concrete norms'. Together with the AVVs, these legal concepts form decisions of general application *(besluiten van algemene strekking*, BAS).

3.2.1. Administrative Decisions in Individual Cases (beschikkingen)

In Article 1:3, paragraph 1, Awb the definition is given of the public law decision. It concerns a juridical act of an administrative organ that intends to externally create a change in the legal status or position of individuals. It is opposed to factual action where there is no intention to create (new) changes in public law (for instance, giving general information to individuals). Factual action related to the preparation of a public law decision dissolves in the decision itself and to this action the same rules apply as to the decision itself. Although an explicit refusal on a request (*aanvraag*) by a person to take a decision is not changing anything in the field of law this is also regarded as a decision (Article 1:3, paragraph 2, Awb). As for the possibility of objections (*bezwaar*)/appeal (*beroep*) the written refusal to decide is a decision as well as the lack of taking a (timely) decision (Article 6:2 under a and b Awb). To make it complex: the refusal to take a decision not to enforce (to condone) is not regarded as such, while the decision not to enforce is regarded as such.[23] Furthermore, a decision on objection (Article 7:1 Awb) is always a decision that can be appealed against irrespective the content of the decision.[24] A vision/statement of the administration in which certain consequences of legal rules are outlined is not considered to cause legal consequences – the rules themselves do so – and are therefore no decisions in the meaning of Article 1:3 Awb, unless it is very unreasonable to postpone the dispute of those rules to the appeal against the actual/concrete (individualized) decision which still has to be taken.[25]

The public law character is related to the exclusive domain (so not the common domain of everybody) of the administration: the competence (*bevoegdheid*). From Article 1:3 Awb also follows that when a public law decision is not issued by an administrative organ it isn't a decision in the meaning of this article.[26]

---

22 In line with this is Article 8:3 Awb, on the basis of which no appeal to the administrative law judge is possible against generally applicable regulations.

23 ABRS 18 June 2003, *AB* 2003, 394.

24 ABRS 24 January 1995, *JB* 1995, 101.

25 ABRS 8 July 2009, *AB* 2009, 363.

26 In principle this could also involve statutes/Acts of Parliament. However, pursuant to Article 1:1, para. 2 (A), Awb, the legislature at the central State level is not an administrative 'organ' (authority) within the meaning of the Awb. Only decisions by organs within the meaning of the Awb fall within the scope of the Awb-provisions.

A further requirement is its written form, although complaints and appeals are possible in case there is no (timely) action (Article 6:2, under b, Awb) or in case specific legal acts indicate that decisions are supposed to be taken in cases the administrative organ does not act (*lex silencio positivo*) or in opposite cases, when these acts indicate that no action within a set time must be regarded as a refusal.

Public law decisions in individual cases are governed by Title 4.1 Awb (procedural aspects of making decisions), which applies to all types of administrative decisions in individual cases. Administrative decisions in individual cases can by subdivided in a number of ways. As follows from the above the Awb or special statutes often apply differently to the various categories. Other titles or sections of the Awb than Title 4.1 contain provisions governing certain types of decisions in individual cases, for instance, Title 4.2 governing subsidies and section 5.3 on enforcement orders. Often, special statutes contain special rules for decisions in individual cases taken by virtue of those statutes (*lex specialis derogat legi generali*).

3.2.1.1. Individual Decisions on Application and *Ex Officio* Decisions in Individual Cases

In Article 1:3, paragraph 3, Awb application (*aanvraag*) is defined as 'a request for a decision by an interested party'. Examples are the application for a (environmental) permit (in the field of prevention of pollution/building/nature conservation or land-use) or social welfare benefits. Often decisions in individual cases are taken *ex officio*, not on application. Examples are tax assessments and decisions by which administrative sanctions are imposed.

3.2.1.2. Individualized Decisions addressed at One or Several Persons and Decisions Relating to Objects

The overwhelming majority of administrative decisions in individual cases are addressed to single persons: the granting of licenses or subsidies, tax assessments, etc. An example of an administrative decision relating to an object was the (former) decision, based on the Housing Act (old) (*Woningwet*), to declare a building unsafe. Also the closing of buildings/houses in cases of public order or offences against the Opium Act (*Opiumwet*) can be mentioned here (Article 174a Municipalities Act/Article 13b Opium Act).

3.2.1.3. Decisions in Personam and Decisions *In Rem*

An administrative decision in individual cases is taken *in personam* if its granting depends in part on the personal qualities of the applicant, for instance, the decision to issue a driver's license. In the case of decisions *in rem*, for instance, the granting of environmental licenses (related to building and pollution) personal qualities are in principle not relevant. The distinction is of particular relevance with regard to the transferability of the decisions.

3.2.1.4. Discretionary and Mandatory Decisions

An important distinction is the one between discretionary and mandatory decisions. It would be more precise, actually, to refer to discretionary and mandatory powers. The distinction is not absolute. Decisions are either more discretionary or more mandatory. The distinction is relevant for the extent of judicial review and also for the possibility of making the decision subject to requirements/provisions. In the case of decisions of a more discretionary nature, the judge must, in principle, respect the discretionary freedom of the administration. The court will examine whether the administrative organ could reasonably have come to the decision and of course will examine whether the principles of due care and of a reasoned decision have been respected.[27]

3.2.1.5. Decisions Granting Rights and Posing Obligations

This distinction is also not absolute. Administrative decisions in individual cases often possess traits of both. For instance, the granting of a license is positive in nature, but the requirements attached to the license are negative. Moreover, the license is (partly) positive as regards the licensee, but negative as to third parties. The distinction is also relevant for the revocability of decisions, as well as for their amendability or retro activeness.

3.2.1.6. Perpetual and Temporary Decisions

Administrative decisions in individual cases are sometimes for a determinate period of time, for instance, some very specific environmental permits based on the Environmental Management Act or the Act on Environmental Licensing and General Provisions. The permission to demonstrate based on the Demonstrations Act (*Wet openbare manifestaties*) is granted for a single occasion only. After the demonstration has been performed, the decision has lost its effect, as it were. An example of a perpetual decision, at least in most cases, is the environmental license for the prevention of pollution, which is granted for an

---

[27] For instance the power for Mayor and Aldermen on the basis of the Environmental Licensing and General Provisions Act to grant a permission to build is mandatory, while the power based on the same Act to deviate by permission from the land-use plan is discretionary.
For instance in the field of traffic-safety (*Wegenverkeerswet*) the withdrawal of drivers licences by the Director of the Service dealing with drivers performances *(Centraal bureau rijvaardigheidsbewijzen*) is mandatory. The same applies with respect to administrative fines by the minister for Social Affairs in the area of working safety (*Arbeidsomstandighedenwet).*

indeterminate period of time, although it can be adapted as a result of a change in circumstances. The distinction is also relevant to the question of revocability. In principle a temporary license cannot be revoked, a perpetual license, on the other hand, is revocable.

The above mentioned classification of decisions is rather abstract. The legal effects related to this classification are especially relevant. Other classifications of decisions are possible related to the purpose of seizure (the duty to tolerate certain public and private activities), financial obligations (tax assessment), orders or prohibitions, declaratory and constitutive decisions, to provide benefits (social security law/subsidies), granting the right to compensation, granting a certain status (the appointment of a public servant) and to provide information pursuant to the Act dealing with public access to information of the administration (*Wet openbaarheid van bestuur).*[28]

3.2.2. Administrative Decisions of General Application (besluiten van algemene strekking)

Decisions of general application (*besluiten van algemene strekking,* BAS) may be subdivided into generally applicable regulations (AVV) and other decisions of general application. The Awb does not provide a definition of the concept of AVV. The case law of the Netherlands Supreme Court on Article 79 Judiciary Organization Act (*Wet op de rechterlijke organisatie*), as formulated at the time, offers some guidance as to what is meant by AVV. 'A legislative act (*wet*)', the Supreme Court held[29],

> 'was any general rule with external effect, i.e. a general rule addressed to the public at large, issued by a public authority, which has derived the power to do so from a statute, meaning a rule enacted by the legislature'.

The adverb 'generally' in generally applicable regulations may refer to time, place, persons and actions or occurrences to which the law attaches legal consequences (*rechtsfeiten*). This generality must be seen as relative; not in all cases, at all times and in all places, are AVVs applicable to the public at large. Their effect is often related to a particular place, time and category. A primary feature of an AVV is that the action or occurrence to which the law attaches legal consequences, the *rechtsfeit*, can be repeated. Each time a certain action or event occurs, the rule applies. For instance, each time a person wishes to carry on a particular business, that person needs a license pursuant to a certain rule or set of rules or falls directly under these rules.

---

28 In the very near future to be replaced by (a broader) *Wet open overheid*. This is not further addressed here.

29 HR 10 June 1919, *Nederlandse Jurisprudentie (NJ)* 1919, 647.

The following decisions of general application (BAS) are not generally applicable regulations (AVV):

1. Decisions relating to the operation of AVVs

Examples are: permissions, annulments, revocations or determinations of the coming into effect of an AVV.

2. Plans are often decisions of general application

A plan may be defined as a body of coherent measures taken by the administration, by which a particular organized situation is sought. One of the most well-known examples is the zoning plan (*bestemmingsplan*) based on the Spatial Planning Act (*Wet ruimtelijke ordening*). By the way this plan has the status of AVV while other plans in the field of environmental law are rather BAS or hold policy rules or even have no (in)direct binding force.

3. Policy rules[30]

Policy rules are established in order to give shape to the exercise of administrative powers. Policy rules contain general rules (not being regulations) about the manner in which the administrative organ has to weigh interests, determine the facts or interpret the applicable legal provisions (see Article 1:3, paragraph 4, Awb). They do not involve a separate power, but are based on existing administrative powers. Pursuant to Article 4:81, paragraph 1, Awb, an administrative organ may draw up policy rules in relation to the execution of powers by itself, powers for the exercise of which it is responsible, or those delegated by it.[31] The administrative organ must act in accordance with its policy rules, unless this would have consequences for one of the interested parties, because of special circumstances, which would be disproportionate to the aims pursued by the policy rules (Article 4:84 Awb). The duty to derogate is an essential feature of the concept of 'policy rule'. In this respect, policy rules are different from AVVs.

4. 'Concrete norms' (decisions to substantiate general norms)

In doctrine the term 'concrete norm' is introduced meaning: an administrative juridical act (*rechtshandeling*), which provides an AVV with concrete content and practical applicability according to time and place. One can think of actions

30 They used to be called 'pseudo-legislation'. They must not be confused with guidelines (*richtlijnen*) enacted by (private) organizations or higher authorities not linked to the execution of administrative powers.

31 By the way: no direct appeal against these rules is possible (Article 8:3 Awb) although of course they can be tested indirectly by the courts in cases where appeal is made against individual decisions in which these rules have been used.

through which AVV's become applicable, such as the placing of a traffic sign through which the underlying AVV becomes applicable in a certain street or area. It goes too far in this respect to elaborate on this.

3.2.3. Administrative Actions and (Possible) Appeal to the Administrative Court

Article 8.1 Awb holds the possibility for an interested person to appeal. Until 2013 it explicitly mentioned the appeal to the District Court (Administrative Law Section) (*rechtbank*).[32] Access to this court, as a general rule – this is also applicable when appealing to the other (appellate) administrative courts (the Judicial Department of the Council of State (ABRS), the Central Appellate Administrative Court (CRvB) and the Corporations Tribunal (CBB)) – is only possible against (written) public law decisions of administrative organs in individual cases. This follows from Articles 8:1 and 1:3 Awb. Two important exceptions in this respect can be distinguished. The first one enlarging the scope of appeal: the action (not necessarily a decision) against a civil servant (Article 8:2, paragraph 1, sub a Awb) and the (factual) actions or non-actions which have been equated with a decision for the purpose of judicial protection (Article 6:2 Awb). The second one restricting the possibility of appeal: the acts specified in Article 8:4 Awb and the so called negative list of Article 8:5 Awb. Although (possibly) a decision or holding decisions in the meaning of Article 1:3 Awb no appeal is possible, for instance, in the field of spatial planning, against several 'policy plans' or the (procedural) decisions by the municipal council or provincial council to coordinate the taking of certain decisions. Sometimes in specific legislative Acts restrictions are made to appeal. An example is Article 1.4 of the Crisis and Recovery Act (*Crisis- en herstelwet*) on the basis of which decentralized legal entities or their administrative organs are excluded to appeal against decisions falling under this Act, in case these decisions are not addressed to them. In other words: although an interested party in the meaning of Article 1:2 Awb no appeal on the basis of Article 8:1 Awb is possible.

Other exceptions exist such as in the case other administrative courts than the District Court are competent. For instance, in certain environmental disputes, like emissions-trading schemes the ABRS is competent in first and final instance. Only since 1 October 2010 the District Courts became competent in most environmental (dealing with pollution) matters. In most matters of social economic decisions the CBB is competent in first and final instance and in social security cases sometimes the CRvB will be competent in first and final instance. See in this respect figure 5.

Decisions holding generally applicable regulations or policy rules (and decisions that deal with annex aspects such as withdrawing, and approving

---

32 Since 2013 this is changed in an appeal to 'the administrative judge' (*bestuursrechter*). This also includes the other administrative judges. See further on this para. 5.3.1.

these regulations/rules) are not open to judicial review (Article 8:3, paragraph 1, sub a, Awb), whereas other juridical decisions of a general import are subject to judicial review in administrative courts but merely because they contain/relate to individual rights/duties, in other words hold 'decisions' in individual cases (in the meaning of Article 1:3 Awb). Although under discussion, the so called 'concrete norms' (see paragraph 3.2.2 under 4) are open for judicial review. Access to the ordinary courts (Civil Law Section) is possible in cases where no action at the administrative court is possible: factual action, AVV's etc. and also in cases where public law decisions dissolve in underlying private law actions, for instance, the public law decision to conclude a private law agreement (Article 8:3, paragraph 2, Awb). This can, for instance, also be the case when the request for damage related to the (illegal) exercise of power by the administration is not linked to an annex decision that can be appealed against at the administrative court.[33] A large category of decisions that only since 2009 can be appealed against at the Administrative Law Section of the District Court (or other administrative law judges) is that in which obligations to pay either by or towards administrative organs are at stake (Title 4.4. of the Awb). See for instance in relation to enforcement: paragraph 6.1.2. Before 1 July 2009 these had to be appealed against at the Civil Law Section of the District Court, because of their private law e.g. factual nature.[34]

3.2.4. Résumé

The administration can act in various ways of a different legal nature in Dutch law. Some of them fall entirely under the scope of the Awb and can be appealed against at the Administrative Law Section of the District Court (in first instance). Against other administrative actions, even that with a public law nature, the civil law judge may (must) be addressed, for instance, in the case of generally applicable regulations. Sometimes both judges – one has to choose – can deal with disputes between the administration and individuals, for instance, in some cases of damage caused by concrete decisions: although the decision which causes the damage itself has to be tested by the administrative judge and if not, in principle the legality of it is given for the civil judge. Differences exist as to the applicable law but also the costs (legal representation/court fees/ number of appellate courts). Although for most decisions in individual cases the administrative law judge is the only one and is addressed, the twofold dimension as to the access to court against actions by the administration from time to time leads to problems of delimitation and of course discussions between scholars. For an overview, see figure 2.

---

33 As for this 'connexity' principle, see the case mentioned in footnote 20.

34 If no decisions are taken, the civil court is still competent, for instance, in tort cases: for an example, where the state was sued for not providing illegal asylum seekers with shelter and care, see Court of Appeal (*Gerechtshof*) Den Haag, 11 January 2011, ECLI:NL:GHSGR:2011:BO9924.

Figure 2. Administrative actions and decisions

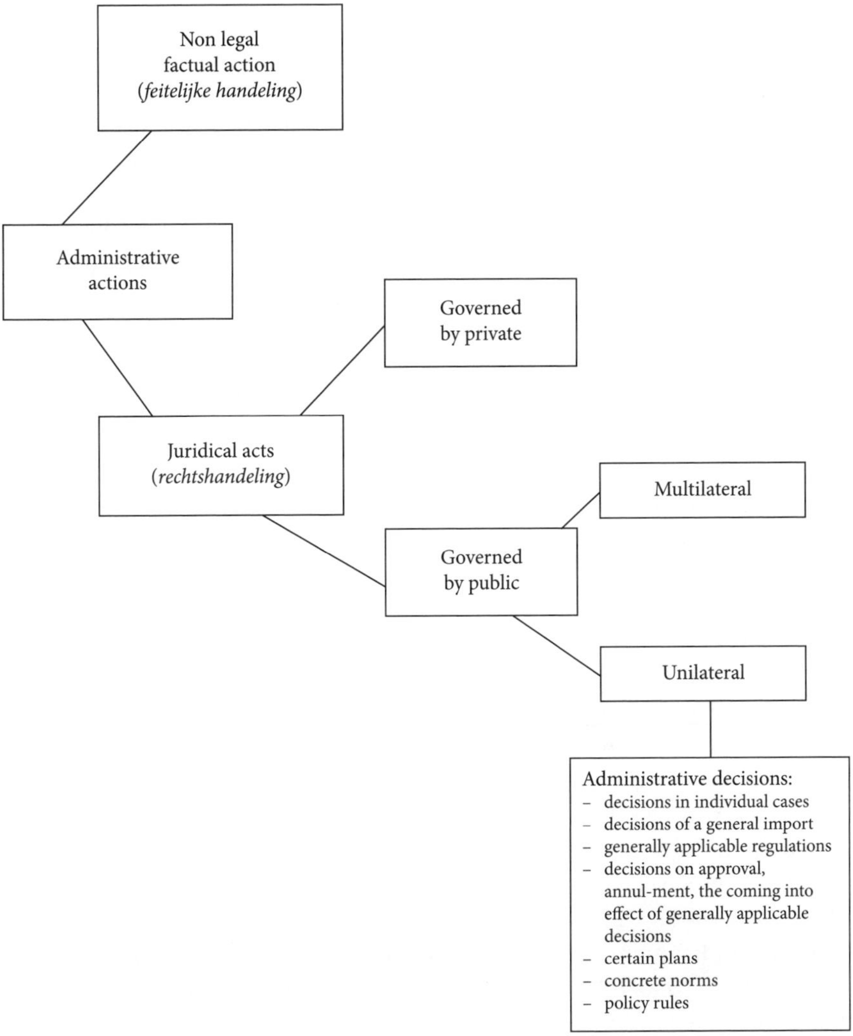

3.3. USE OF PRIVATE LAW BY THE ADMINISTRATION

As discussed in chapter 2, public bodies possess legal personality (under civil law). As a consequence, they may enter into agreements. In the case of disputes relating to such agreements the civil court is competent. In the Netherlands, there is no system, as in France or Germany, which characterizes certain agreements as agreements governed by administrative law (not codified), as a result of which the administrative judge has jurisdiction in these matters. Being this not the case, the civil court is competent. Although in practice (to achieve public goals) the administration uses its public law powers maybe more frequently than its civil law competences it is important to point out (the restrictions to) the latter.

Until 1987, the Supreme Court, the highest court in civil matters, used to treat an administrative legal person the same way as all other legal or natural persons. Until 1990, the Supreme Court's view was that private law could be used by the administration, also in the event of a power governed by public law, in order to achieve the same goal. This was called the two-track doctrine (*tweewegenleer*). The only restriction was that the administration was not to abuse its powers and its effective power position. In the 1987 *Ikon* case[35], the Supreme Court held that administrative acts/actions, which were governed by private law, were also subject to the general principles of proper administration. In this hereditary lease (*erfpacht*) case, the Supreme Court examined whether a public body, in exercising its powers, should act in accordance with the general principles of proper administration, which included the principle of equality (*gelijkheidsbeginsel*). The Municipality of Amsterdam had included conditions in the lease agreement that normally should have been part of a zoning plan on the basis of the Spatial Planning Act (*Wet op de ruimtelijke ordening*). *Ikon Beleidsconsulenten BV* had bought a building, which was used as a dwelling. It planned to convert it into an office building and use it as such. The Municipality of Amsterdam prohibited this, invoking the terms of the hereditary lease agreement, which provided, among other things, that the lessee under a hereditary lease was not allowed to change the use of the grounds and structures to be erected on it without the prior written permission of the Municipal Executive. This theory, developed by the Supreme Court, has been partly codified in the Awb.[36] Since 1994, Article 3:1, paragraph 2, Awb has provided that section 3.2 through 3.4 is applicable to acts other than public law decisions, i.e. factual actions and juridical acts governed by private law, in so far as the nature of the acts does not preclude this.

In 1990, the Supreme Court created some obstacles to the use of private law by the administration, if the administration had powers under public law which could be used to attain the same goal. The Supreme Court argued as follows, concerning the use of an agreement (in literature sometimes called policy agreement)[37]:

> 'to be examined here is the question whether the administration, where certain powers have been granted to it under a public-law rule for the pursuit of certain interests, may also pursue these interests by using powers granted to it, in principle, under private law, such as powers derived from the right of ownership, the power to enter into agreements governed by private law, or the power to institute civil

---

35 HR 27 March 1987, *AB* 1987, 273 and *NJ* 1987, 727.

36 Partly, because not all general principles of proper administration have (yet) been laid down in the Awb. The *Ikon* case therefore still applies where these principles have not been codified.

37 HR 26 January 1990, *AB* 1990, 408 and *NJ* 1991, 393 (*Windmill*).

> proceedings as a result of a tort suffered by it. If the public-law rule in question does not so provide, a decisive factor in answering the question is whether the use of private-law powers unacceptably interferes with the public-law rule. Among others the content and purpose of the rule (which could also be inferred from its history), the way in which and the extent to which the interests of the citizens are protected by the rule, should be taken into account. This should be considered in relation to the remaining written and unwritten rules of public law. Furthermore, it should be examined whether the administration by using the public-rule law is able to achieve a result which compares with the result that could be achieved by using a power under private law, because, if so, it constitutes a major indication that there is no room for taking the private-law route'.

In this case, a manufacturer of fertilizer, Windmill, had deposited waste gypsum in the *Nieuwe Waterweg*, a waterway owned by the State. In its capacity as owner, the State demanded compensation. The Pollution of Surface Waters Act (*Wet Verontreiniging Oppervlaktewateren*), however, provided for the possibility of imposing a charge in such cases. The Act contained rules on the legal foundation of, and the criteria for, the charges. The Supreme Court held that the rules of the Pollution of Surface Waters Act had been unacceptably interfered with, in particular because the State, in so acting, had been able to evade the rules on the charge's legal foundation, the criteria for it and the level of the charge.

After 1990, the Supreme Court rendered many judgements in which the two-track doctrine figured. This case law is rather casuistical. For instance, the Supreme Court assumes that, with regard to spatial planning, the administration may make ample use of private law (based on property rights).[38]

In the area of enforcement by public authorities, the Court, however, more consistently opts for the one-track doctrine. If the administrative organ in question has an administrative enforcement power in conjunction with the power to impose a daily penalty (*dwangsom*), that administration does not have the possibility to bring an action in tort against the offender.[39]

Especially exercise-of-powers agreements may cause legal difficulties. These agreements are made before taking an administrative decision under public law: the administration and the private party (often a legal entity) agree on how the administration will use its power to act. In the majority of cases, the agreement concerns a private party promising financial compensation for something it wishes the administration to do (for instance, granting a permit). In these cases, a tendency towards a more strict approach by the Supreme Court is also observed. In 1962, the Supreme Court argued as follows[40]:

---

38 HR 8 July 1991, *AB* 1991, 659 (*Kunst en Antiekstudio Lelystad*).

39 See, e.g. HR 7 October 1994, *AB* 1995, 47 (*Zomerhuisje Nieuwveen*). This is different when the public body acts as a private party on the basis of its own property rights (and not primarily as administration).

40 HR 13 April 1962, *NJ* 1964, 366 (*Kruseman*).

> 'that the person who, in order to attain a desired and lawful result, needs the co-operation of another person and, gives to that other person, in order to acquire this co-operation, any property negotiated in exchange for his co-operation, does not give without legal basis, and, after having obtained the desired result, what he has given cannot be recovered as being undue, unless there is no lawful ground for what has happened, for instance, where the party who negotiated the property in exchange for his co-operation abused the circumstances of the other party'.

In this case, Kruseman had paid an amount of money to the Municipality of Amsterdam, to be paid into the Fund for the Withdrawal of Residential Accommodation, in order to obtain from the municipal administration a 'certificate of business premises' on the grounds of Article 1, paragraph 6, Residential Accommodation Act (*Woonruimtewet*). Kruseman had bought a house under the subsequent condition that part of the dwelling could be used to carry on a business. The amount paid by Kruseman served as compensation for lost residential accommodation. When Kruseman tried to recover the amount paid on the grounds of undue payment, he was not accommodated by the Supreme Court.

In a more recent judgement, the Supreme Court's attitude was a lot more critical with regard to the concept of exercise-of-powers agreements.[41]

The Municipality of Alkmaar had co-operated in a review of/an exemption from a zoning plan in connection with four houses to be built by Hornkamp. Prior to the review, however, Hornkamp had to enter into an agreement with the Municipality pursuant to which he was obliged to pay the Municipality the sum of NLG 4,000 for the costs of the review. Furthermore, it was negotiated that Hornkamp was to only sell or rent the houses to be built by him (or in any case three of these) to residents of the Municipality or to those who were economically dependent on it. In last-instance proceedings before the Supreme Court, the question arose as to the acceptability of the exercise-of-powers agreement. The Supreme Court answered this question in the negative:

> 'In view of the above, the Court of Appeal did not evidence an incorrect legal opinion by holding that the Municipality, by thus using its powers of refusal, where it did not see any reason to co-operate in granting the exemption requested, so as to effectively make its co-operation contingent on the acceptance of the contractual terms with regard to the selling and renting by Hornkamp exclusively to residents of the Municipality and of those economically dependent on it, used its power for a

---

[41] HR 3 April 1998, *JB* 1998/128 (*Alkemade-Hornkamp*).
HR 2 Mai 2003 *JB* 2002, 234 it was decided that an agreement between a municipality and an individual about who should pay the costs of damage due to land-use plan provisions was an unacceptable overruling of Article 49 Spatial Planning Act on the basis of which the municipality is liable to pay this damage. For such an agreement a specific legal basis is necessary according to the Supreme Court. In 2006 this legal basis is provided for in Article 49a Spatial Planning Act (WRO) and presently in Article 6.4a Spatial Planning Act (Wro).

> purpose other than that for which the power was granted, and that in violating the prohibition against *détournement de pouvoir* the agreed term thus contravenes public order and for that reason is void'.

It should be borne in mind that the administrative judge may also be faced with the above questions. By entering into a policy agreement, the administration refuses to go the public-law route. This implies a refusal to take a decision. The latter is, on the basis of Article 6:2 Awb, open to judicial review. If the case is brought before an administrative judge, he may pronounce on the lawfulness or otherwise of the refusal, and therefore on the lawfulness of following the private-law road.

If a private party refuses, in the context of an exercise-of-powers agreement, to perform his financial obligations and, as a consequence, is faced by a refusal of the administration to use its administrative power (grant the permit), such refusal (the legality of the decision) may be disputed before the administrative court. The administrative judge must then decide whether the statute in question allows for the imposition of an obligation to pay financial compensation. Disputes about the agreement (compliance or financial compensation) have to be settled by the civil court based on the Civil Code (*Burgerlijk Wetboek, BW*).[42]

However, where a statute explicitly states that the administration can make use of private law instruments there is no problem in this respect. This is, for instance, the case under Article 75 of the Soil Protection Act (*Wet Bodembescherming*) when the administration wishes to recover costs made for the remediation of polluted soil.[43] See also (since 2009) chapter 4 Awb on administrative debts.

4. WHAT ARE THE NORMS WITH WHICH THE ADMINISTRATION HAS TO COMPLY?

4.1. INTRODUCTION: HIERARCHY OF NORMS

When taking administrative decisions, the administration has to comply with the law, including the following legal norms (see also figure 3):

- the provisions of the General Administrative Law Code (Awb) and relevant case law;
- the unwritten principles of law, as developed by case law;

---

42 See HR 8 juli 2011, ECLI:HR:2011:BP3057, AB 2011/297 (ETAM/Zoetermeer).

43 Of course the administration should comply with all the necessary requirements under private law, see on this: Seerden, R. & Van Rossum, M., 'Legal Aspects of Soil Pollution and Decontamination in the Netherlands', in: Seerden, R. & Deketelaere, K. (eds.), *Legal Aspects of Soil Pollution and Decontamination in the EU Member States and the United States*, Antwerpen: Intersentia, 2000, p. 326–333.

- the generally applicable regulation (AVV) on which the power to act in question is based[44];
- higher generally applicable regulations, for instance, chapter I of the Dutch Constitution dealing with basic rights;
- *erga omnes* (conferring rights and duties) treaty provisions and decisions by international organizations (Articles 93 and 94 Constitution), human rights as laid down in the ECHR being particularly relevant;
- EU-Treaty provisions and secondary legislation (and decisions) taken by EU organs. The EU is a supranational legal order. As early as 1962, the European Court of Justice held that the European Economic Community constituted a new international legal order, to which the States surrendered sovereignty, be it in limited areas, which not only created rights for Member States, but also for its citizens.[45]

Especially in recent years EU legislation influenced Dutch law (legislation and case law) especially in the field of asylum and migration law.

It should be recalled that the norms addressed to the administration are also norms that the court must apply in judicial review. See for this paragraph 5.3.3 on judicial review. An important point to mention here is that on the basis of Article 120 Constitution the court is not allowed to review the constitutionality of Acts of Parliament, whereas it is obliged to see whether these legislative acts are compatible with *erga omnes* (directly applicable) treaty provisions and EU law. Delegated legislative acts or regulations of lower (administrative) organs, however, can be reviewed by the court. The court can even review whether these acts comply with unwritten principles. The case law as to what extent generally binding regulations can be overruled by general principles of law has yet to be fully crystallized however. But it is clear that it is not impossible for the court to set aside delegated legislation such as Crown decrees/ordinances as far as some principles are concerned.[46]

---

44 This can be an Act of Parliament (statute) but also delegated legislation, such as provincial or municipal ordinances.

45 *Algemene Transport- en Expeditieonderneming Van Gend en Loos* v *Nederlandse Administratie der Belastingen*, Case 26/62 [1963] European Court of Justice 1. Two years later, the Court held that the EEC Treaty had created its own legal order, which was incorporated into the legal order of the Member States at the coming into effect of the Treaty, a legal order which the national judges had to take into account. This implied that, in areas where the Member States have transferred rights and duties under the Treaty provisions to the legal order of the Community, their sovereign rights had been limited definitively, *Costa* v *Ente Nationale per l'Energia Elettrica (ENEL)*, Case 6/64 [1964] European Court of Justice 585. In the 1970's and 1980's case law of the Court of Justice saw the light dealing with the direct application and precedence of EC-secondary legislation (regulations, directives) such as Case 43/71 [1971] 1039 and Case 8/81 [1982] ECR 53 and the place in the legislative hierarchy of treaties concluded by the EC Case 61/94 [1996] ECR 3989 (*International Dairy Arrangement*). See more in detail the contribution in this book by Rolf Ortlep and Rob Widdershoven.

46 See, for instance, HR 16 May 1986, *AB* 1986, 574 (*Landbouwvliegers*). But it is impossible or very difficult for Acts of Parliament (depending on whether the lawfulness of the Act as such

Figure 3. The hierarchy of generally applicable regulations

Erga omnes treaty provisions/EU decisions
(*een ieder verbindende bepalingen*)

⇩

Constitution
(*Grondwet*)

⇩

Statutes
(*wetten in formele zin*)

⇩

General administrative orders/Crown decrees
(*Algemene maatregelen van bestuur/koninklijke besluiten*)

⇩

Ministerial orders
(*ministeriële verordeningen*)

⇩

Provincial ordinances
(*provinciale verordeningen*)

⇩

Municipal ordinances, ordinances issued by water authorities
and ordinances issued by other public bodies

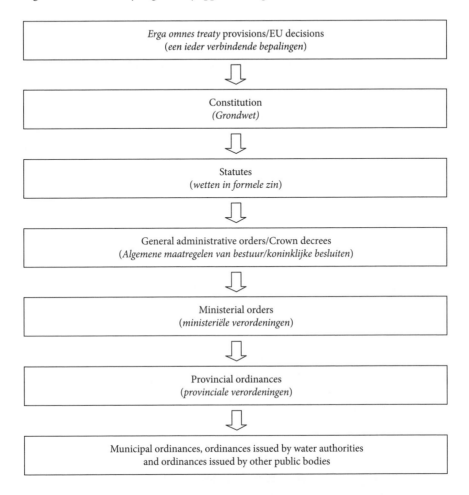

4.2. PRINCIPLES OF PROPER ADMINISTRATION (*ALGEMENE BEGINSELEN VAN BEHOORLIJK BESTUUR*, ABBB)

Below we will discuss the general principles of proper administration, as codified in the General Administrative Law Act (Awb) and the (as yet) uncodified principles of proper administration in more detail.[47]

is questioned respectively the non-application of the Act in a concrete case should be possible; see, for instance, HR 14 April 1989, *AB* 1989, 207 (*Harmonisatiewet*).

47 The allotted space does not allow for a discussion of basic and human rights. In Dutch dogmatics these are deemed to be part of constitutional law.

4.2.1. Prohibition of Bias

An important principle which has been codified in the Awb is the prohibition of bias (*vooringenomenheid*). This principle is laid down in Article 2:4 Awb and has two limbs. Firstly the administration itself has to act without prejudice. Secondly Article 2:4 states that the administrative organ has to ensure that persons working for it or under its responsibility (for instance civil servants or an expert) with a personal interest in the outcome cannot influence the decision-making process. This means that the administration is responsible for ensuring that the decision-making process takes place in a objective manner and improper interests do not play a role in the outcome of this process.

4.2.2. Due Care

Section 3.2 Awb sets out the principle of due care (Article 3:2 Awb, *zorgvuldigheidsbeginsel*) and the weighing of interests (Article 3:4, paragraph 1, Awb, *afweging van belangen*). Article 3:2 Awb is a codification of the essence of the principle of due care and has a formal character. It refers to careful preparation of the decision. Which requirements flow from this principle depends on the nature of the decision and circumstances of a case. If a decision is at hand to grant a permit for a company for activities which have effects on the environment and interests of many people, because it causes pollution of the air or drinking water, the principle requires the administration to do research into these effects before taking a decision or the company itself has to conduct research and then it is up to the administration to review this.

Numerous provisions of the Awb can be considered an elaboration of the principle of due care. For example:

- the provisions governing advice (Articles 3:5 *et seq.* Awb);
- a large number of provisions regarding the (extensive) preparation procedure (paragraph 3.4 Awb);
- provisions governing hearing of applicants when preparing decisions in individual cases (Articles 4:7 and 4:8 Awb);
- the provision of Article 4:5 Awb granting the opportunity to complete an incomplete application.

In addition to this, there are provisions that are closely linked to the principle of due care such as:

- the obligation/duty to forward documents which are obviously linked to the competence of another administrative organ (Articles 2:3 and 6:15 Awb);
- the obligation of the administrative organ to expressly include the possibilities of objection, appeal and judicial review in the decision (Article 3:45 Awb).

4.2.3. *Specificity and détournement de pouvoir*

The legislator not only has to confer a power to take a decision on the administration (legality principle). The limits of this power also have to be specified. The principle of specificity is closely connected to the principle of legality. The administration may only weigh that public interest aspect against the private interests of interested citizens which the statute in question aims to protect. The principle of specificity is laid down in Article 3:4, paragraph 1, Awb. Article 3:3 Awb furthermore contains the prohibition against *détournement de pouvoir*: the administrative organ shall use its power to take decisions for no other purpose than the purpose for which the power has been granted (*specialiteitsbeginsel*). The prohibition against *détournement de pouvoir* has emanated from the principle of specificity.[48] Strictly speaking, the principle of specificity, together with the related prohibition against *détournement de pouvoir*, is not a general principle of administrative law, but a constitutional principle based on the concept of *rechtsstaat*, a state governed by the rule of law.

4.2.4. *Prohibition of Arbitrariness*

The legislator also codified the prohibition to act in an arbitrary manner (*verbod van willekeur*) in Article 3:4, paragraph 2, Awb. This prohibition was developed in case law by the courts and also concerns the constitutional relationship between the courts and the administration. The court can only interfere in the way in which the administration exercises its discretionary power if the decision of the administration is an act of arbitrariness. The courts assume this is the case if the weighing of interests has led to an evidently unreasonable outcome. See further about this paragraph 5.3.3.

4.2.5. *Proportionality*

Article 3:4, paragraph 2, Awb refers explicitly to the principle of proportionality (*evenredigheidsbeginsel*). This norm, addressed to the administration, prescribes that the adverse effects of an administrative decision on one or more interested parties must not be disproportionate to the aims pursued by that decision. In other words, there must be a balanced weighing of the interests involved. This also implies that the administration is not allowed to take measures which will result in needless grave consequences for interested parties (*materiële zorgvuldigheid*). If there are less severe means available the administration is obliged to use these means. Article 3:4, paragraph 2, Awb also contains the principle of *égalité devant les charges publiques* (*gelijkheid voor de openbare*

48 See on this principle Schlössels, R.J.N., *Het specialiteitsbeginsel*, Den Haag: SDU Uitgevers, 1998.

lasten). This principle implies that measures of the administration may not lead to a disproportionate burden for certain individuals in comparison to all others which are affected by the measure.

4.2.6. Reasoning

As in the case of the principle of due care, the principle to state reasons (*motiveringsbeginsel*) is of a formal nature. A decision must be based on valid reasons (Article 3:46 Awb) and the reasons must be stated when the decision is disclosed (Article 3:47, paragraph 1, Awb). The validity of the reasoning concerns the establishment of the facts, the appreciation of the facts, the consistency of the reasoning and whether these elements can lead to the conclusion, i.e. the decision. The principle of reasoned decisions has two major functions. In the first place it increases rational decision-making by the administration. In the second place, it serves as a starting point for the interested citizen who wishes to object to or appeal against the decision.

4.2.7. Legitimate Expectations, Legal Certainty and Equality

(As yet) uncodified principles include the principle of legitimate expectations (good faith) (*vertrouwensbeginsel*), the principle of legal certainty (*rechtszekerheidsbeginsel*) and the principle of equality (*gelijkheidsbeginsel*).

4.2.7.1. Legitimate Expectations

In some instances, the administration's failure to honour legitimate expectations is in violation of the principle of good faith. An important question is who can raise legitimate expectations. It is, of course, first and foremost the administrative organ in question or competent civil servants and individual members of the administrative organ. The legitimacy of the raised expectations also depends on the manner in which the expectations where raised. Was this done explicitly, in a concrete manner concerning the case at hand and in writing? Or could the expectations be derived from a failure to act or general information for the public? Furthermore, the administration has to weigh the interest of the person with legitimate expectations against the general interest and interest of third parties. Under certain (exceptional) circumstances the courts will honour legitimate expectations, even when this would lead to a situation in violation of the law (*contra legem* application). The case law on this subject is not unequivocal. The Judicial Department of the Council of State (*Afdeling bestuursrechtspraak van de Raad van State*) will not rule so in principle, whereas the Central Appellate Administrative Court (*Centrale Raad van Beroep*) and the Supreme Court (*Hoge Raad*) do. A possible explanation for this difference is that in disputes before the Judicial Department of the Council of State often third-party interests are involved, whereas before the Central Appellate Administrative Court and the Supreme Court the dispute, in principle, is between the two parties. In other words, in the latter type of cases third parties are not affected by a *contra legem* decision.

4.2.7.2. Legal Certainty

Closely related to the principle of good faith is the principle of legal certainty.[49] This principle protects existing rights or interests and regulates under which conditions decisions can be altered or revoked (material aspect of the principle of legal certainty). The Judicial Section of the Council of State (*Afdeling Rechtspraak van de Raad van State*, ARRS) one of the predecessors of the present Judicial Department of the Council of State, applied the principle of legal certainty within the context of revoking individual decisions granting rights (positive decisions in individual cases) or the refusal to take such a decision based on decisions in individual cases taken in the past. The latter may occur in large subsidy projects that are being subsidized for a protracted period of time on an annual basis. To stop subsidization from one moment to the next would not be allowed in such cases. The principle not only can imply conditions for the revocation or termination for the future, but it can also imply that termination or revocation with retroactive effect are not possible unless certain requirements are met. In addition, the principle of legal certainty (formal aspect) is applied in order to impose a number of standards on the clarity of a decision; the citizen must know where he/she stands. A case in point is the notice of administrative enforcement. The obligations imposed must have been defined with great accuracy.[50] And finally, the principle of legal certainty may be relevant to the retroactive legal force of generally binding regulations, which put the citizen in a more disadvantageous position.

4.2.7.3. Equality

The principle of equality laid down in Article 1 Constitution (1983) has not often been used as a ground for annulment. This has to do with the fact that two cases are seldom equal and the administration can often rely on grounds for justification of the unequal treatment.[51] There are (exceptional) cases in which the courts have annulled a decision on grounds of violation of the equality

---

49 A number of authors and judges view the principles of good faith and legal certainty as one principle. The principle of good faith in that case is a species of the principle of legal certainty.

50 See, e.g. ARRS 30 January 1979, tB/S III, p. 571.

51 See ABRS 18 June 2003, *AB* 2003, 368; CRvB 30 June 2006, *AB* 2006, 370.

principle.[52] Case law provides more clarity about the circumstances in which invoking the principle of equality cannot lead to success[53]:

- if it would serve as a ground for a decision in contravention of the (written) law and interests of third parties are at stake;
- if it would entail that an incorrect administrative decision issued in an individual case must be repeated;
- if in a similar case the decision was taken not by the defendants, but by a different organ;
- if the policy executed by the administrative organ is consistent or the administrative organ decides to change its policy for the future for good reasons.

4.2.8. Procedures of Decision-Making

In the previous paragraph important principles for decision-making were addressed. Although some of them can be characterized as formal, they must not be confused with Awb-provisions concerning the mere formal procedure for *in primo* decisions, such as:

- how an application for a decision should be drafted by the applicant;
- whether or not a draft decision is necessary;
- whether or not the administration should ask for advice;
- what the time-limits are for making the decision;
- in which way the publication has to be done;
- if there is the possibility for a hearing, etc.

Most of these aspects are dealt with in chapters 3 and 4 of the Awb.[54] Chapter 3 contains the procedural provisions which apply to all decisions of the administration. This chapter does not provide for a general decision-making procedure which has to be followed. It does, however, contain a special procedure which can be declared applicable by the administration or legislature for decisions. Until the middle of 2005 there were several of these special preparation-procedures in this chapter (more or less extensive ones and depending on the question whether the decisions are taken on application or ex officio). Since 2005 the Awb deals with only one more elaborated procedure in chapter 3: the uniform public preparation procedure (*uniforme openbare voorbereidingsprocedure)*. Chapter 4 only concerns decisions for individual and concrete cases and provides for a general preparation procedure for these type of decisions. This procedure is at all times applicable unless the legislator deviates from it in special statutes or the uniform public preparation procedure has been declared applicable by the competent administrative organ. The most important

52 See: ABRS 2 February 2011, *JB* 2011/67; ABRS 14 September 2005, *AB* 2005, 409 (equality principle and principle of reasoned decision violated).

53 ABRS 2 February 2011, *JB* 2011/67.

54 Sometimes specific legislation includes additional or other provisions.

difference between the two is that the uniform public preparation procedure starts with a draft-decision (after an application in most cases) and interested persons can give their views (*zienswijzen*) against it, whereas the procedure in chapter 4 starts with an application but the administration does not provide a draft-decision on which interested persons can give their views before giving its final decision. In some cases, however, the applicant or an interested person must be given the opportunity to give their views if the administration can foresee they will not agree with the decision that will be taken. Furthermore, no objection (*bezwaar)* procedure is possible – one can go straight to court – against the final decision which has been prepared in the uniform public preparation procedure, whereas after the regular procedure in chapter 4 Awb one first has to address the administration before access to court exists.[55]

4.2.8.1. Failure to take a Decision

If the administration fails to take a decision within the statutory time limit appeal will be possible to the administrative judge (Article 6:2 under b Awb). For decisions in individual cases chapter 4 GALA provides for provisions in case the administrative organ fails to take a decision within the statutory time limit. To encourage the administrative organs to act speedily and diligent the GALA automatically imposes a financial penalty on the administrative body for each day it fails to take a decision after the statutory time limit has elapsed. This penalty starts running two weeks after the citizen has sent a default notice to the competent administrative body stating it has breached the statutory time limit (GALA, Articles 4:17 *et seq.*).

4.2.8.2. Decision on Objection

The Awb also contains some specific formal requirements for the decision on objection in chapters 6 and 7. In principle all the requirements for in primo decisions (permits/benefits/enforcement decisions) laid down in chapters 3 and 4 are applicable for decisions on objection but Chapters 6 and 7 can deviate from those.

5. LEGAL PROTECTION AGAINST ADMINISTRATIVE ACTION

5.1. WHICH COURT IS COMPETENT?

As in the case of civil litigation and criminal proceedings, the right of access to an independent and impartial judicial body also exists in the case of administrative

55 See also para. 5.2 and footnote 75.

disputes. In the Netherlands, this right has been recognized by the civil courts since the beginning of the twentieth century. The civil judge deems himself/herself competent in the case of debt recovery claims, even if such claims are rooted in public law.[56] The civil court will, however, not review the content of the claim and declares the citizen's claim inadmissible (*niet ontvankelijk*), if there is the possibility of recourse to an administrative judge covered with sufficient safeguards. The civil judge is sitting as a 'residual' judge, offering additional legal protection.[57]

Until 1985, the civil judge would also refrain from ruling on the content of the claim if there was a possibility of appeal to the Crown (*Kroonberoep*), a special form of administrative appeal provided by over one hundred statutes and protected by specific safeguards. The Administrative Disputes Section of the Council of State (*Afdeling Geschillen van bestuur van de Raad van State*), for instance, had to give an opinion to the minister in the form of a preliminary judgement, which came about after proceedings rather similar to administrative court proceedings. Furthermore, it was difficult for the minister in question to ignore the opinion. The civil court deemed that *Kroonberoep* had so many safeguards that it equated with appeal before an administrative court.

In 1985, the European Court of Human Rights, however, put a stop *to Kroonberoep* as a last instance recourse in administrative matters.[58] The ECtHR held that an environmental license affects the freedom of ownership and the contractual freedom of a licensee/applicant and that, for this reason, 'civil rights and obligations' are affected within the meaning of Article 6, paragraph 1, ECHR. This implies the right of access to an independent and impartial judicial body. The Crown appeal could not be regarded as such. With this judgement, the ECtHR brought a large part of administrative law under the scope of Article 6 ECHR. The judgement in the *Benthem* case has resulted in the abolishment of *Kroonberoep* in the Netherlands.

5.1.1. Towards Enactment of the Awb

In civil and criminal cases things are relatively simple: in the majority of cases there are two instances which examine and assess the facts and the law, namely the District Courts (*rechtbanken*) (and the Courts of Appeal (*Gerechtshoven*) and from which cassation can be lodged with the Supreme Court (*Hoge Raad*) on points of law only. The aforementioned courts belong to the so called judicial power (*rechterlijke macht*).[59]

---

56 See HR 31 December 1915, *NJ* 1916, p. 407 (*Guldemond Noordwijkerhout*).

57 See, for instance, HR 22 February 1957, *NJ* 1957, p. 555 (*Schellen en deuropeners*) in which it was stated that administrative appeal to another administrative organ was not sufficiently covered with these guarantees.

58 ECtHR 23 October 1985, *AB* 1986, 1 (*Benthem*).

59 This judicial power is regulated in the Judiciary Organization Act (*Wet op de Rechterlijke Organisatie*).

In administrative law, such a simple system never existed for the following reasons: first, there is the complexity of administrative law itself. It consists of a large number of different, or 'special', parts. These special parts relate to very different social situations; they were developed at different points in time and their relevant legislation was drawn up by several ministries. It is not so obvious at first sight, therefore, that legal protection with regard to tax assessments, building permits, zoning plans or subsidies is regulated in the same fashion. Furthermore, both scholars and politicians had different views as to how legal protection against administrative action should be best given shape. There were:

- proponents of administrative appeal, in particular *Kroonberoep*. Until the 1985 *Benthem* judgement, administrative appeal was very popular in the Netherlands. It was argued, for instance, that administrative appeal was advantageous to citizens in that a full test was applied (on lawfulness and policy). It should be borne in mind that it was only after the Second World War that the role of the (administrative) judge grew in importance. Only then did courts develop unwritten legal principles on a large scale and began to review more intensively. The lawfulness test as applied in the beginning of the last century offered the citizen only limited protection. Other arguments were the knowledge of the administration and the fact that the administrative appellate proceedings resulted in a new administrative decision. The judge, on the other hand could in general only annul decisions;
- proponents of special administrative jurisdiction. Such jurisdiction is to be taken to mean tribunals competent to give judgement in relation to a particular policy area only, for instance, social security. It was felt that it was an advantage that lay persons could be involved in these cases, for instance, the Social Security Tribunals (*Raden van Beroep*) were composed of a presiding professional judge, an employer representative and an employee representative. An additional advantage, it was felt, was that the professional judges would be able to develop into experts in the particular policy area;
- proponents of general administrative jurisdiction, within or outside the ordinary judiciary. Such jurisdiction was to be taken to mean the situation in which a judge has jurisdiction, in principle, for the entire area of administrative law. Knowledge also played a part here.

The different opinions in science and politics, as well as the gradual development of administrative law, resulted in a particular solution being chosen for a specific topic of administrative law each time. This resulted in a patchwork of legal protection, occurring for the main part outside the ordinary judiciary. Each statute or group of related statutes had its own system, which resulted in the following situation:

- *Kroonberoep* for very important parts of administrative law, such as the environment, environmental planning, nature and education;

- a number of special administrative tribunals, for instance, in the area of social security (Social Security Tribunals, *Raden van Beroep*), for the law governing public servants (Public Service Tribunal, *Ambtenarengerecht*) and for socio-economic administrative law (Corporations Tribunal, *College van Beroep voor het Bedrijfsleven*). Since the 1950s, tax cases were assigned to Tax Chambers of the Courts of Appeal and the Tax Chamber of the Netherlands Supreme Court;
- from 1976 onwards, a general administrative judge, in the form of the Judicial Section of the Council of State pursuant to the Judicial Review of Administrative Action Act *(Wet Administratieve Rechtspraak Overheidsbeschikkingen*, Arob).[60] This judicial body had jurisdiction in a large number of individual administrative decisions. It was sometimes called a complimentary residual administrative judge, because the jurisdiction of the Crown and that of the special administrative judge remained intact;
- the civil court as a sort of unwritten administrative court. If a special statute did not include provisions on legal protection, which was often the case, the citizen affected by the decision could always submit his case to the civil court, bringing an action in tort (the civil court as residual court). The civil court has also contributed significantly to the development of unwritten principles of administrative law (general principles of proper administration).

Nor must the role of the criminal court be forgotten. Administrative law is not only enforced through administrative sanctions, but also by applying criminal law. The special statutes often define acting without a license or, in contravention with the requirements attached to it, as a criminal offence. The criminal court (like the administrative and civil court) has the power to review exceptively, which means that it may test a hierarchically lower generally applicable regulation (AVV) against a higher one. If there is a conflict, the lower AVV is not applied or is declared to have no binding force. This has resulted in the fact that many citizens have been discharged from further prosecution, because the permit system in question conflicted with a higher rule.

5.1.2. Enactment of the Awb

Conceivably, one may get along with such patchwork of legal protection. There are, however, disadvantages attached to it. The system is not clear to the citizens and certainly fails to create legal unity. In order to promote legal unity and legal development, a system is needed that has a single last-instance court at the top of the hierarchy. Inasmuch as a complete reorganization was very comprehensive and drastic, the government, however, opted for a phased approach.

---

60 *Staatsblad* 1975, 284.

As of 1 January 1994, appeal from many administrative decisions can be lodged on the basis of Article 8:1, paragraph 1, Awb with the Administrative Law Section of the District Court (*Rechtbank*).[61] With this, the first phase was achieved: the introduction of administrative law sections at the District Courts charged with first-instance judicial review against administrative acts (*besluiten*), or in any case a large part of it. Appeal from judicial review and last-instance appeal, the integration of socio-economic jurisdiction into the court system and the reorganization of fiscal jurisdiction were to take place at a later stage.[62] This means appeal against the judgement of the District Court is still possible at several bodies: for social security matters the Central Appellate Administrative Court, for social economical matters the Corporations Tribunal and all other administrative disputes end up at the Judicial Department of the Council of State (which acts as a residual appeal court). In 2004 the government concluded that there was no need to reorganize the administrative justice system completely which means part of the patchwork still exists.[63]

On 1 January 2005 tax sections were introduced at the District Court level.[64] In tax disputes from that time onwards appeal has to be made to the District Court and appeal against the judgement of the (Administrative Law Section of the) District Court is possible at the Court of Appeal. Cassation is possible after that at the Supreme Court. Before the present court system is discussed (paragraph 5.3.1 onwards), something has to be said about administrative proceedings first.

5.2. ADMINISTRATIVE PROCEEDINGS

Although it is now widely accepted that an administrative dispute ultimately has to be decided upon by an independent (administrative) court, the general view taken in the Awb is that the court may not be approached immediately. First, the decision in primo must be reconsidered by the administration. Two important considerations underlie this view: the first is the desire to protect the courts against excessive caseloads and the second is that the legislator deemed it important that the administration has the opportunity to review/reconsider the decision and correct possible mistakes.

61 See further para. 5.3.1 and para. 5.3.2. As already mentioned (footnote 32) since 2013 this is an appeal to 'the administrative judge'. Since then it is stated in Article 8:6 Awb that this is, as a general rule, the District Court. See para. 5.3.1.

62 See on this: Stroink, F.A.M., *Rechterlijke organisatie en rechtspraak in beweging*, Zwolle: W.E.J. Tjeenk Willink, 1993.

63 Letter from the minister of Justice and the minister of Interior of 28 April 2004, *Kamerstukken II* 2003/04, 25 425, no. 7. See also para. 5.3.1.

64 Act of 15 December 2004 (*Staatsblad* 2004, 692).

The most important procedure of administrative review is objection (*bezwaar*) to an administrative decision by way of lodging a written notice (*bezwaarschrift*). Article 7:1 Awb prescribes that the person entitled to lodge an appeal with the administrative court must first object to the decision prior to bringing his/her case before the administrative court.[65] The time limit for making an objection is 6 weeks after the publication of the decision *in primo* (Article 6:7 Awb). The most important features of objection are the following:

- the organ which primarily decided, will decide on the written objection;
- the organ which primarily decided, reviews the decision as to its lawfulness and effectiveness (policy);
- review takes place *ex nunc*, so new (relevant) aspects should be considered.

When no court action is taken after the decision on complaint the decision obtains a so-called formal/final status (*formele rechtskracht*) in the sense that the decision is inviolable and the civil and criminal courts in later cases should regard the decision as a legally valid one. Of course this status is also applied by these courts when the administrative court decides that the appeal against the decision is unfounded.

One possible drawback of the objection procedure is that the interested citizen may feel that the administrative organ or procedure will be biased because he has to complain to the same organ that issued the decision. The Awb legislator has prescribed a number of requirements for the procedure, which should ensure objective decision-making. Important guarantees for objective decision-making are the following:

- the administrative organ must exercise its duties without prejudice (Article 2:4, paragraph 1, Awb);
- section 7.2 Awb contains special provisions on objections. A major special provision is the duty to grant a hearing pursuant to Article 7:2 Awb;
- the duty to state the relevant reasons for the decision pursuant to Article 7:12 Awb;
- the possibility to install an advisory committee chaired by an independent chairperson (Article 7:13 Awb). This is often done in practice and often this committee also conducts the hearing;
- if the decision on the objection departs from the committee's opinion/recommendation, the reasons for the departure must be given in the decision and the opinion/recommendation is sent together with the decision (Article 7:13, paragraph 7, Awb);
- Article 10:3, paragraph 3, Awb provides that a mandate to decide on a written objection shall not be granted to the person who has under a mandate taken

[65] On 1 September 2004 Article 7:1a Awb entered into force which makes the administrative review proceedings optional; the parties may skip in certain cases these proceedings by mutual consent.

the decision against which the objection was submitted. This means that the decision on the objection must be taken by a higher officer (under a mandate) or by the administrative organ itself.

The possibility of objecting to a decision is a general rule of the Awb. There are, however, two other administrative review procedures which are nowadays rare, namely administrative appeal (*beroep*) and approval (*goedkeuring*).[66] If a special statute provides for administrative appeal or approval in specific cases, the objection procedure need not be followed (Article 7:1, paragraph 1, Awb). In the system of the GALA only one administrative preliminary procedure has to be followed: either administrative objection, administrative appeal or administrative approval. The nature of administrative appeal is such that the appeal must be lodged with an organ other than the organ, which took the decision. As regards review, there is no difference to administrative objection. In either case, the decisions are fully reviewed. Due to amongst others the *Benthem* case (see paragraph 5.1) this procedure has been gradually replaced by the concept of administrative objection. Approval is a preliminary administrative procedure which is very exceptional. This procedure takes places at a higher administrative level and implies that the act which an administrative organ would like to take can only enter into force after a higher body has given approval to it.

The procedure has a number of drawbacks. If the appeal lies with an organ of another administrative body, for instance, appeal against a decision by a municipal organ may be lodged with a provincial organ, this administrative appellate organ may fully influence the policy of the organ which made the original decision.[67] This contravenes the idea of decentralization. In some instances, administrative appeal is possible against a decision by an executive organ, for instance, the municipal executive (Mayor and Aldermen), with the general legislating administration, for instance, the municipal council. Such general administrative organs are not the most suitable organs to settle actual disputes.

There are two other important exceptions to the rule that administrative review must precede judicial review. First, where the so-called uniform public preparation procedure of paragraph 3.4 Awb applies (*uniforme openbare voorbereidingsprocedure*), – as provided by a legal provision[68] or a decision by

---

66 For several general provisions as to 'approval' see also chapter 10 Awb.

67 Presently, only in a few Acts this administrative appeal is still applicable, for instance in the field of extracting the public character of roads (*Wegenwet*). Already some time ago this was more often so, for instance regarding the withdrawal of a license based on the Liquor and Catering Act (*Drank- en Horecawet*).

68 This is, for instance, the case for the handing out of certain environmental permits on the basis of (Article 3.10 of) the Act on Environmental Licensing and General Provisons.

the administrative organ in question – the objection procedure is not applicable (Article 7:1, paragraph 1 d, Awb), making it possible to lodge one's case directly with the administrative court. This procedure will be applicable in cases in which the administration has a large degree of discretionary freedom and many third-party interests are involved. Preparation of the decision has been so comprehensive in such cases – views (*zienswijzen*) can be brought forward against the draft decision – that a subsequent objection (*bezwaar*) procedure is unlikely to produce a much different result. The applicability of this procedure by law or decision of the administrative organ has increased in recent years. The procedure of objection is particularly useful in the case of decisions of a rather mandatory nature taken in large numbers. Examples are decisions taken in the field of social security or rent support. The objection procedure lends itself very well to correcting mistakes made in the primary decision-making process.[69]

Secondly, if the administration fails to take a decision within the statutory time limit a citizen can directly address the competent court. In that situation there is no need to follow the objection procedure first (Article 7:1, paragraph 1 e, Awb).

Next to these exceptions to the rule that administrative review must precede judicial review the GALA offers the possibility to skip the objection procedure if all parties agree to that (Article 7:1a Awb). In some cases all parties involved (administrative organ and other parties) can feel that the objection procedure does not serve any purpose and will only take up time. In that case an interested party needs to file an objection and if the administrative organ agrees, it can send the notice of objection to the District Court which can treat it as a notice of appeal.

5.3. ACCESS TO THE COURTS

5.3.1. *Present Court System*

It follows from the previous paragraph that the District Court (Administrative Law Section) is the overall judge in first instance in administrative matters

---

[69] Also relevant in this perspective (and especially for the access to courts) is Article 6:13 Awb (amended in 2005) which states that no appeal to the administrative courts is possible for interested parties that reasonably can be blamed not to have brought forward views (*zienswijzen*) or objections (*bezwaren*). In other words, as a general rule: if you do not agree with certain aspects/parts of the decision you have to point that out from the start and if not, the court can deny an appeal related to the aspects that are brought forward later.
It seems that presently the scope of the dispute (*omvang van het geschil*) is less strictly applied between the phases of the administrative proceedings and court proceedings than between the phases of the court in first instance and the court of appeal. See para. 5.3.2.4.

unless there are specific administrative courts. The residual competence of the civil court is obvious in actions where there is no competence for the administrative court, for instance, in cases of generally binding regulations (see section 8:2 Awb), and merely a (problematic) issue in actions for damages against the administration.[70]

From 1994 onwards the Judicial Department of the Council of State, the Central Appellate Administrative Court and the Corporations Tribunal are charged with reviewing cases on appeal (from the District Court). This is logical because little changed with regard to the position of these three administrative judges. The Judicial Department of the Council of State, in fact a fusion of the Judicial Section of the Council of State (*Afdeling Rechtspraak*) and the Administrative Disputes Section of the Council of State (*Afdeling Geschillen*), these days pronounces judgement in a large number of appellate cases, which it judged in first instance in 1994. The position of the Central Appellate Administrative Court has not changed. Prior to 1994, the Court was also the highest instance for social security cases and public-service cases. The bodies judging first-instance cases before 1994, the administrative tribunals (*raden van beroep*) and the tribunals for matters concerning public servants (*ambtenarengerechten*) have been disbanded and their judges have been transferred in large part to the District Courts. The Corporations Tribunal deals with appeals in social economical cases but in a lot of cases acts as a first instance court in these matters. There is a complete separate court branch for tax disputes: the Administrative Law Section of the District Court, the Court of Appeal (tax chamber) and the Supreme Court (tax chamber). For the present organization of the courts, see figure 4.[71] For the most frequent administrative proceedings, see figure 5.

As already mentioned earlier, since 2013 Article 8:1 Awb makes appeal possible to 'the administrative judge' (*bestuursrechter*) (for the definition, see Article 1:4 Awb). Between 1994 and 2013 this was an appeal 'to the District

70 It becomes apparent (from case law of the Judicial Department of the Council of State and the Supreme Civil Court) that the exact division of competences in this field between the administrative and civil court is not (yet) fully crystallized. See, for instance, ABRS 6 May 1997, *JB* 1997/118 (*Zelfstandig schadebesluit Vlodrop*) and HR 17 December 1999, *JB* 2000/4 (*Groningen* v *Raatgever*). See also para. 7.3.

71 Since 2002 some major reforms have taken place in the organization of the Dutch Court system in first instance (*rechtbanken*). The Sub-District courts (judges of the peace) (*kantongerechten*) have been formally abolished and form part of the reduced (at present) 11 District Courts. The appellate administrative judges (ABRS, CRvB and CBB) fall outside the judicial power (*rechterlijke macht*) as regulated in Judiciary Organization Act (*Wet op de Rechterlijke Organisatie*). There is a Coucil for the Judiciary (*Raad voor de Rechtspraak*) that coordinates financial and more substantive aspect of all Districhts Courts. See also footnote 59 and next footnote. Also under the flag of this Act (and the Awb) the digitalization of court proceedings has been taken up (within the socalled KEI-operation), see: *Staatsblad* 2016, 288.

Court'. Due to this change some arrangements had to be made in the Awb as to the delineation of the competent courts in administrative matters.[72] Since 2013 Article 8:6 Awb points out that the appeal can be lounged at the District Court and a technical-legal delineation of jurisdiction between this court and other courts (in first instance) has been arranged as well as between the higher appellate bodies/courts and specific rules about competence (*Bevoegdheidsregeling bestuursrechtspraak*) in Annex 2 to the GALA.

As to the delineation of the first instance appeal chapter 2 of Annex 2 deals with exceptions to the general rule that the District Court is competent. Article 2 of Annex 2 states that in some matters the Judicial Department of the Council of State, the Central Appellate Court or the Corporations Tribunal is competent in first (and only) instance. On the basis of Chapter 3 of this Annex a specific specialized District Court may be competent.

The delineation of appeal from the District Court to the higher appellate administrative judges is as follows. Article 8:105, paragraph 1, Awb provides that in general appeal lies with the Judicial Department of the Council of State, unless according to chapter 4 *Bevoegdheidsregeling bestuursrechtspraak* the appeal against a decision may be lodged with the Central Appellate Court or the Corporations Tribunal. Pursuant to Article 9 and 10 of the afore mentioned Annex 2 the Central Appellate administrative Court (*Centrale Raad van Beroep*) is competent to hear cases concerning public servants and social security cases. The Annex contains further determination of the competence of the Central Appellate Administrative Court. Article 11 of the Annex 2 deals with the competence of the Corporations Tribunal (*College van Beroep voor het Bedrijfsleven*) in appeal. The jurisdiction of the different courts in tax matters has been regulated in the General Act on Taxes (*Algemene wet rijksbelastingen*) and Article 12 of the Annex 2.

5.3.3.1. Further Integration of the Appellate Courts

The mentioned organization of the court system (which was to be a temporary one), hardly promotes uniform application and construction of the Awb, since a large number of judicial bodies (Judicial Department of the Council of State, Central Appellate Administrative Court, Corporations Tribunal, Supreme Court Tax Chamber, Supreme Court Civil Chamber) interpret the Awb at the highest and final instance. A further problem is that this situation was

[72] Before, the Awb-provisions dealing with appeal at the District Court were, as a general rule, also applicable to the proceedings at the CRvB, the ABRS and the CBB. This was stated in the Appeals Act (*Beroepswet*), the Council of State Act (*Wet op de Raad van State*) respectively the Judicial Review Corporations Act (*Wet Bestuursrechtspraak Bedrijfsorganisatie).* Since 2013 these Acts only deal with the organization of these instances and not with procedural rules in appeal, since this is now dealt with in the Awb.

not supposed to last indefinitely, but now probably will. At the moment there seems no political consensus for further integration. In 2016 the Government drafted a Bill to reorganize the system of legal protection in administrative disputes which would lead to maintaining only the Judicial Department of the Council of State, the appellate courts (in tax matters) and the Supreme Court. The Central Appellate Administrative Court and Corporations Tribunal would be abolished and the disputes falling within their competence would fall in the competence of the remaining courts. This proposal was submitted to Parliament but withdrawn by the Government due to political reasons. To remedy the problem of legal unity to some extent in practice judges from one of these appellate courts also act as a honouree judge in the other courts. Some measures to ensure legal uniformity have been taken in the adjustment of the GALA in 2013: in Article 8:12a Awb the legislator created a possibility for the presidents of the different courts to ask the Advocate-General (member of one of the courts) to give a so called 'conclusion' in a concrete dispute which also deals with matters from a legal uniformity perspective. Furthermore the courts sitting as a three judge-chamber (*meervoudige kamer*) may refer a case to a chamber of five judges (*grote kamer*) if warranted by matters of legal unity or legal development. The present appellate court structure will not change in the near future.

Figure 4. Court organization (Articles 112 and 113 Constitution)

Court organization
First instance – District Courts (*Arrondissementsrechtbank*)*
Appeal – Courts of Appeal (*Gerechtshoven*)** – Administrative Courts (Awb decisions)***
Cassation – Supreme Court (*Hoge Raad*)**

* The District Courts (11) deal with civil, penal and administrative matters. The former Sub-District Courts (*kantongerechten*), dealing especially with civil cases in the field of labour law and renting, are in the first decade of the year 2000, integrated in the District Courts (mostly within the civil law section).

** The Courts of Appeal (4) and the Supreme Court, apart from civil and criminal matters, deal also with tax matters.

*** See figure 5 in more detail for the appellate administrative courts (which in certain cases serve as first and final instances).

Figure 5. The most frequent administrative proceedings in the Netherlands (for tax matters, see Figure 4 and the previous text)

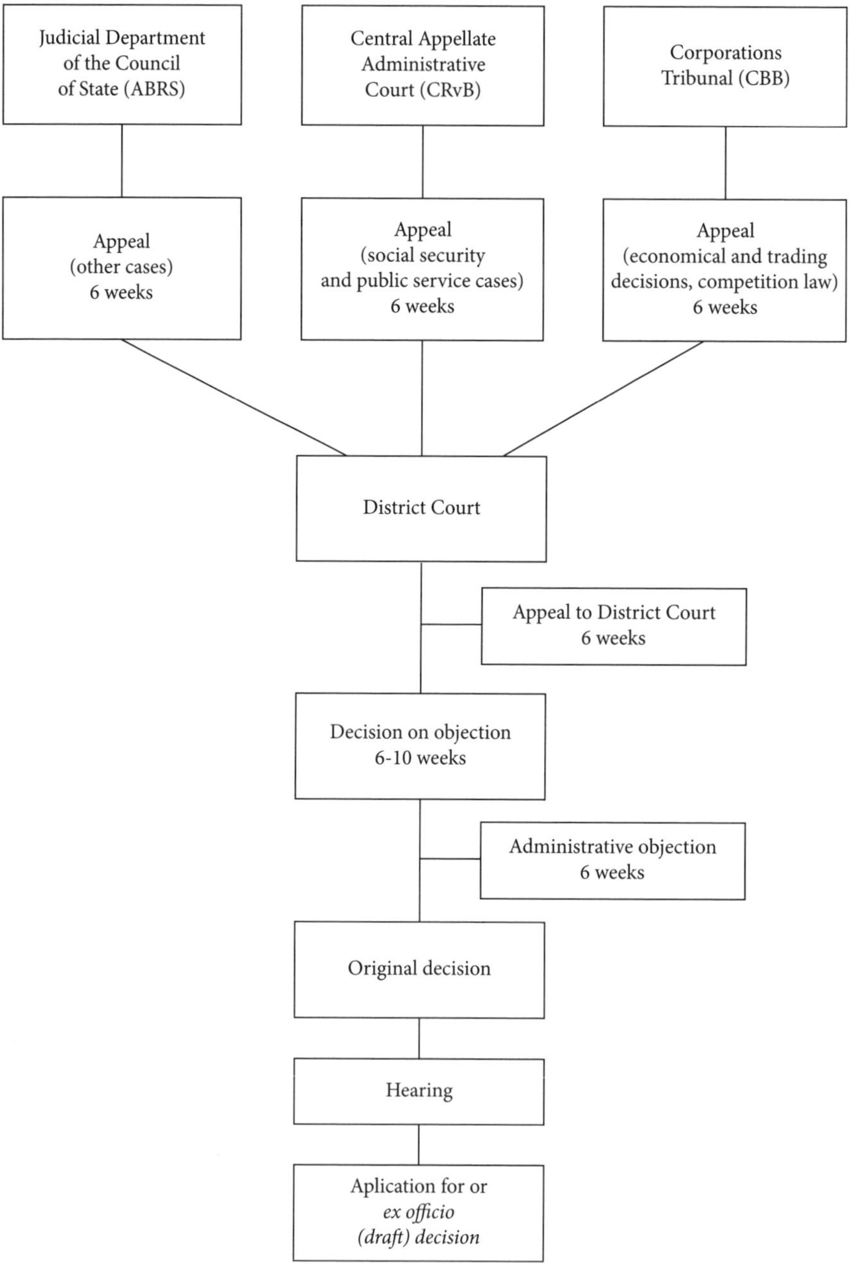

5.3.2. *Appeal to the District Court*

5.3.2.1. Right to Appeal

As already follows from the aforementioned as a general rule appeal – in first instance – to the Administrative Law Section of the District Court on the basis of a written notice is possible against administrative decisions (*besluiten*) on the basis of Article 8:1, paragraph 1, Awb. The appeal has to be brought before the court in six weeks after the announcement of the contested decision (Article 6:7 Awb). In practice in most decisions this possibility is explicitly mentioned (Article 3:45 Awb).

As may follow from paragraph 5.2 of this contribution the appeal in most cases does not concern the decision of the administration 'in primo' but the decision 'on objection'. In general, all decisions (on objection) can be challenged before the court. However, see Article 8:3 Awb: no possibility of appeal against generally applicable regulations as well as policy rules and Article 8:6, paragraph 1, Awb: no possibility of appeal to the District Court, if appeal lies with another administrative court.[73] In addition to decisions all other actions which are equated with decisions on the basis of Article 6:2 GALA, such as refusals to deal with an application and not taking any decision at all within the statutory time limit, can be challenged before the court. Private law acts of the administration, however, have to be brought before the civil court. See also paragraph 3.2.3. Furthermore certain decisions of the administration are excluded from appeal to the (administrative) court (Articles 8:4 and 8:5 Awb).

There are no time limits for the rulings of the court. District Courts try to limit the time between the appeal and the judgement to 1 year, but in some cases this is not possible.[74]

5.3.2.2. Interested Parties

As a general rule only interested parties have access to the administrative court (Article 8:1 Awb). Article 1:2 Awb offers a definition of the concept of 'interested party'.[75]

---

73 For instance, until 2005 regarding taxation decisions not the District Court but the Court of Appeal was competent to decide (in first instance) and until 2010 the same applied concerning environmental pollution permits. Not the District Court but the Judicial Department of the Council of State was made competent to do so.

74 The courts (may) have internal rules dealing with this. There are some exceptions as to time limits for instance in cases where the Crisis and Recovery Act is applicable.

75 Until mid 2005 in some areas like environmental law there was access for almost everybody in administrative proceedings and such participation was sufficient for access to court (actio popularis). Since the amendment of chapter 3.4 Awb in some areas like environmental law still everybody can bring forward views (*zienswijzen*) but access to court is only possible for

Pursuant to paragraph 1, the term 'interested party' is to be taken to mean the person whose interests are directly involved in a decision. Apart from natural persons, legal persons can also be an interested party. From case law it follows that an interested party must demonstrate a direct, personal and objective interest. In addition to this, it must be made plausible that this interest is actually and directly involved in the decision. As regards administrative organs, the interests entrusted to them by the legislator are deemed to be their interests (Article 1:2, paragraph 2, Awb). With regard to legal persons, the general and collective interests, defended in particular by virtue of their objectives and as evidenced by their actual activities, are also deemed to be their interest (Article 1:2, paragraph 3, Awb).[76] The need for an interest is not only necessary in court proceedings but also in the non-contentious phase of decision-making.

To gain access to court it is only necessary that an individual shows that his interest is directly affected by the contested decision. In recent case law the courts are more strict with regard to legal persons/NGOs protecting a general interest. Because of the shift to a more *recours subjectif* approach access to court should be restricted to legal persons which show a directly affected general interest and this means, in order to avoid an *actio popularis*, according to the case law that the criterions have to be interpreted in a (more) narrow manner. These legal persons now have to show actual activities with regard to this general interest next to starting court procedures or administrative preliminary procedures.[77]

5.3.2.3. Schutznorm

Because of the recent emphasis on the *recours subjectif* and more speedily and final settlement of administrative disputes the government also explored the possibility to introduce a stricter criterion: a *Schutznorm* which means that the interest on which the individual relies should be protected by the legal provision or norm which has allegedly been violated. This criterion has been incorporated in the Awb in Article 8:69a since 2013, after first being introduced in Article 1.9 of the Crisis and Recovery Act. It now applies to all administrative court disputes. Furthermore, the criterion does not limit the access to court. The government decided instead that decisions of the administration should not

---

interested persons. Recently the ABRS specified this criterion of interested persons: 16 May 2016, ECLI:NL:RVS:2016:737 and 23 August 2017, ECLI:NL:RVS:2017:2271.

See in a broader European perspective: M. Eliantonio, Ch.W. Backes, C.H. van Rhee, T.N.B.M. Spronken and A. Berlee, Standing up for your (Rights) in Europe, A Comparative Study on Legal Standing (*Locus Standi*) before the EU and Member States' Courts, Intersentia 2013.

[76] See Heldeweg, M.A., Schlössels, R.J.N. & Seerden, R.J.G.H., 'De kwadratuur van de algemeen belangactie', *RM Themis*, 2000 (2), p. 43–58.

[77] See in environmental cases: ABRS 1 October 2008, *AB* 2008, 348. Similar: ABRS 15 October 2008, *JB* 2008, 258 and *AB* 2008, 349 and ABRS 22 October 2008, *AB* 2008, 350 as well as ABRS 22 October 2008, *JB* 2008, 231 and 232.

be annulled by the courts if a legal norm or provision is violated but does not protect the interest of an individual that relies on the norm before the court. For NGO's or legal persons protecting general interests this restriction will not have grave consequences. The general interest they protect will often be the interest or coincide with the interest that the allegedly violated legal norm will protect. In recent case law it is decided that a correction of the Schutznorm may be at hand in cases where the following 2 principles of proper administration are at stake, the principle of legitimate expectations and the equality principle.[78] This criterion is limited to the appeal procedure and does not apply in the objection procedure or any other procedure before the administrative organs.

5.3.2.4. Exhausting Administrative Remedies and the Scope of the Dispute

Article 6:13 Awb contains the obligation for the interested parties to first exhaust all available remedies on the administrative level. If the interested party can reasonably be blamed for not filing an objection (*bezwaar*) or giving his views during the preparation of the decision (*zienswijzen*) then the District Court will declare the appeal inadmissible. This provision, strictly interpreted, implies that objections or views which have not been brought forward in the preliminary administrative procedure and the public preparation procedure against the separate parts of the decisions which can be distinguished will also be declared inadmissible in the appeal procedure as far as the grounds of appeal concern these parts of the contested decision. This is especially so with land-use and environmental permits, that consist of many parts and provisions. It is therefore possible that only part of the appeal is inadmissible. In case law the rule, that there is an obligation to bring forward views or objections in the procedure against (parts of) a decision as early as possible to delimit the dispute as much as possible in appeal, is loosened.[79] The judge has also some discretion in dealing with additional grounds that come up after the (first) written appeal. The case law is that additional grounds or additional reasons to the earlier stated grounds of appeal pending the court proceedings are admissible unless the principle of due process is violated. In general this is the case when at the session (*zitting*) of the court new grounds come up.

5.3.3. Proceedings at the District Court

Article 8:10 Awb states that as a general rule cases are dealt with by a single judge-section (*enkelvoudige kamer*). In practice this is the case. The single judge-section may refer the case to a three judge-section but not too many cases are

---

78 ABRS 16 March 2016 ECLI:NL:RVS:2016:732.

79 See ABRS 9 March 2011, *AB* 2011, 130.

dealt with by a three judge-section (*meervoudige kamer*). In the Netherlands the proceedings are of an informal nature.

5.3.3.1. Principles of Due Process

The most essential principles of procedural law are an independent and impartial judge and the right of access to such a judge, as discussed in the preceding paragraph, in addition to the following:

- right to council[80];
- open-court sessions[81];
- reasoned decisions[82];
- written judgement without undue delay[83];
- enforcement of judicial decisions.[84]

These principles are applicable for all forms of judicial proceedings, be they civil, criminal or administrative. The question as to whether additional criteria should be set for administrative procedure, in view of its special features, will be addressed below.

5.3.3.2. Scope and Grounds of Review

An important power granted to all courts, and therefore also to administrative courts, is the power to review exceptively or indirectly. An example may illustrate what is meant by this. Say the Municipal Executive (Mayor and Aldermen) refuses to grant a license on the grounds of a provision from the General Local Ordinance (*Algemene Plaatselijke Verordening*, APV).[85] In such cases, the administrative judge will, of course, review the conformity of the refusal with

---

80 Legal representation is not obligatory, see, for instance, Article 8:25, para., 1 Awb.

81 Article 121 Constitution; Article 8:62 Awb.

82 Article 121 Constitution and Article 8:77 Awb. Bear in mind that sometimes there are 'exceptions' for instance in appellate courts (see para. 5.3.6.). See for instance Article 91 Aliens Act (*Vreemdelingenwet*) on the basis of which the ABRS can (without an open court session) 'limit' its judgements by (merely) stating 'that the grounds of appeal that are brought forward cannot lead to annulment'. In practice, it is in such judgements added 'that there in the grounds of appeal no questions are raised that, in the interest of legal unity (*rechtseenheid*), legal development (*rechtsontwikkeling*) or legal protection (*rechtsbescherming*), need answering in a general way'.

83 Article 6, para. 1, ECHR; Article 8:66, para. 2, Awb. Notice that this term is the period of time between the hearing and the written decision. The Awb does not provide for a term for the entire judicial proceedings.

84 This has not really been provided for in the Awb. If, however, the court decision is not put into effect by administrative action, pursuant to Article 6:2 (b) Awb the case may again be brought before the judge. He will then undoubtedly use his power to set a term and to impose a per-diem penalty.

85 In a decentralized system such as that of the Netherlands, the Municipal Council is empowered to issue regulations relating to the municipality's economy of its own motion.

the General Local Ordinance. He is also empowered, however, to test the General Local Ordinance against any higher generally applicable regulations (AVV), and therefore against directly applicable treaty provisions, provisions of community law, the Dutch Constitution, Acts of Parliament, general administrative Crown orders, ministerial orders and provincial ordinances (see figure 2). In case of conflict, the judge will rule that the lower provision is not binding or cannot be applied in this case. By the way, the judge in the Netherlands is not allowed to test the constitutionality of Acts of Parliament (Article 120 Constitution).

In addition to reviewing against rules of written law, the judge also tests against rules of unwritten law. For a large part, these rules of unwritten law have now been codified and have been incorporated into the Awb. Some continue to be unwritten law, however. Nor does the Awb prevent the development of new legal principles or the further development of existing principles.

Article 8:77, paragraph 2, Awb prescribes that if a judge decides to grant an appeal, the unwritten or written rule of law or the general principle of law that was deemed to have been violated must be included in the judgement.

The test of the judge is as a general rule *ex tunc*: related to the moment of the decision of the administration, often the decision on objection. Sometimes there are exceptions. For instance, in enforcement cases the primary decision is decisive for whether or not there is a violation of a legislative provision and that is what the judge examines. In for instance asylum cases there may be the necessity to test *ex nunc*: based on the ECHR and EU-legislation: the moment of the judgement of the judge is leading. Such an *ex nunc* test can also be at stake when the judge decides the case and is not merely annulling and referring the decision back to the administration: the decision is tested *ex tunc* but the actual situation is decisive for solving the dispute definitely.

The grounds brought forward by the claimant – for some formal requirements as to the written appeal, see Article 6:4 onwards Awb – are the starting point of the court proceedings and are leading for how the case is dealt with by the judge. Mostly they are brought forward in the beginning of the appeal procedure. Sometimes they follow later and even in the open court session. It is up to the parties and the judge whether or not this may conflict with the principle of due process. Of course (other) general principles of proper judicial review (*beginselen van behoorlijke rechtspraak*) exist, in line with the principles of proper administration, such as the impartiality of the judge, an open public hearing, equality of arms. Some of these are codified in the Awb.

5.3.3.3. Review of Discretionary Power

The standards for administrative action laid down in the first seven chapters of the Awb are also the scrutiny standards for judicial review. There is one exception to having the same standards for administrative action and judicial review, namely the principle of proportionality (when there is discretionary power for the administration) laid down in Article 3:4, paragraph 2, Awb. In the important judgement of 9 May 1996[86] the Judicial Department of the Council of State considered the following:

> 'The Judicial Department of the Council of State cannot agree with the considerations of the District Court as presented above. By thus considering, the District Court displayed an incorrect view of the meaning of the provisions of Article 3:4, paragraph 2, Awb concerning judicial review of the exercise of the power in question by the administration. Article 3:4, par. 2, Awb provides that the adverse effects of an administrative decision shall not be disproportionate to the aim to be served by the decision. This provision, addressed to the administration, was not intended by the legislator as a means of intensifying judicial review with regard to case law which had developed by virtue of, among others, Article 8, par. 1, opening line of the Judicial Review of Administrative Action Act, which was effectively repealed on 1 January 1994. According to the Memorandum of Reply (TK 1990–1991, 21, 221, No. 5, P. 55 ff.) the legislator did not intend for the judge to assess which adverse effects are proportionate and which not, or for the judge to decide which outcome of the weighing of interests must be considered as the most balanced. This view of the legislator is based on the different positions to be taken by the independent judge and the administration politically accountable in the constitutional system. The Memorandum of Reply also reveals that the formulation used in Article 3:4, par. 2, Awb, which contains the double negation 'not disproportionate', is intended to force the judge to exercise restraint in testing the weighing of interests as conducted by the administration.
>
> The District Court has failed to recognise that, since this was in the execution of a discretionary power, correctly characterised as such, it was for the appellants to weigh the interests involved in the exercise of that power and to decide whether to exercise that power.
>
> The District Court should have restricted itself to the question as to whether in the case in hand there has been such disproportional weighing of interests that it warrants the decision that the appellants could not have reasonably decided to grant the exemption requested'.

This judgement neatly defines the constitutional relationship between the administration and the judge in administrative cases.[87] The judge must respect the administration's discretionary (policy) freedom and may only intervene if the weighing of interests was manifestly incorrect and would amount to arbitrariness (prohibition against arbitrariness, *willekeur*).[88]

---

86 ABRS 9 May 1996, *JB* 1996, 158.

87 The question is whether this 'general' judgement to Article 3:4 Awb is also applicable in relation to the application of specific legislative acts. The latter sometimes 'colour' the former, see, for instance, ABRS 21 April 1998, *JB* 1998/133 and ABRS 4 February 1999, *JB* 1999/66 and therefore could leave some extra room for the judge!

88 The prohibition against arbitrariness has been developed by the Supreme Court in its well-known and important judgement in Doetinchem (HR 25 February 1994, *NJ* 1994, p. 558).

Discretion (*beleidsvrijheid*) may be recognized by a so-called 'can'-provision in the regulation at hand. For instance, a provision stating that an environmental permit can be refused in the interest of protecting the environment. Two essential elements of this type of discretion are the duty to weigh interests and the fact that from a legal perspective more than one decision is possible. In case of 'bound' powers there is only one decision possible, for instance, in the case of a decision to give or refuse child or student financial grants; the provision which is the basis for the decision would state that a grant should be refused if certain conditions are met. The weighing of interests is between those of the applicant for/addressee of the decision and those of the public interest as well as third parties (both possibly laid down in the respective legislation). Which interests in particular have to be weighed is dependent on the appropriate legislative act. The fact that all these interests can be weighed differently (according to the legislator) may lead to different decisions by the administration. It is acknowledged that the courts should respect this freedom of the administration (marginal test). Often, however, the administration limits its discretion through the enactment of (self-binding) policy rules. Policy rules could also be used to elaborate on the use of so-called vague legal terms (*vage wettelijke termen*). But as regards these vague legal terms the scrutiny of the court is not marginal but intense. The term discretion may also be used for the situation in which the administration has room to state what the relevant facts are, to qualify these in light of the respective regulation and to apply the regulation to the facts. It depends on the respective regulation whether and to what extent (*beoordelingsruimte*) or not (*beoordelingsvrijheid*) a full/intense legality test by the court is possible. The aforementioned principles with regard to the intensity of review by the court still apply, but in recent case law there has been a development towards more scrutinous review of the way the administration applies policy rules on individual cases and the way it considers the individual circumstances.[89]

5.3.3.4. Recours Subjectif and/or Objectif

It is characteristic for (Dutch) administrative law that administrative decisions (i.e. a juridical act governed by public law) are the central object to review. This has to do with the fact that, in the past, much value was attached to the supervisory role of the administrative judge (*recours objectif*). In the Explanatory Memorandum to the Awb, it is observed that the legal protection of the right of the individual is paramount (*recours subjectif*). This is also evidenced by the introduction of the Schutznorm criterion as mentioned before and the fact that more emphasis has been put on the dispute settlement remedies of the court. However, also in the new legislation of administrative procedure, the administrative decision is the central focus and the remedy is annulment of

[89] ABRS 26 October 2016 ECLI:NL:RVS:2016:2840.

the disputed decision in combination with the obligation for the administrative organ to make a new decision in line with the judgement (and possibly an additional claim for damages). There is often no final solution of the conflict. As a consequence administrative disputes take up a long time period before they are definitively solved and the case can go back and forth to court.

Since the administrative decision remains the core, the object of the dispute, it really does not matter very much whether the supervisory or the legal-protection role is to the fore. In either case, the test is whether the administration is competent and, if so, whether it has exercised that power lawfully. In two respects, however, it may make a difference which role is felt to be more prominent than the other. In the Explanatory Memorandum it is clearly stated that the legal protection function entails two things:

a. the prohibition against *reformatio in peius*;
b. the prohibition against *ultra petita*.[90]

The prohibition against *reformatio in peius* means that the person who lodges an appeal should not be placed in a worse position because of it. The prohibition against *ultra petita* refers to the following: in principle, the judge is not allowed to assess undisputed parts of the decision.

Prior to 1994, the attitude of the judge was characteristically an active one; he used to review *ex officio* on a large scale. Such *ex officio* review is compatible with both the supervisory and the legal-protection function of the judge. It is in the public interest that administrative decisions are lawful and the (less powerful) citizen must be assisted in his protection against the (omnipotent) administration (inequality compensation). It must be borne in mind that in administrative procedure representation by counsel is not required.

After 1994, the Central Appellate Administrative Court continued to follow the old line for the most part. At the Judicial Department of the Council of State, however, a development can be observed towards less *ex officio* review (only dealing with public order (*openbare orde*) provisions)[91] and therefore an assessment that is limited to the grounds/facts submitted by the citizen on appeal (*omvang van het geschil*).[92] In recent case law the courts (at all levels)

---

90 The administrative judge also avoided this prior to 1994.

91 Although public order provisions (this concept is more or less always under development, but it can be linked to key elements of competences of administrative organs and the courts: is the power to decide attributed or delegated to the organ that took the decision, is a decision (in the meaning of the Awb) at hand, is delegated legislation in conformity with higher legislation, is the court competent to judge an appeal against a decision, can somebody be regarded as interested person to raise an objection or appeal, etc.) do not equal mandatory powers for the administration one can say that the ex officio review is somewhat more extensive in cases where these mandatory powers exist than in cases where discretionary powers are executed. See also the next footnote.

92 With the (important) judgement of the CRvB of 17 April 2007 (ECLI:NL:CRVB:2007:BA2955) it seems that this court is about to follow the line of the Judicial Department of the Council of

seem to follow this approach and only examine *ex officio* whether public order provisions have been complied with.

5.3.3.5. (Other) Recent Developments

The mixed functions of the procedural law and remedies in the Awb have one clear disadvantage. Because of the *recours objectif* approach which puts the annulment of the decision at the center of the powers of the court administrative disputes in practice are difficult to settle. After annulment of the decision it will be up to the administration to take a new decision. This decision can be contested before the courts as well and can be annulled which will lead to repetition of the whole process again. The *recours objectif* with the emphasis on the annulment of the decision and the decision-concept as a central notion for the right to access to court has encountered many criticism in literature. The practice can also lead to violation of the reasonable time limit of Article 6 ECHR and the right to a effective remedy of Article 13 ECHR. Due to recent case law of the European Court of Human Rights the Dutch administrative courts have stated in their case law that a right to damages exists if the administrative organs and the administrative courts violate this reasonable time requirement in Article 6 ECHR.[93]

Also relevant, in light of Article 6 ECHR and more specific the principle of equality of arms, is the question whether or not the administrative judge is obligatory to call in an independent medical expert in cases where the administration makes use of its own medical experts, for instance in disability cases (CRvB) and certain migration cases (ABRS).[94]

State. Presently, the latter is also strict in not admitting, as a general rule, new grounds/facts based on EU-law or ECHR-provisions in case these grounds/facts could have been brought forward at the District Court, ABRS 12 June 2006, *AB* 2006, 338 and 21 June 2006, *AB* 2007, 339 (confirming ABRS 2 March 2004, *AB* 2004, 152).

93 Until 2014 there were differences in the case law of the appellate courts (see for instance ABRS 20 Mai 2009, ECLI:NL:RVS:2009:BI4558 – as a general rule a procedure of in total five years (after lodging the objection at the administrative organ) is reasonable (one year for the objection and two years for the first and final court instance) – and see for instance CRvB 26 January 2009, ECLI:NL:CRVB:2009:BH1009 – this period is four years (one half year for the objection, one and a half year for the first court instance and two years for the final instance). If the issue is raised by the claimant he/she receives € 500 for each half year that the reasonable time period is violated.
In the beginning of 2014 – based on a conclusion of the Advocate-General – the ABRS (*grote kamer*) (and also the CBB) decided to follow (in non-punitive administrative matters) the CRvB and the Supreme Court: ABRS 29 January 2014, ECLI:NL:RVS:2014:188. See also the recent (overview) judgement in tax-matters of the Supreme Court, 19 February 2016, ECLI:NL:HR:2016:252. It goes beyond the scope of this contribution to elaborate further on this. For achieving (more) unity between the appellate administrative judges: see para. 5.3.1.1.

94 In light of (especially) the Korosec case of the ECtHR, 8 October 2015 (1008JUD007721212). See the cases of 30 June 2016: ABRS, ECLI:NL:RVS:2017:1674 and CRvB ECLI:NL:CRVB:2017:2226.

Also a hot issue at this moment, but not further addressed here, is the (more objective) way in which cases have to be divided between the judges (*zaaktoedeling*).

5.3.4. *Judicial Dispute-Settlement Powers*

5.3.4.1. Remedies

On the basis of article 8:70 Awb the administrative judge shall rule that he/she lacks jurisdiction, the appeal is inadmissible, the appeal is unfounded, or the appeal is well founded. If the appeal is well founded this automatically leads to the annulment in whole or in part of the administrative decision (Article 8:72 Awb). The power to annul the administrative decision is the central power of the judge in the system of the Awb. Annulment entails that the disputed decision is removed from the legal world *ex tunc*. Usually, as a result of the annulment, the administration will be obliged under the law to take a new decision *ex nunc*. It must, of course, in so doing take the judicial decision into account. But as was stated before in practice a dispute was not often solved by the courts and the case could go back and forth between the administration and the courts in first instance and appeal.

5.3.4.2. Additional Remedies

To remedy this problem to a certain extent, the administrative judge (Administrative Law Section of the District Court) can force the administration to take a new decision (Article 8:74, paragraph 4 under a, Awb) and if the District Court holds that the administrative organ is not prepared to observe the judicial decision the District Court can set a term for the (new) decision to be taken by the administration (Article 8:72, paragraph 5, Awb). In addition, where the administrative organ fails to comply with the judicial decision, the District Court may decide that for so long as it fails to comply, it will forfeit a penalty for each day of non-compliance (Article 8:72, paragraph 7, Awb).

Judicial annulment of a decision entails, of course, the annulment of the legal effects of the decision. The District Court may, however, decide that the legal effects of the decision remain intact in part or in whole (Article 8:72, paragraph 3 Awb). According to the government this power can only be exercised in very specific situations. In the case of an error of form, where it is clear, however, that had the formal requirement been met, this would not have resulted in a different decision, the judge may leave the legal effects intact. In case law, however, the courts have indicated that it is no longer necessary that no other decision would have been taken. If the administration would like to hold on to the decision, it has to sufficiently repair the error, parties should be given the opportunity to give their view on this and the repaired decision is otherwise lawful, the decision will be annulled but the legal effects can stay intact.[95]

In certain cases, the judge may determine that his/her judgement will replace the decision annulled by him/her, instead of ordering the administration to take a new decision (Article 8:72 paragraph 4 under c, Awb). This is often called judicial settlement. This may seem strange at first sight: the judge taking an administrative decision. Would not this be in flagrant violation of the *Trias Politica*, the division of powers? It can be inferred from the Explanatory Memorandum that the setting aside of an administrative decision by taking a new one is only a possibility in a limited number of cases, namely where there is only one legally correct decision. In that case, it is rather efficient, of course, if the judge himself/herself settles the case, saving time and money. If, for instance, the District Court is of the opinion that the administration has incorrectly held that the objection was baseless, because the interested party should have been declared to have *no locus standi*, the administrative judge may pronounce the party's inadmissibility. But even where there can only be one legally correct decision, the judge exercises restraint in providing such a settlement (see also paragraph 5.3.3.3). The Judicial Department of the Council of State, for instance, held that the administrative judge could not, in general, grant or change a building permit (although that can be considered as a mandatory decision).[96] This attitude is understandable. To draft a building permit requires certain technical skills relating to the building which the judge cannot be expected to have, but which the relevant municipal public servants do possess. If the administration possesses discretionary freedom and therefore more than one decision may be legally correct, judicial settlement of the case according to the government in 1994 and case law until 2008 is precluded, since the judge must respect the administration's discretionary power. However, in recent case law the courts also are more inclined to use this power to settle disputes also in cases where the administration does have a discretionary power. The court will have to give other parties the opportunity to give their point of view and has to exercise some restraint keeping the Trias Politica in mind. Furthermore this power can only be used if the case is clear and all the necessary information and evidence is available to the court.[97] In this respect it can be mentioned that judges can call in experts, for instance in environmental cases.[98]

---

95 ABRS 26 March 2008, ECLI:NL:RVS:2008:BC7627; ABRS 10 December 2008, *JB* 2009/39; ABRS 9 February 2011, *AB* 2011, 65; ABRS 27 January 2010, *JB* 2010/77.

96 ABRS 8 July 1996, *JB* 1996, 188.

97 ABRS 30 January 2008, *JB* 2008/59; ABRS 11 February 2009, *AB* 2009, 224 and more recent ABRS 16 November 2016, ECLI:NL:RVS:2016:3054.

98 The Foundation for Advising the Administrative Judges in Environmental Cases (*Stichting Advisering Bestuursrechtspraak*). It is based on the Environmental Management Act (Article 20.2) and the Act on Environmental Licensing and General Provisions (Article 6.5 b). This expert provides impartial technical knowledge and structures facts in complex cases. It can be invoked by only (no other parties) the administrative judges and is financed by the

One has to bear in mind here that the decision tested by the court is the decision on objection and not the decision of the administration *in primo*.[99] Through the enactment of the former the latter is not necessarily withdrawn. The court could do that itself through the application of Article 8:72, paragraph 4 under c, Awb or by an assignment to the administration to do so.

All judicial settlement powers discussed earlier can be found in Article 8:72 Awb. It is worth noting that the Dutch administrative judge does not have the power to render declaratory judgements. There is, however, a growing tendency to characterize judicial decisions in administrative cases as administrative decisions.[100] This means that, if the case is brought before the administrative judge, the judge in effect renders a declaratory judgement.

Next to these powers the legislator decided that in case of an annulment of a fine imposed on an individual by the administration the judge is obligated to settle the dispute. In that case Article 8:72a Awb provides for the power for the judge to impose a fine or decide on the amount of the fine. The reason for this judicial settlement power is Article 6 ECHR. In case of a criminal charge, which a fine can considered to be, the ECtHR stated that national courts need full jurisdiction to review the proportionality of the imposed measure.

5.3.4.3. Judicial Dispute-Settlement Powers during the Procedure

Since the beginning of 2010 the Awb provides the administrative courts with a new instrument to speed up the settlement of administrative law disputes: the administrative loop (*bestuurlijke lus*). If the District Court feels that the decision violates procedural requirements or other legal norms and this violation can be repaired by the administrative authority it can offer the administrative authority a possibility to repair the fault at stake or take a new decision during the court procedure (Article 8:51a Awb). The administration is not obliged to cooperate but if it doesn't annulment of the decision is likely. If the violation is repaired, however, the new or repaired decision will not have to be annulled. This way the procedure will not be delayed, the court is still in charge of the procedure and the court can give clear indications how to repair the decision. The interested parties of course are allowed to bring forward their points of view on the new or repaired decision. After that the court will review this new or repaired decision on its merits. This power is also given to the competent courts in the appeal procedure (ABRS, CRvB and CBB). There is one difference, however, the

central government. The advice of this expert (and other experts) has a strong influence on the outcome of the case.

99 There is one exception: the preliminary ruling pending the decision on objection.

100 See, e.g., ABRS 20 November 1998, *AB* 1999, 82. In this judgement the Judicial Department of the Council of State held that the interpretation of a zoning plan is an administrative judgement constituting an administrative decision within the meaning of the Awb.

administration is obliged to cooperate and it is not given the opportunity but the assignment to repair a fault in the decision (together with clear instructions how to repair it) (Article 8:51d Awb).

5.3.4.4. Sequence of Remedies

Furthermore, in recent case law the appellate courts have established an obligation for each administrative court to examine whether or not it could use its powers to settle the disputes pending before it.[101] The courts are in addition obligated to give reasons for not using their powers to settle the dispute at hand in their judgement.[102] In addition to this, a sequence in which the courts should use their powers granted to them had been established in the GALA in order to settle disputes as soon as possible.[103] This obligation to examine the possible settlement of the dispute and the suggested sequence has been adopted by the Government. It is now incorporated in Articles 8:41a and 8:72 Awb. The sequence is as follows:

1) if the court establishes a violation of a legal norm it first needs to examine whether the decision may be upheld, despite an infringement of a rule or principle. This is possible if it is found that the infringement has not prejudiced the interests of the interested parties (Article 6:22 Awb). If this is possible the appeal will be declared unfounded, the contested decision will not be annulled and the dispute will end there. Originally Article 6:22 Awb was more intended to cover procedural / formal shortcomings but at present also infringements of substantive provisions may fall under its scope[104];
2) if the court, however, concludes that the appeal is founded and the decision has to be annulled (Article 8:72, paragraph 1, Awb), it first has to examine the possibility to leave the legal effects of the decision in tact in whole or in part (Article 8:72, paragraph 3 sub a, Awb). If this is possible this will mean the end of the dispute as well;
3) if it is not possible to leave the legal effects in tact the court has to examine whether it can replace the decision of the administration by its own judgement (Article 8:72, paragraph 3 sub b, Awb). The dispute will come to an end with that judgement.
4) if it is not possible to leave the legal effects intact or replace the decision by a judgement of the court right away the court has to examine whether the administrative loop (*bestuurlijke lus)* can be used and the administration should get the opportunity to repair an error or a fault in the decision

101 ABRS 26 August 2009, *AB* 2009, 368; CRvB 3 November 2010, *AB* 2011, 243.

102 CRvB 3 November 2010, *AB* 2011, 243.

103 See, for instance, Verburg, D.A., 'Finale geschilbeslechting en haar stiefkind, de 'aangeklede' opdracht om een nieuw besluit te nemen', *JBplus*, 2010, p. 153.

104 ABRS 30 November 2016, ECLI:NL:RVS:2016:3167.

(Article 8:51a Awb). After the repair the court can either use the power to leave the legal effects intact or use its power to replace the decision by its own judgement (which power will be used depends on the circumstances of the case and whether or not different legal effects are necessary).

5) if options 1–4 are not possible the court can as a means of last resort, after annulling the decision, order the administration to take a new decision and give as clear as possible indications on the content of this new decision (Article 8:72, paragraph 4, Awb).

In all situations (1–5) cost recovery is possible (see paragraph 5.3.4.6.).

Apart from more juridical changes in this field one sees that courts factually are dealing with methods that accelerate procedures: very timely court sessions in which parties are asked what the real problem is, whether or not the written appeal should be based on more evidence, whether or not the administration is willing to mediate certain aspects etc. (*nieuwe zaaksbehandeling/regiezittingen/* new cases approach and informal sessions).

5.3.4.5. Compensation for (Un)lawful Acts (Financial Liability)

5.3.4.5.1. Compensation for unlawful acts

Until 1 July 2013 the administrative judge was empowered, aside from the power of annulment, to order damages if an appeal was well founded and the decision was annulled due to unlawfulness. This was a very important power, which had been laid down in Article 8:73 Awb, a *novum* for the Awb. Before 1994, only the civil judge was competent to award damages.[105] An important advantage here is that the citizen is able to kill two birds with one stone; he may simultaneously ask for an annulment and for compensation. Prior to 1994, the civil action for damages could only be brought after an annulment by the administrative judge.[106]

However, due to the fact that Article 8:73 Awb did not grant exclusive power to the administrative judge to order compensation if the appeal was granted, the civil judge also had jurisdiction in the matter. This meant citizens had a choice: they address themselves either to the administrative or the civil court. As discussed earlier, it is quite efficient, of course, to apply directly to the

105 Prior to 1994, only the judge competent in public service cases *(Ambtenarengerecht)* could order full compensation. This had to do with the text of the pre-1983 Constitution. This text was interpreted thus that only the civil judge was competent to order compensation. The 1983 Constitution does not prevent the administrative judge from having such competence.

106 The civil judge, however, departed from the assumption that an annulment by the administrative judge was evidence of a wrongful act by the administrative body in question, or in any case that there was fault on the part of that body (improper formal/final status as opposed to the formal/final status referred to in para. 5.3.4.5.2).

administrative judge for compensation. In determining the extent of the damage or loss suffered, the administrative judge applies, in principle, the substantive civil law of compensation.[107]

The injured citizen can therefore not recover more by instituting civil proceedings.

There was also a third way for the citizen to receive compensation for damage suffered as a result of administrative action. After the decision had been annulled by the administrative judge, the citizen could direct him/herself to the administration in question in order to obtain compensation. The administration's reaction to his/her application was seen as a decision subject to appeal. Such decisions were called independent compensation decisions (*zelfstandige schadebesluiten*).[108]

In summation: there was a fairly complicated system in which a citizen had three possibilities to recover damages from the administration in cases of unlawful administrative decisions (in individual cases).[109]

a. by way of applying to the administrative judge for compensation concurrently with his application for annulment;
b. by way of bringing an action for damages before the civil court after the decision has been annulled by the administrative court;
c. by way of claiming compensation from the administration, after the decision has been annulled by the administrative judge. The administration's response is again subject to judicial review.

---

107 Both the administrative and the civil judge depart from the assumption that annulment by the administrative judge implies wrongful acting by the public body, or in any case fault. As a rule, judicial annulment of an administrative decision refers to administrative decisions on objection. The administrative judge exercised more restraint than the civil judge in awarding compensation of the costs incurred in objection proceedings before the administration. In the eyes of the administrative judge, there must be manifest wrongfulness on the part of the administration for the compensation to be awarded. Because of the disparate case law of the civil and administrative courts, an Act (changing Article 7:15 Awb) in line with the case law of the administrative courts has been introduced, *Kamerstukken II* 2000–01, 27 024).

108 There must, therefore, be a relation with an earlier decision which was annulled by the administrative judge. This is called 'substantive connectivity'. 'Formal connectivity' means that the administrative judge who decides on the claim for compensation is the same judge who decided to annul the decision. If, therefore, the damage is caused by generally applicable regulations (AVV) or concrete acts (*feitelijke handelingen*) by the administration, the civil judge has jurisdiction in the matter (because the administrative judge has no competence in these cases).

109 Apart from compensation in case of unlawful action there is also the possibility to receive compensation for lawful actions. In Article 3:4, para. 2, Awb this is recognized in a general way, through the codification of the proportionality principle. In other words: when no compensation is given, the decision could be unlawful. In specific legislation (land-use law and environmental law) explicit provisions exist that make it possible for individuals to claim compensation for lawful decisions. For an elaboration on this see Publication 128 of the Dutch Association for Administrative Law: Hoitink, J.F., Van Maanen, G.E., Van Ravels, B.P.M. & Schueler, B.J., *Schadevergoeding bij rechtmatige overheidsdaad*, Den Haag: Boom Juridische uitgevers, 2002.

Since 1 July 2013 the GALA contains a specific chapter for damages caused by unlawful decisions (section 8.4 Awb *schadevergoeding bij onrechtmatige besluiten*). The goal of the new section in the GALA was to make the system less complicated and create a simple procedure to obtain damages and to allocate competences in a more clear way to the administrative and civil court.

The procedures differ from the regular procedures before the administrative judge. Instead of filing an appeal an injured citizen can file a request to the administrative judge to obtain damages (*verzoekschriftprocedure*). The procedure is limited to damages caused by unlawful decisions (and preparatory actions) of the administration which can be reviewed by the administrative court. During or after an appeal at the administrative court against a decision a request can be done at that court for compensation of damage in case the decision is judged as unlawful. It also may concern a decision of which the administrative organ (on objection) already stated that the decision was unlawful or damages caused by other acts which cannot be reviewed by the administrative court, such as factual acts or regulations (*AVV*). Article 8:88 Awb clarifies against which unlawful decisions and acts a request can be made for damages.

Furthermore in order to obtain damages the person filing the request must be an interested person within the meaning of Article 1:2 Awb. The request must be filed in writing and can only be filed if the injured person has requested damages directly from the administrative organ at least eight weeks before filing the request to the court. If the court grants the request it will award damages (Article 8:95 Awb).

Starting point for damages caused by unlawful decisions is a division of competence between the administrative court and civil court. The delineation of the division of competence is laid down in Article 8:89, paragraph 1 and 2, Awb. In certain cases either the administrative court or the civil court is exclusively competent which means that there no longer exists a choice for the injured citizen. Still room is left for the ordinary courts though (except in cases where the CRvB or the administrative judge in tax matters is competent, since they have an exclusive competence): when the damage is above €25,000 as a general rule only the civil court is competent. Below this amount (except in cases where the CRvB and the administrative tax courts are competent) both the administrative and ordinary court can deal with it. In case the claimant decides to start the procedure at the civil court the administrative court is not competent (anymore) to deal with a request for compensation. In case damage is claimed at the administrative court the ordinary court shall abstain from dealing with it. One can say that this regulation is about a division of competences between the administrative and civil court while for lawful actions the civil court is outside the playing field (see below).

5.3.4.5.2. Criteria for damages for unlawful acts

As stated before, in some cases both the administrative law court and the civil law court are still competent with regard to an action for compensation for an unlawful act of the administration.[110]

In the decision about the duty for the administration to pay compensation the administrative judge (like the civil law judge) makes use of the rules about the general law of torts, dealt with in Article 6:162 BW *et seq.* In this respect often the violation of legal duties is at stake. As to that, apart from the other conditions (accountability, damage and causal connection between unlawfulness and damage), the so-called *Schutznorm* (*relativiteitsvereiste*) is applicable. The courts have to investigate whether the violated legal provision or regulation is intended to protect the interests that have been injured.

Both administrative and civil law judges take as a rule that there is a strict liability: once the administrative judge has quashed the decision the 'accountability' (*schuld*) of the administrative organ is given. The reason for this approach is that the community as a whole can more likely bear the damage than the individual citizen: it is not reasonable to leave the damage caused by an unlawful act to that individual.

When a tort action is initiated the civil court follows the judgement of the administrative judge concerning the (quashed) decision. It would not be efficient and contrary to the principle of legal certainty if the civil judge should give a judgement about the (quashed) decision himself or herself (*formele rechtskracht*).

Once the administrative court is not competent to decide about the action of the administrative organ, the civil court of course has to give a judgement about the legality of the action. As we saw earlier the administrative court, as a general rule, is only competent in cases of individual decisions and not in case of general binding law provisions or factual action (like the factual enforcement (*bestuursdwang*)). As stated in paragraph 5.3.1, in the Netherlands an individual can always go to a judge in cases of disputes with the administration. Once the administrative courts are not competent, the civil courts are.

5.3.4.5.3. Compensation for lawful acts of the administration

In certain cases it is possible to receive financial compensation for lawful acts of the administration. This is based on the principle of *égalité devant les charges publiques*. A decision of the administration can be lawful and necessary in the general interest but it would be unreasonable to leave the (financial) burden to one or more individuals. Sometimes this principle is codified in legislation, for instance, the former Article 49 Act on Land-use Planning (*Wet op de ruimtelijke*

110 See in this respect Article 1:1, paragraph 4, Awb which states that the legal entity (and not the administrative organ) is liable.

ordening) and the present Article 6.1 Act on Land-use Planning (*Wet ruimtelijke ordening*), but it can also function as an unwritten principle for decisions of the administration. In that respect one can always ask the administration for compensation (*bestuurs-/nadeelcompensatie*). The (non)decision is a decision that can be appealed against at the administrative court. Another possibility for compensation is through Article 3:4, paragraph 2, Awb, the principle of proportionality (*evenredigheid*). Not giving compensation may conflict with this. It concerns a so-called *onzelfstandig schadebesluit* because the compensation is part of the decision that causes the damage, like an environmental (building or prevention of pollution) permit. Known in that respect are the *Paul Krugerbrug* cases.[111] The Minister for Traffic and Water Affairs handed out a permit to the municipality of Utrecht to replace a movable bridge for a solid bridge across a canal (De Merwede). That was necessary for a fast tram. The legality of the replacement was not an issue, but the administrative court considered that compensation was necessary for a shipyard that as a result of the new bridge could not use the canal anymore. It took many years to construct the bridge because of this and in that respect a separate decision (*zelfstandig schadebesluit*) about compensation is better.

The division of competences between the administrative and civil courts in cases of lawful actions is and always has been different from that in cases of unlawful acts. In the former only access to the administrative court is available (when the administrative court is also competent in relation to the damaging decision). This was decided by the Supreme Court.[112] It concerned the situation in which a decision was taken by the administration to close a road. As a result a restaurant suffered damage because less people came to eat there. The owner of the restaurant asked for compensation and took action against that decision in the civil court. In the end the Supreme Court decided that the aspect of compensation had to be decided in the decision about the closing of the road. In the meantime that decision, however, had come into effect (and for the civil court that act is irreversible (*formele rechtskracht*). The latter is not the case for the administrative court. Bottom line: One can always ask for a separate decision about compensation but that can only be tested by the administrative court. As we saw earlier, the administrative court, as a general rule, is only competent in cases of individual decisions and not in case of general binding law provisions or factual action.[113] So in that kind of case, the civil courts also are competent. Strange in that respect is that we have no possibility in Dutch law for an action at the civil courts to ask for compensation in case of *lawful* actions

---

111 ARRS 12 January 1982, *AB* 1982, 299 and ARRS 22 November 1983, *AB* 1984, 154.

112 HR 6 December 2002, *JB* 2003, 3 (*Eetcafé-Pannenkoekenhuis De Kabouter*).

113 To make it even more complex: factual aspects (like information given by the administration) that can be linked to the decision form part of that decision and therefore of the *formele rechtskracht*, see HR 9 September 2005, *AB* 2006, 286.

of the administration. The solution is that the civil court addresses an action as *unlawful* because of the refusal of compensation.[114]

5.3.4.5.4. Compensation for lawful acts in the GALA

Some ten years ago a pre-draft for changing the Awb dealing with compensation by the administration was issued. In the spring of 2012 in the First Chamber of Parliament a changed draft was launched and it is not unlikely that it comes into force within a few years. Then the GALA (section 4.5) will contain general rules dealing with compensation in cases of lawful actions of the administration.[115] The highlights are the following. The main rule will be that when an administrative authority acts lawfully and causes damage that goes beyond the normal risk and causes disproportional harm to some in comparison with others the damage, if requested, shall be compensated (*égalité* principle). Legislation will deal with time limits (until when can a claim be done and within what time should the administration deal with it, is a (reimbursable) fee possible etc.). It is in principle linked to all kind of actions (not only decisions) of administrative authorities. Since the request is (formally) dealt with in a decision, this can be appealed in an administrative court (after an objection with the administrative authority). There is no room left for the civil court in this respect.

5.3.4.6. Costs

Apart from damages for an unlawful decision the administrative judge can also order a party (on the basis of Article 8:75 Awb) to pay the costs the other party has reasonably incurred in connection with the court proceedings (and objection proceedings) (*proceskosten*). The types of costs for court proceedings (that also may include costs made in the objection procedure) and their restricted amounts are stated in a General Administrative Order (*Besluit proceskosten bestuursrecht*). In summary: in practice in case the appeal is well founded (this is not a formal requirement) the administrative authority has to pay the costs the claimant makes for legal representation (if the claimant makes use of it because legal representation is not obligatory): being in 2017 in general 2 × €495 (1 point for the written appeal and one point for attending the court session). In case the appeal is well founded also other costs may have to be paid to the claimant by the administrative authority, such as reasonable costs for travelling, experts and unpaid leave. In practice it is mainly applied towards the

114 HR 18 January 1991, *AB* 1991, 241 (*Varkensmestersarrest*).

115 *Kamerstukken II* 2011/12, 32 621A, *Wetvoorstel nadeelcompensatie en schadevergoeding bij onrechtmatige besluiten, Gewijzigd voorstel van wet*. Presently this topic is (more specific) also part of a Bill for a fully new Environment Act (*Omgevingswet*). This is not further addressed here.

administration. However, when a claimant makes abuse of court proceedings (that is never or hardly so) the judge can rule that he/she has to pay the costs of the administration. In principle no costs are reimbursed in case the appeal is unfounded.

When the appeal is well founded (this is a formal requirement) the administrative authority has to pay the before mentioned costs as well as (on the basis of Article 8:74 Awb) reimburse the registry fee paid.[116]

For people with limited means legal aid by registered bar lawyers is available based on the Legal Aid Act (*Wet op de rechtsbijstand).* A specific authority *(Raad voor de rechtsbijstand)* deals with the application of this Act. In recent years the (financial) criteria to receive legal aid have been tightened up.

5.3.5. Right to Provisional Ruling (Interim Relief)

The general rule is that an appeal or objection does not suspend the decision. During the appeal with the District Court – and also when an objection has been raised with the administration against the decision *in primo* –, an application may be made to the summary proceedings judge of the District Court for a temporary ruling, the *voorlopige voorziening* (Article 8:81 Awb, Title 8.3 Awb). These are proceedings on the grounds of urgency (*kort geding*). There are, however, important differences compared to urgency proceedings in the civil court. In the first place, there must have been an objection to (the administrative organ) or appeal (at the court) against the decision (connectivity theory) and in the second place no appeal is possible against the rulings in these urgency proceedings. They only provide the interested parties with a provisional and temporary decision in the case. It is possible, however, for the court, also *ex officio*, to discontinue a preliminary ruling or change it (Article 8:87 Awb). Only in the appeal phase it is also possible for the court to decide the appeal directly when an appeal is lodged and it is requested to give a temporary ruling (*kortsluiting*) (Article 8:86 Awb). A temporary ruling can be given very quickly, even within hours or a few days after the request is made. The court will review and give a provisional judgement on the lawfulness of the decision of the administration. If there are doubts on the lawfulness the court will weigh all interests concerned and decide whether a provisional measure is justified. In this interim relief procedure the relativity requirement (see para. 5.3.2.3) can only be applied during the appeal phase.

---

[116] The registry fee is dealt with in Article 8:41 Awb. For instance, in social security cases it is presently € 46 for natural persons and in other not listed cases it is € 168. When the appeal is lodged by a legal person it is € 333. This also applies to provisional ruling cases, see para. 5.3.5 (Article 8:82 Awb). As already mentioned sometimes the civil court is competent especially concerning damages (see para. 5.3.4.5.1). At the civil court the fees are higher (depending on the requested amount of the damage) and also in case of losing you mostly have to pay the costs of the other party.

5.3.6. *Appellate Court Proceedings (in as far as Different from First Instance)*

5.3.6.1. Function and Scope

In terms of definitions an appellate judge is also an administrative judge and for that reason all rules that are applying for the administrative judge (in first instance) are applicable for the appellate judge, unless this is otherwise stated. This principle is also laid down in Article 8:108 Awb that is part of title 8.5 that deals with higher appeal (*hoger beroep*). There is full review (in fact and in law), an appeal has to be launched within 6 weeks, there is no duty to have legal representation, there is legal aid, etc.[117]

The primary focus in appeal is the (lawfulness of the) judgement of the lower court and not as in first instance the decision of the administration. However, Dutch law is not very clear about the function (and hence also not about the scope) of appeal. The respective appeal courts interpret their role slightly different. The ABRS clearly focusses on her task to control the first instance judge and to unify the application of administrative law. As a consequence, the claimant cannot add new grounds of review which were not discussed in first instance.[118] Furthermore, the ABRS quite quickly rejects new arguments which could have been, but were not brought forward in first instance.[119] Sometimes, but not always (there is no consistent line in that), even evidence is excluded because it could have been brought forward already in first instance.[120]

This is, because of the requirements of article 6 ECHR, only different in appeals against punitive (administrative) sanctions, like administrative fines.

The CRvB and het Supreme Court (in tax law cases) and to quite an extent also the CBB look at the function of appeal differently and acknowledge that the possibility to appeal should offer the appellant a chance of having reviewed the case for a second time. Hence, the appellant may bring forward new grounds, arguments and evidence.[121]

The only limitation is the principle of due process. It is not accepted that the claimant deliberately has kept some grounds of his claim quite to harm the procedural position of one of the other parties. Sometimes parties in appeal agree upon certain things and come to other solutions, for instance during the court session. In that situation the appeal judge has some room to act 'outside the scope of the judgement'?[122]

---

117 The registree fee is somewhat higher: Article 8:109 Awb (see previous footnote).

118 ABRS 21 June 2006, AB 2006, 339.

119 ABRS 29 April 2009, ECLI:NL:RVS:2009:BI2678.

120 ABRS 17 January 2007, ECLI:RVS:2007:AZ6371. However, the opposite was the case in ABRS 9 May 2000, JB 2000, 179.

121 CRvB 14 October 1999, JB 1999, 303; CRvB 4 June 2013, ECLI:NL:CRVB:2013:CA2803; HR 10 December 2010, ECLI:NL:HR:2010:B06786.

122 See for example: ABRS 18 July 2014, ECLI:NL:RVS:2014:2812.

5.3.6.2. Access to the Appellate Courts

Article 8:104, paragraph 1, Awb points out that an interested party and the administrative organ can appeal against specified judgements of the District Court, namely the judgement based on Article 8:66 Awb (the regular judgement to an appeal in first instance), the judgement about an appeal from the interim relief judge of the District Court based on Article 8:86 Awb (in case combined with an appeal), and the judgement of the District Court in which is decided about a request for financial compensation based on Article 8:95 Awb. Article 8:104, paragraph 2, Awb holds the judgements against which no appeal is possible. It concerns mainly the judgements of the District Courts in cases were no oral hearing is held (simplified procedure: Article 8.54 Awb). Against such cases an intern appeal at the District Court is possible (*verzet*). Appeal against judgements in the latter proceedings (*verzet*) is also excluded. Worthwhile mentioning here is that since 1 January 2013, once an appeal is lodged by somebody also the party that could have lodged an appeal may lodge a so-called incidental appeal. This appeal has to be brought forward within six weeks after the appeal judge sent the grounds of the (regular) appeal to this party. The other parties can give their reaction to this incidental appeal. No court fee is obliged for this appeal (Article 8:110 GALA). Articles 8:111 and 8:112 Awb hold some additional rules regarding the admissibility of the incidental appeal. The aim to introduce incidental appeal was twofold. First of all, it is a consequence from the shift from *recours objectif* to *recours subjectif*. The second reason was that the government did want to limit the numbers of appeal in second instance to some extent. Without incidental appeal, a party which did appeal against a decision of the District Court did not run any risk. Now the appeal was limited to its grounds which the District Court had refused, the outcome of the appeal would in any case not be worse for this party. By lodging his appeal on the last day of the period for appeal, the party could, at least to some extent, prevent that the other party also appealed. This now is no longer possible as the other party always can lodge its incidental appeal until six weeks after it received the (regular) appeal. Hence, each party which appeals has to calculate the risk of an incidental appeal of the other party.

5.3.6.3. Procedural Aspects at the Appellate Courts

It follows from the before mentioned that scope and function of higher appeal are comparable with first instance appeal. In that respect the procedural aspects are also comparable. Maybe oral proceedings are somewhat more formal and strict.

5.3.6.4. Grounds of Review (Scope of Judgements) of the Appellate Courts

As to the possible range of judgements of the appellate courts, it is important to mention Article 8:113 Awb. Because, at least as a point of departure, not the administrative decision (as in first instance cases) but the judgement of the lower court is the main focus in appeal, it is stipulated here that this judgement can be confirmed either by upholding or by improving the grounds or that the appellate court does, with quashing in whole or in part the judgement of the District Court, what that court should do. When the judgement of the appellate court has as consequence that the administrative organ has to take a new decision, the appellate court can rule that a new appeal has to be launched directly at the appellate court (and not at the District Court)(judicial loop). Article 8:115 Awb holds 2 situations in which the case has to be referred back to the District Court that dealt with the case in first instance: when the first instance court decided that it was not competent or the appeal was inadmissible (and the appellate court decides that it was competent or the appeal was admissible) and the appellate court finds that there are other reasons that the case has to be done again by the District Court. In the former situation the appellate court can deal with the case itself when it finds that no treatment by the District Court is necessary. Finally the appellate court can decide that in case another District Court was competent the judgement of the incompetent court is healed (Article 8:117 Awb). In Article 8:114 Awb it is indicated that in case of (partial) quashing of the judgement this also means that the court fee has to be refunded by the administrative organ unless it is decided that the court reimburses the court fee itself. Because also administrative organs can appeal to appellate courts Article 8:118 Awb deals with additional provisions in relation to a request for recovery of costs by parties (legal assistance and experts) in cases of withdrawal of appeals by these organs. It follows from the before mentioned that apart from the fact that in appeal cases also the administrative organ can lodge an appeal, there are in principle no differences as to the treatment of first instance and appeal cases although the objective of it is different: the decision of the administration versus the judgement of the court. But in the end that is not really decisive for the test of the court, the remedies, etc.

5.3.7. Complaints at the (National) Ombudsman

Since 1982, the Netherlands has a National Ombudsman. The institution of this Ombudsman, laid down in the National Ombudsman Act (*Wet Nationale Ombudsman*) is not a judicial body, since he/she is not empowered to issue binding decisions. The citizen may lodge a complaint (*klacht*) with the Ombudsman about certain actions by certain public organs.[123] The Ombudsman

[123] This is dealt with in Article 9:18, para. 2, Awb that reads as follows: 'Any person has the right to apply to the ombudsman in writing and request an investigation into the way in which an administrative organ has conducted itself towards a natural or legal person'. Until 2006 this was for the National Ombudsman stated in Article 12, para. 2, National Ombudsman Act, but from that moment on transposed to title 9.2 Awb. This title (Article 9:17–9:36 Awb) deals with (external) complaint procedures by an ombudsman, not only at the national but also

then examines whether the administrative organ has conducted itself properly in the matter under investigation. After the investigation has been concluded, the Ombudsman draws up a report, which reflects his findings and views. In spite of his opinion not being binding, his reports are very influential and prompt the administration to improve public organization. This complaint procedure can be seen as an alternative means of (quasi) judicial protection of the individual which complements the function of judicial review.

In all kinds of matters for which one cannot avail upon the administrative judge the Ombudsman may bring relief.[124] Examples are: failure to reply to letters or to send a timely reply, improper treatment in hearings or in other contact with the administration, but also complaints about police action in maintaining public order. These examples reveal that intervention by the Ombudsman is relevant in relation to factual administrative action (as opposed to legal decisions). Before addressing the Ombudsman, the applicant must first communicate his/her complaints to the administrative organ in question and grant it an opportunity to present its views on the matter.

The Ombudsman applies a broader test when assessing propriety (*behoorlijkheid*) than the administrative judge assessing lawfulness (*rechtmatigheid*). In his annual report of 1990 (and fine-tuned since), the Ombudsman included the following checklist of propriety requirements:

- conformity with written law;
- reasonableness;
- legal certainty;
- equal treatment;
- reasoned decisions;
- due care.

The requirement of due care is subdivided into a number of sub-criteria, namely due care in respect of:

- procedure (for instance, no undue delay);
- service and facilities, for instance, helpfulness and accessibility;
- attitude and conduct of public servants, for instance, correct approach and treatment without prejudice.

---

at the decentralized level (municipalities, provinces and water boards). Article 1a National Ombudsman Act deals with the division of competencies between the national ombudsman and the decentralized ombudsmen. Decentralized authorities may choose to affiliate with the National Ombudsman.

124 The relationship between Ombudsman and judge is rather complex. For instance, the Ombudsman is not competent anymore when the administrative judge already decided about the action and is temporarily not competent as long as judicial review is possible. In practice, however, complaints are mostly related to factual actions and administrative courts are only competent in cases of Awb-decisions in that respect. The purview of this Introduction to Dutch administrative law does not permit further discussion of this relationship.

The above is written from the perspective of the National Ombudsman and time will prove whether or not this will also apply for the ombudsmen at the decentralized level.

Apart from the before-mentioned ombudsman procedures, title 9.1 Awb (Articles 9:1–9:16 Awb) provides for rules related to the right to raise (internal) complaints against actions of the administrative organs to these organs themselves. The general rule in this is that the complaint procedure at the administrative organ has to be followed, before a complaint can be raised at the Ombudsman (Article 9:20, paragraph 1, Awb).

6. ENFORCEMENT OF ADMINISTRATIVE LAW

For the enforcement of administrative law by the administration, of course, administrative law measures are possible and are provided for. Nevertheless civil and penal law enforcements are possible in certain areas to enforce administrative law. In the following the main features of administrative, civil and penal enforcement of administrative law respectively will be addressed with an outlook on the relation between these three types of enforcement.

6.1. ADMINISTRATIVE LAW ENFORCEMENT

6.1.1. Supervision and Sanctioning

When we look at enforcement on the basis of specific legislation, in which the power *to* enforce is provided for, we also have to focus on chapter 5 Awb. Chapter 5 Awb primarily offers general rules on *how to use* administrative instruments for supervision and sanctioning. So mostly the combination of the two offer the applicable rules on enforcement. In principle the competence for enforcement and supervision related to most legislation lies primarily with the licensing authorities e.g. the authorities that grant benefits etc. The enforcement that is dealt with in chapter 5 Awb so far concerns three types of administrative orders.

The first one is the order from an administrative body, competent on the basis of a specific legislative act, stating that the illegal violation of the activity has to be undone and if the offender (owner) fails to do so the competent body can by itself stop the offending activity and recover the costs from the owner of that establishment (*bestuursdwang*).[125] This power can for instance, be used in the field of housing, land-use planning and environmental law in the case of (severe) violations of land-use provisions and environmental permits and general rules.

125 For recovering the actual costs, in case the administration decides to undo the illegal situation, an additional civil law action is needed and can lead to lengthy procedures.

For decentralized authorities this competence is based on articles in the statutes dealing with the organization of the various decentralized authorities, namely municipalities, provinces and district water boards (*Gemeentewet, Provinciewet, Waterschapswet*) in combination with Article 5:22 Awb. For instance, ministers (national government) do not have such general competence but, for instance, for the Minister for the Environment a specific competence exists in Article 5.15 Act on Environmental Licensing and General Provisions.

The second one is the order under penalty (*dwangsom*) on the basis of Article 5:32 Awb. In case of non-compliance with administrative law provisions (licenses, general rules) the offender has to pay a sum of money if he/she remains unwilling to end the violation in accordance with the administrative order that so requires. The competence to issue an order under penalty is an accessory to the abovementioned (general or specific) competence of *bestuursdwang*. A combination of these two orders is not possible (Article 5:32 Awb). Both orders have the aim of restoring the offence, which becomes evident from (as a general rule) the necessity of giving the offender the possibility within a certain period to end the offence (*terme de grace*). Some discretion exists here: as to which order is chosen and how long the period is. In practice in the field of violation of environmental provisions (by the Board of Mayor and Eldermen) often the order under penalty is chosen while in cases where drugs are found in a building (by the Mayor), based on the Opium Act, the order is used to almost immediately close that building for a certain period of time.[126]

The administrative order under penalty should not be confused with the punitive sanction of issuing an administrative penalty (*bestuurlijke boete*). With administrative penalties the aim of the sanction is not primarily to end the offence but to punish the offender. With that aim a change in conduct for the better will not (automatically) result in not having to pay the penalty as would be the case with the administrative order under penalty. In the latter case the penalty is only applied if indeed the offender does not comply with the given order within a certain period of time.

In 2009 a set of rules on administrative penalties (not combined to an order) is introduced in the Awb. So far the administrative penalty is dealt with in social security legislation, for instance, in cases where somebody does not provide the competent body with necessary information for the correct setting of a benefit (*uitkering*) (in case of unemployment, social welfare or the inability to work for medical reasons).[127] In case of (severe) violations the various specific legal

---

126 Very recently (case of 29 November 2017) the ABRS opened up the discussion whether or not *bestuursdwang* in this respect is (maybe) a criminal charge, ECLI:NL:RVS:2017:3251. Recently (1 July 2017) the Mayor, based on the Municipality Act, and to overcome the growing nuisance by neighbours, has become the power to give specific orders about how to behave, *Staatsblad* 2017, 77 and 113.

127 Another area in which it is already for a longer period is used (by the minister for Social Affairs and employment) as a standard sanction: illegal labour by aliens (the employer has to pay the fine). See also footnote 143.

Acts also make the (temporary) withdrawal of such benefits decisions possible and in addition of course a legal basis for the recovery of already paid benefits is provided for. Also in the field of the environment (see also paragraph 6.4) this punitive penalty is introduced.

The measure of 'withdrawal' is also used for environmental permits (building land-use and prevention of pollution (especially based on the Act on Environmental Licensing and General Provisions and not dealt with in the Awb so far).

In this perspective accumulation of enforcements instruments (withdrawal/recovery/penalty) is possible.

As was said earlier, chapter 5 Awb also contains provisions concerning supervisory powers. For instance, the officials appointed by the competent authorities have the power to ask for information, to ask for copies of various documents, to enter all places (except houses) with their equipment and to search vehicles and other property. All these competencies can be exercised insofar as this is necessary for a reasonable fulfilment of the duty of these officials to enforce the law. Supervisors are appointed by a procedure that has a statutory basis (Article 5:11 Awb); for instance, the Environmental Management Act or the Act on Environmental Licensing and General Provisions offer such a basis for supervision with regard to these Acts.

In principle the competence for enforcement and supervision in most Acts lies primarily with the licensing authorities or the authorities that grant benefits.

In most cases there is no statutory link that compels the relevant public authorities to apply the more extensive public preparation procedure of chapter 3.4. Although the authorities themselves can decide to use these procedures (see Article 3:10 Awb) this is not a likely course of action, both because enforcement should be swift and also because the decision on enforcement should not be the moment to review in principle the admissibility of the activity at hand. Naturally with administrative enforcement acts the standard procedure for administrative acts under chapter 4 Awb is applicable.

6.1.2. *Duty for the Administration to Enforce*

An important feature of administrative enforcement especially in the field of environmental law/land-use law, is 'condoning' (*gedogen*). Because competencies for administrative enforcement in this area of law are discretionary powers, the competent authority has, in every case where an administrative sanction is applicable, the duty to weigh the interests involved, for instance, the interest of the environment against the interest of the entrepreneur. If it should turn out, for example, that the illegal activity at hand can be legalized within a short period of time and this activity does no harm to third parties, one could argue that the offence be condoned on the condition that legalization will be effective shortly. Third parties can appeal to a court against such a decision or the refusal to enforce.[128] During the last decade the widespread practice of condoning has met with more critical appraisal. Much aided by case law of the Judicial Department of the Council of State, condoning is now generally regarded as something to be applied only in exceptional cases. When a request for enforcement is made by a third party to the administration, the prospect of legalization has to be clear and the principles of proper administration demand of public authorities that they offer proper motives (not to enforce). Or in other words: Third parties have in principle a right that a measure against a breach of legislative provisions is enforced.[129] Since 2004 the ABRS put it in the following standard criterion: "In the light of the general interest that is served with enforcement in cases of violation of a legal provision the administrative organ that has the power to give orders (*bestuursdwang*) or to give orders under penalty (*dwangsom*) should as a rule make use of this power. Only in special circumstances can it be asked from the administrative organ not to do so. This can be the case when a concrete expectation of legalization exists. Furthermore enforcement can be so unreasonable in relation to the interests served by it that in that concrete situation, it should be refrained from."[130] Of course when a request is not made by a third party the practice of condoning – the administration knows of the illegal situation but does not act – could still be at hand.

6.1.2. Execution

In 2009 the GALA was changed in the way that also a part (not everything) of the financial execution came within the field of administrative law (before, that was a civil law issue). It primarily concerns title 4.4 dealing with administrative financial debts. In the field of enforcement it mainly concerns the reclaiming of costs in case the administration itself executes the rectification order (*kostenverhaal*) or claims the penalty that is combined with the order under penalty (*invordering*). Separate Awb-decisions (*beschikkingen*) are necessary in this respect (see also chapter 5). Especially in relation to claim the penalty – this penalty is for the administration and for instance not for the third party that made the request for the enforcement – various formal requirements exist. Bear in mind that the penalty is related to the *terme de grace* and is directly lost / forfeited (*verbeurd*) within 6 weeks after that time limit and should in principle

---

128 See, for instance, ABRS 11 April 1997, *JB* 1997, 152.

129 See for this principle of the duty to enforce (*beginselplicht tot handhaving*) ABRS 2 February 1998, *AB* 1998, 181. For a slightly changed criterion, which leaves some more room for policy of the administration, see ABRS 5 October 2011, ECLI:NL:RVS:2011:BT6683.

130 For one of the first cases in which this standard criterion was introduced, see ABRS 30 June 2004, *JB* 2004, 293. For some minor adjustments, see ABRS 5 October 2011, ECLI:NL:RVS:2011:BT6683.

be reclaimed within a one year (*verjaring*). The claim for the cost-recovery of the rectification order expires after 5 years: Articles 5:33 and 5:35 Awb.

It goes beyond this contribution to elaborate further on this. Important to mention is that third interested persons (mostly the ones that requested the administration to enforce) can also ask the administration to reclaim the costs. For these third persons and off course the offenders the same procedures and judicial review possibilities exist as in relation to the enforcement decisions itself. For efficiency reasons legal provisions exist in which it is stated that procedures about (not) enforcement and (not) reclaiming penalties should be combined (Article 5:39 Awb). As for the enforcement also for the execution there is in principle a duty for the administration to claim and do that fully.[131] If the administration is reluctant to do that a decision can be provoked under a penalty and appeal is possible (*beroep en dwangsom niet tijdig beslissen*). This penalty is for the person who asks for the decision (Article 4:17 and 8:55a onwards Awb). By the way: case law exist in which the requirements are formulated for the enforcement decision and the reclaiming decision (how should an – ongoing – violation be reported, documented etc.).[132]

6.1.3. *Preventative Assessments*

A (new) element worthwhile mentioning here and of a very preventative nature is the Act dealing with the promotion of integrity assessments by the administration (*Wet bevordering integriteitsbeoordelingen door het openbaar bestuur*, or Wet Bibob).[133]

On the basis of this Act and delegated legislation (Crown Decree), administrative authorities can, as far as they have been given the power, grant a permit or withdraw a permit. This competence, linked to specific Acts such as the Environmental Management Act and the Liquor and Catering Act, is available in case danger (*gevaar*) exists that the applicant/holder of the permit will take advantage of committed criminal actions (*strafbare feiten*), the permit is/will be used to commit criminal actions or that for obtaining the permit a criminal action is committed, in short in cases where there is a link between the permit and criminal actions (Article 3 Wet Bibob).

When making the assessment administrative authorities can ask for advice from the (national) Bibob Office. Some administrative authorities have made policy rules in that perspective. Because the use of the Bibob powers can have great impact, the following principles of proper administration especially apply, due care, reasoning and proportionality.

---

131 See ABRS 24 December 2013, ECLI:NL:RVS:2013:2626.

132 See ABRS 3 May 2017, ECLI:NL:RVS:2017:1179.

133 This Act came into force on June 1 2003 (*Kamerstukken II* 1999–00, 26 883).

6.2. CIVIL LAW ENFORCEMENT[134]

Actions under civil law are in principle used by individuals against other individuals. Especially in non-contractual liability cases, the violation of administrative law provisions can be of major importance for a successful action. One can think of an action under tort law in the case where somebody acts contrary to an environmental license. Under Dutch civil law such an action is not only open for individuals but also action groups, i.e. legal persons.[135] Here it is more important to look at the possibility for government bodies to commence civil law proceedings. Articles 6:162 *et seq.* Dutch Civil Code deal with this non-contractual civil liability. The essential requirements for the successful application of Article 6:162 *et seq.* BW are; unlawfulness, accountability (*culpa*/ risk), (impending) damage and a causal connection between unlawful actions and the damage. Concerning the civil liability, the unlawfulness is the key element here. The other requirements will only be addressed when they are relevant in this matter. Article 6:162, section 2, BW points out that there is unlawfulness in the case of a breach of (subjective) rights, when the action (or lack of an action) violates legal duties or when a violation of unwritten law or failure to take due care (*maatschappelijke onzorgvuldigheid*) is at stake.

Governmental bodies can be declared justiciable fairly easily in Awb procedures and on Awb appeal on the basis of Article 1:2, paragraph 2, Awb. For governmental actions under civil law, a similar system applies as to the civil law actions by action-groups under Article 3:305a BW. On the basis of Article 3:305b BW governmental legal persons can raise claims for the protection of interests of other persons as far as the promotion of these interests is entrusted to them. However, there is a legal action in which the government can raise any civil law claim on the basis of the promotion of the general interest (*algemeen belang*), as stated in the Supreme Court's judgement in the *Staat*/*Kabayel* case; if there is a sufficient interest (a legal position or interest is at stake and the civil action can in fact serve to protect or compensate this interest).[136] This case may well open up the way to give the administration an almost unlimited power to raise civil law claims. But in situations in which the administration, in order to promote or protect public aims and interests, wants to make use of competencies under civil law parallel to or instead of existing public law competencies, the Supreme Court

134 In para. 3.3 of this contribution the use of private law by the administration is addressed. What is written here is partly the same but is more linked to enforcement.

135 Civil law action is also possible when no violation of legislative provisions is at hand. In that perspective the problem of the (non)indemnifying character of a permit/license occurs. When violation of administrative law provisions is at stake, civil law action by an individual against the wrongdoer is possible next to the request by that individual to the administration for administrative law enforcement.

136 HR 18 February 1994, *NJ* 1995, 718.

has set some limitations.[137] One of the leading cases concerning the possibility of using private law competencies parallel to or instead of public law competencies in order to realize public aims is the *Windmill* case.[138] In this case the Supreme Court decided that when public law provisions do not deal with the matter – this is the use of private law competencies parallel to or instead of public law competencies – public law provisions may not be crossed out in an unacceptable way. In this respect, the content and meaning of the public law regulation and the way in which and the extent to which this public law regulation protects the rights of citizens (in the light of other written and unwritten rules of public law) has to be taken into account. Also important is whether the government could achieve a similar result by exercising the public law competencies as by exercising the civil law competence. If so, this is a major indication that there is no place for a civil law action by the government. After the *Windmill* case several other judgements were given by the Supreme Court in which the *Windmill* standards were used. This implies that, for instance, where administrative authorities have a public law competence to give an order under penalty (for instance, under Article 5:32 Awb) the use of the civil law competence to do this in combination with an action for injunction based on tort law is excluded. The government then has to follow the public law provisions.[139] This also implies that if, for instance, a specific Act contains explicit provisions for government action under civil law the use of civil law is possible. For instance, on the basis of the Soil Protection Act (*Wet bodembescherming*) the government is free to start a civil law action to seek compensation from the polluter for pollution of the soil that is or will be cleaned up by the government (Article 75 Soil Protection Act; see also Article 5.26 Act on Environmental Licenses and General Provisions).

6.3. PENAL LAW ENFORCEMENT

Just like the relation between public and private law, the relation between public (in the meaning of administrative) and penal (criminal) law is especially relevant where it concerns enforcement. Apart from the administrative law competencies to enforce the law against the violation of environmental legal provisions (administrative penalties, withdrawal of permits etc.), there are also penal law competencies to punish such violations. It is not the competent administrative body but the public prosecutor (*officier van justitie*) who initiates the criminal prosecution. Just like the administrative bodies, the prosecutor has the competence to initiate the sanctioning of the violation of legal (administrative

137 For instance, making agreements, exercising property rights and starting procedures under the law of torts.

138 HR 26 January 1990, *AB* 1990, 408.

139 HR 22 October 1993, *M&R* 1994, 1 (*Staat* v *Magnus*).

law) provisions. The public prosecutor is not obliged to do this, although a complaint can be made at the Court of Appeal (*Gerechtshof*) against a refusal (Article 12 *Wetboek van Strafvordering*, Sv) by individuals and legal entities that have a direct interest in the matter. Under penal law (as is the case under civil law) the ordinary courts are competent (District Court, Court of Appeal and Supreme Court). In principle criminal courts also rely on interpretations of the administrative court.

It goes beyond the scope of this chapter to address in depth the penal law. The most important issues will be pointed out. No attention will be given to the following (procedural) aspects of penal environmental law: the organization of investigating and prosecuting, the problems related to evidence, the possibility of the liability under criminal law of legal persons and governmental bodies etc.

In recent years, this perspective on penal law as an *ultimum remedium* has become less dominant, especially in the field of environmental law. The public prosecutor is more active and increasingly makes it his/her own responsibility to enforce laws. One of the main reasons for this change of heart is possibly the fact that at this moment most of the administrative action in the field of administrative law making (and certainly in fields as environmental law), licensing, etc., is complete and the enforcement stage has been reached and needs to be activated on all fronts.

Penal law enforcement of administrative law can fall within the Economic Offences Act (*Wet Economische Delicten*, Wed). A lot of social-economic (administrative) legislation falls within its scope, for instance, land-use planning law, environmental law etc. Article 1a Wed contains an enumeration of administrative law provisions, the violation of which can be regarded as Wed offences. There are several categories of Wed offences of varying seriousness.

The Wed contains a standard regime for punishment, for competencies related to investigating and prosecuting and also for the competencies of the judge concerning the penal enforcement of administrative law provisions. Because the substantive provisions are found in administrative law and not in the specific penal law provisions, one can in this respect speak of the penal law's dependency on administrative law. Sometimes this causes problems because of the specific characteristics of penal law in general.

Apart from the Wed offences, the Penal Code (*Wetboek van strafrecht*, Sr) allows for the criminalization of offences. Also general offences, such as committing forgery, can be the basis for the criminalization of offenders.

The most important difference between the Economic Offences Act and the Penal Code is that for the applicability of powers for the prosecution etc. in the latter case you need to be a suspect, while this is not the case for the Wed (where there is a broad scope of prosecution actions).

The third category of penal offences is becoming very rare, namely in the specific legislation itself.

6.4. CRIMINAL ENFORCEMENT BY ADMINISTRATIVE AUTHORITIES[140]

The administrative penalty (*bestuurlijke boete*) can already be regarded as a punitive sanction (rather than a repairing sanction) in the hands of the administration and in some areas of administrative law the merger between administrative and penal law enforcement goes further. Some years ago an experiment was started in which a small number of administrative authorities (mainly municipalities) received the power to come to an agreement with the offender for simple and frequently occurring environmental offences.[141] Normally this criminal law competence is only vested within the public prosecutor since it is related to penal law and more specifically the prevention of penal prosecution. This is in 2012 integrated in a Crown Decree with a broader perspective for the public prosecutor to deal with enforcement and also some administrative authorities have a similar competence for this type of decision, the so called criminal order (*bestuurlijke strafbeschikking*) but only in minor / not serious cases.[142]

The use of penal competencies by administrative authorities and *vice versa*[143] can in our view give rise to certain problems, since in penal law more than in administrative law, certain safeguards are guaranteed (in the light of Article 6 ECHR), such as *ne bis in idem / una via* and *nemo tenetur*. The same is applicable in the relation between more classic penal law and penal law as laid down, for instance, in the Wed, which is meant to be used in a more effective and efficient way (where, for instance, for many of the powers it is not necessary that there is 'suspicion'). While this goes beyond the contents of our chapter, we think that the possibilities and restrictions in this respect will become more clear in future years. The broad introduction in the Awb of the competence to issue

---

140 Bear in mind that there are also possibilities to hold administrative authorities and/or their civil servants liable under penal law and that at the moment this is still under debate in the Netherlands. This is, however, not further addressed here.

141 Crown Decree of 8 July 2000 (*Transactiebesluit milieudelicten, Staatsblad* 2000, 320 and Crown Decree of 4 July 2007, *Stb.* 2007, 255 (linked to *Stb.* 2006, 330 (*Besluit Om-afdoening en bestuurlijke strafbeschikking*).

142 See previous footnote and *Stb.* 2012, 150 as well as *Staatscourant* 2012, 8384 dealing with this competence of issing criminal orders.

143 For instance, in the Netherlands in the field of (simple and frequently occurring) traffic offences the public prosecutor enforces the relevant provisions not as a penal body but as an administrative authority (the decisions, however, are decided by the ordinary courts). A similar instrument (*bestuurlijke strafbeschikking*) is introduced to enforce 'offences in the public space'.

administrative penalties does not really change that because in this respect many people use the word 'punitive' penalties. Relevant in the perspective of administrative fines (*una via /ne bis in idem)* is that in Article 5:44 Awb a coordination mechanism is provided for between the administration and the public prosecutor.

7. CONCLUSION

The introduction of the Awb in the Netherlands has resulted in a fresh strong scholarly interest in (general) administrative law and an improvement in the quality of the administration. The adoption of the Awb in 1994 and the case law based on it, has led to many scholarly activities. The administration has taken the Awb seriously from the start. It apparently prefers a clearly defined statute to serve as a guideline as opposed to case law and fragmented procedural legislation. It follows from the previous chapters that the Awb – it almost has its 25th anniversary – has not yet been completed. New chapters are added all the time.[144]

In 2009, for instance, rules on administrative penalties, financial decisions, direct appeal (without objection at the administrative organ) and appeal in case of not timely decisions came into force. In 2013 the judicial dispute-settlement powers have been adjusted and a new section on damages in case of unlawful administrative acts has entered into force. Also chapter 8 of the Awb was reformed because of the introduction there of the appellate court proceedings. It is the question whether or not the review of the judicial organization and especially the appellate administrative judges/courts will ever take place. A state of affairs that was supposed to be temporary, could now last indefinitely. In such a case, the Netherlands has a curious system, by which judicial review of administrative action, as a general rule, in the first instance is vested in the District Courts, whereas there are more appellate bodies/courts for most administrative action in the form of individual decisions and the Supreme Court in certain administrative law cases (taxes). Next to that there is the Supreme (Civil) Court, that in last resort can deal with compensation issues between authorities and private parties or comes in when general regulations are at stake. This undermines in some way the position of the Awb which was intended to bring more unity to administrative law. It seems logical that in a country which has a General Administrative Law Act/Code there should be a single last-instance body with jurisdiction to interpret this Act/Code.

For the coming years at least new rules about compensation (also related to lawful acts) will see the light. Furthermore thought will be given to introduce a

[144] That makes this Dutch contribution somewhat complex, but we thought it necessary to show as much developments as possible.

more complete system for final dispute settlement (especially in cases where no third parties are at stake or when that is the case parties agree) and mediation. Maybe also rules about the burden of proof will see the light. The topics lending themselves for inclusion into the Awb and the level of detail needed are part of an on-going discussion. The relation between the general Awb and procedural rules in specific legislative Acts should not be forgotten and also the fact that new legislation very often requires transition rules and time is needed to crystallise.

It is the question whether or not all changes of the Awb are for the better. It has become more formal and (technically) complex. One should also not forget that there is EU-legislation that more and more influences general administrative law. In recent years, for instance in the field of asylum law, EU (primary and secondary) legislation touched more and more the national proceedings at the administration and in the administrative courts: Concerning the latter for instance related to the moment (*ex nunc*) and intensity of the testing of administrative decisions. The same applies to the ECHR.

Part of the changes deal with the on-going discussion about the relationship between administration and judge. At the end of 1997, the *Van Kemenade* Committee sounded the alarm bell on behalf of the administration. The Committee published a report entitled: *Bestuur in Geding*, which translates roughly into 'Administration under Fire', a report on the need to reign in the growing legal complexity of the administration. The committee was gravely concerned about this tendency and the concomitant use by the citizen of his legal protection options. The report deals with many topical and important issues, such as:

- the degree of judicial review;
- the issue of unnecessarily complex regulation and deregulation;
- the quality of public administration which must have so much expertise and so many experts in order to perform its many and complex duties properly.

One can see that apart from the introduction of more juridical dispute-settlement powers and the possible introduction of a *Schutznorm* other less juridical means see the light such as the new cases approach by the courts.

It is not yet clear what the consequences will be of further digitalization of procedures, recently introduced in the Awb / certain areas such as asylum law.

The most essential thing in administrative law is: a fairly easy access to procedures at the administration and especially the courts. That is still the case (in most matters) in the Netherlands due to low court fees and the fact that no legal representation is required, legal aid is still available, and the informal and more and more pragmatic proceedings.

BIBLIOGRAPHY

Barkhuysen, T., Polak, J., Schueler, B., Widdershoven, R., *AB Klassiek*, 7th ed., Deventer: Wolters Kluwer, 2016.

Bröring, H.E., de Graaf, K.J., *et al.*, *Bestuursrecht 1 Systeem, Bevoegdheid, Bevoegdheids-uitoefening, Handhaving*, 5th ed., Den Haag: Boom Juridische uitgevers, 2016.

De Haan, P., Drupsteen, Th.G. & Fernhout, R., *Bestuursrecht in de sociale rechtsstaat*, 4th ed., Deventer: Kluwer, part I 1996, part II 1998 (see also: Schlössels, R.J.N., Zijlstra, S.F., *Bestuursrecht in de sociale rechtsstaat*, part I, Wolters Kluwer, 2016.

Heldeweg, M.A., Seerden, R.J.G.H., Environmental Law in the Netherlands, Wolters Kluwer, 2013.

Heringa, A.W., Verhey, L., Van der Velde, J., Van de Woude, W., *Staatsrecht*, 12th ed., Deventer: Wolters Kluwer, 2015.

Konijnenbelt, W. & Van Male, R.M., *Hoofdstukken van bestuursrecht*, 16th ed., Deventer: Wolters Kluwer, 2016.

Marseille, A.T., Tolsma, H.D., *et al.*, *Bestuursrecht 2 Rechtsbescherming tegen de overheid*, 6th ed., Den Haag: Boom Juridische uitgevers, 2016.

Michiels, F.C.M.A., *Hoofdzaken van het bestuursrecht*, 8th ed., Deventer: Wolters Kluwer, 2016.

Schlössels, R.J.N., Albers, C.L.G.F.H., Bots, A.A.M.M., Kole, M.S.D.P., *JB Select*, 3rd edition, Den Haag: Sdu Uitgevers, 2014.

Schlössels, R.J.N., Schutgens, R.J.B., Peters, J.A.F., Feteris, M.W.C., Snijders G., Keus, L.A.D. (ed.), *De burgerlijke rechter in het publiekrecht*, Deventer: Wolters Kluwer, 2015.

Seerden, R. & Van Rossum, M., 'Legal Aspects of Soil Pollution and Decontamination in the Netherlands', in: Seerden, R. & Deketelaere, K. (eds.), *Legal Aspects of Soil Pollution and Decontamination in the EU Member States and the United States*, Antwerpen: Intersentia, 2000, p. 289–337.

Seerden, R., Heldeweg, M. & Deketelaere, K. (eds.), *Public Environmental Law in the European Union and the United States. A Comparative Analysis*, Comparative Environmental Law and Policy Series, London-The Hague-Boston: Kluwer Law International, 2002.

Stroink, F.A.M., *Rechterlijke organisatie en rechtspraak in beweging*, Zwolle: W.E.J. Theenk Willink, 1993.

Stroink, F. & Van der Linden, E. (ed.), *Judicial Lawmaking and Administrative Law*, Antwerpen-Oxford: Intersentia, 2005.

Tak, A.Q.C., *Het Nederlands Bestuursprocesrecht, in theorie en praktijk*, 5th ed., Oisterwijk: Wolf Legal Pubishers, 2014.

Wenders, D.W.M., *Doorwerking van de beginselen van behoorlijke rechtspleging in de bestuurslijke voorprocedures*, Deventer: Kluwer, 2010.

WEBSITES

Legislation:

- <www.overheid.nl>
- <www.justitie.nl/awb>

Parliamentary documents:
- <www.parlement.nl/>
- <www.tweedekamer.nl/>
- <http://parlando.sdu.nl>

Case Law:
- <www.rechtspraak.nl>
- <www.raadvanstate.nl>

ANNEX: KEY PROVISIONS GENERAL ADMINISTRATIVE LAW ACT (*ALGEMENE WET BESTUURSRECHT*)

CHAPTER 1: INTRODUCTORY PROVISIONS

Title 1.1 Definitions and scope

Article 1:1 (administrative authority/*bestuursorgaan*)

1. 'Administrative authority' means:
   a. an organ of a legal entity which has been established under public law, or
   b. another person or body which is invested with any public authority.
2. The following authorities, persons and bodies are not deemed to be administrative authorities:
   a. the legislature;
   b. the First and Second Chambers and the Joint Session of the States General;
   c. independent authorities established by law and charged with the administration of justice as well as the Council for the judiciary and the Board of representatives
   d. the Council of State and its departments;
   e. the General Chamber of Audit;
   f. the National Ombudsman and Deputy Ombudsmen as mentioned in Article 9, para. 1 National Ombudsman Act and ombudsmen and ombudscommissions as mentioned in Article 9:17, part b;
   g. the chairmen, members, registrars and secretaries of the authorities referred to at (b) to (f), the Procurator General, the Deputy Procurator General and the Advocates General to the Supreme Court, and committees composed of members of the authorities referred to at (b) to (f);
   h. the commission of inspection concerning intelligence and safety services, mentioned in Article 64 Intelligence and Safety Services Act 2002.
3. An authority, person or body excluded under subsection 2 is nonetheless deemed to be an administrative authority in so far as it takes decisions or performs actions in relation to a public servant referred to in Article 1 Public Service Act, his surviving

relatives or his successors in title, with exclusion for a public servant appointed for live working at the Council of State and its departments and the General Chamber of Audit.

4. The consequences with respect to property rights of an action of an administrative organ touch the legal entity to which the organ belongs.

Article 1:2 (interested party/*belanghebbende*)

1. 'Interested party' means: a person whose interest is directly affected by a decision.
2. As regards administrative authorities, the interests entrusted to them are deemed to be their interests.
3. As regards legal entities, their interests are deemed to include the general and collective interests which they particularly represent in accordance with their objects and as evidenced by their actual activities.

Article 1:3 (decision/*besluit*)

1. 'Decision' means a written decision of an administrative authority constituting a public law act. (*besluit*).
2. 'Administrative decision in an individual case' means a decision which is not of a general nature, including rejection of an application for such a decision. *(beschikking).*
3. 'Application' means a request by an interested party to take a decision. (*aanvraag*).
4. 'Policy rule' means: a rule laid down in a decision, not being a generally binding regulation, about the weighing of interests, the determination of facts or the interpretation of statutory regulations, when exercising a power of an administrative authority.(*beleidsregel*).

Article 1:4 (administrative judge/*bestuursrechter*)

1. 'Administrative judge' means: an independent organ, instituted by Act, that deals with administrative judicial review (*bestuursrechtspraak*).
2. 'Higher appellate court' (*hoger beroepsrechter*) means: an administrative judge ruling in higher appeal.
3. A court belonging to the judiciary (*rechterlijke macht*) is considered to be an administrative judge if chapter 8 or the Act on administrative enforcement of trafic provisions (*Wet administratiefrechtelijke handhaving van verkeersvoorschriften),* except chapter VIII, is applicable.

(...)

CHAPTER 3: GENERAL PROVISIONS CONCERNING DECISIONS (*BESLUITEN*)

Division 3.1 Introductory provisions

Article 3:1

1. Decisions being generally binding regulations:
   a. shall only be subject to the provisions of division 3.2 in so far as their nature does not impose to that;
   b. shall not be subject to the provisions of division 3.6 and 3.7.
2. Divisions 3.2 to 3.4 shall apply *mutatis mutandis* to other actions of administrative authorities than decisions in so far as their nature does not impose to that.

Division 3.2 The duty of care and the weighing of interests

Article 3:2

When preparing a decision an administrative authority shall gather the necessary knowledge concerning the relevant facts and the interests to be weighed.

Article 3:3

An administrative authority shall not use the power to make a decision for a purpose other than that for which it was conferred.

Article 3:4

1. When making a decision the administrative authority shall weight the interests directly involved in so far as no limitation on this duty derives from a statutory regulation or the nature of the power being exercised.
2. The adverse consequences of a decision for one or more interested parties may not be disproportionate to the purposes to be served by the decision.

(…)

Division 3.4 Uniform public preparation procedure

Article 3:10

1. This division is applicable for the preparation of decisions when this is stated in a legal provision or is decided for by an administrative authority.

(…)

Division 3.7 Reasons (motivering)

Article 3:46

A decision shall be based on proper reasons.

Article 3:47

1. The reasons shall be stated when the decision is notified.
2. If possible, the statutory regulation on which the decision is based shall be stated at the same time.
3. If, in the interests of speed, the reasons cannot be stated immediately when the decision is notified, the administrative authority shall give communication of them as soon as possible thereafter.
4. In such a case, Articles 3:41 to 3:43 inclusive shall apply *mutatis mutandis*.

Article 3:48

1. The reasons need not be stated if it can reasonably be assumed that there is no need for this.
2. If, however, an interested party asks within a reasonable period to be informed of the reasons, they shall be communicated as quickly as possible.

Article 3:49

For stating the reasons of a decision or part of a decision, it is sufficient to refer to an opinion (advise)(*advies*) drawn up in this connection if the opinion itself contains the reasons and communication of the opinion has been or is given.

Article 3:50

If the administrative authority makes a decision which derogates from an opinion drawn up for this purpose pursuant to a statutory regulation, this fact and the reasons for it shall be stated in the reasons of the decision.

(…)

CHAPTER 4: SPECIAL PROVISIONS CONCERNING DECISIONS

Division 4.1 Decisions (beschikkingen)

(…)

CHAPTER 6: GENERAL PROVISIONS ON OBJECTIONS (*BEZWAAR*) AND APPEAL (*BEROEP*)

Division 6.2 Other General Provisions

Article 6:4

An objection shall be lodged by a notice of objection at the administrative authority that has taken the decision.

(…)

Article 6:13

No appeal to the administrative judge is possible for an interested party that reasonably can be blamed not to have brought forward views in the meaning of article 3:15, or did not make an objection or an administrative appeal.

Article 6:22

A decision against which an objection or appeal is made, can, despite the violation of a written or unwritten rule or general principle, be upheld by the organ that decides on the objection or appeal when it is likely that the interested persons are not aggrieved.

CHAPTER 7: SPECIAL PROVISIONS CONCERNING OBJECTIONS (*BEZWAAR*) AND ADMINISTRATIVE APPEALS (*ADMINISTRATIEF BEROEP*)

Division 7.1 Notice of objection preceding appeal to an administrative court

Article 7:1

1. The one who has the right to appeal against a decision to the administrative judge shall lodge an objection against the decision before lodging an appeal, unless the decision:
   a. has been made in respect of an objection or an administrative appeal;
   b. is subject to approval;
   c. is one approving another decision or refusing such approval; or
   d. is prepared in accordance with division 3.4,
   e. the decision is taken based on a judgement of the administrative judge in which is stated that division 3.4 is (partly) not used,
   e. the appeal is against a not timely taken decision,
   g. the decision is taken based on a provision in this Act that deals with direct appeal. (*Regeling rechtstreeks beroep*).
2. An appeal can be lodged against the decision on the objection in accordance with the provisions that govern the lodging of an appeal against the decision against which the objection was made.

Article 7:1a

1. In the notice of objection a request can be made at the administrative authority to agree with a direct appeal to the administrative judge (in contradiction with article 7:1) …
2. …

(…)

CHAPTER 8: SPECIAL PROVISIONS CONCERNING APPEALS TO THE ADMINISTRATIVE JUDGE (*BEROEP BIJ DE BESTUURSRECHTER*)

Title 8.1 General provisions about appeal in first instance

Division 8.1.1 Jurisdiction

Article 8:1

1. An interested party can appeal to the administrative judge against a decision.

Article 8:2

1. With a decision shall be equated:

(...)

Article 8:3

1. No appeal can be lodged against:
   a. a decision containing a generally binding regulation or a policy rule,
   b. a decision repealing or laying down the entry into force of a generally binding regulation or policy rule,
   c. a decision approving a decision, containing a generally binding regulation or a policy rule or repealing or laying down the entry into force of a generally binding regulation or a policy rule.

(...)

Article 8:6

1. The appeal can be lodged at the District Court (*rechtbank*) unless another administrative judge is competent on the basis of the rules of chapter 2 of this Act (*Bevoegdheidsregeling bestuursrechtspraak*).

(...)

Title 8.2 Court proceedings (behandeling van het beroep in eerste aanleg)

Division 8.2.1a General Provison

Article 8:41a

The administrative judge as much as possible settles the dispute definitively.

Division 8.2.2a Administrative loop

Article 8:51a

The administrative judge can give the administrative authority the opportunity to restore a shortcoming in the contested decision unless interested persons who are not participating as interested parties in the appeal can be aggrieved unproportionally.

(...)

Division 8.2.6 Judgement

Article 8:69

1. The administrative judge shall give judgement on the basis of the notice of appeal, the documents submitted, the proceedings during the preliminary inquiry and the hearing.
2. The administrative judge shall supplement the legal basis on its own initiative.
3. The administrative judge can supplement the facts on its own initiative.

Article 8:69a

The administrative judge does not quash a decision on the ground that it is contrary to a written or unwritten rule or a general principle, in case this rule or principle is not intended to protect the interests of the person who invokes it.

Article 8:70

The judgement states that:

a. the administrative judge is not competent (*bevoegd*),
b. the appeal is inadmissible (*niet-ontvankelijk*),
c. the appeal is unfounded (*ongegrond*), or
d. the appeal is well founded (*gegrond*).

Article 8:72

1. If the administrative judge states that the appeal is well founded, he shall annul all or part of the disputed decision.
2. If a decision or part of a decision is annulled, this implies that the legal consequences of the (part of the) decision are void.
3. The administrative judge can determine that:
   a. the legal consequences of the annulled decision or the annulled part of the decision shall be allowed to stand, or
   b. his judgement replaces the decision or the annulled part of the decision.
4. The administrative judge can, when application of paragraph 3 is not possible, order the administrative authority to take a new decision or another action, in accordance with his judgement: He can:
   a. determine that legal provisions about the preparation of the new decision or other action are not applicable;

b. set the administrative authority a time limit for issuing a new decision or performing another action,
5. The administrative judge can, if necessary, take a provisional ruling. In that case he determines the time when the provisional ruling ceases.
6. The administrative judge can determine that, as long as the administrative authority does not comply with a judgement, it has to pay a penalty, to be fixed in the judgement, to a party designated by him. (...).

Article 8:72a

When the administrative judge quashes a decision holding an administrative fine he decides about the administrative fine himself and orders that his judgement replaces the annulled decision.

Article 8:75

1. The administrative judge has the exclusive jurisdiction to order a party to pay the costs which another party has reasonably incurred in connection with the appeal and the objection procedure (...). A natural person can be ordered to pay costs only in case of a manifestly unreasonable use of the right of appeal. In a Crown Decree further rules are set concerning the costs to which an order as referred in the first sentence may exclusively relate and how the amount of the costs is to be fixed in the judgement.

ADMINISTRATIVE LAW IN THE UNITED KINGDOM

Katharine THOMPSON

1. INTRODUCTION

1.1. WHAT IS ADMINISTRATIVE LAW?

The use of the term 'administrative law' in England remains relatively new. More than a century ago the eminent constitutional lawyer Professor A.V. Dicey suggested that there was no such subject within English Law.[1] By this Dicey meant to draw a distinction between the arrangements for subjecting government to judicial control as he believed them to exist in continental civil law countries, as compared with England. The fact that England did not possess an institutionally and doctrinally separate system of *droit administratif* on the continental pattern was regarded by Dicey as a considerable virtue. For Dicey the ideal of the 'rule of law' meant that government in all its various manifestations should be answerable for its actions before the *ordinary* courts, presided over by the *ordinary* independent judges, and applying the *ordinary* laws of the land.

Dicey's views appear to have hindered the development in the United Kingdom of a refined body of administrative law. For many years the term was viewed with some suspicion, suggesting a body of rules and procedures set to undermine the ordinary common law rights of the citizen. It was commonly viewed as a body of rules likely to confer powers of decision on contentious matters between citizen and the state on Ministers, and on specially created tribunals, rather than on the ordinary judges.

However, over the past fifty years 'administrative law' has come to be viewed in a more positive light: as the study of rules and procedures that on the one hand serve to promote good administrative practice in governmental agencies, and on the other hand provide mechanisms of redress, judicial or otherwise, when grievances have arisen as a result of decisions or actions of government.

---

1 'The words 'administrative law', which are its (*droit administratifs*) most natural rendering, are unknown to English judges and courts, and are in themselves hardly intelligible without further explanation', Dicey, A.V., *An Introduction to the Study of the Law of the Constitution*, 10th ed., London: Macmillan, 1987.

In very general terms administrative law covers specialist subject areas as diverse as planning law, immigration law and revenue law. However, the administrative lawyer cannot hope to have a detailed knowledge of all these areas of law. Rather, his or her concern is with the *administrative process*, at the levels of central, local and at European Union level; and with the means by which *grievances in respect of governmental actions may be examined and, where appropriate redressed*. In particular, the procedure for what is technically known as 'judicial review' must be understood.

To place administrative law in England in its correct context, we must first understand how the United Kingdom operates at a constitutional level.

1.2. THE CONSTITUTIONAL CONTEXT

1.2.1. Terminology

The 'United Kingdom' consists of Great Britain and Northern Ireland; and 'Great Britain' is made up of England, Scotland and Wales. Within the United Kingdom there are three distinct legal systems and it is wrong therefore to refer to *British* law. However, it is common practice to think in terms of *British* constitutional law, although more properly we mean the constitution of the United Kingdom of Great Britain and Northern Ireland.

The Parliament of the United Kingdom, consisting of the House of Commons[2], the House of Lords[3] and the Queen, is based in London (Westminster) and save where legislative power has been devolved to Scotland, Northern Ireland and Wales has power to legislate for the whole of, or any part of, the United Kingdom. There is no separate legislative body for England alone, but Scotland, Wales and Northern Ireland do all now have some element of devolved legislative and administrative power.

England and Wales were effectively integrated in 1536 and since then the two countries have shared a common legal system, usually referred to as the English legal system. Under the government of Wales Act 1998 the National Assembly of Wales was established, with certain administrative (but not primary law making) powers devolved to it. However, since Part 4 of the Government of Wales Act 2006 was brought into force[4] the Assembly does now have some primary law making powers.

---

2 The House of Commons consists of 650 elected representatives, known as Members of Parliament (MPs). There is provision under the Parliamentary Voting System and Constituencies Act 2011, s 11 to reduce the number to 600.

3 The House of Lords is a non-elected body. It is made up hereditary peers, life peers and Bishops of the Church of England. It is undergoing reform but there are no proposals to make it a fully elected chamber. However, there are proposals, albeit controversial, to make it substantially elected.

4 Following a referendum held on 3 March 2011.

The legal system in Scotland has throughout its history differed from that in England, and this despite the unification of the two nations by the Act of Union 1707. Since the Scotland Act 1998, when Scotland was granted a large measure of devolved legislative and administrative power the two countries' laws have diverged even further. In Scotland, therefore, administrative law in general, and the rules on judicial review in particular are in some significant respects different to that in England and will not be considered in this chapter.[5]

Northern Ireland emerged as a result of the partition of Ireland in the 1920s. Under the Government of Ireland Act 1920 a parliamentary system of government was established for Northern Ireland, and this continued until the early 1970s. Since then Northern Ireland has been predominately governed by direct rule from London, albeit with various attempts having been made over those years to set up some form of devolved locally elected legislature. The most recent attempts at devolved power, under the Northern Ireland (Elections) Act 1998 has had a chequered history, with the Northern Ireland Assembly and Executive being suspended on a number of occasions. Following elections held on 8 May 2007 the Northern Ireland Assembly and Executive were restored. However, although Northern Ireland is ultimately ruled from 'Whitehall' and the Westminster Parliament it does have a distinct legal system, with its own courts and legal profession. In terms of administrative law, judicial review in Northern Ireland has followed the English and Welsh model and although English case law is not binding, it is normally followed.[6]

1.2.2. Supremacy of Parliament

The fundamental features of the United Kingdom's constitutional law need now to be considered, since these have a significant bearing on the scheme of administrative law which has developed. At the heart of our constitutional law is the doctrine of 'legislative supremacy', or as it is sometimes described the 'sovereignty of parliament'.

Dicey described this fundamental constitutional doctrine as follows:

> 'The principle of Parliamentary sovereignty means neither more nor less than this, namely that Parliament … has … the right to make or unmake any law whatever; and, further, that no person or body is recognised by the law … as having a right to override or set aside the legislation of Parliament'.[7]

This means that, at least in theory, the United Kingdom's Parliament can by ordinary legislation do the sort of things which elsewhere might require a special

---

5 For Scotland, see further Supperstone, M., Goudie, J. & Walker, P., *Judicial Review*, 5th ed., London: LexisNexis, 2014, ch. 21.

6 See Anthony, G., *Judicial Review in Northern Ireland*, 2nd ed., Oxford: Hart Publishing, 2014.

7 Dicey, *supra* note 1, p. 39–40.

procedure, or even amendment to the Constitution. Parliament has for example altered the duration of its own life[8], legislated retrospectively[9], conferred judicial and legislative powers on organs of the executive[10], and excluded rights of access to the courts to challenge allegedly unlawful governmental action.[11] Almost by definition the only thing which parliament cannot do is to bind its successors, for if it could do so it would no longer be supreme as an ongoing institution.

However, it may be the case that a new constitutional hypothesis is emerging, whereby it is conceivable that the courts might review and set aside legislation in certain extreme circumstances.[12] This far-reaching possibility has emerged as a result of the House of Lords decision in 2006 in *Jackson* v *Attorney-General.*[13] The case concerned a challenge to the validity of the Hunting Act 2004. The passage of the Act caused much controversy and it was eventually passed using the procedures set out in the Parliament Acts 1911 and 1949, which under certain conditions permit an Act to be passed into law without the acceptance of the House of Lords.[14] For our purposes the importance of the case lies in the obiter statements made by their Lordships as to whether they have any general power to review the validity of an Act of Parliament. Take, for example the following statements:

Lord Steyn:

> 'The classic account given by Dicey of the doctrine of the supremacy of Parliament, pure and absolute as it was, can now be seen to be out of place in the modern United Kingdom. Nevertheless, the supremacy of Parliament is still the *general* principle of our constitution. It is a construct of the common law. The judges created this principle. If that is so, it is not unthinkable that circumstances could arise where the courts may have to qualify a principle established on a different hypothesis of constitutionalism. In exceptional circumstances involving an attempt to abolish judicial review or the ordinary role of the courts, the Appellate Committee of the House of Lords or a new Supreme Court may have to consider whether this is a constitutional fundamental which even a sovereign Parliament acting at the behest of a complaisant House of Lords cannot abolish'.[15]

---

8 Parliament Act 1911.

9 See for example the War Damages Act 1965.

10 See the extensive powers to make delegated legislation, which have been granted.

11 See for example the Interception of Communications Act 1985, s 7(8).

12 Jowell, J., 'Parliamentary Sovereignty under the New Constitutional Hypothesis', *Public Law*, 2006, p. 562 and Gordon, M., 'The Conceptional Foundations of Parliamentary Sovereignty: Reconsidering Jennings and Wade', *Public Law*, 2009, p. 519.

13 [2006] 1 AC 262.

14 Before the Constitutional Reform Act 2005 the House of Lords was both a court of law and a legislative chamber. The Parliament Acts relate to the House of Lords as a legislative chamber.

15 [2006] 1 AC 262 at para. 102.

Lord Hope:

> 'Our constitution is dominated by the sovereignty of Parliament. But Parliamentary sovereignty is no longer, if it ever was, absolute ... It is no longer right to say that its freedom to legislate admits of no qualification whatever. Step by step, gradually but surely, the English principle of the absolute legislative sovereignty of Parliament which Dicey derived from Coke and Blackstone is being qualified'.[16]

Baroness Hale:

> 'The courts will treat with particular suspicion (and might even reject) any attempt to subvert the rule of law by removing governmental action affecting the rights of the individual from all judicial powers'.[17]

It is important to remember that despite these statements the traditional notion of supremacy remains reasonably intact. However, there does now seem a real possibility that at some point in the future the bold decision will be taken to assert that '[t]he rule of law enforced by the courts is the ultimate controlling factor on which our constitution is based'.[18]

1.2.3. Human Rights Act 1998

One of the earliest legislative acts of the Labour Government elected in 1997 was to enact the Human Rights Act 1998. The constitutional status of this piece of legislation should be explained. Although it does attempt to incorporate the rights set out in the European Convention on Human Rights and Fundamental Freedoms into United Kingdom domestic law its constitutional status is that it is just an ordinary Act of Parliament. It is not in any way a fundamental law. It is not constitutionally entrenched. The government did consider, when drawing up the legislation, whether there should be some change to the doctrine of supremacy but it rejected the idea.[19] Nonetheless, and notwithstanding that it is only a piece of ordinary legislation, it has had a significant impact.

Under section 3[20] of the Act all legislation, whenever passed, must be interpreted, if at all possible, in a way which is compatible with Convention

16 *Ibid.* at para. 104.
17 *Ibid.* at para. 159.
18 *Ibid.*, Lord Hope at para. 107.
19 *Rights Brought Home: The Human Rights Bill*, Cm 3782, 1997, para. 2.16. This was a command paper (Cm), the name given to papers presented to Parliament by Ministers, technically at the command of Her Majesty. Command papers began in 1833 and have been published in six separately numbered series. To distinguish the six series, a different form of the abbreviation for the word 'Command' has been used i.e. Cmd, Cmnd and Cm. For a discussion of the impact of the 1998 Act on the constitution see Feldman, D., 'The Human Rights Act 1998 and constitutional principles', *Legal Studies*, 1999, vol. 19, p. 165.
20 Acts of Parliament are divided into sections and subsections.

rights.[21] This is the primary remedy under the Act to deal with incompatibility. As a last resort section 4 of the Act gives power to judges to declare that an Act of Parliament is incompatible with Convention Rights. However, importantly, they do not have any power to declare an Act *invalid*. Making such a declaration amounts to a statement that parliament has acted wrongly, and gives to Ministers the power under the 1998 Act, but not any duty, to change the law with some immediacy by means of a delegated legislative instrument.[22]

One of the most significant impacts of the Human Rights Act has been the need for courts to apply the test of proportionality in almost every case when a claim for judicial review is based on an infringement or restriction of a Convention Right.[23]

1.2.4. Supremacy and the EU

The Human Rights Act 1998 was drafted to sit neatly alongside the notion of legislative supremacy. However, we should note that that very doctrine of supremacy had undergone some revision in the previous decade or so. Following the European Communities Act 1972, and by ratification of the accession treaty, the United Kingdom became a member of what is now the European Union. As is well known, the European Court of Justice has long considered that where there may be found a conflict between European law and domestic law, European law should prevail.[24] In short there have become now two law-making bodies for the United Kingdom, the UK Parliament and the European Union's own legislative mechanisms. Inevitably there would in due course come

---

21 The powers under s. 3 to interpret legislation were used most radically in *R* v *A* [2002] 1 AC 45 concerning s 41 of the Youth Justice and Criminal Evidence Act 1999. Section 41 excluded evidence relating to prior sexual behaviour of the complainant (subject to narrow exceptions), during the trial of a sexual offence. This was held to be incompatible with Art. 6 but their Lordships concluded that s 41 could be construed in a compatible way by 'reading in' an implied provision that evidence required to ensure a fair trial should not be excluded. See Kavanagh, A., 'Unlocking the Human Rights Act: The "Radical" Approach to section 3(1) Revisited', *European Human Rights Law Review*, 2005, p. 259.

22 Up to the end of July 2016 there have been 22 final declarations of incompatibility. All of the declarations have been remedied (or are still under consideration with a view to being remedied), usually by primary legislation, see *Responding to Human Rights judgements: Report to the Joint Committee on Human Rights on the Government's response to Human Rights judgements 2014–16*, Ministry of Justice, 2016 at p 45. See, for example, *A and others* v *Secretary of State for the Home Department* [2004] UKHL 56 where provisions of the Anti-terrorism and Security Act 2001 were declared incompatible with Arts. 5 and 14 and as a result repealed and replaced by the Prevention of Terrorism Act 2005; and *R (on the application of F and Thompson)* v *Secretary of State for the Home Department* [2010] UKSC where section 82 of the Sexual Offences Act 2003 was declared incompatible with Art. 8. This incompatibility was remedied by the Sexual Offences Act 2003 (Remedial) Order 2012.

23 The status of proportionality as a ground for judicial review and the impact of the Human Rights Act in UK law is considered in detail at paragraph 5.8.2 below.

24 See for example Case 6/64 *Costa* v *ENEL*, ECR, 1964, 585.

before the courts a conflict of legal provisions, notwithstanding the best efforts of the courts, over a number of years, to deny conflicts (and so any clash of supremacies) through their broad powers of interpretation. Eventually, however, in *R* v *Secretary of State for Transport, ex parte Factortame Ltd*[25] the question had to be squarely faced: which was to prevail where there was direct conflict between domestic law and European law. Following a preliminary ruling from the European Court of Justice[26], the House of Lords accepted that provisions of a United Kingdom Act of Parliament should – notwithstanding the doctrine of sovereignty of parliament – be 'disapplied' where there is a conflict not resolvable by judicial interpretation.[27]

The UK's decision to leave the EU has been formally signified by the passage of the European Union (Notification of Withdrawal) Act 2017 and the notification under Article 50(2) of the Treaty on the European Union. There is to be a 'Great Repeal Bill' which will repeal the European Communities Act on the day that the UK exits the EU. Once this happens the Government has stated that the 'UK Parliament will unquestionably be sovereign again. Our courts will be the ultimate arbiters of our law.'[28]

1.2.5. Separation of Powers

The United Kingdom's constitution does not display much noticeable regard to the rigid separation of powers. There are, of course, recognizable legislative, executive and judicial bodies but there are many overlaps in terms of both personnel and functions between the bodies.[29]

---

25 [1990] 2 AC (Law Reports Appeal Cases) 85. A note on case names: This form of case name was the usual form for cases in the Divisional Court of the Queen's Bench by way of judicial review. The 'R' stands for Regina: i.e. the Crown or Queen. The name given '*ex parte*' is that of the applicant. The 'R' appears in the name because the Crown is the nominal claimant, although in practice it is a private body or person who brings the claim. In December 2000 there was a modernization of case names. If this case were heard now it would be called *R (on the application of Factortame Ltd)* v *Secretary of State for Transport*. If there is an appeal the name of the case can change and any reference to 'R' is dropped. The name then becomes *Factortame Ltd* v *Secretary of State for Transport*. In criminal cases the State, in the name of the Queen brings the actions and the name would appear as '*R* v *name of the defendant*'.

26 Case C-213/89, ECR, 1990, 1–2433.

27 [1991] 1 AC 603. For a discussion of the constitutional impact of EU membership on the doctrine of supremacy see Munro, C., *Studies in Constitutional Law*, 2nd ed., London: Butterworths, 1999, Chapter 6 and Elliott, M., 'The Principle of Parliamentary Sovereignty in Legal, Constitutional, and Political Perspective', in: Jowell, J., & Oliver, D. & O'Cinneide, C., (eds.), *The Changing Constitution*, 8th ed., Oxford: Oxford University Press, 2015.

28 Legislating for the United Kingdom's withdrawal from the European Union, Cm 9446, 2017, p. 7.

29 Until quite recently the office of the Lord Chancellor showed these overlaps well. The Lord Chancellor was the head of the English judiciary, and occasionally sat as a judge in the House of Lords. He also presided, over the House of Lords as a deliberative and legislative chamber. In addition, he was a prominent member of the executive, as a Cabinet Minister. The Lord Chancellor's role was radically reformed under the Constitutional Reform Act 2005

1.2.6. *The 'Rule of Law'*

The 'rule of law' has many different meanings. According, however, to Dicey the 'rule of law' included three distinct concepts: the absence of arbitrary power; equality before the law; and that the protection of the liberty of subjects was the result of ordinary statutes and judicial decisions, rather than the subject of *a priori* constitutional guarantees of rights.[30]

In a quite broad way these principles of the rule of law do describe the fundamentals of the British Constitution. However, as we have already noted, the supremacy of parliament, as it currently applies, means that our parliament is subject to no limits, and in this sense the *constitution* is not subject to the rule of law, in the way that systems which recognize a judicial power to hold legislation unconstitutional may so be regarded.

Nevertheless, the Human Rights Act 1998 has reinvigorated the significance of the rule of law to the constitution as the courts have shown an increased willingness to give weight to the doctrine. This was highlighted in *A* v *Secretary of State for the Home Department*[31], a case involving the Anti-Terrorism, Crime and Security Act 2001 and its powers to detain without trial. Here the majority of their Lordships were willing to question the government's view of what was necessary in the interests of national security. It has been noted that this is all the more remarkable because prior to this decision whenever 'the government played the national security card … it almost always resulted in something approaching judicial surrender.'[32] As Lord Nicholls observed, 'indefinite detention without charge or trial is anathema in any country which observes the rule of law'.[33]

In the context of administrative law we may also suggest that the concept of the rule of law should go beyond Dicey's rather formal definition, and require that legislation conferring powers on the executive should be intelligible, define powers with maximum precision, and be available to public scrutiny; that there should be judicial and other mechanisms for ensuring that the executive acts within those powers, and does not exceed or abuse them; that such judicial mechanisms should be impartial and independent of government; that access to the courts should be reasonably affordable and as simple as practically possible; and that any special governmental privileges and immunities should be restricted to such as are genuinely necessary in the public interest.

---

to formally recognize the importance in this particular context of securing a separation of powers. The significant overlap between the legislature and the judiciary in the form of the House of Lords (both a court and a legislative chamber) was also removed under the 2005 Act with the formation of a separate Supreme Court, removing the right of the most senior judges to sit and vote in the House of Lords, sitting as a branch of Parliament.

30 Dicey, *supra* note 1, see Chapter 10.

31 [2005] 2 W.L.R 87.

32 Elliott, M. & Varuhas, J.N.E., *Administrative Law: Text and Materials*, 5th ed., Oxford: Oxford University Press, 2017, p. 293.

33 [2005] 2 W.L.R. 87, para. 74.

1.2.7. Royal Prerogative

The final aspect of the constitution which should be noted is the 'royal prerogative', as its position in administrative law remains of some importance. The royal prerogative is the collective name given to the unique legal powers, duties and privileges possessed at common law by the Crown. These powers include the granting of royal assent to legislation, the appointment and dismissal of ministers, the ratification of treaties and the granting of passports. It should be noted that these prerogative powers, by constitutional convention[34], are exercised now not by the Monarch according to personal whim, but rather 'on the advice of her Ministers'. In reality, therefore, these powers are controlled and exercised by the elected government.

Traditionally the courts took the view that it was not within their powers to question the way in which an admitted prerogative power was exercised.[35] However, given that in reality it is Ministers who usually exercise prerogative powers, this resulted in a not insubstantial area of governmental discretionary power which was not subject to judicial review. In1984, in *Council of Civil Service Unions* v *Minister for Civil Service*[36], the House of Lords finally asserted a willingness to review the exercise of many (although not all) prerogative powers.

2. THE DISTRIBUTION OF ADMINISTRATIVE POWERS

2.1. INSTITUTIONS OF GOVERNMENT

In the United Kingdom there is a wide variety of what may be regarded as 'governmental' institutions. Indeed in this 'post-privatization' era the borderline between institutions of government and private law institutions is, as will be seen below, by no means clear.

At the heart of the United Kingdom's Government are the Prime Minister, the Cabinet and the Central Government Departments of State. The Queen appoints the Prime Minister and by convention she will choose the leader of the majority party in the House of Commons. In recent decades the role of the Prime Minister within the governmental apparatus appears to have become more powerful, and the role of the cabinet and its individual ministers has in consequence diminished. The Cabinet, consisting of the most senior ministers, certainly used to be the body which determined (or at least contributed to the

34 Constitutional conventions are non-legally-binding rules of political importance which are understood to reflect constitutionally correct behaviour.

35 See for example *Hanratty* v *Lord Butler*, (115) *Solicitor's Journal*, 1971, p. 386.

36 [1985] AC 374. The case is most commonly referred to as the *GCHQ* case.

determination of) the general policy decisions of the government. However, in recent times the full Cabinet meets less often and for less long than formerly, and Cabinet Committees and Sub-committees have proliferated and become more influential in formulating government strategies and decisions. The consequence has been to render ministers more directly accountable than formerly to the Prime Minister.[37]

Within each government department there will be a ministerial 'head', usually called the 'Secretary of State', assisted by 'junior' ministers. Civil servants, headed by a Permanent Secretary, will staff the department. The precise number of, and the division of functions between, Departments may change from time to time very much in keeping with the latest views on whether departments should be large or small, and which areas of governmental responsibility should be grouped together. In modern times, for example, 'education' and 'employment' have been separate departments, merged together and then again divided. In 2016 a new government department was created, the Department of Business, Energy and Industrial Strategy. This was created as a result of a merger between the Department of Energy and Climate Change and the Department of Business, Innovation and Skills. Following the UK's vote to leave the EU, 2016 also saw the creation of the Department for Exiting the European Union, which is charged with overseeing negotiations to leave the EU and establishing the future relationship between the UK and the EU.

In many instances legislation gives to 'the Minister' or the 'Secretary of State' power to act or to make decisions. However, in reality many of these decisions must be, and are, made by civil servants because ministers simply do not have the time to take each and every one of these decisions personally. The 'reality' of this is, moreover, recognized in law. In *Carltona* v *Commissioners of Works*[38] Lord Greene MR[39] noted that the powers granted to ministers are usually exercised by officials but that 'the decision of such an official is [in law] … the decision of the minister, the minister is responsible. It is he who must answer before parliament for anything his officials have done under his authority …'.

Thus, for example, a decision relating to deportation may validly be taken by a civil servant in the Home Office, acting on behalf of the Home Secretary and without any reference to the minister personally.[40] Although ultimate responsibility and accountability to parliament lies with the minister under the convention of 'ministerial responsibility', it is a debatable matter whether in reality parliament is effective in calling ministers to task for the actions of their departments. Certainly there are a few examples of ministers who have resigned

---

37 See Hennessy, P., *Whitehall*, London: Fontana Press, 1990 and Hennessy, P., *The Prime Minister: The Office and its Holders since 1945*, London: Allen Lane, 2000.

38 [1943] 2 All ER (*All England Law Reports*) 563.

39 MR stands for Master of the Rolls, who is the leading judge dealing with the civil work of the Court of Appeal.

40 *Oladehinde* v *Secretary of State for the Home Department* [1990] 3 All ER 383.

because of failings in their departments[41] but the list of ministers who have not resigned – pleading that they had no personal involvement in the matters under criticism – is very much longer.

The shape of the civil service has changed dramatically since the late 1980s.[42] In 1988 a report, *Improving Management in Government: The Next Steps*[43], had a radical effect on the organization of Central Government. The report drew a firm distinction between issues of (i) policy formulation and (ii) matters of mere administration or service delivery. It could see no role for ministers in the day-to-day administration of government. Therefore, where civil servants far removed from the policy-forming centre of government did no more than carry out functions of government, those functions could be removed from the department and given to an executive agency, headed by a non-civil servant chief executive. As a result around 100 agencies have been established, with responsibilities for areas as diverse as passports, social security, tax, highways, customs and excise and the prison service.

These new agencies give rise to problems of 'accountability'. There is concern that ministers can now all too easily disassociate themselves from errors which previously would have been made within their departments. A much-cited example of this occurring concerned the Prison Service and the role of the Home Secretary. In 1994 and 1995 there were a number of well-publicized lapses of prison security, including the escape of some prisoners, but despite parliamentary criticism the Home Secretary refused to accept any blame. The Prison Service had become an executive agency in March 1994 and its Director General made day-to-day operational decisions. Under a framework document, which set out areas of responsibility, it was stated that the Home Secretary was accountable broadly to parliament for the prison service but that he had no involvement in day-to-day management, although he was to be consulted on operational matters which gave rise to grave public or parliamentary concern. Although there was some evidence to suggest that the Home Secretary had at least attempted to interfere in operational matters during this troubled time for prisons, he never accepted any responsibility for what went wrong and in the end it was the Director General of the Prison Service who was sacked (by the Home Secretary!). What the whole incident showed was the very artificiality of the policy/operational distinction, particularly in an area of high political sensitivity.[44] Loveland has argued that not only has the *Next Steps* initiative

---

41 See for example the resignation of the Foreign Office Ministers in 1982 following the Argentine invasion of the Falkland Islands.

42 See Wade, H.W.R. & Forsyth, C.F., *Administrative Law*, 11th ed., Oxford: Oxford University Press, 2014, pp. 40–48.

43 Her Majesty's Stationery Office (HMSO).

44 Drewry, G., 'The Executive: Towards Accountable Government and Effective Governance?', in: Jowell, J, & Oliver, D. (eds.), *The Changing Constitution*, 7th ed., Oxford: Oxford University Press, 2011, p 204.

weakened an already weak system of ministerial accountability but also that as political accountability has declined there has been no reciprocal increase in legal or other regulation. Accordingly there has become, in aggregate, less political or other accountability for the actions of civil servants.

On the fringes of 'government' are bodies sometimes called Quangos (quasi-autonomous-non-governmental-organizations) or NDPBs (non-departmental public bodies).[45] These are non-elected bodies whose members are usually appointed by Ministers and their number has grown quite substantially in the last twenty years. Much of the growth of these organizations can be associated with the policy in recent years of privatization and deregulation. Out of the privatization of the public utilities have sprung bodies like OFWAT (Office of Water Services) and OFCOM (Independent regulator and competition authority for the UK communication Industry), whose roles are to act as 'watchdogs' over the provision of the privatized services. National Health Service (NHS) Foundation Trusts and NHS trusts providing ambulances services, emergency care services, or mental health services, have emerged following reforms of the National Health Service. These are then overseen by NHS Improvement. Such has been the growth of these bodies that the Public Bodies Act 2011 was passed with the intention of allowing government ministers to abolish or merge many such bodies, with a view to saving cost.

Again, there are concerns about the accountability of these bodies, for, as with Executive Agencies the traditional model of ministerial responsibility does not fit. Some element of accountability can be exercised through the parliamentary Select Committee system, judicial review and the ombudsman system (on which see later). The Labour Government, from 1997, tried to enhance the accountability of these bodies by increasing public participation in the work of the bodies, and by trying to encourage a more open approach to the dissemination of information about the work of the bodies.[46]

Finally, the role of directly elected *local authorities* must be noted. These carry out a wide range of governmental functions. Local authorities are bodies created by Acts of Parliament, and as such their powers and duties can be scrutinized by the courts, through the mechanism of judicial review.[47] The structure of local government is rather complex and has undergone significant reform in recent times. In England as a whole there are; county councils, metropolitan districts, district councils, unitary authorities – and in London there is a Greater

---

45 It should be noted that there is no agreement on what terminology should be used and when. The Government's consultation paper, *Opening up Quangos, A Consultation Paper*, Cabinet Office, 1997 excluded many bodies like NHS Trusts and regulatory agencies, although many would include these under the heading Quangos.

46 See *Quangos: Opening the Doors*, Cabinet Office, 1998.

47 The Local Government Acts 1972 and 1974 and the Local Government Finance Act 1988, as amended, form the main basis of local authority law, although there are many other relevant pieces of legislation.

London Authority, along with London boroughs. Scotland and Wales only have unitary districts. In some parts of England there is a two-tier structure of local government (each area within served by two councils) and in others a unitary system (a single council performing all functions).

Local authorities in modern times have rather less functions and power than in earlier decades. The Conservative governments of the 1980s believed that many of the functions of local authorities should be opened up to market competition (and that much discretionary decision-making should lie with central Ministries rather than with locally elected councillors). As a result many local authority services were put out to competitive tender, tenants were given the right to buy their council houses and local authority control over education was reduced. However, local authorities are still responsible for such matters as public sector housing, schools, public health and sanitation, welfare services, and town and country planning. The Cities and Local Government Devolution Act 2016 does give the Secretary of State for Communities and Local Government the power to devolve powers from central government to combined local authorities, which would be led by a directly elected mayor. The first of these mayors, heading combined authorities, were elected in May 2017.

Figure 1. United Kingdom's State Structure

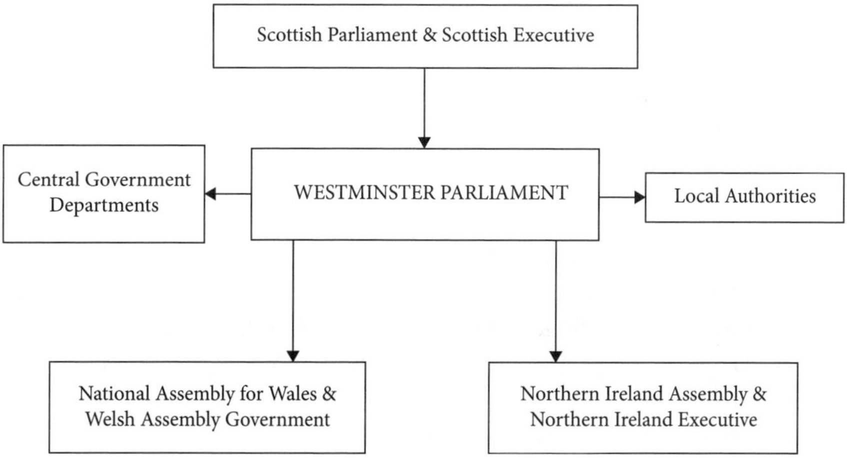

3. HOW ARE ADMINISTRATIVE DECISIONS MADE?

Most public administration is carried out under statutory powers granted to public authorities under Acts of Parliament. Because of the legislative supremacy of parliament, and because the executive, in the form of the government, controls parliament, the executive can in effect give itself such powers as it may desire. Subject to conformity with EU law requirements[48] (and to a lesser extent conformity with the Human Rights Act 1998 – see above) the validity of the Act conferring that power cannot be questioned. The role for the reviewing court is rather different, to establish the parameters of the power granted, by seeking the intention of parliament as it has been expressed in the legislation (or as may be inferred). The principles of judicial review of administrative may therefore be considered to reflect the approaches taken by the judges to the interpretation of such empowering legislation.

3.1. SOURCES OF POWER

3.1.1. Parliamentary Legislation[49]

Interpretation of the scope of statutory functions

A statutory power granted to a public authority will be construed not only according to its express terms, but also as impliedly authorizing anything that is considered to be incidental or consequential to the power itself.

Lord Selbourne made the classic formulation of this principle in *Attorney-General v Great Eastern Railway Co.*[50]

> '... the doctrine ought to be reasonably ... understood and applied, and ... whatever may fairly be regarded as incidental to, or consequential upon those things which the legislature has authorized, ought not (unless expressly prohibited) to be held, by judicial construction to be *ultra vires*'.

A good example of this principle can be seen in *Attorney-General* v *Crayford Urban District Council*[51] where the council used its express powers and duties under the Housing Act 1957 in relation to the 'general management, regulation and control' of houses provided by the local authority, to act as an agent for a private insurance company providing household belongings insurance. There was no express power to act in this way, but the local authority's activities were held to be lawful on the basis that if its tenants had such insurance, then

48 Until the UK leaves the EU, it is still required to comply with EU obligations.

49 The official text of an Act of Parliament is known as the Queen's Printer Copy. The Act will be printed and issued a few days after Royal Assent. The Acts are subsequently reissued as annual bound volumes. The Office of Public Sector Information (OPSI) website provides the full text of all Acts of Parliament from 1988, <www.legislation.gov.uk/ukpga (accessed 18 April 2017). Information on Bills before parliament can be found at the following website: <www.parliament.uk/about/how/laws/bills/public/> (accessed 18 April 2017).

50 (1880) 5 *App Case* 473 at 478, HL (House of Lords). This abbreviation is used for Appeal Cases where the case was reported between 1875 and 1880.

51 [1962] 2 All ER 147.

should they suffer a personal disaster like damage from flooding, they would be less likely to become rent defaulters. The local authority's promotion of private insurance was therefore reasonably incidental to the performance of its duties in the context of housing management.

3.1.2. Delegated Legislation

In the modern world it is not practical for any parliament itself to make all the detailed legislation which is a practical necessity. In the United Kingdom parliament has increasingly delegated its law-making powers to ministers (power to make regulations and other orders) and to local authorities (powers to make bye-laws).

There are, however, some concerns about the proliferation of such 'subordinate' legislation. It has become increasingly common for parliament to legislate in only very general terms and for the powers given to the executive to be not merely to 'fill in technical details, but also to decide broad issues of policy, thereby leading to a consequential shift in the balance of power between Parliament and the Executive'.[52] Because of concerns about the quantity of powers being delegated a House of Lord Select Committee on Delegated Powers and Regulatory Reform has been established: one of its central roles being to assess whether the provisions of any bill seem inappropriately to delegate legislative power. The presence of the Committee ensures at least that government proposals to introduce particularly broad delegated powers require some reasoned justification.

Under the European Communities Act 1972 the Crown, by Order in Council[53], and any designated minister or department, have power by regulations to make most of the changes to domestic law necessary for the purpose of implementing community obligations. As European law becomes more prolific, these powers of delegated legislation have become an importance source of administrative legislative power.

A type of delegated legislation which has come in for recent criticism is what is known as a 'Henry VIII' clause, allowing Ministers to amend primary legislation through delegated legislation. Some such clauses are uncontroversial: for example the one in the Human Rights Act 1998, which allows (but does not oblige) Ministers quickly to alter legislation that a court has indicated to be in

---

52 Craig, P.P., *Administrative Law*, 8th ed., London: Sweet & Maxwell, 2016, p. 436.

53 Where the enabling power in an Act is delegated to the Crown rather than to a minister, the delegated legislation made under the Act is made by the Sovereign in the Privy Council, as an Order in Council. The Privy Council is a remnant from the time when the monarchy rather than Parliament governed the country. It was a select group of royal officials and advisers. In modern times it has no real power and its role is to give a rather more solemn legal form to certain decisions of the government.

conflict with the European Convention of Human Rights.[54] Other provisions, such as those to be found in the Legislative and Regulatory Reform Act 2006 are far more controversial. Section 1 of the Act confers power on a Minister to make any provision by order which he considers would serve the purpose of removing or reducing any burden, or removing or reducing the overall burdens, to which any person is subject as a direct or indirect result of any legislation, which includes Acts of Parliament. This is an extremely wide ranging power.[55]

The Statutory Instruments Act 1946 lays down quite complex procedural rules for the making of statutory instruments (i.e. ministerial regulations, rules and orders) and requires the publication of most such legislation.[56]

Parliamentary scrutiny of delegated legislation is in reality quite limited.[57] Many pieces of delegated legislation have to be 'laid before parliament', and this can take a number of different forms. Which procedure is to be used is determined by the enabling Act. Simple laying merely requires the instrument to be laid before parliament and is a procedure seldom used in modern times. The most common procedure is the 'negative resolution procedure' which requires an instrument to be laid before parliament after being made but prior to it coming into operation. Provided no Member of either House, within a period of 40 days, successfully moves an annulment resolution it will remain in force. The 'affirmative resolution' procedure requires each House to pass a resolution that the instrument be brought into force. This procedure does provide effective control by parliament but it is rarely used because of the pressures it imposes on parliamentary time.

The Parliamentary Joint Committee on Statutory Instruments is charged with the task of considering every general statutory instrument required to be laid before parliament, with a view to determining whether the special attention

---

54 Under s 4 of the Human Rights Act the English courts which can declare an Act of Parliament incompatible are the Supreme Court, the Court of Appeal and the High Court.

55 The Act has been described as 'one of the most constitutionally significant Bills' for years. (House of Commons Regulatory Reform Committee, Legislative and Regulatory Reform Bill, First Special Report of Session 2005–06, HC 878, para. 5.) Provisions in the Deregulation and Contracting Out Act 1994, which did not go as far at the 2006 Act, were described at the time as 'unprecedented in the time of peace'. (Select Committee on the Scrutiny of Delegated Legislation, *Eighth Report*, HL (House of Lords) 60 of 1993–94 at para. 1).

56 The official text of a statutory instrument (SI) is published by Her Majesty's Stationery Office (HMSO). The SIs are issued individually on a daily basis by HMSO and they equate to the Queen's Printer copies of Acts of Parliament. There appears to be no particular policy on what form the SI should take and it makes no legal difference whether the SI is termed an 'order', 'rule' or 'regulation'. However, how one refers to the numbered parts of the instrument varies according to its title. If the SI is an Order they are called paragraphs, if it is a Regulation they are referred to as regulations (reg) 1, 2 etc. and if they are rules they are referred to as rules (r) 1, 2 etc.

57 For a critical assessment of Parliamentary scrutiny of delegated legislation see Hansard Society, *Making the Law: The Report of the Hansard Society Commission on the Legislative Process*, 1993 at paras. 364–387 and Hayhurst, J. & Wallington, P., 'The Parliamentary Scrutiny of Delegated Legislation', *Public Law*, 1988, p. 547.

of either House should be drawn to it on any of a number of grounds, including its imposition of a tax or charge, that it is retrospective in operation or that by virtue of its enabling Act it is excluded from challenge in the courts. The Committee is not, however, concerned with the merits of, or the policy behind, any instrument and therefore its task is of a somewhat technical nature.

One means of exercising some degree of control over delegated legislation is by way of pre-legislative consultation. It is common for parent Acts to require the subordinate legislator to consult with certain bodies, either named specifically or described in general terms, before exercising the power to legislate.

What exactly does consultation mean? The High Court has stated:

> 'Firstly, that consultation must be at a time when proposals are still at a formative stage. Second, that the proposer must give sufficient reasons for any proposal to permit intelligent consideration and response. Third, that adequate time must be given for [such] consideration and response and ... fourth, that the product of the consultation must be conscientiously taken into account in finalising statutory proposals'.[58]

Whilst clearly the relevant minister is not under an obligation to accept the advice of consultees, if the parent statute requires a consultative process, a failure properly to consult is likely to invalidate any subsequent delegated legislation made (unless, unusually, there may be exceptional circumstances, which in the public interest require the legislation to remain intact).[59]

Delegated legislation can also be challenged in the courts on the substantive ultra vires ground that it goes beyond the powers conferred by on the rule-making agency by the parent Act. This issue is considered in more detail below[60] but we may note here that the courts will expect clear words in the parent Act before delegated legislation can be made which purports to impose a charge[61] or in some way seriously invades the constitutional rights or liberties of the individual.[62] The courts have, however, been slow in general terms to

58 Per Hodgson J in *R* v *Brent London Borough Council, ex parte Gunning* (1985) 84 Local Government Reports (LGR) 168 at 189. See also *Rollo* v *Minister of Town and Country Planning* [1948] 1 All ER 13.

59 See for example Webster J in *R* v *Secretary of State for Social Services, ex parte Association of Metropolitan Authorities* [1986] 1 WLR (*Weekly Law Reports)* 1 where housing benefit legislation was declared *ultra vires* due to lack of proper consultation but left in place as the 'regulations [had] been in force for about six months and, although their implementation creates difficulties for some at least of the housing authorities who have to administer them, those authorities must by now have adapted themselves as best they can to those difficulties'.

60 See *infra* section 5.

61 *Attorney-General* v *Wilts United Dairies* (1922) 38 TLR (*Times Law Reports)* 781.

62 *Chester* v *Bateson* [1920] 1 KB (*Law Reports: King's Bench Division)* 829. A Defence of the Realm Regulation stated that no one could sue for possession of a munitions worker's house without the permission of a minister. This was held to be ultra vires as it took away from subjects their normal rights of access to the courts and that such an extreme measure could only be imposed by express words in the enabling legislation.

hold that statutory instruments are invalid on the ground that they are merely 'unreasonable'[63], and even more reluctant to do so where the instruments have been the subject of some form of parliamentary approval, such as a resolution of the House of Commons.[64]

3.1.3. Delegated Legislation and Exiting the EU

Although the UK has begun the formal process of exiting the EU, leaving is far from straightforward. As the Government has acknowledged, 'Simply repealing the [European Communities Act 1972] would lead to a confused and incomplete legal system.'[65] The intention is for a 'Great Repeal Bill' to convert EU law into domestic law. However, it is anticipated that despite this, there will still be many gaps left and the intention is that these should be filled by delegated legislation. A House of Lords Select Committee has considered how this could be achieved without giving too much unchecked power to the government.[66] At present it is not clear what the nature of the power will be. Although the government has indicated that it is mindful of the need to have limits on the power it is also conscious that the power must be 'broad enough to make all of the necessary amendments to the statute book within the time frame determined by the EU withdrawal process.'[67]

Figure 2. Hierarchy of legislation

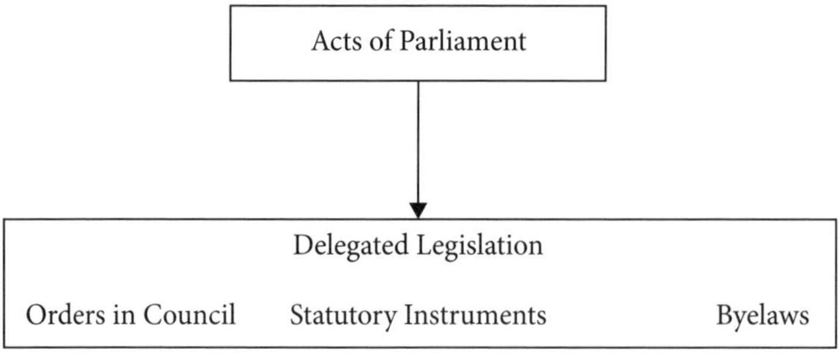

---

63 See *McEldowney* v *Forde* [1971] AC 632.

64 See *R* v *Secretary of State for the Environment, ex parte Nottinghamshire County Council* [1986] AC 240 and *R* v *Secretary of State for the Environment, ex parte Hammersmith and Fulham London Borough Council* [1990] 1 AC 521.

65 Legislating for the United Kingdom's withdrawal from the European Union, Cm 9446, 2017, para. 2.4.

66 See Constitution Committee, *The 'Great Repeal Bill' and delegated powers*, 7 March 2017, HL 123 2016–17.

67 Legislating for the United Kingdom's withdrawal from the European Union, Cm 9446, 2017, p. 23.

3.2. INQUIRIES

Government bodies conduct inquiries into a wide variety of matters and these inquiries take one of two main forms: statutory and non-statutory inquiries. The Inquiries Act 2005 has replaced the Tribunals of Inquiry (Evidence) Act 1921, under which even over quite a long period fewer than 30 inquiries were held. Recent examples of Tribunals of Inquiry included the Cullen Report into the shootings at Dunblane primary school[68], the Smith Reports into the issues arising from the case of mass murderer Dr Harold Shipman and the Saville Report into the 'Bloody Sunday' events in Northern Ireland.[69] The 2005 Act was introduced to replace over 30 different pieces of legislation on inquiries and to codify past practice for inquiries.

The Inquiries Act 2005 allows an inquiry to compel any information that could be compelled in normal civil proceedings and a judge is permitted to be a member of an inquiry panel.

Inquiry findings are not legally binding upon any governmental body but they are usually influential. There is an expectation that recommendations will be followed or if not, that reasons will be offered for choosing a different course of action. Two very critical and influential reports on the conduct of government in recent years have been the Scott Inquiry into the 'Arms to Iraq' affair[70] and the Inquiry into BSE and new variant-CJD.[71] What became clear from the Scott Inquiry was that government policy on arms dealing was secretly changed and that members of parliament and parliament itself were misled about those changes. Scott concluded that although it may be impossible to give every fact on such matters to parliament, there should be a fair summation of the full picture given in response to requests about policy. To this general principle Scott indicated that there could be, however, exceptions, such as matters relating to security, but that such exceptions should only be made where there are cogent reasons for so acting, and that the general principle should be that ministerial accountability requires that where a minister speaks in parliament, or to a select committee, or answers a parliamentary question, this is done under an obligation to give full information, 'for otherwise the legislature cannot hold the executive fully to account'. This view has been accepted and can now been seen reflected in the Code of Conduct for Ministers.[72]

---

68 Cm 3386.

69 See Hadfield, B., '*R v Lord Saville of Newgate, ex parte* anonymous soldiers: What is the purpose of a Tribunal of Inquiry', *Public Law*, 1999, p. 663.

70 Inquiry into the Export of Defence Equipment and Dual-Use Goods to Iraq and Related Prosecutions, HC (House of Commons) 115 (1995–96).

71 More commonly known as the Phillips Inquiry or the BSE Inquiry. The Report of the inquiry was published in October 2000.

72 It is worth noting that views on the impact of the Scott Inquiry are mixed. For example Leigh, I. & Lustgarten, L., 'Five Volumes in Search of accountability: the Scott Report', *Modern Law Review*, 1996 (59), p. 695–724 argue 'The process by which Ministers responded to the Report

The Inquiry into BSE also found evidence of secrecy in policymaking, and failure by the government to have kept the public informed of a possible risk. Unusually this rt named not only ministers but also individual civil servants who were considered to be to blame for policy failures. The report pointed to a number of problems with the way the main government department involved, the Ministry of Agriculture, Fisheries and Food (MAFF) operated, and indicated that the relationship between it and other government departments was not as close as it should have been. Partly as a result of this report MAFF was dismantled and its responsibilities combined with 'environment' and 'rural affairs' within the Department for the Environment, Food and Rural Affairs (DEFRA).

A much more common type of inquiry is the public local inquiry in the context of land use decisions. A number of Acts of Parliament provide for such local inquiries and they are a means of giving a fair hearing to objectors before a final decision is taken which affects a citizen's rights or interests. Planning inquiries are the most common type of inquiry under this heading. They must be held before the adoption of planning schemes of general character and also in many cases of individual appeals against refusal of planning permission or against conditions imposed by a local planning authority. A difference between these land use inquiries and the ones referred to in earlier paragraphs is that whereas the earlier discussed inquiries operate only where government chooses to establish an inquiry, the 'land use' inquiries are a mandatory part of the planning and compulsory purchase administrative processes.

3.3. INSPECTIONS

In many branches of government provision is made for the appointment of inspectors, who are responsible for checking the manner in which a particular activity is being carried out. Some inspections concern the activities of private individuals, such as inspections by environmental health inspectors; other inspections are carried out by a governmental body on some other organ of the administration. For example, the Office of Standards in Education, Children's Services and Skills (OFSTED) inspects state schools so as to ensure the maintenance of certain standards throughout the country.

Where an inspection is followed by an adverse report a variety of consequences may follow, although it is anticipated that usually the mere fact of regular inspection in itself will ensure attention to the maintenance of standards. In the case of schools, OFSTED aims to visit most schools at least once every five

---

and by which Parliament considered it could hardly have been a more graphic illustration of the central lesson of the entire Arms for Iraq episode; the futility and ineffectiveness of parliamentary scrutiny'.

years and a report is prepared following the inspection. If a school is found to have serious weakness, the school must prepare an action plan and is given a year to overcome its weaknesses. Where a school is found to be failing to give its pupils an acceptable standard of education, the school is put on what is known as 'special measures' and the local education authority has to prepare an action plan.[73]

Also of relevance here is the question of the *financial* inspection of central and local government. The Audit Commission reviews expenditure decisions of local authorities and ensures that the authority's records are in order and that proper arrangements have been made for securing economy and efficiency in the use of resources.[74] Central government spending is subject to inspection by the Comptroller and Auditor General and also subject to scrutiny by the Public Accounts Committee of the House of Commons.

3.4. LICENSING

Many activities are the subject of some form of governmental licensing control. Although this is usually to seek to enforce or maintain standards, in some cases the main purpose may simply be to raise revenue or perhaps just to regulate the *number* of persons engaged in an activity. Licensing is normally of a local nature and amongst the activities which are licensed at a local level are the provision of taxi services, selling alcohol, and running a public cinema or theatre or a sex shop. At national level examples include the licensing of drivers and the operation of air passenger routes. There is also much permitting in the context of environmental pollution. Here responsibilities divide between central government, local government and the Environment Agency (a body with some degree of independence from government).

Conditions may be imposed both as to standards that must be satisfied before a license will be issued, and as to the manner in which the particular activity may subsequently be carried out under the license. For example, a full driving license will not be issued unless the applicant has passed his driving test. As a general rule a government body may not require any payment as a condition precedent to the issue of the license unless this is provided for expressly by statute. There is a strong presumption against a statute conferring a taxing power in the absence of a clear statement to that effect.[75] However, parliament does often specifically authorize the charging for a license and these powers are utilized to seek to cover

73 See Education Act 2005 and Education and Inspections Act 2006.

74 Local Government Finance Act 1982.

75 See *Attorney-General* v *Wilts United Dairies* (1922) 38 TLR 788 and *McCarthy & Stone* v *Richmond Upon Thames London Borough* [1982] 2 AC 48.

administrative costs. For example, local authorities may impose a charge on any person to whom it issues a pet shop license.[76]

Statutes imposing licensing requirements often provide a right of appeal against the refusal of a license, and also against any condition that may be imposed on the grant of a license. Such appeals may lie (as the particular statute may provide) to a court (usually the magistrates' court), a statutory tribunal or to a superior agency within the administration, such as the Minister. It may also be possible to seek judicial review, following the refusal or revocation of a license.[77]

The legislation under which the relevant license is issued will normally contain provisions for the enforcement of licensing control. Usually the legislation provides for some criminal offences (conviction for which can result in a fine, a term of imprisonment or both), powers of closure in respect of licensed premises and in some circumstances the power to revoke a license.[78]

3.5. PUBLIC PARTICIPATION AND OPEN GOVERNMENT

Governments are, of course, much interested in 'public opinion' and account is taken of this in decision-making.[79] In a number of ways provision is made, in certain areas of public administration, for public participation in decision-making. This is most marked in cases where consultation takes place with interested parties, and in situations where public local inquiries are held at which objectors may formally state their views. Such public participation is an important feature of the town and country planning process, and also of a wide variety of other matters in the property rights context, such as the making of compulsory purchase orders.

Of course 'public participation' may amount to little if there is no 'open government'.

> 'If the principle of open government is to be maintained, there must be ... public access to information about government activities and decisions. Openness in government is necessary if Parliament, groups and the public are to be able to

[76] See Pet Animals Act 1951, as amended.

[77] See *infra* section 5. But note that judicial review may not be allowed where there is an adequate alternative remedy by way of appeal.

[78] See for example, Manchester, C., *Manchester on Alcohol and Entertainment Licensing Law*, 3rd ed., Leeds: Woods Whur Publishing, 2012, chapter 11.

[79] The Labour Party, when in government, made extensive use of focus groups to gauge public opinion on its policy proposals, see Gould, P., *The Unfinished Revolution: How the Modernisers Saved the Labour Party*, London: Little Brown & Co, 1998 and Tony Blair, when Prime Minister, was reported to start most weeks by talking to his pollster, see Hennessy, *supra* note 37, p. 484.

> contribute to the making of policy, and if the actions of government are to be properly scrutinized and evaluated, and the decision-makers held accountable'.[80]

British government has traditionally tended towards secrecy. However, since the early 1990s there have been some moves towards more open government. In 1993 the Conservative Government issued a White Paper on *Open Government*[81] proposing the introduction of a non-statutory, non-legally binding code of practice on public access to government information. *The Code of Practice on Access to Government Information* came into effect in 1994, with a revised edition being issued in 1997. The Code applied to all government departments, agencies and authorities that were subject to the jurisdiction of the Parliamentary Commissioner for Administration (the Parliamentary Ombudsman). The Code required much information, although not documents, to be put into the public domain, but it contained numerous exceptions and 'the fact remained that if a government minister decided to keep secret an embarrassing piece of information, even if the information revealed unlawful actions by government officials or minister, there was no means by which parliament or an individual citizen could force the minister to disclose that information'.[82]

The Labour Government, which came to power in 1997, was committed in its manifesto to introduce a Freedom of Information Act, something rather radical for the United Kingdom, but common-place in many other countries. Before the year was out the Cabinet Office's Freedom of Information Unit had produced a White Paper containing proposals for statutory freedom of information, unless disclosure would cause substantial harm to specified public interests.[83] The White Paper was not greeted with universal approval and it was not until towards the middle of 1999 that a draft Freedom of Information Bill was published for consultation.[84] The Bill which was finally introduced into the House of Commons in November 1999 was a rather 'watered down' version of earlier proposals. The Bill was finally passed in November 2000.[85] One commentator, Austin, has expressed the not uncommon view that the final Act 'is not only a sheep in wolf's clothing but a fraud on democratic accountability' because 'in reality, what the government has enshrined in this Act is a discretionary power

80 Turpin, C. & Tomkins, A., *British Government and the Constitution*, 7th ed., Cambridge: Cambridge Press, 2012, p. 556.

81 Cm 2290.

82 Austin, R., 'The Freedom of Information Act 2000 – A Sheep in Wolf's Clothing', in: Jowell, J. & Oliver, D., *The Changing Constitution*, 5th ed., Oxford: Oxford University Press, 2004, p. 404.

83 Your Right to Know: The Government's Proposals for a Freedom of Information Act, Cm 3818.

84 Freedom of Information: Consultation on Draft Legislation, Cm 4355.

85 The Environmental Information Regulations 2004 (SI 2004/3391) lay down broadly parallel, but not identical, rules on access to environmental information.

to choose what information to disclose'.[86] Not everyone would agree with this view. Lord Lester, a prominent supporter of freedom of information, has noted the danger of conferring a right that is 'illusory; not a real or effective right but something written in water'[87] but has concluded that the Act, as finally passed, is not open to that objection. The House of Common Justice Committee considers that the legislation has been a 'significant enhancement to our democracy'.[88]

The limits of the powers under the Freedom of Information Act were tested in the very high profile case concerning access to letters written by the Prince of Wales to government ministers. The Attorney General asserted his right under s 53 to issue a certificate to stop the disclosure of the letters. However, his certificate was challenged on the basis that his withholding of the information was not justifiable and therefore unlawful. The Supreme Court agreed with this view in *R (on the application of Evans) v Attorney General*[89] emphasising that the Attorney General could not attempt to withhold information just because he did not agree that it should not be disclosed.

3.6. THE USE OF PRIVATE LAW BY THE ADMINISTRATION[90]

3.6.1. Contractual Powers

Government, and local government in particular, needs to enter into many ordinary commercial contracts for the procurement of goods and services, and the recent trend of contracting out the performance of public services has ensured that modern government enters ever more contracts. Powers to contract may be conferred specifically by statute, generally by such statutory provisions as section 111 of the Local Government Act 1972[91], or by the common law.

86 *Supra* note 82 at p. 414.

87 *Hansard HL*, vol. 619, col 136.

88 1st Report, HC 96-I of 2012–13, p. 3.

89 [2015] UKSC 21.

90 The discussion below focuses on the *contractual* powers of government. It will be noted that in the main the position of government equates with the position of private individuals, subject only to government needing to possess legal authority to enter into the contractual relationship in question. Some special rules apply in the local Government context under which those who deal with local authorities need not make inquiries about the authority's capacity to contract. Certain common principles which seemed at one time to confer powers on government to breach contracts with impunity 'in the public interest' (the so-called *Amphitrite* principle) no longer seem to be regarded as having substance. Equally the Government may sue and be sued in tort (subject only to the quite limited 'public interest' defence of Act of State – a defence which cannot be pleaded in relation to alleged wrongs to British subjects or alleged wrongs done within United Kingdom territory. With only slight modifications the ordinary rules of property ownership apply to government.

91 Under this provision local authorities can incur expenditure 'which is calculated to facilitate, or is conducive or incidental to, the discharge of any of their functions'.

The power to determine with whom it will contract has at times been used by government as an 'extra-legal' means of advancing governmental policies. Thus for example governments in the past have imposed a 'fair wage' condition on government contractors; and in the late 1970s the Labour Government used its contractual powers to award contracts to support a counter-inflation policy on wages; and in pre-EU membership days contractual favouritism was sometimes bestowed upon British companies.[92] Less controversially, government contracts will typically include clauses like the requirement that the contractor refrains from unlawful discrimination.

Prior to the Crown Proceedings Act 1947 the private individual was at a substantial disadvantage as a litigant against the Crown.[93] In medieval times the King *was* government and all government was conducted in the name of the King. In time, the personal influence of the monarch diminished and the functions of government were carried out by bodies on behalf of the Crown, such as the central departments of state. The problem this presented arose from the medieval principle that 'the King can do no wrong', and could not be proceeded against in the courts, as they were his courts.

If the King could do no wrong, did those who represented the Crown share this immunity? The answer, until the Crown Proceedings Act (CPA) 1947, was that the Crown could not be proceeded against (for example in tort or for breach of contract); although certain practices did develop to try to mitigate against the unfairness of the situation: such as the so called *petition of right*. None of these devices was able, however, to overcome the basic problem of Crown immunity.

The matter was put on a more modern footing by the CPA 1947 Act. The 1947 Act now provides that the Crown can be sued in those circumstances in which a 'petition of right' could have been brought prior to the Act. As a general rule the Crown is now liable for breaches of contract in circumstances where any other defendant would be liable under the ordinary law. There is no special law relating to government contracts; their interpretation and enforcement is governed by the ordinary rules of contract that apply to contracts made between private individuals.

3.6.2. Enforcement of Standards

Public authorities are much concerned with the enforcement of statutory standards. Local authorities have many duties to secure compliance with standards imposed in the public interests. For example, the Environmental Protection Act 1990 imposes a duty on local authorities to take action where

---

92 Favouritism towards national companies is no longer possible under EU law.

93 For a discussion of the position of the Crown in proceedings both pre and post the 1947 Act, see Lord Woolf's speech in *M* v *Home Office* [1993] 3 All ER 537.

premises within their area are 'in such a state as to be prejudicial to health or a nuisance'.[94]

Although it is normally the express duty of the authority to enforce the standard in question, it is usually left to the authority to decide for itself what steps it should take, if any, to ascertain whether the standard has been complied with. However, on some occasions the statute may *require* the local authority to inspect its area and to ascertain whether standards are being observed; for example to carry out a review of housing conditions.[95]

Where an official of a local authority discovers that statutory standards are not being observed a report will be made to the local authority for its consideration. A decision will then have to be made by the local authority members, or by a committee or by an officer with delegated power. The decision will normally be to serve a notice on the person concerned, requiring him to comply with the prescribed standards. On some occasions the statute authorizes the immediate commencement of criminal proceedings, although it is normal first to issue an informal warning. If a notice has to be served, the responsible officer will prepare it. It must be in writing and in some cases in a prescribed form.[96] Officers must be very careful to follow procedures correctly, as a failure to adhere to the procedures is likely to invalidate the decision.[97] Any rights of appeal against the notice must be stated.[98] If the notice requires works to be carried out, only the minimum necessary to secure compliance with the standard may be specified[99], and a reasonable time must be stated within which the works must be carried out.

If the requirements of the notice are not complied with, the local authority, under the statute, may have power to act in default. The authority must first ensure that the time prescribed by the notice has expired and it may only carry out the minimum work necessary for compliance with the terms of the notice. The statute normally provides that the local authority has a right to recover its expenses reasonably incurred in acting in default. In addition to the cost of having the work carried out, the authority can usually add interest,

---

94 See Environmental Protection Act 1990, section 79.

95 Housing Act 2004, section 3.

96 See for example the Detention of Food (Prescribed Forms) Regulations 1990 (SI 1990/2614, which prescribe the form to be used in connection with the detention of foodstuffs under the Food Safety Act 1990, if it is believed that the food does not comply with the food safety standards.

97 See, for example, *Bexley London Borough* v *Gardner Merchant PLC* [1993] COD (Crown Office Digest) 383 where an improvement notice served under section 10 of the Food Safety Act 1990 was found not to fully comply with the provision's requirements. The Court of Appeal held that where the notice was not served in accordance with the statute it had to be cancelled and it could not at a later date be amended or modified. In these situations the criminal charges can be dismissed by the trial court or there could be claim for judicial review.

98 See *Rayner* v *Stepney Corporation* [1911] 2 Law Reports Chancery Division (Ch) 312.

99 See *Welton* v *North Cornwall District Council* [1997] 1 WLR 570.

at a prescribed rate, and the interest can run from the date of the demand.[100] These expenses are normally recoverable as a civil debt summarily before the local magistrates or alternatively before the ordinary civil courts. Statutes often provide that expenses incurred as a consequence of taking action in default of compliance with a statutory notice, shall be registrable as a charge on the land.

As an alternative to requiring the service of a notice, the statute may empower the local authority to prosecute an offender who has not complied with the particular statutory standard. In some cases the authority may be empowered to bring a prosecution at the same time as it serves a statutory notice[101], and in others a prosecution may only be brought (perhaps as well as taking default action) in respect of a failure to comply with the statutory notice in due time.[102]

In exercising these powers the local authorities may also need to exercise other powers. For example, most of the relevant statutes will permit officers of the local authority to effect entry onto property where this is necessary for them to carry out their statutory functions. The use of these powers is, however, strictly regulated as the laws of England have long protected private property, as is demonstrated in the following statement from Lord Camden in the famous case of *Entick* v *Carrington*[103]:

> 'By the laws of England, every invasion of private property, be it ever so minute, is a trespass. No man can set his foot upon my property without my licence, but he is liable to an action, though the damage be nothing ... If he admits the fact he is bound to show by way of justification, that some positive law has empowered or excused him'.

Local authorities may, on occasion, seek private law injunctions to prevent the infringement of rights of the public – such as a public nuisance affecting the health of the district, or the continued flouting of a byelaw, or other legislation. These actions can be brought in the public interest by the local authority, provided that it deems it expedient to bring the action 'for the promotion or protection of the interests of the inhabitants of their area'.[104] Alternatively the local authority (or other person) may acquire standing by acting in conjunction with the Attorney-General. Where the Attorney-General brings the action at the relation of the authority this is known as a *relator action*. If an injunction which has been obtained is ignored this will involve a contempt of court, which at the court's discretion can be punished by imprisonment or by a fine.

---

100 See, for example, Public Health Act 1936, section 291.

101 See, for example, section 290(6) of the Public Health Act 1936.

102 See, for example, the Environmental Protection Act 1990, section 80 with regard to abatement notices.

103 (1765) 19 St Tr (State Trials) 1030.

104 Section 222, Local Government Act 1972. See Hough, B., 'Local Authorities as the Guardians of the Public Interest', *Public Law*, 1992, p. 130.

An example will serve to illustrate this procedure. In *Stoke-on-Trent City Council* v *B & Q Retail Ltd*[105] a company was trading on a Sunday in breach of the Shops Act 1950 despite warnings from the local authority not to do so. Under section 7(1)(b) of the Act the authority was under a 'duty … to enforce within their district' the provisions of the Act. The authority sought an injunction restraining the company from trading in breach of the Act on the basis that this was necessary to protect the interests of the inhabitants. The injunction was granted and the company appealed against them on the ground that the local authority's power to claim injunctive relief under section 222 of the Local Government Act 1972 was limited to circumstances where the acts complained of were likely to cause a public nuisance. The House of Lords upheld the injunctions, making it clear, however, that local authorities could only use the power if they could show that the offending behaviour was deliberate and that the law was being flagrantly flouted. On the facts of the case their Lordships were satisfied that the authority could take the view that the company intended to continue to flout the law and would not be deterred by the maximum fine that could be imposed under the Shops Act. Accordingly, there was sufficient justification for the grant of the injunction.

4. NON JUDICIAL REDRESS OF GRIEVANCES

4.1. OMBUDSMEN

'Ombudsmen' or 'grievance men' are, as is well known, a Scandinavian idea, and it is, as implemented in the UK, their role to consider not the *merits* of a decision, but to review the *process* by which decisions may have been taken. The first ombudsman was established in the United Kingdom by the Parliamentary Commissioner for Administration Act 1967 establishing an ombudsman in relation to central government departments. Since then Commissioners for Local Administration[106], for the health service[107] and for public services in Scotland, Wales and Northern Ireland[108] have been established. The principle has spread also outside the sphere of 'government' into the private sector, and there is for example, a Pensions Ombudsmen and an ombudsman in the area of financial services.

The Parliamentary Ombudsman (PCA) has jurisdiction to hear complaints of injustice resulting from *maladministration* on the part of central government departments and bodies (or their modern equivalents).[109] As Wade and Forsyth

---

105 [1984] AC 754.

106 Local Government Act 1974.

107 Health Service Commissioners Act 1993.

108 Scottish Public Services Ombudsman Act 2002, Public Services Ombudsman (Wales) Act 2005 and Public Services Ombudsman Act (Northern Ireland) 2016.

109 See Parliamentary Commissioner Act 1967, section 4 and schedule 2 (as amended) for a full list of the departments, corporations and bodies which are subject to the PCA's jurisdiction.

note, 'the establishment of executive agencies and the "contracting out" of some government services has not affected the Commissioner's jurisdiction, since he may investigate actions whether taken by or "on behalf of" a body subject to his jurisdiction'.[110]

Complaints to the PCA must be made through an MP and the number of complaints received has steadily increased to around 1,500 a year, although a good many of these have to be rejected as not falling within the PCA's jurisdiction. The main exclusions to the PCA's jurisdiction are cases where the complainant has a right of appeal or review before a tribunal or court of law or has a remedy by way of proceedings in court, complaints about the commercial or contractual dealings of government, and complaints which are more than twelve months old. There is, however, some overlap between the jurisdiction of the PCA and that of the courts and tribunals. Under section 5(2) of the 1967 Act the PCA has a discretion to investigate a complaint where the person does have a right of appeal, review or remedy before a court or tribunal where he is 'satisfied that in the particular circumstances it is not reasonable to expect him to resort or have resorted to it'.

Maladministration is not defined in the legislation: but during the passage of the legislation through parliament it was stated – in oft-repeated words – to include 'bias, neglect, inattention, delay, incompetence, ineptitude, arbitrariness and so on'.[111] The Act makes it clear that the PCA may not investigate the merits of a decision taken without maladministration and the courts have indicated that they will intervene if an ombudsman interferes with the merits in the absence of maladministration.[112] Nonetheless the PCA has adopted a fairly generous interpretation of maladministration. For example, he is willing to investigate injustice resulting from 'bad rules' on the basis that if a bad rule causes injustice there will probably have been maladministration in failing to have monitored the rule's application and to have modified it in the light of the hardship discovered to have been caused. Similarly, the PCA has taken the view that he may *infer* maladministration in the case of a decision which is 'thoroughly bad in quality'.

The types of complaints that have led to findings of maladministration include complaints of misleading statements and advice, and complaints of unjustified delay in making a decision. Once the PCA has investigated a complaint, reports will be sent to the MP who forwarded the complaint and also to the head of the department subject of the complaint. Where a finding of maladministration has been made, the PCA normally recommends some compensation be paid to the complainant, or recommends that some other action be taken to relieve the injustice. Although departments are under no

110 Wade, H.W.R. & Forsyth, C.F., *Administrative Law*, 11th ed., Oxford: Oxford University Press, 2014, p. 72.

111 734 HC Deb (House of Commons Debates) col 51 (18 October 1966).

112 *R* v *Local Commissioner for Administration, ex parte Eastleigh Borough Council* [1988] QB (*Law Reports Queen's Bench Division)* 855.

obligation to act upon these recommendations[113], departments have a very good record of acting upon them. This is best illustrated by reference to what has been the PCA's most famous success. The *Barlow Clowes* affair[114] involved an investigation into a brokerage business, which lost the life savings of many of its investors. The Department of Trade and Industry was accused of having persistently disregarded evidence of serious malpractices and the PCA concluded that there was on its part maladministration, which had resulted in loss to the investors. It was therefore recommended that compensation should be paid by the DTI. While the government did not accept that there was maladministration, it was prepared to offer a substantial pay-out, partly out of respect for the Commissioner's office. In all around £ 150 million was paid out in compensation.

Whilst it is very rare for the PCA's reports not to be followed, the PCA has powers to report to parliament where it is believed that complainants have suffered maladministration leading to injustice 'and the injustice has not been, or will not be, remedied'.[115] This power has been used only seven times, most recently in July 2014, when the PCA laid a report into the way the Electoral Commission had considered donations to the Liberal Democrat Party in 2005.[116] A report laid by the PCA in 2006 on the government's maladministration involving the winding up of final salary occupational pension schemes resulted in the complainants seeking to get redress through other avenues.[117] The failure of the government to act upon this report resulted in four of those adversely affected seeking judicial review to challenge the Government's decision to reject the PCA's findings. The Court of Appeal concluded that the Secretary of State's rejection of the findings that Government information had been potentially misleading and amounted to maladministration had been irrational.[118] Apart from securing redress for the individual in particular cases, the PCA places great emphasis on the extent to which investigations may result in the alteration and improvement of departmental procedures, standing instructions, published information and the content of forms.[119]

---

113 This has most recently been confirmed by the Court of Appeal in *R (on the application of Bradley)* v *Secretary of State for Work and Pensions* [2008] 3 WLR 1059.

114 See Gregory, R. & Drewry, G., 'Barlow Clowes and the Ombudsman', *Public Law*, 1991, p. 192 and p. 408.

115 Parliamentary Commissioner Act 1967, section 10(3).

116 'A report by the Parliamentary Ombudsman on an investigation into a complaint about the Electoral Commission', H.C. 540 2014–2015.

117 'Trusting in the pensions promise: government bodies and the security of final salary occupational pensions', H.C. (2005–2006) 984.

118 *R (on the application of Bradley)* v *Secretary of State for Work and Pensions* [2008] 3 WLR 1059.

119 See for example *The Principles of Good Administration*, 2009, <www.ombudsman.org. uk/ improving-public-service/ombudsmansprinciples/principles-of-good-administration> (accessed 3 May 2017).

The PCA's office has been the subject of recent review[120] and serious proposals for reform have been made.[121] If new legislation is passed, the intention is to create a new Public Service Ombudsman. The new Ombudsman would cover government departments and a range of other public bodies including local government and the NHS in England. It is proposed that there would be direct access to the Ombudsman, although complainants could go through an MP, should they so wish.

4.2. TRIBUNALS

In the modern age, when there are so many potential disputes between individuals and the administration, members of the public want cheap, speedy and informal methods by which they can have their grievances dealt with. For this reason a very large number of relatively informal adjudicatory tribunals have been created. They aim to provide cheaper, speedier, more accessible justice, freer from procedural technicality, and more expert in their knowledge of the subject matters within their remit, than the ordinary courts. A further benefit derived from these tribunals is that they assist the court system by diverting cases away, which might otherwise have had to be dealt with by the ordinary judicial process. The decision-making function of any tribunal depends on the legislation by which it has been established. This will indicate the kinds of cases it may hear, its composition and the procedures to be followed, and also whether its role is to reach a decision fully on the merits of the issues before it, or is simply to consider whether an earlier decision displays some error of law or error of fact (or both). In this way, depending on the nature of the tribunal, decisions can simply turn on the facts of the case or they can focus alone on what may be quite complex legal arguments.

For most of the first half of the 20th Century tribunals were created on a rather ad hoc basis, and there was no set pattern as to how they operated. This resulted in many criticisms of tribunals, which were often said to lack independence from the administration. In 1957 the influential Franks Committee Report on Tribunals and Enquiries[122] was published. The Report laid much stress upon the potential *advantages* of the tribunal system. However, it also took note of the criticisms of the system and made numerous recommendations to improve the actual workings of tribunals. In particular the Report placed great importance on the attainment of 'openness, fairness and impartiality', explaining these concepts as follows:

---

120 Gordon, R., *Better to Serve the Public: Proposals to restructure, reform, renew and reinvigorate public service ombudsmen*, October 2014; Cabinet Office, *A Public Service Ombudsman: A Consultation*, 2015; and Cabinet Office, *A Public Service Ombudsman: Government Response to Consultation*, 2015.

121 *Draft Public Service Ombudsman Bill*, Cm 9374, 2016.

122 Cmnd 218.

> '*Openness* appears to us to require the publicity of proceedings and knowledge of the essential reasoning underlying the decisions; *fairness* to require the adoption of a clear procedure which enables parties to know their rights, to present their case fully and to know the case which they have to meet; and *impartiality* to require the freedom of tribunals from the influence, real or apparent, of Departments concerned with the subject matter of their decisions'.[123]

The Report was followed almost immediately by the Tribunals and Inquiries Act 1958[124], which implemented many of the recommendations, and established a Council on Tribunals: a body which exercised a general supervision over most tribunals and inquiries.

Whilst it was hoped that tribunals would provide a much more informal and legally less complex forum than do the courts, in practice this has not always proved possible. A number of factors have been identified which inhibit informality.[125] Firstly, the subject matters of tribunal decisions tend often to involve complex legal rules and case law. Secondly, too much informality can lead claimants to have false expectations as to what can be achieved.[126] Thirdly, unrepresented claimants are at a disadvantage and tribunal panels are seldom in a position to take a less adversarial approach in order to afford substantial help to the unrepresented claimant. Legal representation or other representation before a tribunal is permitted and evidence does suggest that a person's chances of success before a tribunal are significantly increased if represented, and that they significantly decrease where the claimant is unrepresented and the respondent is legally represented.[127] However, there has only ever been quite limited state-funded financial assistance for taking complaints to tribunals (in comparison, until recently at least, with such support for cases before the ordinary courts).

If legislation provides for a right to appeal against an administrative decision before a tribunal, then there is usually a requirement that the administrative body should draw this right to the attention of the person at the time the decision is made. A failure to do so will amount to a challengeable procedural error. Obviously, if an appeal hearing is to be worthwhile the individual needs to know what arguments the administration will put forward in defence of the decision being challenged. Most tribunals have established detailed procedural rules requiring such prior disclosure.

Tribunal hearings are normally open to the public. However, a tribunal can sit *in camera* for reasons of national security or where the evidence is of a very personal nature. Most tribunals have no power to administer an oath to

---

123 *Ibid.* at para. 42.

124 See now Tribunals and Inquiries Act 1992.

125 See Genn, H., 'Tribunals and Informal Justice', *Modern Law Review*, 1993 (56), p. 393.

126 *Ibid.* at p 401.

127 See Genn, H. & Genn, Y., *The Effectiveness of Representation at Tribunals*, London: The Lord Chancellor's Department, 1989.

witnesses giving evidence, and the formal legal rules on admissibility of evidence do not normally apply. Therefore 'hearsay' evidence can be accepted and the tribunal may also rely on its own general knowledge and experience to a rather greater extent than is permitted a court of law.

In 2001 a Review of Tribunals Report (Chair, Sir Andrew Leggatt) was published.[128] The Review's central recommendation was that there should be a common administrative support system with responsibility vested in the Lord Chancellor's Department. It also recommended that the Lord Chancellor should assume responsibility for appointments to tribunals in order to give tribunal users real confidence that appeals are decided by people genuinely independent of government departments. It was felt that in general tribunals needed to function in more 'user friendly' ways, so that it would be more practicable for users to prepare and present cases themselves. The Review made several recommendations for the future role of the Council on Tribunals, including monitoring the development of the new tribunals system and championing the cause of users as its primary duty.

In response to the Review the government issued a White Paper which proposed a number of major reforms to the administrative justice system.[129] These proposals were largely reflected in the Tribunals, Courts and Enforcement Act 2007. This Act, along with the Tribunals and Inquiries Act 1992 now provides the statutory framework for the tribunal system.

The 2007 Act created a new unified two-tier tribunal system by establishing two new tribunals: the First-tier Tribunal and the Upper Tribunal (appellate tribunal).[130] These tribunals now exercise the jurisdiction of most of the tribunals previously administered by central government.[131] Both the First-tier and Upper Tribunals are divided into chambers and both have jurisdiction to review their own decisions.[132] Where the First-tier Tribunal sets aside one of its own decisions, it must either re-decide the matter or refer it to the Upper Tribunal. There is generally a right of appeal on a point of law from the First-tier Tribunal to the Upper Tribunal[133] and from the Upper Tribunal to the Court of Appeal.[134] This right is subject to the need for permission from either the First-tier or Upper Tribunal in the case of appeals from the First-tier Tribunal and

128 Tribunals for Users – One System, One Service.

129 Independent Tribunals Service: Complaints, Redress and Tribunals, Cm 6243.

130 Legal aid is not generally available for tribunals because it is considered that representation is not required. Generally each party will bear their own cost before a tribunal and there is no shifting of costs onto the losing party, see *Costs in Tribunals,* Report by the Costs Review Group to the Senior President of Tribunals, December 2011.

131 The exceptions are the employment tribunals and the Employment Appeal Tribunal, because of the nature of the cases that come before them, which involves one party against another, rather than hearing appeals against decisions of the state.

132 Tribunals, Courts and Enforcement Act 2007, sections 9 and 10.

133 Tribunals, Courts and Enforcement Act 2007, section 11.

134 Tribunals, Courts and Enforcement Act 2007, section 13.

from either the Upper Tribunal or the Court of Appeal, where the appeal is from the Upper Tribunal.

Section 10 of the 1992 Act requires tribunals to give reasons for their decisions, with some exceptions, such as national security or where the disclosure of reasons would be contrary to the interests of any person primarily concerned. In reaching a decision tribunals are not bound by precedent but it seems that in many cases they do follow previous decisions.[135]

Section 43 of the 2007 Act established the Administrative Justice and Tribunals Council (AJTC), a replacement for the Council on Tribunals. Its principal functions were to keep under review, and report on, the constitution and working of listed tribunals[136] and statutory inquiries and to keep under review the administrative justice system. As an austerity measure, the AJTC was abolished in 2013[137] and instead an Administrative Justice Forum has been established, an advisory body reporting to the Ministry of Justice. The Public Administration Select Committee strongly questioned the rationale of this decision[138] and it has been suggested that 'the ability to look across the whole administrative justice system and identify ways of improving the experience for citizens has been weakened'.[139]

5. JUDICIAL REVIEW

5.1. GENERAL POINTS

The supervisory jurisdiction of the courts, the power to ensure that public bodies observe the law, fulfil their public duties, and do not act beyond the scope of their powers goes back to medieval times, when the Courts of the Kings Bench at Westminster carried out this task. In the 19th Century this power became vested in the High Court and a branch of that court, the Administrative Court[140], now possesses this important jurisdiction. For the English Court structure, see figure 3.

135 Buck, T., 'Precedent in Tribunals and the Development of Principle' *Civil Justice Quarterly*, 2006, 458.

136 Listed tribunals are the First-tier Tribunal and Upper Tribunals established by the Tribunals, Courts and Enforcement Act 2007 and tribunals listed by orders made by the Lord Chancellor, the Scottish Minister and the Welsh Ministers.

137 Public Bodies (Abolition of Administrative Justice and Tribunals Council) Order 2013/2042.

138 Public Administration Committee, *Future Oversight of Administrative Justice: the Proposed Abolition of the Administrative Justice and Tribunals Council*, 21st Report, 2012.

139 Skelcher, C., 'Reforming the oversight of administrative justice 2010–2014: does the UK need a new Leggatt Report?', *Public Law*, 2015, p.215 at p. 223.

140 The Administrative Court was established in 2000. It consists of judges specializing in administrative law. The change reflected what was already happening in practice, where judicial review cases were given to specialists in the Queen's Bench Division of the High

Figure 3. The English court structure

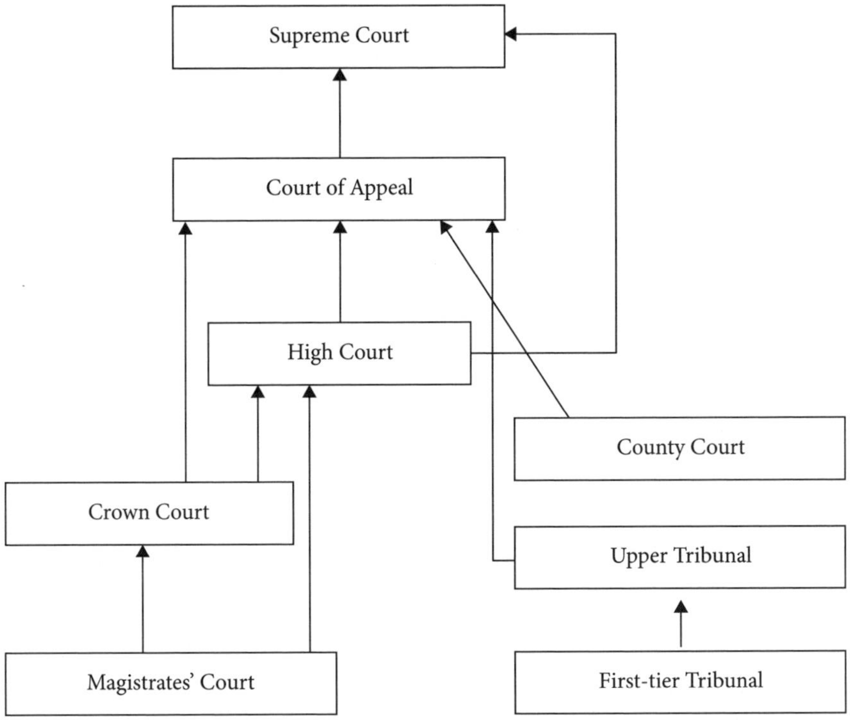

The role of the court is to ensure, by applying the ultra vires doctrine, that administrative bodies are kept within the law. This role is linked to the notion of the separation of powers, requiring the judges to be independent of the executive. The process of judicial review also brings into focus the doctrine of legislative supremacy. This provides the constitutional justification for the courts engaging in judicial review of the exercise of statutory power. In ruling that a particular power has been exceeded, the courts are merely enforcing the will of parliament. This is well illustrated in the following statement from Sir John Donaldson MR in *R* v *Boundary Commission for England, ex parte Foot*:

> 'It is the essence of parliamentary democracy that those to whom powers are given by Parliament shall be free to exercise those powers, subject to constitutional protest and criticism and parliamentary and other democratic control. But any attempt by Ministers or local authorities to usurp powers which they have not got or to exercise their powers in a way which is unauthorised by Parliament is a quite

---

Court. The court sits in London and since 21 April 2009 also in Birmingham, Cardiff, Leeds and Manchester. See Nason, S., Hardy, D. & Sunkin, M., 'Regionalisation of the Administrative Court and Access to Justice', *Juridical Review*, 2010 (15), p. 220.

different matter ... If asked to do so, it is then the role of the courts to prevent this happening'.[141]

There is an important distinction between the role of the courts on *review* and on *appeal*. This distinction was stressed by Lord Hoffman in *Kemper Reinsurance Company* v *Minister of Finance*:

'judicial review is quite different from appeal. It is concerned with legality rather than the merits of the decision ...'.[142]

Likewise, in *R* v *Secretary of State for the Home Department, ex parte Launder*, Lord Hope stated:

'It cannot be stressed too strongly that the decision rests with the Secretary of State and not at all with the court. The function of the court in the exercise of its supervisory jurisdiction is that of review. This is not an appeal against the Secretary of State's decision on the facts'.[143]

Judicial review is a remedy of last resort and so all other possible remedies must first be exhausted. So, for example, if a statute has created an appeal procedure to another executive body, such as from a local authority to a minister, this may affect the availability of judicial review. This is well illustrated by the statement from Lord Scarman in *R* v *Inland Revenue Commissioners, ex parte Preston*:

'... a remedy by way of judicial review is not to be made available where an alternative remedy exists. This is a proposition of great importance. Judicial review is a collateral challenge: it is not an appeal. Where Parliament has provided by statute appeal procedures ... it will only be very rarely that the courts will allow the collateral process of judicial review to attack an appealable decision ...'[144]

Before proceeding further it is necessary to explain the English court structure. The Administrative Court is part of the High Court. If the Administrative Court has granted or refused judicial review at a substantive hearing of the claim there may be an appeal to the Court of Appeal. The Court of Appeal consists of two Divisions, Civil and Criminal, and an appeal would lie to the Civil Division. Permission to appeal is required in judicial review cases. Permission can be sought from the Administrative Court at which the decision to be appealed was made. If the Administrative Court refuses an application for permission to appeal, a further application for permission to appeal can be made to the Court

141 [1983] 2 WLR 458 at 468.
142 [2001] 1 AC 1 at 14–15.
143 [1997] 1 WLR 839 at 847.
144 [1985] AC 835 at 852.

of Appeal. Under the CPR permission to appeal will only be granted if the court considers that the appeal would have a real prospect of success or there is some other compelling reason why the appeal should be heard.[145]

A further appeal may be possible from the Court of Appeal to the Supreme Court[146], but not in respect of a refusal of permission to appeal to the Court of Appeal. An appeal to the Supreme Court must have leave of either that court or the Court of Appeal. It is possible, on very rare occasions, to 'leapfrog' over the Court of Appeal and appeal directly to the Supreme Court[147] A certificate is needed from the High Court judge that the case is suitable for the Supreme Court to hear and the Supreme Court must give leave to appeal. All the parties must consent and the case must be one which involves a point of general public importance about a matter of statutory interpretation or be one where the contentious issue is one on which the Court of Appeal is bound by a precedent of the Court of Appeal or the Supreme Court.

The cost of bringing even a straightforward judicial review claim is estimated to be in the region of £ 10,000 to £ 20,000. If the case is lost, costs are likely to be awarded against the claimant and the legal bill would then be higher.[148] Although in theory claimants can represent themselves in judicial review hearings the complexity of the law in this area means that this does not happen often. Community Legal Service Funding (Legal Aid) is available but this dependent upon the claimant's income and it has become increasingly difficult to obtain.[149]

Under the Civil Procedure Rules (CPR) all courts have an 'overriding objective' of ensuring that courts deal with cases 'justly and at a proportionate cost'. This includes, so far as is practicable:

'(a) ensuring that the parties are on an equal footing;
(b) saving expense;
(c) dealing with the case in ways which are proportionate –
  (i) to the amount of money involved;
  (ii) to the importance of the case;
  (iii) to the complexity of the issues; and
  (iv) to the financial position of each party;
(d) ensuring that it is dealt with expeditiously and fairly;

145 For an example of permission to appeal being granted because of the importance of the issue rather than the prospects of success, see *R (on the application of Ben-Abdelaziz)* v *Haringey London Borough Council* [2001] 1 WLR 1485.

146 Under section 23 of the Constitutional Reform Act 2005 the House of Lords, as the final court of appeal, was replaced by a Supreme Court. The change took place on 1 October 2009.

147 Administration of Justice Act 1969, sections 12–15.

148 See Bondy, V., Platt, L. & Sunkin, M., *The Value and Effects of Judicial Review: The Nature of Claims, their Outcomes and Consequences*, Public Law Project, 2015.

149 See 'How to apply for Legal Aid funding for Judicial Review', *Public Law Project, Short Guide 05*, 2016.

(e) allotting to it an appropriate share of the court's resources, while taking into account the need to allot resources to other cases; and
(f) enforcing compliance with rules, practice directions and orders.'[150]

5.2. FILING A CLAIM FOR JUDICIAL REVIEW

Part 54 of the Civil Procedure Rules (CPR) sets out the means by which a claimant may make a claim to review the lawfulness of an enactment or a decision, action or failure to act in relation to the exercise of a public function.[151]

The claim form must be filed promptly and the general time limit is no later than three months after the grounds to make the claim first arose (CPR 54.5(1)).[152] The leading case on the meaning of these words under the old procedure for judicial review was *R* v *Dairy Produce Quota Tribunal for England and Wales, ex parte Caswell*.[153] In that case the House of Lords made it clear that although ordinarily any application must be made promptly and in any event within three months, where the court was satisfied that there was a good reason for delay, an extension of time could be granted. It is evident from *R (on the application of Melton)* v *School Organization Committee*[154] that the administrative court's procedure under the new Rules is no less rigorous than under the old procedures and that the principles in *Caswell* are still to be followed.

The first hurdle that the claimant must overcome is to get permission from the court to proceed (CPR 54.10–12).[155]

The application for permission to proceed will be considered in one of two ways – on the papers or at an oral hearing in open court. Normally a judge will decide whether to grant permission without hearing oral submissions, so that the matter is dealt with speedily and without unnecessary delay. If permission

150 Civil Procedure Rules (CPR), Rule 1.1.

151 See www.justice.gov.uk/courts/procedure-rules/civil/rules/part54 (accessed 25 July 2017). These rules replaced Order 53 of the Rules of the Supreme Court in December 2000.

152 There are exceptions to the general time limit. Planning law judicial review claims, for example must be made no later than six weeks after the grounds for complaint arose (CPR 54.5(5). See also CPR 54.5(6) and 54.7A for further exemptions. A fee of £ 154 is payable when an application for judicial review is lodged. Generally there are no fees to be paid for bringing a case to a tribunal. There are some exceptions with regard to some immigration cases and a controversial fee system has been introduced for employment tribunals, see *Review of the introduction of fees in the Employment Tribunals: Consultation on proposals for reform*, Ministry of Justice, 2017. In July 2017 the Supreme Court declared that the fee system for employment tribunals was unlawful because it has the effect of preventing access to justice, see *R (on the application of Unison) v Lord Chancellor* [2017] UKSC 51.

153 [1990] 2 WLR 1320.

154 [2001] EWHC (England and Wales, High Court) 245. The case concerned a lack of promptness in challenging school reorganization.

155 If permission is granted and the claim is to be pursued a fee of £ 385 is payable at this stage.

is refused, or is granted subject to conditions or on certain grounds only[156], the claimant may request that the decision be reconsidered at an oral hearing.[157] If permission is still refused, the claimant can appeal within seven days by lodging an application with the Court of Appeal for permission to appeal. At an oral hearing a claimant may appear in person or be represented by Counsel. An oral permission hearing is allocated 30 minutes of court time, unless there are special reasons why this may be insufficient.[158]

In the last few years some important changes have been made to the considerations that the High Court should take into account when deciding whether or not to grant leave. In 2013 the Government announced that it was 'concerned by the use of unmeritous applications of judicial review to delay, frustrate or discourage legitimate executive action.'[159] Amendments were made to the discretion that a judge has under s. 31 of the Senior Courts Act 1981 on whether or not to grant permission by s. 84 of the Criminal Justice and Courts Act 2015. Under the amended s. 31 the High Court is empowered to consider of its own motion whether the outcome for the applicant would have been substantially different if the conduct complained of had not occurred, and it must consider that question if the defendant asks it to do so.[160] If the court considers that it is 'highly likely that the outcome for the applicant would not be substantially different, the court must refuse to grant leave'[161], unless it considers that it would not be appropriate to do so 'for reasons of exceptional public interest'[162] and certifies that this is the case.[163]

5.3. REMEDIES IN JUDICIAL REVIEW

If a claim is upheld, the court has a wide range of discretionary remedies available.[164] There are three orders unique to public law: *quashing order,*

156 In these circumstances the arguments which the claimant can put forward at the substantive hearing will be limited. For example the court may state that there would be no merit in a challenge based on irrationality but that the claim can proceed on the basis of illegality.

157 Such a request must be filed within 7 days after serving of the notification of the decision. However, if permission was refused because the application was' totally without merit', such a request cannot be made (CPR 54.12(7). Totally without merit has been defined broadly and applies to a case that is 'bound to fail' or 'hopeless', *Samia W v Secretary of State for the Home Department* [2016] EWCA Civ 82.

158 *The Administrative Court Judicial Review Guide 2016,* HM Courts & Tribunal Service, 2016 at para. 8.5.

159 *Judicial Review: proposals for further reform*, Cm 8703, para. 7.

160 Senior Courts Act 1981, s. 31(3C).

161 *Ibid*, s. 31(3D).

162 *Ibid*, s. 31(3E).

163 *Ibid*, s. 31(3F).

164 As with granting leave, amendments to s. 31 of the Senior Courts Act 1981 have restricted the discretion available. A court must now refuse to grant relief or make an award of damages where 'it appears to the court to be highly likely that the outcome for the applicant would not

prohibition order and *mandatory order*.[165] A quashing order is issued to an 'inferior court' or a person or body exercising 'judicial' or 'quasi judicial' functions to have its decision quashed. What is an inferior court for this purpose, or whether a person or body exercises powers of a judicial or quasi judicial nature is a question for the High Court to decide. The order of prohibition is used to prevent an inferior court or tribunal from exceeding or continuing to exceed its jurisdiction or infringing the rules of natural justice. An order of prohibition cannot be issued once a final decision has been given. Where a final decision has been made a quashing order would be used. A quashing order and a prohibition order can be granted together, for example to quash a decision already made and to prevent the body from continuing to exceed or abuse its jurisdiction. A mandatory order may be issued to any person or body commanding him or it to carry out some public duty.

In addition, the court may occasionally restrain unlawful action by means of an injunction, or it may simply state what the legal position is, in what is called a declaration. Damages, restitution or recovery of a sum due can be claimed in judicial review, although this is not common and it is not possible to claim damages etc. alone (CPR 54.3(2)).[166] As Baroness Hale observed in *R (Quark Fishing Ltd)* v *Secretary of State for Foreign and Commonwealth Affairs:*

> 'Our law does not recognise a right to claim damages for losses caused by unlawful administrative action (although compensation may sometimes be available to the victims of maladministration). There has to be a distinct cause of action in tort or under the Human Rights Act 1998'.[167]

If the sole reason for the claim was the recovery of damages, then an ordinary private law claim should be brought.

5.4. STANDING

Both at the permission stage and at the hearing of the judicial review, the claimant must be able to show that he has a 'sufficient interest' in the subject

have been substantially different if the conduct complained of had not occurred' (s. 31(2A)). This may be disregard if the court considers it appropriate to do so 'for reasons of exceptional public interest' (s. 31(2B)) and certifies that this is the case (s. 31(2C)).

165 These remedies were previously known as *certiorari, prohibition* and *mandamus.*

166 Section 31(4) of the Senior Courts Act 1981 sets out the circumstances in which the court may award damages etc. in a claim for judicial review. Tribunals have no power to award damages. Effectively a tribunal is being asked whether a departmental or council decision was correct. So for example in a dispute over the payment of social security benefits the appellant will be claiming that a benefit should be paid or should not have been stopped. If the appellant wins the department or council is told that they must start to make the payment etc.

167 [2006] 1 A.C. 529 at para. 96. For a fuller discussion on the position of damages for administrative wrong doing see below at section 6.

matter.[168] This requirement is sometimes justified, somewhat curiously, as a means of weeding out frivolous or vexatious applicants.

The term 'sufficient interest' is not defined. The wider the interpretation given to the term the more people who will be able to challenge decisions, and conversely a narrow interpretation will restrict the number of potential challengers. The parties cannot confer standing by consent[169], but it is not clear to what extent standing is a matter of discretion for the court or is determined according to principles of law.[170]

The leading case on the interpretation of 'sufficient interest' is *Inland Revenue Commissioners* v *National Federation of Self Employed and Small Businesses*[171] where the House of Lords relaxed certain technical restrictions which had for long bedevilled the common law. Lord Diplock noted:

> 'It would ... be a grave lacuna in our system of public law if a pressure group ... or even a public spirited taxpayer, were prevented by outdated technical rules of locus standi from bringing the matter to the attention of the courts to vindicate the rule of law and get the unlawful conduct stopped'.[172]

More recently in *R (Feakins)* v *Secretary of State for the Environment, Food and Rural Affairs* Lord Justice Dyson stated:

> 'In recent years, there has unquestionably been a considerable liberalisation of what is required to found a sufficiency of interest for the purposes of standing'.[173]

This liberal approach has extended to benefit individual claimants[174], groups affected, and public interest challenges.[175]

---

168 This is required by section 31(3) of the Senior Courts Act 1981.

169 See Woolf LJ in *R* v *Secretary of State for Social Services, ex parte Child Poverty Action Group* [1990] 2 QB 540 at 556: 'we make it clear that in our view the question of *locus standi* goes to the jurisdiction of the court ... The parties are not entitled to confer jurisdiction, which the court does not have, on the court by consent'.

170 There are conflicting views as to how much discretion the court has in determining standing. Compare for example Lord Wilberforce in *R* v *Inland Revenue Commissioners, ex parte Self-Employed and Small Businesses Ltd* [1982] AC 617 at 631: 'the test ... of sufficient interest ... does not remove the whole ... question of *locus standi* into the realm of pure discretion' and Watkins LJ in *R* v *Felixstowe Justices, ex parte Leigh* [1987] QB 582 at 598: 'the court has a large measure of discretion in determining whether sufficient interest has been established'.

171 [1982] AC 617.

172 *Ibid.* at 644.

173 [2004] 1 WLR 1761 at para. 21.

174 See, for example, *R* v *Somerset County Council, ex parte Dixon* [1998] Env LR (*Environmental Law Reports)* 111, where an environmentally concerned individual had standing to challenge a grant of planning permission.

175 See, for example, *R* v *Sefton Metropolitan Borough Council, ex parte Help the Aged* [1997] 4 All ER 532, where a charity was able to bring a test case to challenge the way care for the elderly in nursing homes was paid for.

However, notwithstanding such change 'sufficient interest' does have some substantive content, and not every claimant is entitled to judicial review as of right. The balance to be struck was highlighted by Lord Fraser in *Inland Revenue Commissioners* v *National Federation of Self Employed and Small Businesses*:

> 'On what principle, then is sufficiency to be judged? All are agreed that a direct financial or legal interest is not now required ... There is also general agreement that a mere busybody does not have sufficient interest. The difficulty is, in between those extremes, to distinguish between the desire of the busybody to interfere in other people's affairs and the interest of the person affected by or having a reasonable concern with the matter to which the [claim] relates'.[176]

Lack of sufficient interest came to the fore in *R* v *Secretary of State for the Environment, ex parte Rose Theatre Co*[177], where a group of people formed a company to try to stop redevelopment on the site of the former Rose Theatre in London. Schiemann J. held:

> 'Merely to assert that one has an interest does not give one an interest ... The fact that some thousands of people join together to assert that they have an interest does not create an interest if the individuals do not have an interest ... The fact that those without an interest incorporate themselves and give the company in its memorandum power to pursue a particular object does not give the company an interest'.[178]

In practice, however, the courts have become quite liberal in granting standing, particularly where a group appears to be a well-placed challenger in terms of its awareness of the issues involved in the case. So, for example, Otton J in *R* v *Her Majesty's Inspectorate of Pollution, ex parte Greenpeace Ltd*[179] [1994] 4 All ER 329 at 350 granted standing to Greenpeace because it was

> 'an entirely responsible and respected body with a genuine concern for the environment ... [w]ith its particular experience in environmental matters, its access to experts in the relevant realms of science and technology (not to mention law) [it] is able to mount a carefully selected, focused, relevant and well-argued challenge'.

5.5. PUBLIC/PRIVATE DIVIDE

Judicial review operates in the broad context of public law and public bodies. The importance of the distinction between public and private law for judicial

176 [1982] AC 617 at 646.
177 [1990] 1 QB 504.
178 *Ibid.*, at p 521.
179 [1994] 4 All ER 329 at 350.

review came to the fore in the House Lords decision in *O'Reilly* v *Mackman*[180], concerning the vexed question of 'procedural exclusivity'.

The concern of the courts has been that cases which should be dealt with by judicial review, with all the safeguards and benefits that this brings to public bodies, like strict time limits and an expert body of judges, might be side-stepped by challenging governmental decisions by means of an ordinary private law action (for example, an injunction or a declaration). In the *O'Reilly* case their Lordships held that as a general rule proceedings challenging actions by public bodies and asserting public law rights should be commenced by judicial review proceedings, and that to proceed by means of an ordinary action was an abuse of process. The difficulty with this statement has been that it is not at all easy to identify what is a matter of 'public' law or what is a 'public' body: and these problem questions have subsequently taken up much space in both the law reports and in academic journals.[181]

In deciding whether a body is or is not amenable to judicial review the prime focus is not now so much on the status and nature of the decision-making body itself as on the particular function being exercised by that body.[182]

The leading decision on this matter is *R* v *Panel on Takeovers & Mergers, ex parte Datafin plc.*[183] This involved a decision of a non-statutory, unincorporated association, without legal personality. The Takeover Panel was the City of London's self-regulatory body for overseeing the processes of takeovers and mergers. It had no statutory or common law powers, and at first glance it might appear that such a body would not be subject to public law. However, the Panel's important public protection role was recognized and was in fact supported by certain statutory powers. The Court of Appeal concluded that in all the circumstances the Panel should be regarded as subject to judicial review. Sir John Donaldson MR described it as 'performing a public duty' and said that there was a 'public element' to its work. Lloyd LJ asked: was the body 'exercising public law functions' and did the 'exercise of its functions have public law consequences'. If in either case it did, that might be 'sufficient to bring the body within the reach of public law'. This approach can, however, raise as many questions as it answers. What, for example, should be regarded as public law consequences?

Apart from obvious examples of public bodies like local authorities and government departments a wide variety of bodies have been held to be subject

---

180 [1983] 2 AC 237.

181 See for example Woolf, H., 'Public Law – Private Law, Why the Divide?', *Public Law*, 1986, p. 220; Pannick, C., 'Who is subject to Judicial Review and in Respect of What?', *Public Law*, 1992, p. 1; Bamforth, N., 'The Scope of Judicial Review: Still Uncertain', *Public Law*, 1993, p. 239; Fredman, S. & Morris, G.S., 'The Costs of Exclusivity: Public and Private Re-examined,' *Public Law*, 1994, p. 69; Emery, C., 'Public Law or Private Law? – The Limits of Procedural Reform', *Public Law*, 1995, p. 450; De la Mare, T., 'Procedural Exclusivity: Slaying the Procedural Bugbear', *Judicial Review*, 1998, p. 133.

182 Fordham, M., *Judicial Review Handbook*, 6th ed., Oxford: Hart Publishers, 2012, para. 34.1.

183 [1987] QB 815.

to judicial review. These include the Broadcasting Complaints Commission[184], the Advertising Standards Authority[185], the National Trust[186], a privatized water company exercising statutory functions[187] and the Independent Committee supervising premium rate telephone services.[188]

What, then, makes a body public or private for the purposes of judicial review? Some general principles can be drawn from the cases. Bodies whose sole source of power is a consensual (contractual) submission to its jurisdiction will not be susceptible to review. This was noted in *Datafin*, and this view has excluded from judicial review bodies like the Jockey Club[189], the Football Association[190], the Insurance Ombudsman Bureau[191] and the Association of British Travel Agents.[192]

The courts may be influenced by whether or not they believe a statutory body would be established if it were not for the existence of the non-statutory body in question. It was such an underpinning and the belief that if it did not exist the government would have created such a body that influenced some of the judges in *Datafin* to hold the Panel on Takeovers and Mergers reviewable. Conversely, the Chief Rabbi was said not to be susceptible to judicial review because it could not 'be suggested … that … but for his offices the government would impose a statutory regime'.[193] However, the judges' conclusions applying this 'test' are not always consistent, as can be seen in the *Jockey Club* case where Hoffman LJ took the view that if there was no Jockey Club the government would not set up a statutory body, while Sir Thomas Bingham felt that the government would probably be driven to establish such a body!

What the cases show is that there is no universal test applicable to all circumstances. As Lord Justice Dyson has observed:

> 'It seems to me that the law has now developed to the point where, unless the source of the power clearly provides the answer, the question whether the decision of a body is amenable to judicial review requires careful consideration of the nature of the power and function that has been exercised to see whether the decision has

---

184 *R* v *Broadcasting Complaints Commission, ex parte Owen* [1985] QB 1153.

185 *R* v *Advertising Standards Authority, ex parte The Insurance Service Plc* (1990) 2 *Administrative Law Reports* (Admin LR) 77.

186 *Scott* v *National Trust for Places of Historic Interest* [1998] 2 All ER 705.

187 *R* v *Northumbria Water Ltd., ex parte Newcastle and North Tyneside Health Authority* [1999] Env LR 715.

188 *R* v *Independent Committee for the Supervision of Telephone Information Services, ex parte Firstcode Ltd* [1993] COD 325.

189 *R* v *Disciplinary Committee of the Jockey Club, ex parte Aga Khan* [1993] 1 WLR 909.

190 *R* v *Football Association Ltd, ex parte Football League Ltd* [1993] 2 All ER 833.

191 *R* v *Insurance Ombudsman Bureau, ex parte Aegon Life Assurance Ltd* [1993] The Times, 7 January.

192 *R* v *Association of British Travel Agents, ex parte Sunspell Ltd* [2001] Administrative Court Digest (ACD) 88.

193 *R* v *Chief Rabbi, ex parte Wachmann* [1992] 1 WLR 1036 per Simon Brown J at 1041.

> a sufficient public element flavour or character to bring it within the purview of public law. It may be said with some justification that this criterion for amenability is very broad, not to say question-begging. But it provides the framework for the investigation that has to be conducted'.[194]

If trying to establish whether a body is a public body for the purpose of judicial review is hard, trying to determine whether a matter of public law is at issue which must be dealt with by way of judicial review (rather than by private law action) has been described as a 'procedural minefield'. However, Fordham has noted that recent judicial trends indicate that judicial attachment to the principle of 'exclusivity' stated in *O'Reilly* is fast reducing. It aspired at one time to a strictness which proved unworkable and undesirable. It has subsequently become a much more flexible principle, which, in effect, only insists on judicial review where there is some real reason to consider that an ordinary private law form action would involve an abuse of process.[195]

The leading case on whether an issue *must* be challenged by judicial review is now *Clark* v *University of Lincolnshire and Humberside*[196] where the Court of Appeal and Lord Woolf MR in particular, sought to offer some practical guidance. The case concerned a student in dispute with her university over the marking of a paper that she had submitted for her final examination. The work had been given a mark of zero because of plagiarism, although subsequently the university did not give this as the reason for the final mark awarded. The student brought proceedings for breach of contract against the university, alleging that the university had not dealt with the matter properly under the university's regulations. The university sought to have this private law claim in contract stuck out as an abuse of process, claiming that the matter should have been challenged by way of judicial review, and that the time limits for judicial review had expired by the time the private law action had been launched.

The Court of Appeal decided that there was a claim in contract, although the claim would have been brought more appropriately by judicial review. They refused to strike out the claim merely because of the procedure which had been adopted. Lord Woolf emphasized that what is important is that there should be clear evidence of an abuse of process by having sought to have avoided proceedings by way of judicial review, but that this will not *automatically* follow from using the private law procedure. Instead the courts need to be flexible in their approach. What will be important will be whether there has been an unjustified delay in bringing the proceedings by means of an ordinary action when the claim should normally have been made (more promptly) by way of judicial review. The nature of the claim is also relevant. For example, 'if that

194 *R (Beer (t/a Hammer Trout Farm))* v *Hampshire Farmers' Ltd* [2004] 1 WLR 233.

195 Fordham, M., *Judicial Review Handbook*, 6th ed., Oxford: Hart Publishers, 2012, para. 27.3.

196 [2000] 3 All ER 752.

which is being claimed could affect the public generally, the approach of the court will be stricter than if the proceedings only affect the immediate parties'.[197]

5.6. EXCEPTIONS TO 'PROCEDURAL EXCLUSIVITY'

Even when the doctrine of 'exclusivity' was being applied most strongly it was accepted that there were some exceptions to the rule: as noted by Lord Diplock in *O'Reilly*:

> 'there may be exceptions, particularly where the invalidity of the decision arises as a collateral issue in a claim for infringement of a right of the [claimant] arising under private law ...'[198]

The term 'collateral issue', or 'collateral challenge', is used in connection with 'many forms of incidental challenge and has been recognized for over 300 years'.[199] For example, arguments raised by way of defence to a criminal charge, or by way of defence to a demand for some payment. So, for example, in *Wandsworth London Borough Council* v *Winder*[200] a tenant of a council house was able to defend himself, in eviction proceedings for rent arrears, by claiming that the council was acting ultra vires in seeking to evict him and that the rent rise which he had refused to pay was 'illegal'.

The matter was considered by the House of Lords in *Boddington* v *British Transport Police*.[201] According to Lord Steyn:

> 'Since *O'Reilly* ... decisions of the House of Lords have made it clear that the primary focus of procedural exclusivity is situations in which an individual's sole aim was to challenge a public law act or decision. It does not apply in a civil case where an individual seeks to establish private law rights, which cannot be determined without the examination of the validity of a public law decision. Nor does it apply where the defendant in a civil case simply seeks to defend himself by questioning the validity of the public law decision'.[202]

Boddington allowed the defendant to raise as a defence to a criminal charge a contention that a byelaw, or more precisely an administrative decision made pursuant to powers conferred by the bye-law, was ultra vires. The court stated that a defendant would only be prevented from raising such a defence where a

197 [2000] 3 All ER 752 at 761.
198 [1983] 2 AC 237 at 285.
199 Craig, *supra* note 52, p. 760.
200 [1984] 3 All ER 976.
201 [1999] 2 AC 143.
202 [1999] 2 AC 143 at 172.

clear statutory intention indicated that such a challenge could only be made by judicial review, and this was not such a case.

5.7. MATTERS WHICH ARE NOT REVIEWABLE

The courts today are quite reluctant to say that a matter is not justiciable. This was made clear in the words of Simon Brown J in *R* v *Ministry of Defence, ex parte Smith*:

> 'To my mind only the rarest cases today will be ruled strictly beyond the court's purview – only cases involving national security properly so-called and where in addition the courts really do lack the expertise or material to form a judgement on the point at issue'.[203]

As we will see below, the courts have sought to bring even the exercise of wide discretionary power within the ambit of judicial review. Nevertheless, there do exist some matters which are regarded by the courts as unsuitable for review. Lord Roskill in the *GCHQ* case indicated the nature of some prerogative powers and the reasons for their non justiciability:

> '... the making of treaties, the defence of the realm, ... the grant of honours, the dissolution of Parliament, and the appointment of Ministers ... are not, I think, susceptible to judicial review because their nature and subject matter are such as not be amenable to the judicial process. The courts are not the place wherein to determine whether a treaty should be concluded or the armed forces deployed in a particular manner ...'.[204]

As stated above, the courts are sometimes reluctant to engage in close review of decisions which have been justified on the grounds of 'national security'. The courts will require a minimum evidential base to be shown for the decision taken, but will not otherwise intervene. As the *GCHQ* case demonstrated this may have the effect of depriving a claimant of a remedy which the courts might, depending on the evidence and the court's assessment of security considerations, otherwise have granted. In *GCHQ* it was accepted that the employees should have been consulted before their right to belong to a trade union was removed, but ultimately the court refused to grant relief simply because it was satisfied that concern for national security lay behind the decision not to consult.

In some contexts review is not so much excluded but may be simply less intense than is generally the case. This can be illustrated by *R* v *Harrow London*

---

203 [1995] 4 All ER 427 at 446.

204 *Council of Civil Service Unions* v *Minister for the Civil Service* [1985] AC 374 418.

Borough Council, ex parte D[205] where it was held that review of a decision of a council to put the name of a child on its register of children at risk would be rare and exceptional, and only to be undertaken when the decision was wholly unreasonable.

One final area of non justiciability should be considered. This is where parliament may have sought to prevent the courts from engaging in review by its use in the governing legislation of what are called 'ouster' or 'preclusive' clauses.

'Ouster' clauses are a means by which jurisdiction purports to be ousted completely; a 'preclusive' clause allows review but only within a short time frame (e.g. six weeks).

It might be thought that the doctrine of the legislative supremacy of parliament would ensure that the wishes of parliament would be upheld and that ouster provisions would be applied unquestioningly. However, the courts are zealous to preserve their constitutional function of scrutinizing the legality of executive action, and therefore construe such clauses extremely restrictively. In *Anisminic* v *Foreign Compensation Board*[206] the House of Lords held that the Board had acted ultra vires by making an error of law as to its powers, despite the fact that the statute in question, the Foreign Compensation Act 1950, stated that any 'determination' of the Board should not be called into question in 'any proceedings'. The House of Lords reasoned that since the action of the Board was ultra vires, and thus a nullity, there was, in law, no 'determination' to question.

The courts have, however, been distinctly more willing to apply preclusive (i.e. time limit) clauses[207] and it may well prove possible for parliament, with ingenuity, to draft an ouster provision which cannot be evaded by the courts.[208]

The legitimacy of ouster clauses was raised very controversially in the government's attempts to exclude the possibility of judicial review of the Asylum and Immigration Tribunal's decisions by the higher courts in the Asylum and Immigration (Treatment of Claimants, etc.) Bill in 2004. The proposal led to enormous criticism and in the end the government was forced to drop the clause from the Bill in view of the political and judicial protests.[209] The reaction to the ouster clause was a reminder that 'the right of access to justice is a fundamental and constitutional principle of our legal system'[210] and that it should not be given up easily.

---

205 [1990] 3 All ER 12.

206 [1969] 2 AC 147.

207 See for example *R* v *Cornwall County Council, ex parte Huntington* [1992] 3 All ER 526.

208 See for example section 67(8) of the Regulation of Investigatory Powers Act 2000 which provides that 'Except to such extent as the Secretary of State may by order otherwise provide, determinations, awards, orders and other decisions of the Tribunal (including decisions as to whether they have jurisdiction) shall not be subject to appeal or be liable to be questioned in any court.'

209 Rawlings, R., 'Review, Revenge and Retreat', *Modern Law Review*, 2005 (63), p. 378.

210 Lord Steyn in *R* (*Anufrijeva*) v *Secretary of State for the Home Department* [2003] 3 WLR 252.

5.8. LEGITIMATE EXPECTATIONS

Judicial review is not concerned only with the protection of rights. In recent years the concept of *legitimate expectation* 'has increasingly informed the reviewing function of the Court'.[211]

What are legitimate expectations? The *GCHQ* case can perhaps be regarded as a classic example of a legitimate expectations case. The workers in that case had no right to be consulted before their terms of employment were altered, but there was a well-established practice of consultation, such that the workers had a legitimate expectation of being consulted, which would have been protected by the court, but for the fact that in the circumstances of the case the reason for the absence of consultation decision was 'national security'.

According to Wade and Forsyth[212] legitimate expectations can be broadly defined into two groups. Firstly, a procedural expectation 'where a procedure not otherwise required has been promised', as in *GCHQ*. Secondly, where 'what is expected may be a particular or favourable decision by the authority'. This is known as a substantive expectation. The protection afforded by judicial review to substantive expectations is somewhat more limited than that provided for procedural expectations.

The difficulty that some judges find with protecting substantive legitimate expectations is that it sits awkwardly with the rule that a decision-maker should not fetter the exercise of his or her discretion and that decision-makers should not, by such substantive protection be prevented from changing their policies where the public interest may so require.

These concerns are apparent in the Court of Appeal decision in *R* v *Department of Education and Employment, ex parte Begbie*.[213] The case concerned the Secretary of State's refusal to retain a publicly funded assisted place for the applicant child to attend a private school. The school place had been offered under Conservative legislation. However, following the general election in May 1997 the Labour Government abolished the assisted places scheme. Under the new legislation there was some discretion to permit a child to continue with an assisted place if the Secretary of State was satisfied that 'it was reasonable in any particular circumstances', but the child in this case did not benefit from the discretion being exercised in her favour. It was contended by the applicant that the refusal to exercise the discretion in her favour was inconsistent with pre- and post-election promises, and that the Secretary of State had a duty to adhere to such promises because they had given rise to a substantive legitimate

---

211 Fordham, M., *Judicial Review Handbook*, 3rd ed., Oxford: Hart Publishers, 2001, p. 646. See also Knight, C.J., 'Expectations in Transition: Recent Developments in Legitimate Expectations', *Public Law*, 2009, p. 15.

212 Wade & Forsyth, *supra* note 110, p. 457.

213 [2000] 1 WLR 1115.

expectation. However, judicial review was refused because '[i]t is common ground that any expectation must yield to the terms of the statute under which the Secretary of State is required to act'[214] and the Secretary of State had to act in accordance with section 2 of the Education (Schools) Act 1997. Moreover, his exercise of discretion could not be fettered by holding that he was bound by pre-election promises.

In *Thoburn* v *Sunderland City Council* it was made clear that no legitimate expectation could arise solely from a statement in parliament giving a false impression as to the effect of a Bill.[215]

Not all claims to protection of substantive expectations are, however, unsuccessful. A case which illustrates such an expectation being protected is *R* v *North and East Devon Health Authority, ex parte Coughlan*[216], concerning long-term care arrangements for a woman with severe physical handicaps. Because the council had promised the woman that the 'home' she was in would be her permanent home, a substantive legitimate expectation arose which the council could only depart from if there was an 'overriding public interest', which did not exist here because of the small numbers to whom such assurances had been given. The Court of Appeal took time to consider the court's role where what is at issue is a promise by a public body as to how it would behave in the future, when exercising a statutory function:

> 'Policy being (within the law) for the public authority alone, both it and the reasons for adopting or changing it will be accepted by the courts as part of the factual data – in other words, as not ordinarily open to judicial review. The court's task … is then limited to asking whether the application of the policy to the individual who has been led to expect something different is a just exercise of power'.[217]

The court placed great emphasis on fairness, and considered that it would be an abuse of process if the authority were allowed to go back on its promise.

5.9. GROUNDS FOR JUDICIAL REVIEW

Lord Diplock in *GCHQ* classified the broad grounds of judicial review under three main headings: *illegality* (unlawfulness), *irrationality* (unreasonableness) and *procedural impropriety* (unfairness).

This has become an accepted starting point for a consideration of the grounds for review. However, it is important to appreciate that Lord Diplock's formulation was a distillation of a great many legal principles developed on a

214 *Ibid.* at 1125.
215 [2003] QB 151 at para. 76, per Lord Justice Laws.
216 [2000] 3 All ER 850.
217 *Ibid.* per Lord Woolf at 880.

case-by-case basis over a good many years. His trilogy are not in themselves grounds of review, they are merely convenient headings within which to describe a more complex web of potentially successful lines of challenge.

5.9.1. Illegality

This ground is concerned with ensuring that power has in substance been exercised as permitted by parliament or the common law. It is a ground that would be relatively simple if it were not for the granting of discretionary powers to public bodies. When parliament gives a discretionary power to a Minister or a local authority how can the exercise of that power be illegal? If a local authority has a power to act 'as it sees fit' how can this be questioned? The task for the court in this situation is to seek to apply what is perceived to be the intent and purpose inherent in the legislative scheme: and this may expressly or impliedly limit the scope of discretion afforded to the recipient of the power in its exercise of the statutory discretion. This is by no means a straightforward task and much may turn, context by context, on judicial perceptions as to what are the proper limits of judicial intervention.

The most famous case on the exercise of discretion is *Associated Provincial Picture Houses* v *Wednesbury Corporation*.[218] This case has become well known for Lord Greene MR's classic statement on the review of the exercise of discretionary powers: what have become known as the 'Wednesbury principles'. The case concerned a statutory power to license Sunday entertainment, which permitted local authorities to attach such conditions as they sought fit. Wednesbury Corporation granted a license to a company to open cinemas on Sundays but imposed a condition prohibiting the admission of children under the age of 15. When this condition was challenged the Corporation argued that it was legitimate for it to have taken the moral welfare of children into account.

The Court of Appeal, on appeal from the High Court, concluded that the Corporation had acted within its powers and in doing so Lord Greene indicated that the exercise of discretion could not be questioned if the following principles were observed:

> 'The exercise of such a discretion must be a real exercise of discretion. If, in the statute conferring the discretion, there is to be found, expressly or by implication, matters which the authority exercising that discretion ought to have regard, then in exercising that discretion, it must give regard to those matters ... [and] disregard irrelevant collateral matters ... Bad faith, dishonesty ...unreasonableness, attention given to extraneous circumstances, disregard of public policy...'.[219]

218 [1947] 2 All ER 680.
219 *Ibid.* at 682.

What is clear is that when a public body is exercising discretion it must take into account all relevant matters and disregard irrelevancies.[220] What, though, are relevant considerations? The answer appears to depend upon the court's construction of the whole purpose and scheme of the legislation. In *Roberts* v *Hopwood*[221], a local council was held to have acted unlawfully in taking other than economic factors into account in setting the wage rate for its workforce. The council had decided to grant its employees a pay increase, which was considerably higher than inflation, and which did not take account of the sex of the employee or the nature of the work done. The House of Lords concluded that the council had been guided, in the words of Lord Atkinson, by 'eccentric principles of socialist philanthropy, or by feminist ambition to secure the equality of the sexes in the matter of wages' which was an irrelevant consideration.[222] What the council had a legal duty to take into account, and what it had failed to do, was the burden of the wage increase upon the ratepayer. Their decision, therefore, was unlawful.

A more recent example of taking into account irrelevancies can be seen in *R* v *Secretary of State for the Home Department, ex parte Venables*[223], which concerned the tariff, set by the Home Secretary for two boys aged ten, who were convicted of the murder of a two year old boy. The trial judge had recommended that the boys should spend some eight years in detention, which the Lord Chief Justice[224] had subsequently suggested to the Home Secretary should be increased to ten years. However, following a public petition, a newspaper campaign, and the receipt of many letters, the Home Secretary used his statutory discretion to impose a sentence of 15 years. The majority in the House of Lords concluded that taking into account public feeling about the length of sentence was irrelevant and unlawful and affirmed the decision of the Court of Appeal to quash the decision of the Home Secretary.

In reality, when reaching a decision, many decision-makers will be found to have taken into account both relevant and irrelevant considerations. Does this mean that the decision is ultra vires? This has been considered in several cases and several different tests have at different times emerged. The issue has been described by one commentator as a 'legal porcupine bristling with difficulties'. The better view is that the test to be applied is the one found in *R* v *Broadcasting Complaints Commission, ex parte Owen*[225] and *R* v *Inner London*

---

220 This was reiterated by the House of Lords in *R* (*on the application of Alconbury Developments Ltd*) v *Secretary of State for the Environment Transport and the Regions* [2001] 2 WLR 1389.

221 [1925] AC 578.

222 *Ibid.* at 594.

223 [1997] 3 All ER 97.

224 The Lord Chief Justice is the senior permanent judge in the country. His main functions are to preside over the Queen's Bench Division and the criminal work of the Court of Appeal. In cases where defendants are sentenced to life imprisonment he must advise on how long defendants should serve before they become eligible for parole.

225 [1985] 2 All ER 522.

Education Authority, ex parte Westminster City Council[226]: Did the unauthorized purpose or the irrelevant considerations materially influence the final decision of the decision-maker? Only if it may have exerted a material influence will the ultimate decision be unlawful and be quashed.

This brings us to another important element of the Wednesbury principles, which is that power must be exercised for a proper purpose. Clearly there is a strong link between 'proper purpose' and 'relevance' of considerations taken into account. This can be seen, for example, in *R* v *Ealing London Borough Council, ex parte Times Newspapers Ltd*[227] where a local authority banned some of the publications of the Times Newspaper group from their libraries. The action was aimed at providing encouragement and support for some dismissed print workers of Times Newspapers, who were engaged in a long and bitter industrial dispute, which had attracted a lot of political support. The main reason for the ban was to hurt the newspaper group. The authority had a duty under the Public Libraries and Museums Act 1964 to provide a 'comprehensive and efficient library service ... and for that purpose ... to provide ... books and other materials ... as may be requisite'. It was held that the ban was inspired by political views and that the use of the statutory powers for such a purpose could not have been within the contemplation of parliament. The case can equally be explained on the basis that in deciding to ban the publications from the library irrelevant considerations had been taken into account, namely that the publishing group was involved in the industrial dispute.

5.9.2. Irrationality

Irrationality is sometimes referred to as 'perversity', or as Lord Greene MR termed it, 'unreasonableness'. There has been some inconsistency over the terminology used. Sir John Donaldson in the Court of Appeal in *R* v *Secretary of State for the Environment, ex parte Hammersmith and Fulham London Borough Council*[228] described irrationality as not only including Wednesbury unreasonableness but also situations where the decision-maker had failed to have regard to relevant matters or used the powers in a way that would frustrate the purposes of the enabling Act. This was not the approach taken by Lord Bridge in the House of Lords, who adopted the more conventional categorization – confining the concept of 'irrationality' to its narrow meaning of unreasonableness.

Wade and Forsyth have expressed their dissatisfaction with the term 'irrationality', preferring to refer to the principle of reasonableness.[229] In

226 [1986] 1 All ER 19.
227 [1987] Industrial Relations Law Reports (IRLR) 129.
228 [1990] 3 WLR 898.
229 Wade & Forsyth, *supra* note 110, p. 295.

R v *Devon County Council, ex parte G* Lord Donaldson MR expressed his dissatisfaction also with the term on the basis that it is 'widely misunderstood by politicians ... and even more by their constituents, as casting doubt on the mental capability of the decision-maker'.[230]

The difficulty, whatever term is used, is to define what it means. How does a court decide whether a body has acted irrationally or unreasonably? There appear to be two possible approaches to this question. Firstly, the decision-maker may have considered all the right considerations and disregarded all the irrelevant considerations and yet a court may still conclude that the ultimate decision is irrational in that it bears no relation to those considerations. Alternatively, the court may conclude that whatever considerations may appear to have been taken into account, the final decision is so unreasonable in relation to those considerations that the decision-maker must in fact have been motivated by other considerations. Both of these approaches are consistent with Lord Greene's statement in Wednesbury. In *R* v *Chief Constable of Sussex, ex parte International Trader's Ferry Ltd*, Lord Cooke expressed his own discontent with the development of this ground of challenge, indicating a preference for what he termed a 'simple test', 'whether the decision in question was one which a reasonable authority could reach'.[231]

More recently in the important House of Lords decision of *R* v *Secretary of State for the Home Department ex parte Daly*, Lord Cooke observed:

> 'And I think the day will come when it will be more widely recognised that the *Wednesbury* case was an unfortunately retrogressive decision in English administrative law, in so far as it suggested that there are degrees of unreasonableness, and that only a very extreme degree can bring an administrative decision within the legitimate scope of judicial invalidation. The depth of judicial review and the deference due to administrative discretion vary with subject matter. It may well be, however, that the law can never be satisfied in any administrative field merely by a finding that the decision under review is not capricious or absurd'.[232]

What does this mean for irrationality as a ground of review? What is clear now is that there is a

> 'sliding scale of review, more or less intrusive according to the nature and gravity of what is at stake ... The more the decision challenged lies in what may inelegantly be called the macro-political field, the less intrusive will be the court's supervision'.[233]

230 [1989] AC 573 at 577.
231 [1999] 1 All ER 129 at 157.
232 [2001] 3 All ER 433 at 442.
233 *R* v *Department of Law for Education and Employment, ex parte Begbie* [2000] 1 WLR 1115, per Laws LJ at 1130.

This can be best illustrated by *R* v *Ministry of Defence, ex parte Smith*[234], which reviewed the then Ministry of Defence policy that homosexuals should not be permitted to serve in the armed forces. A number of ex-service men and women who had been discharged from the services because of their sexual orientation sought judicial review of this policy, on the ground of irrationality. Ultimately the policy was upheld by the Court of Appeal, but Sir Thomas Bingham MR explained this 'sliding scale' approach:

> 'The greater the policy content of a decision, and the more remote the subject matter of a decision from the ordinary judicial experience, the more hesitant the court must necessarily be in holding a decision to be irrational. That is good law and, like most good law, common sense. Where decisions of a policy-laden, esoteric or security based nature are in issue, even greater caution than normal must be shown in applying the test, but the test itself is sufficiently flexible to cover all situations'.[235]

Context is clearly important and therefore there is not too much value in trying to draw many general lessons from findings of irrationality. However, a few examples of cases will serve to give a flavour. In *R (on the application of Wagstaff)* v *Secretary of State for Health*[236] it was held to be irrational in all of the circumstances for an inquiry investigating how Dr Shipman, a general practitioner, had murdered so many of his patients, to sit in private. Dr Shipman was convicted of 15 counts of murder and was perhaps responsible for the deaths of many more. As the inquiry was to consider how he had managed to kill so many of his patients without any suspicions being aroused by those in authority, it was unreasonable for it to be heard in private. In *R* v *Secretary of State for the Home Department, ex parte Bostanci*[237] a freelance interpreter in the Turkish language was not permitted to interpret on behalf of an asylum seeker undergoing an asylum interview because her father was a well-known Turkish political activist. The immigration officers feared that she might encounter asylum seekers who did not support her father's political beliefs and who might therefore be fearful of her. However, this decision was found to be irrational. There was no evidence at all that the daughter shared the perceived political views of her father, or that asylum seekers would be aware of who she was. In *R (on the application of B)* v *Worcestershire County Council*[238] a local authority's decision to close a day care centre, without having conducted a detailed analysis of whether the needs of its service users could be met at other centres, was said to be irrational.

---

234 [1996] 1 All ER 257.

235 *Ibid.* at 264.

236 [2001] 1 WLR 292.

237 [1999] *Immigration Appeal Reports* (Imm AR) 411.

238 [2009] All ER (D) 51 (Apr).

An important recent debate in the context of review of discretionary powers has been whether or not 'disproportionality' should be considered a ground for review. Proportionality is well established in the administrative law jurisprudence of continental Europe and is one of the general principles of EC law. Nevertheless, the English courts have treated the principle with some great caution and suspicion.[239]

In *GCHQ* Lord Diplock, in setting out the grounds for review, indicated that he thought the principle might at some point be adopted as a ground of review. However, in *Brind* v *Secretary of State for the Home Department*[240] the House of Lords clearly rejected the argument put forward that the courts could strike out the actions of a decision-maker simply because they were 'disproportionate'. So to do, it was feared, would involve the courts in inquiring too nearly into the *merits* of the decision. It has, however, been argued that there is no need to introduce proportionality into English law because where a decision is disproportionate it is also likely to be irrational. This argument was put forward by Lord Donaldson MR in the Court of Appeal decision in *Brind*.

Does proportionality amount to an assessment of the merits of a decision, and involve the court deciding the issue as if it, and not the administrators, was the recipient of the statutory power? It has been explained that this is to misunderstand the concept. 'The short answer to that question is no. Judges are not being set free to second-guess administrators on the merits of their policies'.[241] However, there appears to be no clear understanding of how a doctrine of review for disproportionality might operate. Woolf, Jowell and Le Sueur have observed that 'under proportionality different margins of appreciation apply in different circumstances. Varying levels of intensity of review will be appropriate in different categories of case and this will, in turn, correspond to the different formulas of the test'.[242] This means that the test is adapted to meet the needs of the situation. Where, for example, fundamental rights are at issue the margin of appreciation will be lower and the intensity of review at its greatest. Wade and Forsyth note: 'In the adoption of a context-sensitive or relative approach to necessity we may note a proper reluctance for the test of proportionality to destroy the distinction between merits and review'.[243]

Where does 'proportionality' as a ground of review stand at present? It seems not at all out of the question that in the not too distant future proportionality

---

239 The English courts have applied proportionality in respect of directly effective EU law, see for example *R* v *Chief Constable of Sussex, ex parte International Trader's Ferry Ltd* [1999] 1 All ER 129 and *R* v *Secretary of State for Health, ex parte Eastside Cheese Co* [2000] EHLR (*Environmental Health Law Reports)* 52.

240 [1991] 1 All ER 720.

241 Jowell, J., 'Beyond the Rule of Law: Towards Constitutional Judicial Review', *Public Law*, 2000, p. 671–681.

242 De Smith, S.A., Woolf, H.K., Jowell, J.L. & Le Sueur, A.P., *De Smith, Woolf and Jowell's Principles of Judicial Review*, London: Sweet & Maxwell, 1999, p. 509.

243 Wade & Forsyth, *supra* note 110, p. 315.

may be fully accepted as a ground for review.[244] The Human Rights Act 1998 has meant that the English courts now have to think about proportionality on a more regular basis.

Their gradual 'acclimatization' to the concept can also be seen in a case like *Daly*, where the House of Lords reviewed the distinction between irrationality and proportionality. The case involved a challenge to a blanket policy of searching legal correspondence in prison cells in the prisoners' absence. Although their Lordships applied ordinary principles of judicial review they also considered whether or not the impact of the Secretary of State's decision was disproportionate. Applying either approach the Secretary of State's policy was found to be unlawful. It was noted that although most cases would be decided in the same way whichever approach was adopted, the differences in approach could sometimes yield different results, because the intensity of review is rather greater under the 'proportionality' approach. Lord Steyn indicated that there were at least three significant differences with the approaches:

> 'First, the doctrine of proportionality may require the reviewing court to assess the balance which the decision maker has struck, not merely whether it is within the range of rational or reasonable decisions. Secondly, the proportionality test may go further than the traditional ground of review in as much as it may require attention to be directed to the relative weight accord to interests and considerations. Thirdly, even the heightened scrutiny developed in [*ex parte Smith*] is not necessarily appropriate to the protection of human rights ... the intensity of review, in similar cases, is guaranteed by the twin requirements that the limitation of the right was necessary in a democratic society ... and the question whether the interference was really proportionate to the legitimate aim being pursued'.[245]

The court was, however, very keen to stress that whatever approach is taken there will be no shift to *merit* review and that the respective roles of 'judge' and 'administrator' will remain fundamentally distinct.

5.9.3. Procedural Impropriety

'Procedural impropriety' is an expression which covers two areas of review: (i) procedural *ultra vires* – where a body fails to comply with express statutory procedural requirements, and (ii) the common law rules of natural justice.

Some express procedural requirements are said by the courts to be 'mandatory', and non-compliance will then result in the decision or action taken being void. However, where the requirement is categorized as merely 'directory' the decision will normally stand. Typical examples of procedural *ultra vires* would be where a decision-maker fails to comply with an obligation to

244 See Olley, K., 'Proportionality at Common Law', *Judicial Review*, 2004, p. 197.

245 [2001] 3 All ER 433 at 446.

consult before he makes his decision, or gives no reasons for a decision despite a statutory requirement to do so.

R v *Secretary of State for Social Services, ex parte Association of Metropolitan Authorities*[246] is a good illustration both of procedural *ultra vires* and the problems that may be encountered in trying to grant an effective remedy. The case concerned a duty to consult the Association before making regulations. The Secretary of State had made some effort to consult but the conclusion of the court was that in all the circumstances there was not sufficient consultation to meet the statutory obligations. However, although the judge was willing to grant a declaration to the effect that the Secretary of State had failed to consult, he refused to exercise his discretion to revoke the regulations. A variety of reasons were given, including the procedural rather than substantive nature of the challenge, the fact that other bodies which should have been consulted had not complained, and most importantly because the regulations had been applied nationally for several months before then being consolidated in what were now clearly valid regulations. The administrative burden on local authorities of having to re-open benefit cases in respects of those earlier months was clearly very influential in respect of the decision to decline to revoke the regulations.

Apart from express statutory procedural requirements the *common law* sometimes implies procedural standards into certain types of action or decision-making. The standards that have been implied have historically been known as the principles of natural justice and they have been encapsulated in two Latin maxims: *audi alterem partem* and *nemo judex in causa sua potest*: hear both sides and do so in the absence of apparent bias.

In the early part of the 20th Century these principles were only applicable where the body under review was engaged in adjudicatory functions. This involved the courts in the difficult task of having to try to classify functions as either 'judicial' or 'administrative'. However, in 1965, in *Ridge* v *Baldwin*[247], the House of Lords declared (reverting to older doctrine) that instead of concentrating on the classification of functions, the courts should look to the effect of what was being done. If what was being done was affecting a person's rights then the body was acting under a duty to act judicially and should therefore act in accordance with the principles of natural justice. This proposition has since been extended to include decisions affecting legitimate expectations as well as those affecting rights.[248]

In recent times procedural impropriety has become synonymous with the notion of 'procedural fairness'. In general terms, what does fairness require? Firstly, there must be an absence of apparent bias in the decision-making process. Clearly where a person has a direct pecuniary interest in a decision

246 [1986] 1 WLR 1.

247 [1963] 2 All ER 66.

248 See *supra* para. 5.8.

he should not take part in it. The leading authority on this point remains the old case of *Dimes* v *Grand Junction Canal Properties*[249], which was recently applied and clarified in *R* v *Bow Street Metropolitan Stipendiary Magistrates, ex parte Pinochet Ugarte (No 2)*, a case actually concerning non-pecuniary direct interest.[250] *Pinochet* involved a House of Lords judge who had sat as part of a judicial panel determining whether or not the ex Head of State of Chile was immune from extradition. Following the decision that Pinochet was eligible to be extradited it was discovered that the judge, Lord Hoffman, was a director of a charitable company which had links to Amnesty International, which was an intervening party in the case, and the decision was challenged by Pinochet on the ground of bias. Should Lord Hoffman have sat on the case? The House of Lords concluded that he should not, given the very close links between the two organizations and 'that there must be a rule which automatically disqualifies a judge who is involved, whether personally or as a director, in promoting the same causes in the same organization as is a party to the suit'.[251]

Lord Bingham summed up the position on automatic disqualification in *Davidson* v *Scottish Ministers*:

> '[A] judge will be disqualified from hearing a case (whether sitting alone, or as a member of a multiple tribunal) if he or she has a personal interest which is not negligible in the outcome, or is a friend or relation of a party or witness, or is disabled by personal experience from bringing an objective judgement to bear on the case in question. Where a feature of this kind is present, the case is usually categorized as one of actual bias. But the expression is not a happy one, since "bias" suggests malignity or overt partiality, which is rarely present. What disqualifies the judge is the presence of some factor which could prevent the bringing of an objective judgement to bear, which could distort the judge's judgement'.[252]

The test to be applied where no actual bias is proved but there is an allegation of *apparent* bias is to be found in Lord Hope's speech in the House of Lords decision in *Porter* v *Magill*[253], which supported, with modifications, the formulation put forward by the Court of Appeal in *In re Medicaments and Related Classes of Goods (No 2)*:

> 'The court must first ascertain all the circumstances which have a bearing on the suggestion that the Judge was biased. It must then ask whether those circumstances would lead a fair-minded and informed observer to conclude that there was a real possibility, or a real danger, the two being the same, that the tribunal was biased... The court does not have to rule whether the explanation should be accepted or

249 (1852) 3 *House of Lords Cases* (HL Cas) 759 HL.
250 [1999] 1 All ER 577.
251 *Ibid.* per Lord Browne-Wilkinson at 588.
252 2004 *Scots Law Times* 895 at para. 6.
253 [2002] AC 357.

rejected. Rather it has to decide whether or not the fair-minded observer would consider that there was a real danger of bias notwithstanding the explanation advanced'.[254]

Lord Hope said of the test:

> 'It represents in clear and simple language a test which is in harmony with the objective test which the Strasbourg court applies when it is considering whether the circumstances give rise to reasonable apprehension of bias. It removes any possible conflict with the test which is now applied in most Commonwealth countries and in Scotland. I would delete however from it the reference to "a real danger". Those words no longer serve a useful purpose here, and they are not used in the jurisprudence of the Strasbourg court. The question is whether the fair-minded and informed observer, having considered the facts, would conclude that there was a real possibility that the tribunal was biased'.

A fundamental aspect of procedural fairness is the 'right to be heard'. However, what a fair hearing actually must comprise in order to be fair varies according to circumstances. The concept of a formal courtroom type hearing, with procedures to match, is by no means always essential, 'all that is required is that [the hearing] must be fair to all those who have an interest in the decision'.[255] It is clear that normally a person should be told the case against him, as illustrated by Lord Morris' dictum in *Ridge* v *Baldwin*:

> 'It is well established that the essential requirements of natural justice at least include that before someone is condemned he is to have an opportunity of defending himself, and in order that he may do so that he is to be made aware of the charges or allegations or suggestions which he has to meet ... My Lords, here is something which is basic to our system: the importance of upholding it transcends the significance of any particular case'.[256]

It is obvious also that a person needs to be given notice in reasonable time of the case against him.[257]

To what extent is legal representation at a hearing required? Procedural fairness does not as a matter of course encompass a right to be represented, legally or otherwise. Whether a person is entitled to be represented depends

---

254 [2001] 1 WLR 700.

255 *Bushell* v *Secretary of State for the Environment* [1980] 2 All ER 608, per Lord Diplock at 612–613.

256 [1963] 2 All ER 66 at 102. It should be noted that where national security is an issue these standards of procedural fairness may be modified, as was made clear in *R* v *Secretary of State for the Home Department, ex parte Hosenball* [1977] 3 All ER 452.

257 See for example *R* v *Secretary of State for Education and Employment, ex parte National Union of Teachers* 14 July 2000, unreported, where four days notice was found to be wholly insufficient.

on the circumstances of the case, as was made clear in *R* v *Board of Prisoners of HM Prison, the Maze, ex parte Hone* where Lord Goff declared 'though the rules of natural justice may require legal representation before a board of visitors [the prison disciplinary body], I can see no basis for [the] ... submission that they should do so in every case as of right. Everything must depend on the circumstances of the particular case'.[258]

The last aspect of procedural fairness to consider, and one which has assumed greater importance in recent times is whether there is a duty to state reasons for a decision. The advantages and disadvantages of the provision of reasons were very clearly articulated by the Privy Council[259] in *Stefan* v *General Medical Council*:

> 'The advantages ... relate to the decision making process, in strengthening that process itself, in increasing the public confidence in it, and in the desirability of the disclosure of error where error exists. They relate also to the parties immediately affected by the decision, in enabling them to know the strengths and weaknesses of their respective cases, and to facilitate appeal where that course is appropriate. But there are also dangers and disadvantages in a universal requirement to give reasons. It may impose an undesirable legalism into areas where a high degree of informality is appropriate and add to delay and expense'.[260]

It is certainly the case that many individual statutes do impose a clear requirement to give reasons, and where this is so this obligation must be complied with.[261] What, though, is the position where there is no such express obligation imposed?

At first sight it might seem strange that the courts could claim a decision-maker was acting illegally for failing to state its reason when under no express obligation to do so. However, the courts have been quite inventive in this area. In *Padfield* v *Minister of Agriculture, Fisheries and Food* Lord Reid stated:

> 'It was argued that the Minister is not bound to give reasons for refusing to refer a complaint to the committee, that if he gives no reasons his decisions cannot be questioned, and that it would be unfortunate if giving reasons put him in a worse position. But I do not agree that a decision cannot be questioned if no reasons are given. It is the Minister's duty not to act so as to frustrate the policy and objects of

---

258 [1988] 1 All ER 321 at 327.

259 In this context the Privy Council is a court composed of the Justices of the Supreme Court. It is the final court of appeal for some Commonwealth countries and it also hears appeals from a number of professional disciplinary bodies.

260 [1999] 1 WLR 1293 at 1300. See also Justice-All Souls, Administrative Justice: Some Necessary Reforms, Oxford, 1988, Chapter 3 and *R* v *Higher Education Funding Council, ex parte Institute of Dental Surgery* [1994] 1 WLR 242.

261 It should be noted that where there is a duty to give reasons, the reasons do not have to be in writing, see *R* v *Criminal Injuries Compensation Board, ex parte Moore* [1999] 2 All ER 90.

> the Act, and if it appears from all the circumstances ... that that has been the effect of the Minister's refusal, then it appears to me that the court must be entitled to Act'.[262]

Lord Upjohn went further:

> '... if he does not give any reasons for his decision it may be, if the circumstances warrant it, that a court may be at liberty to come to the conclusion that he had no good reason for reaching that conclusion'.[263]

More recent decisions would seem to indicate that the law may be moving towards a general duty to give reasons in certain, as yet not closely defined, contexts or circumstances. The Court of Appeal in *R* v *Civil Service Appeal Board, ex parte Cunningham*[264] acknowledged that the common law imposed no general duty to give reasons. However, it did conclude that a public body, carrying out judicial functions, such as determining whether or not a dismissal was fair, was required to give reasons. In *R* v *Secretary of State for the Home Department, ex parte Doody*[265] the House of Lords went further. The case concerned the rights of mandatory life sentence prisoners to make representations about, and to know the reasons for, the determination of the tariff element of their sentences, as decided by the Home Secretary. Their Lordships were unanimous in their decision that the Minister was under a duty to give reasons. This view was reached on two alternative grounds. Firstly, the more orthodox ground that in order to challenge the Home Secretary's decision effectively by judicial review, reasons were required to determine the legality of the decision. The alternative ground was to 'ask simply: Is refusal to give reasons fair. I would answer without hesitation that it is not ...'.[266]

Whilst there is still no general, across the board, duty placed upon administrators to give reasons we may conclude with the words of the Privy Council in *Stefan*:

> 'The trend of the law has been towards an increased recognition of the duty upon decision-makers of many kinds to give reasons. This trend is consistent with current developments towards an increased openness in matters of government and administration. But the trend is proceeding on a case by case basis... There is certainly a strong argument for the view that what were once seen as exceptions to a rule may now be becoming examples of the norm, and the cases where reasons are not required may be taking on the appearance of exceptions'.[267]

262 [1968] 1 All ER 694 at 701.
263 *Ibid.* at 719.
264 [1991] 4 All ER 310.
265 [1993] 3 All ER 92.
266 *Ibid.*, per Lord Mustill at 110.
267 [1999] 1 WLR 1293 at 1300–1301.

6. LIABILITY OF PUBLIC AUTHORITIES

It is important to note that under English law there is no remedy in damages for a breach of a public law right *per se*. Over the years strong arguments have been put forward as to why damages should be payable for administrative wrongdoing but no change to the law has resulted.[268] This has been viewed by some as a sign of immaturity in the legal system.[269]

Through the ombudsman system compensation may be obtained for maladministration but any payments are made *ex gratia* and the ombudsmen have no power to order payment. Compensation will be recommended where it seems that the maladministration has caused injustice to the complainant of such a kind that compensation is an appropriate remedy. However, the recommendation of compensation is not automatic and often other remedies are considered more appropriate, such as the substitution of a fresh decision.

Where a right to damages seems to exist under private law (e.g. for a commission of a tort, a breach of contract, or under the law of restitution) it is possible to include that claim for damages, debt or restitution in judicial review proceedings, but it is not possible to seek such a remedy alone under CPR 54.3 (2). Moreover:

> 'In practice, where there is a claim for damages as part of an otherwise appropriate claim for judicial review, the claim for damages would normally be left over to be dealt with as a discrete issue, if still relevant, after the main issue of public law had been determined. Even if dealt with under CPR Part 54, rather than transferred out of the Administrative Court, it would still generally be subject to directions bringing it broadly into line with a damages claim commenced in the normal way'.[270]

If judicial review has been sought solely to underpin a claim for damages, the claim is likely to be rejected. That is because it is considered wrong to invoke the Administrative Court's jurisdiction 'to establish that which not only can, but can more conveniently, be established elsewhere'.[271]

In the absence of 'a much-needed statutory or public law solution' to the problem of monetary remedies, 'claims for reparation have to fit within established causes or rights of action'.[272] Claims for damages for breach of contract can be and are brought against public bodies in the ordinary way.

---

268 See for example Justice/All Souls Report, *Administrative Justice: Some Necessary Reforms*, Oxford: Clarendon Press, 1988, chapter 11.

269 Fordham, M., 'Reparation for Maladministration: Public Law's Final Frontier', *Judicial Review*, 2003, p. 104.

270 Per Richard J in *R* (*Kurdistan Workers Party*) v *Secretary of State for the Home Department* [2002] EWHC 644 (Admin) at para. 87.

271 *R* v *Northavon District Council, ex parte Palmer* (1994) Admin LR 195.

272 Fordham, *supra* note 182, p. 284.

In principle a public body is also liable in tort. The extent to which public authorities are liable in negligence in the way that they perform their duties is a matter of considerable judicial debate and is too big a subject to be considered here.[273] Public authorities can also be liable for torts such as nuisance, false imprisonment, occupier's liability and defamation. One tort of particular note is misfeasance in public office. This tort was considered in detail by the House of Lords in *Three Rivers Council* v *Governor and Company of the Bank of England (No 3)*.[274] The case concerned the Bank of England's supervision of the Bank of Credit and Commerce International (BCCI). According to Lord Steyn the 'rationale of the tort is that in a legal system based on the rule of law executive or administrative power may only be exercised for the public good and not for ulterior and improper purposes'.[275] The ingredients of the tort are: (1) the defendant must be a public officer; (2) there must be an exercise of power as a public officer; (3) the state of mind of the defendant must demonstrate either targeted malice on the part of the public officer or that the officer acts knowing that he has no power to do the act complained of and that it will probably injure the claimant; (4) provided that the claimant has sufficient interest to sue, there is no separate requirement of proximity; (5) causation is a necessary element of the claimant's cause of action; and (6) any claims are in respect of actually foreseen or probable damage.[276]

Under the Human Rights Act 1998 it is possible for a victim of a European Convention of Human Rights violation by a public authority to claim monetary 'just satisfaction', which is an equivalent of damages. However, under s 8(2) 'damages may be awarded only by a court which has power to award damages, or to order the payment of compensation, in civil proceedings'. An award of damages will not be made unless the court is satisfied that the award is necessary to afford just satisfaction to the victim. It has also been noted that in a human rights claim 'the concern will usually be to bring the infringement to an end and any question of compensation will be of secondary, if any, importance'.[277]

As is the case in all EU member states there is the possibility of claiming *Francovich*[278] reparation in the English courts.[279] A good illustration of such a claim being attempted can be seen in the *Three Rivers* case.

Public authorities may sometimes be required to pay compensation, even where no tort or breach of contract has been committed. The duty to pay compensation will here be imposed by statute: the classic example

273 See Booth, C. & Squires, D., *The Negligence Liability of Public Authorities*, Oxford: Oxford University Press, 2006.
274 [2003] 2 AC 1.
275 *Ibid.* at p 190.
276 *Ibid.* at p 191–196.
277 *Anufrijeva* v *London Borough of Southwark* [2004] 2 WLR 603 at para. 53.
278 *Francovich* v *Republic (Italy)* [1995] ICR 722.
279 De la Mare, T., 'Bringing a *Francovich* Claim in English Courts', *Judicial Review*, 1997, p. 143.

is compensation payable – according to principles set out in the Land Compensation Acts 1961 and 1973 – where land has been acquired by compulsory purchase.[280] However, it is important to note that supremacy of parliament means that legislation can be passed to provide for expropriation of property of other assets without compensation – and this has occurred on a small number of occasions.[281] Nonetheless, it is an established principle relating to the interpretation of statutes that 'an intention to take away the property of a subject without giving him a legal right to compensation is not to be imputed to the legislation unless the intention is expressed in unequivocal terms'.[282] Since the enactment of the Human Rights Act 1998 there may also, in certain instances, be issues of compatibility between a taking away of property without compensation and Article 1 of Protocol 1 to the European Convention on Human Rights.

In addition to statutory compensation where land is compulsorily acquired it is in some cases possible for adversely affected parties to get compensation where the value of an interest in land is depreciated by physical factors caused by adjacent public works. The 'physical factors' are noise, smell, fumes, smoke, artificial lighting and the discharge of any substance onto the land.[283] In addition, in some quite limited circumstances, it is also possible for a landowner to get compensation for restrictions imposed by the Town and Country Planning Act on the use of the land.[284] However, the basic principle upon which the planning legislation has operated, since its introduction in its modern form in 1947, is that the right to develop land is subject to requirement of governmental permission, and that a decision not to allow permission to develop land is not therefore a matter in respect of which compensation for loss of development opportunity should follow.

Statutory compensation schemes have also been established in some situations where government may, for reasons of public interest, require property to be destroyed. This applies, for example, to farming livestock which may have to be destroyed to prevent the spread of disease.[285]

---

280 For a detailed account of how compensation is awarded see *Compulsory Purchase and Compensation*, ODPM Publications, 2004. Any dispute over compensation is dealt with by the Lands Tribunal, from which an appeal lies direct to the Court of Appeal.

281 See for example War Damage Act 1965, which reversed the House of Lords decision in *Burmah Oil Co. Ltd.* v *Lord Advocate* [1965] A.C. 75; and the Leasehold Reform Act 1967.

282 *Central Control Board (Liquor Traffic)* v *Cannon Brewery Co. Ltd.* [1919] A.C. 744, per Lord Atkinson at 752.

283 See Land Compensation Act 1973.

284 See Parts IV and V of the Town and Country Planning Act 1990.

285 See for example Cattle Compensation (England) Order 2012 and TSE (England) Regulations 2010.

7. CONCLUSION

It is hoped that the discussion above has described reasonably clearly the main features of the British system of Administrative Law. Inevitably in that discussion many matters of detail have been simplified, but hopefully not to the point of distortion. The fundamentals of judicial review have been shown to date back several centuries, although the last fifty years have – with some 'stops' and 'starts' – witnessed a quite remarkable period of judicial activism as regards the willingness of the judges to subject the administration to scrutiny as regards both its procedures and the substantive legality of its decisions.

These developments in the substantive doctrine of judicial review look set to continue as the judges come to terms also with their rather newer role of scrutinizing governmental actions in the light of the Human Rights Act 1998.

Alongside the judicial developments of these past decades there should also be noted the very substantial improvements in the workings of the system of tribunals and inquiries, and also the emergence of the Ombudsman-style remedy. Of course, complacency is not in order, and much remains to be done if substantial criticisms of present arrangements for securing the redress of grievances are to be met. Moreover, familiarity with one's own system can breed complacency. It is often through the reflections prompted by comparative legal study that new perceptions of the quite familiar can suddenly be gained. It is hoped that this volume may serve to indicate, by comparison with other systems described, the matters upon which English public lawyers might well pay closest attention as regards future reforms.

BIBLIOGRAPHY

Anthony, G., *Judicial Review in Northern Ireland*, 2nd ed., Oxford: Hart Publishing, 2014.

Austin, R., 'The Freedom of Information Act 2000 – A Sheep in Wolf's Clothing', in: Jowell, J. & Oliver, D., *The Changing Constitution*, 8th ed., Oxford: Oxford University Press, 2004, p. 401–415.

Bamforth, N., 'The Scope of Judicial Review: Still Uncertain', *Public Law*, 1993, p. 239–248.

Booth, C. & Squires, D., *The Negligence Liability of Public Authorities*, Oxford: Oxford University Press, 2006.

Bradley, A.W., Ewing, K.D. & Knight, C.J.S., *Constitutional & Administrative Law*, 16th ed., Harlow: Pearson, 2014.

Buck, T., 'Precedent in Tribunals and the Development of Principle' *Civil Justice Quarterly*, 2006, p. 458–484.

Committee of the Justice-All Souls Review of Administrative Law in the United Kingdom, *Administrative Justice: Some Necessary Reforms*, Oxford: Clarendon Press, 1988.

Craig, P.P., *Administrative Law*, 8th ed., London: Sweet & Maxwell, 2016.

Dicey, A.V., *An Introduction to the Study of the Law of the Constitution*, 10th ed., London: Macmillan, 1987.

Drewry, G., 'The Executive: Towards Accountable Government and Effective Governance?', in: Jowell, J. & Oliver, D. (eds.), *The Changing Constitution*, 7th ed., Oxford: Oxford University Press, 2011.

Elliott, M., 'The Principle of Parliamentary Sovereignty in Legal, Constitutional, and Political Perspective', in: Jowell, J., Oliver, D. & O'Cinneide, C., (eds.), *The Changing Constitution*, 8th ed., Oxford: Oxford University Press, 2015.

Elliott, M. & Varuhas, J.N.E, *Beatson, Matthews and Elliott's Administrative Law: Text and Materials*, 5th ed., Oxford: Oxford University Press, 2016.

Emery, C., 'Public Law or Private Law? – The Limits of Procedural Reform', *Public Law*, 1995, p. 450–461.

Feldman, D., 'The Human Rights Act 1998 and Constitutional Principles', *Legal Studies*, 1999 (19), p. 165–206.

Fordham, M., 'Reparation for Maladministration: Public Law's Final Frontier', *Judicial Review*, 2003, p. 104–108.

Fordham, M., *Judicial Review Handbook*, 6th ed., Oxford: Hart Publishers, 2012.

Fredman, S. & Morris, G.S., 'The Costs of Exclusivity: Public and Private Re-examined,' *Public Law*, 1994, p. 69–85.

Genn, H., 'Tribunals and Informal Justice', *Modern Law Review*, 1993 (56), p. 393–411.

Genn, H. & Genn, Y., *The Effectiveness of Representation at Tribunals*, London: The Lord Chancellor's Department, 1989.

Gordon, M., 'The Conceptional Foundations of Parliamentary Sovereignty: Reconsidering Jennings and Wade', *Public Law*, 2009, p. 519–543

Gould, P., *The Unfinished Revolution: How the Modernisers Saved the Labour Party*, London: Little Brown & Co., 1998.

Gregory, R. & Drewry, G., 'Barlow Clowes and the Ombudsman', *Public Law*, 1991, p. 192–215

Hadfield, B., 'R v Lord Saville of Newgate, ex parte Anonymous Soldiers: What is the Purpose of a Tribunal of Inquiry', *Public Law*, 1999, p. 663–681.

Hayhurst, J. & Wallington, P., 'The Parliamentary Scrutiny of Delegated Legislation', *Public Law*, 1988, p. 547–576.

Hennessy, P., *Whitehall*, London: Fontana Press, 1990.

Hennessy, P., *The Prime Minister: the Office and its Holders since 1945*, London: Allen Lane, 2000.

Hough, B., 'Local Authorities as the Guardians of the Public Interest', *Public Law*, 1992, p. 130–149.

Jowell, J., 'Beyond the Rule of Law: Towards Constitutional Judicial Review', *Public Law*, 2000, p. 671–681.

Jowell, J., 'Parliamentary Sovereignty under the New Constitutional Hypothesis', *Public Law*, 2006, p. 562–579.

Kavanagh, A., 'Unlocking the Human Rights Act: The "Radical" Approach to section 3(1) Revisited', *European Human Rights Law Review*, 2005, p. 259–275.

Knight, C.J., 'Expectations in Transition: Recent Developments in Legitimate Expectations', *Public Law*, 2009, p. 15–24.

Leigh, I. & Lustgarten, L., 'Five Volumes in Search of accountability: the Scott Report', *Modern Law Review*, 1996, Volume 59, p. 695–724

Loveland, L., *Constitutional Law, Administrative Law and Human Rights: A Critical Introduction*, 7th ed., Oxford: Oxford University Press, 2015.

Manchester, C., *Manchester on Alcohol and Entertainment Licensing Law*, 3rd ed., Leeds: Woods Whur Publishing, 2012.

De la Mare, T., 'Bringing a *Francovich* Claim in English Courts', *Judicial Review*, 1997, p. 143–149.

De la Mare, T., 'Procedural Exclusivity: Slaying the Procedural Bugbear', *Judicial Review*, 1998, p. 133–139.

Munro, C., *Studies in Constitutional Law*, 2nd ed., London: Butterworths, 1999.

Nason, S., Hardy, D. & Sunkin, M., 'Regionalisation of the Administrative Court and Access to Justice', *Judicial Review*, 2010, p. 220–227.

Olley, K., 'Proportionality at Common Law', *Judicial Review*, 2004, p. 197–201.

Pannick, D., 'Who is Subject to Judicial Review and in Respect of What?', *Public Law*, 1992, p. 1–7.

Parpworth, N., *Constitutional & Administrative Law*, 9th ed., Oxford: Oxford University Press, 2016.

Rawlings, R., 'Review, Revenge and Retreat', *Modern Law Review*, 2005 (63), p. 378–410.

De Smith, S.A., Woolf, H.K., Jowell, J.L., & Le Sueur, A.P., *De Smith, Woolf and Jowell's Principles of Judicial Review*, London: Sweet & Maxwell, 1999.

Supperstone, M., Goudie, J. & Walker, P., *Judicial* Review, 4th ed, London: LexisNexis, 2010.

Turpin, C. & Tomkins, A., *British Government and the Constitution*, 7th ed., Cambridge: Cambridge Press, 2012.

Wade, H.W.R. & Forsyth, C.F., *Administrative Law*, 11th ed., Oxford: Oxford University Press, 2014.

Woolf, H., 'Public Law – Private Law, Why the Divide?', *Public Law*, 1986, p. 220–2.

ANNEX: SENIOR COURTS ACT 1981, SECTION 31

31 Application for judicial review

(1) An application to the High Court for one or more of the following forms of relief, namely –
 (a) a mandatory, prohibiting or quashing order;
 (b) a declaration or injunction under subsection (2); or
 (c) an injunction under section 30 restraining a person not entitled to do so from acting in an office to which that section applies,

 shall be made in accordance with rules of court by a procedure to be known as an application for judicial review.

(2) A declaration may be made or an injunction granted under this subsection in any case where an application for judicial review, seeking that relief, has been made and the High Court considers that, having regard to –

(a) the nature of the matters in respect of which relief may be granted by mandatory, prohibiting or quashing orders;
(b) the nature of the persons and bodies against whom relief may be granted by such orders; and
(c) all the circumstances of the case,

– it would be just and convenient for the declaration to be made or of the injunction to be granted, as the case may be.

(2A) The High Court –
(a) must refuse to grant relief on an application for judicial review, and
(b) may not make an award under subsection (4) on such an application if it appears to the court to be highly likely that the outcome for the applicant would not have been substantially different if the conduct complained of hand not occurred.

(2B) The court may disregard the requirements in subsection (2A)(a) and (b) if it considers that it is appropriate to do so for reasons of exceptional public interest.

(2C) If the court grants relief or makes an award in reliance on subsection (2B), the court must certify that the condition in subsection (2B) is satisfied.

(3) No application for judicial review shall be made unless the leave of the High Court has been obtained in accordance with rules of court; and the court shall not grant leave to make such an application unless it considers that the applicant has a sufficient interest in the matter to which the application relates.

(3C) When considering whether to grant leave to make an application for judicial review, the High Court –
(a) may of its own motion consider whether the outcome for the applicant would have been substantially different if the conduct complained of had not occurred and
(b) must consider that question if the defendant asks it to do so.

(3D) If, on considering that question, it appears to the High Court to be highly likely that the outcome for the applicant would not have been substantially different, the court must refuse to grant leave.

(3E) The court may disregard the requirement of subsection (3D) if it considers that it is appropriate to do so for reasons of exceptional public interest.

(3F) If the court grants leave in reliance on subsection (3E), the court must certify that the condition in subsection (3E) is satisfied.

(4) On an application for judicial review the High Court may award to the applicant damages, restitution or the recovery of a sum due if –
(a) the application includes a claim for such an award arising from any matter to which the application relates; and
(b) the court is satisfied that such an award would have been made if the claim had been made in an action begun by the applicant at the time of making the application.

(5) If, on an application for judicial review, the High Court quashes the decision to which the application relates, it may in addition –

(a) remit the matter to the court, tribunal or authority which made the decision, with a direction to reconsider the matter and reach a decision in accordance with the findings of the High Court, or

(b) substitute its own decision for the decision in question.

(5A) But the power conferred by subsection (5)(b) is exercisable only if –

(a) the decision in question was made by a court or tribunal,

(b) the decision is quashed on the ground that there has been an error of law, and

(c) without the error, there would have been only one decision which the court or tribunal could have reached.

(5B) Unless the High Court otherwise directs, a decision substituted by it under subsection (5)(b) has effect as if it were a decision of the relevant court or tribunal.

(6) Where the High Court considers that there has been undue delay in making an application for judicial review, the court may refuse to grant –

(a) leave for the making of the application; or

(b) any relief sought on the application,

if it considers that the granting of the relief sought would be likely to cause substantial hardship to, or substantially prejudice the rights of, any person or would be detrimental to good administration.

(7) Subsection (6) is without prejudice to any enactment or rule of court which has the effect of limiting the time within which an application for judicial review may be made.

(8) In this section '*the conduct complained of*', in relation to an application for judicial review, means the conduct (or alleged conduct) of the defendant that the applicant claims justifies the High Court in granting relief.

EUROPEAN ADMINISTRATIVE LAW

Rolf Ortlep and Rob Widdershoven

1. INTRODUCTION

1.1. WHAT IS EUROPEAN ADMINISTRATIVE LAW?

In this chapter attention will be paid to European administrative law. European administrative law is concerned with the implementation and application of Union law in a broad sense.[1] This application takes place by means of cooperation between institutions, bodies, offices and agencies at the Union and at the national level. This cooperation can be characterized as *shared or composite government.*[2] At the Union level, EU institutions lay down rules of a general nature – the Treaty on the European Union (hereafter: TEU), the Treaty on the Functioning of the EU (hereafter: TFEU), regulations and directives – and decisions. These instruments of Union law, which will be examined in more detail in paragraph 3.2, are sometimes directed towards specific individuals. This may be the case, for instance, in European competition and civil servants law, in which the Commission takes decisions towards companies and civil servants. Usually, however, the addressees of Union law are the Member States. The implementation of Union law, so that it is applied *vis-à-vis* individuals, by means of Acts of Parliament, delegated or lower legislation, individual decisions, factual acts etc., takes place by national authorities at the Member State level.

1 See in general J.H. Jans, S. Prechal & R.J.G.M. Widdershoven (eds.), *Europeanisation of Public Law*, Europa Law Publishing, Groningen 2015; K. Lenaerts, I. Maselis & K. Gutman, *EU Procedural Law*, OUP, Oxford 2014; P. Craig, *EU Administrative Law*, OUP, Oxford 2012; J.P. Terhechte (Hrsg.), *Verwaltungsrecht der Europäischen Union*, Nomos, Baden-Baden 2011; T. Von Danwitz, *Europäisches Verwaltungsrecht*, Springer Verlag, Berlin/Heidelberg 2008; J.-B. Auby & J. Dutheil de la Rochère (eds), *Droit Administratif Européen*, Bruylant, Brussels 2007; J. Schwarze, *European Administrative Law*, 2nd ed. Thomson/Sweet, Andover 2006; E. Schmidt-Assman & B. Schöndorf-Haubold (Hrsg.), *Der Europäsche Verwaltungsverbund*, Mohr Siebeck, Tübingen, 2005.

2 J. Bridge, 'Procedural Aspects of the Enforcement of EC Law through the Legal Systems of the Member States', *European Law Review*, 1984, pp. 28–42; Jans *et al. (eds.), supra* note 1, p. 79; R.J.G.M. Widdershoven, *Naar een bestuurs(proces)rechtelijk Ius Commune in Europa* (*Towards a Ius Commune in administrative law*), VAR-reeks 116, Samsom H.D. Tjeenk Willink, Alphen a/d Rijn, 1996, p. 100; L.F.M. Besselink, *A Composite European Constitution*, Europa Law Publishing, Groningen 2007.

For this purpose, the Member States make use of their national administrative organization and their national (administrative) law.

European administrative law studies both the Union and national component of this process of shared government. Thus, in the first place, it is concerned with the administrative law of the Union itself, more in in particular with the law applicable to action of EU institutions, bodies, offices and agencies.[3] This law can be found in the TEU and TFEU, including the Charter of Fundamental Rights of the European Union (hereafter: Charter or CFR), attached to both Treaties, in secondary Union legal instruments such as directives, regulations and decisions, but also in the case law of the Court of Justice of the European Union (hereafter: CJEU or Court). This Court is the judicial institution of the European Union and of the European Atomic Energy Community (Euratom). It is made up of two courts: the Court of Justice and the General Court. Within the case law of the CJEU one can distinguish the influences of the legal order of especially the larger Member States: France, Germany and the United Kingdom.[4] In the second place, European administrative law is concerned with the national component of the application of Union law. In this respect, special attention will be paid to the question of to what extent national administrative law is influenced by the fact that it is used for the application of Union law. This European influence is closely connected with the concept of shared government. As within this concept the effective application of Union law depends, to a considerable extent, on the legal order of the Member States, it is not strange that the national legal orders must meet some European requirements. Therefore, national administrative law is becoming increasingly Europeanized.[5] In this chapter these requirements and this development will be studied in depth.

On 1 December 2009, the Lisbon Treaty entered into force. Since that date, the European Union is based on two treaties, the TEU and the TFEU. The TEU contains the basic constitutional principles on which the Union is based, establishes the EU institutions and regulates the – still intergovernmental – area of the Common Foreign and Security Policy. The TFEU is the successor to the

---

3 See M.P. Chiti & G. Greco (eds.), *Trattato di diritto amministrativo comunitario*, Giuffré, Milano: 2007; Auby & Dutheil de la Rochère (eds.), *supra* note 1; Von Danwitz, *supra* note 1; Craig, *supra* note 1.

4 Whether the probable Brexit of the United Kindom out of the EU will reduce the UK influence on the CJEU's case law in future, remains to be seen.

5 See J. Schwarze, 'Tendencies Towards a Common Administrative Law in Europe', *European Law Review*, 1991, pp. 3–19; R. Caranta, 'Judicial Protection against the Member-States: a New Ius Commune Takes Shape', *Common Market Law Review*, 1995, pp. 702–726; W. van Gerven, 'Bridging the Gap between Community and National Laws', *Common Market Law Review*, 1995, pp. 679–702; J. Schwarze (Hrsg.), *Das Verwaltungsrecht under Europäischem Einfluss. Zur Convergenz der mitgliedstaatlichen Verwaltungsrechtsordnungen in der Europäischen Union*, Baden-Baden, Nomos, 1996; K.H. Ladeur, *The Europeanisation of Administrative Law*, Dartmouth, Aldershot 2002; Widdershoven, *supra* note 2, pp. 97–200; J.-B. Auby, 'About Europeanization of Domestic Judicial Review', *Review of European Administrative Law*, 2014/2, pp. 19–34; Jans *et al.* (eds.) *supra* note 1, chapters 1 & 8.

former Treaty on the European Community (TEC) and contains the substantive policy areas in which the Union can be active. As a consequence, the European Community no longer exists and has been 'replaced' by the European Union. Moreover, the old terms EC or Community law are no longer applied and have been replaced by EU or Union law. In this chapter, the post Lisbon terminology, Union or EU law, will be used as much as possible. Only when unavoidable, for instance, when citing a pre-Lisbon judgement of the CJEU, the old terms EC or Community law are used.

1.2. LEADING PRINCIPLES OF THE EUROPEAN LEGAL ORDER

Within the European legal order the relationship between Union law and national (administrative) law is governed by three leading principles, the principle of the supremacy of Union law, the principle of sincere cooperation and the principle of subsidiarity.[6]

1.2.1. Principle of Supremacy

The most important leading principle is the principle of the supremacy of EU law. As opposed to normal international treaties and other obligations imposed by public international law, the application of Union law in the national legal order is not governed by national constitutional law, but by Union law itself. In its case law the CJEU has determined that the Union Treaties constitute a new legal order, which in turn is incorporated into the legal order of the Member States.[7] Union law is moreover an independent source of law: it is Union law itself and not the national law of the Member States which determines under which conditions it applies in the territory of the Member States. For this reason, Union law also enjoys primacy over conflicting rules of national law.

The principle of supremacy applies to Union law as a whole: this includes the Union Treaties, including the CFR, secondary Union law (regulations, directives, and decisions) and unwritten Union law (general principles). Moreover, the principle of supremacy applies retroactively, which means in relation to older national legislation, as well as to the future, in relation to legislation at a later date. In the case of a conflict between a rule of Union law and a rule of national law, the national rule should not be applied. In paragraph 3.3 the instruments by

6 S. Prechal, 'Europeanisation of National Administrative Law', in: Jans *et al* (eds.) *supra* note 1, pp. 39–43.

7 Case 26/62, *Van Gend & Loos*, ECLI:EU:C:1963:1; Case 6/64, *Costa*, ECLI:EU:C:1964:66. See R. Barents, *The Autonomy of Community Law*, Kluwer Law International, The Hague-London-Boston, 2004; B. de Witte, 'Direct Effect, Supremacy and the Nature of the Legal Order', in: P. Craig & G. de Burca (eds.), *The Evolution of EU Law*, OUP, Oxford 1999, pp. 323–362.

which the principle of supremacy is realized in the national legal order, namely the instruments of direct and indirect effect of Union law, are examined in more detail.

1.2.2. Principle of Sincere Cooperation

The second leading principle, which is of importance for the relationship between national and Union law, is the principle of sincere or loyal cooperation.[8] This principle is codified in Article 4, third paragraph TEU, which contains two positive obligations and one negative obligation for the Member States. In the first place, the Member States shall take all appropriate measures, whether general or particular, to ensure the fulfilment of the obligations arising out of the Treaty or resulting from action taken by the institutions of the Union. Secondly, the Member States are obliged to facilitate the achievement of the Union tasks. Thirdly, they shall refrain from any measure which could jeopardize the attainment of the objectives of the Treaties. Furthermore, Article 4, third paragraph TEU prescribes, both the Union and its Member States, to assist each other in carrying out tasks which flow from the Treaties.

In spite of the relatively vague wording of this Article, it offers – according to the case law of the CJEU – a legal basis for several, quite concrete, obligations on the part of (the administrative authorities and courts of) the Member States. These obligations have one common purpose that is to ensure an effective application of EU law in the Member States. Thus, Article 4, third paragraph TEU is the legal basis for the obligation of Member States to ensure an equivalent, effective and dissuasive enforcement of Union law[9]; for the Member States' obligation to arrange effective judicial protection[10]; for the general principle of Union law whereby a Member State must be liable for any loss and damage caused to individuals as a result of breaches of Union law for which the State can be held liable[11], etc. A more specific means of cooperation between the national courts and the CJEU is the preliminary ruling procedure of Article 267 TFEU. This procedure is discussed in paragraph 6.3.2.

---

8 M. Klamert, *The Principle of Loyalty in EU Law*, OUP, Oxford, 2014; R.J.G.M. Widdershoven, 'The Principle of Loyal Cooperation: Lawmaking by the European Court of Justice and the Dutch Courts', in: F. Stroink & E. van der Linden (eds.), *Judicial Lawmaking and Administrative Law*, Intersentia, Antwerpen-Oxford, 2005, pp. 3–35; J. Temple Lang, 'The Core of the Constitutional Law of the Community – Article 5', in: L.W. Gormley (ed.), *Current and Future Perspectives on EC Competition Law*, Kluwer Law International, London-The Hague, 1997, pp. 41–72.

9 Case 68/88, *Greek maize*, ECLI:EU:C:1989:339. See paragraph 4.2, below.

10 Case 222/86, *Heylens*, ECLI:EU:C:1987:442, Case C-97/91, *Borelli*, ECLI:EU:C:1992:491, Case C-432/05, *Unibet*, ECLI:EU:C:2007:163. See paragraph 6, below.

11 Joined cases C-6/90 & C-9/90, *Francovich and Bonifaci*, ECI:EU:C:1991:428. See paragraph 7.3, below.

1.2.3. *Principle of Subsidiarity*

The third and final leading principle is the principle of subsidiarity, which is codified in Article 5, third paragraph TEU.[12] According to this Article the Union shall take action, in areas which do not fall within its exclusive competence[13], only if and insofar as the objectives of the proposed action cannot be sufficiently achieved by the Member States and can therefore, by reason of the scale or effects of the proposed action, be better achieved by the Union. In practice this principle means that the Union, if it is considering taking action in a specific area, must first ask itself whether this topic can be better regulated at Union level or at national level.[14] The principle of subsidiarity is above all a political principle. The CJEU only exercises 'marginal review': it is sufficient if it appears from the justification of the Union act concerned that the question which level of action is the better, national or Union, has been considered.[15] Nevertheless, the principle is of importance, because it can be considered as the ideological background to the autonomy of the Member States in institutional and procedural matters. This autonomy is examined in the next paragraph.

1.3. EUROPEAN CONSTRAINTS ON NATIONAL ADMINISTRATIVE LAW: EQUIVALENCE AND EFFECTIVENESS

As mentioned in paragraph 1.1, the application and enforcement of Union law mainly takes place within the national legal order. The same is true for legal protection. How this application and legal protection is organized and which procedures are applicable to these activities is in principle a matter for the Member States. Thus, it is the Member State, which determines whether a Union act will be applied and enforced by the central government, by decentralized authorities or by a specialized agency. It is also the Member State which determines how the national judiciary is organized, which court is competent in Union matters and which procedural law is applicable to proceedings before this court. The Member States enjoy institutional and procedural autonomy.

---

12 T. Koopmans, 'The Quest for Subsidiarity', in: D. Curtin & T. Heukels (eds.), *Institutional Dynamics of European Integration, Essays in Honour of Schermers*, vol. II, Nijhoff, Dordrecht, 1994, pp. 43–55; see Craig, *supra* note 1, pp. 390–399.

13 Areas which fall within the exclusive competence of the EU are (Art. 3 TFEU): customs; competition; monetary Euro policy; the conservation of marine biological recourses under the common fisheries policy, common commercial policy.

14 See for the obligations under the subsidiarity principle in this respect, Protocol (No. 2). On the application of the principles of subsidiarity and proportionality, attached to the Lisbon Treaty.

15 Cf. Case C-233/94, *Germany* v *EP and Council*, ECLI:EU:C:1997:231, Case C-84/94, *UK* v *Council*, ECLI:EU:C:1996:431.

This autonomy is not absolute however. In order to ensure an effective and more or less uniform application of Union law in the Member States, the CJEU has formulated two requirements, the so-called *Rewe* requirement, which national law must meet in procedures in which Union rights are at stake.[16]

a. The *principle of equivalence (non-discrimination)*: according to this principle the (procedural) rules governing actions for safeguarding Union rights must not be less favourable than the rules governing actions for safeguarding similar domestic rights. Or, in other words: Union claims must be treated equally to similar claims based on national or domestic law.
b. The *principle of effectiveness*: according to this principle the rules governing procedures in which rights conferred by Union law are at issue, must not render the exercise of these rights virtually impossible or excessively difficult. Whether a procedural provision is incompatible with this requirement must be determined by reference to the role of that provision in the procedure. In the light of that determination the basic principles of the domestic judicial system, such as the protection of the rights of defence, the principle of legal certainty and the principle of the proper conduct of proceedings, must be taken into consideration.[17] A national provision of procedural law that limits the application of Union law in a given case is contrary to the effectiveness requirement when the provision cannot be reasonably justified by these basic principles (procedural rule of reason).

Whether a rule of national law is in accordance with these principles has to be assessed by the national courts. Questions concerning the application of the principles can be referred to the CJEU in a preliminary ruling procedure.

In addition to the *Rewe* requirements, the Member States' procedural and institutional autonomy may also be limited by fundamental rights and general principles of EU law (see paragraph 5), and by means of secondary sectoral Union law, regulating issues of the national institutional organization, single case decision-making, enforcement actions or legal protection in a specific area

---

16 Case 33/76, *Rewe*, ECLI:EU:C:1976:188, Case 45/76, *Comet*, ECLI:EU:C:1976:191. See F. Grashof, *National Procedural Autonomy Revisited*, Europa Law Publishing, Groningen, 2016; Lenaerts *et al.*, *supra* note 1, chapter 4; H.-W. Micklitz & B. de Witte (eds.), *The European Court of Justice and the Autonomy of the Member States*, Intersentia, Cambridge, 2012; D.U. Galetta, *Procedural Autonomy of EU Members States: Paradise Lost?*, Springer, Heidelberg, 2010; M. Dougan, *National Remedies before the Court of Justice*, Hart Publishing, Oxford-Portland (Oregon), 2005; S. Prechal, 'Judge-made Harmonisation of National Procedural Rules: a Bridging Perspective', in: J. Wouters & J. Stuyck (eds.), *Principles of Proper Conduct for Supranational, State and Private Actors in the European Union, Essay in Honour of Walter van Gerven*, Intersentia, Antwerp-Groningen-Oxford, 2001, pp. 39–58; S. Prechal, 'Europeanisation of National Administrative Law', in: Jans *et al* (eds.) *supra* note 1, pp. 39–43.

17 Case C-430/93, *Van Schijndel*, ECLI:EU:C:1995:441, Case 312/93, *Peterbroeck and others*, ECLI:EU:C:1995:437. See S. Prechal, 'Community Law in National Courts: the Lessons from Van Schijndel', *Common Market Law Review*, 1998, pp. 681–706.

of law. A random example of such regulatory influence is the Aarhus Directive, which provides for binding obligations in respect of *inter alia* legal protection in the area of environmental law.[18] Hereafter, other examples will be mentioned as well.

1.4. THE USE OF ADMINISTRATIVE POWERS IN THE EUROPEAN LEGAL ORDER

In the concept of shared government, the use of administrative powers is governed and limited by two principles of legality, a Union one – usually referred to as the principle of conferral or the principle of the legal base – and a national one.

1.4.1. Union Level

The European legal order is governed by the rule of law.[19] Therefore, measures and activities of the EU institutions must be compatible with 'the constitutional charter on which the [Union] is founded, the Treaty'.[20] According to the TEU, and different from the Member States, the Union does not enjoy general powers to interfere in society, but enjoys only specific powers: the Union may exercise its power only insofar as the Treaties contain an explicit legal basis to do so. This basic assumption is codified in Article 5, second paragraph TEU: the Union shall act within the limits of the powers conferred upon it by the Member States in the Treaties to attain the objectives set out therein. It is referred to as the principle of conferral or the principle of the legal base.[21]

This principle of conferral is closely connected with the principle of legality. Both principles are similar in the sense that they offer a guarantee that the administration may only take binding decisions against individuals, if and insofar as it is explicitly empowered to do so by an Act. However, the principle of conferral has a wider scope in three respects:

---

18 Directive 2003/35, *OJ* 2003, L 165/17. See paragraph 6.3.2.1, below.

19 L. Pech, "A Union Founded on the Rule of Law": Meaning and Reality of the Rule of Law as a Constitutional Principle of EU Law', *European Constitutional Law Review*, 2010/3, pp. 359–396; K. Lenaerts, 'The Basic Constitutional Charter of a Community Based on the Rule of Law', in: M.P. Maduro & L. Azoulai (eds.), *The Past and Future of EU Law*, Hart Publishing, Oxford, 2010, pp. 295–315; W.T. Eijsbouts, 'In Defence of EC Law', in: T.A.J.A. Van Damme. & J.H. Reesman (eds.), *Ambiguity in the Rule of Law*, Europa Law Publishing, Groningen, 2001, pp. 35–50; W. van Gerven, *The European Union. A Polity of States and Peoples*, Hart Publishing, Oxford-Portland (Oregon), 2005, chapter 3.

20 Case 294/83, *Les Verts*, ECLI:EU:C:1986:166.

21 R.H. van Ooik, *De keuze der rechtsgrondslag voor besluiten van de Europese Unie* (*The Choice of Legal Base for Decisions of the European Union*), Europese Monografieën (63), Kluwer, Deventer, 1999.

a. *Limitation of the competence of the Union*: the Union is only empowered to take measures in a certain policy area, if this power is explicitly attributed to it in the Treaties. In recent years, the number of areas in which the Union is empowered to take measures has increased considerably. In some areas, like customs and the common commercial policy, the Union enjoys exclusive competence (Article 4 TFEU). In other policy areas – for instance, the internal market, environment, transport, consumer protection, energy and the area of freedom, security and freedom – the Union shares its competence with the Member States (Article 5 TFEU). In several areas, like culture, education, civil protection and administrative cooperation, the Union is only competent to carry out actions to support, coordinate or supplement the actions of the Member States (Article 7 TFEU). However, areas that are not mentioned in the Treaties are outside the Union competence and remain with the Member States (Article 5, second paragraph, TEU).
b. *Influence of the Member States*: the legal basis of a Union measure is also decisive for the applicable voting requirement in the legislative procedure in the Council and therefore for the influence of the Member States on EU legislation. The Treaties provide for three different voting requirements. The general rule is Council voting by qualified majority (Article 16 TEU). In some important areas – for instance, foreign policy, security and defence policy, the right to vote in European and national elections (Article 22 TFEU), police cooperation (Article 89 TFEU) and the harmonization of tax legislation (Article 113 TFEU) – the Treaties prescribe voting by unanimity. Finally, in a few mainly procedural matters the Council decides by simple majority (see, for instance, Article 48 TEU. It is obvious that each Member State enjoys the greatest degree of influence on EU-legislation when unanimity is prescribed. Therefore, in practice there have been a number of proceedings before the CJEU concerning the question of whether the Union has chosen the correct legal basis for a certain act or measure. In these cases, the Commission tends to choose in favour of a legal basis, which allows for decision-making by qualified majority, while the Member States in the Council favour a legal basis, which prescribes unanimity.[22]
c. *Influence of the European Parliament*: finally, the legal basis is of importance for the involvement of the European Parliament in the EU legislative process. Depending on the legal basis of a specific policy area, the Parliament is co-legislator with a right of amendment and the right to veto an act, enjoys an advisory function only (for instance, regarding the harmonization of tax legislation) or enjoys no competence at all (for instance, regarding the

---

22 See, for instance, Case C-176/03, *Commission* v *Council*, ECLI:EU:C:2005:542, regarding the Proposal of a Directive on the Protection of the Environment through Criminal Law. See paragraph 4.3.

conclusion of international trade agreements between the Union and third countries, cf. Article 28 TEU).

After the foregoing the importance of the legal basis will be clear. As mentioned above the question of the correct legal basis is frequently the subject of proceedings before the CJEU. In its case law the CJEU has demonstrated that it is quite strict concerning the question of whether a legal basis can be indicated in the Treaty. Thus, the court, for instance, (also) demands a legal basis for the decision to grant a subsidy for financing certain projects.[23] The mere existence of a budget is considered to be insufficient. However, if a legal basis exists, the CJEU is quite flexible in its interpretation. In this respect in several judgements the CJEU has favoured the doctrine of implied powers[24]: According to this doctrine the CJEU accepts that when the Treaty explicitly confers a certain power to the Union, the EU institutions are also allowed to exercise powers which are not in fact conferred to it, but can be considered to be necessary for the effective application of the power explicitly conferred.

1.4.2. National Level

As mentioned above the implementation, application and enforcement of Union law mainly takes place within the Member States. The Member States will apply their national legal instruments thereto, such as Acts of Parliament, general binding rules, individual decisions etc. The use of these instruments is governed by the principle of legality of the Member States. The content and meaning of this principle in each Member State is described in other chapters of this book.[25] These national principles of legality also apply in principle to the application of Union law in the Member State[26], at least insofar as such an application results in obligations which are imposed upon individuals. In that case, national authorities should be empowered by national law to apply the EU law in question. If the Union confers rights on individuals, these rights may, in certain circumstances, be directly enforced before the national courts and the national administration by means of the instrument of direct effect. See for this instrument, paragraph 3.3.

---

23 Case C-106/96, *United Kingdom* v *Commission*, ECLI:EU:C:1998:218.

24 For instance, case C-240/90, *Commission* v *Germany (Sheepmeat)*, ECLI:EU:C:1992:408.

25 Cf. for the principle of legality in Germany, France and the Netherlands, M.J.M. Verhoeven, *The Costanzo Obligation. The Obligations of National Administrative Authorities in the Case of Incompatibility between National Law and European Law*, Intersentia, Antwerp, 2011, chapter 4.

26 See however Joined Cases C-383/06 and C-385/06 *Vereniging Nationaal Overlegorgaan Sociale Werkvoorziening*, ECLI:EU:C:2008:165, and Case C-599/13, *Somvao*, ECLI:EU:C:2014:2462, from which it may be derived that a regulation may provide for a legal base for a recovery decision of a national authority. Cf. Jans *et al.* (eds.) *supra* note 1, pp. 28–29, for a critical assessment of this case law.

2. WHO HAS ADMINISTRATIVE POWERS?[27]

2.1. ADMINISTRATIVE POWERS IN THE EUROPEAN UNION

The highest institution of the European Union is the *European Council* (Article 15 TEU). The European Council brings together the Heads of State or Government of the Member States and the President of the Commission. The High Representative of the Union for Foreign Affairs and Security Policy takes part in its work. When the agenda so requires, the members of the European Council can be assisted by a minister, and the President of the Commission by a member of the Commission. The European Council meets at least four times a year, under the chairmanship of its President which is elected by the European Council for a term of two and a halve years (renewable once). At the moment of writing the President is Donald Tusk. The function of the European Council is to provide the Union with the necessary impetus for its development and to define general political guidelines thereof. In practice, it decides about all fundamental matters concerning the Union, such as the enlargement of the EU and the establishment of measures against the financial crisis. However, the European Council does not exercise legislative functions.

Legally the most important institution of the European Union is the *Council* (of Ministers). It consists of representatives of the 28 Member States at the ministerial level. They should be authorized to commit the Government of the Member State in question. The Council exercises, jointly with the *European Parliament* (see paragraph 1.4), the legislative and budgetary functions of the Union. Moreover, it carries out policy-making and coordinating functions in the areas in which the Union is *competent*. In some areas, the Council enjoys the competence to take individual decisions.

As regards the execution of administrative powers, the most important Union institution is the *European Commission*. This institution consists of 28 members, one national of each Member State, including its President, at the moment of writing Jean-Claude Junker (Luxembourg). They are chosen on the ground of their general competence and European commitment from persons whose independence is beyond doubt. The Commission promotes the general interest of the Union. In this respect, it exercises several functions.

- In the first place, the Commission is responsible for the preparation of policy issues and of legislation (right of initiative).
- Secondly, the Commission supervises Member States' compliance with EU law (Articles 258–260 TFEU). If the Commission considers that a Member State has failed to fulfil an obligation under the Treaty, and the

[27] See also figure 1, Organization of the European Union.

State concerned does not comply with this opinion, the Commission may bring the matter before the CJEU. Such failure may, for instance, concern the non- or incorrect transposition of a directive, the incorrect application of a directive or regulation by the national administration in an individual case or the non-enforcement of EU law in a Member State. If the CJEU agrees with the opinion of the Commission, the State is obliged to take the necessary measures to comply with the judgement of the CJEU. If the Member State fails to take these measures, the CJEU in a new procedure may impose a lump sum (administrative fine) or a penalty payment on the Member State in question. In its case law, the CJEU has ruled that, in principle, it is possible to impose on a Member State as sanctions both a penalty payment and the liability to pay a lump sum. The imposition of a penalty payment induces the Member State to put an end to the infringement, and is therefore directed to the future. The lump sum can be regarded as a sanction against the infringement in the past. The basic criteria the CJEU applies for establishing a lump sum and/or a penalty payment are: the duration of the infringement; the seriousness of the infringement; and the ability of the Member State to pay.
- Finally, the Commission exercises the powers, which are attributed to it by the Treaties or delegated to it in secondary legislation. The latter powers may concern the taking of decisions as regards individuals. Delegated powers may also concern the power to establish (delegated) rules for the application of the Council's legislation (cf. Article 290 TFEU).

A relatively new phenomenon in the European administrative structure are the so-called *agencies*.[28] In recent years the Council has established a considerable number of agencies in its legislation. They are considered bodies of the Union and may possess legal personality. Therefore, they enjoy a certain degree of independence from the main EU institution, in particular from the European Commission. The highest organ within an agency is usually the Management or Administrative Board, which is composed of persons who are appointed by the Governments of the Member States and by the EU institutions.

The functions and tasks of agencies are diverse. Some of them – the so-called regulatory agencies – have the power to adopt legally binding decisions as regards individuals. Examples are the Office for Harmonisation in the Internal Market (Trade Marks and Designs), which has been given the power to determine the registration of trademarks, the European Plant Variety Office, which takes decisions on the granting of plant variety rights, and the European

28 See Craig, *supra* note 1, chapter 6; R.H. van Ooik, 'The Growing Importance of Agencies in the EU: Shifting Governance and the Institutional Balance', in: D. Curtin & R. Wessel (eds.), *Good Governance and the European Union*, Intersentia, Antwerpen-Oxford-New York, 2005, pp. 125–152.

Securities and Market Authority, which enjoys enforcement powers over credit rating agencies and trade repositories. The decisions of these agencies may be challenged before the CJEU. Other agencies lack the power to take binding decisions as regards individuals. The majority have as their primary task the gathering and processing of information with respect to the subject matter for which the agency was created. Examples from this group are the European Environment Agency, and the European Agency for Health and Safety at Work. Others combine an independent research function with inspection powers, but leave the possible follow up measures to the Commission or the Member States. Examples from this group are the European Medicine Agency and the European Food Safety Authority.[29] The final group of agencies are the so-called operational agencies. They assist the European Commission by implementing particular EU programmes and policies.

2.2. NATIONAL ADMINISTRATIVE POWERS IN THE EUROPEAN LEGAL ORDER

As mentioned in paragraph 2.1, the Commission in particular and sometimes the Council and even some agencies may be empowered to take binding decisions as regards individuals. Usually however, Union law must be applied and enforced as regards individuals in the Member States. Which organ or authority within the Member State is empowered to exercise this task is a matter for the institutional law of the Member States. According to the principle of institutional autonomy the Union does not, in principle, interfere in the national choices, which have been made in this respect.

In practice a variety of national authorities may be responsible for the application of Union law. Which authority is responsible, is determined by the constitutional law of the Member State. Thus, in many Member States the most important tasks involving the application of EU law are carried out by the administrative authorities of the central government, mostly the ministers. In other countries, however, parts of EU law have been devolved to local government bodies. In this case Union law is applied by organs of, for instance, municipalities, provinces or *Länder*. Sometimes a Member State will delegate the application of a part of EU law to an agency, a regulator or to another more or less autonomous public authority. From the point of view of the European Union all these institutional arrangements are in principle allowed. However, in particular in the area of market regulation, the Union legislator increasingly obliges the Member States to set up national authorities which should meet

[29] Cf. M. Scholten & M. Luchtman (eds.), *Law Enforcement by EU Authorities. Political and judicial accountability in shared enforcement*, Edward Elgar, Cheltenham, 2017.

certain institutional requirements of independence. Well-known examples are the National Regulatory Authorities in the area of Telecommunication and Energy, which should be independent, not only from the market parties, but from political influence as well.[30]

However, in spite of the institutional freedom of the Member States, it is the Member State, which is responsible to the European Union for the correct application of EU law within that Member State. After all, it is the Member State which is a party to the Treaties and which is the addressee of most of the Treaties' provisions and other EU legislation. Therefore, the responsibility of the Member State also concerns the (mis)application of EU law by decentralized authorities and agencies. Thus, it is the Member State, which will be brought before the CJEU by the Commission, and this is (also) the case when a decentralized authority has not complied with the Treaties or with any other EU legislation. This procedure may eventually lead to the imposition of a fine or a penalty payment on the Member State by the CJEU (cf. paragraph 2.1). It is also the Member State, which is financially responsible to the EU for the irregularities committed by decentralized authorities or agencies in the application of Union subsidy rules. Whether it is possible for the Member State to recover an imposed fine or penalty payment from the decentralized authority or agency that committed the irregularity is a matter of national law.

In proceedings before the CJEU the Member State cannot raise the defence that national constitutional law does not provide the necessary instruments in order to interfere in the (mis)application of EU law by a decentralized authority or agency. The EU respects the institutional autonomy of the Member States, but does not allow them to 'hide under the skirts' of their national constitutional law in order to escape Union obligations. Therefore, it seems a sound policy that Member States give themselves the necessary authority to interfere in the activities of decentralized authorities and agencies if and when these authorities neglect their Union tasks.[31]

30 Framework Directive 2002/21, as amended by Directive 2009/140. See on this development, S. Lavrijssen & A.M. Ottow, 'The Legality of Independent Regulatory Authorities', in: L.F.M. Besselink *et al* (eds.), *The Eclips of the Legality Principle in the European Union*, Kluwer Law International, Alphen a/d Rijn, 2011, pp. 73–96.

31 Verhoeven, *supra* note 25, pp. 249–283; B. Hessel, 'European integration and the supervision of local and regional authorities. Experiences in the Netherlands with the requirements of European Community Law', *Utrecht Law Review*, June 2006, available at <www.utrechtlawreview.org/>.

Figure 1. Organization in the European legal order

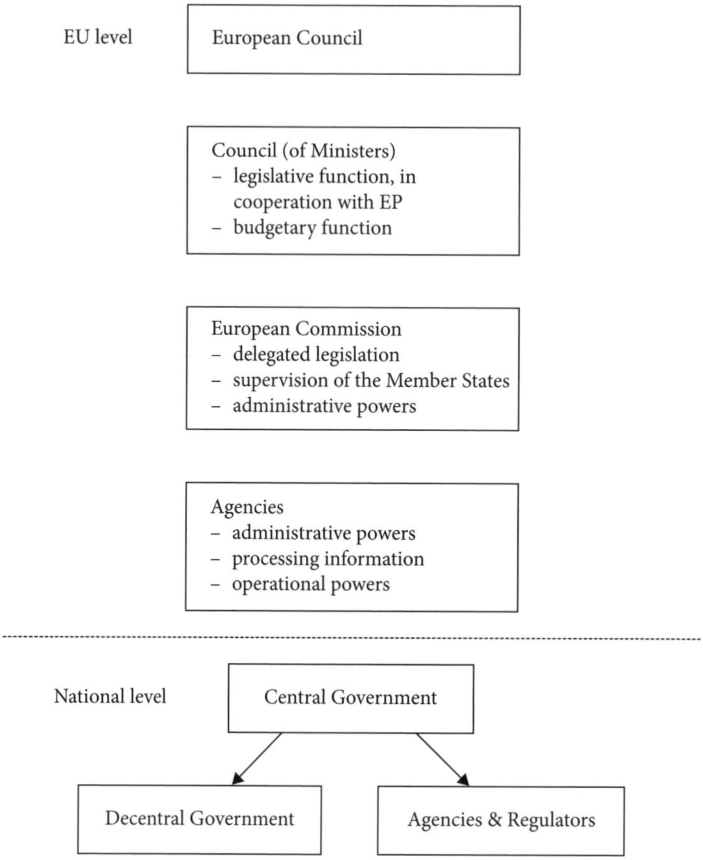

3. WHAT INSTRUMENTS ARE AVAILABLE IN THE ADMINISTRATION?

3.1. LEGAL INSTRUMENTS AT THE EU LEVEL

3.1.1. The Treaties

The Union's most important legal instruments are the TEU and the TFEU. As already indicated in paragraph 1.1 the TEU contains the basic constitutional principles on which the Union is based and establishes the Union institutions. The TFEU contains the substantive policy areas in which the Union can be active. Important provisions of the TFEU are concerned with Union citizenship (Articles 20 and 21 TFEU) and the four freedoms: the free movement of goods

(Article 28 TFEU), the free movement of persons (Articles 45 and 49 TFEU), the free movement of services (Article 56 TFEU) and the free movement of capital (Article 63 TFEU). These freedoms contain a prohibition on restricting free movement between the Member States, although exceptions can be made. Besides the four freedoms the Treaty contains provisions concerning competition (Articles 101 and 102 TFEU) and state aid granted by the Member States (Articles 107 and 108 TFEU). Furthermore, the Treaty provides the legal basis for Union legislation and other Union action in specific policy areas such as agriculture, transport, the environment, social policy, consumer protection and the area of freedom, security and justice (which includes policies on asylum and immigration and the judicial cooperation in civil and criminal matters).

Since the coming into force of the Lisbon Treaty on 1 December 2009 the Charter of Fundamental Rights of the EU, although not incorporated in the Treaties, has the same legal value as the Treaties (Article 6, first paragraph, TEU). The Charter contains a large number of fundamental rights and can be described 'as a creative distillation of the rights contained in the various European and international agreements and national constitutions'.[32] Its most important source of inspiration is the European Convention for the Protection of Human Rights and Fundamental Freedoms (hereafter: ECHR). The Charter is not only binding for the EU institutions, but also for the Member States when 'they are implementing Union law' (Article 51, first paragraph, Charter). Which actions of the Member States qualify as `implementing Union law' is discussed in more detail in paragraph 5.3, below. Article 288 TFEU contains the necessary legal instruments by which the Union institutions can take measures in specific policy areas. The most important are: regulations, directives and decisions. Hereafter, these instruments and also instrument of soft law will be examined. Attention is also devoted to the instruments by means of which the Member States must implement and apply these Union legal instruments.

3.1.2. Regulations

A regulation has general application. It is binding in its entirety as far as the Member States and individuals are concerned and is directly applicable in the Member States. Regulations are mainly used in the fields of agriculture, structural funds, customs and transboundary activities. They prescribe in detail the way in which the authorities of the Member States have to act in a specific area, for instance, under which conditions the authorities may grant a subsidy or permit. In their structure and content regulations are quite similar to Acts of Parliament and other generally binding national rules. However, they do not originate from a national legislator, but from the European legislator.

---

32 P. Craig & G. de Búrca, *EU Law. Text, Cases and Materials*, 5th ed., OUP, Oxford, 2011, p. 395.

To achieve an effective application of a regulation in the national legal order, the regulation should be 'incorporated' into national law. In this respect, it is necessary for national law to appoint a national administrative authority, which is responsible for the application of the regulation in the Member State. Moreover, additional legal arrangements usually have to be made in order to ensure the application of the regulation. One may think of the establishment of rules for the procedure, which will ensure the application of the regulation or rules, which are necessary to ensure the effective enforcement of that regulation.

3.1.3. Directives[33]

A directive is (only) binding, as to the result to be achieved, upon each Member State to which it is addressed, but leaves to the national authorities the choice of form and methods. It is given full effect in the Member States because it is transposed in national legislation and thereby subsequently applied by the competent national authorities. The time limit, within which the transposition of the directive must have taken place, is prescribed in the directive itself. This time limit may not be exceeded.

In transposing a directive, the Member States in principle enjoy freedom to choose the necessary forms and methods in order to obtain the directive's objectives. In practice this freedom is usually quite limited because many directives leave the Member State with little, if any, discretion. Furthermore, the CJEU subjects the transposition of directives to certain strict conditions. Concerning form, the Court demands that transposition should take place in 'binding provisions of national law'. Thus, it should be legally guaranteed that the directive will be effectively applied. Moreover, the transposition must be accurate, clear and complete. Or, as the CJEU has stated it in its case law[34]: to transpose a directive correctly,

> 'it is essential for national law to guarantee that the national authorities will effectively apply the directive in full, that the legal position under national law should be sufficiently precise and clear and that individuals are made fully aware of their rights and, where appropriate, may rely on them before the national courts'.

The requirement that transposition should take place by means of 'binding provisions of national law' limits the choice of national legal instruments by which the Member States may transpose a directive. This requirement demonstrates a clear preference for the use of generally binding rules. The CJEU is not an advocate of alternative transposition instruments, which have a less legally binding effect. In its case law the CJEU tends to usually (dis)qualify these

---

33 S. Prechal, *Directives in EC Law*, 2nd ed., OUP, Oxford, 2005.

34 For instance, Case C-144/99, *Commission* v. *the Netherlands*, ECLI:EU:C:2001:257.

instruments as 'mere administrative practices, which by their nature may be altered at the whim of the administration'.[35] Therefore they do not guarantee the full application of the directive. Moreover, individuals cannot rely on these instruments before the national courts.

For this reason, directives cannot be transposed by, for instance, policy rules or soft law arrangements: the administration is after all empowered to depart from them in special circumstances. Furthermore, the CJEU in principle does not accept the transposition of a directive by means of voluntary agreements (covenants).[36] This instrument is sometimes used in the field of environmental law: in order to achieve a certain environmental goal – for instance, the reduction of a certain emission – the administration enters into an agreement with the group of polluting companies. The problem with voluntary agreements from the point of view of Union law is that they are entered into by these companies on a purely voluntary basis. Therefore, there is no guarantee that every company, which is responsible for the pollution in question, is a party to the voluntary agreement. Moreover, the companies are free to leave the voluntary agreement. An effective enforcement of the directive is therefore not guaranteed.

3.1.4. Decisions

A decision is binding in its entirety. Sometimes decisions are addressed to a specific individual, for instance, the decision of the Commission to impose a fine upon an undertaking, which has violated EU competition rules. This decision is, of course, binding for the undertaking. Most decisions, however, address one (or more) Member State(s). The Member State is subsequently obliged to implement the decision in its national legal order. This implementation sometimes implies that an individual decision (addressed to a specific individual) has to be taken. This is, for instance, the case when the Commission, by means of a decision, imposes an obligation on the Member State to recover subsidies or aids from an undertaking when such subsidies/aids have been granted by the Member State contrary to the state aid rules of Articles 107 and 108 TFEU. In other cases, decisions have to be implemented in the Member States by means of generally binding rules. This is, for instance, the case if the EU decision obliges the Member States to prohibit imports of certain goods from a third country for reasons of public health. This prohibition must be implemented in a national Act of Parliament or in national legislation of a lower status and must subsequently be applied by the national authorities in a specific case.

---

35 For instance, Case C-97/81, *Commission* v. *the Netherlands*, ECLI:EU:C:1982:193.

36 J.A.E. van der Jagt, *Milieuconvenanten gehandhaafd* (*Environmental Voluntary Agreements Enforced*), Boom Juridische uitgevers, Den Haag, 2006, pp. 52–67.

Figure 2. Simplified representation of the hierarchy of generally applicable rules in the European legal order

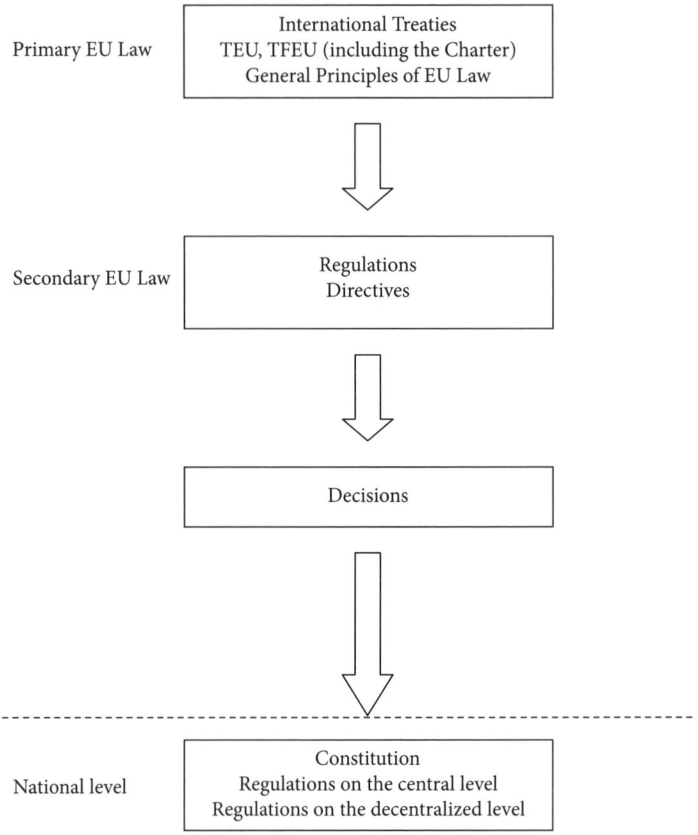

3.1.5. Union Soft Law Instruments

Union law also includes soft law instruments.[37] Examples of soft law in the TFEU are: recommendations and opinions (Article 288, fifth paragraph, TFEU), general action programmes (Article 191 TFEU) and multi annual framework programmes (Article 182 TFEU). In addition to these instruments, there exist a large number of soft law instruments which lack a legal basis in the Treaties, such as resolutions, guidelines, declarations, codes of conduct etc. These instruments

37 L.A.J. Senden, *Soft Law in European Community Law*, Hart Publishing, Oxford-Portland (Oregon), 2004. Cf. O. Stefan, 'Hybridity before the Court: a Hard Look at Soft Law in the EU Competition and State Aid', *European Law Review*, 2012/1, pp. 49–69; O. Stefan, *Soft law in Court – Competition Law, State Aid, and the Court of Justice of the European Union*, Kluwer Law International, Alphen aan den Rijn, 2012.

share one common feature, namely they are not completely binding from a legal point of view.

This does not mean, however, that these instruments are legally irrelevant. For instance, when the Commission assesses the lawfulness of aids granted by a Member State (Article 107 TFEU) it is obliged – under the general principles of Union law (see paragraph 5) – to follow the guidelines which it has established concerning the application of discretionary powers in this area. In addition, the CJEU sometimes uses recommendations as a tool for interpreting Union rules.[38] In such a case national authorities and national courts are also obliged to take these recommendations into consideration.

It is, however, difficult to provide a general opinion on the binding force of soft law instruments: this will depend on the wording of the instrument in question and on the particular field in which it is being used.

3.2. LEGAL INSTRUMENTS AT THE NATIONAL LEVEL

The Member States have an obligation to ensure the effective application of Union legal instruments in the Member States. In the foregoing text, it has generally been indicated which legal instruments can be used. Hereafter, the most important national legal instruments are examined in an integrated way.

Firstly, in order to ensure the effective application of Union law it is usually necessary to implement its provisions by means of generally binding national rules. In the case of the transposition of directives it is almost always necessary to make use of this instrument, because transposition should take place by means of 'binding provisions of national law'. As has already been stated Union law is not an advocate of alternative transposition instruments, which are not so legally binding, such as policy rules and voluntary agreements (see paragraph 3.1). Regulations and many decisions should also be usually incorporated in generally binding national rules. Within these rules a national administrative authority must be empowered to apply the regulation or decision *vis-à-vis* individuals, procedural rules must be established in order to apply these instruments, additional arrangements concerning, for instance, the enforcement of the regulation or decision must be taken etc.

It is, however, not always necessary that *new* generally binding rules are established in order to implement Union legal instruments. In many cases, it is possible to incorporate directives, regulations and decisions within existing generally binding rules. This should be done, however, in a precise and accurate manner: a completely effective application of the instruments in the national legal order should be guaranteed. The choice of a specific type of generally binding (national) rules in order to implement a Union instrument

---

38 Case 322/88, *Grimaldi*, ECLI:EU:C:1989:646.

is a matter for the Member State. Implementation may take place by means of an Act of Parliament, but also by way of generally binding rules of a lower status, for instance, in ministerial regulations. It is also possible that Union legal instruments are implemented in the form of legislative acts by decentralized authorities.

In the second place, the national legislation in which the Union instruments are implemented or incorporated must apply to individuals. Many regulations and some directives contain specific provisions on the national legal instruments, which may be used. Thus, a regulation may prescribe that the national authorities have to impose a levy on individuals, to grant subsidies or restitution etc. In some directives, it is prescribed that the substantive norms, which have to be achieved, should be stated in the terms of a permit or a license. In other directives, the establishment of rules of a general nature is prescribed, for instance, assigning a certain area as a protected habitat area.

If the Union instrument does not contain any specific provision, every legal instrument, which is available in the legal order of the Member State, can in principle be applied. Usually the application of Union instruments as far as individuals are concerned will take place by means of single case administrative decisions. Administrative decisions, which frequently have (at least partly) a Union background, are:

- decisions imposing a financial obligation: mainly in the field of customs and tax law;
- decisions granting subsidies and restitutions: mainly in the field of agricultural law and the structural funds;
- permits and concessions: for instance, in the field of environmental law, water management, transport, telecommunication and energy.

3.3. THE DIRECT AND INDIRECT EFFECT OF UNION LAW

If everything operates as the founding fathers of the European Economic Community had planned, Union law is applied in the national legal order in a correct manner by means of the national legal instruments mentioned. In reality, however, this is not always the case. In fact, breaches of EU law by the authorities of the Member States are quite common. Directives are not transposed in due time or in an incorrect manner; Treaty provisions are violated by national legislation or national decisions; regulations are not or are incorrectly applied etc. For these situations, Union law provides two instruments by which an individual can nevertheless enforce the rights conferred upon him by Union law: the instruments of direct effect and of indirect effect or consistent interpretation.[39] Both instruments are closely connected to the principle of supremacy: they can be seen as a means by which this principle can be realized in the national legal order.[40]

As will be detailed below, the instruments of direct and indirect effect have their own possibilities and limitations. In some situations, both can be used to remedy the violation of the Union rules concerned. According to the CJEU, in such situation the national court should first try to remedy the violation by means of the instrument of indirect effect, before proceeding to the instrument of direct effect.[41] Nevertheless, hereafter we will first discuss the possibilities and limitations of direct effect, because that instrument was developed by the CJEU first, and the CJEU's `invention' of indirect effect is partly due to the limitations of direct effect.

3.3.1. Direct Effect

A Union law provision has direct effect if it can be directly relied on by individuals in proceedings before the national courts and can be applied by these courts. In other words, the provision should be `justiciable'. If a provision is justiciable (has direct effect), the national courts are obliged to apply them, setting aside any national law which is contrary to that provision. The obligation to apply directly effective Union law not only rests with the courts. Administrative (decentralized) authorities are also under an obligation to apply such provisions and to refrain from applying any national provision which conflicts with them.[42]

The main condition under which a provision has direct effect is that the Member State enjoys no discretion when implementing it. The provision must thereby be unconditional and sufficiently precise.[43] According to these criteria the most important rights and freedoms in the TFEU, as well as the provisions of regulations in general, have direct effect. Provisions of a directive have direct effect when they are unconditional and sufficiently precise, after the expiration of the time limit within which the transposition of the directive in the national legal order should have taken place. Before the expiration of the transposition time limit provisions of a directive have no direct effect. However, this does not

---

39 If both instruments cannot be applied because of their specific limitations, the party injured as a result of domestic law not being in conformity with EU law can in principle rely on the instrument of state liability in order to obtain compensation for the loss sustained. See paragraph 7.3.

40 See concerning both instruments, Prechal, *supra* note 33; Jans *et al.* (eds.) *supra* note 1, chapter 3.

41 Case C-282/10, *Dominguez*, ECLI:EU:C:2012:33.

42 Case 103/88, *Fratelli Costanzo*, ECLI:EU:C:1989:256, Case C-243/09, *Fuss*, ECLI:EU:C:2010:609. See for the obligation of the administrative authorities extensively, Verhoeven, *supra* note 25.

43 Case 8/81, *Becker*, ECLI:EU:C:1982:7.

mean that these provisions are legally irrelevant. In its case law the CJEU has stipulated that – on the ground of Article 4, third paragraph, TEU (principle of sincere cooperation) in conjunction with Article 288 TFEU – during the transposition period the Member States 'must refrain from taking any measures liable seriously to compromise the result prescribed by the directive'.[44] According to *Inter-Environment Wallonia* it is inconsistent with this obligation to refrain, if the Member State, during the transposition period, lays down new legislation, intending to implement the directive definitively, and this implementing legislation is inconsistent with the directive. In addition, the obligation may be violated if the Member State, during the transposition period, establishes new legislation, without assessing whether this new legislation might seriously compromise the result prescribed by the directive concerned.[45]

The direct effect of a Union provision applies first and foremost to the vertical relationship between an individual and an administrative authority: the individual may rely on its Union rights against the authority. In other words: the provision has vertical direct effect. Regulations and some Treaty provisions may also directly impose obligations on individuals in their relationship with an administrative authority (reverse vertical direct effect) or with other individuals (horizontal direct effect). However, the direct effect of directives only exists – according to Article 288 TFEU – in relation 'to the Member State to which it is addressed'. Therefore, a directive, which has not been (correctly) transposed in national law, may not in itself impose any obligation upon individuals.[46] This has two consequences:

- In the first place, administrative authorities cannot rely on a directive against an individual. Thus, it is, for instance, forbidden to impose a levy upon an individual on the basis of a directive which has not been transposed, or when this has been done incorrectly (prohibition of reverse vertical direct effect).
- In the second place, individuals may not rely on the provisions of a directive, which has not or incorrectly been transposed in their relationship with other individuals (prohibition of horizontal direct effect).

The prohibition of reverse vertical direct effect does not apply in triangular situations. In such situations, the obligation of the national court or authority to apply a directive provision with direct effect at the request of an individual (for instance, an environmental NGO) has negative effects for another individual (for instance, a company). According to the CJEU in the case of *Wells* 'mere reverse repercussions on the rights of third parties, do not justify preventing an individual from invoking the provision of the directive against the Member State

44 Case C-129/96, *Inter-Environnement Wallonia*, ECLI:EU:C:1997:628, Case C-144/04, *Mangold*, ECLI:EU:C:2005:709.

45 Case C-138/04, *Stichting Zuid-Hollandse Milieufederatie*, ECLI:EU:C:2005:678.

46 Case 152/84, *Marshall*, ECLI:EU:C:1986:84, Case 80/86, *Kolpinghuis*, ECLI:EU:C:1987:431.

concerned'.[47] Or, in different wording, the negative effects for a third party (the company) are considered as 'collateral damage' resulting from the right of the other party (the environmental NGO) to rely on the direct effective directive provision against the State, and are therefore allowed.

3.3.2. Indirect Effect or Consistent Interpretation

The second way in which the application of Union rights can be enforced in the national legal order is by means of the instrument of indirect effect, also called the principle of consistent interpretation.[48] This instrument is usually applied to directive provisions. According to the case law of the CJEU the authorities of the Member States – i.e. the administration as well as the courts – are obliged to interpret their national law, as far as possible, in the light of the wording and the purpose of a directive in order to achieve the result pursued by that directive. This obligation applies to both national provisions dating from before the directive, as well as to provisions of a later date. The principle of indirect effect is frequently applied in order to remedy relative minor defects in the transposition of a directive. In such a case a national court or an administrative authority will interpret a national provision which is not completely in line with the directive, in such a way that it is in conformity with this directive. Similar to direct effect, the obligation of indirect effect only applies after he expiry of the transposition period of a directive.[49] However and similar to direct effect as well, during the transposition period the national courts must refrain as far as possible from interpreting domestic law in a manner which might seriously compromise, after the period for transposition has expired, attainment of the objective pursued by the directive.

Compared to the instrument of direct effect, the instrument of indirect effect offers additional possibilities for the correct application of Union directives. In the first place, the instrument is not limited to provisions that have direct effect – in other words: that are unconditional and sufficiently precise – but it can also be applied to provisions without direct effect.[50] In the second place, the instrument can be used in horizontal relationships, i.e. in disputes between two individuals.[51] The prohibition of horizontal effect does not apply to the instrument of indirect effect. In the third place, the instrument is not limited

---

47 Case C-201/02, *Wells*, ECLI:EU:C:2004:12, Joined cases C-152/07 to C-154/07, *Arcor and others*, ECLI:EU:C:2008:426. See also J.H. Jans & M.J.M. Verhoeven, 'Europeanisation via Consistent Interpretation and Direct Effect', in: Jans *et al.* (eds.) *supra* note 1, pp. 111–117, and Verhoeven, *supra* note 25, pp. 29–31.

48 Case 14/83, *Von Colson and Kamann*, ECLI:EU:C:1984:153, Case C-106/89, *Marleasing*, ECLI:EU:C:1990:395, Case C-397/01, *Pfeiffer*, ECLI:EU:C:2004:584.

49 Case C-212/04, *Adeneler*, ECLI:EU:C:2004:443.

50 See case 14/83, *Von Colson and Kamann*, ECLI:EU:C:1984:153.

51 See case C-106/89, *Marleasing*, ECLI:EU:C:1990:395, Case C-397/01, *Pfeiffer*, ECLI:EU:C:2004:584.

by the prohibition of reverse vertical effect. A Member State 'may, in principle, impose on individuals an interpretation of national law in keeping with a directive'.[52]

On the other hand, the application of the instrument of indirect effect is also limited in two ways.

- Firstly, the application may not lead to the situation 'that a directive, of itself and independently of a national law adopted by a Member State for its implementation, has the effect of determining or aggravating the liability in criminal law of persons who act in contravention of the provision of that directive'.[53] According to the CJEU this would be contrary to the principles of legal certainty and non-retroactivity. The latter principle is now codified in Article 49, first paragraph, of the Charter. As this provision also applies to administrative sanctions of a criminal nature (see paragraph 4.2), the same limitation probably applies to the imposition of such sanctions as well.
- Secondly, the obligation to interpret a national provision in conformity with a directive may not lead to a *contra legem* application of the national provision.[54] Thus, if the wording of the national provision shows considerable differences from the directive's provision, this deviation cannot be remedied by consistent interpretation. This limitation, however, only applies if consistent interpretation would be contrary to the wording of the national provision, and not if it only would be inconsistent with the interpretation of the national provision by the highest national court.[55] Thus, in respect of the prohibition of *contra legem* consistent interpretation, the interpretation by the national courts is not considered to be a part of the '*legem*'.

4. HOW IS EUROPEAN ADMINISTRATIVE LAW ENFORCED?[56]

4.1. INTRODUCTION

As stated in paragraph 2.1, in some policy areas Union institutions are empowered to apply and enforce EU rules towards individuals. This is, for

52 Case C-53/10, *Mücksch*, ECLI:EU:C:2011:585.

53 Case 80/86, *Kolpinghuis*, ECLI:EU:C:1987:431, Case C-168/95, *Arcaro*, ECLI:EU:C:1996:363.

54 Case C-105/03, *Pupino*, ECLI:EU:C:2005:386, Case C-282/10, *Dominguez*, ECLI:EU:C:2012:33.

55 Case C-441/14, *Danski Industri*, ECLI:EU:C:2016:278.

56 A.J.C. de Moor-van Vugt & R.J.G.M. Widdershoven, 'Administrative Enforcement', in: Jans *et al.* (eds.), *supra* note 1, chapter 5; J.A.E. Vervaele (ed.), G. Betlem, R. de Lange & A.G. Veldman (co-eds.), *Compliance and Enforcement of European Community Law*, Kluwer Law International, The Hague-London-Boston, 1999; A.J.C. de Moor-van Vugt, 'Administrative Sanctions in EU Law', *Review of European Administrative Law*, 2012/1, pp. 5–41; O. Jansen

example, the case in European competition law: in this area, the Commission is competent to enforce violations of Articles 101 and 102 TFEU by imposing financial fines and periodic penalty payments.[57] These sanctions can be challenged before the CJEU. However, generally Union law is applied in the Member States by national authorities. In that case, also the enforcement of EU law takes place at the national level. It is the task of the Member States to ensure the effective enforcement of EU law. In doing so, they have to monitor compliance with EU law within their territory, investigate possible violations and impose sanctions for infringements of EU law.

In principle, the Member States decide which authorities are empowered to enforce Union law and which system of enforcement is used (they enjoy 'enforcement autonomy'). They may opt for enforcement by means of *administrative law*. In that case, the Member State applies the administrative law sanctions which are present in its national law. These may be sanctions of a reparatory nature – such as a direct enforcement action, the withdrawal of a favourable decision or the recovery of an unlawfully received subsidy – but may also be sanctions of a punitive or criminal nature, such as an administrative fine. These sanctions are imposed by national administrative authorities and may be challenged before the national administrative courts. The Member States can also enforce Union rules using *criminal law*, either in addition to administrative enforcement or instead of it. In that case violations of Union law may also be punished by the sanction of imprisonment. The criminal prosecution is initiated by the national public prosecutor and sanctions are imposed by the national criminal courts. Finally, Member States may opt to enforce Union law by means of *civil law*. In that case, the European rules are not enforced by a public law (administrative or criminal) authority, but by private individuals whose interests have been affected by an infringement of EU law by another individual.[58] Such private law actions – which are, for instance, common in the area of European competition law[59] – are brought before the national civil courts by the first individual against the latter.

It is common knowledge that the enforcement by the Member States of Union law has been and still is quite feeble. At a regular base one can read in the newspapers articles about fraud with European subsidies, about violations of the European fisheries rules, about value added tax fraud schemes, about non-compliance with the European environmental rules etc. In response to this

(ed.), *Administrative Sanctions in the European Union*, Cambridge, Antwerp, Portland, Intersentia, 2013.

57 The Commission competence to impose fines and penalty payments is provided for in Article 103, second paragraph, sub a, TFEU, in conjunction with Regulation 1/2003, *OJ* 2003, L 1/1.

58 Case C-253/00, *Munoz*, ECLI:EU:C:2002:497.

59 See, for example, Case C-453/99, *Courage* v *Crehan*, ECLI:EU:C:2001:465, Joined cases C-295/04 to C-298/04, *Manfredi*, ECLI:EU:C:2006:461.

European enforcement deficit, the European Union has increasingly intervened in the enforcement process in the Member States. By doing so, the existing national enforcement autonomy is gradually being limited. The European influence on national enforcement of EU law is exercised in two ways. In the first place, it is through the case law of the CJEU. With due regard to the Member States' own responsibility for enforcement of Union law, it is now settled case law that national enforcement measures must fulfil various European quality requirements. These requirements will be discussed in paragraph 4.2. In the second place, the Union has employed *legislative instruments* to lay down general rules to be applied in the national process of enforcement in specific policy areas. These rules are concerned with the monitoring by the Member States of compliance with Union law, with investigating violations and with the imposition of sanctions. These legislative instruments are elaborated further in paragraph 4.3.

4.2. JUDGE-MADE RULES FOR NATIONAL ENFORCEMENT OF EU LAW

In its case law the CJEU has ruled that the enforcement of EU law by the Member States should meet several quality requirements. These requirements are of an instrumental nature on the one hand, and of a protective nature on the other.

The *instrumental requirements* are based on Article 4, third paragraph, TFEU (principle of sincere cooperation). In a series of judgements – of which the case of *Greek Maize* must be mentioned in particular – the Court has ruled that this provision implies not only an obligation to implement EU law, but also to enforce it.[60] More specifically the national enforcement of EU law should meet the principle of equivalence and must be effective, dissuasive and proportionate. Partly these requirements are the same as the general requirements the Member States should meet when *applying* EU law (see paragraph 1.3). In the context of enforcement these requirements can be described as follows[61]:

a. *Equivalence (non-discrimination)*: according to this principle Member States must, in the first place, punish infringements of Union law under conditions, both procedural and substantive, which are analogous to those applicable to infringements of national law of a similar nature and importance. In the second place, a Member State's efforts to actually enforce European rules must also be equivalent: the national authorities must proceed with the same diligence against infringements of Union law as against infringements of corresponding national laws.

60 Case 68/88, *Commission* v *Greece (Greek Maize)*, ECLI:EU:C:1989:339.

61 The protective requirement of proportionality is dealt with below.

b. *Effectiveness*: as regards this principle, it is not sufficient that national legislation contains sanctions for infringements of Union law; the national authorities must also actually enforce the rules in order to ensure they are effectively applied.[62] Where there is a conflict between the requirement of effectiveness and the requirement of equivalence, the former takes precedence[63]: consequently Member States cannot claim in their defence against a complaint that Union law has not been effectively enforced, that similar national rules are not effectively enforced either.
c. *Dissuasiveness*: according to this principle the Member States are obliged to impose sanctions for violations of EU law in such a manner that individuals are prevented from infringing European rules. In other words, the imposed sanctions should be so severe that they have a deterrent effect.

The instrumental requirements apply not only to the national enforcement of directives and regulations (positive integration), but also to the enforcement of the TFEU's freedoms (negative integration). The latter became clear in the case of *Spanish Strawberries*.[64] In this case the Court ruled that the prohibition on restricting the free movement of goods of (now) Article 34 TFEU, also implies that Member States adopt enforcement measures against obstacles to the free movement of goods which are not caused by the State. Because France took no enforcement measures against the obstruction by French farmers of the free movement of certain products from other Member States (amongst others, Spanish strawberries) on its territory over a number of years, this Member State failed to fulfil its obligations under (now) Article 34 TFEU, in conjunction with Article 4, third paragraph, TEU.

In addition to the instrumental requirements based on Article 4, third paragraph, TFEU, the Court also requires national enforcement measures to meet criteria which stress the *protective function* of the law. Three groups of protective requirements can be distinguished:

a. *General principles of Union law*: these principles will be discussed in depth in paragraph 5.2. As regards the enforcement of Union law, the most important general principles are the principle of proportionality and the rights of defence. In the context of enforcement, the principle of proportionality requires that the severity of a sanction is proportionate to the seriousness of the violation.[65] The right of defence requires *inter alia* that, before a national authority imposes a sanction, the individual should have the opportunity to make its point of view known as regards the facts on which the sanction is based.

---

62 Case C-42/89, *Commission* v *Belgium (Verviers Drinking Water)*, ECLI:EU:C:1990:285.

63 Case 199/82, *San Giorgio*, ECLI:EU:C:1983:318.

64 Case C-265/95, *Commission* v *France (Spanish Strawberries)*, ECLI:EU:C:1998:595.

65 See for an application of the principle of proportionality in the context of a national sanction imposed for a violation of EU rules, Case C-210/10, *Urbán*, ECLI:EU:C:2012:64.

b. *Fundamental rights*: as will be elaborated in more detail in section 5.3, Member States, when enforcing Union law, must observe the fundamental rights as codified in the Charter, and which, in so far as they are also guaranteed by the European Convention on Human Rights (hereafter: ECHR), still constitute general principles of Union law as well (Article 6, third paragraph, TEU). Judgements in which national enforcement measures were limited by fundamental rights are for example the cases of *Schmidberger* – which is discussed below – and *Roquette Frères*.[66] In the latter, the CJEU ruled that searching business premises by a national competition authority in the course of a Commission inspection, without prior authorization of a national court was in the circumstances of the case a disproportionate breach of at that time Article 8 ECHR (now Article 7 Charter)..[67] In addition, Articles 48 to 50 Charter provide for specific criminal law guarantees – such as the presumption of innocence, the principle of legality and the principle of *ne bis in idem* – which must be observed by the Member States when imposing criminal law sanctions or administrative sanctions of a criminal nature. To decide whether an administrative sanction qualifies as a sanction of a criminal nature, the CJEU applies the criteria that have been developed by the European Court of Human Rights (hereafter: ECtHR) in respect of a 'criminal charge' in the meaning of Article 6 ECHR, in the case of *Engel* and subsequent case law[68], the qualification of the sanction under national law, the nature of the offence, and the punitive and deterrent purpose of the sanction imposed. On the ground of these criteria administrative fines generally qualify as 'criminal'.[69]
c. *Treaty freedoms*: national enforcement measures must also be compatible with the Treaty freedoms, for instance, the free movement of persons or services. An example can be found in the case of *Calfa*. In this case, the CJEU ruled that the Greek penalty of expulsion for life from Greece in case of obtaining and being in possession of drugs constitutes an obstacle to the freedom to provide services which is not justified by the public policy exception provided in (now) Article 52 TFEU.[70]

In practice, it is possible that the instrumental and protective European enforcement requirements lead to a different conclusion. In that case both

---

66 Case C-94/00, *Roquette Frères*, ECLI:EU:C:2002:603.

67 See however Case C-583/13 P, *Deutsche Bahn*, ECLI:EU:C:2015:404, from which can be derived that in respect of such searches a prior authorization by a national court is not necessary as a rule.

68 Case C-489/10, *Bonda*, ECLI:EU:C:2012:319, with reference to ECtHR 8 June 1976, *Engel*, no. 5100/71. See e.g. also, ECtHR 21 February 1984, *Öztürk*, no. 8544/79.

69 Case C-45/08, *Spector Photo Group*, ECLI:EU:C:2009:806, Case C-617/10, *Åkerberg Fransson*, ECLI:EU:C:2013:105.

70 Case C-348/96, *Calfa*, ECLI:EU:C:1999:6.

requirements must be reconciled. An example of such reconciliation is offered by the case of *Schmidberger*.[71]

This judgement is the fundamental rights sequel to the above mentioned *Spanish Strawberries* case. In *Schmidberger* the free movement of goods was restricted by environmental protesters effectively closing the Brenner Pass for a 30-hour period. The question referred to the Court was whether the Austrian authorities had contravened Union law by failing to prevent the blockade. In its answer, the Court first followed the line of the *Spanish Strawberries* case. It ruled that Austria, by not banning the blockade, in principle had failed to take all necessary and appropriate measures to ensure the free movement of goods on its territory. So far, the conduct of Austria was incompatible with its obligation to enforce this Treaty freedom. However – and this is where the Court departed from its line in *Spanish Strawberries* – this failure could under certain circumstances be 'objectively justified': more specifically, the protection of fundamental rights may be a legitimate interest which, in principle, justifies a restriction of a Treaty freedom such as the free movement of goods. In this case, the environmental protestors were exercising their fundamental rights of expression (Article 10 ECHR) and assembly (Article 11 ECHR). The Court continued:

> 'as the requirement of the protection of fundamental rights provided strong arguments in justification of Austria's failure to enforce, whereas the requirement of ensuring freedom of movement would produce the opposite result, these two requirements needed to be reconciled'.

The question to be answered is whether the restrictions placed upon intra-Union trade are proportionate in the light of the legitimate objective pursued, namely the protection of fundamental rights. In the *Schmidberger* case the CJEU decided in favour of the latter. The reasons for this were, *inter alia*: the demonstration in this case took place following a request for authorization and after the competent authorities had decided not to ban it; the blockade of the Brenner Pass lasted only 30 hours and the obstacle to the free movement of goods was therefore only minor; the Austrian authorities in *Schmidberger* had taken various measures to limit the disruption of free movement as far as possible. For example, an extensive publicity campaign had been launched well before the date on which the demonstration was due to take place and various alternative routes had been designated. Consequently, the fact that the national authorities did not ban the demonstration was not incompatible with (now) Articles 34 and 35 TFEU, in conjunction with Article 4, third paragraph, TEU.

---

71 Case C-112/00, *Schmidberger*, ECLI:EU:C:2002:333.

4.3. LEGISLATIVE MEASURES CONCERNING NATIONAL ENFORCEMENT OF UNION LAW

The enforcement of Union law in the Member States is also Europeanized by legislative measures. Different from the judge-made requirements discussed above – which apply to the enforcement of EU law in general – these legislative requirements are only relevant for national enforcement in the specific policy area regulated by the Union rules concerned.[72] The legislative influence relates both to the national monitoring of compliance with Union law, to national investigation actions and to the imposition of sanctions.[73] The requirements prescribed may be very detailed, but can also be more general. As regards the latter, it should be noted that, starting from the beginning of the nineties, the Union legislator has prescribed in most secondary Union rules that the national enforcement of the rules concerned should meet the *Greek Maize* requirements of equivalence, effectiveness, dissuasiveness and proportionality (see paragraph 4.2).In respect of combating fraud and other illegal activities affecting the financial interests of the Union, these requirements have been codified in Article 325 TFEU. A large number of Union regulations and some directives impose specific requirements on Member States' activities concerning the monitoring of compliance with Union law and the investigation of possible sanctions. The purpose of these rules is to ensure an adequate and equivalent level of supervision in the Member States. The standard of supervision required by regulations may be very detailed indeed. For instance, in the regulations in the area of agricultural subsidies, one can find detailed rules on administrative inspection, on the minimum amount of physical checks on the spot which have to be exercised and even on the inspection with satellites. The Bathing Water Directive 2006/7/EC provides for a minimum frequency of sampling operations, and contains all kinds of detailed provisions concerning methods of analysis and inspection of the water.

An increasing number of Union regulations and some directives describe in detail the sanctions the Member States must impose when the Union rules in question are infringed.[74] These sanctions may be of a *reparatory nature*. For example, Union legislation often provides for an action to recover European subsidies that have been wrongly paid. In other Union regulations, the imposition of *administrative sanctions of a criminal nature*, such as administrative fines, is

---

72 Cf. A.M. Keessen, *European administrative Decisions. How the EU Regulates Products on the Internal Market*, Europa Law Publishing, Groningen, 2009, pp. 86–137.

73 See De Moor-van Vugt & Widdershoven, *supra* note 56, pp. 281–293, for more examples of regulatory influence on national monitoring activities, investigation acts and the imposition of sanctions.

74 See e.g. on sanctions prescribed in the area of environmental law, A.B. Blomberg, 'European Influence on National Environmental Law Enforcement', *Review of European Administrative Law*, 2008/2, pp. 39–82.

prescribed. Of more general importance is Regulation 2988/95 on the protection of the EU's financial interests.[75] This horizontal regulation applies to both the revenue's side of the financial EU interests (customs, value added tax), and to the expenses (European subsidies), and contains an overview of the different administrative penalties the Member States may have to impose if an economic operator commits intentionally or as a result of negligence, an irregularity having the effect of prejudicing the budget of the Union. They include: payment of an amount greater than the amounts wrongly received or evaded; exclusion from the advantage for a period subsequent to that of the irregularity; temporary withdrawal of the approval or recognition necessary for participation in a Union aid scheme; and the loss of a security or deposit provided for the purpose of complying with conditions. In the case of *Bonda*[76], the CJEU has determined that these penalties, although they go further than reparation only, do not qualify as sanctions of a criminal nature (or as criminal charge in the meaning of Article 6 ECHR). The Court came to this decision, because their main purpose is not punitive, but the protection of the management of the EU funds, and because they do not apply to all citizens but only to a specific group of individuals who have entered a subsidy scheme voluntary. As a result, the principle of *ne bis in idem* does not apply to the combined imposition of (one of) these penalties and a national criminal law sanction.

The next step in the Europeanization of national sanctions is that the Union increasingly prescribes the imposition of *criminal sanctions* for the infringement of sectoral Union rules. In the pre-Lisbon era, it was uncertain whether the (then) Community was competent to prescribe to the Member States criminal enforcement of harmonized EC rules, for instance, of European environmental rules. In the landmark case *Commission versus Council* in 2005, the CJEU ruled in favour of the Community competence in this regard, at least where 'the application of effective, proportionate and dissuasive criminal penalties is an essential measure to ensure' that the environmental rules 'are fully effective'.[77] Since the coming into force of the Lisbon Treaty the Union's competence to prescribe criminal enforcement is no longer disputed. According to Article 83, second paragraph TFEU the Union is competent to establish by means of directives minimum rules with regard to the definition of criminal offences and sanctions in policy areas which have been subject to harmonization measures. Such directives are adopted by the same legislative procedure as was followed for the adoption of the harmonization measure in question. As a rule, this implies decision-making in the Council by qualified majority. Moreover, the Union is also competent to establish by means of directives minimum rules concerning

75 Regulation 2988/95, *OJ* 1995, L 312/1. See J.A.E. Vervaele (ed.), *Transnational Enforcement of the Financial Interests of the EU*, Intersentia, Antwerpen/Groningen/Oxford, 1999.

76 Case C-489/10, *Bonda*, ECLI:EU:C:2012:319. In the same vein, Case C-210/00, *Käserei Champignon Hofmeister*, ECLI:EU:C:2002:440.

77 Case C-176/03, *Commission* v. *Council*, ECLI:EU:C:2005:542.

the definition of criminal offences and sanctions in the areas of particularly serious crimes with a cross-border dimension, like terrorism, trafficking of human beings, illicit drugs trafficking, money laundering, corruption and organized crime (Article 83, first paragraph, TFEU).

5. WHAT ARE THE NORMS WITH WHICH THE ADMINISTRATION HAS TO COMPLY?

5.1. INTRODUCTION

The European administration and national administrations should, in the first place, comply with written rules of law. In addition, the European administration in general, and the national administrations when 'acting within the scope of Union law' are bound by the general principles of Union law and the – partly overlapping – fundamental rights codified in the Charter (see paragraph 5.2 and 5.3 for details). Together these sources of law constitute the legal framework, which is applied by the CJEU and the national courts if they have to review the acts and decisions of Union institutions and national authorities.

Rules of *written law* that are of importance for the European institutions can be found in the Treaties, in regulations and directives and in international treaties to which the European Union is a party. For the national administration, the relevant written law is Union law (the Treaties, regulations, directives and decisions), international law and national law. It should be noted that the national authorities, when applying EU law, must also comply with the rules of national law, at least insofar as they are not incompatible with EU law. After all, the application of EU law within the national legal order occurs by means of national law (see paragraph 1.3). Thus, for instance, a decision to grant an environmental permit, which is compatible with EU law, but inconsistent with additional national norms or national provisions concerning e.g. the procedure, will be overturned by the national court.

There exists a hierarchy between the several European and national norms with which the administration must comply.[78] Highest in rank is the so-called primary Union law. To this group belong the Treaties (including the Charter), the general principles of Union Law and the (directly effective provisions of) international treaties to which the European Union itself is a party. Whether a provision of an international treaty has direct effect in the European legal order, is decided by the CJEU. Lower in rank is the secondary Union law, i.e. regulations, directives and decisions. These legal instruments have to be consistent with primary Union law. Thus, regulations, directives and decisions

[78] See figure 2.

contrary to the Treaties (including the Charter), a general EU principle or an international treaty to which the Union is a party are unlawful. In principle regulations and directives enjoy the same legal status. The choice between both legal instruments depends on the legal basis in the Treaties (see paragraph 1.4). Decisions are subordinate to the provision of the Treaty, and to a regulation or directive on which they may be based. Lowest in rank is the national legislation implementing the EU legal instruments. Whether there exists a hierarchy between the different national legislative instruments, is a matter of national constitutional law.

5.2. GENERAL PRINCIPLES OF UNION LAW[79]

The general principles of Union law are the most important unwritten source of Union law. General principles have been developed by the CJEU from the early years of the European cooperation.[80] They differ from written law in the sense that they have an open character and apply `in general'. Therefore, they offer a standard for the assessment of measures in the various fields of law. The meaning of rules of written law is usually limited to a certain area of law. For instance, a directive concerning CO_2 emissions is only of importance in the field of environmental law. Similarly, a regulation concerning European subsidies for farmers is only relevant in agricultural law. General principles, however, must be complied with in environmental, agricultural and all other fields of law

The somewhat hidden legal basis for the application of general principles in the Union legal order is Article 19, first paragraph TEU. According to this Article the CJEU shall 'ensure that in the interpretation and application of the Treaties the law is observed'. From this Article, it is clear that there is 'law' which is additional to that in the Treaties. This 'extra' law is the general principles of Union law. The most important general principles of Union law, which will be discussed in more detail in paragraph 5.4 and further, are: the principle of equality; the principle of proportionality; the principle of respect fort rights of defence; the principle of legitimate expectations; the duty to state reasons and the principle of transparency.

Although initially developed by the CJEU as unwritten law, general principles are not unwritten by definition. Not only in the Treaty, but in some regulations and directives as well, several general principles are (partly) codified. For instance, the prohibition of discrimination on grounds of nationality is codified in several articles of the TFEU, such as Articles 18, 45, second paragraph

79 T. Tridimas, *The General Principles of EC Law*, 2nd ed., Oxford: Oxford University Press, 2006; Craig, *supra* note 1, chapters 17–20; Van den Brink *et al*, 'General Principles of Law', in: Jans *et al.*, *supra* note 1, chapter 4.

80 See Joined Cases 7/56 and 3 to 7/57, *Algera*, ECLI:EU:C:1957:7, for the 'discovery' by the CJEU of the first general principle of Union law, the principle of legal certainty.

and 49 TFEU. Article 219 Regulation 952/2013 (Union Customs Code) contains a codification of the principle of legitimate expectations in customs matters. Moreover, several general principles, such as the principle of equality (Chapter 3), several aspects of the rights of defence (Article 41) and the principle of proportionality (Article 52), are (partly) codified in the Charter.

Fundamental rights constitute a special group of general principles of Union law. In the founding Treaty of the European Economic Community there was no mention of fundamental rights. To fill in this gap, the CJEU has recognized them as 'an integral part of the general principles of law', the observance of which the Court ensures.[81] To establish the precise content of a fundamental right, the CJEU draws inspiration from the constitutional traditions of the Member States and from international law. A special source of inspiration in this respect was (and is) the ECHR. Its privileged position is explicitly recognized in Article 6, third paragraph, TEU. Before the coming into force of the Charter on 1 December 2009, the CJEU frequently applied specific ECHR rights – such as the right to effective judicial protection (Article 6 and 13 ECHR), the right to private life (Article 8), the freedom of expression (Article 10 ECHR) and the freedom of assembly (Article 11 ECHR) – as general principles of Union law.[82] The interpretation of these principles by the CJEU was (and is) tuned to the case law of the ECtHR regarding the ECHR rights mentioned, to which the CJEU regularly referred (and refers).

Most other general principles, developed in the case law of the CJEU, are derived from and inspired by the laws of the Member States.[83] One article of the Treaty, namely Article 340, second paragraph, TFEU even explicitly prescribes that a Union principle must be 'in accordance with general principles common to the law of the Member States'. That the CJEU case law on general principles has been inspired by national law, is not strange considering that the judges of the CJEU also originate from the Member States. Thus, the principles of Union law are quite similar to the general principles which are applied in the Member States. The existence of similarities between Union and national general principles of law does not mean, however, that a Union principle is consistent in every detail with the equivalent principle in each of the Member States.[84] This

---

81 Cf. Case 29/69, *Stauder*, ECLI:EU:C:1969:57, Case 11/70, *Internationale Handelsgesellschaft*, ECLI:EU:C:1970:114, Case 4/73, *Nold*, ECLI:EU:C:1974:51.

82 See e.g., Case 222/86, *Heylens*, ECLI:EU:C:1987:442, Case C-97/91, *Borelli*, ECLI:EU:C:1992:491 (both Articles. 6 and 13 ECHR), Case C-94/00, *Roquette Frères*, ECLI:EU:C:2002:603 (Article 8 ECHR), and Case C-112/00, *Schmidberger*, ECLI:EU:C:2002:333 (Articles. 10 and 11 ECHR).

83 X. Groussot, *General Principles of Community Law*, Europa Law Publishing, Groningen, 2006.

84 Cf. as regards the similarities and differences between the Union and Dutch general principles of law, R.J.G.M. Widdershoven & M. Remac, 'General Principles of Law in Administrative Law under European Influence', *European Review of Private Law*, 2012, pp. 381–407.

would be impossible because of the differences, which exist between the specific principles in the Member States. Therefore, the CJEU has given its own Union meaning to its general principles. Usually the Union principle offers a wise compromise between the variety of national principles.

General principles of Union law are of course binding as far as EU institutions are concerned. Furthermore, national authorities have to comply with them when acting 'within the scope of Union law'.[85] The precise meaning of this phrase will be discussed in depth in paragraph 5.4 below, as the same scope applies to the Charter rights as well and the phrase has been developed in more detail in the context of the Charter. Problems may occur where a general principle of Union law deviates from the national equivalent. After all, the application of EU law in the Member States occurs by means of national law, including the national general principles (see paragraph 1.3). If a national principle is not consistent with the Union principle, the national administrative authority therefore has to choose between both principles. In making this choice, two situations should be distinguished.

a. The Union principle offers more protection to individuals than the national equivalent: in this situation the principle of the supremacy of Union law requires that the Union principle is applied. The national principle must be set aside.
b. The Union principle offers less protection to individuals than the national equivalent: according to the principle of procedural autonomy it is in principle possible to apply the national principle, as long as the requirements of equivalence and effectiveness are met (see paragraph 1.3). The result, which this assessment may lead to, is demonstrated in paragraph 5.6 where the application of the principle of legitimate expectations is examined.

5.3. CHARTER OF THE FUNDAMENTAL RIGHTS OF THE EU[86]

Since 1 December 2009 the EU has its own binding fundamental right catalogue, the EU Charter of Fundamental Rights. The Charter contains a large number of fundamental rights, which are partly equivalent to the ECHR rights and partly go beyond them. It is divided in six substantive chapters, which are headed:

- *Dignity*: this chapter includes, for instance, the right to life (Article 2), the right to integrity of a person (Article 3) and the prohibition of torture and inhuman treatment (Article 4).

---

85 Cf. Case 5/88, *Wachauf*, ECLI:EU:C:1989: 321, Case 260/89, *ERT*, ECLI:EU:C:1991:254, Case 309/96, *Annibaldi*, ECLI:EU:C:1997:631.

86 See extensively, S. Peers, T. Hervey, J. Kenner & A. Ward (eds.), *The EU Charter of Fundamental Rights – A Commentary*, Hart Publishing, Oxford, 2014.

- *Freedoms*: this chapter contains for example the right to private and family life (Article 7), the freedom of thought, conscience and religion (Article 10), the freedom of expression and information (Article 11), the freedom of assembly and of association (Article 12); the right to education (Article 14) and the right to property (Article 17).
- *Equality*: this chapter contains, for instance, the right of equality before the law (Article 20), the prohibition of discrimination (Article 21), equality of women and men (Article 22) and the rights of the child and the elderly (Articles 23 and 24).
- *Solidarity*: this chapter includes for example workers' rights to information and consultation within the undertaking (Article 26), the right of collective bargaining and action (Article 27), access to services of general economic interests (Article 35) and environmental and consumer protection (Articles 37 and 38).
- *Citizens' rights*: this chapter includes, for instance, the right to vote and stand as a candidate at elections for the European Parliament and at municipal elections (Articles 39 and 40), the right to good administration (Article 41), the right of access to documents (Article 42) and the right to petition (Article 44). The right to good administration of Article 41 is of special importance for administrative law as it codifies several (aspects of) general principles of administrative law, such as the principles of impartiality, fairness and reasonable time, the right to be heard, the right to have access to the file and the obligation of the administration to state reasons.
- *Justice*: this chapter contains the right to an effective remedy and to a fair trial (Article 47), the presumption of innocence (Article 48), the principles of legality and proportionality of criminal offences and penalties (Article 49) and the principle of *ne bis in idem* (Article 50).

The Charter is not only binding for the EU institutions, but also for the (legislative, administrative and judicial authorities of the) Member States, be it 'only when they are implementing Union law' (Article 51, first paragraph). At first sight, this phrase seems more restrictive than the phrase the CJEU applied in respect of the application by the Member States of general principles of Union law, 'acting within the scope of' (see paragraph 5.2, above). However, in the landmark case of *Åkerberg Fransson*[87], the Court has determined that `implementing Union law' in the meaning of Article 51 Charter should be interpreted as 'acting within the scope of Union law'. As a result, the scope of the Charter rights is identical to the scope of general principles of Union law.

In particular, since the coming into force of the Charter in 2009, the CJEU in many cases has clarified in which situation Member States are 'acting within

87 Case C-617/10, *Åkerberg Fransson*, ECLI:EU:C:2013:105. See also Case C-198/13, *Hernandez*, ECLI:EU:C:2014:2055, Case C-206/13, *Siragusa*, ECLI:EU:C:2014:12.

the scope of Union law'. Point of departure of the CJEU's case law is that Charter provisions (and thus general principles of Union law as well) are applicable in all situations governed by European Union law, but not outside such situations.[88] To be governed by Union law the situation should have 'a certain degree of connection with Union law above and beyond the matters covered being closely related to one of those matters that has an indirect impact on the other'.[89] In this regard it is not sufficient that a national measure comes within an area in which the EU is in principle competent to regulate on the basis of the TFEU.[90] It is required that the Union has actually used this power and has imposed obligations on the Member States that are applicable to the national situation..[91] In general, one may say that a Member State is acting within the scope of Union law and has to respect the Charter (and general principles of Union law), if, in the case at hand, there is *another EU law provision* than the provision of the Charter relied upon.[92] Charter provisions cannot, of themselves, trigger their own application. In the case law of the Court one can distinguish three categories of national measures and situations that fall within the scope of Union law and are therefore protected by the Charter.[93]

a. *Agent situation*: Member States act within the scope of Union Law when they are implementing *specific* Union obligations and thus act as an agent of Union law. In most cases, such obligations are prescribed by secondary Union law. In this respect, this category includes the national operationalization and application of specific provisions of EU regulations and decisions[94], the transposition of EU directives[95] and the application of – in itself correct – national transposition legislation.[96] In addition, Member States act as an EU agent when they are applying certain specific Treaty obligations, such as the competition rules of Articles 101 and 102 TFEU and the state aid provisions of Articles 107 and 108 TFEU. In all these agent situations Member States should observe the Charter and general principles of Union law.
b. *Derogations of the free movement and Union citizenship rights*: Secondly, national acts fall `within the scope of Union law' when Member States

88 Case C-617/10, *Åkerberg Fransson*, ECLI:EU:C:2013:105, Case C-483/12, *Pelckmans*, ECLI:EU:C:2014:304.

89 Case C-206/13, *Siragusa*, ECLI:EU:C:2014:126, Case C-299/95, *Kremzov*, ECLI:EU:C:1997:254.

90 Case C-198/13, *Hernandez*, ECLI:EU:C:2014:2055.

91 Case C-206/13, *Siragusa*, ECLI:EU:C:2014:126, Case C-144/95, *Maurin*, ECLI:EU:C:1996:235, Case C-265/13, *Marcos*, ECLI:EU:C:2014:187.

92 S. Prechal, ''The Court of Justice and Effective Judicial Protection: What has the Charter Changed?', in: C. Paulussen *et al* (eds.), *Fundamental Rights in International and European Law, Public and Private Law Perspectives*, T.M.C. Asser Press, 2016.

93 Cf. Van den Brink *et al*, *supra* note 79, pp. 150–155.

94 E.g. Case C-349/07, *Sopropé*, ECLI:EU:C:2008:746, Case C-568/11, *Agroferm*, ECLI:EU:C:2013:407.

95 E.g. Case C-144/04, *Mangold*, ECLI:EU:C:2005:709, Case C-201/08, *Plantanol*, ECLI:EU:C:2009:539.

96 Case C-62/00, *Marks & Spencer*, ECLI:EU:C:2002:435.

derogate from the free movement rights (free movement of goods, persons, services, and capital) and from the provisions on Union citizenship (Articles 20 and 21 TFEU). This implies that Charter rights and general EU principles have to be respected when determining whether a particular restriction of these rights can be justified on grounds provided by Union law.[97] To come within the scope of Union law, the restriction of the free movement right should, however, not be too uncertain and indirect.[98] Moreover, as free movement rights and EU citizenship provisions, in principle, only apply in cross-border situations, the same goes for the Charter rights and general principles. Therefore, they do not have to be observed in so-called purely internal situations in which all elements of the dispute are confined within a single Member State.[99]

c. *Remedial context of a) and b)*: thirdly, national acts are 'within the scope of Union law' if they relate to the remedial context of the aforementioned categories. The remedial context includes all national rules that are not specifically regulated by secondary and primary Union rules, but are necessary for an effective application and enforcement of these rules.[100] Hence, these rules belong to the procedural or enforcement autonomy of the Member States (paragraph 1.3). An example of the application of the Charter in the situation of procedural autonomy is offered in *Toma*.[101] In this case the CJEU ruled that Article 47 Charter, in principle, applies to a national decision not reviewing an earlier decision which was inconsistent with Union law, although the Union legislation concerned did not contain any provision in respect of such review. In this regard, it was of importance that the individual concerned could rely on another EU law provision than the Charter, namely Article 4, third paragraph, TEU. In respect of the enforcement of Union law, the CJEU applies a similar line of reasoning in *Åkerberg Fransson*.[102] In this case the Court ruled that the imposition of national sanctions for the evasion of value added tax, was 'within the scope of Union law', although the Union rules in question did not prescribe any specific sanctions. The Court based its opinion on, *inter alia*, Article 4, third paragraph, TEU, and Article 325 TFEU

---

97 E.g. Case C-260/89, *ERT*, ECLI:EU:C:1991:254, Case C-112/00, *Schmidberger*, ECLI:EU:C:2003:333. Concerning Union citizenship, see f.i. Case C-135/08, *Rottmann*, ECLI:EU:C:2010:104.

98 Case C-483/12, *Pelckmans*, ECLI:EU:C:2014:304.

99 E.g. Case C-245/09, *Omalet*, ECLI:EU:C:2010:808, Case C-268/15, *Ullens de Schooten*, ECLI:EU:C:2016:874.

100 R.J.G.M. Widdershoven, 'Developing Administrative Law in Europe: Natural Convergence or Imposed Uniformity?', *Review of European Administrative Law*, 2014/2, pp. 9–31, in particular p. 20.

101 Case C-205/15, *Toma*, ECLI:EU:C:2016:499. By the way, the decision not reviewing the earlier one was not considered to be inconsistent with Article 47 Charter. See for this topic more extensively, paragraph 6.3.3.5, below.

102 Case C-617/10, *Åkerberg Fransson*, ECLI:EU:C:2013:105.

> which obliges the Member States to counter fraud affecting the financial interests of the EU through measures that are dissuasive, effective and equivalent. As already stated in paragraph 4.2 and 4.3, these enforcement requirements are derived from the CJEU's case of *Greek Maïze*[103], and have, since the nineties, been prescribed to the Member States in most secondary Union legislation. Therefore, national enforcement of all this legislation is 'within the scope of Union law' as well.[104] Possibly national enforcement of Union rules might even be within scope of Union law, if the Union rules concerned do not contain these requirements. After all, also in that situation the requirements apply to the national enforcement of the EU rules, namely on the basis of *Greek Maïze* itself. Therefore, it seems a small step to extent the *Åkerberg Fransson* reasoning to the enforcement of Union law in general. Whether the Court is willing to take this step, future case law will tell.

The exercise of the Charter's rights may be limited. Any limitation must be provided for by law and respect the very essence of the rights. Moreover, limitations may be made only if they are necessary and genuinely meet objectives of general interest recognized by the Union or the need to protect the rights and freedoms of others (Article 52, first paragraph).

As far as Charter rights correspond to the rights laid down in the ECHR the meaning and scope of the Charter rights are to be the same as those laid down by the ECHR (Article 52, third paragraph). The meaning and scope of the guaranteed rights must be determined not only by reference to the text of the ECHR, but also by reference to the case law of the ECtHR.[105] However, this does not preclude the CJEU from granting wider protection under EU law. In practice the CJEU assesses cases primarily in the light of the Charter provision involved.[106] This provision is interpreted in conformity with the ECHR and the case law of the ECtHR, to which the CJEU generally explicitly refers. Sometimes in order to confirm or support its finding as regards a Charter provision[107], in other cases to guide the interpretation of such provision.[108] According to Article 6, second paragraph, TEU, it is the intention of the Treaties legislator that the Union shall accede to the ECHR. However, the negative Opinion 2/13 of the CJEU on the draft agreement between the Council of Europe and the

---

103 Case 68/88, *Commission* v *Greece (Greek Maize)*, ECLI:EU:C:1989:339.

104 See e.g. Case C-418/11, *Textdata Software*, ECLI:EU:C:2013:588. In Joined cases C-387/02, C-391/02 and C-403/02, *Berlusconi*, ECLI:EU:C:2005:270, the criminal enforcement of Union rules was even considered to be 'within the scope of Union law', although the Union rules concerned prescribed the imposition of 'appropriate sanctions' only.

105 See Explanations relating to the Charter, Article 52. See more extensively, S. Peers & S. Prechal, 'Art. 52 – Scope of Guaranteed Rights', in: Peers *et al* (eds.) 2014, pp. 1455–1521.

106 Case 199/11, *Otis*, ECLI:EU:C:2012:684.

107 E.g. Case C-205/15, *Toma*, ECLI:EU:C:2016:499.

108 E.g. Case C-279/09, *DEB*, ECLI:EU:C:2010:811.

EU concerning the accession[109], has delayed the accession seriously. Whether, when and how the accession will take place – and what consequences it will have for the relationship between the CJEU and the ECtHR – is therefore as yet unclear.

EU law recognizes the importance of national fundamental rights as a source of inspiration for the Union fundamental rights of the Charter (cf. Article 6, third paragraph, TEU, and Article 52, fourth paragraph, Charter). However, because Member States may recognize different fundamental rights or apply similar fundamental rights in a different way, this does not prevent tensions between EU law and national fundamental rights of particular Member States.[110] This raises the question whether national fundamental rights that deviate from EU fundamental rights may be applied in cases 'within the scope of Union law'. This question has been decided in the case of *Melloni*[111], in which the Court ruled that Article 53 Charter (the provision which regulates the matter):

> 'confirms that, where an EU legal act calls for national implementing measures, national authorities and courts remain free to apply national standards of protection of fundamental rights, provided that the level of protection for by the Charter, as interpreted by the Court, and the primacy, unity and effectiveness of EU law are not thereby compromised.'

From this statement, it is clear that the Charter not only offers a minimum standard of fundamental rights protection, but also a maximum standard, namely in the situation that the application of a national fundamental right, offering a higher standard of protection than the Charter, would compromise the primacy, unity or effectiveness of Union law. In *Melloni*, the relevant issue – whether Spain, in accordance with its constitutional law, was entitled to make the surrender from Spain to Italy of Melloni, who had been convicted in Italy *in absentia*, conditional upon a retrial in Italy – had been regulated exhaustively by Union law.[112] Therefore the CJEU considered the application of the more generous Spanish fundamental right to be inconsistent with the requirements of unity and effectiveness. When the right at issue is not completely determined by Union law, the CJEU will probably offer the Member States more leeway in applying more generous fundamental rights.[113]

---

109 Opinion 2/13, ECLI:EU:C:2014:2454.

110 L.F.M. Besselink, 'FIDE 2012 General Report: The Protection of Fundamental Rights post Lisbon. The Interaction between the EU Charter of Fundamental Rights, the European Convention of Human Rights (ECHR) and National Constitutions', available at www.fide2012.eu.

111 Case C-399/11, *Melloni*, ECLI:EU:C:2013:107.

112 Framework Decision 2002/584, as revised by Framework Decision 2009/299.

113 Case C-617/10, *Åkerberg Fransson*, ECLI:EU:C:2013:105.

5.4. PROPORTIONALITY[114]

The principle of proportionality is perhaps the most important principle of Union law. It is partly codified in Article 5, fourth paragraph, TEU ('The content and form of Union action shall not exceed what is necessary for the objectives of the Treaties'). In a more general definition the principle requires that the adverse consequences of a certain measure for one or more interested individuals may not be disproportionate in relation to the purposes and objectives served by that measure. The prohibition of disproportionality expresses the principle of administrative 'restraint': intervention by the administration in social life may be necessary and useful from the viewpoint of a general interest, but at the same time it should not extend beyond that which is necessary to serve this interest in a proper manner.

To assess whether the principle of proportionality has been violated, the CJEU distinguishes three questions:

- Is the measure *suitable* in order to achieve the objective of the measure?
- Is the measure *necessary* in order to achieve the objective? Or can the objective also be achieved by another measure, which is less aggravating for individuals.
- Is the measure proportionate *in sensu stricto*? To assess this question, the court must examine whether a measure, which is as such suitable and necessary, may damage the interests of a specific group of individuals in a disproportionate manner.

The principle of proportionality is applied in three different situations. The intensity, with which the CJEU or national courts may examine whether the principle has been violated, depends on the margin of discretion enjoyed by the authorities when implementing the measure concerned.

In the first place, the principle is applied by the CJEU when reviewing the legislative measures taken by the Union institutions. In general, the EU institutions have a wide margin of discretion when establishing legislation. The Council and Commission are also politically responsible for their legislation. Therefore, the CJEU exercises restraint reviewing these measures. Legislation is only declared void if the measure is 'manifestly disproportionate'.[115]

Secondly, the principle is an important standard in assessing the justification of a national restriction on the free movement rights, such as the free movement of goods (Article 34 TFEU). As such, Member States are allowed to restrict the free movement of goods as long as the restriction can be justified on the

114 N. Emiliou, *The Principle of Proportionality in European Law, A Comparative Study*, Kluwer Law International, London-The Hague-Boston, 1996; Tridimas, *supra* note 79, chapters 3–4; Craig, *supra* note 1, chapters 19–20; Van de Brink *et al*, in: Jans *et al* (eds.), *supra* note 1, pp. 183–207.

115 Case 331/88, *Fedesa*, ECLI:EU:C:1990:391.

grounds mentioned in Article 36 TFEU (amongst others: public morality, public policy or public security; the protection of health and life of humans, animals or plants; the protection of industrial and commercial property). In assessing the question whether a specific measure can be justified according to a certain ground the court will subject the proportionality of the restriction to quite intense examination. This examination will be carried out by the national court before which the national measure is challenged. The national court may refer the question to the CJEU in the preliminary procedure.

Thirdly, and finally, proportionality is applied by the CJEU and the national courts when assessing law enforcement actions, in particular the imposition of sanctions (see paragraph 4.2). The CJEU is the competent court if the sanction has been imposed by a Union institution, for instance, in the field of European competition law, the Commission. Sanctions imposed by national authorities because of violations of Union law in the Member States must be challenged before the national courts. In both procedures, the main question is whether the severity of the sanction is proportionate to the seriousness of the violation. This review of proportionality is fairly intense.[116] In the area of competition law the Union courts even enjoy 'unlimited jurisdiction' when assessing the amount of a competition fine or penalty payment imposed by the Commission.[117] Therefore, they are entitled to substitute their own appraisal for the Commission's and, consequently, to cancel, reduce or increase the fine or penalty payment imposed.

5.5. EQUALITY

The principle of equality or non-discrimination requires that cases are to be treated equally and that unequal cases are treated unequally.[118] Different treatment may be allowed but – as will be indicated hereafter – only to the extent that such different treatment can be objectively justified, i.e. with reference to accepted legal reasons. This principle is an unwritten fundamental principle of Union law, but is codified in written Union law as well. First, the principle and the prohibition of non-discrimination on several grounds are codified in Title 3 of the Charter. Secondly, the TFEU contains several prohibitions of discrimination, for instance, on the grounds of nationality – see for example Articles 18, 45, second paragraph, and 49 TFEU – and of gender (Article 157 TFEU). Prohibitions of discrimination are also prescribed in several directives.[119] When Union institutions and national authorities apply EU law,

[116] Cf. Case C-210/10, *Urbán*, ECLI:EU:C:2012:64.

[117] Case C-389/10 P, *KME*, ECLI:EU:C:2011:816.

[118] Tridimas, *supra* note 79, chapter 2; Craig, *supra* note 1, chapter 17.

[119] For instance, Directive 2006/54, on equal treatment of men and women as regards access to employment, *OJ* 2004, L 158/77; Directive 2000/43, to combat race discrimination, *OJ* 2000, L 180/22; Directive 2000/78, general framework directive as regards equal treatment in

they should comply with the non-discrimination provisions laid down in written law as well as with the unwritten equality principle.

The distinction between direct and indirect discrimination is typical of the Union principle of equality.

- In the case of direct discrimination, the different treatment of two situations is explicitly based on a forbidden criterion, for instance, on nationality or gender. This is only allowed if there are specific grounds which can justify the different treatment. Such grounds can, for instance, be found in Article 45, fourth paragraph, TFEU: the prohibition of discrimination on the ground of nationality does not apply to employment in the public service.
- In the case of indirect discrimination, a measure will have discriminating effects for a certain group while not applying an explicitly forbidden criterion. The measure may, for instance, make use of a gender-neutral criterion, but in practice it nevertheless has adverse consequences for women. Indirect discrimination may be allowed if the measure in question is objectively justified. To be objectively justified the measure must have a justified or legitimate purpose. Moreover, the measure must comply with the principle of proportionality: it must be suitable and necessary in order to achieve the required aim.

An example of the way in which the principle of equality is examined, can be found in the case of *Pastoors*.[120] This case concerned the Belgian legislation on the enforcement and sanctioning of violations of several EU regulations relating to road transport. When these regulations were infringed, the Belgian legislation imposed an obligation on non-residents who did not opt for immediate payment of the prescribed fine, to lodge by way of security in respect of each offence a fixed sum higher than that provided for in the case of immediate payment. According to the CJEU, the national legislation in question did not directly discriminate on the (forbidden) ground of nationality, since the obligation to lodge a sum of money by way of security was imposed on any offender who was not resident in Belgium, irrespective of nationality. However, the criterion of non-residence was liable to operate mainly to the detriment of nationals of other Member States, and thus to constitute indirect discrimination by reason of nationality. The CJEU continued by establishing that this difference of treatment between residents and non-residents was justified by a legitimate purpose, namely to ensure the enforcement of the measures in question: after all, there is 'a real risk that enforcement of a judgement against a non-resident would be impossible or, at least, considerably more difficult and onerous' than the enforcement of judgements against residents. Nevertheless, the legislation

employment and occupation on the ground of religion or belief, disability, age and sexual orientation, *OJ* 2000, L 303/16.

120 Case C-29/95, *Pastoors*, ECLI:EU:C:1997:28.

was declared inconsistent with EU law, because the obligation imposed on non-residents to lodge a fixed sum higher than provided in case of immediate payment and in respect of each offence, was held to be disproportionate and excessive.

5.6. THE RIGHTS OF DEFENCE

The principle of respect of the rights of defence is a fundamental right of Union law.[121] It has mainly been developed in the case law of the CJEU in relation to European competition law. This is not strange, because in this field the Commission is empowered to impose administrative fines and penalty payments on undertakings, which violate European competition rules. However, the scope of the principle is not limited to sanctions in this field. According to the case law of the CJEU, the principle should be respected in all proceedings 'which are liable to culminate in a measure adversely affecting the individual'.[122] The principle applies both to the administrative procedure which may lead to the measure adversely affecting the individual, and to the judicial procedure in which the measure is challenged. Certain rights, which are implied in the principle, must even be respected in preliminary investigations.[123] Because of the fact that the case law of the CJEU is usually concerned with Commission decisions, these rights are generally formulated as rights *vis-à-vis* the Commission. However, they must also be respected by the national authorities whenever they act `within the scope of Union law' (see paragraph 5.3, above), for instance, when they apply and enforce a regulation, a decision or (the national transposition of) a directive.[124]

Several rights of defence have been codified in Article 41, second paragraph, Charter, as part of the right to good administration, be it only in respect of institutions, bodies, offices and agencies of the Union. However, the substance of these codified rights also applies in the relation between a Member State and individuals, as the CJEU has ruled that these rights 'reflect a general principle of EU law'[125], and this general principle applies to Member States as well, at least when they act 'within the scope of Union law'. In addition, the rights of defence

---

121 Groussot, *supra* note 83, pp. 228–234; O. Jansen & P. Langbroek (eds.), *Defence Rights during Administrative Investigations*, Intersentia, Antwerpen-Oxford, 2007; A.J.C. de Moor-van Vugt, 'The Ghost of Criminal Charge: the EU Rights of Defence in Dutch Administrative Law', *Review of European Administrative Law*, 2012/2, pp. 5–16.

122 Case C-32/95 P, *Lisretal*, ECLI:EU:C:1996:402.

123 Joined cases 46/87 and 227/88, *Hoechst*, ECLI:EU:C:1989:337.

124 See explicitly, Case C-349/07, *Sopropé*, ECLI:EU:C:2009:746, Joined Cases C-129–130/13, *Kamino & Datema*, ECLI:EU:C:2014:2041 (both application of a regulation), and Case C-28/05, *Dokter*, ECLI:EU:C:2006:408 (application of a directive).

125 Case C-604/12, *H.N.*, ECLI:EU:C:2014:302, Case C-166/13, *Mukarubega*, ECLI:EU:C:2014:2336.

are codified in Article 47, second paragraph, Charter (in the context of judicial protection) and in Article 48, second paragraph (in the context of criminal charges).

In its case law the CJEU has formulated various sub-categories of rights, which are implied in the rights of defence:

- *The right to be heard*: before a national or Union authority may take an individual measure 'adversely affecting' the interests of an individual, the individual should have the opportunity to make effectively known its view on the evidence on which the decision is based. The 'hearing' may take place in writing. If the Commission wants to impose a competition fine, however, the individual has the right to an oral hearing. An individual who is given a hearing must be granted sufficient time to prepare his defence.[126]
- *The right to be informed about the facts on which the measure is based*: in order to adequately exercise the right to be heard the individual should be informed about the essential facts on which the objections against the individual are based.
- *Access to the file*: the individual must be granted access to the documents, that are to be used as evidence of the measures concerned. Some documents, however, are confidential and are therefore not accessible, for instance, the business secrets of third parties.
- *Protection against self-incrimination*: an individual cannot be compelled to provide the Commission with information, which involves an admission on its part of the existence of an infringement, which the Commission has to prove.[127] This right must already be respected in preliminary investigations. Nowadays this right is probably implied in Article 48, second paragraph, Charter. It only applies if the infringement may lead to the imposition of a criminal sanction or administrative sanction of a criminal nature (see paragraph 4.2).
- *The right to legal assistance*: this right must also be respected already in preliminary investigations. Therefore, the Commission is obliged to wait for the individual to have access to a lawyer before an investigation of the premises may take place.
- *Legal privilege*: the confidential nature of correspondence between an independent lawyer and his client should be respected.[128] Confidentiality also applies to this correspondence when it is in the possession of the client, and to the internal documents of the client containing the advice received from an independent legal adviser.[129]

126 Case C-349/07, *Sopropé*, ECLI:EU:C:746.

127 Case 374/87, *Orkem*, ECLI:EU:C:1989:387.

128 Case 155/79, *AM&S*, ECLI:EU:C:1982:29, Case C-550/07 P, *Akzo & Akcros*, ECLI:EU:C:2010:512.

129 Case T-30/89, *Hilti*, ECLI:EU:T:1990:70.

Finally, it should be noted that not every infringement of the rights of defence by an Union or national authority should necessarily lead to the annulment of the decision concerned. In respect of violations of in particular the right to be heard, the CJEU has determined that such violation should only result in an annulment 'if, had it not been for such an irregularity, the outcome of the procedure might have been different'.[130]

5.7. THE PRINCIPLE OF LEGITIMATE EXPECTATIONS[131]

The principle of legitimate expectations has long been recognized by the CJEU as a general principle of Union law.[132] It requires that the administrative authorities must, if possible, fulfil the legitimate or justified expectations created by them. Legitimate expectations can be created by generally binding rules (for instance: regulations) or individual decisions, at least to the extent that one may have confidence in the fact that they will not be abruptly changed, although they are sometimes also created by promises and assurances on the part of the administration or by soft law instruments (see paragraph 3.1). The protection of the principle is not absolute in so far that legitimate expectations must always be fulfilled come what may. In a concrete case, it will ultimately always be necessary to balance, on the one hand, the interests which one or more individuals have in seeing the principle fulfilled and, on the other, the possible conflicting general interests or conflicting interests of third parties.

Successful appeals based on this principle are quite scarce in the case law of the CJEU. An important reason for this is that the CJEU has, to date, consistently rejected the application of the principle *contra legem*. Therefore, an appeal based on this principle cannot be upheld by the (Union and national) courts if this would lead to a decision which is contrary to EU law. Or, in the words of the CJEU[133]: 'Neither wrongful promises given by national or Community authorities, nor a practice or policy rules of these authorities which are contrary to a Community regulation, may give rise to a situation protected by Community law'.

Furthermore, the possibility of a successful appeal based on this principle is limited, because legitimate expectations cannot be created by incorrect information provided by the administration, if this incorrectness could have been detected by an 'attentive trader' or a 'diligent businessman'. Therefore,

---

130 Case C-383/13, *M.G. & N.R.*, ECLI:EU:C:2013:533, Joined Cases C-129–130/13, *Kamino & Datema*, ECLI:EU:C:2014:2041.

131 Schønberg, S., *Legitimate Expectations in Administrative Law*, OUP, Oxford, 2000; Tridimas, *supra* note 79, chapter 5; Craig, *supra* note 1, chapter 18; Groussot, *supra* note 83, pp. 189–212.

132 Case 112/77, *Töpfer*, ECLI:EU:C:1978:94.

133 Case 5/82, *Maizena*, ECLI:EU:C:1982:439;,Case 316/86, *Krücken*, ECLI:EU:C:1988:201, Case 188/82, *Thyssen*, ECLI:EU:C:1983:329.

in the view of the CJEU it is not unreasonable, for instance, to expect the undertaking to consult the relevant Official Journals to order to discover the applicable customs tariffs; the undertaking may not rely on any possible incorrect information provided by the administration concerning these tariffs.[134]

The Union principle of legitimate expectations must be complied with by both the EU institutions and the national authorities when acting in the scope of EU law. The national authorities must in principle also comply with their national laws and principles, amongst which may be a national principle of legitimate expectations. As long as the Union principle offers more (or the same) protection to individuals than the national principle, the Union principle must be applied (see paragraph 5.2). In some Member States, however – for instance, Germany and the Netherlands – the national principle offers more protection.[135] In that case the question can be raised whether the national principle can still be applied in Union cases.

The conflict between the national principle of legitimate expectations and Union law is often at issue in cases concerning the recovery, by a national authority, of a subsidy which has been granted to an undertaking contrary to EU law. In the countries mentioned this recovery might be contrary to the national principle of legitimate expectations. From the point of view of Union law, however, these expectations may not be justified because the undertaking is expected to know that the subsidy was contrary to EU law. In the CJEU's case law this conflict has been solved as follows.

According to the CJEU the national authority is, in principle, allowed to apply the national principle as long as the *Rewe* requirements of equivalence and effectiveness are adhered to.[136] However, the application of the national principle is increasingly restricted by the requirement of effectiveness, as upholding an appeal based on the principle would be contrary to the effective application of the Union rules concerned.[137] This is for instance so in cases concerning the recovery of state aid, which was granted by a national authority contrary to Article 107 TFEU. As regards the recovery of unlawfully granted European subsidies, the CJEU in the past used to leave some (limited) space for the application of a national principle of legitimate expectations. In fairly exceptional circumstances – one has to think of the combination of a considerable period of time having elapsed since the payment of the subsidy in question, negligence of the national authorities and the good faith of the recipient – the application of

134 Case 161/88, *Binder*, ECLI:EU:C:1989:312.

135 See for the Dutch principle, J.B.J.M. ten Berge & R.J.G.M. Widdershoven, 'The Principle of Legitimate Expectations in Dutch Constitutional and Administrative Law', in: E.H. Hondius (ed.), *Netherlands Report to the Fifteenth International Congress of Comparative Law, Bristol 1998*, Intersentia, Antwerpen/Groningen, 1998, pp. 421–452.

136 Joined cases 205/82 to 215/82, *Deutsche Milchkontor*, ECLI:EU:C:1983:233.

137 For instance, Case 5/89, *BUG Alutechnik*, ECLI:EU:C:1990:320, and Case C-24/95, *Alcan*, ECLI:EU:C:1997:163.

the national principle was not limited by the effectiveness principle.[138] Therefore, in such a case it was not necessary to recover the unlawfully paid subsidy. In recent years, the CJEU's approach has become stricter.[139] In some cases the test on effectiveness tailors the protection of national principle to the level of the stricter Union principle.[140] In others, the national principle vanishes even completely and is replaced by the Union principle.[141]

5.8. OTHER GENERAL PRINCIPLES OF UNION LAW

At the end of this paragraph two other general principles of Union law must be briefly mentioned: the duty to state reasons and the principle of transparency.

The Union's *duty to state reasons* is codified in Article 296 TFEU: regulations, directives and decisions shall state the reasons on which they are based and shall refer to any proposals, initiatives, recommendations, requests or opinions required by the Treaties. In addition, Article 41, second paragraph, sub c, Charter provides for the same obligation in respect of decisions only. The duty applies to the Member States when acting within the scope of Union law as well, as part of both, the right/principle to good administration, and the principle of effective judicial protection.[142] According to the CJEU the duty to state reasons is 'an essential procedural requirement'. The absence or insufficiency of the reasons required leads to the annulment of the decision. The duty serves three functions. In the *Brennwein* case, the CJEU described them as follows[143]:

> The duty to state reasons 'seeks to give an opportunity to the parties of defending their rights (1), to the Court of exercising its supervisory functions (2) and to the Member States and to all interested nationals of ascertaining the circumstances in which the EC institution has applied the Treaty (3)'.

In order to serve these functions detailed reasoning is not always required. It is often sufficient to state in a concise and clear manner the principal issues of law and of facts upon which the decision is based and which are necessary to understand the reasoning which has led the EU institution to its decision.

---

138 Case 366/95, *Steff-Houlberg*, ECLI:EU:C:1998:216.

139 P. Boymans & M. Eliantonio, 'Europeanization of Legal Principles? The Influence of the CJEU'S Case Law on the Principle of Legitimate Expectations in the Netherlands and the United Kingdom', *European Public Law* 2013, pp. 715–738.

140 Case C-383/06 to C-385/06, *Vereniging Nationaal Overlegorgaan Sociale Werkvoorziening*, ECLI:EU:C:2008:165.

141 Case C-568/11, *Agroferm*, ECLI:EU:C:2013:407.

142 Cf. Case 222/86, *Heylens*, ECLI:EU:C:1987:442.

143 Case 24/62, *Brennwein*, ECLI:EU:C:1963:14.

A second general principle, which has been 'discovered' by the CJEU fairly recently, is the *principle of transparency*.[144] The principle refers to the openness of government and is concerned with the availability, accessibility and clearness of governmental information. It offers the basis for public access to information legislation[145], but is also applied in the context of restrictions of the free movement rights, in the area of state aid and – especially – in procedures of competitive distribution of so-called scarce economic rights.[146] Scarce economic rights are rights such as permits, concessions or subsidies, which are limited in numbers and for which there are more applicants than rights to be granted. A well-known example of a system of competitive distribution of such rights is the tendering procedure in the area of public procurement. However, also other distribution systems, like auctions and beauty contests, qualify as such.

The principle of transparency was first recognized by the CJEU as a principle of public procurement law, but has gradually been developed into a general principle of EU law which also applies outside the scope of public procurement.[147] In this respect it is of importance that the CJEU considers the principle as a pre-condition for the restriction of the freedoms of establishment and services (Articles 49 and 56 TFEU)[148], so that the principle has also a basis in primary Union law. Moreover, the principle has been codified in more or less detail in several Union acts, such as the Framework Directive for electronic communications networks and services, the Services Directive and the public procurement directives.[149] The precise meaning of the transparency principle depends on the context in which it is applied. So, in the area of public procurement the precise obligations which can be derived from it are more detailed than in other areas. However, in all areas the principle includes

144 S. Prechal & M. de Leeuw, 'Dimensions of Transparency: The Building Blocks for a New Legal Principle, *Review of European Administrative Law*, 2007/1, pp. 51–62; A.W.G.J. Buyze, *The principle of transparency in EU law*, BOXPress, Den Bosch, 2013.

145 See Regulation 1049/2001. See for explicit references to the principle of transparency in the context of this regulation, Joined cases C-541/11P and C-605/11P, *LPN & Finland v. Commission*, ECLI:EU:C:2013:738, and Case C-127/13 P, *Strack v. Commission*, ECLI:EU:C:2014:2250.

146 C.J. Wolswinkel, 'The Allocation of a Limited Number of Authorisations: Some General Requirements from European Law', *Review of European Administrative Law*, 2009/2, pp. 61–104.

147 Cf. Case T-297/05, *IPK International IPK* v *Commission*, ECLI:EU:T:2011:185, in which the General Court recognizes the principle of transparency as a fundamental principle for the award of subsidies.

148 Case C-231/03, *Coname*, ECLI:EU:C:2005:487, Joined cases C-203/08 and C-258/08 *Betfair and Ladbroke*, ECLI:EU:C:2010:307.

149 Directive 2002/21 (common regulatory framework for electronic communications networks and services), *OJ* 2002, L 108/33; Directive 2006/123 (services in the internal market), *OJ* 2006, L 376/36; Directive 2014/24 (concerning the award of public supply contracts), *OJ* 2014, L 94/65, and Directive 2014/25 (concerning the award of public supply contract in the areas of water, energy, public transport and postal services), *OJ* 2014, L 94/243, respectively.

the following obligations[150]: the use of clear and unambiguous language, equal opportunities for all applicants to compete (including equal access to information), the duty to make public distribution standards and the consistent interpretation of such standards.

6. WHAT LEGAL PROTECTION IS THERE AGAINST ADMINISTRATIVE ACTION?

6.1. EFFECTIVE JUDICIAL PROTECTION AGAINST SHARED GOVERNMENT

The legal protection granted to individuals within the European legal order is governed by the principle of effective judicial protection.[151] This principle is derived from the constitutional traditions of the Member States and from Article 6 and 13 ECHR, and has now been codified in Article 47 Charter. According to the principle individuals must be able to enforce the rights, which are conferred on them by Union law before an independent court. In order to comply with this principle, it is first necessary that individuals have *effective access* to a court. Secondly, the (process before the) court must meet several *institutional and procedural requirements*, such as impartiality and independence, fair trial, reasonable time and public hearing. Thirdly, these courts should have at their disposal *effective remedies*, i.e. remedies by which Union law can be enforced and violations of Union law can be effectively restored. In the European legal order, which is characterized by the concept of shared government between Union and national authorities, the principle of effective judicial protection is realized at two levels.

a. *The Union level*: at this level, several remedies exist. The most important for individuals are the action for review of the legality of acts taken by a Union institution (Article 263 TFEU), the action for failure to act (Article 265 TFEU) and the action for non-contractual liability concerning damage caused by a EU institution (Article 268 in conjunction with 340, second paragraph, TFEU). The competent court is the CJEU. Furthermore, citizens of the European Union are entitled to submit complaints concerning instances of maladministration in the activities of the Union institutions or bodies to the European Ombudsman (Article 228 TFEU). The Ombudsman is appointed by the European Parliament and shall conduct inquiries either on his own initiative or on the basis of complaints. Although the decisions

150 Prechal & De Leeuw, *supra* note 144; Buijze, *supra* note 144, p. 260 *et seq.*

151 Jans *et al.*, *supra* note 1, chapters 2 & 6; Groussot, *supra* note 83, pp. 235–249. See case C-50/00 P, *Unión de Pequeños Agricultores*, ECLI:EU:C:2002:462, Case C-263/02 P, *Jégo-Quéré*, ECLI:EU:C:2004:210, Case C-432/05, *Unibet*, ECLI:EU:C:2007:163.

of the Ombudsman are formally not binding, the institutions concerned in general comply with them.[152]

b. *The national level*: as mentioned in paragraph 1.1, the application of EU law as far as individuals are concerned usually occurs at the national level by the national authorities. Legal protection against this application is granted by the national courts. In this respect, Article 19 TFEU states that the Member States shall provide remedies sufficient to ensure effective protection in the fields covered by Union law. Which national court is competent and what procedural rules and principles are applicable, is in principle a matter for national (procedural) law. The national courts can be considered as *juge de droit commun*. They have the task of ensuring an effective application of EU law in the Member State. To guarantee a uniform application of EU law, national courts have the opportunity or obligation to refer preliminary questions concerning the validity and interpretation of EU law to the CJEU (Article 267 TFEU).

Hereafter in paragraph 6.2, the action for review of legality (including the action for failure to act) at the Union level is studied. The action for Union liability is dealt with in paragraph 7.2. In paragraph 6.3 the role of the national courts as *juge de droit commun* is examined.

6.2. REMEDIES AT THE UNION LEVEL[153]

6.2.1. The Court of Justice of the European Union

According to Article 19, first paragraph, TEU, the Court of Justice of the European Union is the judicial institution of the European Union. It is made up of two courts: the Court of Justice and the General Court (hereafter: GC). The Court of Justice consists of 28 judges, one from every Member State. Eleven Advocates Generals assist it. The judges are chosen from persons whose independence is beyond doubt and who possess the qualifications required for appointment to the highest judicial courts in their respective countries or who are *jurisconsults* of recognized competence. They are appointed by a common accord of the Governments of the Member States for a term of six years. The tasks of the Court of Justice are threefold. First, it hears appeals against decisions of

152 Cf. Craig, *supra* note 1, chapter 24. See S. Schoenmaekers, 'The Increasing Influence of the Ombudsman in the Institutional System of the European Union', in: M. de Visser & A.P. van der Mei (eds.), *The Treaty on European Union 1993–2013: Reflections from Maastricht*, Intersentia, Antwerp 2013, pp. 177–200.

153 See R. Barents, *Remedies and Procedures before the EU Courts*, Wolters Kluwer, Alphen aan den Rijn 2016; R. Ortlep & R.J.G.M. Widdershoven, 'Judicial Protection', in: Jans *et al.*, *supra* note 1, chapter 6.

the GC. Secondly, it gives preliminary rulings on questions referred by national courts under Article 267 TFEU. Finally, under Articles 259 and 260 TFEU it has jurisdiction in first and last instance in actions against the Member States for failure to fulfil their Treaties' obligations.

The GC consists of 47 judges. In 2019, this will be increased to 56 (2 judges from each EU country). They are chosen from persons whose independence is beyond doubt and who possess the ability required for appointment to judicial office. The GC rules on actions for review of legality (see below) and actions for non-contractual liability of the EU (see par. 7.2). In general such actions are brought before the GC by natural and legal persons. As regards substance, most cases are concerned with competition law, civil servants law, State aid, product regulation and trademarks. The judgements of the GC may be appealed against before the Court of Justice on points of law only. The time limit for lodging an appeal is two month.

Provisions concerning the competence and organization of the CJEU (Court of Justice and GC) can be found in the Treaties, but also in the Statute of the CJEU. Provisions concerning the proceedings before these Union courts can be found in the Statute and in the Rules of Procedure of both courts. See figure 3 for an overview of legal protection within the shared European legal order.

Figure 3. Organization of legal protection in the shared European legal order

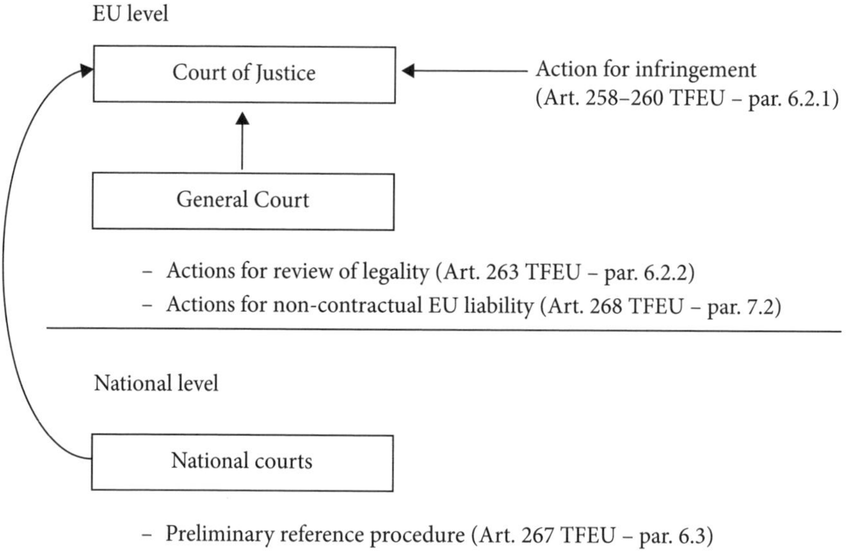

6.2.2. *Review of Legality*[154]

6.2.2.1. General Aspects

The remedy of review of legality of Union acts is regulated in Article 263 TFEU. Its purpose is to declare an illegal act void. The time limit for instigating an action for review is two months (Article 263, sixth paragraph TFEU). As stated above, in first instance actions are decided by the GC. The appeal against a GC judgement may brought before the Court of Justice within two month as well. Hereafter, both courts are referred to as CJEU. The procedure before the CJEU is free of charge. Natural and legal persons must be represented by a lawyer.

The grounds for review are: (1) lack of competence, (2) infringement of an essential procedural requirement, (3) infringement of the Treaties or of any rule of law relating to its application, and (4) misuse of powers (Article 263, second paragraph TFEU). The third ground is interpreted by the CJEU as an 'infringement of law' (in general). Under this category, the general principles of Union law, discussed in paragraph 5, are also implied.

If an action is well founded, the CJEU shall declare the act concerned to be void (*ex tunc*). However, it may – if it considers this necessary, for instance, in order to protect the legitimate expectations of individuals – state that the (or certain) effects of the act which have been declared void shall be considered as definite (Article 264 TFEU). Moreover, violations of procedural requirements, such as the rights of defence, do only lead to the annulment of the contested act if the violation may possibly affect the content of the decision.[155] The judgement on an action for review should contain a decision as to the costs. In this respect unsuccessful parties, including unsuccessful individuals, should in principle pay the costs of the successful party, in particular the lawyer's costs. As a result, an action for review is not without financial risk.

The institution whose act had been declared void is required to take the necessary measures to comply with the judgement of the CJEU within a reasonable time (Article 266 TFEU). In general, the Court is not competent to issue a replacing decision after the original one has been declared void. Only with regard to penalties – which can, for instance, be imposed by the Commission in competition cases – the Court exercise 'unlimited jurisdiction' (Article 261 TFEU).

6.2.2.2. Object of Review

In principle, the action for review of legality can be brought against every act of every EU institution intended to produce legal effects *vis-à-vis* third parties.

---

154 Cf. Lenaerts *et al.*, *supra* note 1, chapter 7.

155 Cf. Case 30/78 *Distillers Company*, ECLI:EU:C:1980:1862229, and Case C-12/87 *Belgium* v *Commission*, ECLI:EU:C:1988:298.

In practice the most important objects of appeal are decisions, regulations and directives.

An action for review of legality is also possible against an institution's failure to act (Article 265 TFEU). A failure to act is only unlawful if the institution was under a duty to act. The duty to act must derive from superior Union law. An action for failure to act is only admissible if the institution concerned has first been called upon to act. That is when the time limit starts to run within which the institution must define its position or possibly face an action for failure to act. Moreover, the call to act determines the subject-matter of the action. It is therefore important that the appellant concerned clearly indicates what action he wants the institution to take.

Union law does not prescribe a time limit within which the call to act must be made. In general, this will have to be made within a reasonable period after it has become apparent that the institution is showing no sign of acting. What is reasonable depends on the specific case. After the call to act, the institution has two months in which to define its position. If it does nothing, the action must be brought before the CJEU within a further period of two months. If the institution does define its position but the appellant disagrees, he must bring an action for review of legality against this act under Article 263 TFEU. Where the failure to act is held to be unlawful, the Court will rule that Union law has been infringed, as no other decision – for instance, an order addressed to the institution – is possible.

6.2.2.3. Standing

According to Article 263, second paragraph, TFEU several EU institutions and the Member States are considered to be 'privileged applicants' and are entitled to instigate an appeal before the CJEU against every act of an EU institution also, for instance, against regulations and directives.

The right of appeal against an EU act or a EU failure to act of *natural and legal persons* is subjected to quite strict standing requirements, which will be discussed hereafter. Therefore, individuals usually cannot contest regulations and directives before the Court. An individual who wishes to challenge the validity of these generally binding rules is usually obliged to start proceedings before a national court: in the lawsuit against a national decision which is based on the regulation or directive, the national court may refer the question of the act's validity to the CJEU.

The right of natural or legal persons to instigate proceedings before the CJEU is limited to three groups of acts (Article 263, fourth paragraph TFEU).

a. *Acts addressed to the person*: these acts are quite rare because Union law is usually applied *vis-à-vis* individuals by the authorities of the Member States. An important exception is to be found in European competition law. In this area, the Commission is competent to take decisions, such as the imposition of fines and periodic penalty payments, addressed to undertakings because of violations of European competition law. Against these decisions, the person to which the act is addressed can bring an action for annulment before the CJEU. However, third parties do not fall within this group, because the act concerned is not addressed to them.

b. *Acts which are of direct and individual concern to the person*: the term 'act' includes in principle regulations, directives and decisions. However, to have standing against these acts the person involved must – in the first place – be *individually* affected by the act 'by reason of certain attributes which are peculiar to him or by reason of circumstances in which he is differentiated from all other persons, and by virtue of these factors distinguishes him individually just as in the case of the person addressed'.[156] Therefore the act should relate to one specific person or to a closed group of individuals which can be determined in advance. Even in theory the possibility that other persons may join the group in the future must be excluded. In the second place the act must be of *direct* concern to the person. To be of *direct* concern it is necessary that the national authorities are bound to apply the act both strictly and mechanically. The authorities should not have any discretionary power when applying it.

   Because of these strict requirements, individuals' appeals against *regulations* and *directives* are nearly always inadmissible. Because of their general nature, they do in principle not affect a person individually in a way which differentiates him from other persons. In addition, directives are in general not of direct concern to individuals because they first have to be transposed by the Member States. Whether an individual can bring an action against a *decision* which is not addressed to him but to a Member State[157], depends on the substance of it. If the decision is of a general nature, persons are not individually affected by it and cannot instigate proceedings. If the decision (indirectly) relates to a specific person and the Member State has no discretionary powers when implementing it, the individual may challenge it before the CJEU. A well-known example of a decision addressed to the Member State which may be challenged by an individual before the Court, is the decision of the Commission addressed to the Member State in which it declares that state aid granted to a specific undertaking by the Member State is not compatible with the common market and therefore has to be recovered from this undertaking by the Member State (cf. Articles 107 and 108 TFEU).[158]

---

156 Case 25/62, *Plaumann*, ECLI:EU:C:1963:17.

157 A decision addressed to an individual resort under group a, and is therefore 'appealable' by the individual.

158 Cf Case 132/12 P, *Woonpunt*, ECLI:EU:C:2014:100.

c. *A regulatory act which is of direct concern to a person and does not entail implementing measures*: sometimes a regulation does not entail any national implementing measures.[159] In the pre-Lisbon era the only manner by which a person could challenge the validity of such regulation was to disregard it and to raise the question of validity in a subsequent national criminal procedure. Because this is a not very attractive option, the Lisbon Treaty has filled in the gap by adding this third group of acts against which persons can instigate proceedings before the CJEU. As regards this group – and different from group b – individuals do not have to meet the requirement of individual concern. In *Inuit Tapiriit Kantami* the CJEU has ruled that the term 'regulatory act' must be interpreted restrictively and does not include legislative acts which have been adopted in the legislative procedure of Article 294 TFEU, but only non-legislative acts of general application in the meaning of Article 290 TFEU. This implies that in respect of legislative acts individuals must still meet the requirement of individual concern to have access to the CJEU. From other case law, it appears that also the condition that the act should 'not entail implementing measures', may constitute a serious obstacle for admissible appeals, because most regulatory acts have to be implemented by EU institutions or national authorities to be effective.[160] Thus, in practice the Lisbon Treaty's extension of the possibility to directly challenge general applicable EU acts before the CJEU is of limited importance.

From the foregoing, it is clear that the rules for standing before the CJEU are quite strict as far as individuals are concerned. Only individuals to which a decision is addressed and individuals for whom a decision is of direct and individual concern are entitled to instigate an appeal before the Court. Third parties and NGOs generally have no right to access. An illustration of the limited admissibility of these groups before the Court, is provided for by the judgement in *Greenpeace and some inhabitants of the Canary Islands against the Commission*.[161] The appeal was directed against a decision of the Commission to co-finance the construction of two power stations on the islands. The applicants claimed that this construction was incompatible with EU law, because, contrary to Directive 85/337, no environmental assessment

---

159 E.g. Case C-50/00 P, *Unión de Pequeños Agricultores*, ECLI:EU:C:2002:462, and Case C-263/02 P, *Jégo-Quéré*, ECLI:EU:C:2004:210.

160 For instance Case T-221/10, *Iberdrola*, ECLI:EU:T:2012:112; Case T-381/11, *Eurofer*, ECLI:EU:T:2012:273, Case C-274/12 P, *Telefónica SA*, ECLI:EU:C:2013:852, Case C-133/12 P, *Stichting Woonlinie*, ECLI:EU:C:2014:105. See A. Kornezov 'Shaping the New Architecture of the EU System of Judicial Remedies: Comment on Inuit', *European law* review, 2014/2, pp. 251–263.

161 Case C-321/95 P, *Greenpeace*, ECLI:EU:C:1998:153. See for another example Case C-362/06 P, *Markku Sahlstedt*, ECLI:EU:C:2009:243.

procedure had taken place.[162] The inhabitants were denied standing, because the decision to co-finance the construction was not of individual concern to them. After all, they were affected by the decision in the same way as 'various categories of person and in fact any person residing or staying temporarily in the area concerned' (such as any other local residents, fishermen, farmers or tourists) were affected. Greenpeace was denied standing because the decision of the Commission only affected the general – and not the individual – interests of this NGO. According to the CJEU this lack of standing at the Union level was not contrary to the principle of effective judicial protection, because the inhabitants and Greenpeace could challenge the permits, which had been granted for the construction of the power stations before the Spanish administrative court. In this procedure, the possible infringement of Directive 85/337 could be referred to the CJEU.

In order to comply with the obligations arising under Article 9, third paragraph, of the Aarhus Convention as regards the access to justice in environmental matters, the Council has extended the admissibility of environmental NGOs in the so-called Aarhus Regulation.[163] With regard to such access, Article 10, first paragraph, of the regulation grants environmental NGOs, meeting certain requirements, the right to make a request for internal review of an administrative act under environmental law to the EU institution concerned. It follows from Article 12 of the regulation, that in the event the review does not produce the desired results, the NGO can initiate proceedings before the CJEU 'in accordance with the relevant provisions of the Treaty'. Because the decision on internal review is *addressed* to the NGO, the NGO may challenge this decision without meeting the requirements of direct and individual concern. However, whether the Aarhus route will substantively enlarge NGOs access to justice at Union level may be doubted, because the regulation has considerably reduced the scope of the review procedure (and thus the access to the CJEU), in particularly by restricting it to administrative acts 'of individual scope'. Therefore, as yet most NGO's applications for the review procedure have been declared inadmissible by the Commission.[164] Furthermore, in *Vereniging Milieudefensie* the Court has ruled that the validity of the restrictions, provided for in the Aarhus regulation, cannot be assessed in the light of Article 9, third paragraph, of the Aarhus Convention, because this article is not unconditional and sufficiently precise and, therefore, lacks direct effect.[165] Thus, it seems not very likely that the limited admissibility of environmental NGOs will be enlarged substantively for the years to come.

162 Directive of 27 June 1985, *OJ* 1985, L 175 40.

163 *OJ* 2006, L264/13.

164 Cf. G.J. Harryvan & J.H. Jans, 'Internal Review of EU Environmental Measures', *Review of European Administrative Law*, 2010/2, pp. 53–65.

165 Case C-401–403/12 P, *Vereniging Milieudefensie*, ECLI:EU:C:2015:4.

6.2.2.4. Judicial Assessment

The intensity of the judicial control exercised by the CJEU depends on the object of appeal (legislation or individual decision) and the margin of discretion or appreciation the EU institution enjoys. When establishing regulations and directives the institutions in general have a wide margin of discretion. Therefore, the CJEU exercise restraint when reviewing these acts. They are declared void only in case they are considered to be 'manifestly disproportionate'.

As regards individual decisions the intensity of judicial control varies. If the institution enjoys limited or no discretion, judicial scrutiny is quite strict. Most strict is the judicial assessment of penalties in the area of competition law to which the Court exercise 'unlimited jurisdiction', and is is entitled to substitute its own appraisal for the Commission's and to cancel, reduce or increase the fine or penalty payment imposed.[166] If the institution enjoys a wide margin of discretion or appreciation the CJEU use the two-stage approach which was applied for the first time in the case of *Tetra Laval*.[167] In this approach the judicial assessment differentiates between the establishment of the relevant facts by the institution, and the institution's appraisal of the facts. The correctness of the establishment of the facts is fully scrutinized by the Court. By contrast the Court only marginally check whether the ensuing appraisal stage meets the appropriate standards of soundness. The reason for this is that the Court cannot take the place of the institution when the latter exercises (political) discretion or must carry out complex economic, ecological or technical assessments. Therefore, as regards the content of the decision, the Court confines himself to a test on 'manifest' errors. In addition – and to offer some compensation – the Court verifies quite strict whether the applicable procedural guarantees have been fully observed.

The CJEU can be characterized as a passive court. Its assessment is restricted to the factual and legal grounds which have been put forward by the parties. The Court is not obliged to *ex officio* (of their own motion) apply the appropriate legal provisions to the factual grounds the applicant has raised. In addition, *ex officio* application outside the scope of the dispute is limited to rules of public order. These rules are mainly concerned with the competence of the CJEU and the admissibility of the appeal. The CJEU may order that an expert's report be obtained (Article 70 Rules of Procedure of the Court of Justice). The order appointing the expert shall define his task and set a time-limit within which the expert is to submit his report. In practice, this competence is hardly ever applied by the Court.

---

166 Case C-389/10 P, *KME*, ECLI:EU:C:2011:816.

167 Case C-12/03 P, *Tetra Laval,* ECLI:EU:C:2005:87. See M. Schimmel & R.J.G.M. Widdershoven, 'Judicial Review after *Tetra Laval*: Some Observations from a European Administrative Law Point of View', in: O. Essens, A. Gerbrandy & S. Lavrijssen, *National Courts and the Standard of Review in Competition Law and Economic Regulation*, Europa Law Publishing, Groningen 2009, pp. 51–77.

6.2.2.5. Interim Relief

Actions brought before the CJEU have no suspending effect. The individual is, however, entitled to request the Court to order the application of the contested act to be suspended (Article 278 TFEU), or to prescribe any necessary interim measure (Article 279 TFEU). The most important criterion, which the Court applies in this procedure, is the *fumus boni iuris* criterion: is the application legally and factually *prima facie* justified? In addition, there should be an urgent need for the application: the interim measure should be necessary to avoid serious and irreparable damage being caused to the party seeking the relief. Purely financial damage cannot in principle be regarded as irreparable because this damage can be subsequently compensated. In the third place, the measure requested should retain the character of an interim measure: it should be aimed at the conservation of the legal position of the parties in question.[168]

6.2.2.6. Interference with Remedies at the National Level

Although the rules for standing for (legal) persons before the CJEU are strict, it is possible in certain circumstances that the right to appeal to the Court interferes with a right of judicial review before a national court. This is the case where an individual first is directly and individually affected by a Union decision addressed to a Member State and subsequently by the decision of the Member State in which the Commission decision is implemented. In that case, the individual may instigate proceedings against the Commission decision which addresses the Member State before the Court, while the implementing decision by the Member State can be challenged before a national court. The question can be raised as to what extent both appeals influence each other? This question was answered in *Textilwerke Deggendorf (TWD)*.[169]

This case concerned a decision by the Commission which was addressed to Germany and which ordered this country to recover aid, which had been illegally granted by Germany to TWD. This aid was to be recovered directly from TWD. It was clear that TWD could instigate proceedings against this decision before the Court, because the decision was of direct and individual concern to the undertaking in question. Moreover, TWD had been informed by the German Government of the possibility to appeal. Nevertheless, TWD did not make use of this right to appeal. Afterwards, however, TWD challenged the national decision, which implemented the Commission decision before the national court. In this case TWD argued that the national decision was invalid

168 See Lenaerts *et al.*, *supra* note 1, no. 13.31 *et seq.*

169 Case C-188/92, *Textilwerke Deggendorf*, ECLI:EU:C:1994:90. See also Case C-178/95, *Wiljo*, ECLI:EU:C:1997:46, Case C-239/99, *Nachi Europe*, ECLI:EU:C:2001:101, Joined cases C-346/03 and C-529/03, *Atzeni*, ECLI:EU:C:2006:130. See R. Schwensfeier, 'The TWD principle post-Lisbon', *European Law Review*, 2012/2, pp. 156–175.

because it was based on a decision of the Commission, which was in its opinion unlawful. In a preliminary question the national court asked the Court whether TWD could still raise this question of the lawfulness of the Commission decision before the national court when the undertaking did not make use of the opportunity to contest this decision before the CJEU. The Court answered in the negative. In this answer three aspects were of importance. Firstly, an affirmative answer would enable the person concerned to overcome the definitive nature, which the Commission decision assumes as against that person once the time limit for bringing an action has expired. This would be incompatible with the requirement of legal certainty. In the second place, TWD's appeal under (now) Article 263 TFEU would undoubtedly have been admissible. Finally, TWD was informed of the existence of the Commission decision and of the fact that it could instigate proceedings against this decision before the Court.

Two conclusions can be drawn from this judgement. In the first place, an individual who has standing before the CJEU to challenge a decision of the Commission addressed to a Member State should in principle use this possibility to appeal. In this respect it is of importance, however, that the individual is informed of the existence of the decision and that his appeal is undoubtedly admissible. In the second place, if a national court is asked to review the national decision by which the decision of the Commission is implemented and the individual has not instigated proceedings before the Court, the national court is then bound by the non-contested Commission decision.

6.3. REMEDIES AT THE NATIONAL LEVEL

As EU law is usually applied in the Member States, most lawsuits concerning EU law are heard before the national courts. Which court is competent and what procedural rules are applicable is in principle a matter for national law. However, because of the fact that EU law is at issue, the judicial organization and procedure is to a certain extent influenced by Union law.[170] In the following paragraph this influence is examined.

6.3.1. Preliminary Rulings

6.3.1.1. Introduction

The first European influence on the national judicial procedure can be found in Article 267 TFEU, which contains the preliminary ruling procedure.[171]

170 See in general, W. van Gerven, 'Of rights, remedies and procedures', *European law review*, 2000/3, pp. 501–536; Craig, *supra* note 1, chapter 23; R. Ortlep & R.J.G.M. Widdershoven, 'Judicial Protection', in: Jans *et al.*, *supra* note 1, chapter 6.

171 See in general, M. Broberg, 'Judicial Coherence and the Preliminary Reference Procedure', *Review of European Administrative Law*, 2015/2, pp. 9–37; R. Grimbergen, 'How Boundaries

According to this article the CJEU has jurisdiction to give preliminary rulings concerning both the interpretation of the Treaties and other acts by Union institutions, as well as the validity of Union acts. In the case of a question of interpretation a national court asks the Court in what way a provision of Union law should be interpreted, usually in order to establish whether a rule of national law is compatible with this provision. In the case of a question of validity the referring national court wishes to know whether a Union act – for instance, a regulation or decision – on which a national decision is based is legally sound. In these cases, there is doubt on the part of the national court as to whether the Union act is compatible with, for instance, the Treaties (including the Charter) or a general principle of Union law.

The preliminary ruling procedure offers an important instrument for co-operation between the national courts and the CJEU. It is the exclusive right of the national courts to refer a preliminary question. The parties to the dispute are not empowered to refer questions to the Court. The legal basis for the procedure is exclusively Article 267 TFEU; the power to refer to the CJEU cannot be limited by national law.

Since the first preliminary question in 1961 the preliminary ruling procedure has become quite a success. In the period from 1961 until the end of 2016 the national courts referred 9616 questions to the CJEU. German courts (numerically) asked the most questions, namely 2300, followed by Italy (1388) and the Netherlands (975).[172]

6.3.1.2. Discretion or Obligation to Refer to the CJEU

According to Article 267 TFEU preliminary questions may or shall be referred to the CJEU by a 'court or tribunal of a Member State'. It is a matter for the CJEU to decide whether a body is a court or tribunal for the purpose of this Article. The Court will take a number of factors into account when making its determination, including[173]: whether the body has been established by law, whether it is permanent, whether its jurisdiction is compulsory, whether its procedure is adversarial, whether it applies rules of law, and whether it is independent. According to these factors the administrative courts of the Member States are empowered to refer a question to the Court. However, administrative bodies

Have Shifted. On Jurisdiction and Admissibility in the Preliminary Ruling Procedure', *Review of European Administrative Law*, 2015/2, pp. 39–70; M. Broberg & N. Fenger, *Preliminary References to the European Court of Justice*, OUP, Oxford, 2014; Lenaerts *et al.*, *supra* note 1, chapters 3 & 6; M. Schönemeyer, *Die Pflicht des Bundesverfassungsgerichts zur Vorlage an den Gerichtshof der Europäischen Union gem. Art. 267 Abs. 3 AEUV*, Duncker & Humblot, Berlin 2014.

172 See www.curia.europa.eu, The Annual Report, Statistics of judicial activity of the CJEU 2016.

173 For instance, Case 246/80, *Broekmeulen*, ECLI:EU:C:1981:218. See more recent, Case C-377/13, *Ascendi Beiras Litoral e Alta*, ECLI:EU:C:2014:1754, Case C-555/13, *Merck Canada*, ECLI:EU:C:2014:92.

which in some Member States are charged with the administrative review of a decision before an individual can instigate proceedings before a court – one has to think, for instance, of the procedure for objections or for appeal to a higher administrative authority – are not considered to be 'a court or tribunal' for the purpose of Article 267 TFEU, because they are not independent. Therefore, they cannot refer questions to the CJEU.

Article 267 TFEU draws a distinction between (lower) courts or tribunals, which have the discretion to refer to the CJEU, and courts and tribunals 'against whose decision there is no judicial remedy under national law'. In the latter instance the court is in principle under an obligation to refer, provided – of course – that a decision on a question is necessary to enable the court or tribunal to render a judgement. In two situations, however, the highest national court is not obliged to refer a question.[174]

- In the first place, when the question concerns a so-called *acte éclairé* (precedent). This exception includes two situations: (a) the situation in which the question raised is materially identical with a question which has already been the subject of a preliminary ruling in a similar case, and (b) the situation where previous decisions of the CJEU have already dealt with the point of law in question, even though the questions at issue are not strictly identical. Previous judgements of the CJEU can therefore be considered to be a precedent in future cases.
- In the second place, when the question concerns an *acte clair*. In this case, the correct application of Union law is so obvious as to leave no scope for any reasonable doubts as to the manner in which the question raised is to be answered. The fact that a lower court has referred a question to the CJEU, does not in itself preclude a higher court from concluding that the question concerns an *acte clair*.[175] The national court should not however be too quick to assume that a matter is obvious.[176] Not only should it be obvious to the national court that there is no scope for reasonable doubt, it must also be convinced that the matter is equally obvious to the courts of the other Member States and to the CJEU. Moreover, it must also take into account the specific characteristics of Union law, such as the existence of authentic versions of judgements in various languages, and the fact that certain concepts used in Union law do not necessarily have the same meaning in Union law as they do in national law.

On the other hand, lower (and higher) national courts are under an obligation to refer questions of validity to the CJEU, at least whenever they are of the opinion that a Union act is invalid. National courts cannot themselves determine a Union

174 Case 283/81, *CILFIT*, ECLI:EU:C:1982:335.
175 Joined Cases C-72/14 and C-197/14, *X & Van Dijk*, ECLI:EU:C:2015:564.
176 Case C-160/14, *Ferreira da Silva and others*, ECLI:EU:C:2015:565.

act to be invalid[177], only the Court has the power to do this. This is to ensure a uniform application of Union law in the Member States. The requirement of uniformity is particularly imperative when the validity of a Union act is in question. Divergences between the courts in the Member States as to the validity of Union acts would be liable to place the very unity of the EU legal order in jeopardy and would detract from the fundamental requirement of legal certainty. So whenever a national court suspects a Union act to be invalid, it should refer the validity question to the CJEU.[178] National courts are, however, competent to *reject* a party's claim that a Union act is invalid.

To the foregoing, it can be added that national courts are empowered to temporarily suspend the application of a Union act in the Member State in a procedure for interim relief. This power is subjected to quite strict, uniform Europeanized conditions, however. One of these conditions is that the national court has to refer the question to the CJEU. See paragraph 6.3.2.2 for details.

6.3.1.3. Procedural Aspects

In the national procedure, referring a preliminary question to the CJEU has the character of a procedural incident. Questions are generally asked by means of an interim judgement. After referring the matter to the CJEU the national proceedings are suspended until the Court delivers its judgement. While the case is pending, the national court may take all the necessary measures to ensure the full effect of Union law; it may, for instance, suspend the application of the national decision, which is allegedly contrary to EU law. After the CJEU has answered the preliminary question, the national court will then resume hearing the case. The national court has to decide on the legal consequences of the Court's judgement for the dispute in question.

The CJEU is *dominus litis* in the preliminary proceedings. The parties to the national procedure cannot influence these proceedings. They are, however, – together with the Member States, the Commission and (in certain circumstances) the Council and the European Parliament – empowered to file written remarks. The session before the Court is open to the public. In the session experts and witnesses may be heard. The parties can only plead through their lawyer. Whether they are entitled to legal aid, is a matter of national law.[179] The preliminary ruling procedure is as such free of charge.

The preliminary rulings are binding from the day on which the judgement is delivered. A ruling on the validity of a Union act has *erga omnes* effect: every court in the EU has to comply with the judgement. The legal effect of judgements

177 Case 314/85, *Foto Frost*, ECLI:EU:C:1987:452.

178 Even if the question of validity concerns an *acte éclairé*. See Case C-461/03, *Gaston Schul*, ECLI:EU:C:2005:742.

179 Case C-472/99, *Clean Car Autoservices*, ECLI:EU:C:2001:663.

concerning questions of interpretation is in theory limited to the case in question. In practice, however, its effect reaches beyond this case because the judgement is a *de facto* precedent in other similar cases.

Judgements of the CJEU concerning the interpretation or validity of a Union provision have retroactive effect: the Court explains in which way the provision had to be understood from the moment it entered into force. Sometimes this leads to the consequence that in retrospect a large number of decisions taken by national authorities during a long period of time must be considered to be incompatible with a provision of Union law. Overturning all of these decisions may in certain circumstances, however, be contrary to the principle of legal certainty. The CJEU is therefore empowered to limit the retroactive effect of a judgement if this is in the interest of legal certainty.[180]

6.3.2. *Effective Judicial Protection in the Member States*

The principle of effective judicial protection governs legal protection in the European legal order as a whole and therefore also in the Member States (see paragraph 6.1). In general, the Member States are obliged to ensure an effective system of judicial protection in cases where Union rights are violated. From this principle, several requirements can be derived.[181] They are concerned with:

- *effective access to court*: requirements concerning access to justice will be discussed in paragraph 6.3.2.1. Incidental the Union legislator has laid down specific requirements as regards access to justice in certain areas of Union law, for instance, in the area of environmental law (standing of NGOs) and in the area of services (*silencio positivo*).[182] This legislative influence will also be examined briefly.
- *institutional and procedural guarantees*: the national courts and court proceedings should meet the requirements of fair trail, independence and impartiality, reasonable time and public hearing (Article 47, second paragraph Charter). In respect of these requirements, Article 47 Charter corresponds to Article 6 ECHR. Therefore, their meaning is the same as Article 6 ECHR as interpreted in the case law of the ECtHR (Article 52, third paragraph, Charter). However, the scope of Article 47 Charter differs from Article 6 ECHR. While the latter only applies to the determination of civil rights and obligations or criminal charges, the Charter also applies in administrative law cases within the scope of Union law. This includes for instance migrant law and tax cases

180 For instance, Case 43/75, *Defrenne*, ECLI:EU:C:1976:56, and Case C-262/88, *Barber*, ECLI:EU:C:1990:209.

181 See in general, F.K. Brockmann, *Effektiver Rechtsschutz – Das Recht der Europäischen Union*, Peter Lang, Frankfurt am Main, 2014; K. Kulms, *Der Effektivitätsgrundsatz. Eine Untersuchung zur Rechtsprechung des Europäischen Gerichtshofs*, Nomos, Baden-Baden, 2013.

182 See also Directive 89/655, modified by Directive 2007/66, on legal protection in the area of public procurement, which prescribes to the Member States the existence of several remedies (annulment, interim relief, liability) in this area.

within this scope, cases which are not protected by Article 6 ECHR. Finally, Article 47, third paragraph, Charter contains a right to legal aid for those who lack sufficient resources in so far as such aid is necessary to ensure effective access to justice. 'Legal aid' may cover both assistance by a lawyer and dispensation from payments of the costs of proceedings. The requirement is interpreted by the CJEU in line with the case law of the ECtHR.[183]

- *effective remedies*: national courts should have to their disposal remedies by which EU law can be enforced and violations can be restored. In order to respect this right, the Member States must *inter alia* provide for immediate legal protection in a remedy for interim relief (paragraph 6.3.2.2); and for the remedy for State liability. The latter is discussed separately in paragraph 7.

As holds true for all fundamental Union rights, the principle of effective judicial protection

> 'does not constitute unfettered prerogatives and may be restricted, provided that the restrictions in fact correspond to objectives of general interest pursued by the measure in question and that they do not involve, with regard to the objectives pursued, a disproportionate and intolerable interference which infringes upon the very substance of the right guaranteed'.[184]

In *Alassini* the CJEU had to examine the question of whether the establishment of a mandatory out-of-court settlement procedure as a condition for the admissibility of actions before the national courts was compatible with the right to effective judicial protection.[185] The Court recognized that such a condition amounts to an additional step in accessing the courts and might prejudice the principle of effective judicial protection. However, in the case at hand the Court ruled that the imposition of the out-of-court settlement procedure was not inconsistent with the principle, because the requirement was not disproportionate in relation to the objective pursued, namely to offer a quicker and less expensive settlement of disputes.

6.3.2.1. Access to the National Courts

Creation of access to the national courts

An individual should have the opportunity to enforce those rights which have been conferred by EU law before an independent court. As has been shown in

183 Case C-279/09, *DEB*, ECLI:EU:C:2010:811, with reference to *inter alia* ECtHR 9 October 1979 (*Airey*), Series A, Vol. 32.

184 Joined cases C-317 to 320/08, *Alassini*, ECLI:EU:C:2010:146. Under the Charter a similar restricting clause is provided for in Article 52, first paragraph, Charter.

185 Joined cases C-317 to 320/08, *Alassini*, ECLI:EU:C:2010:146.

paragraph 6.2, individuals enjoy a limited right of access to the CJEU. In this case, the right of access is guaranteed at the Union level. Insofar as it is not possible to enforce one's Union rights before the Court, individuals should have a right of access to a national court. The *Borelli* case is interesting in this respect.[186]

In this case the Commission had, in line with the negative advice provided by the Italian authorities, refused *Borelli*'s request for a subsidy. According to the Community regulation in question the Commission could only grant a subsidy in the case of positive advice from the Member State. Borelli instigated proceedings against this refusal before the CJEU claiming that the negative advice by the Italian authority had been illegal. However, according to Italian procedural law, this advice could not be challenged before an Italian court. The Court rejected the appeal because the Commission was legally bound by the negative Italian advice. The possible illegality of this advice had to be assessed by a national court. If this was not possible under Italian procedural law, then Italy had to change this law. The Court based its opinion upon the principle of effective judicial protection.

Another important case as regards the Member States' obligation to create access to a court in Union matters is *Unibet*.[187] In this case the question was raised whether the principle of effective judicial protection requires it to be possible in the legal order of the Member State to bring a free-standing action for an examination as to whether national legislation was compatible with (now) Article 56 TFEU. The CJEU stated as a principle that Union law does not intend to create new remedies in the national courts to ensure observance of Union law other than those already laid down by national law. However, this would be otherwise 'if it were apparent from the overall scheme of the national legal system in question that no legal remedy existed which made it possible to ensure, *even indirectly*, respect for an individual's rights under' Union law (emphasis added).[188] In *Unibet* the Court examined the Swedish legal system and found that the question of incompatibility of national legislation with Union law could be raised as a preliminary issue in the context of a claim for damages and in a procedure for judicial review against the application of the law concerned. Therefore, Union law did not require Sweden to provide for a free-standing action against national legislation. However, if these indirect remedies do not exist in a certain Member State, it must provide for a free-standing action.

186 Case C-97/91, *Borelli*, ECLI:EU:C:1992:491. See also Case C-50/00 P, *Unión de Pequeños Agricultores*, ECLI:EU:C:2002:462, Case C-263/02 P, *Jégo-Quéré*, ECLI:EU:C:2004:210, and Case C-562/12, *Liivimaa Lihaveis MTÜ*, ECLI:EU:C:2014:2229. See further, F. Brito Bastos, 'The Borelli Doctrine Revisited: Three Issues of Coherence in a Landmark Ruling for EU Administrative Justice', *Review of European Administrative Law*, 2015/2, pp. 269–298.

187 Case C-432/05, *Unibet*, ECLI:EU:C:2007:163.

188 Case C-432/05, *Unibet*, ECLI:EU:C:2007:163, point 41.

STANDING BEFORE THE NATIONAL COURTS

The principle of effective judicial protection also influences the access to a national court in another way. Although it is, in principle, for national law to determine an individual's standing and legal interest in bringing proceedings, Union law requires that, whenever EU law confers rights on individuals, those individuals should have the opportunity to rely on them before a national court (*ubi jus, ibi remedium*).[189] Most EU acts only confer rights on specific individuals. Sometimes however, especially in the field of environmental law, the *ratione personae* of an EU act is much wider as some directives in this field confer rights to a large group of individuals in a certain area. This is, for instance, the case with several environmental directives on air quality limit values. In order to protect human health these directives contain limit values for, for instance, sulphur dioxide and lead in the air.[190] Because, exceeding of these limits can endanger potentially the health of many individuals, a wide group of individuals should be able to rely on the limits before a national court and, therefore, should have access to a court against national decisions implementing these limits.[191]

In general, the CJEU does not impose on the Member States obligations as regards standing of NGOs.[192] However, such obligations can be found in the Aarhus Directive in the area of environmental law.[193] This directive implements the obligations arising under the Aarhus Convention as regards the wide access to justice in environmental matters in the Member States. Briefly put, the directive allows the Member States to restrict standing of individuals to those having sufficient interest, or those maintaining the impairment of a right (the so-called *Schutznorm* requirement). However, as regards NGOs the directive states that their interest shall be deemed sufficient, and that NGOs shall be deemed to have rights capable of being impaired. In *Trianel*[194] and *Commission/Germany*[195] the CJEU has ruled that the directive precludes the application of

[189] Joined cases C-87/90-C-89/90, *Verholen and others*, ECLI:EU:C:1991:314, Case C-174/02, *Streekgewest Westelijk Noord-Brabant*, ECLI:EU:C:2005:10.

[190] Directive 80/779/EEC, on air quality limit values and guide values for sulphur dioxide, *OJ* 1980, L 229 30; Directive 82/884/EEC, on a limit value for lead in the air, *OJ* 1982, L 378.

[191] Case C-361/88, *Commission v Germany*, ECLI:EU:C:1991:224, Case C-59/89, *Commission v Germany*, ECLI:EU:C:1991:225. See also, Case C-237/07, *Janecek*, ECLI:EU:C:2008:447.

[192] See in general, M. Eliantonio & Ch.W. Backes, 'Access to Courts for Environmental NGOs at the European and national level: Improvements and room for improvement since Maastricht', in: M. de Visser & A.P. van der Mei (eds.), *The Treaty on European Union 1993–2013: Reflections from Maastricht*, Intersentia, Cambridge, 2013, pp. 557–580.

[193] Directive 2003/35, *OJ* 2003, L 165/17. In Case C-243/15, *Lesoochranárske zoskupenie VLK*, ECLI:EU:C:2016:838, the CJEU has, by means of an Article 47 Charter consistent interpretation of the directive, extended the scope of the directive requirements to the area of the Habitat Directive.

[194] Case C-115/09, *Trianel*, ECLI:EU:C:2011:289.

[195] Case C-137/14, *Commission/Germany*, ECLI:EU:C:2015:683.

the strict German *Schutznorm* requirement under which environmental NGOs are not permitted to rely before the national courts on several rules of Union environmental law on the ground that these rules protect only the interests of the general public and not the interests of individuals. Although the Member States are empowered to determine the conditions under which an environmental NGO has the right of appeal, these conditions must ensure 'wide access to justice'. In *Djurgården* the CJEU ruled a national provision which reserved the right to bring an appeal to environmental associations which have at least 2000 members, contrary to this requirement.[196]

EFFECTIVE ACCESS AND THE EXCEEDING OF TIME-LIMITS FOR DECISION-MAKING

Union acts only sporadically prescribe a specific time-limit for single decision-making by national administrative authorities. If an EU regulation or directive contains such time-limit, national law should – on the ground of the principle of effective judicial protection – provide for a judicial remedy in case the administration fails to decide in time.[197] A possible remedy is the right to appeal against the (fictitious) refusal which legally comes into being as a result of the exceeding of the time-limit.

The system of *silencio positivo* – in which 'administrative silence' is converted in a (fictional) positive decision (which can be challenged before to courts by third parties) – is only obligatory in Union matters, where it is explicitly prescribed by an EU regulation or directive.[198] A well-known example is offered by the Services Directive.[199] According to Article 13, fourth paragraph of the directive, a services authorization is considered to be granted in case the authorities have exceeded the prescribed time-limit.[200]

6.3.2.2. Interim Relief

Effective judicial protection implies immediate judicial protection. Where a Union right is at issue in a national judicial procedure, the national court should have the power to grant interim relief. This implies both the power to suspend the contested act as well as the power to prescribe a positive interim measure. The right to interim legal protection exists in two situations:

a. *Cases concerning questions of interpretation*: in this situation, interim relief is requested by an applicant because a national measure is, in its opinion, inconsistent with EU law. In the famous *Factortame* judgement the CJEU declared that in order to ensure the full effect of Union law a national court

196 Case C-263/08, *Djurgården*, ECLI:EU:C:2009:631.

197 Case C-186/04, *Housieaux*, ECLI:EU:C:2005:248.

198 Case C-245/03, *Merck, Sharp & Dohme*, ECLI:EU:C:2005:41.

199 Directive 2006/123/EC, on services in the internal market, *OJ* 2006, L376/36.

200 See K.J. de Graaf & N.G. Hoogstra, 'Silence is golden? Tacit Authorizations in the Netherlands, Germany and France', *Review of European Administrative Law*, 2013/1, pp. 7–34.

should have the power to suspend a national measure which is incompatible with Union law.[201] The consequence of the judgement was that the United Kingdom had to overturn the rule of national law under which national courts were forbidden to grant an interim junction against the Crown. The conditions for granting interim relief in cases concerning questions of interpretation have not been Europeanized[202]: the national courts are allowed to apply their domestic rules governing procedures for interim legal protection, provided that the principles of equivalence and effectiveness are met.

b. *Cases concerning questions of validity*: in this situation, interim relief is requested against a national decision because it is based on an allegedly invalid Union act. The Union act – usually a regulation or a decision – is said to be contrary to, for instance, a general principle of Union law or the Treaties. In *Zuckerfabrik Süderdithmarschen* and *Atlanta* the CJEU recognized both, the power of a national court to suspend, by way of an interim measure, the application of national administrative measures based on allegedly invalid Union acts, and the power to take a positive interim measure.[203] However, because of the fact that in these cases the application of a Union act in a Member State is at issue, the Court has prescribed several uniform, quite strict European conditions which the national court must observe when deciding on the request for interim relief.
    - the national court should entertain serious doubts as to the validity of the Union act;
    - the judgement of the national court should retain the character of an interim measure. Therefore, the interim relief may only be granted until such time as the CJEU has delivered its ruling on the question of the validity of the contested Union act. Where this question is not already an issue before the Court, the national court should refer it to the Court in the preliminary procedure under Article 267 TFEU;
    - there should be urgency and a threat of serious and irreparable damage to the applicant in question. Purely financial damage is in general not irreparable unless the enforcement of the contested decision will probably lead to the bankruptcy of the undertaking in question;
    - the national court should take due account of the Union interests: if the interim relief measure implies a financial risk for the EU, the national court must be in a position to require that the applicant provides adequate guarantees, such as the deposit of a sum of money and other securities;
    - in assessing these conditions, the national court should respect any decision of the CJEU on the lawfulness of the Union act in question in another similar case.

---

201 Case C-213/89, *Factortame*, ECLI:EU:C:1990:257.

202 Case C-432/05, *Unibet*, ECLI:EU:C:2007:163.

203 Joined cases C-143/88 and C-92/89, *Zuckerfabrik Süderdithmarschen and Soest*, ECLI:EU:C:1991:65, and Case C-465/93, *Atlanta*, ECLI:EU:C:1995:369.

Only if all these conditions are met, the national court is allowed to grant the request for interim relief. In practice, this is seldom the case.

6.3.3. *Application of National Procedural Law in Union Matters*

6.3.3.1. General

In the foregoing, it has become clear that Union law influences legal protection in the Member States in two ways: (a) it has created the preliminary ruling procedure, and (b) the legal protection has to comply with the principle of effective judicial protection, which implies *inter alia* the right to access to a court and the right to a procedure for interim legal protection. Except for these influences, national proceedings concerning the application of Union law in the national legal order are in principle governed by national law (principle of procedural autonomy). This national law, however, must be in accordance with the minimum requirements of equivalence and effectiveness. These principles were already mentioned in paragraph 1.3. In this paragraph, we will examine some examples of the application of these requirements in the Court's case law.[204]

According to the *principle of equivalence* (non-discrimination) the national procedural rules governing actions to safeguard Union rights must not be less favourable than the national rules governing actions to safeguard similar domestic rights. The domestic rights concerned must be similar as regards 'purpose, cause of action and essential characteristics'.[205] Union law does not require the Member States to apply their most favourable procedural rule. The case law of the CJEU demonstrates several examples in which this requirement has been violated. One of them is the case of *Deville*[206]: in this case the Court declared a French law, according to which the recovery of taxes which had been imposed upon individuals contrary to Union law was governed by much shorter time-limits than the recovery of taxes imposed upon individuals contrary to national law, to be incompatible with the equivalence requirement.

The *principle of effectiveness* implies that a national provision governing procedures in which rights conferred by Union law are at issue, must not render the exercise of these rights virtually impossible or excessively difficult. When assessing this principle the national court has to take into consideration 'the role of the provision in the procedure, its progress and its special features, viewed as a whole', and 'the basic principles of the domestic judicial system such as the protection of the right of defence, the principle of legal certainty and the principle

---

204 S. Prechal, 'Community Law in National Courts: the Lessons from Van Schijndel', *Common Market Law Review*, 1998/3, pp. 681–706.

205 Case C-63/08, *Pontin*, ECLI:EU:C:2009:666.

206 Case 240/87, *Deville*, ECLI:EU:C:1988:349.

of the proper conduct of procedure'.[207] The main question to be answered in this respect is the following: can a national law provision which limits the application and enforcement of Union law in the Member State reasonably be justified by these basic principles (procedural rule of reason)?[208] The case law of the CJEU offers many examples of this test.

6.3.3.2. Fatal Time Limits and Principle of *Res Judicata*

Sometimes a Union right can no longer be enforced by an individual before a national court because the individual has not challenged an administrative decision within a fatal time-limit, prescribed by national law. In the case law of the CJEU the question has been raised whether the application of such time limits is contrary to the effectiveness requirement. According to the Court this is not the case as long as the time limit is reasonable.[209] After all, the application of time limits can be justified by the basic principle of legal certainty. This principle protects the interests of the competent authorities and of other (third) parties. However, a fatal time limit cannot be applied when exceeding the time limit by the individual is the result of misleading conduct by the competent authorities.[210]

As regards final judicial decisions, the Court applies a similar approach. In this respect, the principle of *res judicata* is of relevance, according to which a judicial decision becomes final after all rights of appeal have been exhausted or after the expiry of the time limits provided for in that regard. In its case law the CJEU has ruled that the principle of *res judicata* in principle also applies in Union cases, even if the judicial decision is contrary to Union law: to ensure stability of the law and legal relations, as well as the sound administration of justice, it is important that judicial decisions which have become final can no longer be called in question.[211] Therefore Union law does not require as a matter of principle that a national final judicial decision is reviewed (or revoked) when it is contrary to Union law, provided that the principles of equivalence and

---

207 Case C-430/93, *Van Schijndel*, ECLI:EU:C:1995:441, Case 312/93, *Peterbroeck and others*, ECLI:EU:C:1995:437.

208 Cf. S. Prechal & R.J.G.M. Widdershoven, 'Redefining the Relationship between "Rewe-effectiveness" and Effective Judicial Protection', *Review of European Administrative Law*, 2011/2, pp. 31–50.

209 Case 33/76, *Rewe*, ECLI:EU:C:1976:188, Case 45/76, *Comet*, ECLI:EU:C:1976:191, Case C-310/97 P, *AssiDomän Kraft*, ECLI:EU:C:1999:407.

210 Case C-208/90, *Emmott*, ECLI:EU:C:1991:333, as interpreted in Case C-231/96, *Edis*, ECLI:EU:C:1998:401. See also Case C-452/09, *Tonina Enza Iaia*, ECLI:EU:C:2011:323.

211 Cf. Case C-126/97, *Eco Swiss*, ECLI:EU:C:1999:269, Case C-234/04, *Kapferer*, ECLI:EU:C:2006:178, Case C-213/13, *Impresa Pizzarotti*, ECLI:EU:C:2014:2067, Case C-69/14, *Târsia*, ECLI:EU:C:2015:662. In the exceptional Case C-119/05, *Lucchini*, ECLI:EU:C:2007:434, the *res judicata* of a national judicial decision was set aside by the principle of primacy of, in particular, Article 108 TFEU, as it prevented the recovery of state aid of which the Commission had already established in a final decision that it was incompatible with the internal market.

effectiveness are met. An obligation to revoke a final judicial decision contrary to Union law may be derived from the principle of equivalence, if and to the extent such obligation exists in respect of judicial decisions contrary to national law as well.[212]

In its case law the Court is more critical about the binding authority of the *res judicata* of a judicial decision contrary to Union law in another judicial dispute. This appears from *Olimpiclub*, in which it had to rule about the wide Italian application of the principle, according to which a final decision as regards a value added tax decision in one tax period (which was contrary to Union law) had binding authority in respect of similar value added tax decisions in future tax periods.[213] According to the Court this application of the principle of *res judicata* was contrary to the effectiveness principle, as such extensive obstacles to the effective application of the Union rules could not reasonably be regarded as justified in the interests of legal certainty. A similar approach is applied in *Klausner Holz Niedersachsen*.[214] In that case the CJEU ruled that a national rule which prevents the national court from drawing all the consequences of a breach of the stand-still obligation of Article 108, third paragraph, TFEU because of a decision of a national court, which has *res judicata*, given in a dispute which does not have the same subject-matter and which did not concern the State aid characteristics of the contracts at issue, must be regarded as being incompatible with the principle of effectiveness. According to the Court such a significant obstacle to the effective application of EU law and, in particular, a principle as fundamental as that of the control of State aid, cannot be justified either by the principle of *res judicata* nor by the principle of legal certainty.

6.3.3.3. *Ex Officio* Application of Union and the Prohibition of *Reformatio in Pejus*

In several cases the question has been raised whether a national procedural rule which prohibits the national court from applying Union law *ex officio* (of its own motion), where the parties to the dispute have not relied thereon, is incompatible with the effectiveness requirement. In the *Van Schijndel* case the CJEU declared that this is not the case in actions before a civil court because this prohibition can be justified by the principle of passivity, a concept which prevails in civil cases in most of the Member States.[215] This principle safeguards the right of defence and it ensures the proper conduct of proceedings. In the case of *Van der Weerd* the Court has ruled that the same applies to administrative courts. Thus, national limitations on the *ex officio* application of the law (including Union

212 Case C-213/13, *Impresa Pizzarotti*, ECLI:EU:C:2014:2067.
213 Case C-2/08, *Fallimento Olimpiclub*, ECLI:EU:C:2009:506.
214 Case C-505/14, *Klausner Holz Niedersachsen*, ECLI:EU:C:2015:742.
215 Case C-430/93, *Van Schijndel*, ECLI:EU:C:1995:441.

law) by administrative courts are not contrary to the effectiveness principle.[216] According to the Court the taking into consideration by the national court of its own motion of issues not put forward by the parties to the proceedings is capable of infringing the rights of defence and the proper conduct of proceedings and, in particular, of leading to the delays inherent in the examination of new pleas.

From the foregoing, it cannot be concluded that national courts are never under an obligation to apply Union law *ex officio*. In the first place this obligation may result from the principle of equivalence. If and to the extent national law requires *ex officio* application of binding domestic rules, the same applies to similar Union rules. For example, in the context of arbitration awards, the CJEU ruled in *Eco Swiss that – as an application of the principle of equivalence*[217] – Article 101 TFEU is considered to be of public order (*order public*) and therefore must be applied *ex officio* by the national courts.[218]

Moreover, an obligation to apply Union law *ex officio* also exists where national law confers (only) *discretion* to do so in domestic cases.[219] Thus, national discretion as regards *ex officio* application of national law implies a Union obligation to do so in respect of Union law.

In the second place, it is consistent case law of the CJEU that the national courts must determine of their own motion whether provisions of consumer directives, in particular Directive 93/13, on unfair terms in consumer contracts, have been complied with.[220] According to the Court, this is necessary to ensure effective protection of the rights this directive confers on consumers. The case law is based on the premise that a consumer is the weaker party to a consumer contract and that therefore the judge should assist him or her in effectuating the directive's consumer protection. Thus, if a consumer has failed to challenge a term as being unfair, for example because of ignorance of the law, the national court is obliged to evaluate the term of its own motion. However, this line of reasoning is limited to the field of consumer protection. Outside this field it is not applicable.[221]

The *prohibition of reformatio in pejus*, according to which an individual who brings an action before an administrative court cannot find himself in a less favourable position than he would have been in, if the action had not been brought, exists probably in every administrative law system. According to the CJEU in the case of *Heemskerk & Schaap* this prohibition can also be applied

216 Joined cases C-222/05 to C-225/05, *Van der Weerd*, ECLI:EU:C:2007:318.

217 Joined Cases C-222/05 to C-225/05 *Van der Weerd*, ECLI:EU:C:2007:318.

218 Case C-126/97, *Eco Swiss*, ECLI:EU:C:1999:269, as interpreted in Joined cases C-295/04-C-298/04, *Manfredi*, ECLI:EU:C:2006:461.

219 Case C-430/93, *Van Schijndel*, ECLI:EU:C:1995:441.

220 See Joined Cases C-240/98 to C-244/98, *Océano Grupo Editorial*, ECLI:EU:C:2000:346, Case C-473/00, *Cofidis*, ECLI:EU:C:2002:705, Case C-168/05 *Mostaza Clara*, ECLI:EU:C:2006:675, Case C-429/05, *Rampion & Godard*, ECLI:EU:C:2007:575, Case C-40/08, *Asturcom*, ECLI:EU:C:2009:615, Case C-618/10, *Banco Español de Crédito*, ECLI:EU:C:2012:349, Case C-488/11, *Asbeek Brusse*, ECLI:EU:C:2013:341, Case C-497/13, *Faber*, ECLI:EU:C:2015:357.

221 See Joined Cases C-430/93 and C-431/93, *Van Schijndel and Van Veen*, ECLI:EU:C:1995:441.

in Union cases.[222] It can be justified by the principles of respect for the rights of defence, legal certainty and legitimate expectations, and the principle of effective judicial protection.

6.3.3.4. Judicial Scrutiny and Evidence

Up until recently the Union influence on the intensity of national courts' review of decisions in Union cases was rather limited. As Union legislation did not contain any specific provision in that respect, it was for the Member States to determine the detailed rules for judicial review in accordance with the principles of equivalence and effectiveness.[223] Within these minimum requirements, both the marginal test of the English courts (on Wednesbury unreasonableness)[224] and the more intensive scrutiny of decisions by the German courts, were – and probably in general still are – allowed.[225]

Fairly recently, Union's influence on the intensity of national courts' review of decisions in Union cases has enlarged. In some areas, the Union legislator has laid down binding rules harmonizing the standard of review in a specific area. Article 46, third paragraph of the Recast Directive, on common procedures in asylum cases, for example, prescribes a *full and ex nunc examination of both facts and points of law* in judicial review procedures against asylum decisions before a court or tribunal of first instance.[226] Such review goes much further than the *ex tunc* judicial assessment which is common standard in the administrative law systems of most Member States. In addition, in *Samba Diouf* also the CJEU seems to intensify its grip on the national judicial assessment in Union cases.[227] In this case the Court derives from the principle of effective judicial protection, as codified in Article 47 Charter, an obligation of the national courts to exercise in asylum cases a 'thorough review' as regards both the fact and the law. Moreover, the Court prescribes a strict judicial test of the reasons of an asylum decision: It states:

> 'The right to an effective remedy is a fundamental principle of EU law. In order for that right to be exercised effectively, the national court must be able to review the merits of the reasons which led the competent administrative authority to hold the application for international protection to be unfounded or made in bad faith, there being no irrefutable presumption as to the legality of those reasons.'

---

222 Case C-455/06, *Heemskerk & Schaap*, ECLI:EU:C:2008:650.

223 Case C-120/97, *Upjohn*, ECLI:EU:C:1999:14, Case C-55/06, *Arcor*, ECLI:EU:C:2008:244.

224 English Court of Appeal 7 November 1947, *Associated Provincial Picture Houses* v *Wednesbury Corporation* [1948] 1 KB 223.

225 Compare the English Case C-120/97, *Upjohn*, ECLI:EU:C:1999:14, with the German Case C-55/06, *Arcor*, ECLI:EU:C:2008:244.

226 Recast Directive 2013/32, *OJ* 2013 L 180/60. See M. Reneman, *EU Asylum Procedures and the Right to an Effective Remedy*, Hart Publishing, Oxford, 2014.

227 Case C-69/10, *Samba Diouf*, ECLI:EU:C:2011:524.

Also in respect of evidence, it is the general rule that, as long as the Union legislator has prescribed specific evidential rules in a specific area of law by means of secondary Union law, the Member States are allowed to apply their national rules of evidence, albeit within the limits of equivalence and effectiveness and of the principle of effective judicial protection (Article 47 CFR). In several cases the CJEU has ruled that national rules of evidence were incompatible with the effectiveness principle, as rules concerned rendered excessively difficult the exercise of rights conferred by Union law. They contained, for instance, a reversal of the burden of proof to the detriment of the individual who wanted to enforce its Union right; or they contained a limitation on the means of evidence – non-written evidence was excluded – to prove a Union right.[228]

6.3.3.5. Review of Final Administrative Decisions

Finally, some attention is paid to the question to what extent EU law obliges a national final administrative decision to be reviewed (or revoked) if that decision does not comply with Union law. This question was raised for the first time in *Kühne & Heitz*[229], in the situation where the decision had become final as a result of judgement of a national court, adjudicating at final instance, a judgement which was contrary to Union law as well. In its answer the Court observed, first, that Union law does not require that administrative authorities be placed under the obligation, in principle, to review (or to revoke) a national administrative decision which has become final after the expiry of reasonable time limits for legal remedies or by exhaustion of these remedies. After all, finality of administrative decision contributes to legal certainty, a general principle recognized by Union law. However, according to the Court, a EU obligation to review a national final administrative decision does exist, where the following cumulative conditions are met:

- under national law, the administrative authority has the power to review final administrative decisions. Where such power does not exist, Member States are not obliged to create it;
- the administrative decision in question has become final as a result of a judgement of a national court ruling at final instance.
- that judgement is, in the light of a decision given by the CJEU in a later preliminary procedure, based on a misinterpretation of EU law which was adopted without a question being referred to the Court for a preliminary ruling under Article 267 TFEU; and
- the person concerned complained to the administrative authority immediately after becoming aware of that decision of the Court. In this

---

228 See for both examples, Case 199/82, *San Giorgio*, ECLI:EU:C:1983:318. Furthermore, national rules of evidence must be consistent with Art. 6 ECHR. See Case C-276/01, *Steffensen*, ECLI:EU:C:2003:228.

229 Case C-453/00, *Kühne & Heitz*, ECLI:EU:C:2004:17.

respect, the Member States are free to set reasonable time-limits within which an application for review should be made in a manner consistent with the principles of effectiveness and equivalence.[230]

In subsequent case law, the Court has made clear that the conditions of *Kühne & Heitz* only apply in the exceptional situation where the administrative decision has become final as a result of an incorrect judgement of a national court adjudicating in last instance.[231] If the administrative decision has become final because the individual did not exhaust the available national remedies, the question whether the decision must be reviewed when contrary to Union law should be answered within the framework of the principle of national procedural autonomy, as limited by the principles of equivalence and effectiveness. An obligation to review (and revoke) a final decision contrary to Union law may result from the equivalence principle[232], if and to the extent such obligation exists under national law in respect of final decisions contrary to national law.

If such national obligation does not exist in a Member State, the decision not reviewing a final decision contrary to Union is generally consistent with the effectiveness principle, as it may be justified by the principle of legal certainty. An exception to this rule is the case of *Byankov*[233], in which the administrative decision at issue – prohibiting Byankov from leaving Bulgaria on account of his failure to pay a private debt – not only constituted a clear breach of the fundamental right laid down in Article 21 TFEU to move and reside freely within the territory of the Member States, but was also adopted for an unlimited period and continued to produce legal effects with regards to Byankov for eternity. In these particular circumstances, the decision not to revoke it could, according to the Court, not reasonably be justified by the principle of legal certainty and was therefore contrary to the principles of effectiveness and sincere cooperation.

7. NON-CONTRACTUAL LIABILITY

7.1. INTRODUCTION

In the European legal order, which is characterized by the concept of shared government, questions concerning the non-contractual (financial) liability of the administration can be raised at two levels, at the Union level and at the national level. At the Union level, non-contractual liability is governed by Article 340,

230 Case C-2/06, *Kempter*, ECLI:EU:C:2008:78.

231 See already Joined cases C-392/04 and 422/04, *i-21 and Arcor*, ECLI:EU:C:2006:586, and more clear Case C-249/11, *Byankov*, ECLI:EU:C:2012:608.

232 Joined cases C-392/04 and 422/04, *i-21 and Arcor*, ECLI:EU:C:2006:586.

233 Case C-249/11, *Byankov*, ECLI:EU:C:2012:608. See Case 161/06, *Skoma-lux*, ECLI:EU:C:2007:773.

second paragraph, TFEU. The competent court is the CJEU (at first instance, the GC). This Union liability is primarily concerned with acts of Union institutions, but may in specific circumstances be of importance for the application of Union law by an authority of a Member State (paragraph 7.2). However, in general actions concerning the non-contractual liability for the national application of Union law must be brought before the national courts. In that case, the substantive conditions are to a certain extent Europeanized by the case law of the CJEU (paragraph 7.3).

7.2. NON-CONTRACTUAL LIABILITY OF THE UNION[234]

According to Article 340, second paragraph, TFEU, the Union shall, in the case of non-contractual liability, make good any damage caused by its institutions or its servants in the performance of their duties. Article 268 TFEU declares that the CJEU has jurisdiction in any dispute relating to compensation for damage. In the first instance these disputes are decided by the GC. An appeal may be lodged before the Court of Justice. Actions for damages are subject to a limitation period of five years. The procedure is as such free of charge. However, individual claimants shall be represented by a lawyer and if their claim is unsuccessful they should not only bear their own cost, but will in principles be ordered by the CJEU to pay the costs of the successful party as well.

The Union liability of Article 340 TFEU is only concerned with damages caused to individuals by means of *unlawful* acts of EU institutions. In the case of *FIAMM* the CJEU has rejected the existence of a general principle under which the Union can be held liable for damages caused by *lawful* acts, in particular where these acts are of a legislative nature.[235] The main reason for the rejection is that only few Member States recognize the possible liability for lawful legislation. Therefore, there is insufficient convergence of the national legal system as regards this form of liability.

The non-contractual liability of the Union is first and foremost of importance when individuals are directly confronted with an unlawful act of an EU institution or with wrongful conduct by an EU civil servant. However, this liability can also be relevant when EU law is applied *vis-à-vis* an individual by an authority of a Member State.[236] In its case law the CJEU has ruled that the

234 See Lenaerts *et al.*, *supra* note 1, chapter 11; Craig, *supra* note 1, pp. 681–704; P. Aalto, *Public Liability in EU Law*, Hart Publishing, Oxford, 2011.

235 Joined cases C-120/06 P and C-121/06 P, *FIAMM and Fedon*, ECLI:EU:C:2008:476.

236 T. Heukels & A. McDonnell, 'The Action for Damages in a Community law perspective', in: T. Heukels, & A. McDonnell (eds.), *The Action for Damages in Community Law*, Kluwer Law International, The Hague-London-Boston, 1997, pp. 1–9; A.W.H. Mey, 'Article 215 EC and Local Remedies', in: T. Heukels & A. McDonnell (eds.), *The Action for Damages in Community Law*, Kluwer Law International, The Hague-London-Boston, 1997, pp. 273–284; Craig, *supra* note 1, p. 681 *et seq.*

liability regime of Article 340 TFEU is applicable to the national application of Union acts, if the national authority 'is bound to strictly and mechanically apply' an Union act which is contrary to higher Union law.[237] In practice these cases are always concerned with the application of EU regulations or decisions, which are incompatible with the Treaties (including the Charter) or with a general principle of Union law. In these cases, the unlawfulness of the national decision implementing the regulation or decision is attributed to the EU institution, that established the unlawful Union act (causation theory).

The background to this case law is that the authorities of the Member States are obliged to apply Union acts as long as they have not been declared invalid in a procedure before the CJEU.[238] This duty also exists if the national authority is of the opinion that the Union act is invalid. Therefore, it is not strange that the Union institution establishing the invalid act is held to be liable and not the national authority which correctly applied this (unlawful) act. The exclusion of national liability, which is the result of this case law, only concerns the situation in which the national authority was legally forced by the Union act to take the unlawful decision. The national authority is, however, liable for its own deficiencies in the implementation and application of Union acts. Paragraph 7.3 examines the European influence on this liability.

The conditions governing Union liability are derived from the general principles, which are common to the laws of the Member States (Article 340, second paragraph, TFEU). They are the same as the European minimum conditions governing the liability of the Member States for breaches of Union law.[239] According to them the Union incurs liability for damage caused to individuals by a breach of higher-ranking rules of Union law were three conditions are met[240]: the rule of law infringed must be intended to confer rights on individuals; the breach must be sufficiently serious; and there must be a direct causal link between the breach of Union law and the damage sustained by the injured party. These conditions are discussed in paragraph 7.3.

7.3. MEMBER STATE LIABILITY[241]

In the famous *Francovich* judgement in 1991 the CJEU declared that it is a general principle of Union law that a Member State must be liable for any loss or

237 Case C-165/84, *Krohn*, ECLI:EU:C:1986:507, Joined cases C-106–210/87, *Asteris*, ECLI:EU:C:1988:457, Joined cases C-104/89 & C-37/90, *Mulder*, ECLI:EU:C:1992:217.

238 Case 314/85, *Foto Frost*, ECLI:EU:C:1987:452.

239 W. van Gerven, 'Bridging the Unbridgeable: Community and national Tort Law after Francovich and Brasserie', *International & Comparative Law Quarterly*, 1996, pp. 507–544.

240 Case C-352/98 P, *Bergaderm*, ECLI:EU:C:2000:361.

241 Tridimas, *supra* note 79, pp. 321–327; Craig, *supra* note 1, p. 727 *et seq*; J.H. Jans & A.P.W. Duijkersloot, 'State Liability', in: Jans *et al.* (eds.), *supra* note 1, chapter 7.

damage caused to individuals as a result of breaches of Union law for which the State can be held liable.[242] According to the Court this principle of State liability is inherent to the system of the Treaties. A further legal basis can be found in (now) Article 4, third paragraph, TEU (principle of sincere cooperation) and in the principle of effective judicial protection.

The principle of State liability applies to every possible violation of Union law by the authorities of the Member States, for instance: the non-transposition (in due time) of a directive; the incorrect transposition of a directive; legislation or individual decisions contrary to the Treaty; the incorrect application of a regulation, and even breaches of Union law by a national court adjudicating in last instance.[243] It does not matter whether the Union provision in question has direct effect. Furthermore, this principle holds true in any case in which a Member State breaches EU law, whichever State body is responsible for the breach. This may be the central or decentralized administration, the Parliament as the legislator or a lower legislator, and a court adjudicating in last instance. Actions concerning state liability for breaches of EU law must be brought before the national court. It is for the legal system of each Member State to designate the competent court and to lay down rules of procedure.

The CJEU has also defined the minimum conditions under which the Member State may incur liability for breaches of Union law.[244] These conditions are the same as those governing the liability of Union institutions under Article 340, second paragraph, TFEU (see paragraph 7.2)[245]: the rule of law infringed must be intended to confer rights on individuals; the breach must be sufficiently serious; direct causal link between the breach of Union law and the damage sustained by the injured party.

- The rule of law infringed must be intended to confer rights on individuals: whether this is the case depends on the Union rule in question. Union rules that clearly confer rights on individuals are, for instance, the right to compensation for arrears of wages (*Francovich*), the right to refund of money paid to an insolvent tour operator (*Dillenkoffer*) and the right to cancel a contract (*Facini Dori*).[246] In addition, the CJEU has ruled that the fact that a Union rule primarily serves the general interest does not exclude the possibility that it also confers rights on individuals. In this respect, individual

242 Joined cases C-6/90 & C-9/90, *Francovich and Bonifaci*, ECLI:EU:C:1991:428.

243 Case C-224/01, *Köbler*, ECLI:EU:C:2003:513, Case C-173/03, *Traghetti del Mediterraneo*, ECLI:EU:C:2006:391. Cf. Z. Varga, 'In Search of a 'Manifest Infringement of the Applicable Law' in the Terms set out in Köbler', *Review of European Administrative Law*, 2016/2, pp. 5–40.

244 T. Tridimas, 'Liability for Breach of Community Law; Growing up and Mellowing Down?', *Common Market Law Review*, 2001, pp. 301–332.

245 Joined cases C-46/93 and C-48/93, *Brasserie du Pêcheur and Factortame*, ECLI:EU:C:1996:79.

246 Joined cases C-6/90 & C-9/90, *Francovich and Bonifaci*, ECLI:EU:C:1991:428, Joined cases C-178–179/94 and C-188–190/94, *Dillenkoffer*, ECLI:EU:C:1996:375, Case C-91/92, *Facini Dori*, ECLI:EU:C:1994:292.

rights may also be derived from detailed obligations of the administrative authorities to act in a certain way.[247] Thus, in the case of *Danske Slagterier* specific EU standards for testing male pigs, were converted into liability rights of individuals to market in another state male pigs which complied with these Union standards. Moreover, from the case of *Leth* it appears that procedural administrative obligations may confer rights on individuals as well.[248] In the case Ms. Leth held Austria liable for the pecuniary damage (the decrease of the value of her property) she had suffered because the country had granted consent for the expansion of an airport without any environmental impact assessment having been performed as prescribed by Directive 85/337. According to the CJEU this pecuniary damage was covered by the objective of the protection pursued by the directive, to the extent that the damage was the direct economic consequence of the environmental impact of the project. This may be the case if the exposure to the noise caused by the airport has major consequences for human beings, in the sense that their environment, quality of life and possibly their health are affected.

However, to confer rights on individuals it is necessary that the rule concerned *specifically* aims at protecting these rights. This appears from *Peter Paul*.[249] In this case Peter Paul and others brought proceeding against the Republic of Germany for the loss of their deposits, claiming that they would not have lost the deposits if Germany had transposed Directive 94/19, on the supervision of financial markets, in due time. The national supervisor, the *Bundesaufsichtsamt*, would then have been competent to take supervisory measures. The decisive question to be answered was whether the directive conferred liability rights on individuals. Although one of the objectives of the Directive was to protect depositors, the CJEU found several reasons for a negative answer to the question: the directives did not contain explicit provisions conferring rights on depositors in the event their deposits became unavailable as a result of defective supervision; coordination of the national provisions on liability in the event of defective supervision did not seem necessary in view of the harmonization the directives aim to achieve; and the complexity of banking supervision.

- The breach of Union law by the Member State must be sufficiently serious: whether a breach is sufficiently serious depends on the margin of discretion enjoyed by the Member State when exercising the power, which has violated EU law. If there is no discretion at all – for instance, in the case of the transposition of a directive in due time – then the mere infringement of the Union obligation is sufficient to establish the existence of a sufficiently

[247] Case C-445/06, *Danske Slagterier*, ECLI:EU:C:2009:178.

[248] Case C-420/11, *Leth*, ECLI:EU:C:2013:166.

[249] Case C-222/02, *Peter Paul*, ECLI:EU:C:2004:606.

serious breach.[250] If the Member State enjoys wide discretion, the decisive test for finding that a breach of Union law is sufficiently serious, is whether the State concerned has manifestly and gravely disregarded the limitations on its discretion. Factors which the competent national court may take into consideration when assessing this test include, are amongst others[251]: the clarity and precision of the rule breached, the measure of discretion left by that rule to the national authorities, whether any error of law was intentional or involuntary, whether the error of law was excusable or inexcusable etc. Moreover, if the CJEU has already established that a certain national act infringes Union law, and the Member State nevertheless continues the infringement, this will constitute a sufficiently serious breach. Finally, it should be noted that in case of infringements of Union law by a national court adjudicating in last instance the CJEU has prescribed, in the *Köbler* case, an even more strict condition: state liability for these infringements can incur only in the exceptional case where the court has *manifestly* infringed Union law.[252]

- Direct causal link between the breach of the Union obligation and the damage sustained by the injured parties: from the scares case law regarding this condition it seems that breaches of procedural Union requirements, as far as they do not have substantive consequences, have in general no direct causal link with the damage sustained. Thus, in the *Leth* case, mentioned above, the CJEU doubted whether the violation of the Environmental Impact Assessment Directive was as such the actual cause of the loss of value, as the infringed rules, procedural by nature, only prescribed an assessment of the environmental impact, but did not lay down substantive rules in respect to the balancing of the environmental effects with other interests or prohibit the completion of the project concerned (the expansion of the airport).[253] In different words, if the Austrian authorities would not have violated the EIA Directive, the project concerned could still have been carried out and the loss of value would have occurred as well.

In its case law the CJEU has Europeanized the legal basis of Member State liability for breaches of EU law – since 1991 this has been the general principle of EU law as 'found' in the *Francovich* judgement – and the conditions under which this liability occurs. This does not mean, however, that national law is no longer relevant for this liability.

In the first place, it should be noted that the liability conditions developed by the CJEU are necessary and sufficient to give individuals the right to obtain

250 Joined cases C-178–179/94 and C-188–190/94, *Dillenkoffer*, ECLI:EU:C:1996:375, point 26.

251 Joined cases C-46/93 and C-48/93, *Brasserie du Pêcheur and Factortame*, ECLI:EU:C:1996:79, point 56.

252 Case C-224/01, *Köbler*, ECLI:EU:C:2003:513.

253 Case C-420/11, *Leth*, ECLI:EU:C:2013:166.

redress, but they do not preclude a State from incurring liability under less strict conditions on the basis of national law.[254] If a Member State has – from the point of view of individuals – a more favourable regime in place for cases of State liability for breaches of national law, this regime should also be applied in cases concerning a breach of Union law. In other words: the Europeanization of liability regimes for breaches of EU law must be considered as minimum harmonization.

In the second place, it is of importance that, with the exception of the legal basis and the conditions for State liability, all other substantive and procedural matters concerning this remedy are still governed by domestic liability law, provided that the principles of equivalence and effectiveness are met (cf. paragraph 1.3). This means that the conditions for the reparation of loss and damage laid down by national law relating to claims based on Union law must not be less favourable than those relating to similar domestic claims and must not be such as to make it impossible or excessively difficult to obtain reparation in practice. Matters that are governed by national law are for instance: the competent national court, the rules concerning the procedure (time limits, rules of evidence), the relation between the liability action and the utilization of a national remedy for annulment[255], and the division of liability between the central or federal State and decentralized authorities.[256] The case of *Ferreira da Silva e Brito* offers an example of a limitation of national procedural autonomy in a liability procedure by means of the effectiveness requirement.[257] The CJEU ruled that the *Köbler* liability for violations of Union law by a court adjudicating in final instance cannot be made conditional upon the judicial decision that caused the damage having first been set aside, as this precondition may make it excessively difficult to obtain reparation of the damage and cannot be justified by the principles of *res iudicata* and legal certainty.

8. CONCLUSION

In the foregoing, we have studied European administrative law. This area of law is concerned with both the Union and the national component of the shared application of Union law. The most important conclusion may be that national administrative law is increasingly becoming influenced by Union law. This

---

254 Joined cases C-46/93 and C-48/93, *Brasserie du Pêcheur and Factortame*, ECLI:EU:C:1996:79, point 66.

255 According to Case C-445/06, *Danske Slagterier*, ECLI:EU:C:2009:178, the Member States are in principle allowed to apply a rule according to which the injured party must bear the loss and damage himself in case he did not avail himself in time of all legal remedies available in order to avoid loss and damages or limit its extent.

256 Case C-302/97, *Konle*, ECLI:EU:C:1999:271.

257 Case C-160/14, *Ferreira da Silva e Brito*, ECLI:EU:C:2015:565.

process can be seen in the several topics, which we have discussed. The extent to which each topic is already influenced by Union law differs, however. The influences are most intense in the areas of fundamental rights and general principles of law (paragraph 5), legal protection (paragraph 6) and state liability (paragraph 7). In the area of the organization of the administration Union influences are, as yet, not very important (paragraph 2). Nevertheless, one can say that a common administrative law or a *Ius Commune* is gradually taking shape in Europe.[258]

The Europeanization of administrative law is especially the result of and is enforced by the CJEU. In its case law the Court has developed several general principles of Union law, such as the principles of proportionality, equality, defence etc., as well as the very important principle of effective judicial protection, which also includes the principles of state liability and immediate legal protection. Administrative authorities and national courts have to comply with these principles when acting within the scope of Union law. This compulsory influence may be labelled as *direct reception* of Union law influences.[259] In addition, direct reception of Union law may occur if and to the extent the Union legislator has regulated, by means of sectoral secondary Union law, specific issues of e.g. national enforcement or legal protection in a specific area of law.

The development towards a common administrative law in Europe is also favoured by the phenomenon of *indirect reception* or *voluntary adoption* of Union standards in the legal order of the Member States. This phenomenon – which was not discussed in this chapter – implies that the Member States apply, on a voluntary basis, the Union standards and principles in purely domestic cases. An example of this Europeanization from bottom up is the judgement of the English House of Lords in *M.* v *Home Office*.[260] This case dates from after the CJEU judgement in the *Factortame* case. As discussed in paragraph 6.3.3, the Court declared in *Factortame* that a national court should have the power to suspend a national measure which is incompatible with EU law. The consequence of this judgement was that the United Kingdom had to set aside the rule of national law by which national courts were precluded from granting an interim junction against the Crown, at least in cases where Union law was at issue. In *M.* v *Home Office* the House of Lords extended this rule to purely domestic cases: since that time the English courts have had complete jurisdiction to issue interim orders against the Crown. The argument for this judgement was the avoidance of discrimination against purely domestic claims. The House of Lords wanted to

258 Jans *et al (eds.)*, *supra* note 1, chapter 8; Groussot, *supra* note 83; Caranta, *supra* note 5; Van Gerven, *supra* note 5; Schwarze, *supra* note 5; Ladeur, *supra* note 5.

259 M.L. Fernandez Esteban, 'National Judges and Community law: The Paradox of the Two Paradigms of Law', *Maastricht Journal of European and Comparative Law*, 1997 (4), pp. 143–151.

260 *Weekly Law Reports* (WLR), 1993, 3, pp. 433–448.

end 'the unhappy situation that while a citizen is entitled to obtain injunctive relief against the Crown to protect its interest under Community law, he cannot do so in respect of other (national) interests which may be just as important'.

Other examples of indirect reception of Union standards and principles can e.g. be found in Spain[261], where the *Factortame* principle of immediate legal protection was also extended to purely domestic cases, in Belgium[262], where the Constitutional Court, on the ground of its constitutional equality principle, adopted the *Köbler* conditions for liability for violations of EU law by national courts adjudicating in last instance in purely domestic cases, and in the Netherlands[263], where the Council of State has, in the context of the distribution of scarce or limited public rights, recognized the EU principle of transparency as a national principle as well, so that it also applies to such distribution outside the scope of Union law. Obviously, this process of indirect reception promotes the development of a *Ius Commune*. Moreover, it avoids the situation where two sets of principles have to be applied within one legal order, one in Union cases and one in domestic cases.

Finally, the development towards a common European administrative law may be enhanced by the European mandate, imposed by Article 298 TFEU, of adopting necessary provisions to achieve 'an open, efficient and independent European administration'. The provision aims to ensure that the Union legislator develops, through legally binding rules, the fundamental rights enshrined in Article 41 Charter. In 2016, the European Parliament has, on the basis of Article 298 TFEU, submitted a proposal for a Regulation on the Administrative Procedures of the European Union's institutions, bodies, offices and agencies.[264] It contains detailed rules regarding initiation, management and conclusion of procedures for single case decision-making. In addition, the preamble of the proposal contains definitions of the general principles of Union law which are operationalized in the proposal and should function as a source of inspiration when interpreting the proposal provisions. The proposed regulation only applies to decision-making of EU institutions, bodies, etc., and not of national authorities, even when they are acting within the scope of Union law. Nevertheless, when adopted it might gain binding force in the Member States, if and in so far EU sector-specific law will render it applicable to acts of the Member States in the specific sector. In addition, it should not be excluded that the CJEU will draw inspiration from the (proposed) regulation when

---

261 See for this and other examples, R. Caranta, 'Learning from our Neighbours: Public Law Remedies Homogenization for Bottom Up', *Maastricht Journal of European and Comparative Law*, 1997 (4), pp. 220–247.

262 Belgium Constitutional Court 30 June 2014, nr. 5611. See paragraph 7.3, on the *Köbler* conditions.

263 Dutch Council of State 2 November 2016, ECLI:NL:RVS:2016:2927. See paragraph 5.8, on the EU principle of transparency.

264 DV/10812532EN.doc.

further developing its case law regarding Article 41 Charter and the principle of good administration codified in it.[265] In that case elements of the proposal may become binding for the Member States when they are acting within the scope of Union law.

The content of the EP proposal is considerably influenced by book III of the Model Rules on EU Administrative Procedures of the *Research Network on EU Administrative Law (ReNEUAL).*[266] This academic network has published the model rules in September 2014. They exist of six books on more or less every part of general administrative law with an exception for judicial review. The titles of the books are: General Provisions (I); Administrative Rulemaking (II); Single Case Decision-Making (III); Contracts (IV) Mutual assistance (V); Information management (VI). Book II, III, and IV are applicable only to administrative action of EU institutions, bodies etc. Nevertheless, they might become relevant for the Member States in a similar way as the EP proposal. Moreover, ReNEUAL encourages the Member States to use its model rules as guidance when they are implementing Union law in accordance with their national procedural law.[267] Book V and VI are applicable to the Member States in their relation with other Member States and the EU. Obviously, it remains to be seen whether the ReNEUAL Model Rules will be transformed into binding EU rules ever.

BIBLIOGRAPHY

Aalto, P., *Public Liability in EU Law*, Hart Publishing, Oxford, 2011

Auby, J.-B., 'About Europeanization of Domestic Judicial Review', *Review of European Administrative Law*, 2014/2, pp. 19–34.

Auby, J.-B. & Dutheil, J., de la Rochère (eds.), *Droit Administratif Européen*, Bruylant, Brussels, 2007.

Barents, R., *Remedies and Procedures before the EU Courts*, Wolters Kluwer, Alphen aan den Rijn 2016.

Barents, R., *The Autonomy of Community Law*, Kluwer Law International, The Hague-London-Boston, 2004.

ten Berge, J.B.J.M. & Widdershoven, R.J.G.M., 'The Principle of Legitimate Expectations in Dutch Constitutional and Administrative Law', in: Hondius, E.H. (ed.), *Netherlands Report to the fifteenth International Congress of Comparative Law, Bristol 1998*, Intersentia, Antwerp/Groningen,1998, pp. 421–452.

265 Widdershoven 2014, *supra* note 100, pp. 25–31.

266 The Model Rules are published on www.reneual.eu. Cf. H.C.H. Hofmann, J.-P. Schneider & J. Ziller, 'The Research Network on European Administrative Law's Project on EU Administrative Procedure – Its Concepts, Approaches and Results, *Review of European Administrative Law*, 2014/2, pp. 64–64; M. Ruffert, *The Model Rules on EU Administrative Procedures: Adjudication*, Europa Law Publishing, Groningen, 2016.

267 Article 1–3 Book 1.

Besselink, L.F.M., *A Composite European Constitution*, Europa Law Publishing, Groningen, 2007.

Besselink, L.F.M., 'FIDE 2012 General Report: The Protection of Fundamental Rights post Lisbon. The Interaction between the EU Charter of Fundamental Rights, the European Convention of Human Rights (ECHR) and National Constitutions', available at www.fide2012.eu.

Blomberg, A.B., 'European Influence on National Environmental Law Enforcement, *Review of European Administrative Law*, 2008/2, pp. 39–82.

Boymans, P. & Eliantonio, M., 'Europeanization of Legal Principles? The Influence of the CJEU'S Case Law on the Principle of Legitimate Expectations in the Netherlands and the United Kingdom', *European Public Law*, 2013, pp. 715–738.

Bridge, J., 'Procedural Aspects of the Enforcement of EC Law through the Legal Systems of the Member States', *European Law Review*, 1984, pp. 28–42.

Van den Brink, J.E., Den Ouden, W., Prechal, S., Widdershoven, R.J.G.M., Jans, J.H., 'General Principles of Law', in: Jans *et al*, chapter 4.

Brito Bastos, F., 'The Borelli Doctrine Revisited: Three Issues of Coherence in a Landmark Ruling for EU Administrative Justice', *Review of European Administrative Law*, 2015/2, pp. 269–298.

Broberg, M., 'Judicial Coherence and the Preliminary Reference Procedure', *Review of European Administrative Law*, 2015/2, pp. 9–37.

Broberg, M. & Fenger, N., *Preliminary References to the European Court of Justice*, OUP, Oxford, 2014.

Brockmann, F.K., *Effektiver Rechtsschutz – Das Recht der Europäischen Union*, Peter Lang, Frankfurt am Main, 2014.

Buyze, A.W.G.J., *The principle of transparency in EU law*, BOXPress, Den Bosch, 2013.

Caranta, R., 'Judicial Protection against the Member-States: a New Ius Commune Takes Shape', *Common Market Law Review*, 1995, pp. 702–726.

Caranta, R., 'Learning from our Neighbours: Public Law Remedies Homogenization for Bottom Up', *Maastricht Journal of European and Comparative Law*, 1997 (4), pp. 220–247.

Chiti, M.P. & Greco, G. (eds.), *Trattato di diritto amministrativo comunitario*, Giuffré, Milano, 2007.

Craig, P., *EU Administrative Law*, OUP, Oxford, 2012.

Craig, P. & de Búrca, G., *EU Law. Text, Cases and Materials*, 5th ed., OUP, Oxford, 2011.

Von Danwitz, T., *Europäisches Verwaltungsrecht*, Springer Verlag, Berlin/Heidelberg, 2008.

Dougan, M., *National Remedies before the Court of Justice*, Hart Publishing, Oxford-Portland (Oregon), 2005.

Eijsbouts, W.T., 'In Defence of EC Law', in: Van Damme, T.A.J.A. & Reesman, J.H. (eds.), *Ambiguity in the Rule of Law*, Europa Law Publishing, Groningen, 2001, pp. 35–50.

Eliantonio, M. & Backes, Ch.W., 'Access to Courts for Environmental NGOs at the European and national level: Improvements and room for improvement since Maastricht', in: De Visser, M. & Van der Mei, A.P. (eds.), *The Treaty on European Union 1993–2013: Reflections from Maastricht*, Intersentia, Cambridge, 2013, pp. 557–580.

Emiliou, N., *The Principle of Proportionality in European Law, A Comparative Study*, Kluwer Law International, London-The Hague-Boston, 1996.

Fernandez Esteban, M.L., 'National Judges and Community law: The Paradox of the Two Paradigms of Law', *Maastricht Journal of European and Comparative Law*, 1997 (4), pp. 143–151.

Galetta, D.U., *Procedural Autonomy of EU Members States: Paradise Lost?*, Springer, Heidelberg, 2010.

Van Gerven, W. , 'Bridging the Gap between Community and National Laws', *Common Market Law Review*, 1995, pp. 679–702.

Van Gerven, W. , 'Bridging the Unbridgeable: Community and National Tort Law after Francovich and Brasserie', *International & Comparative Law Quarterly*, 1996, pp. 507–544.

Van Gerven, W. , 'Of Rights, Remedies and Procedures', *European Law Review*, 2000, pp. 501–536.

Van Gerven, W., *The European Union. A Polity of States and Peoples*, Hart Publishing, Oxford-Portland (Oregon), 2005.

Grashof, F., *National Procedural Autonomy Revisited*, Europa Law Publishing, Groningen, 2016.

Grimbergen, R., 'How Boundaries Have Shifted. On Jurisdiction and Admissibility in the Preliminary Ruling Procedure', *Review of European Administrative Law*, 2015/2, pp. 39–70.

Groussot, X., *General Principles of Community Law*, Europa Law Publishing, Groningen, 2006.

Harryvan, G.J. & Jans, J.H., 'Internal Review of EU Environmental Measures', *Review of European Administrative Law*, 2010 (2), pp. 53–65.

Hessel, B., 'European integration and the supervision of local and regional authorities. Experiences in the Netherlands with the requirements of European Community Law', *Utrecht Law Review*, June 2006, available at <www.utrechtlawreview. org/>.

Heukels, T. & McDonnell, A. (eds.), *The Action for Damages in Community Law*, Kluwer Law International, The Hague-London-Boston, 1997.

Hofmann, H.C.H., Schneider, J.-P. & Ziller, J., 'The Research Network on European Administrative Law's Project on EU Administrative Procedure – Its Concepts, Approaches and Results', *Review of European Administrative Law* 2014/2, pp. 64–64.

Van der Jagt, J.A.E., *Milieuconvenanten gehandhaafd* (*Environmental Voluntary Agreements Enforced*), Boom Juridische uitgevers, Den Haag, 2006.

Jans, J.H. , Prechal, S. & Widdershoven, R.J.G.M. (eds.), *Europeanisation of Public Law*, Europa Law Publishing, Groningen, 2015 (second edition).

Jans, J.H. & Duijkersloot, A.P.W., 'State Liability', in: Jans *et al.* (eds.), chapter 7.

Jans, J.H. & Verhoeven, M.J.M., 'Europeanisation via Consistent Interpretation and Direct Effect', in: Jans *et al.* (eds.), chapter 3.

Jansen, O. (ed.), *Administrative Sanctions in the European Union*, Intersentia, Cambridge, Antwerp, Portland, 2013.

Jansen, O. & Langbroek, P. (eds.), *Defence Rights during Administrative Investigations*, Intersentia, Antwerp-Oxford, 2007.

Keessen, A.M., *European administrative Decisions. How the EU Regulates Products on the Internal Market*, Europa Law Publishing, Groningen, 2009.

Klamert, M., *The Principle of Loyalty in EU Law*, OUP, Oxford, 2014.

Koopmans, T., 'The Quest for Subsidiarity', in: Curtin, D. & Heukels, T. (eds.), *Institutional Dynamics of European Integration, Essays in Honour of Schermers*, vol. II, Nijhoff, Dordrecht,1994, pp. 43–55.

Kornezov, A., 'Shaping the New Architecture of the EU System of Judicial Remedies: Comment on Inuit', *European law* review, 2014/2, pp. 251–263.

Kulms, K., *Der Effektivitätsgrundsatz. Eine Untersuchung zur Rechtsprechung des Europäischen Gerichtshofs*, Nomos, Baden-Baden, 2013.

Ladeur, K.H., *The Europeanisation of Administrative Law*, Aldershot, Dartmouth, 2002.

Lavrijssen, S. & Ottow, A.M., 'The Legality of Independent Regulatory Authorities', in: Besselink, L.F.M. *et al* (eds.), *The Eclips of the Legality Principle in the European Union*, Kluwer Law International, Alphen a/d Rijn, 2011, pp. 73–96.

Lenaerts, K., 'The Basic Constitutional Charter of a Community Based on the Rule of Law', in: Maduro, M.P. & Azoulai, L. (eds.), *The Past and Future of EU Law*, Hart Publishing, Oxford, 2010, pp. 295–315.

Lenaerts, K., Maselis, I. & Gutman, K., *EU Procedural Law*, OUP, Oxford 2014.

Meij, A.W.H., 'Article 215 EC and Local Remedies', in: Heukels, T. & McDonnell, A. (eds.), *The Action for Damages in Community Law*, Kluwer Law International, The Hague-London-Boston, 1997, pp. 273–284.

Micklitz, H.-W. & De Witte, B. (eds.), *The European Court of Justice and the Autonomy of the Member States*, Intersentia, Cambridge, 2012.

De Moor-van Vugt, A.J.C. & Widdershoven, R.J.G.M., 'Administrative Enforcement', in: Jans *et al.* (eds.), chapter 5.

De Moor-van Vugt, A.J.C., 'Administrative Sanctions in EU Law', *Review of European Administrative Law*, 2012/1, pp. 5–41.

De Moor-van Vugt, A.J.C., 'The Ghost of Criminal Charge: the EU Rights of Defence in Dutch Administrative Law', *Review of European Administrative Law*, 2012/2, pp. 5–16.

Ortlep, R. en Widdershoven, R.J.G.M., 'Judicial Protection', in: Jans *et al.* (eds.), chapter 6.

Van Ooik, R.H., *De keuze der rechtsgrondslag voor besluiten van de Europese Unie* (*The Choice of Legal Base for Decisions of the European Union*), Europese Monografieën (63), Kluwer, Deventer, 1999.

Van Ooik, R.H., 'The Growing Importance of Agencies in the EU: Shifting Governance and the Institutional Balance', in: Curtin, D., & Wessel, R., (eds.), *Good Governance and the European Union*, Intersentia, Antwerp-Oxford-New York, 2005, pp. 125–152.

Pech, L., "A Union Founded on the Rule of Law": Meaning and Reality of the Rule of Law as a Constitutional Principle of EU Law', *European Constitutional Law Review*, 2010/3, pp. 359–396.

Peers, S., Hervey, T., Kenner, J., Ward, A. (eds.), *The EU Charter of Fundamental Rights – A Commentary*, Hart Publishing, Oxford, 2014.

Peers, S. & Prechal, S., 'Art. 52 – Scope of Guaranteed Rights', in: Peers *et al* (eds.) 2014, pp. 1455–1521.

Prechal, S., 'Community Law in National Courts: the Lessons from Van Schijndel', *Common Market Law Review*, 1998, pp. 681–706.

Prechal, S., 'Judge-made Harmonisation of National Procedural Rules: a Bridging Perspective', in: Wouters, J. & Stuyck, J. , (eds.), *Principles of Proper Conduct for*

Supranational, State and Private Actors in the European Union, Essay in Honour of Walter van Gerven, Intersentia, Antwerp-Groningen-Oxford, 2001, pp. 39–58.

Prechal, S., *Directives in EC Law*, 2nd ed., OUP, Oxford, 2005.

Prechal, S., 'Europeanisation of National Administrative Law', in: Jans *et al.* (eds.), chapter 2.

Prechal, S., ''The Court of Justice and Effective Judicial Protection: What has the Charter Changed?', in: Paulussen, C. *et al* (eds.), *Fundamental Rights in International and European Law, Public and Private Law Perspectives*, T.M.C. Asser Press 2016.

Prechal, S. & De Leeuw, M., 'Dimensions of Transparency: The Building Blocks for a New Legal Principle', *Review of European Administrative Law*, 2007/1, pp. 51–62.

Prechal, S. & Widdershoven, R.J.G.M., 'Redefining the Relationship between 'Rewe-effectiveness' and Effective Judicial Protection', *Review of European Administrative Law*, 2011/2, pp. 31–50.

Reneman, M., *EU Asylum Procedures and the Right to an Effective Remedy*, Hart Publishing, Oxford, 2014.

Ruffert, M., *The Model Rules on EU Administrative Procedures: Adjucation*, Europa Law Publishing, Groningen, 2016.

Schimmel, M. & Widdershoven, R.J.G.M., 'Judicial Review after *Tetra Laval*: Some Observations from a European Administrative Law Point of View', in: Essens, O., Gerbrandy, A., Lavrijssen, S., *National Courts and the Standard of Review in Competition Law and Economic Regulation*, Europa Law Publishing, Groningen, 2009, pp. 51–77.

Schmidt-Assman, E. & Schöndorf-Haubold, B. (Hrsg.), *Der Europäsche Verwaltungsverbund*, Mohr Siebeck, Tübingen, 2005.

Schoenmaekers, S., 'The Increasing Influence of the Ombudsman in the Institutional System of the European Union', in: De Visser, M. & Van der Mei, A.P. (eds.), *The Treaty on European Union 1993–2013: Reflections from Maastricht*, Intersentia, Antwerp 2013, pp. 177–200.

Schönemeyer, M., *Die Pflicht des Bundesverfassungsgerichts zur Vorlage an den Gerichtshof der Europäischen Union gem. Art. 267 Abs. 3 AEUV*, Duncker & Humblot, Berlin 2014.

Senden, L.A.J., *Soft Law in European Community Law*, Hart Publishing, Oxford-Portland (Oregon), 2004.

Scholten, M. & Luchtman, M. (eds.*), Law Enforcement by EU Authorities. Political and judicial accountability in shared enforcement*, Edward Elgar, Cheltenham, 2017.

Schønberg, S., *Legitimate Expectations in Administrative Law*, OUP, Oxford, 2000.

Schwarze, J., 'Tendencies towards a Common Administrative Law in Europe', *European Law Review*, 1991, pp. 3–19.

Schwarze, J. (Hrsg.), *Das Verwaltungsrecht under Europäischem Einfluss. Zur Convergenz der mitgliedstaatlichen Verwaltungsrechtsordnungen in der Europäischen Union*, Nomos Verlag, Baden-Baden, 1996.

Schwarze, J., *European Administrative Law*, 2nd ed., Thomson/Sweet, Andover, 2006.

Schwensfeier, R., 'The TWD principle post-Lisbon', *European law review*, 2012/2, pp. 156–175.

Stefan, O., 'Hybridity before the Court: a Hard Look at Soft Law in the EU Competition and State Aid', *European Law Review*, 2012/1, pp. 49–69.

Stefan, O., *Soft law in Court - Competition Law, State Aid, and the Court of Justice of the European Union*, Kluwer Law International, Alphen aan den Rijn, 2012.

Terhechte, J.P. (Hrsg.), *Verwaltungsrecht der Europäischen Union*, Nomos, Baden-Baden 2011.

Tridimas,T., 'Liability for Breach of Community Law; Growing up and Mellowing Down?', *Common Market Law Review*, 2001, pp. 301–332.

Tridimas, T., *The General Principles of EU Law*, 2nd ed., OUP, Oxford, 2006.

Temple Lang, J., 'The Core of the Constitutional Law of the Community - Article 5', in: L.W. Gormley (ed.), *Current and Future Perspectives on EC Competition Law*, Kluwer Law International, London-The Hague, 1997, pp. 41–72.

Varga, Z., 'In Search of a 'Manifest Infringement of the Applicable Law' in the Terms set out in Köbler', *Review of European Administrative Law*, 2016/2, pp. 5–40.

Verhoeven, M.J.M., *The Costanzo Obligation, The Obligations Of National Administrative Authorities in the Case of Incompatibility between National Law and European Law*, Intersentia, Antwerp, 2011.

Vervaele, J.A.E. (ed.), *Transnational Enforcement of the Financial Interests of the EU*, Intersentia, Antwerp/Groningen/Oxford, 1999.

Vervaele, J.A.E. (ed.), Betlem, G., De Lange, R. & Veldman, A.G. (co-eds.), *Compliance and Enforcement of European Community Law*, Kluwer Law International, The Hague-London-Boston, 1999.

Wolswinkel, C.J., 'The Allocation of a Limited Number of Authorisations: Some General Requirements from European Law', *Review of European Administrative* Law, 2009/2, pp. 61–104.

Widdershoven, R.J.G.M., *Naar een bestuurs(proces)rechtelijk Ius Commune in Europa* (*Towards a Ius Commune in administrative law*), VAR-reeks (116), Samsom H.D. Tjeenk Willink, Alphen a/d Rijn, 1996.

Widdershoven, R.J.G.M., 'The Principle of Loyal Cooperation: Lawmaking by the European Court of Justice and the Dutch Courts', in: Stroink, F., Van der Linden, E. (eds.), *Judicial Lawmaking and Administrative Law*, Intersentia, Antwerp-Oxford, 2005, pp. 3–35.

Widdershoven,R.J.G.M., 'Developing Administrative Law in Europe: Natural Covergence or Imposed Uniformity?', *Review of European Administrative Law*, 2014/2, pp. 9–31.

Widdershoven, R.J.G.M. & Remac, M., 'General Principles of Law in Administrative Law under European Influence', *European Review of Private Law*, 2012, pp. 381–407.

De Witte, B., 'Direct Effect, Supremacy and the Nature of the Legal Order', in: Craig, P. & De Burca, G. (eds.), *The Evolution of EU Law*, OUP, Oxford 1999, pp. 323–362.

WEBSITES

- European legislation and case law: <www.eur-lex.europa.eu/>
- Recent case law: <www.curia.europa.eu/>
- Information on the legislation process: <www.ec.europa.eu/prelex/apcnet.cfm>

ADMINISTRATIVE LAW IN THE UNITED STATES

Jeffrey S. LUBBERS*

1. WHAT IS ADMINISTRATIVE LAW IN THE UNITED STATES?

1.1. WHAT IS ADMINISTRATIVE LAW?

Administrative law is the group of requirements and restrictions on how administrative agencies take actions that affect members of the public. While this is a simple, straightforward description, virtually every word or phrase needs elaboration to impart its full impact:

- Administrative law is not a single, compact body of law, but rather is a collection of a number of principles that are contained in the Constitution, the Administrative Procedure Act (APA), the substantive statutes that agencies administer, opinions of the courts, and duties imposed by the President and others in the Executive Branch.
- Administrative law governs both what agencies must do and what they may not do when taking actions, as well as the judicial review of their actions.
- Administrative law is concerned with the *process* by which agencies take actions, not the substance of those actions, although the substantive issues may influence what procedure is appropriate.
- Administrative law applies to government agencies that exercise delegated power; thus it is not directly concerned with the decision-making of the President, Congress, or the courts, although each of the three play large roles in administrative law.
- Administrative law addresses the relationship between the government and the private sector; it is not concerned with the internal management of government except as it affects the public (thus, ironically, administrative law is not about administration).

* I wish to recognize the contribution by my friend Philip J. Harter, whose chapter in the third edition of this volume formed the basis for this revised chapter. However, any mistakes, and opinions expressed herein are mine.

While the nominal duties and procedures of administrative law apply consistently across a vast range of agencies and activities at the federal, state, and local levels, their actual application vary somewhat depending on the circumstances. For example, if an agency is faced with a decision in which it has an inherent conflict of interest[1] or if the agency itself is viewed sceptically, then the procedures are likely to be enforced with considerable rigor. If, on the other hand, the agency enjoys broad political support and the decision to be made is not of fundamental importance, they may be relaxed. To an extent, the rigor with which the nominal procedures are enforced is proportional to the magnitude of the decision to be made.

1.2. THE ROLE OF ADMINISTRATIVE AGENCIES

Agencies are the instrumentalities by which government authority is exercised on a day-to-day basis, and consequently administrative law is focused primarily with *how* they function. The fifteen Departments are part of the President's Cabinet and hence are viewed as closely aligned with the President and his policies. Examples are the Department of Labor, Department of Health and Human Services, Department of State, and the Department of Defense. Each of these cabinet agencies contains other agencies as subparts. For example, the Food and Drug Administration is part of the Department of Health and Human Services (HHS) and regulates the safety and efficacy of food, drugs, and medical devices. HHS also contains the Centers for Disease Control, which protects our nation against health threats, and responds when they arise, and it contains another agency called the Centers for Medicare and Medicaid Services, which finances health care for qualified individuals. The major medical research institution, the National Institutes of Health, is likewise part of HHS. Thus, the single agency holds a number of sub-agencies that together span a variety of activities – from regulation, to enforcement, to payments of benefits, to research.

Some agencies are free-standing executive agencies in that they are not part of a department but report directly to the President, and the President has a significant amount of power over them. A primary example of such an agency is the Environmental Protection Agency (EPA). A third type is the independent regulatory agencies. These agencies are normally headed by a multi-member board or commission. Although part of the executive branch, these agencies are often regarded as reporting more to Congress than to the President, and usually (but not always) the President can only remove a member of the agency for cause, such as malfeasance in office, but not for policy disagreements.[2] Examples are the Securities and Exchange Commission and the Federal Trade Commission.

---

1 For example, one mission of the Department of Agriculture is to promote the interests of US farmers and another is to promote animal welfare. Decisions or regulations concerning the enforcement of animal welfare laws might be opposed by the poultry farming industry.

2 Nor does Congress have the authority to remove a member of the agency. What is meant by saying that the agency reports to Congress and not the President, is that the President's

Each of these, agencies, regardless of whether they are called departments, commissions, or administrations, or whether they are part of another agency, are 'agencies' within the terms of the APA and are governed by administrative law.

Figure 1. Federal administrative organization in the United States

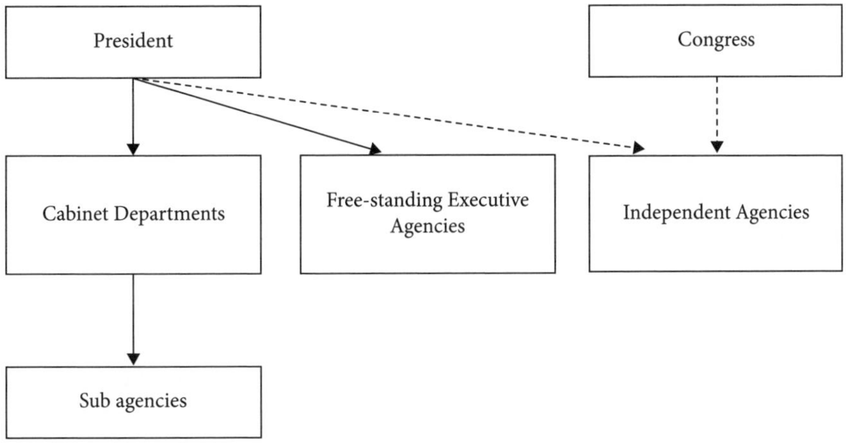

This review will primarily focus on administrative law at the federal level, and hence will be concerned with federal agencies. The same overall concepts generally apply at both the state and local levels, although the actual implementation and emphasis differ jurisdiction from jurisdiction. Generally speaking, the administrative process tends to become more informal the further down in the governmental hierarchy one goes. The allocation of responsibilities between the federal government and the states and between the states and local governments within the states is usually analysed in 'constitutional law' and in 'state and local government law'.

Two issues are worth noting here, however. The first is that the federal government has the authority under the Constitution to regulate interstate commerce. When exercising that authority, the federal government can 'pre-empt' inconsistent state and local laws. This ability is frequently an issue in many regulatory programs. In some instances, Congress is quite explicit that it is pre-empting the field so that states may not regulate at all in the area; in other instances, however, the preclusion is implied from the comprehensive nature of the federal statute. Sometimes the decision is for regulatory programs to co-exist. For example, a state cannot impose additional requirements on the design of

influence over the agency is minimal, consisting largely of the power to select which of the members of the agency will serve as chair. It does not mean that Congress exerts any direct managerial control over the agency.

automobiles, but Congress has explicitly provided that many environmental regulations are a 'floor' that can be supplemented by the states.

The second point is that even though a particular matter might be beyond its control, the federal government might condition the granting of funds on a state's meeting certain requirements. An example of this conditioning is the federal government's refusing to pay for highways unless the state's minimum age for drinking alcohol is 21; the federal government cannot control that directly but has achieved its goal through the 'power of the purse'.[3]

1.3. BRIEF HISTORY OF ADMINISTRATIVE LAW

Although there were some important antecedents[4], modern American administrative law begins in the late 19th century with the creation of the Interstate Commerce Commission to regulate railroads. The Populist movement was designed to curb the growing power of corporations. While administered by agencies, the procedures used were largely based on a judicial model, with formal hearings in individual cases. This era evolved into the Progressive Era where the rhetoric was still populist, but there was a much greater willingness to use the power of the federal government to accomplish its ends. A number of important agencies were created during this era of the early 20th century to protect the public from such things as adulterated food and drugs or monopolies; banking regulation was strengthened, and transportation more tightly controlled. As the power of agencies was growing, courts became suspicious of them and tended to limit their incursion into private autonomy unless explicitly authorized to do so by Congress and with the courts themselves fully in control of the ultimate judicial power.[5]

With the coming of the Great Depression and the New Deal of the Roosevelt Administration came a burst of activity in the area of administrative law. Many new agencies were established to bolster and regulate economic development. Agencies continued to function largely on a case-by-case basis and did not issue many generally applicable rules. But, considerable thought was also given as to how they function, with two theories competing for supremacy concerning how the administrative process should work and why the body politic should accept it as legitimate. The earlier one sought to protect private autonomy from incursion by agencies, and hence would limit their activity to only those specifically authorized by Congress; further, agencies were to function much like courts and enforcement actions were to be taken in courts and not decided

---

3 *See South Dakota v. Dole*, 483 U.S. 203 (1987).

4 *See* J.L. Mashaw, 'Administration and "The Democracy": Administrative Law from Jackson to Lincoln, 1829–1861' (2008) 117 *Yale Law Journal* 1568, 1628–66 (describing the implementation of the Steamboat Safety Act of 1852).

5 *See Crowell v. Benson*, 285 U.S. 22 (1932).

by agencies themselves. This movement reached its apex when Congress passed the Walter-Logan Act that would codify this theory. President Roosevelt vetoed the legislation, however, in favour of the competing idea that was based on the notion that government agencies are 'experts' in their respective fields and could be trusted to make the proper decisions with a minimum of procedural requirements. A corollary was that politics, and in particular the President, should not play a role in administrative decisions since that would conflict with the exercise of the agency's expertise. This view eventually prevailed with the enactment of the APA in 1946.[6] As a result, a number of 'independent' agencies were established that did not report to the President; these agencies would, like an appellate court, have multiple commissioners and the formal decisions of the agency would be made by a majority of them. In an abrupt turnabout, the courts switched from being suspicious of agency power to embracing it fully: courts would sustain agency decisions if virtually any potential set of facts would make the decision 'rational' – an extraordinarily deferential standard of review. This period lasted until about 1964.

That year Congress enacted the Civil Rights Act, which focused on a particular social outcome across the full range of the economy instead of addressing a single sector as most administrative action had before. Many other regulatory programs were enacted in short order, to protect consumers, workers, and the environment. This produced an extensive growth of rulemaking in which agencies issued commands that applied generally to all parts of the economy. Although there was no change in the general statutes that defined administrative law, the courts began to play a greater role during this period and required agencies to develop far more information and explain their reasoning far more than had been the case in the past. Thus, public participation in rulemaking was encouraged and agencies had to be concerned about producing an administrative record that would satisfy judicial review.

The great expansion of regulation and administrative law then switched again in the late 1970s as a consolidation and reform movement took place. This brought with it an accepted, if initially controversial, direct role for the White House in rulemaking, and a refinement of the procedures that developed alongside of the expansion of the federal presence in the economy. Several of the efforts were directed to controlling administrative agencies and ensuring that they adequately considered their effects on favoured constituencies, such as small businesses or state and local governments. We nominally remain in this era, although some of the recent efforts that are putatively directed at improving the regulatory process are also intended to slow it down and curtail the imposition of new regulatory requirements. Regulatory policy has undeniably become more politicized, with the Democrats generally favouring stronger regulation,

6 *See* Shepherd, G.B., 'The Administrative Procedure Act Emerges from New Deal Politics' (1996) 90 *Northwestern Law Review* 1557.

especially in the health, safety, environmental, and consumer protection areas, and the Republicans favouring less federal regulation across the board. With the election of Donald Trump and Republican control of Congress, the latter attitude is ascendant.

2. THE CONSTITUTIONAL STRUCTURE

2.1. CONGRESS

The administrative process necessarily begins with Congress. Article I of the Constitution provides that 'all legislative power herein granted shall be vested in a Congress of the United States, which shall consist of a Senate and House of Representatives'.[7] Both houses must agree on the exact language of a bill before it can become law. The bill must then be presented to the President for signature, and it does not become law until he signs it. The President may, instead, veto the legislation, but Congress can override the rejection by a two-thirds majority vote of both Houses in which case the bill becomes law without the President's concurrence. Congress therefore establishes the agency, the program, and the processes by which the program is administered. Congress cannot authorize an agency to exercise unfettered discretion; however, since the Supreme Court held in two cases in the 1930s that this was an impermissible delegation of legislative authority.[8] Thus, Congress must at least provide an 'intelligible principle' that courts can use to determine whether the agency is acting within the bounds defined by Congress.[9] Although this is hardly a high bar for Congress to meet, this non-delegation doctrine however, does serve as somewhat of a check on the breadth of an agency's authority. In addition, Congress may not 'veto' action taken by an agency or the President without following the procedures for enacting legislation.[10]

---

7 Article I, § 1.

8 Panama Refining Co. v. Ryan, 293 U.S. 388 (1935); A.L.A. Schecter Poultry Corp. v. United States, 295 U.S. 495 (1935).

9 The Supreme Court recently reaffirmed this doctrine. The court of appeals had held a provision of the Clean Air Act was unconstitutional because it conferred too much discretion on the Administrator of the EPA without sufficiently defined standards to guide that decision. The Supreme Court reversed the decision, saying that the phrase in question, 'requisite to protect the public health,' was enough of an intelligible principle to constrain the agency's choice. *Whitman* v *American Trucking Associations, Inc.*, 531 U.S. 457 (2001).

10 *INS v. Chadha*, 462 U.S. 919 (1983). In response to this decision, in 1996, Congress enacted the Congressional Review Act, 5 U.S.C. §§ 801–808, which allows Congress to disapprove agency regulations through a legislative process that requires presidential approval. It had been used successfully only once until 2017, when a carry-over provision allowed the new Congress to overturn fourteen 'midnight' rules of the Obama administration.

Figure 2. Government organization in the United States

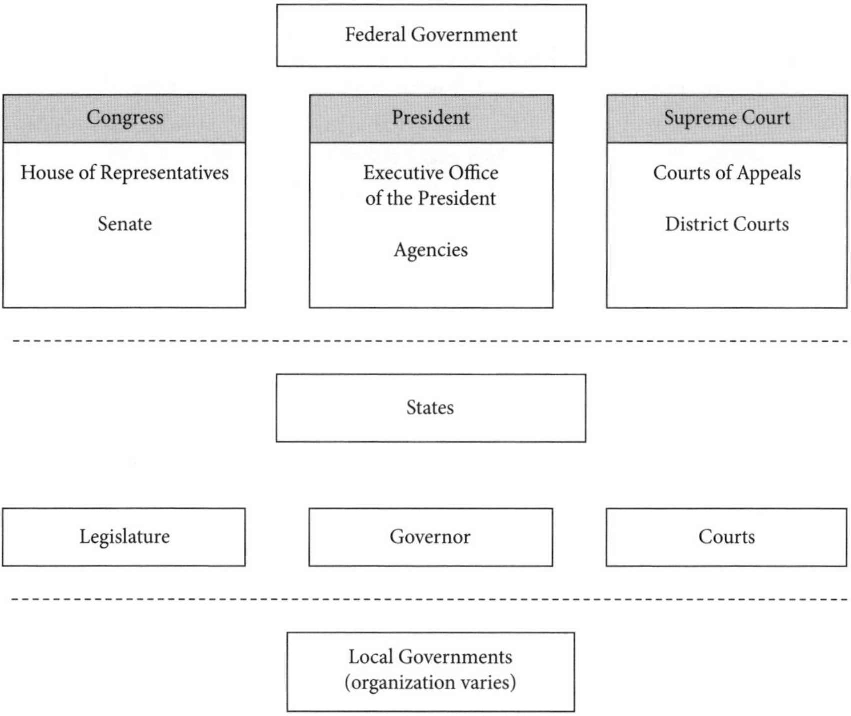

2.2. THE PRESIDENT

Article II of the Constitution provides that 'The Executive Powers shall be vested in a President of the United States of America'.[11] Usually, the President is an active participant in the development and refinement of legislation before Congress. Significant governmental actions, which include the establishment of government policy and regulatory actions that have a coercive effect, can only be taken by an 'Officer of the United States'.[12] All principal Officers must be nominated by the President and confirmed by the Senate. Thus, the President appoints the heads of the agencies and those within agencies who have significant power. He can also remove most, but not all, agency heads.[13] 'Inferior' officers (those who are supervised by principal officers, but who still exercise 'significant authority pursuant to the laws of the United States') do not require Senate confirmation and may be appointed

11 Article II, § 1.

12 *Buckley v. Valeo*, 424 U.S. 1 (1976).

13 For some independent agencies, Congress has provided that the agency head or members of the commission can only be removed only "for cause," i.e., not for policy differences.

by the President, head of a department, or a court of law.[14] The President and his immediate staff also review proposed rulemakings by the executive agencies to make sure they are compatible with the Administration's program. If a proposal is not, the President can direct the agency head to change it, but in most instances he cannot change the action directly. That is because Congress authorized the agency, not the President, to implement the statute so that at least theoretically the President is powerless to effect the change. As a practical matter, however, the agency head is very likely to accede to a direct request of the President.

Figure 3. Hierarchy of legal sources

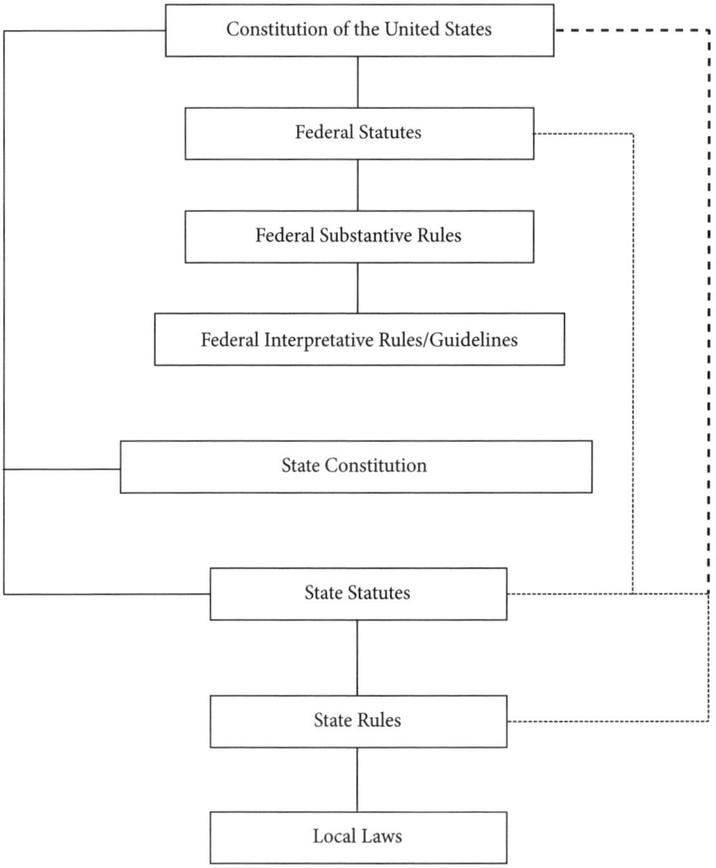

[14] Article II, § 2, cl. 2. *See Buckley v. Valeo*, 424 U.S. at 126; *Freytag v. Commissioner*, 501 U.S. 868 (1991).

2.3. COURTS

Article III of the Constitution establishes the Supreme Court and authorizes Congress to create such lower courts as it deems necessary.[15] Congress has done so by establishing trial courts, called federal district courts, in each state and twelve geographical circuit courts of appeals. In addition, there is one additional specialized circuit court in Washington and a Court of International Trade in New York. The judges of these courts are nominated by the President and must be confirmed by the Senate; once in office, to assure their independence, the judges enjoy life tenure and a protected salary.

Although the Supreme Court has some mandatory jurisdiction in which it must hear a case presented to it, for the most part it chooses the cases it wishes to resolve by issuing a *writ of certiorari* to the court whose decision is to be reviewed; the petition for the writ is filed by a party seeking the review. The Supreme Court may also review decisions by the highest court of a state 'where the validity of a … statute of the United States is drawn in question or where the validity of a statute of any State is drawn in question on the ground of its being repugnant to the Constitution, treaties, or laws of the United States …'.[16]

The courts of appeals have appellate jurisdiction over decisions of the district courts generally and as otherwise assigned, as is the case for many administrative actions. The federal district courts are the trial courts. They have jurisdiction over 'all civil actions arising under the Constitution, laws, or treaties of the United States'.[17]

Unfortunately, there is no hard-and-fast formula that can be used uniformly to determine which court – court of appeals or district court – is the one to review a particular type of administrative action. One leading text contains the following description:

> 'A sensible system of judicial review would allocate to circuit courts review of all agency actions that are likely to raise major issues of law or policy and that can be reviewed based exclusively on the record created at the agency. All agency legislative rules meet these criteria, as do orders issued in adjudications conducted by agencies that adjudicate a relatively small number of major disputes. … A sensible system of review would allocate to district courts all agen cy actions that are numerous, i.e., orders issued by an agency that resolves thousands of adjudications each year, all actions in which specific factual disputes tend to dominate disputes over law or policy, and all actions that require the reviewing court to be prepared to take evidence. …

15 Article III, § 1.
16 28 U.S.C. (United States Code) § 1257(a).
17 28 U.S.C. § 1331.

> Generally, the statutory allocation of review jurisdiction corresponds reasonably well with the comparative advantages of circuit courts. The problems arise primarily from Congress' tendency not to exercise care in drafting statutory provisions governing judicial review and not to amend statutes when intervening changes in law and practice render obsolete the initial allocation of review jurisdiction.'[18]

In addition to these 'Article III' courts, Congress has created some specialized courts to decide matters relating to tax disputes, bankruptcy, veterans benefits, and money claims against the government. Judges of these courts, also called 'Article I courts', are not required to have life tenure. The Supreme Court has held that Article I courts may not exercise the full range of judicial powers, such as conducting jury trials and making final decisions in disputes between private parties.[19]

The United States, unlike many other countries, does not have an 'administrative court' whose jurisdiction is solely to review decisions of the government, whether adjudicatory or policymaking. Rather, appeals from agency decisions go to the general courts and follow the established procedures of those courts. As the quote above indicates, the 'rule of thumb' is that appeals from formal agency adjudication and appeals of rules that are primarily based on the rulemaking record and involve questions of law are generally directed by statute to be filed in the courts of appeals and reviews of high-volume or informal agency adjudications go to the district courts. However, this is only a rough benchmark, so the specific statutory provisions for any particular action needs to be consulted. If the statute is silent on the reviewing court, any challenge must be brought as an action for injunctive or declaratory relief in the appropriate district court.

18 K.C. Davis & R. Pierce, *Administrative Law Treatise, 3d ed.*, Little, Brown, 1994, § 18.2.

19 *Northern Pipeline Co. v. Marathon Pipe Line Co.*, 458 U.S. 50 (1982).

Figure 4. American judicial system

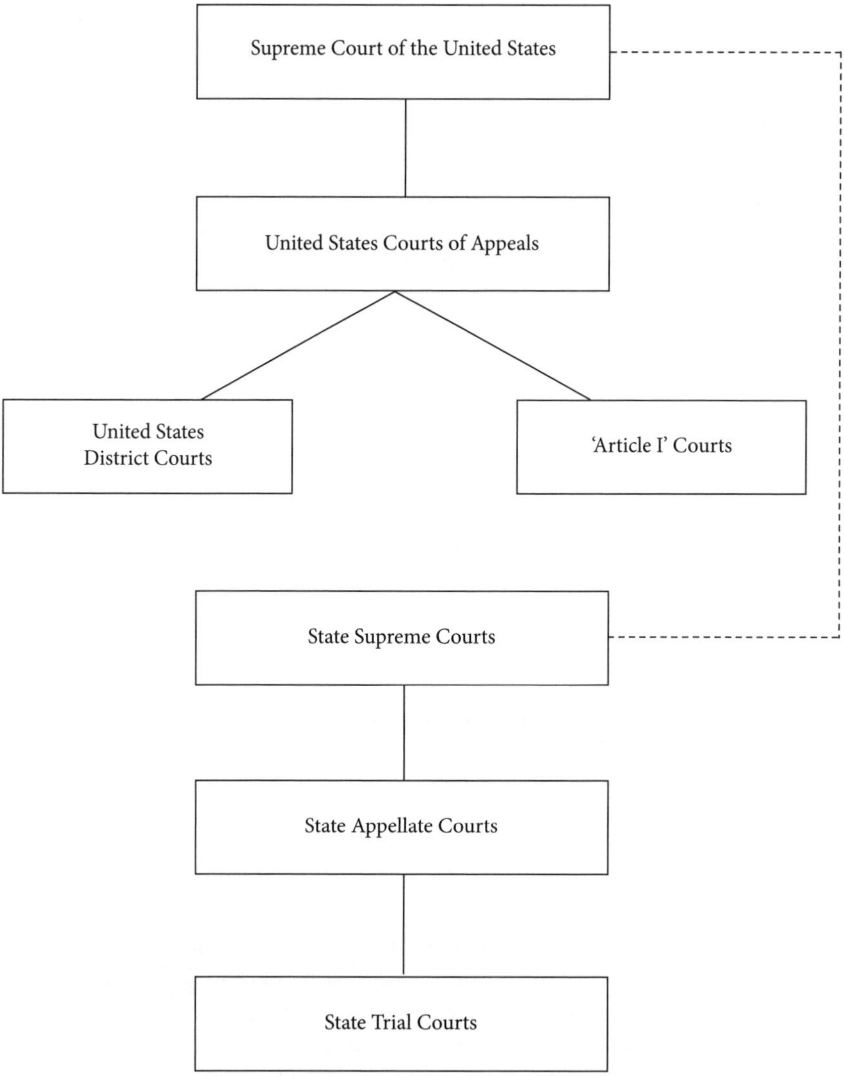

2.4. SEPARATION OF POWERS GENERALLY

As this section indicates, the Constitution separates the three powers of government – legislative, executive, and judicial – into distinct branches. Nevertheless, it is clear that the three types of powers shade one into another, and programs may be far more effective if some of them are shared. Although the Constitution is now more than 200 years old, there has been considerable litigation over the past 40 years over separation-of-powers issues in which the question is what types of actions each of the branches can undertake and which duties they may not yield to any other branch. By and large, the Court has been fairly tolerant of programs in which they work together and share functions that are explicitly assigned to only one; the Court has used a 'functional' approach that has been quite accommodating so long as one branch is not seen as 'self-aggrandizing' at the expense of another branch.[20] On the other hand, if one branch is encroaching on another or frustrating its ability to function, the Court switches into a 'formal' mode and tends to read the Constitution quite literally. Several programs have been struck down as a result of one branch exercising powers that belong to another under the structure of the Constitution.[21]

3. THE AMERICAN ADMINISTRATIVE PROCESS

The following synopsis of American administrative law describes the powers that agencies have and the means by which they are exercised. As such, it highlights the relationship between government and those in the private sector.

3.1. ACQUISITION OF INFORMATION

The Fourth Amendment to the US Constitution provides:

> 'The right of the people to be secure in their persons, houses, papers and effects against unreasonable searches and seizures, shall not be violated, and no warrants shall issue, but upon probable cause, support by oath or affirmation, and particularly describing the place to be searched, and the persons or things to be seized'.

The government, at all levels, relies on an enormous number and variety of physical inspections to enforce compliance with the law. These range from houses and automobiles to workplaces, nuclear plants, and drug manufacturers. The question naturally arises in some cases as to whether an agency may have conducted an inspection that violated the Fourth Amendment. Although the plain language of the Constitution seems to contemplate that the agency must have 'probable cause' to believe that a violation is occurring at a particular location before it could conduct an inspection, the courts have accommodated these requirements from the criminal law to the realities of administrative law. It is sufficient if the particular inspection is authorized by legislative or

20 See, for example, *Mistretta v. U.S.*, 488 U.S. 361 (1989); *Commodity Futures Trading Commission v. Schor*, 478 U.S. 833 (1986).

21 See, for example, *Bowsher v. Synar*, 478 U.S. 714 (1986); *INS v. Chadha*, 462 U.S. 919 (1983).

administrative standards that are based on neutral principles.[22] Thus, the agency must develop an overall plan as to how it will conduct inspections, and, absent probable cause, it may not decide ad hoc which entities it will inspect. Moreover, the inspection itself must be reasonable. There are exceptions to this limitation on agency authority for those enterprises that are pervasively regulated or are required by law to be inspected on a regular basis.[23]

Outside of individual investigations, an agency can also seek information from regulated entities so long as the information is germane to a legitimate subject of regulation by the agency. Before doing so, however, the agency must secure the approval of the Office of Management and Budget[24] (OMB), which implements the Paperwork Reduction Act.[25] The Act is designed to minimize the paperwork burden on individuals and businesses while still ensuring that the government can get the information it legitimately needs. Thus, for example, a company can be required to maintain records that document its air emissions and to provide those records to the EPA upon request.

Further, if authorized by legislation, agencies may compel testimony or the production of documents for use by the agency in investigations and enforcement proceedings.[26] As with physical inspections, the courts had to struggle to reconcile this administrative need with the Fourth Amendment. After a restrictive early interpretation, the current standard for issuing a subpoena demanding information is[27]:

- the topic to be investigated must be *arguably* within the agency's jurisdiction (that is, it is not plainly outside the scope of its authority);
- the description of what is demanded must not be too indefinite; that is, the recipient must be able to determine what is sought;
- the amount of information requested must not be too broad; in practice, a subpoena must be extremely oppressive before enforcement would be denied;
- the information must be potentially relevant to an authorized investigation; it is sufficient, however, for the agency to seek the information to determine whether or not the recipient is complying with the law, instead of the agency's having to have some reason to suspect that that is the case;
- as a whole, the subpoena must be reasonable; and
- the requirement must be issued in good faith; demonstrating that the agency had some ulterior motive is a high, difficult standard.

---

22 *Marshall v. Barlow's Inc.*, 436 U.S. 307 (1978).

23 *Donovan v. Dewey*, 452 U.S. 594 (1981).

24 The Office of Management and Budget is part of the Executive Office of the President, which is known collectively as 'The White House'. As its title indicates, it is responsible for preparing the President's budget, which he submits to Congress for its consideration and for managing the Executive Branch of the government. The Office of Information and Regulatory Affairs (OIRA) is the part of OMB that deals with regulatory and paperwork reduction issues.

25 44 U.S.C. § 3501 *et seq.*

26 Most, but not all, federal agencies have this authority.

27 *Oklahoma Press Publishing Co. v. Walling*, 327 U.S. 186 (1946).

Only a court can order compliance with a subpoena, although usually it will enforce an agency's demand with only a cursory review unless the recipient mounts a strong case that one of the standards has been violated.

3.2. OPEN GOVERNMENT

The 'multi-member agencies' – those boards and commissions that are headed by more than one person – are required by the Sunshine Act[28] to conduct the meetings of the members of the agency in public. Thus, anytime a majority of the members meets to decide agency business, the meeting 'shall be open to public observation'.[29] While there are exceptions to this rule[30], as a general matter, collegial agencies must conduct their affairs subject to public observation.

Before any agency may seek the collective advice of a committee that has at least one member of the private sector, it must first comply with the Federal Advisory Committee Act.[31] FACA requires that the membership of the committee must be fairly balanced in terms of the points of view represented, that the committee operate for only a fixed period of time, and that its duties are only advisory. At the outset, the agency must consult with the General Services Administration; this bureaucratic requirement has been responsible for delays in establishing committees and has caused a number of agencies to avoid creating them. The meetings of a committee must be announced in the Federal Register[32] 15 days in advance, and the public must be able to attend subject to the same exceptions as the Sunshine Act. Committee documents are subject to the Freedom of Information Act, described below. Agencies use advisory committees to gain insights into complex issues and to help them resolve difficult policy matters. Many, however, are required by statute, and since they are imposed, the agency may or may not pay much attention to them.

While the details vary, many states have similar requirements.

---

28 The full title of the Act is the 'Government in the Sunshine Act', 5 U.S.C. § 552b.

29 5 U.S.C. § 552b(b). The requirement does not apply when the meeting is simply to seek information. *FCC v. ITT World Communications, Inc.*, 466 U.S. 463 (1984).

30 5 U.S.C. § 552b(c).

31 5 U.S.C. Appendix 2. These restrictions do not apply to meetings initiated by individual members of the private sector or to meetings with groups where collective advice is not sought.

32 The Federal Register is the federal government's daily publication that contains announcements such as new rules, proposed rules, Presidential announcements and orders, major regulatory filings, and notices of meetings. See, for example, www.federalregister.gov/articles/current.

3.3. FREEDOM OF INFORMATION ACT

The heart of the Freedom of Information Act, generally known as FOIA, is the provision: 'each agency, upon any request which reasonably describes such records … shall make the records promptly available to any person'.[33] Thus, anyone – without restriction – may request a particular record, and the agency is required to furnish it 'promptly'.[34] An agency need not comply, however, if one of nine exemptions to the general duty applies.[35] The exemptions, which have produced a lot of case law, are:

- information that is authorized to be kept secret in the interest of national defence or foreign policy; internal personnel rules of an agency;
- matters specifically exempted from disclosure by a statute that requires the information be withheld from the public;
- trade secrets and commercial or financial information obtained from a person that is privileged or confidential;
- internal government memoranda and papers that are privileged or are both pre-decisional and deliberative;
- personnel files the disclosure of which would cause an unwarranted invasion of privacy;
- law enforcement records if revealing them would compromise enforcement or a fair trial;
- regulatory reports on financial institutions, and
- geological and geophysical information concerning wells.

If part of a document is exempted and part is not, the agency must furnish the non-exempt portion if it is reasonably segregable.

Other provisions of FOIA require agencies to affirmatively publish, either in the Federal Register, or in some cases on agency websites, all generally applicable final rules, policy statements, and adjudicative opinions. Final rules are then codified in the Code of Federal Regulations.

3.4. THE DICHOTOMY BETWEEN ADJUDICATION AND RULEMAKING

A pair of Supreme Court decisions early in the 20th century defined the great divide of American administrative law between rulemaking and adjudication.

[33] 5 U.S.C. § 552(a)(3). The Act does not apply to the President, Vice President or components of the Executive Office of the President that exist solely to advise the President. There is a separate law, the Presidential Records Act of 1978, 44 U.S.C. §§ 2201–2207, that provides for delayed release of presidential records.

[34] While FOIA contemplates a very short period of 20 working days, in fact the response rate runs a year or more for many agencies because of the volume of requests and agencies' lack of resources to meet the prompt compliance dates.

[35] 5 U.S.C. § 552(b).

Although one of the cases contains some language that has caused some ambiguities, the law has followed the distinction developed in the cases. The first entailed the paving of a street, which in time became one of the main avenues of Denver. The question presented was whether an individual landowner who abutted the road was entitled to a hearing on the proportion of the total cost of the operation that that person would be required to pay.[36] The second, decided seven years later, involved whether individual citizens of Denver were entitled to hearings when everyone's property taxes were raised by 40 per cent.[37] In the first case, the Court held that:

> 'where the legislature of a State, instead of fixing the tax itself, commits to some subordinate body the duty of determining whether, in what amount, and upon whom it shall be levied, and of making its assessment and apportionment, due process of law requires that at some stage of the proceedings before the tax becomes irrevocably fixed, the taxpayer shall have an opportunity to be heard, of which he must have notice, either personal, by publication, or by a law fixing the time and place of the hearing. … [A] hearing in its very essence demands that he who is entitled to it shall have the right to support his allegations by argument however brief, and, if need be, by proof, however informal'.

In the second, the Court posited that everyone's property was valued at the same percentage of its fair market value since there were procedures in place for such corrections. The question, therefore, was whether an individual citizen was entitled to a hearing when the decision affected everyone equally. The court held that this was a generalized policy judgement and that individual hearings were not necessary.[38]

The distinction drawn by the Court is that a hearing is required when the government is making a decision that applies existing law or policy based on someone's individualized circumstances. These are adjudicatory decisions. Individual hearings are not required, however, if decision is to make policy that applies generally, as opposed to a specific individual, and has future effect. In administrative law, this is rulemaking. This distinction is embodied in the Administrative Procedure Act[39] (APA), which forms the basis for modern administrative procedure at the federal level; states tend to adhere to the same distinction.[40] The procedures followed in the two types of decisions vary.

---

36 *Londoner v. Denver*, 210 U.S. 373 (1908).

37 *Bi-Metallic Investment Co. v. State Bd. of Equalization of Colorado*, 239 U.S. 441 (1915).

38 Note that the Court held that the Constitution's Due Process Clause did not require a hearing in this situation; however, the Administrative Procedure Act, and its state equivalents, may require additional procedures when making such a decision.

39 5 U.S.C. § 551 *et seq*. The APA was adopted in 1946 following a comprehensive study of agency procedures in use during the 1930s by a Committee headed by the Attorney General.

40 See, for example, the Model State Administrative Procedure Act (2010) <www.uniformlaws.org/shared/docs/state%20administrative%20procedure/msapa_final_10.pdf> accessed 08.04.2017.

Initially, the procedural distinction between the two was quite significant, but many aspects of the two have grown closer together over the years.

Figure 5. Administrative activity

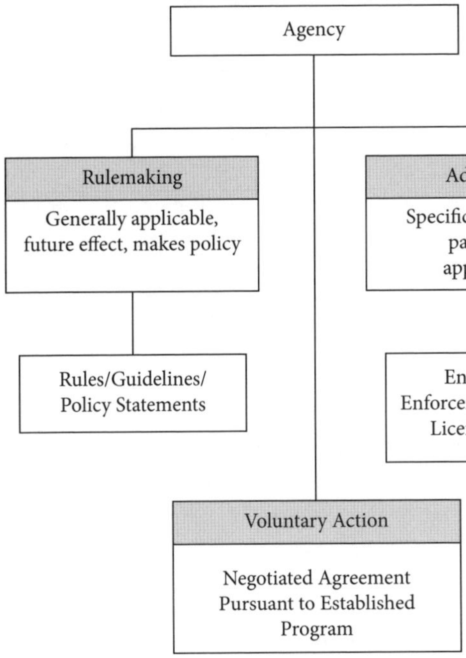

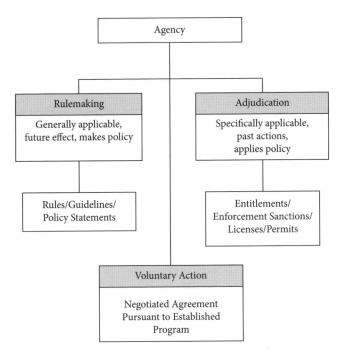

3.5. RULEMAKING

A rule is defined by the APA as an agency statement of general … applicability and future effect designed to implement, interpret, or prescribe law or policy.[41] The procedures set out in the APA for developing rules are quite streamlined: An agency must publish a general notice of proposed rulemaking in the Federal Register that sets out the legal authority for the agency's action and the terms or substance of the proposed rule.[42] The agency must then give the public the opportunity to submit comments on the proposed rule. The agency is directed to consider all relevant matter that was submitted by the public. When it issues the final rule, the agency is required to publish it in the Federal Register at

41 5 U.S.C. § 551(4). The definition also includes, somewhat confusingly, statements of 'particular applicability'. While this would seem to include as rules issues that would normally be treated as adjudications under the traditional doctrine, in fact this definition was included to ensure that ratemakings are treated as rulemakings and not as adjudications.

42 5 U.S.C. § 553(b).

least 30 days before its effective date[43], and it must include in the publication a 'concise general statement of [the rule's] basis and purpose'.[44] Not surprisingly, given the nature of the process, this is called 'informal' or 'notice-and-comment' rulemaking.[45] The agency was directed to consider all relevant matter that was presented during the rulemaking procedure, but it was not required to base the decision on a 'record'; that is, the agency could rely on facts and information that was not submitted by anyone in the proceeding nor explicitly revealed by the agency in any of the publications. Courts would sustain rules if there were any 'rational basis' for it and the court would 'presum[e] the existence of facts justifying' the rule.[46] In short, agencies were given wide leeway to develop rules through a highly flexible process that could be implemented in a short time frame.

But, notwithstanding precatory language from the Supreme Court to use rulemaking[47], the vast bulk of policymaking came through case-by-case adjudications; rules were not widely used. That began changing in the 1960s, however, when Congress started enacting new regulatory statutes. Moreover, rules were seen as a more open, participatory, and precise way to develop policy. In addition, the minimal requirements of the APA were expanded by the courts[48], and as a result, new procedures emerged that agencies must follow when issuing rules. Also, the courts expanded judicial review to ensure that the agencies adhered to the procedures and that the rules were well-grounded in the facts presented by the agency. By and large, there was a great push to

---

43 5 U.S.C. § 553(d). The agency need not publish the final rule 30 days in advance if there is good cause not to or if it is an interpretative rule or statement of policy, i.e., guidance that does not impose a duty but rather either interprets a rule or statute or indicates how the agency might exercise its discretion on a matter.

44 5 U.S.C. § 553(c).

45 In part, these names are to distinguish this process from the other rulemaking procedure that is set out in the APA, which is called 'formal' or 'trial type' rulemaking. If the statute requires the agency to develop the rule 'on the record' after an opportunity for an agency hearing, then the APA requires a procedure similar to that used for adjudication. 5 U.S.C. § 553(c), 556 and 557. Very few statutes do so, however, and the Supreme Court has held that unless the statute is quite explicit about the use of the formal procedures, the agency may use the informal process. *Florida East Coast Railway Co., v. United States*, 410 U.S. 224 (1973). As a result, formal rulemaking is very rarely used.

46 *Pacific States Box & Basket Co. v. White*, 296 U.S. 176 (1935).

47 *SEC v. Chenery Corp.*, 332 U.S. 194 (1947).

48 See, J.S. Lubbers, *A Guide to Federal Agency Rulemaking*, 4th ed., Chicago: III, Section of Administrative Law and Regulatory Practice, American Bar Association, 2012 p. 6–12. As is explained more fully below, the timing and nature of judicial review of rules also changed with their greater use. Whereas previously a rule could only be challenged as part of an enforcement action, the Supreme Court allowed challenges to come soon after a rule was issued if its command was clear and complete. *Abbott Laboratories v. Gardner*, 387 U.S. 136 (1967). Thus, the court's review would be based on the reasoning of the agency in developing the rule and on the factual basis underlying the rule, as opposed to its application in a particular case. In most instances, however, someone can still challenge the validity of a rule as a defense to an enforcement action.

make the rulemaking process more *rational*. The courts required that agencies explain the basis for their rules far more than had previously been the case. As a result, the 'concise general statement' of the APA has now become a 'preamble' that may run for hundreds of pages in the small type of the Federal Register. Moreover, to the extent the factual basis of a rule can actually be developed, the agency is required to do so; it must generate the scientific and technical information that supports the agency's position and explain any contrary evidence. Of course, in some instances some facts are not determinable and the agency must extrapolate from what is known to support the rule. In any event, the agency is required to place its information in the rulemaking file that may be examined by the public.[49] Also, the agency needs to explain how it progressed from the facts to the rule. As a result of these requirements, if someone submits comments that cast significant doubt on the factual predicate of an agency's proposal, the agency is required to change it before issuing the final rule.

It should be noted that, as with many aspects of modern life, rulemaking has become e-rulemaking, and the great majority of comments are filed (and stored) electronically on the federal government's centralized portal, www.regulations.gov. This has not only made it easier for interested persons to file comments, it has created some new challenges for agencies in terms of privacy issues, the volume of comments, and handling comments with copyrighted material or confidential business information.

The courts also began taking a 'hard look' at what the agency did to make sure the agency has engaged in reasoned decision-making.[50] While the courts required agencies to conduct necessary research and explain themselves in much greater detail as a means of complying with the APA, the Supreme Court made it clear that courts were not to require agencies to use trial type procedures.[51] Thus although the courts greatly expanded the process by which agencies make policy – even reversing who has the burden of proof with respect to the underlying facts – they did not erase the long held dichotomy between court and agency: the only powers a court has are to either deny the petition for review (and thus affirm the rule's legality) or set aside an illegal or unsupported rule and then remand it to the agency to remedy whatever was wrong. The court may give direction to the agency, but it cannot itself fix the problem.[52] Indeed, this

49 One of the major recent developments in rulemaking is the use of the internet. The regulatory file is now available online, and the public can submit comments on proposed rules electronically. The central access point is <www.regulations.gov>.

50 *Greater Boston Television Corp. v. FCC*, 444 F.2d 841 (D.C. Cir. 1970), *cert. denied*, 403 U.S. 923 (1971).

51 *Vermont Yankee Nuclear Power Corp. v. Natural Resources Defense Council, Inc.*, 435 U.S. 519 (1978).

52 If the rule is declared to be *ultra vires*, the court will vacate it. If the rule is deemed to lack factual support, the remedy is to send it back to the agency. In the latter situation, the court might allow the rule to stay in effect while the agency addresses the issue.

illustrates a general point about judicial review – in most cases, the courts do not accept new evidence, but rather review the evidence and reasoning offered by the agency to see whether it supported the result.

3.5.1. Presidential Involvement in Rulemaking

Since rulemaking clearly became the more significant means of developing government policy, it is not surprising that it also became seen as a political undertaking, and hence the White House became more involved than it had been under the original structure of the APA. Through a series of executive orders issued by successive Presidents[53], an agency must submit a proposed rule to the Office of Information and Regulatory Affairs (OIRA), which is part of the Office of Management and Budget, which in turn is part of the Executive Office of the President, generally known collectively as 'the White House'. OIRA reviews the proposal to make sure it is consistent with the President's regulatory policy, that it is the most cost effective means to achieve the regulatory objective, that alternatives (including economic incentives and other non-regulatory approaches) have been considered, and that the rule imposes the least burden on society that is consistent with achieving the goal of the action.[54] If the rule is deemed a 'significant regulatory action'[55], then the agency must also prepare a Regulatory Impact Analysis that analyses the costs and benefits of the proposed rule. If OMB believes the submission does not meet these standards, a negotiation between it and the submitting agency ensues until it does; in the rare case when the two cannot reach an agreement, the matter is submitted to the President for resolution. The agency must again submit the final rule for OMB clearance before publishing it in the Federal Register. Thus, the President and his immediate office have become far more involved in regulatory decision-making than was the case 40 years ago.[56] As part of this 'mood' of extending the President into rulemaking, currently, major regulatory developments are often publicly announced as

---

53 President Carter issued Ex. Or. 12044, which provided for White House review of major agencies rules as well as imposing various management requirements on agencies. That review and involvement was extended by President Reagan in Ex. Or. 12291. President Clinton continued the practice by substituting his Ex. Or. 12866. President Bush made some minor amendments in Ex. Or. 13258. President Obama reinstated the original Ex. Or. 12866 in Ex. Or. 13497, and then issued a supplemental order with some additional emphases, Ex. Or. 13563. President Trump has so far retained the Clinton and Obama orders but issued Ex Or. 13771, which requires that for 2017 the gross cost of every new rule issued must be offset by the repeal of at least two existing rules.

54 Section 1(b), Ex. Or. 12866. Note, however, that independent agencies are not covered by these requirements.

55 These are generally those rules that have an annual effect on the economy of more than $100 million or adversely affect a sector of the economy. Ex. Or. 12866 § 3(f).

56 P.L. Strauss, 'Overseer, or "The Decider"? The President in Administrative Law' (2007) 75 *George Washington Law Review* 696.

being issued by the President, when in fact they are issued by the agency (and it was previously the custom to attribute the new rules to the agency and not the President).

These developments converted a flexible, abbreviated process into one that is far more complex, and one that in many ways has assumed some of the characteristics of adjudication. For example, there is now a 'record' that underlies the factual predicate of the rule[57] and the agency must demonstrate the factual basis for the rule, as opposed to the courts' simply assuming it. Further, those affected have far greater means of participating directly and substantially in the formulation of the rule.

3.5.2. Negotiated Rulemaking

In part in response to the increasingly formal and adversarial rulemaking and in part on the theory that 'better' rules would result, Congress authorized agencies to engage in 'negotiated rulemaking'.[58] In negotiated rulemaking, known informally as *reg-neg*, the agency seeks to identify representatives of the interests that will be substantially affected and empanel them into an advisory committee, including a senior representative of the agency itself, that is charged with developing a consensus on a proposed rule. The agency then bases its proposed rule on the consensus and follows through with the normal rulemaking process of taking comments and making revisions when required or appropriate. The process has been successful in addressing rules that are complex and that have become politically controversial. Such rules are often difficult for agencies to issue by the traditional means. It has been well received politically[59] and by participants.[60] It has also proven to be faster than traditional rulemaking when appropriately used and has reduced judicial challenges.[61] For various reasons, the negotiated rulemaking process has not been widely used by most agencies.[62] It has, however, had a major effect on rulemaking in that agencies now routinely use a far more significant means of 'public participation'

---

57 *Ass'n of Data Processing Service Organizations, Inc. v. Bd. of Governors of the Federal Reserve System*, 745 F.2d 677 (D.C. Cir. 1984).

58 Negotiated Rulemaking Act, 5 U.S.C. § 561 *et seq.*

59 For example, section 6(a)(1) of Ex. Or. 12866 provides: 'Each agency ... is directed to explore and, where appropriate, use consensual mechanisms for developing regulations, including negotiated rulemaking'.

60 J. Freeman, & L. Langbein, 'Regulatory Negotiation and the Legitimacy Benefit', (2000) 9 *New York University Environmental Law Journal* 60.

61 P.J. Harter, 'Assessing the Assessors: The Actual Performance of Negotiated Rulemaking' (2000) 9 *New York University Environmental Law Journal* 32. Others have argued, however, that it saves neither. C. Coglianese, 'Assessing Consensus: The Promise and Performance of Negotiated Rulemaking' (1997) 46 *Duke Law Journal* 1255.

62 *See* J.S. Lubbers, 'Achieving Policymaking Consensus: The (Unfortunate) Waning of Negotiated Rulemaking' (2008) 49 *South Texas Law Review* 987.

in the development of rules, generally through some sort of informal advisory committee or public meetings. The distinction between this and negotiated rulemaking is that in 'public participation' the goal of the agency is to become informed about the concerns of the public and to learn any facts they believe are relevant; the decision remains exclusively that of the agency in that no consensus or decision by the public is sought.

3.5.3. Petitions for Rulemaking

The actions of the private sector significantly changed the nature of rulemaking from one virtually completely within the control of the agency to one that must conform to fairly detailed procedures in which the agency must make changes in a proposal if significant comments are submitted in response to the notice of proposed rulemaking.

Moreover, the APA also provides that 'each agency shall give an interested person the right to petition for the issuance, amendment, or repeal of a rule'.[63] An agency is required to respond to such a petition 'promptly' (although that stricture is difficult to enforce) and provide a brief explanation for its actions. But the courts are highly deferential to the agencies in allowing them to control their own agenda and allocate their inherently scarce resources; further, the agency may decide how it wants to evolve its policy and how to reconcile competing priorities. However, where an agency denies a petition on the grounds that it lacks jurisdiction or where the petition asserts that an agency rule needs to be modified due to changed conditions, courts are more likely to review with more intensity. The Supreme Court has confirmed the limited nature of review of denials of petitions for rulemaking, but it did so in a high-profile case rejecting the EPA's decision in the Bush II administration to deny a petition to regulate greenhouse gases emitted by motor vehicles.[64]

Normally when a court finds the agency's denial lacking, it orders that agency to reconsider its decision – as did the Court in the greenhouse gas case. Thus, it is rare for a court to order an agency to grant a petition for rulemaking, but it does happen occasionally.[65]

---

63 5 U.S.C. § 553(e).

64 Massachusetts v. Environmental Protection Agency, 549 U.S. 497 (2007).

65 *See, e.g., American Horse Protection Assoc., Inc. v. Lyng*, 812 F.2d 1 (D.C. Cir. 1987).

Figure 6. The rulemaking process

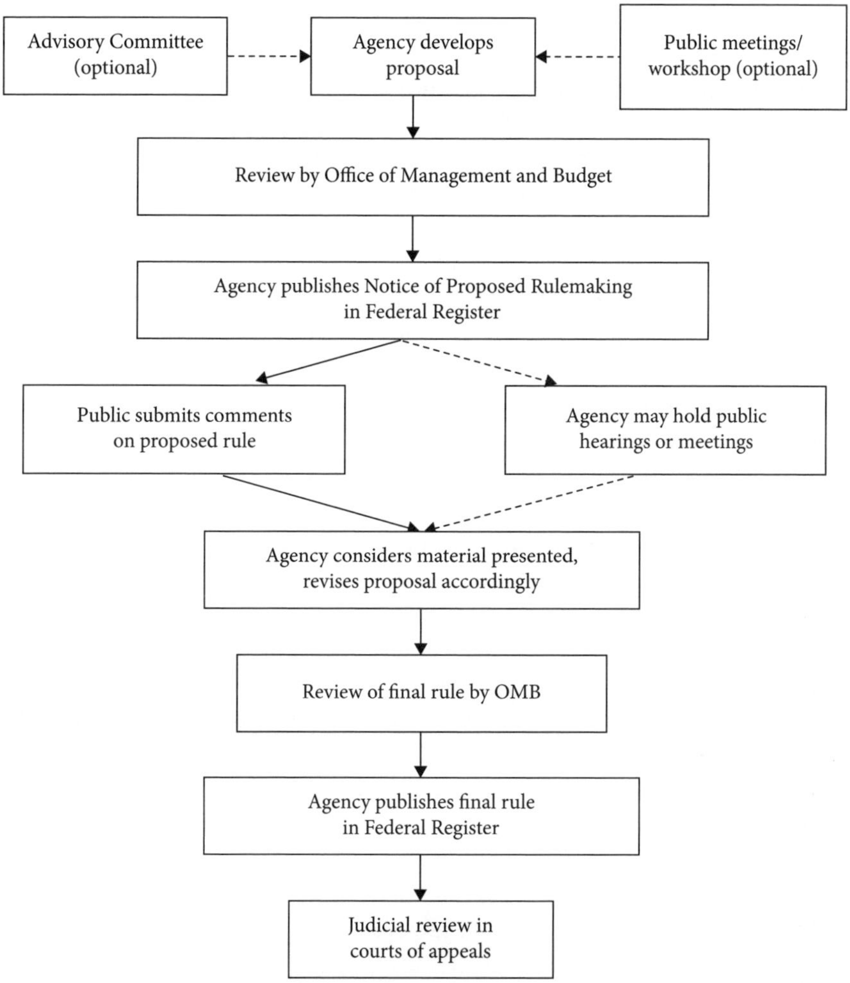

3.6. NON-LEGISLATIVE RULES, POLICY STATEMENTS, AND GUIDELINES

Substantive or 'legislative' rules (sometimes informally referred to as 'regulations') are an exercise of authority delegated by Congress to make law. Assuming they have been properly issued and have withstood any judicial review, they have the same force and effect as a statute. Thus, they are binding on those to whom they apply.

In addition, agencies also issue a variety of guidance documents that have varying practical effects. One type is an 'interpretive rule' in which the agency provides the public with its views as to the meaning of a statutory or regulatory term. Another is a statement of general policy in which the agency describes how it plans to exercise its discretion in the future or provides guidance on how to comply with a requirement. In order to encourage agencies to provide the public with information as to its thinking and means of complying with its requirements, these types of policy statements are not required to be published for notice and comment[66] nor be published at least 30 days before they become effective[67]; they are, however, required to be published in the Federal Register.[68]

While there may be a clear conceptual difference between legislative and non-legislative rules, determining when a policy statement is or is not a legislative rule is not always easy.[69] Agencies frequently argue that its issuance is a non-legislative policy statement in order to avoid complying with the rigors of the rulemaking process, but then turn around and ask a court to defer to it in an enforcement action, which would, as a practical matter, give binding effect to something that purportedly was not binding. Courts are then pressed to decide whether the statement was in fact a legislative rule, which should have complied with the notice-and-comment procedures.

As the procedures for rulemaking have grown more complex and arduous, agencies frequently turn to these alternative means to clarify general requirements. Some of these issuances clearly impose new, detailed requirements beyond the duties otherwise applicable. In many instances, the practice can be quite helpful in letting the subject of the requirements know in advance what the agency is thinking and what actions it may take. On the other hand, the practice has been opposed in some quarters as having been abused by the agencies in the form of imposing new duties without the benefit of the rulemaking process. For these reasons, in 2007, OMB issued a memorandum setting forth good practices for issuing guidance documents[70], and an executive order also made significant guidance documents subject to OMB review.[71]

---

66 5 U.S.C. § 553(b).

67 5 U.S.C. § 553(c).

68 5 U.S.C. § 552(a)(1).

69 For a discussion of disagreements among sophisticated academics, see W.F. Funk, 'A Primer on Non legislative Rules' (2001) 53 *Administrative Law Review* 1321.

70 Office of Management and Budget, *Final Bulletin for Agency Good Guidance*, issued 18 January 2007, 72 Fed. Reg. 3432 (25 January 2007).

71 Section 7, Executive Order 13422, 72 Fed. Reg. 2763 (23 January 2007). A guidance document is defined as 'an agency statement of general applicability and future effect, other than a regulatory action, that sets forth a policy on a statutory, regulatory, or technical issue or an interpretation of a statutory or regulatory issue. § 3(g). The requirements as to what constitutes a 'significant' guidance are then set out, but essentially, they are ones that are expected to have a major impact.

3.7. ADJUDICATION UNDER THE APA

Prior to 1965, the focus of administrative law was primarily on agency adjudication and judicial review since that was largely how agencies functioned. As a result, the Administrative Procedure Act is replete with details as to how the hearings specified under the Act are to work. Agency adjudications most often occur when statutes or regulations are being enforced, and the respondent seeks a hearing, or when a private party applies for a benefit (such as social security) or a license, and it is denied. Basically, the APA procedures apply to 'every case of adjudication required by statute to be determined on the record after opportunity for any agency hearing'.[72] Interestingly, the APA is silent as to what procedures are to be followed if the governing statute does not contain this command.[73] As will be discussed subsequently, the question as to whether a hearing must be held in adjudications under such statutes and, if so, what type of hearing, is determined by the Due Process Clause of the Constitution.[74] In administrative law literature, hearings 'on the record' are called 'formal adjudication' and the rest are considered 'informal'.

3.7.1. *Formal Adjudication*

Although the APA provides many details as to just how formal adjudication proceedings are conducted, what follows is a brief overview of the process and the relationship among the various actors. The process begins by the agency providing a notice of (1) the time, place, and nature of the hearing; (2) the legal authority and jurisdiction under which the hearing is to be held; and (3) the matters of fact and law that are asserted.[75] The agency must then give all parties the opportunity to present facts, arguments, and offers of settlement.[76]

---

72 5 U.S.C. § 554(a). This triggering language, or something equally explicit, must be present before an agency is required to follow the formal procedures in §§ 556–57. Courts have construed the provision to mean that the 'record', which consists of the evidence and testimony adduced in the hearing, will form the exclusive basis for the decision; all factual matters must be resolved based on the information contained in the record. There are various limited exceptions to this requirement. One is for matters subject to a trial de novo in court, which means that the court decides the issue on its own without regard to what the agency decided, as opposed to reviewing the decision in an appellate mode. Statutes prescribing de novo review are rare, however.

73 Even where statutes do not explicitly trigger the adjudicatory sections of the APA, agencies often, nevertheless, voluntarily comply with most of those provisions. They frequently do not, however, use Administrative Law Judges to preside over the hearings and instead use other hearing officers. ALJs have a more rigorous selection process, more guarantees of independence within the agency, and higher salaries than the others.

74 The Fifth Amendment to the U.S. Constitution provides: 'No person shall be ... deprived of life, liberty, or property, without due process of law'.

75 5 U.S.C. § 554(b).

76 5 U.S.C. § 554(c).

An Administrative Law Judge (ALJ) then presides over the hearing.[77] ALJs are judicial officers within agencies who are independent of the policymaking and enforcement parts of the agency. The ALJ has the normal judicial authority to regulate the hearing[78] and make the initial or recommended decision in the case.[79] Typically, the agency will also provide at least one and sometimes more levels of appeal or review within the agency itself.[80] In addition, the APA provides for 'separation of functions', meaning that staff engaged in investigation or prosecution may not communicate with decision-makers about a case while it is in progress.[81] The formal rules of evidence do not apply in agency proceedings, and hearsay evidence is normally allowed.[82] Agencies often take 'official notice' of broad general facts, but they are required to allow a party to demonstrate that the assumption is not accurate if the unproven fact is material to decision.[83] *Ex parte* communications – those between the decision-maker and fewer than all of the parties – are prohibited.[84] Agencies and agency officials are allowed to have a particular point of view or general bias. Thus, for example, it is fully appropriate for a Federal Trade Commission that is avowedly pro-competition to hear a case in which it is charging a company with anti-competitive activity.[85] And, it is similarly acceptable for a state medical board to investigate whether or not there is probable cause to bring an action and then to sit in judgement as to whether or not the offence occurred; here there was a commingling of investigation and adjudication.[86] There are limits, however, and courts will disqualify an adjudicator if the person has a specific, personal bias, such as having already decided major issues of fact[87], animus against a litigant, or a personal interest in the outcome.[88]

Note that there are some different limits in rulemaking proceedings. For example, ex parte communications are not barred in informal rulemakings,

77 5 U.S.C. § 556(b); the agency itself or one of the members of the collegial body governing the agency may also preside.
78 5 U.S.C. § 556(c).
79 5 U.S.C. § 557(b).
80 See, for example, 5 U.S.C. § 557 and *Darby v. Cisneros*, 509 U.S. 137 (1993).
81 5 U.S.C. § 554(d).
82 5 U.S.C. § 556(d).
83 5 U.S.C. § 556(d).
84 5 U.S.C. § 557(d)(1).
85 *FTC v. Cement Institute*, 333 U.S. 683 (1948).
86 *Withrow v. Larkin*, 421 U.S. 35 (1975).
87 *Texaco, Inc. v. FTC*, 336 F.2d 754 (D.C. Cir. 1964); the Chairman of the Federal Trade Commission made a speech that clearly indicated that he had already decided central issues of fact in a case that was currently pending before his agency.
88 In *Gibson v. Berryhill*, 411 U.S. 564 (1973), the Court concluded that the composition of a state licensing agency was unacceptably biased as having too substantial a pecuniary interest in the outcome.

absent agency self-imposed prohibitions, and it is much more difficult to disqualify rulemaking officials for bias.[89]

Figure 7. Typical agency hearing process

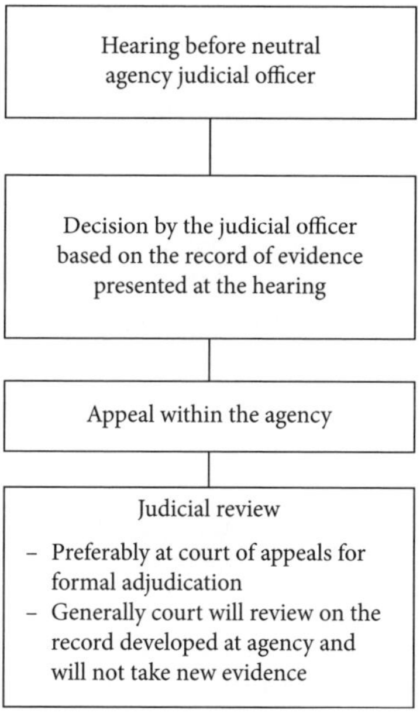

3.7.2. Raising Issues in Adjudicatory Proceedings

Interested members of the public who have 'standing' (which is described more fully below) may intervene in agency adjudicatory proceedings and participate to ensure that significant issues are addressed.[90] Agencies had argued that they themselves represented the 'public interest' and therefore private parties were neither needed nor welcome. The courts rejected that view of government and decided instead that the best way to ensure that the multiple issues that must be resolved are in fact litigated is to allow those who will be directly affected to do so, subject to the agency's ability to manage the proceeding.

3.7.3. Due Process and Informal Adjudication

If the governing program statute does not require a hearing, the question arises whether an agency must hold one before taking action that someone views as

89 The test for disqualification of rulemakers is 'a clear and convincing showing of an unalterably closed mind on matters critical to the proceeding'. *Ass'n of National Advertisers, Inc. v. FTC*, 627 F.2d 1151, 1154 (D.C. Cir. 1979).

90 *Office of Communication of the United Church of Christ v. FCC*, 359 F.2d 994 (D.C. Cir. 1966).

adverse to their interests.[91] The Fifth Amendment to the U.S. Constitution provides, 'No person shall be … deprived of life, liberty, or property, without due process of law'.[92] The issue then becomes when does the 'Due Process Clause' apply and when it does, what does it require?

The Supreme Court has recognized that property interests extend well beyond the ownership of tangible things such as land. Rather, the Due Process Clause safeguards the security of interests a person has. To be property, a person must have more that an abstract need or desire for it or a unilateral expectation of acquiring or maintaining it. Instead, there must be a legitimate claim of entitlement that arises from existing statutes, rules, contracts, or understandings. Thus, for example, someone who is hired on a year-to-year basis has no 'property interest' in being hired the next year, and hence no due process right to a hearing of any sort.[93] Contrariwise, if the employee and employer have an agreement that the employee will be retained during good behaviour, then the employee has a legitimate claim of continued employment that amounts to property and can only be terminated by due process of law, which requires a hearing of some sort.[94]

Liberty goes beyond freedom from detention and includes 'the right of the individual to contract, to engage in any of the common occupations of life, to acquire useful knowledge … generally to enjoy those privileges long recognized … as essential to the orderly pursuit of happiness'.[95] Thus, liberty could be impaired if a charge were made that would damage a person's standing in the community, such as an allegation of dishonesty or immorality or by a government action that imposed a stigma that would interfere with the person's ability to secure employment.

Once it is established that someone has a property or liberty interest at stake, the next issue that must be decided is 'what process is due' under the Due Process Clause. The Court has determined that it depends on the circumstances and requires the balancing of three factors, known as the '*Mathews* balancing test'[96]: (1) the nature of the private interest that will be affected by the official action; (2) the risk of erroneous deprivation of such interest though the procedures used by the government, and the probable value if any of additional procedural safeguards; and, (3) the government's interest, including the function

91 In some instances, the action might be taken before a hearing so long as the person adversely affected can raise the appropriate issues, such as compensation, afterwards. *North American Cold Storage Co. v. Chicago*, 211 U.S. 306 (1908) (need to take immediate action against allegedly putrid poultry; owner could sue subsequently to demonstrate the poultry was not in fact putrid and, if successful, be compensated for it).

92 The Fourteenth Amendment applies these duties to the states: '… nor shall any State deprive any person of life, liberty, or property, with due process of law …'.

93 *Board of Regents v. Roth*, 408 U.S. 564 (1972).

94 *Perry v. Sindermann*, 408 U.S. 593 (1972).

95 *Board of Regents v. Roth*, 408 U.S. 564 (1972).

96 *Mathews v. Eldridge*, 424 U.S. 319 (1976).

involved and the fiscal and administrative burden that the additional procedures would cause. Thus, unlike formal adjudication where the procedures are specified, the process of informal adjudication under the Due Process Clause is rather variable and ad hoc. Hearings in these instances are sometimes extremely brief: an opportunity for the adversely affected person to tell her side of the controversy and present whatever evidence she may have to support it. In one famous case, it was required that a public high school student be able to tell his side of a playground dust-up before he could be expelled from school for 10 days.[97]

In sum, the process for 'formal' adjudication is quite detailed in the APA, but applies only when the statute in question has the requisite triggering language. If the statute lacks such language, because the APA lacks an 'informal adjudication' provision, the procedures of any resulting adjudications are in effect governed by the *Mathews* balancing test and thus can range from cursory 'paper' proceedings to close-to-formal trial-like proceedings, depending on the circumstances. One element of due process, the right to be represented by counsel in all federal administrative proceedings, is provided for in the APA.[98]

3.7.4. Alternative Dispute Resolution

Congress has authorized agencies to use alternative means of dispute resolution to resolve issues if all the parties agree to do so. Thus, instead of relying solely on adjudication, either formal or informal, the parties may use mediation and arbitration to resolve their dispute. The Administrative Dispute Resolution Act (ADRA)[99], which amended the APA, also provides that communications provided in confidence between the neutral mediator or arbitrator and a party are to remain confidential unless all parties to the communication waive the right or a court determines that disclosure is necessary and is of sufficient importance in the individual case to outweigh the integrity of dispute resolution proceedings in general. Such confidential communications are also exempt from disclosure under the Freedom of Information Act. Many complex matters are now routinely mediated by agencies, using both public and private mediators. Arbitration[100] has been used less frequently, although it is finding its place in resolving disputes over government contracts.[101]

---

97 *Goss v. Lopez*, 419 U.S. 565 (1975).

98 5 U.S.C. § 555((b). Agencies may also allow parties to be represented by non-attorneys. *Id.*

99 5 U.S.C. § 571 *et seq.*

100 Like a mediator, the arbitrator may be anyone who is acceptable to the parties and may be either a government employee or someone in the private sector.

101 Although Congress was initially reluctant to cede authority to a private arbitrator to issue an award that would be binding on the government, 5 U.S.C. § 580 (1990), when it reauthorized ADRA it also empowered the arbitrator to make decisions binding on the agency 5 U.S.C. § 580 (1996). To control the discretion of the arbitrator, the parties may specify the issues that are subject to arbitration and the range that any award must be within. 5 U.S.C. § 575.

3.8. AGENCY DISCRETION TO CHOOSE RULEMAKING OR ADJUDICATION TO MAKE POLICY

Agencies have broad discretion in choosing the procedural means of achieving their goals and in the use of their resources.

3.8.1. Choice of Process

If an agency has the statutory authority to develop its policy either through rules or through a series of case-by-case decisions, the Supreme Court has made it clear that the choice is for the agency alone.[102] This choice is limited only by unusual circumstances in which the decision would be an abuse of discretion, such as imposing liability in an adjudicatory proceeding for past actions that were taken in good faith reliance on the then-current state of the law as developed by the agency.

3.8.2. Relationship of Rules to Adjudication

A party may have a statutory right to a hearing before an agency may make a decision involving it, such as denying an application for a license or for benefits or changing an authorized method of business, but if the agency has issued a valid rule that provides a general policy that would resolve the matter, the agency need not hold the hearing. It may, however, be required to allow the private party to either show that the rule does not or should not apply to the particular situation. Thus, for example, the Federal Communications Commission had a rule that prohibited anyone from owning more than a certain number of radio stations. A company applied for permission to own one more than the maximum permitted by the rule under a statute that said the agency could deny ownership permission only after a hearing. The agency was justified in not holding a hearing since the outcome was foreordained[103]: authorization would not be granted. This doctrine that general rules could preclude individual hearings was then extended when an agency was upheld for deciding issues in a rule that had recurred in disability hearings; the Supreme Court sanctioned the process since it said the rule would not apply if the facts did not merit it, and otherwise there was no point to relitigating similar facts in multiple cases.[104]

---

102 *NLRB v. Bell Aerospace Co.*, 416 U.S. 267 (1974); *SEC v. Chenery Corp.*, 332 U.S. 194 (1947).

103 *United States v. Storer Broadcasting Co.*, 351 U.S. 192 (1952).

104 *Heckler v. Campbell*, 461 U.S. 458 (1983).

4. JUDICIAL REVIEW OF ADMINISTRATIVE ACTION

In general, judicial review is based on the administrative record assembled by the agency in the proceeding that is being challenged. So, normally, reviewing courts do not allow new evidence to be admitted. They also do not consult outside experts in making their decisions, whereas agencies can and do consult experts, but the procedures are a bit different in agency adjudications and rulemakings. In an agency adjudication, any such consultations would have to be on the record and the parties would be given a chance to challenge the experts' testimony. In a rulemaking, agencies are freer to consult experts, but if they want to rely on their views, they would have to be disclosed and included in the rulemaking record.

The judicial review of actions taken by administrative agencies has several components that are provided by the APA, the Constitution, and decisions by the courts. They are:

- whether the action is judicially reviewable at all;
- who may bring the action;
- when can they bring it; and
- what is the scope of review for the factual, legal, and policy issues?[105]

4.1. AVAILABILITY OF JUDICIAL REVIEW

The judicial review section of the APA begins by saying that it applies 'except to the extent that – (1) statutes preclude judicial review; or (2) agency action is committed to agency discretion by law'.[106]

Implicit in the first provision is the recognition that Congress may prohibit a court from reviewing the actions taken under a particular program.[107] Not surprisingly, however, courts do not favour such limitations and have developed a 'strong presumption that Congress intends judicial review of administrative action'.[108] And, indeed, courts have been highly creative in interpreting statutes that would seemingly limit judicial review to allow some review.[109] Thus, unless a statute is overwhelmingly clear and forceful that judicial review is not to be had, the courts are likely to find it appropriate.

105 'Scope of review' is the term used in the APA, 5 U.S.C. § 706, to describe the standards that the court will apply in conducting its review. As such, it defines the relationship between the court and the agency.

106 5 U.S.C. § 701(a).

107 *Block v. Community Nutrition Institute*, 467 U.S. 340 (1984).

108 *Bowen v. Michigan Academy of Family Physicians*, 476 U.S. 667 (1986).

109 *See, e.g., McNary v. Haitian Refugee Centre*, 498 U.S. 479 (1991); *Lindahl v. Office of Personnel Management*, 470 U.S. 768 (1985).

The second clause – 'committed to agency discretion by law' – means that Congress has not provided any standards by which the action is to be gauged by a court; in short, there is no law to apply. An agency determination whether or not to take an enforcement action is usually deemed exempt from review.[110] The Court also applied this provision in a case challenging the dismissal of an employee of the Central Intelligence Agency when the statute authorized its director to terminate anyone whenever 'he shall deem' such termination in the interests of the United States.[111]

As a result, with relatively rare exceptions, some sort of judicial review is available, provided the other, following, conditions are met.

4.2. STANDING TO SUE

If judicial review is available, the question then becomes, who can invoke it? The US Constitution limits the jurisdiction of the courts to 'cases' and 'controversies.'[112] Thus, courts are not authorized to provide advisory opinions, but rather they may only resolve actual disputes. This limitation undergirds the law of standing, which has frequently been interpreted and applied by the Court in various factual situations. To have standing, the plaintiff must allege an 'injury in fact'[113] that is fairly traceable to the defendant's allegedly unlawful conduct that is distinct and palpable, and hence not abstract, conjectural, or hypothetical.[114] Further, the court must be in a position that it can redress the wrong if the plaintiff is successful.[115] Moreover, that person must also be arguably within the 'zone of interests' that are sought to be regulated or protected by the law in question.[116]

Several examples will help illuminate these abstractions: Someone may not sue solely on the ground that the government is violating the law; rather that person must show a direct injury that has resulted from the transgression.[117]

---

110 *Heckler v. Chaney*, 470 U.S. 821 (1985).

111 *Webster v. Doe*, 486 U.S. 592 (1988). In this case, however, the Court did permit the plaintiff to raise the issue that his termination was unconstitutional. Thus, the preclusion of judicial review extended only to the allegation that the termination was not in the best interests of the US; it did not reach the constitutional issues.

112 Article III, § 2.

113 *Ass'n of Data Processing Service Organizations v. Camp*, 397 U.S. 150 (1970).

114 *Allen v. Wright*, 468 U.S. 737 (1984).

115 *Simon v. Eastern Kentucky Welfare Rights Organization*, 426 U.S. 26 (1976). In this case, the plaintiff alleged that a change in the tax code caused a local hospital to stop providing services to indigent people. The court reasoned that even if it were to invalidate the change in the tax code, it was by no means clear that the hospital would resume its services.

116 *Clarke v. Securities Industry Association*, 479 U.S. 388 (1987). This part of the test for standing derives from the APA provision that 'A person suffering legal wrong because of agency action or adversely affected or aggrieved by agency action within the meaning of a relevant statute, is entitled to judicial review thereof.' 5 U.S.C. § 702.

117 *Allen v. Wright*, 468 U.S. 737 (1984).

A public interest organization, such as an environmental advocacy group, cannot sue to vindicate its particular cause, no matter how well established or well known the organization may be[118]; it may, however, represent the bona fide interests of its members.[119] Nor may someone sue to enforce an Act that requires agencies to consult with the Secretary of the Interior before taking action that might harm endangered species when the allegation in the complaint was that the petitioners might travel to locations where threatened species lived.[120] The Court thought the nexus between the alleged failure to consult and the plaintiff was too vague and remote to constitute an injury.[121] An example of excluding standing under the 'zone of interests' test is when the Court denied a challenge by a union of postal employees to a new regulation by the Postal Service that authorized private carriers to take mail to Europe; the Court reasoned that the purpose of the underlying statute was to protect the revenue of the Postal Service, not provide for its employees.[122]

4.3. TIMING OF JUDICIAL REVIEW

When an action may be brought is determined by three interrelated, and often overlapping, doctrines: ripeness, exhaustion of remedies, and finality.

4.3.1. Ripeness

Ripeness is a determination as to whether the agency's action is suitable for judicial resolution at the present time; whether it is 'ready' for the court or whether more is needed. In deciding whether an issue is ripe for decision the Court balances whether the legal issue is currently fit for judicial resolution and the hardship to the parties for withholding judicial review until further developments. Thus, for example, an agency regulation that requires companies to comply immediately is 'ripe' for judicial review when it is issued since the agency has done everything it will do to define the duty and there is nothing more to be done.[123]

---

118 The question of who has standing to challenge agency action does not depend on whether the plaintiff is a natural person, corporation, or some other legal entity. The issue is whether that entity was adversely affected.

119 *Sierra Club v. Morton*, 405 U.S. 727 (1972).

120 *Lujan v. Defenders of Wildlife*, 504 U.S. 555 (1992).

121 The Court acknowledged in *Lujan* that standing is more difficult for one who is not directly regulated. *Id.* at 562.

122 *Air Courier Conference of America v. American Postal Workers Union, AFL-CIO*, 498 U.S. 517 (1991).

123 *Abbott Laboratories v. Gardner*, 387 U.S. 136 (1967). Prior to this case, rules were customarily only challenged when the agency sought to enforce them; this case ushered in 'pre-enforcement' review so that rules are often considered ripe for review as soon as they are issued. The Court made clear that the reviewing court could allow the rule to remain in effect

Contrariwise, a regulation that prescribes inspections that an agency plans to make in the future is not ripe for resolution since the reasonableness can only be judged in the context on a particular inspection and the new rule does not have a direct and immediate effect on the company; thus, more is needed before the matter is suitable for court action.[124] Nor can someone challenge an agency when it expresses its intent to take future action on the grounds that that action would violate a statute; instead, the putative challenger must wait until the agency actually takes action and may not challenge the program as a whole.[125] The Court reasoned that more was needed before anyone was actually harmed sufficient for judicial review.

4.3.2. Exhaustion of Administrative Remedies

The APA specifies that if the agency has a multi-step internal appeals process, and specifies by rule that a party must complete all the steps before seeking judicial review, courts should honour that.[126] This is known as 'exhausting your administrative remedies'. It is based in part on the allocation of responsibility between the agency and the court, in that the agency should be given the opportunity to address the issue and perhaps remedy it so that a court challenge would be moot. Further, the agency's views of the facts and law of the case may well be important to the resolution of the case and not within the purview of the court to supply. For example, in one early famous case, the petitioner argued that it was not subject to the jurisdiction of a particular agency, and hence it should not have to go through a hearing before it; the Supreme Court disagreed, saying that the agency's views as to the particular facts would be important in deciding whether the agency had jurisdiction.[127]

Exhaustion is not jurisdictional, however, so that in appropriate situations courts may waive its application, such as when the matter presented is purely a question of constitutional law where the agency's views are not relevant, where the agency cannot grant the relief sought, or where the petitioner would be prejudiced by the delay.[128] Note that one important consequence of the

---

while the challenge was being litigated or it could, on motion, stay its effectiveness pending the outcome of the review. And, indeed, in some instances a rule or other action is reversed by the court and remanded to the agency, but the rule or other action will remain in effect pending the agency's further action.

Although the practice has been limited by statute in some instances, usually the validity of a rule may still be challenged when an agency brings a case to enforce the rule or otherwise takes action based on the rule.

124 *Toilet Goods Association, Inc. v. Gardner*, 387 U.S. 158 (1967).

125 *Lujan v. National Wildlife Federation*, 497 U.S. 871 (1990).

126 5 U.S.C. § 704, as interpreted by *Darby v. Cisneros*, 509 U.S. 137 (1993). The rule must also specify that the agency action is inoperative during the appeal process.

127 *Myers v. Bethlehem Shipbuilding Corp.*, 303 U.S. 41 (1938).

128 *See McCarty v. Madigan*, 503 U.S. 140 (1992).

exhaustion doctrine is that an issue may not be raised for the first time in front of a court when challenging an action taken following an agency hearing. Even in challenges to agency rules, courts may prevent a challenger from raising an issue that had not been presented to the agency first in the comment period.[129]

4.3.3. *Finality*

For reasons similar to the policy underlying exhaustion, and because the APA so stipulates[130], courts will only review 'final' agency actions.[131] The courts do not want to become ensnared in an issue that is still evolving in the agency. Under the allocation of responsibilities, an agency normally should complete its decision before the court begins its review; the agency might moot the issue, it may be settled, or the legal issues may be sharpened and the facts better defined if the agency completes its work. But, it is not always easy to determine just what is and what is not 'final' for these purposes. For example, in an early influential decision, a formal opinion by the administrator of a program as to its applicability was held 'final' for these purposes even though he had not taken any specific action.[132] The court reasoned that it was an 'authoritative determination' following a 'structured controversy' and hence was not an informal guidance issued by the staff; rather, it was controlling. However, since then, the Supreme Court has laid down a more restrictive test for finality:

> 'As a general matter, two conditions must be satisfied for agency action to be "final": First, the action must mark the "consummation" of the agency's decisionmaking process – it must not be of a merely tentative or interlocutory nature. And second, the action must be one by which "rights or obligations have been determined," or from which "legal consequences will flow."'[133]

The Supreme Court recently extended the notion of finality procedurally. The Environmental Protection Agency had ordered a family to take particular action under a statute that provided significant penalties for each day ($75,000) of non-compliance after receiving such a notice. The lower courts would not entertain a challenge to the determination since it was not "final" agency action. The

129 J.S. Lubbers, 'Fail to Comment at Your Own Risk: Does Issue Exhaustion Have a Place in Judicial Review of Rules?' (May 2015) Report to the Administrative Conference of the United States, <https://www.acus.gov/sites/default/files/documents/Final%20Issue%20Exhaustion%20Report%2005052014_1.pdf> accessed 08.04.2017, to be published in (2018) 70 *Administrative Law Review* 1 (forthcoming).

130 5 U.S.C. § 704.

131 The Administrative Procedure Act provides 'Agency action made reviewable by statute and final agency action for which there is no other adequate remedy in a court are subject to judicial review'. 5 U.S.C. § 704.

132 *National Automatic Laundry & Cleaning Council v. Schultz*, 443 F.2d 689 (D.C. Cir. 1971).

133 *Bennett v. Spear*, 520 U.S. 154, 177–78 (1997).

Supreme Court decided, however, that EPA had made its determination and was not going to do anything further so that the action was, in fact, final.[134]

4.4. THE APPEAL

As is explained above at footnote 18, there is not a single rule that determines which court will hear a particular category of appeals. The APA simply leaves the matter to be dictated in particular statutes; but it also provides that if the relevant statute fails to specify the reviewing court, then challengers must file for declaratory or injunctive relief in the appropriate federal district court.[135] Thus, appeals from formal agency adjudications and appeals of rules that are primarily based on the rulemaking record and involve questions of law are generally directed by statute to be filed in the courts of appeals and reviews of high-volume or informal agency adjudications go to the district courts. But, this is only a rough benchmark, so the specific statutory provisions requirements for any particular action needs to be consulted.

The filing fees for making an appeal are modest. It costs $400 to file a case in the district court and $500 for an appeal to the court of appeals.[136] Most filings are done electronically, usually in the form of attached PDF versions of briefs and attachments.

Although in the American system, each party pays its own expenses and is not awarded those expenses from the other parties if they prevail, Congress has modified that general rule in certain circumstances. The Equal Access to Justice Act (EAJA) provides that in an administrative adjudication, an agency is to 'award, to a prevailing party ... fees and other expenses incurred by that party ... unless the adjudicative officer of the agency finds that the position of the agency was substantially justified or that special circumstances make an award unjust.'[137] The purpose of EAJA is to protect the private party from unjustified behaviour by the government. However, the Act only allows for the award of fees to individuals with a net worth of less than $2 million, small businesses as defined by the Act,

---

134 *Sackett v. EPA*, 132 S. Ct. 1367 (2012). The case is interesting inasmuch as the order charged that the Sacketts filled wetlands illegally and ordered them to restore the land to a way specified in the order. The Sacketts were left in limbo: they could defend against the order if EPA brought an action but the agency had not done that; instead the fines kept mounting. They then turned to the courts, which ruled the decision wasn't final since it was only a charge. Nonsense, ruled the Court: the agency had made its decision that affected the rights of the Sacketts – it was final; nothing more was going to happen.

135 5 U.S.C. § 703.

136 *See* <www.dcd.uscourts.gov/fee-schedule> and <https://www.cadc.uscourts.gov/internet/home.nsf> (search for 'fee summary') accessed 08.04.2017. Note that there is typically no filing fee for an administrative hearing or appeal within an agency, although some agencies are authorized to assess fees for certain types of applications.

137 5 U.S.C. § 504(a)(1).

and charitable organizations.[138] EAJA also authorized courts to award fees and expenses, including attorneys' fees, in civil litigation brought by or against the United States, unless the court finds that the position of the United States was substantially justified or that special circumstances make an award unjust.[139]

4.5. SCOPE OF REVIEW

The Administrative Procedure Act[140] defines the scope of review as directing the reviewing court to:

1. compel agency action unlawfully withheld or unreasonably delayed; and
2. hold unlawful and set aside agency action, findings, and conclusions found to be –
   A. arbitrary, capricious, an abuse of discretion, or otherwise not in accordance with law[141];
   B. contrary to constitutional right, power, privilege, or immunity;
   C. in excess of statutory jurisdiction, authority, or limitations, or short of statutory right;
   D. without observance of procedure required by law;
   E. unsupported by substantial evidence in a case subject to [the formal adjudication provisions of this Act]; or
   F. unwarranted by the facts to the extent that the facts are subject to trial de novo by the reviewing court.

4.5.1. Review of the Facts

The APA provides that an agency's decision made in a formal adjudication must be supported by 'substantial evidence'.[142] The courts have interpreted this term as meaning the kind of evidence on which responsible people rely in making serious decisions or, in another way, such relevant evidence as a reasonable mind

---

138 5 U.S.C. § 504(b)(1)(B).

139 28 U.S.C. §§ 2412(a)(1), 2414(d)(1)(A). A similar restriction as to who can be awarded such fees applies here as well. § 2412(d)(2)(B).

140 5 U.S.C. § 706.

141 While the terms 'arbitrary', 'capricious', or an 'abuse of discretion' sound quite harsh and hence it appears that courts would likely find such a violation only rarely, they have in fact become terms of art in American administrative law that define a process, which is described below, by which courts review policy and legal determinations by agencies, and they do not indicate total waywardness by an agency.

142 The APA itself only applies this standard to those cases that are determined on a record developed by the trial type procedures of §§ 556 and 557 of the APA. Congress has occasionally imposed similar requirements for review of informal rulemakings; however, courts have found that in review of rules the test converges with the normally applicable 'arbitrary and capricious' test under § 706(2)(A). *See Ass'n of Data Processing Service Organizations, Inc. v. Bd. of Governors of the Federal Reserve System*, 745 F.2d 677 (D.C. Cir. 1984).

might accept as adequate to support a conclusion. In deciding whether a record contains substantial evidence, the court looks at the evidence that supports the proposition as discounted by the evidence that fairly detracts from it.[143] Thus, the court looks to the totality of the record (including both the ALJ's decision and the final agency decision) when determining whether the agency's factual determination is supported by substantial evidence.

For informal agency actions, including informal adjudications and most rulemakings, the substantial evidence test normally does not apply. The Supreme Court has made clear that de novo review is not to be used except in the handful of situations in which a statutory or constitutional guarantee outside of the APA requires such treatment. Instead, the factual basis for rules and informal decisions is reviewed under the arbitrary and capricious test. As mentioned in relation to judicial review of rules[144], if the adjudicative order is declared to be *ultra vires*, the court will vacate it, but if the order is deemed to lack factual support, the remedy is to remand it to the agency. In such cases the agency may still prevail if it can re-do the adjudication and meet its evidentiary burden, but in many cases the court's opinion will make that difficult and the non-enforcement of the agency's order will end the proceeding.

The Court set out the process it will use in reviewing agency informal decisions in the case of *Citizens to Preserve Overton Park v. Volpe*.[145] In reviewing a decision by the Department of Transportation to grant funds to build a highway through a park, the Court determined that it should apply the arbitrary-and-capricious test by conducting a 'searching and careful' review of the facts, but it cautioned that its role was limited to ensuring that the decision was supported in the materials before the Administrator and that the court is not authorized to substitute its judgement for that of the Administrator. This mode of review has also been applied to the review of the factual basis for rules as well.

4.5.2. Review of Law and Policy

In reviewing agency applications of law or choice of policy, whether made in adjudication or rulemaking, the Court has made clear that such decisions will also be reviewed according to the arbitrary-and-capricious test. This review has several components:

- whether the decision was based on the consideration of the relevant factors set out in the legislation;

143 *Universal Camera Corp. v. NLRB*, 340 U.S. 474 (1951).
144 See note 52, *supra*.
145 401 U.S. 402 (1971).

- whether any impermissible factors might have entered into the calculus of the decision, and
- whether there was a clear error of judgement.[146]

Thus began the intense judicial review of agency policy decisions and the application of law. This evolved into courts taking a 'hard look', as the process became known, at whether the agency had engaged in reasoned decision-making.[147] In particular, the agency must consider the relevant factors, inclusively and exclusively, and must explain the basis for its decision. That is, it must describe the facts, and the evidence supporting the facts, and the relationship between the facts found and the choice made.[148] The intensity increased if the agency was changing direction. These cases were largely directed at making the administrative process more rational and open.

The question remained, however, as to who – agency or court – should decide the questions of law that might arise from the agency's interpretation of its own statute. Traditionally, courts looked at the text and legislative history of the statute and would then impose their views on the agencies. The Supreme Court redefined that relationship in a case that has become one of the most cited cases in American legal history, the *Chevron* case:

> 'When a court reviews an agency's construction of the statute which it administers, it is confronted with two questions. First, always, is the question whether Congress has directly spoken to the precise question at issue. If the intent of Congress is clear, that is the end of the matter; for the court, as well as the agency, must give effect to the unambiguously expressed intent of Congress. If, however, the court determines Congress has not directly addressed the precise question at issue, the court does not simply impose its own construction on the statute, as would be necessary in the absence of an administrative interpretation. Rather, the question for the court is whether the agency's answer is based on a permissible construction of the statute'.[149]

The Court reasoned that a gap in the legislation, meaning that Congress had not addressed the issue in question, should be treated as an express delegation of authority by Congress to the agency to elucidate by regulation.[150] The Court

146 An example of such an error might be that an agency had consistently decided an issue in a particular manner, but suddenly and without explanation changed course and decided a similar case in a very different way.

147 *Greater Boston Television Corp. v. FCC*, 444 F.2d 841 (D.C. Cir. 1970), *cert. denied*, 403 U.S. 923 (1971).

148 *Motor Vehicle Manufacturers Ass'n v. State Farm Mutual Automobile Insurance Co.*, 463 U.S. 29 (1983).

149 *Chevron U.S.A. Inc. v. Natural Resources Defense Council, Inc.*, 467 U.S. 837 (1984). Footnotes omitted.

150 Since the focus of the case was on the role of the agency in implementing a statute it is charged with administering, *Chevron* deference does not apply to interpretations of statutes that are administered by more than one agency, such as the Administrative Procedure Act

also pointed out in a footnote that the judiciary is the final authority on statutory construction so that in determining whether Congress had addressed the issue and whether the agency's construction of the statute is reasonable, the courts are to employ traditional tools of statutory construction. This process of review has become known as the '*Chevron* two step'. In step one the court should decide whether Congress's intent is clear as to the interpretative issue. If it is not clear, then step two requires the court to defer to a reasonable agency interpretation. The resulting acceptance of the agency's filling of the gaps is called '*Chevron* deference'. While experts still argue about the case's jurisprudential significance, it clearly has had an important effect on the relationship between agencies and courts, with the courts sustaining agency interpretations of their statutes more than previously.

The Supreme Court subsequently decided several cases that indicate *Chevron* deference is not appropriate for *all* agency pronouncements that fill gaps in their statutes. The full reach of the decisions continue to be hotly debated in the academic literature and will likely have to evolve in additional decisions. The first case held that *Chevron* deference is inapplicable to interpretations contained in an opinion letter.[151] The second generalized and limited *Chevron* deference to cases in which it appears that Congress delegated authority to the agency to make rules and decisions having the force of law and that the agency decision for which *Chevron* deference is claimed was promulgated in the exercise of that authority.[152] That process need not be notice-and-comment rulemaking or formal adjudication, but it does need to reflect a similar law-making intent. Thus, the Court refused to defer to an agency's assessment of a customs duty since they are typically done at the staff level in multiple regions involving thousands of individual decisions. The Court emphasized that even though the strong *Chevron* deference will not be granted to these types of decisions, the weaker '*Skidmore*' deference continues to apply.[153] Thus, *Chevron* appears to be now limited to the exercise of relatively formal decisions by agencies in which the agency purports to speak with the force of law.

It should be noted that, among some conservative Justices on the Supreme Court including its newest Justice (Gorsuch), there is an increasing scepticism about judicial deference to agency legal interpretations.[154] The Republican-

---

or the Wilderness Act. Nor is deference given to the interpretation of criminal statutes since courts make the final decisions there.

151 *Christensen v. Harris County*, 529 U.S. 576 (2000).

152 *United States v. Mead Corp.*, 533 U.S. 218 (2001).

153 This type of deference comes from *Skidmore v. Swift & Co.*, 323 U.S. 134, 140 (1944) ('The weight of such judgement in a particular case will depend upon the thoroughness evident in its consideration, the validity of its reasoning, its consistency with earlier and later pronouncements, and all those factors which give it the power to persuade, if lacking power to control'.).

154 See, e.g., the dissenting opinion by Chief Justice Roberts and two others in *City of Arlington, Tex. v. F.C.C.*, 133 S.Ct. 1863, 1877 (2013), and *Gutierrez-Brizuela v. Lynch*, 834 F.3d 1142, 1149 (10th Cir. 2016) (Gorsuch, J., concurring).

controlled House of Representatives has even recently passed a bill to forbid courts from giving such deference, though passage by the Senate is doubtful.[155]

4.6.1. Role of Private Parties in Forcing and Enforcing Government Duties

Whether or not someone in the private sector can force an agency to address a particular issue has an important bearing on the nature of the relationship between the public and private sectors and the nature of government. Private parties might take a variety of actions other than judicial review of agency action to hold government agencies accountable for complying with legal requirements. They might, for example petition the agency to issue, repeal, or modify a rule; go to court to force an agency to follow a non-discretionary statutory mandate; or even in some cases pressure agencies to take an enforcement action against someone whom they believe is violating the law. They also might be able to take action themselves against the malefactor to enforce compliance with an existing standard. If they felt the government had overstepped its bounds, they might sue in tort for a remedy or they might claim that the government had illegally seized their property. These issues are explored in this section.

4.6.1. Judicial Review of Agencies' Failure to Act

Under the APA, a reviewing court may 'compel agency action unlawfully withheld or unreasonably delayed'.[156] However, the Supreme Court has held that an agency's decision on a petition to initiate an enforcement action is committed to the agency's discretion by law.[157] Hence, there is a presumption that the courts will not review the agency's decision not to take enforcement action. The Court said that this presumption may be rebutted by showing that: the underlying statute either provides a duty to enforce[158] or guidelines the agency must follow in enforcement; the agency has simply refused to enforce the law; or the agency has adopted a policy that is so extreme as to amount to an abdication of its statutory responsibility. Moreover, in an another case, the Supreme Court rejected a challenge to an agency's failure to take appropriate action to enforce a programmatic statute – protecting public lands from environmental harm caused by off-road vehicles. The Court held that such suits could 'proceed only where an agency failed to take a discrete agency action that it is required to take'.[159]

---

155 The Separation of Powers Restoration Act, H.R.4768, 114th Congress.
156 5 U.S.C. § 706(1).
157 *Heckler v. Chaney*, 470 U.S. 821 (1985).
158 *Dunlop v. Bachowski*, 421 U.S. 560 (1975).
159 Norton v. Southern Utah Wilderness Alliance, 542 U.S. 55 (2004).

In short, unless a statute imposes an explicit duty to take some sort of action, which is rare, agencies control their own agendas, and it is difficult for members of the private sector to force an agency to either enforce a rule or write a new one.

4.6.2. *Judicial Review of Undue Delay*

When challengers challenge an undue delay by an agency in a matter such as conducting a rulemaking, the courts have propounded four factors to be considered:

1. The court should ascertain the length of time that has elapsed since the agency came under a duty to act. Although there is no per se rule as to how long is too long, inordinate agency delay would frustrate congressional intent by forcing a breakdown of regulatory processes.
2. The reasonableness of the delay must be judged in the context of the statute that authorizes the agency's action.
3. The court must examine the consequences of the agency's delay. Delays that might be altogether reasonable in the sphere of economic regulation are less tolerable when human lives are at stake.
4. The court should give due consideration in the balance to any plea of administrative error, administrative convenience, practical difficulty in carrying out a legislative mandate, or need to prioritize in the face of limited resources.[160]

4.6.3. *Citizen Suits to Enforce Regulatory Compliance*

Some environmental statutes authorize private citizens to bring a civil action against any person, including the United States or a governmental agency, who is alleged to have violated or to be in violation of statutory limitations or standards.[161] To commence an action, the citizen must provide a written 'Intent to Sue' notice to the agency, the state in which the offence occurred, and the alleged violator. This notice provides the agency with an indication that a violation is or will occur, and also provides an opportunity for the violator to investigate and resolve the violation. Consequently, the agency or state must investigate whether an actual violation is occurring, and the violator has the opportunity to remedy any ongoing violations. If such efforts fail, the citizen may file a civil action demanding injunctive relief and civil penalties. In general, these statutes provide for a waiting period before the commencement of a

160 *In re International Chemical Workers Union*, 958 F.2d 1144, 1149 (D.C. Cir. 1992) (citations and internal quotation marks omitted).

161 *See, e.g.*, 33 U.S.C. § 1365 and 42 U.S.C. § 7604 – provisions in the Clean Water Act and Clean Air Act, respectively. A somewhat similar provision is included in the procedures of the Equal Employment Opportunity Commission. 29 C.F.R. § 1601.28(e). The details of precisely how this power to private citizens' works varies according to the specific Act in question.

citizen suit. For example, the Clean Water Act requires the action not begin less than sixty days from the date of a notice of violation. In addition, the statutes prohibit any action by a citizen in situations where the Administrator or state is 'diligently prosecuting' the offender.[162]

The Supreme Court has held that an 'ongoing' violation was a prerequisite for a citizen suit under the Clean Water Act.[163] This serves to prohibit any civil action for purely past violations. In regards to possible future violation, the Court held that a plaintiff must show the possibility by 'adducing evidence from which a reasonable trier of fact could find a continuing likelihood or a recurrence in intermittent or sporadic violations'.[164] Once an action has begun, the EPA Administrator retains the right to intervene in the case.[165] If any civil money penalties are assessed, the moneys are deposited in the federal Treasury.[166] Private plaintiffs may, however, receive an award of attorney fees.[167]

4.6.4. Qui Tam Suits under the False Claims Act

In addition to citizen suit provisions in regulatory statutes, an old law that was passed in 1863, the False Claims Act[168], allows private citizens to file actions against federal contractors claiming fraud against the government, such as in health care, military, or other government spending programs. Persons filing under the Act, known as relators, bring a lawsuit, on behalf of the United States under the '*qui tam*' provision of the law. The complaint is filed under seal to prevent the target from knowing about it at the outset although the U.S. Department of Justice is notified; it has the option to intervene in the suit. If the Department does intervene, it will notify the company or person being sued that a claim has been filed. In such cases, if the government prevails in the suit, the relator is entitled to a portion of the proceeds between 15 and 25 percent. If the government decides not to participate in a *qui tam* action, the relator may proceed alone without the Department of Justice, though such cases historically have a much lower success rate. Relators who do prevail in such cases will get a

162 D.F. Buckman, 'Requirement that there be Continuing Violation to Maintain Citizen Suit under Federal Environmental Protection Statutes-Post-Gwaltney Case' (1999) 158 *American Law Reports Federal* 519.

163 *Gwaltney v. Chesapeake Bay Foundation, Inc.*, 484 U.S. 49 (1987).

164 *Id.* at 65.

165 42 U.S.C. § 6972(d) (2000).

166 A.K. Wooster, 'Actions Brought Under Federal Water Pollution Control Act (Clean Water Act) Amendments of 1972' (2000) 163 *American Law Reports Federal* 531.

167 The Equal Access to Justice Act provides that 'An agency that conducts an adversary adjudication shall award, to a prevailing party other than the United States, fees and other expenses incurred by that party in connection with that proceeding, unless the adjudicative officer of the agency finds that the position of the agency was substantially justified or that special circumstances make an award unjust'. 5 U.S.C. § 504(a)(1). Attorneys' fees for civil litigation are provided by 28 U.S.C. § 2412(b).

168 31 U.S.C. §§ 3729–3733.

higher relator's share, between 25 and 30 percent. Numerous law firms specialize in these *qui tam* actions.

4.6.5. Money Damages against the Government

As a general matter, the doctrine of sovereign immunity – the King can do no wrong – holds that the United States government may not be sued without its consent. Thus, without consent given by the Congress, the government could not be sued for any injuries it may have caused through erroneous conduct. But for these purposes, there is at least partial consent. In the Federal Tort Claims Act[169], Congress authorized tort suits against the federal government for any 'negligent or wrongful act or omission of any employee of the Government while acting within the scope of his office or employment, under circumstances where the United States, if a private person, would be liable to the claimant' to the same extent as a private individual under like circumstances.[170] There are, however, numerous exceptions to this general acceptance of applying the private law of torts to impose liability of the government for the actions of its officials. The most significant for our purposes is the 'discretionary function' exception – that this liability does not extend to:

> 'Any claim based upon an act or omission of an employee of the Government, exercising due care, in the execution of a statute or regulation, whether or not such statute or regulation [is] valid, or based upon the exercise or performance or the failure to exercise or perform a discretionary function or duty on the part of a federal agency or an employee of the Government, whether or not the discretion involved [is] abused'.[171]

The first Supreme Court decision that construed this provision made its limited reach clear: It was not 'intended that the constitutionality of legislation [or] the legality of regulations ... should be tested through the medium of a damage suit for tort.'[172]

Thus, a private person may not recover when the contention is that the government[173] made (or did not but should have made) a policy determination that caused the injuries.[174] The injured party may collect, however, if the

169 28 U.S.C. §§ 1346(b), 2671–80.
170 28 U.S.C. § 1346(b).
171 28 U.S.C. § 2680(a).
172 *Dalehite v. United States*, 346 U.S. 15, 27 (1953), quoting from the hearings on the Federal Tort Claims Act.
173 The immunity extends to government employees acting in the course of their employment. Such suits may only be brought against the United States. 28 U.S.C. § 2679(b)(1)(1988).
174 *United States v. S.A. Empresa de Viacao Aerea Rio Grandense (Varig Airlines)*, 467 U.S. 797 (1984).

decision made by the government violated a clear duty provided by a statute or regulation, in which case there was no discretion to be exercised.[175]

4.6.6. Suits for Damages against Officials

Although the government may be liable for some tortious conduct under the Federal Tort Claims Act, the question would still remain whether someone who was injured could recover damages arising from the violation of their constitutional rights at the hands of a particular government official. The competing contentions are that on the one hand, someone who is injured should be compensated for the injury and that action will serve as a check on illegal behaviour. The contrary argument is that officials must be able to exercise their duties free of concerns over subsequent liability and that, in any event, errors on their part may be corrected through judicial proceedings. The Supreme Court held:

> '[I]n a suit for damages arising from unconstitutional action, federal executive officials exercising discretion are entitled to ... qualified immunity ... subject to those exceptional situations where it is demonstrated that absolute immunity is essential for the conduct of public business. ... Federal officials will not be liable for mere mistakes in judgement, whether the mistake is one of fact or one of law'.[176]

Thus, an official with only qualified immunity may *not* exercise that official duty in a way that is known to violate constitutional rights or in a way that 'transgresses a clearly established constitutional rule'[177], or with a malicious intent to cause a deprivation of constitutional rights.[178] Any such malice must be specifically pled so that 'government officials performing discretionary functions generally are shielded from liability for civil damages insofar as their conduct does not violate clearly established statutory or constitutional rights of which a reasonable person would have known'[179] Judges, including administrative law judges in the executive branch, have absolute immunity, as do prosecutors.

As a result, money damages are not available for routine regulatory or administrative decisions even if they cause injury and are later proven wrong.

4.6.7. Compensation for Regulatory Takings

The Fifth Amendment to the US Constitution provides in part that 'private property [shall not] be taken for public use, without just compensation'.[180] The

175 *Berkovitz v. United States*, 486 U.S. 531 (1988).
176 *Butz v. Economou*, 438 U.S. 478 (1978).
177 *Id.*
178 *Harlow v. Fitzgerald*, 457 U.S. 800 (1982).
179 *Id.*
180 U.S. Const. amend. V.

Supreme Court expanded the nature of what constitutes a 'taking' when it ruled that 'while property may be regulated to a certain extent, if regulation goes too far it will be recognized as a taking'.[181] Generally, regulations are considered Fifth Amendment *per se* takings in two circumstances: when an owner's property is permanently invaded physically because of a government regulation, or when regulations fully divest an owner of all economically beneficial uses for the owner's property.[182]

Beyond these circumstances, the criteria in determining whether a regulation affects property to the degree that it constitutes a taking are 'the regulation's economic impact on the claimant, the extent to which it interferes with distinct investment-backed expectations, and the character of the government action'.[183]

The remedies available to a plaintiff for a regulatory taking are decided, not by the courts, but by the legislature or agency responsible for the regulation.[184] Once a court determines that a taking has occurred, the government retains the whole range of options already available – amendment of the regulation, withdrawal of the invalidated regulation, or exercise of eminent domain. Regardless of which of these actions the government decides to take, it is still liable for the 'temporary' taking that occurred between the regulation's coming into effect and the government's remedying the damage.[185]

Typically, takings cases arise with government action asserting 'eminent domain' over private property for a public use.[186] However, property owners who believe that government action has 'taken' their property can seek compensation through an 'inverse condemnation' action. Although most takings cases involve state or local government action, and are decided in state or local courts or agencies, takings actions can be filed against the federal government, normally in the Court of Federal Claims.

4.7. NON-JUDICIAL MEANS OF ACCOUNTABILITY

Much of the attention of American administrative law has been concerned with ensuring that agencies are held accountable for their actions. That means they adhere to the law established by Congress, operate by means of acceptable procedures, and make decisions that are legitimate. Certainly, the courts play the

181 *Lingle v. Chevron U.S.A. Inc.*, 544 U.S. 528, 537 (2005), citing *Pennsylvania Coal Co. v. Mahon*, 260 U.S. 393, 415, (1922).

182 *Id.* at 538.

183 *Id.* at 528, citing *Penn Central Transp. Co. v. New York City*, 438 U.S. 104, 124 (1978); these criteria are, therefore known as the *Penn Central* factors.

184 *First English Evangelical v. County of Los Angeles*, 482 U.S. 304, 321 (1987).

185 *Id.* at 318, stating that '"temporary" takings which, as here, deny a landowner all use of his property, are not different in kind from permanent takings, for which the Constitution clearly requires compensation'.

186 *See Kelo v. New London*, 545 U.S. 469 (2005).

primary role in providing that accountability. But there are other mechanisms as well that bear mentioning.

4.7.1. Oversight Hearings

Committees of Congress often hold public hearings in which they call representatives of the administration to testify. The committee might summon White House officials, politically appointed officials in an agency, or career agency employees. The purpose of such hearings is to inquire into how the agency is administering a particular program or why it has taken particular actions. The witnesses are instructed to address the questions that are set out by the committee. The witnesses make prepared presentations and are then questioned by members of the Committee who frequently also make a statement about the issue. The major purpose of the enterprise is to highlight what is happening and to provide Congress with the opportunity to comment on whether it agrees with what is being done – or disagrees, as is more frequently the case, since that is what sparks hearings in the first place. The hearings serve as a political check on agencies, and if Congress disagrees sufficiently, it might change the underlying legislation. While the hearings lack power to force agency changes in administration – at least directly – they are an important means of raising an issue politically. As such, they can have a considerable practical effect.

The decision as to whether or not to hold hearings is made by the chair of the Committee. As a result, when Congress and the President are of the same political party, hearings are not nearly as frequent or as intense as when the two branches have divided loyalty.

4.7.2. Ombuds

Unlike many countries, the federal government does not have a national ombudsman (often called an 'ombuds' in America) that is designated as such. One major reason for this is that members of Congress like to think of themselves as serving that role for their own constituents. When Senators and Representatives receive complaints and inquiries from their constituents, their designated staff members address these issues by making inquiries of agencies, helping the person navigate through a bureaucratic maze to get what they need, or suggesting to an agency that it accommodate the request.

Nevertheless, Congress or the agencies themselves have established ombuds offices in numerous federal programs, specifically to hear complaints from affected citizens.[187] For example, the National Taxpayer Advocate in the Internal

[187] For a comprehensive list of such programs, see Carole Houk, et al., 'The Ombudsman in Federal Agencies – Master List of Federal Ombuds Offices' (2016) prepared for the Administrative Conference of the United States (ACUS) <https://www.acus.gov/appendix/ombudsman-federal-agencies-master-list-federal-ombuds-offices> accessed 08.04.2017.

Revenue Service (IRS) has offices all over the country to assist taxpayers with their problems with the IRS and recommends administrative and legislative changes to IRS policies and operations. The Consumer Financial Protection Bureau Ombudsman assists consumers who experience problems with the agency's supervisory and examination activities. There are also programmatic ombuds in the areas of immigration and small business regulation, among others.

Congress has created several other entities in both the legislative and executive branches that also enhance government accountability.

4.7.3. Government Accountability Office

The website for the Government Accountability Office provides a succinct view of its role: 'The U.S. Government Accountability Office (GAO) is an independent, nonpartisan agency that works for Congress. Often called the "congressional watchdog," GAO investigates how the federal government spends taxpayer dollars'.[188] GAO gathers information to help Congress determine how well executive branch agencies are doing their jobs. GAO's work routinely answers such basic questions as whether government programs are meeting their objectives or providing good service to the public. To that end, GAO provides Senators and Representatives with the best information available to help them arrive at informed policy decisions – information that is accurate, timely, and balanced. GAO supports congressional oversight by:

- auditing agency operations to determine whether federal funds are being spent efficiently and effectively;
- investigating allegations of illegal and improper activities;
- reporting on how well government programs and policies are meeting their objectives;
- performing policy analyses and outlining options for congressional consideration; and
- issuing legal decisions and opinions, such as bid protest rulings and reports on agency rules.[189]

ACUS adopted a recommendation that urged federal agencies to 'consider creating additional ombuds offices to provide places perceived as safe for designated constituents to raise issues confidentially and receive assistance in resolving them without fear of retribution.' ACUS Recommendation 2016-5, 'The Use of Ombuds in Federal Agencies' (adopted 14 December 2016), 81 Fed. Reg. 94316 (23 December 2017). See also the American Bar Association's (ABA's) 'Standards for the Establishment and Operation of Ombuds Offices' (2004), accessible, with accompanying report as a link at <www.abanet.org/dch/committee.cfm?com=AL322500>. Both the ABA and ACUS use the term 'ombuds' instead of the more customary 'ombudsman' so as to reflect gender neutrality. While 'ombudsman' is still likely a more prevalent term, at least one statute uses the term 'ombuds'. The Administrative Dispute Resolution Act specifically authorizes agencies to use 'ombuds' to 'resolve issues in controversy'. 5 U.S.C. § 571–572.

188 <www.gao.gov/about/index.html> accessed 08.04.2017.

189 *Id.*

Unlike ombuds, however, GAO does not respond to inquiries and complaints by individual citizens, but rather to members of Congress as well as on its own initiative. As with congressional hearings, a GAO inquiry and report does not compel a result, but rather analyses what an agency has been doing and makes recommendations for its improvement. Any change in the program comes from the resulting political process.

4.7.4. Inspectors General

Congress has established offices of Inspector General in all departments and most large agencies. 'IGs' as they are called, are independent officials (meaning they cannot be removed by the agency).[190] Their main role is to protect against 'waste, fraud, and abuse'. But in some instances and in some agencies their role is broader and includes ensuring that the agency is administering its duties legitimately. Over time, they have become important and independent anti-corruption and pro-accountability power centres within the executive branch.

4.7.5. Administrative Conference of the U.S.

The Administrative Conference of the United States (ACUS) is an independent federal agency in the Executive Branch, established in 1968 as an advisory agency in administrative law and procedure.[191] ACUS has broad authority to conduct studies and make recommendations for improving the efficiency, adequacy, and fairness of the procedures agencies use in carrying out administrative programs and to collect data and publish reports useful for evaluating and improving administrative procedures.

ACUS is composed of a Chairman, a Council, and an Assembly. The Chairman is appointed by the President and serves as the chief executive of the Conference. The Council is composed of the Chairman and ten members who serve as a 'board of directors.' The Assembly is comprised of approximately 100 members, consisting of representatives of federal agencies and private citizens, including lawyers, law professors, and others knowledgeable about administrative law and practice. The Assembly ordinarily meets twice a year in plenary session to consider the adoption of formal ACUS recommendations. All members serve on standing committees that develop proposed recommendations in their subject matter areas (for example, adjudication, rulemaking, judicial review, and so on).

The Office of the Chairman contains a small permanent staff of lawyers and support personnel whose responsibility is to administer the day-to-day

---

190 See the Inspector General Act of 1978, Pub. L. No. 95–452, 92 Stat. 1101 (now codified as amended at 5 U.S.C. App. §§ 1–12).

191 ACUS's statutory authorization is found at 5 U.S.C. §§ 591–96.

operations of the agency, organize a research program, serve the membership and committees of the ACUS, and pursue the implementation of adopted recommendations.

ACUS recommendations are non-binding, but are influential because they are consensus-based, and based on objective research. Its budget is quite small, but it serves as a forum for discussing agency procedural problems. Its past recommendations and current activities can be found at ACUS.gov.

5. MEANS OF ENFORCEMENT

There is no overarching, generally applicable theory or authorization for how agencies enforce their mandates. Rather, each program has its own means of doing so, and they vary widely. Traditionally agency statutes provided for an enforcement action brought in federal district court. In such cases, the Department of Justice would prosecute the case and defendants would have a right to a jury trial under the Seventh Amendment.[192] Because such a procedure is cumbersome, especially for small penalties, Congress has provided in many statutes that agencies can enforce their civil penalties through agency adjudication. In such cases, the respondent defends itself in a hearing before an administrative law judge, with an appeal to the agency head and then to the courts – usually directly to the courts of appeals.[193] In a few statutes, the enforcement action must be brought before a separate agency.[194] Substantively, the remedies vary from orders directing the respondent to correct the problem, to civil money penalties, and, in egregious cases, criminal prosecutions.

5.1. REMEDIAL ACTION

Certainly one of the classic responses an agency may have is simply to ensure that the situation is rectified. The agency will therefore issue an order directing that specific action be taken to bring the situation into compliance.[195] A company that fails to do so may then be fined or otherwise penalized. In some instances, most notably our 'Superfund' law that is designed to clean up toxic waste sites,

---

192 For example, under the Clean Water Act, enforcement actions must be brought in a federal district court.

193 For example, a violation of unfair competition rules enforced by the Federal Trade Commission is resolved in such a proceeding.

194 For example, a citation for a violation of a rule issued by the Occupational Safety and Health Administration (OSHA) is heard by the Occupational Safety and Health Review Commission (OSHRC) – a separate, independent agency.

195 For example, the Occupational Safety and Health Act provides: 'Any employer who fails to correct a violation for which a citation has been issued … within the period permitted for its correction … may be assessed a civil penalty of not more than $7,000 for each day during which such failure or violation continues'. 29 U.S.C. § 666(d).

the agency itself may take the remedial action and then charge those who are responsible the costs of doing so.[196]

5.2. MONETARY PENALTIES

Federal statutes provide a vast array of potential penalties. Some statutes provide that anyone who has violated the statute or a regulation carrying out the statute is responsible for a 'civil penalty'[197] of an amount not to exceed a specified amount. That is probably the most common enforcement tool. But Congress can be much more directive in specifying factors to be considered by the agency in enforcement. Many are included in a single paragraph of the Clean Air Act:

> 'In determining the amount of any penalty to be assessed under this section ... the Administrator or the court, as appropriate, shall take into consideration (in addition to such other factors as justice may require) the size of the business, the economic impact of the penalty on the business, the violator's full compliance history and good faith efforts to comply, the duration of the violation as established by any credible evidence (including by evidence other than the applicable test method), payment by the violator of penalties previously assessed for the same violation, the economic benefit of non-compliance, and the seriousness of the violation. ... A penalty may be assessed for each day of violation'.[198]

This statute clearly authorizes the agency or court to impose whatever monetary penalty may be appropriate to provide a significant deterrence and to remove any economic benefit that may accrue from non-compliance. While this section is undoubtedly one of the most comprehensive in describing these considerations, it demonstrates the range of enforcement strategies that may be used by Congress. Note that only Congress can authorize penalties and specify the penalty assessment procedures; that is not within the discretion of the agency.

5.3. CRIMINAL SANCTIONS

Only Congress can make some types of conduct a crime. Thus, an agency cannot issue a rule that says that a violation of one of its rules would constitute criminal

---

196 Comprehensive Environmental Response, Compensation and Liability Act, 42 U.S.C. § 9604.

197 The term 'civil penalty' is used to distinguish the monetary charge from a criminal fine. If it were a criminal proceeding, the US Constitution would require an opportunity for a jury trial under the Sixth Amendment. Moreover, where Congress has assigned the matter (involving 'public rights' rather than a suit at common law) to an agency for adjudication, the Seventh Amendment's right to a jury trial is not violated either. *Atlas Roofing Co., Inc. v. OSHRC*, 430 U.S. 442 (1977).

198 Clean Air Act, 42 U.S.C. § 7413 (e).

conduct. Congress can, however, provide that the violation of an agency's rules constitutes a criminal offence. In such circumstances, the agency can in fact define the nature of the crime by how it sets the rule. Thus, for example, the Clean Air Act provides:

> 'Any person who knowingly violates any requirement or prohibition of … a requirement of any rule, order, waiver, or permit promulgated or approved under [designated sections of the Act] shall be punished by a fine pursuant to [the criminal law] or by imprisonment for not to exceed 5 years, or both'.[199]

Until the early 1980s, criminal enforcement of regulatory requirements was relatively rare. Since then, however, there has been an expansion of criminal sanctions, with numerous regulatory statutes including them.[200] One difficulty is that criminal sanctions have been imposed inconsistently and the actual offences for which criminal prosecutions have been used vary extraordinarily in terms of the severity of the harm resulting from the transgression and the culpability of the defendant. On the other hand, undoubtedly, the stigma of criminal sanctions and the threat of prison have also had a significant effect in securing compliance when previously paying civil penalties was viewed as merely a cost of doing business.

If an agency has statutory authority to impose criminal sanctions, e.g., for a particularly egregious violation, the agency must forward the case to the Department of Justice for prosecution. The DOJ retains the ultimate control of that prosecution – although it will of course give some deference to the agency's wishes.

6. REVIEW AND PROGNOSIS

Until 2017, American administrative law had, on the whole, been remarkably stable for the past 40 years. It took a while for the great upheavals of the 60s and 70s to be refined, but they were integrated into the framework provided by the APA. One period that tested this stability occurred following the election of 1994 and the Republican takeover of the Congress, when some major procedural 'reforms' were advocated. The most radical proposals were blocked, but two new procedural statutes were enacted, one part of which suddenly became important in 2017.

The Small Business Regulatory Enforcement Fairness Act (SBREFA) was enacted in 1995 to amend and strengthen the Regulatory Flexibility Act of

---

199 42 U.S.C. § 7413(c)(1). Other criminal provisions do not require that the offence be 'knowing'.

200 *See* D.K. Brown, 'Criminal Law's Unfortunate Triumph over Administrative Law' (2011) 7 *Journal of Law, Economics & Policy* 657.

1980.[201] This Act requires agencies to consider the impact of their regulations on small entities and for the first time, the amendments authorized small entities who are 'adversely affected or aggrieved by final agency action' to seek judicial review of the agency's analysis.[202] In addition, SBREFA incorporated a separate law, called the Congressional Review Act, which requires that all agencies must submit new rules and their supporting analyses to Congress.[203] The Act provides for an elaborate process by which Congress can undertake to disapprove a rule by passing a statute (technically a 'joint resolution of disapproval') on an expedited basis.[204] In practice, the disapproval provision only is likely to be effective when the Act's carryover provision applies. It provides that rules issued at the end of a session of Congress can be disapproved early in the next session. This has traction when the new Congress (and President) are from a different party than the previous administration. One 'midnight rule" issued at the end of the Clinton Administration was disapproved this way, and, before the opportunity for doing this ended in May of 2017, fourteen Obama administration rules were disapproved by the 115th Congress and President Trump.[205]

The second statute to emerge from the 'regulatory reform wars' of the mid-90s was the Unfunded Mandates Reform Act.[206] It too requires additional analyses of the costs and benefits of regulation and of alternative approaches to achieving the agency's goals that extend and codify those that had been performed for years. But it provides for limited judicial review of those analyses, largely only for whether or not the agency complied with the duties.[207]

Other analytical requirements have been included over the years in executive orders and memoranda in which the President or OMB directs agencies to focus especially on particular issues.[208] These orders were by-and-large retained by the Clinton, Bush II, and Obama administrations. For example, the Obama administration, building on its predecessors, issued an Executive Order that require agencies to review their existing rules to weed out those that are "outmoded, ineffective, insufficient, or excessively burdensome."[209]

201 5 U.S.C. §§ 601–612.

202 5 U.S.C. § 611. Previously, these 'reg-flex analyses' were not judicially reviewable, but rather were explicitly for internal review purposes only.

203 5 U.S.C. § 801.

204 5 U.S.C. § 802. Unlike the legislative veto, which was declared unconstitutional in *INS v. Chadha*, 462 U.S. 919 (1983), this resolution of disapproval must pass both Houses of Congress and be presented to the President for signature (or veto). It is, therefore, fully consonant with the Constitution's bicameralism and presentment requirements for legislation.

205 *See* http://progressivereform.org/assaultscratargets.cfm.

206 5 U.S.C. § 1531 *et seq.*

207 5 U.S.C. § 1571. It also provides explicitly that the information in the analyses is part of the rulemaking record during judicial review of the rule.

208 For example, Ex. Or. 13132, 64 Fed. Reg. 43255 (10 August 1999) directs agencies to pay special attention to issues of federalism and the allocation of responsibilities between the federal government and the states.

209 Section 6(a), Ex. Or. 13563, 76 Fed. Reg. 3821 (21 March 2011).

It then issued an Executive Order directing agencies to facilitate international regulatory cooperation and harmonization[210] and repeated the call for a retrospective analysis of regulations, while emphasizing that OIRA is in charge of that effort.[211]

It can be argued that these demands for new analyses have had only a marginal effect on the day-to-day operations of agencies since they were already required to consider all relevant information both by the courts interpreting the APA and by the string of Executive Orders on rulemaking. But these new duties did contribute to a feeling on the part of agencies of being under siege, under increasing layers of management. Perhaps because of this, perhaps because most regulatory statutes are now relatively mature and hence the 'easy' rules have been issued and the more difficult ones remain, there is a perception among those who are supportive of regulation that it has become overly difficult and time consuming for agencies to issue new regulations. That in turn has led to an increasing use of non-legislative rules such as guidelines, interpretations, letters, and the like by agencies.

On the other hand, despite the four decades of 'regulatory reform' efforts that have resulted in increasing procedural and analytical rigor in the regulatory process, there continued to be a strong campaign led by the business community and conservatives in Congress for adding even more rigor and, indeed, for reducing what they call the 'regulatory burden'. With the election of Donald Trump, these campaigners are now in the driver's seat. One of the President's senior advisers announced that one of the Administration's top priorities is the 'deconstruction of the Administrative State'.[212] Thus, it was not surprising that in the first weeks of the Trump Administration the President issued a series of executive orders mandating that agencies consider how to rescind specific high-profile regulations issued by the Obama Administration, and requiring that, going forward, for every new regulation issued by an agency, at least two regulations with equivalent total (gross) cost on the economy be rescinded.[213] A follow-up order required agencies to appoint internal 'Regulatory Reform Task forces' to 'evaluate existing regulations ... and make recommendations to the agency head regarding their repeal, replacement, or modification'.[214] A third order required agencies to report on ways to reorganize themselves – designed

210 Ex. Or. 13609, 77 Fed. Reg. 26413 (4 May 2012).

211 Ex. Or. 13610, 77 Fed. Reg. 28469 (14 May 2012). In its review of significant proposed and final regulations OIRA is making more of the policy decisions or at least controlling them by making sure they comport with OIRA's views of administrative policy.

212 P. Rucker & R. Costa, 'Bannon vows a daily fight for 'deconstruction of the administrative state', *Washington Post*, (23 February 2017) <www.washingtonpost.com/politics/top-wh-strategist-vows-a-daily-fight-for-deconstruction-of-the-administrative-state/2017/02/23/03f6b8da-f9ea-11e6-bf01-d47f8cf9b643_story.html?utm_term=.ad1a7b04d661> accessed 08.04.2017.

213 Ex. Or. 13771, issued 30 January 2017, 82 Fed. Reg. 9339 (3 February 2017).

214 Ex. Or. 13777, issued 24 February 2017, 82 Fed. Reg. 12285 (1 March 2017).

to lead to an OMB plan 'to reorganize the executive branch in order to improve the efficiency, effectiveness, and accountability of agencies'.[215] These measures, coupled with aggressive use of the Congressional Review Act to quickly abolish rules issued at the end of the Obama Administration[216], draconian proposed budget cuts for EPA[217] and other regulatory agencies, and numerous bills in Congress that would eliminate judicial deference to agencies and dismantle the APA's rulemaking provisions, portend potentially large changes in American administrative law.

However, there are still limits, inherent in our system of checks and balances, to what a President can do himself. New laws have to pass both houses of Congress and the Senate's filibuster rules still require a super-majority of 60 votes to cut off debate on legislation. Nor can agencies rescind rules willy-nilly. Amending or repealing rules constitutes 'rulemaking' under the APA, and agencies will find it difficult to produce an about-face on rules they have just spent years justifying. Supporters of regulation will doubtless seek judicial review of agency attempts to do that.

How these challenges fare in the courts depends on several variables. Now that President Trump has succeeded in replacing Justice Scalia with the equally conservative Justice Gorsuch, the Court is back to its divided state with Justice Kennedy being a swing vote on many issues. If he or one of the more four more liberal justices were to depart the Court in the next few years, the balance would shift decisively in favour of a Court that would be more sceptical of regulation. This shift was already beginning to happen with respect to the weakening of judicial deference for agency legal interpretations and it might spread to less deference to agency expertise more generally. For now, the lower courts are dominated by Obama nominees, but this will gradually change as President Trump begins to fill the vacancies kept open for him by the Republicans in the last Congress.

The crystal ball is cloudy. Much depends on the elections in 2018 and 2020, but it appears sure that in the next four years, there will be many fewer new rules (not counting rescissions) by executive agencies. Give the difficulty of rulemaking, some agencies might begin to shift back to making policy less visibly through case-by-case adjudication. There will certainly be battles over the enforcement of existing regulatory frameworks in most substantive areas of regulation – and over legislation that would heavily encumber the rulemaking process and reject the consensus that has protected the basic terms

215 Ex. Or. 13781, issued 13 March 2017, 82 Fed. Reg. 13959 (16 March 2017).

216 See text at note 205, *supra*.

217 See Environmental Protection Network, 'Analysis of Trump Administration Proposals for FY2018 Budget for the Environmental Protection Agency' (22 March 2017) <www.4cleanair.org/sites/default/files/Documents/EPA_Budget_Analysis_EPN_3-22-2017.pdf> accessed 08.04.2017.

of the Administrative Procedure Act for seventy years. Shortly after the Act was enacted, the Supreme Court said, 'The Act … represents a long period of study and strife; it settles long-continued and hard-fought contentions, and enacts a formula upon which opposing social and political forces have come to rest.'[218] The political forces have now alighted once more, and the APA is in danger of being discarded.

It is also likely that more responsibility will be shifted away from federal regulation with more reliance on the states, on voluntary measures, and on the 'market'. Examples of such decentralized approaches might be:

- an agency contracts with a firm to achieve certain regulatory goals;
- an agency entrusts a regulated firm to put in place audits and management programs to ensure compliance with specified performance goals, or
- the agency and a company or group of companies jointly undertake to achieve a desired goal.

The procedures by which such programs would work need to be developed. Issues that need to be considered are:

- the ability of the public, or at least parts of the public to participate in shaping the duties;
- how are the standards to be set;
- how are the standards to be enforced;
- how are disagreements between the participants to be resolved.

If this predication is right, an important question in American administrative law (if it is not 'deconstructed' by the Trump Administration) will be how to develop the relationship between the public and private sectors in achieving decentralized regulation and the achievement of broader goals. While the public's faith in corporations is currently very low in the wake of continual revelations of wrong-doing by both the companies and those who putatively were ensuring their compliance with the law, the current governmental leadership is not likely to turn to government agencies to provide all the essential decisions and enforcement of governmentally imposed duties. Instead, we will likely enter a great debate over the proper allocation of power between the public and private sectors and the means by which these decisions are made and, critically important in the current environment, enforced. That is likely to be the next frontier of American administrative law.

218 *Wong Yang Sung v. McGrath*, 339 U.S. 33, 40 (1950).

BIBLIOGRAPHY

ABA Section of Administrative Law & Regulatory Practice, *A Blackletter Statement of Federal Administrative Law*, (2d ed.) (2013) (1st ed. originally published at 54 Admin. L. Rev. 1 (2002)).

Aman, A.C., *Administrative Law and Process* (3d ed.) (2014 Lexis-Nexis).

Aman, Jr. A.C & Mayton, W.T. *Hornbook on Administrative Law* (3d ed.) (2014 West Academic)

Asimow, M & Levin, R.M., *State and Federal Administrative Law* (4th ed.) (2014 West Academic).

Breyer, S., Stewart, R., Sunstein, C., Vermeule, A., & Herz, M., *Administrative Law and Regulatory Policy*, 7th ed., New York: Aspen Publishers, 2011.

Brown, D.K., 'Criminal Law's Unfortunate Triumph over Administrative Law' (2011) 7 *Journal of Law, Economics & Policy* 657.

Buckman, D.F., 'Requirement that there be Continuing Violation to Maintain Citizen Suit under Federal Environmental Protection Statutes-Post-*Gwaltney* Case' (1999) 158 *American Law Reports Federal* 519.

Cass, R.A., Diver, C.S., Beermann, J.M. & Freeman, J., *Administrative Law: Cases and Materials* (6th ed.) (2011 Aspen).

Clark, T.C., *Attorney General's Manual on the Administrative Procedure Act*. U.S. Department of Justice (1947), reprinted in Funk, W.F., & Lubbers, J.S. (eds.), *Federal Administrative Procedure Sourcebook*, 5th ed., Chicago: III, Section of Administrative Law and Regulatory Practice, American Bar Association, 2016.

Coglianese, C. 'Assessing Consensus: The Promise and Performance of Negotiated Rulemaking' (1997) 46 *Duke Law Journal* 1255.

Davis K.C. & Pierce, Jr., R.J., *Administrative Law Treatise*, New York: Aspen Law & Business, 2002.

Fox, W.F., *Understanding Administrative Law* (6th ed.) (2012 LexisNexis Publishing).

Freeman, J. & Langbein, L., 'Regulatory Negotiation and the Legitimacy Benefit', (2000) 9 *New York University Environmental Law Journal* 60.

Funk, W.F., 'A Primer on Non-legislative Rules' (2001) 53 *Administrative Law Review*, 1321.

Funk, W.F. & Lubbers, J.S., *Federal Administrative Procedure Sourcebook: Statutes and Related Materials* (5th ed.) (2016 ABA Book Publishing).

Funk, W.F. & Seamon, R.H., *Administrative Law: Examples and Explanations*, (4th ed.) (2011 Aspen).

Funk, W.F., Shapiro, S.A. & Weaver, R.L., *Administrative Procedure and Practice: Problems and Cases* (5th ed.) (2014 West Academic).

Glicksman, R.L., & Levy, R.E., *Administrative Law: Agency Action in Legal Context* (2d ed.) (2015 Foundation Press).

Harter, P.J, 'Assessing the Assessors: The Actual Performance of Negotiated Rulemaking' (2000) 9 *New York University Environmental Law Journal* 32.

Herz, M., Murphy, R., & Watts., K, eds., *A Guide to Judicial and Political Review of Federal Agencies*, (2d ed.) (2015 ABA Book Publishing).

Hickman, K & Pierce, Jr., R.J., *Federal Administrative Law, Cases and Materials* (2d ed.) (2014 Foundation Press).

Houk, C., et al., 'The Ombudsman in Federal Agencies – Master List of Federal Ombuds Offices' (2016) prepared for the Administrative Conference of the United States (ACUS) <https://www.acus.gov/appendix/ombudsman-federal-agencies-master-list-federal-ombuds-offices> accessed 08.04.2017.

Koch, Jr., C.H., Jordan, III, W.S., Murphy, R.M., & Virelli, III, L.J., *Administrative Law: Cases and Materials* (6th ed.) (2010 LexisNexis).

Lawson, G., *Federal Administrative Law* (7th ed.) (2016 West Academic).

Levin, R.M. & Lubbers, J.S., *Administrative Law and Process in a Nutshell* (6th ed.) (2017 West Nutshell Series).

Litwak, J., ed., *A Guide to Federal Agency Adjudication* (2012 ABA Book Publishing).

Lubbers, J.S. 'Achieving Policymaking Consensus: The (Unfortunate) Waning of Negotiated Rulemaking' (2008) 49 *South Texas Law Review* 987.

Lubbers, J.S., *A Guide to Federal Agency Rulemaking*, 5th ed., Chicago: III, Section of Administrative Law and Regulatory Practice, American Bar Association, 2012.

Lubbers, J.S., 'Fail to Comment at Your Own Risk: Does Issue Exhaustion Have a Place in Judicial Review of Rules?' (May 2015) Report to the Administrative Conference of the United States, <https://www.acus.gov/sites/default/files/documents/Final%20 Issue%20Exhaustion%20Report%2005052014_1.pdf> accessed 08.04.2017; to be published in (2018) 70 *Administrative Law Review* 1 (forthcoming).

Mashaw, J.L., 'Administration and "The Democracy": Administrative Law from Jackson to Lincoln, 1829–1861' (2008) 117 *Yale Law Journal* 1568.

Mashaw, M., Merrill, R., Shane, P., Magill, E, Cuellar, M., & Parillo, N, *Administrative Law: The American Public Law System – Cases and Materials* (7th ed.) (2014 West Academic).

Pierce, Jr., R.J., *Administrative Law Treatise* (5th ed.), (2009 Aspen) (formerly by Davis & Pierce). (Supplemented annually).

Pierce, Jr., R.J., Shapiro, S.A., & Verkuil, P.R., *Administrative Law and Process* (6th ed.) (2014 Foundation Press).

Popper A.F., McKee, G.M., Varona, A.E., Harter, P.J., Niles, & M., Pasquale, F., *Administrative Law: A Contemporary Approach* (3d ed.) (2016 West Academic).

Rogers, J.M., Healy, M.P. & Krotoszynski, R.J., *Administrative Law*, (3d ed.) (2012 Aspen).

Schuck, P.H., *Foundations of Administrative Law* (3d ed.) (2012 LexisNexis).

Schwartz, B., Corrada, R.L. & Brown, Jr., J.R., *Administrative Law: A Casebook*, (7th ed.) (2010 Aspen).

Seamon, R.H., *Administrative Law – A Context and Practice Casebook* (2013 Carolina Academic Press).

Shepherd, G.B., 'The Administrative Procedure Act Emerges from New Deal Politics', 90 *Northwestern Law Review* 1557 (1996).

Strauss P.L., ed., *Administrative Law Stories* (2006 Foundation Press).

Strauss, P.L., *Administrative Justice in the United States* (3d ed.) (2016 Carolina Academic Press).

Strauss, P.L., 'Overseer, or "The Decider"? The President in Administrative Law', 75 *George Washington Law Review* 696 (2007).

Strauss, P.L., Rakoff, T., Farina, C.R., & Metzger, *Gellhorn and Byse's Administrative Law, Cases and Comments, 11th*, (2011 University Case Book Series, Foundation Press).

Werhan, K.M., *Principles of Administrative Law* (2d ed.) (2014 West Academic).

Wooster, A.K., 'Actions Brought Under Federal Water Pollution Control Act (Clean Water Act) Amendments of 1972' (2000) 163 *American Law Reports Federal* 531.

WEBSITES

ABA Administrative Procedure Database. Developed and maintained with the cooperation and support of the American Bar Association's Section of Administrative Law and Regulatory Practice and the Florida State University College of Law. Contains links to federal agency home pages, state resources, historical materials (such as Attorney General's manual on the APA), and other useful links. <http://fall.fsulawrc.com/admin/>

Administrative Conference of the United States. Contains links to past (1968–95) and current activities. <www.acus.gov>

Congress.gov – Congress's website: <www.congress.gov>

Government Accountability Office (GAO) Reports <www.gao.gov>

Government Printing Office. Official gov't documents <www.gpo.gov/fdsys> [To be replaced soon by <https://www.govinfo.gov/>]

Louisiana State University's government website. A comprehensive link to federal agencies and subunits from all three branches. <www.lib.lsu.edu/gov/index.html>

Office of the Federal Register. Contains (searchable) Federal Register (1994 forward), Code of Federal Regulations, Semiannual Regulatory Agenda, Public Laws (1994 Forward), U.S. Government Manual (1995-forward), Weekly Compilation of Presidential Docs. (1993-forward) <www.archives.gov/federal-register>

Regulations.gov – the federal government's "one-stop shop" for filing comments in rulemaking. <www.regulations.gov>

Regulatory Information Service Center, (Unified Agenda of Regulations – 1995-present, and information about OIRA reviews) <www.reginfo.gov>

Small Business Association Office of Advocacy. Lots of useful links about Regulatory Flexibility Act <www.sba.gov/advo>

The Center for Regulatory Effectiveness, Business-oriented group site with a wealth of useful information on regulation, especially the Data Quality Act. <http://thecre.com>. Has extensive archive of "Inside Administration" papers at <www.thecre.com/ombpapers/centralrev.html>

U.S. Supreme Court < www.supremecourt.gov>

COMPARATIVE REMARKS

René SEERDEN

1. INTRODUCTION

In this chapter some comparative remarks will be made on the basis of the contributions in the previous chapters. The reason for making these remarks is to give some further insight into the main structure and features of administrative law in the European Union, the EU Member States and the United States of America, and to determine whether these developments are in tune with one another or whether they are clearly divergent.

As already mentioned in the introductory remarks to this book, it is not the purpose of this comparative chapter to make an extensive analysis of all the possible similarities and differences in the field of administrative law between the various EU Member States, the USA and at the level of the EU.

In the first place, I think that it is very difficult for anybody to give such an overall analysis. To fully understand the administrative law system of a country it is absolutely necessary to have full information and knowledge about the historical, political, social and economic context in which this system is incorporated. It is not easy to have this information and knowledge for one's own home country, let alone for more than five other legal systems. So, the 'real comparison' I leave to the readers of this book. They can make their 'in depth' comparisons on those topics in which they are most interested and specialized.

Secondly, as is also indicated in the introductory remarks, this book is meant as a (first) step for subsequent discussions, research and further writings. As in the previous editions of this book I do not want to give this process too strong a direction by overemphasizing the comparative aspects.

A third reason for the absence of very detailed comparison here is that, although I could make use of the contributions of the first three editions, and by making editorial comments on the draft updates for this fourth edition, this compatibility has (still) not always been achieved. Of course, this is logical in the light of the fact that we are dealing with many countries, many authors with different backgrounds, some new authors, different approaches, different timetables, etc. Further study of legislation, case law and the comments and proposals by academic writers would be necessary. This clearly goes beyond the scope of this book, which is meant as an introductory step and is especially written for educational purposes, towards one or more of those studies.[1]

The main question here will be whether it can be said that we are witnessing something of the rise of a *ius commune* in administrative law. This seems especially relevant to the EU, but in this age of 'globalization' it is also relevant in relation to the USA. I will make summary comparative remarks (by pointing out the most remarkable similarities and discrepancies) related to the most central items of administrative law that are addressed in the various contributions. Thereby I hope to shed some light on the main trends. In the following paragraphs, the framework for the contributions will also be the framework for making these comparative remarks. In this respect, the enumeration of countries (whether or not between brackets) in the comparative remarks is merely intended as an illustration and is not necessarily meant to be exhaustive.

2. COMPARATIVE REMARKS

2.1. ADMINISTRATIVE LAW

In most of the contributions to this book a division is made between general administrative law and more specific administrative law. The general part is concerned with rules and principles common to the entire field of administrative action (decision-making process and access to court), while the special parts deal with policy areas such as the environment, land-use planning, social security, tax, education, migration, etc. The latter have their own statutes and (delegated) legislation, which deal with the rights and duties of individuals towards the government *(vice versa)*, mostly executed through decisions of the administration. The focus of administrative law is really that of the administration towards the individual and often concerns the execution of legislation through an individual decision. The latter, however, does not mean that the making of generally binding rules (legislation) that may affect the rights and duties of individuals is not a part of administrative law, but in practice the main field of administrative law deals with individual decision-making, such as the issuing of permits, grants, administrative sanctions, etc.

It seems that the general part of administrative law is for a large part (originally) developed by the courts and not the legislator, although in Germany the Constitution (*Grundgesetz*) plays a large role as well. For instance, in France, which is characterized by a clear division between administrative and

1 One of these studies, partly based on this book, is the forthcoming (May 2018): *Cases, Materials and Text on Judicial Review of Administrative Action*, edited by Chris Backes and Mariolina Eliantonio (Series: Ius Commune Casebooks for the Common Law of Europe), Hart Publishing.

private law, the *Conseil d'Etat* has developed general principles. In the United Kingdom this development is less present or clear, because the ordinary courts are competent in administrative matters and as a general rule the administration is subject to common law. On the other hand it is still recognized, certainly in the last twenty to thirty years, that administrative (procedural) law is a separate branch of law and that the Administrative Court as part of the High Court – until 2000 named the Queen's Bench of the High Court – is more an administrative than an ordinary court when it deals with applications for judicial review. It should also be mentioned here that in the UK tribunals play an important role and were reformed in 2007 and since then are part of the court system. In the USA, like the UK a common law system exists but unlike the UK there is a written Constitution, the Constitution deals with the Judicial Branch and in that perspective judicial review (see further paragraph 2.5).

Also in the Netherlands the ordinary courts and the administrative courts developed the general principles of proper administration (*algemene beginselen van behoorlijk bestuur*), that are a relevant tool for review by the courts. In addition, however, there was a major codification in 1994 of these principles in the General Administrative Law Act (*Algemene wet bestuursrecht*) in combination with rules about procedures of decision-making and access to administrative courts. The latter occurred even earlier in Germany with the codifications of the *Verwaltungsverfahrensgesetz* and the *Verwaltungsgerichtsordnung*. For the United States the Administrative Procedure Act can be mentioned and for France the *Code de Justice Administrative*. One has to bear in mind that the scope of this codification of general administrative law differs and that it is always possible that more specific legislative acts (*lex specialis derogat legi generali*) derogate from these general legislative acts. Some of the contributions are very clear in that respect (Netherlands). What you see is that the (further) codification of general administrative law often results in a fresh and strong scholarly interest and the improvement of the quality of the administration and court-proceedings. Especially for students the availability of (general) legislation makes the comparison of systems more easy. To some contributions (Netherlands) key-provisions are added. In the other contributions reference is made to relevant websites.[2]

The question is whether or not the State form – unitary or federal – is of relevance for the development of general administrative law. Of course a division between federal and State matters could also give rise to the use of different administrative law. One often sees that federal administrative law is also applied by the constituent States (Germany and the United States). It seems that the highest courts play a more important role here and in that perspective it must

---

2 For the European continent and the States addressed here, it is worthwhile to refer to *The Maastricht Collection, Volume II: Comparative Public Law, Part II (Administrative Law)*: edited by S. Hardt and N. Kornet, 5th edition, Europa Law Publishing, 2017.

be noticed that in federal States – which are more likely to have constitutional courts – the constitutional courts are the highest courts, although the competence of these courts may differ (see further paragraph 2.5).

One can see that in the European countries the dimension of 'Europe' is becoming more part of their systems. One should not forget that the Court of Justice of the European Union (Luxembourg) but also the European Court of Human Rights (Strasbourg) are the highest courts concerning the application of the EU-Treaties and secondary EU-legislation and the European Convention of Human Rights respectively and in that respect can overrule national law and (therefore) national courts. It cannot be said yet how, due to the recent coming into force at the EU level of the Charter of Fundamental Rights, the relation between the two courts will develop.

2.2. THE ADMINISTRATION

One could argue about whether the question of who is administrating is really part of administrative law or not. Some will say, since it is concerned with the allocation of competencies at the central or decentralized State level, that it is part of constitutional law. Apart from the fact that in my opinion constitutional law and administrative law merge more and more and certainly in this respect, I think it is worthwhile to give the reader an idea of who is administrating, in order to illustrate who is opposed to the individual. Is it an organ at the local level and maybe part of an elected body, is it a Minister, is it an agency within such a public body or belonging to another body or acting independently, etc.? In addition, generally, not one but many organs are involved in the entire decision-making process throughout all its phases: the initial decision, the decision on objection and/or in appeal. For this reason it is interesting to give a glance to the 'administration' also from the perspective that with the shift in competent administrative organs different rules may become applicable.

In some contributions there is not so much said about the administration (who hands out permits, who is enforcing etc.) for instance, in the chapter on the United States of America. The reason for this could be that it is seen as something outside administrative law or because only the federal administrative law is addressed and there agencies are the main organs, that are more or less strongly related to national ministries. In Germany (more so than in the United States?) in addition to federal administrative agencies, national ministries themselves and also organs of the constituent States and even local authorities play an important role in executing federal competencies. In addition to State organs and agencies, administrative organs of local authorities (municipalities and provinces) play a role. It becomes clear from most of the contributions that if the local authorities have competencies these are often delegated to them on the basis of specific statutes and that there is not much more room for real autonomous rule-making.

In the unitary States addressed here (the Netherlands, France and United Kingdom) one also sees that competencies for various administrative organs exist at all the levels of the State. In addition to dividing administrative powers over the traditional territorial entities, functional decentralization is also at stake or independent bodies are set up. Both functionally decentralized bodies and independent administrative organs have very specific powers limited to one topic of public policy. The difference between the two is that functional authorities, for instance, the water authorities in the Netherlands, (just as the traditional territorial authorities) have their basis in elections by the population, while independent bodies don't have that basis.

At the EU level this abundance of numbers and forms of the administration is almost a non-issue since in most matters the execution of EU legislation towards individuals is not applied by organs of the EU itself but through the administration of the Member States. In some fields (e.g. competition law) the European Commission can be regarded as an administrative organ that directly acts towards individuals. Of course it also acts towards the Member States themselves. This latter internal relationship, which obviously exists in every State between 'higher' and 'lower' administrative bodies/organs, is not addressed further here: there is – as a general rule – no external effect that directly touches the rights of individuals.

The previous part deals with administrative organs that take the initial decision. As to which body within or outside 'the administration' is competent to decide on objections or appeals against these decisions, see paragraph 2.5.

2.3. LEGAL INSTRUMENTS

It is obvious that the administration mainly acts on the basis of explicit administrative law competencies that are found in specific statutes and delegated legislation. The forms of these actions may differ from individual decisions (permits, grants, administrative sanctions) to generally applicable rules. Mostly the latter are made by elected organs or at a more central level. Besides this classical form of administrative action other instruments are used that often have a more indirect effect towards individuals: plans, circulars, policy rules etc. One of the main questions is what their exact legal force is and whether or not they can be directly and singularly challenged in (an administrative) court.

Which court is competent is really apparent when the administration makes use of private law instruments. Just as private persons and private legal entities public legal entities take part in daily life by buying supplies, etc. that are necessary for their operations. There is no need to address these activities differently and there is no reason why in these cases different judges should be competent to settle disputes. That may be different where public bodies do not act in the same way as private persons. For instance, where they clearly serve the general interest or where they try to achieve public law goals through private law instruments instead or in addition to the use of private rights: by using property rights, starting actions under tort law or to conclude agreements.

For instance, in the Netherlands it has been decided by the Supreme Court, competent in civil matters, that there are restrictions in this perspective for the administration. The use of private law is forbidden where this would result in an unacceptable non-application of public law. Where private law action is possible public law principles like the principles of proper administration remain applicable. In other States, such as France, you see that agreements in which the public authorities participate (concessions, public services etc.) are dealt with in legislation and do not fall under general private law. This does not only concern contracts that can be concluded by every other party but also agreements that are really of a public law nature, namely those in which a public authority restricts itself in its use of administrative law competence. An example of the latter is the so-called administrative law agreement (*öffentlich-rechtlicher Vertrag*) in Germany, provided for by legislation and that can only be opposed in administrative courts and not in the ordinary courts (unlike the real private law agreements of 'buying and selling'). In the common law systems of the USA and the UK there seems to be much more room for the administration to use private law instruments (common law) as extra legal means: anything which is not forbidden is permitted. However, also in the common law systems questions of 'demarcation' may arise, for instance, concerning procedural exclusivity or in other words when is a body susceptible to judicial review and, if so, if there is still room for private claims. And what is the justification, not only in these common law systems but also in other States addressed here, that the sole recovery of damages even in case of public law decisions often lies with a private claim, which has to be addressed by the ordinary courts and not the administrative courts?

By the way, in some States the relation between administrative and private law and especially the use of private law instruments to achieve public goals instead of or in addition to administrative law competencies seems to be more of an issue than that of the combination of administrative and criminal law. That is, in my view, somewhat strange because more and more in the field of enforcement of legislation – see, for instance, Germany and the Netherlands – the accumulation of competencies within both fields seems to be possible and these competencies are within the remit of one and the same State organ. An exception may be the United Kingdom, where on the basis of the case law mentioned in the contribution to this book, one sees that the application for judicial review is often at stake where competencies of a criminal law nature are at issue. Whether or not something is within the field of administrative or criminal law could have consequences for aspects such as rights for parties (*nemo tenetur, una via* and *ne bis in idem*) rules of evidence, the test made by the judges etc.

2.4. RULES AND PRINCIPLES

Legality is the founding principle of administrative law: no unilateral public law action that involves rights and duties of individuals (in a negative way) is possible without an explicit and specific legal basis. This means that for positive actions it is not necessarily a prerequisite and as we have seen action under private law, at least in some States, doesn't require an explicit legal basis either. Especially in Germany the principle of legality – in the constitutional framework of human rights – is extensively elaborated. By the way, it seems that more than in any other state in Germany the doctrine (opinion of writers) plays a very important role in the development and interpretation of (administrative) law.

Administrative action needs to be in conformity with the 'law'. Ultimately it is of course up to the courts to decide on the lawfulness of administrative action. Primarily this is a test on the basis of written law, but they make use of unwritten law.

As to written law one sees that in dualistic systems (like the United Kingdom, the United States and to a great extent also Germany) international law will only be applied when it is transformed into national law. The Netherlands and France are examples of States that are more open to international law. Of course this concerns traditional international law and not supranational EU law, since the European Court of Justice has made it very clear that directly applicable EU law has supremacy over the national law of the Member States. Where no international or supranational law exists only national law is part of the test. The sovereignty of Parliament, for instance, in the UK, although a new constitutional hypothesis is emerging, makes it difficult for the courts to test the legality of Acts of Parliament. In this respect the application of the Human Rights Act in the UK seems to be becoming more important. At this moment the consequences of the Brexit are not clear yet. In some States a constitutionality test is possible and mostly constitutional courts decide on this but not necessarily.

Unwritten law also forms part of the test. A clear example of that is France where unwritten general principles of law (*principes généraux du droit*) play an important role in the case law of the administrative courts. In Germany such principles are derived from the Constitution. In the Netherlands some unwritten principles of proper administration still play a role in the case law of the courts (like the principles of legitimate expectations and legal certainty) but many (formal) principles have been codified, such as the principle of due care and the duty to give reasons. The proportionality principle, also as a result of its application on the EU level, plays an important role in many legal systems (France and Germany). In England the proportionality principle (due to the European dimension) has only recently appeared. There the principle of reasonableness leaves more room for the administration to use its discretion (see further paragraph 2.5).

All the countries addressed in this book are, regardless of their possible differences in State form, the competent courts and procedural law, democratic States adhering to the Rule of Law. It already follows from the above that administrative law is based on identical principles. From a procedural perspective one can mention *audi et alteram partem* and *nemo iudex in sua causa*. More recent phenomena are the ombudsman and the principle of openness of the administration and its decision-making.

As already mentioned under 1 in some States (large parts of) general administrative law has (have) been codified. Germany is an example where the decision-making procedures by the administration (*Verwaltungsverfahrensgesetz*) and access to the courts in administrative matters (*Verwaltungsgerichtsordnung*) is laid down in legislation. Almost 25 years ago – since then many times adjusted – this was done in the Netherlands (*Algemene wet bestuursrecht*). Of course differences exist between these General Administrative Law Codes especially concerning the organization of the courts (see paragraph 2.5). In addition to the two major topics of the German codification the Dutch code also deals with other items, such as enforcement and supervision. France is an example where several legislative acts especially dealing with the organization of and proceedings before the administrative courts have been systematically compiled in the *Code de Justice Administrative*. Consequently it is not really comparable with the German and Dutch codification, unlike the American Administrative Procedure Act for the process of decision and rule making and to some extent the Civil Procedure Rules in England concerning the procedures of the application for judicial review. Is codification of administrative law at the level of the EU the next phase?

2.5. ACCESS TO COURT AND (PRIOR) OUT-OF-COURT PROCEEDINGS

Before one can go to court against decisions of the administration in every State *prior out-of-court proceedings* exist. The reasons for these proceedings are various.

Sometimes one has to lodge an objection with the same administrative body that took the initial decision. In the Netherlands this *bezwaar* is the general rule on the basis of the *Algemene wet bestuursrecht*. In that procedure there is room for a hearing before an independent commission. In France such a complaint procedure is only the case where a specific statute obliges it, so is generally not required for the *recours pour excès de pouvoir*. Moreover in France if you voluntarily ask the administration to withdraw the decision or to change it, the time limit for commencing court action is suspended.

In Germany there is also an objection procedure (*Widerspruch)* on the basis of the *Verwaltungsgerichtsordnung*. The same administrative organ that took the initial decision is competent if the complaint is justified. In other cases the supervising authority gives the ruling and in my view the term 'appeal' would be more suited. Here the focus is on self-regulation by the (same) administration. In the United States of America one sees that a more independent board/tribunal within or outside the administration has adjudicating powers. In the United Kingdom that may be the case as well but also many tribunals have been established by statute in specific areas, more and more acting as independent 'courts', partly due to general legislation dealing with these tribunals, rather than being dependent on the administration. Despite the fact that they are not part of the administration not only the lawfulness (legality) but also the merits of the case are tested. It must be mentioned that some years ago a reform has been made to come to a new unified tribunal system forming part of the court system.

In the common law systems it seems that the use of the available prior out-of-court proceedings is not a prerequisite for an application for judicial review, although the instrument of 'leave' could be used to decide otherwise. In most of the other States addressed objection or appeal procedures are obligatory and are a formal necessity for court action to be admissible. For that reason generally a kind of interest is needed to be accessible in these prior out-of-court proceedings (similar for access to court.

For a case (in light of an individual decision) to be admissible some kind of interest is necessary. In the Netherlands *standing* in administrative matters is dealt with in Article 1:2 in combination with Article 8:1 of the *Algemene wet bestuursrecht*: the person in question must have an interest that is directly involved with the decision at hand. The administrative courts employ a broad interpretation in this respect. Some specific statutes make it possible for everybody, without the need of showing some kind of interest, to participate in administrative decision-making and until 2005 merely the participation sufficed to have standing in court. Since then for court proceedings – except in cases of access to public documents – an interest is required. In France the administrative courts, due to the fact that they operate as a kind of supervisor in the general interest (*recours objectif*) also have a very wide view as to the spectrum of the *intérêt pour agir*. In the United Kingdom sufficient interest is required on the basis of the Civil Procedure Rules and on the basis of the UK-chapter in this book one can say that this test does not cause too many difficulties as regards access to courts. Maybe as in the Netherlands and France this is because of the fact that judicial review originally was about supervision by the King of courts and the administration. Although some differences may occur between the remedies (*Klagen*) stated in the *Verwaltungsgerichtordnung* at hand, in Germany access to court against administrative decisions is more a matter of the protection of subjective rights. One could say that the test here is maybe somewhat more stringent than in the other countries – in the Netherlands the introduction in 2013 of the *Schutznorm* in court procedures follows the German system – mentioned so far. By the way, as the German and EU-contribution shows, one has to notice that EU legislation may give rise to the extension of rights of actions in administrative courts. In some specific matters, like environmental protection, on the basis of statutory provisions an *actio popularis* has to be foreseen. In the United States a group may only sue for interests of its members and not solely for its particular cause. Generally the issue of standing seems to be interpreted somewhat more strictly there.

The rules for standing for individuals before the courts at the level of the EU are very strict, mainly because most legal instruments are regulations and directives, which have a broad range of potentially affected people but are not addressed to them directly and do not individually concern them.

Under 1 it was already said that *constitutional courts* in federal States may play an important role in administrative law since they may be the highest courts: The Supreme Court in the United States and the *Bundesverfassungsgericht* in Germany. In addition there are (highest) administrative courts (the *Bundesverwaltungsgericht* in Germany and the Supreme Court in the United States). France is an example of a unitary State with a constitutional court (*Conseil Constitutionnel*) and a (highest) administrative court (*Conseil d'Etat*). In the following a description is given about the relation between these constitutional courts and the (other) administrative courts as well as the position of the administrative courts in the other countries, of which the highest are: the Supreme Court, the former House of Lords, (United Kingdom) and (because of competencies in different matters) the *Afdeling bestuursrechtspraak van de Raad van State*, the *Centrale Raad van Beroep* and the Supreme Court (the Netherlands).

As to the *competence* of the various courts, one may see striking differences. For instance, in the Netherlands and Germany the competence of the administrative courts is based on whether or not there is a public law decision for an individual case (*besluit*/*Verwaltungsakt*). This means that for private law and factual actions of the administration the ordinary courts are still competent. That may also be so for the recovery of damages in case of (un)lawful administrative decisions and certainly in the Netherlands for the possibility to challenge directly generally applicable legislation (statutes and delegated legislation). (As an aside, in the Netherlands the constitutionality of Acts of Parliament may not be tested). In Germany there is – depending on the *Länder* – the possibility for individuals to question legislative measures below the level of *Landesgesetz* in the administrative courts (*Normenkontrollverfahren* at the *Oberverwaltungsgericht*).

Such a dual system may of course lead to different approaches and the need for coordination. For instance, in the Netherlands the ordinary courts deny jurisdiction where an action can be brought in the administrative courts against actions of the administration and where that possibility exists (regardless of whether it has been used): the legality of the decision of the administration can no longer be reviewed (*formele rechtskracht*). This thinking is also applied in Germany (*Bestandskraft*) but their formal rules as to conflicts of jurisdiction between the administrative courts and ordinary courts have been codified in the *Gerichtsverfassungsgesetz*.

In the common law systems of the UK and USA no separate administrative courts exist. They form part of the ordinary courts, which could be, but is not necessarily, a guarantee for more coordination. As follows from part 54 of the Civil Procedures Rules court access in the United Kingdom is less formal than under Dutch or German law: 'claims can be made to review the lawfulness of an enactment, decision or action or failure to act in relation to the exercise of a public function'. On the other hand one also sees here that discussions of the division between public and private law arise. (In the beginning) courts decided that in administrative matters the ordinary remedies could not be requested outside the formal procedure of an application for judicial review (and the other way around: a private case cannot be dealt with through an application for judicial review).

In France the range of actions of the administration that may lead to access to an administrative court is even broader because of its competence to decide on certain contracts (*contrats administratifs)* in which the administration participates and matters of liability. Because of the divide between administrative courts and ordinary courts in cases where the administration is involved a special court has been developed to decide which court should handle the issue, namely the *Tribunal de Conflits*, consisting of members of the *Conseil d'Etat* and the *Cour de Cassation.*

The relevancy of whether an administrative or ordinary court is competent is related to such aspects as which law has to be applied, the procedural costs etc.

The *(administrative) court systems* differ strongly. For instance, in the United Kingdom (High Court, Court of Appeal and Supreme Court) and the United States of America (District Court, Court of Appeal and Supreme Court) the ordinary courts decide about applications for judicial review, while in France administrative courts are competent (*Tribunaux Administratifs, Cours Administratives d'Appel* and *Conseil d'Etat*). In the United States the Supreme Court is also a constitutional court and has a very broad competence, such as discretional review over decisions by the highest court of each State where the validity of a federal statute is questioned or where a question involving the constitution arises. In France there is a separate constitutional court with a very restricted competence. The *Conseil Constitutionnel* is only competent to test the constitutionality of Acts of Parliament before they are enacted and on behalf of one of the parties involved in the legislative process. No direct appeal is therefore possible against Acts of Parliament before the French Council of State. No appeal is possible in the United Kingdom against Acts of Parliament. In the United Kingdom – to some extent this is also the case in the United States with the system of adjudication – many statutes provide for statutory appeal to tribunals. The existence of these – it seems that the distinction between the administration and these tribunals is not so big – may explain why the application for judicial review (on the basis of common law) is applied less than is the case in France. Germany like France also has specific administrative courts in addition to other branches (*Verwaltungsgericht, Oberverwaltungsgericht, Bundesverwaltungsgericht*). Unlike the United States the judicial system is a unitary one, in which the same courts administer the federal and State law. One should bear in mind that the Federal administrative court only decides upon federal law. It is interesting to mention here that in the interests of the unity of administrative law the Federal administrative court may also interpret the general administrative law of the *Länder* where this is identical to the *Verwaltungsverfahrensgesetz*.

As in France but contrary to the United States a separate constitutional court (*Bundesverfassungsgericht*) exists in Germany. Apart from, amongst others, resolving disputes between the *Bund* and the *Länder*, the constitutional court is also competent to decide on the constitutionality of a *Bundesgesetz* or *Landesgesetz* where questions are asked by the lower courts, since the latter are not competent to nullify that kind of legislation themselves. More important here is the fact that also individuals can go to the constitutional court if the administration infringes their constitutional rights (only after exhaustion of the normal courts and after leave has been granted). This does not mean that constitutional rights don't play a role in the normal courts (Netherlands, France). In the past years no important changes in the court systems are made. In the Netherlands the effort to integrate some higher administrative courts did not succeed. Some more informal ways are made available to cooperate.

It is already some years ago, that at the EU level the Court of Justice has become a general court (without a court in first instance) Also the creation of special courts is introduced such as for civil service matters.

It is interesting to notice that in Germany some form of consultation is institutionalized between the (administrative) courts (*gemeinsamer/großer Senat*), for instance, in order to prevent discrepancies in case law, but of course the only court that can bind all the other courts is the Constitutional Court.

It is interesting to point out here that in France and the Netherlands the position of the Councils of State is not really at stake anymore, because it was somewhat fragile in light of the so-called *Procola* case of the Court of Human Rights. On the basis of this case the (comparable) Council of State of Luxembourg was deemed not to be an independent court within the meaning of Article 6 ECHR. For that reason about 10 years earlier (on the basis of the *Benthem* case) the appeal to the Crown in the Netherlands had to be abolished.

In most States, in most administrative cases, two *instances* are available: a court of first instance and a court of appeal. Sometimes a third instance is possible. As Dutchman I am really pleased that through legislation in 2010 in many environmental cases the Council of State (*Afdeling bestuursrechtspraak van de Raad van State*) is made competent to hear appeals from the administrative law section of the District Court (*rechtbank*) and is not anymore the competent judge in first and only instance, just as in cases where an appeal to the Central Appellate Administrative Court (*Centrale Raad van Beroep*) as second and final instance is possible. There is a form of informal consultation between these two highest administrative courts and the Supreme Court, that is competent in final (third) instance in tax matters As said earlier in some matters like damages (as in Germany) and actions against legislative measures the ordinary courts are competent. In France one sees that the administrative courts are competent regarding legislative measures at the local level and that for certain legislative measures (such as governmental decrees and ordinances) the Council of State has jurisdiction in first and only instance. More instances of administrative courts therefore do not always mean that all these instances have jurisdiction in all matters.

In this respect it should be mentioned that in some States a leave system exists. You may expect such a system to function between the courts of appeal and the highest courts, as in Germany, where the decision of the appeal court is not in conformity with earlier decisions of the highest court. But is also possible that already in first instance a kind of leave must be obtained of the court, like in the United Kingdom. There it serves as an instrument to determine whether a case is arguable. Of course special proceedings exist for the refusal to obtain leave. Also worth mentioning here is the fact of the possibility in France of the so-called preliminary rulings of the Council of State in *questions de droit nouvelles*, asked by the lower administrative courts and the possibility in Germany to go directly from the *Verwaltungsgericht* to the *Bundesverwaltungsgericht* (*Sprungrevision*).

The following peculiar, but noteworthy point may merit a mentioning here in the historical (and not always rational) development of things. As already may follow from what is said earlier, in tax matters in the Netherlands the Court of Appeal and Supreme Court (*Gerechtshof* and *Hoge Raad*, within the ordinary courts) act as an administrative court. Since 2004 for tax cases the districts courts (administrative law sections) are competent in first instance. In France there is a division: matters of indirect taxation fall within the jurisdiction of the civil courts and questions of direct taxation fall under judicial review in the administrative courts. Is tax law therefore regarded there administrative law? In Germany fiscal law is more or less seen as an autonomous branch and this is also reflected in a separate court system (*Finanzgericht*, *Bundesfinanzhof*). In addition to the rules about the division of competencies between administrative courts and the ordinary courts, where there may be multiple competent administrative courts explicit rules (about reference) may also apply (France, Germany).

Often these rules have a formal dimension (who should deal with a case) and do not deal with substantive solutions (unity of administrative law).

Of course one should bear in mind that in matters where the interpretation of EU law is at stake the (highest) national (administrative) courts, are obliged to ask for a preliminary ruling from the European Court of Justice. For individuals who fall under the scope of the European Convention of Human Rights – also the UK with the Human Rights Act seems to be showing less reluctance – there is, after exhaustion of the national remedies, a final recourse to the European Court of Human Rights.

The United Kingdom and the United States of America have a system of (common law) *remedies* related to the application for judicial review. There is the choice of asking to quash the decision or to prohibit the action but also to ask the court to oblige the administration to do something or to give a declaratory ruling and to ask (as an accessory) for damages. In Germany similar *Klagen* exist in order to address the administrative action. It is up to the plaintiff to make a choice and in this respect substantive differences sometimes go hand in hand with procedural differences. As said earlier damages have to be recovered in the ordinary courts. In the Netherlands this is also the case but since 1994 (and changed again in 2013) it is also possible to ask for damages in the proceedings before the administrative courts (which apply the rules on damages as developed in the ordinary courts). See paragraph 2.7.

Compared to the States mentioned here the Netherlands originally had a less refined system and the main tool for the administrative court was to grant or not grant the appeal and in the first case to (partly) quash (*vernietiging*) the decision. In recent years there dispute-settlement powers have become more elaborated. Except for the declaration, in practice, the outcome of the Dutch proceedings can be the same as in the UK, the USA and Germany, for instance, combined with the annulment of the decision the court can rule that within a certain period a new decision has to be taken. What one can also see is that in the Netherlands, more than in the other States, court proceedings aim at finalizing the dispute. In that respect other tools are given to the administrative judge than merely quashing the decision (administrative loop, leave aside (formal) breaches of law, etc.). In this respect, the focus is more pragmatic than formal.

Recourse to the courts is often also possible where the administration fails to act. In addition, whilst the action or appeal is pending the plaintiff can request provisional relief or for the decision to be suspended (*voorlopige voorziening/schorsing*). Only since 2000 in France the possibility of *mesures nécessaires* has been substantially broadened. Like in the Netherlands as a general rule, commencing a court action does not automatically suspend the decision. The opposite is the case in Germany, even where a judgement is appealed in a higher court.

In France a distinction is made between *recours pour excès de pouvoir* (quashing, *annulation*) and *recours de plain juridiction* (damages, *responsabilité*). As to the former: in the mid-1990s more room has been given for injunctions thanks to legislation. As to the latter: the Council of State has developed a system of compensation of damages specifically for administrative (un)lawful actions.

The *grounds for review* are in my view very open and stated in general terms. That makes it difficult to come to a real comparison in this respect. Only further study of comparable case law may give rise to more detailed reflections in this respect. So just a few observations here, also because I have already said something about rules and principles under 2.4 and these more or less also serve as testing materials for the courts and I discussed above the possible claims of the plaintiffs.

In the United Kingdom judicial review is done within the framework of the so-called *ultra vires* doctrine, which means that the administration should act within its authority. Apart from the legal framework, aspects like improper purposes, irrelevant consideration, mixed motives and unreasonableness come into play. The latter plays a role as regards discretion (see further below). In France the grounds of appeal are the grounds for review: *incompétence, vice de forme/procédure, violation de la loi* and *vices de motifs*. As a general rule the plaintiff has to state the grounds except for incompetence. There the court has to act *ex officio*. This aspect and also whether or not one can add other grounds further on in the proceedings are really issues that would merit further investigation. It follows already that some differences may occur related to the fact of whether the focus of legal protection is more subjective or objective. For instance, when the claim is decisive a full review of grounds is carried out (Germany).

For the EU (apart from having more instances) several of the elements addressed above are also relevant: the application of general principles, the possibility of interim relief, precedents, enlargement of standing, liability of the State, effective legal protection, protection of constitutional rights, etc. But of course it deals far more with the Member States, who have to apply European law directly towards individuals. But through this application it also becomes part of national administrative law and may influence it, for instance, in the field of specific areas of administrative law, such as environmental law where several directives lead to the adjustment of national law, as to standing, access to public information etc. In recent year also asylum law within the Member States is for the largest part based on EU legislation. It is not unlikely that in the future also (parts of) general administrative law will be codified at the EU level in order to achieve more uniformity in the Member States.

When the competencies of the administration are 'bound' the *test* of the court can be very strict. In practice, however, the administration has some 'discretion' and there is room to weigh the interests at hand. In principle discretion means that the administration has the final say. But one sees that through a more than marginal test, especially on the basis of the proportionality principle, the court limits in some way the discretion of the administration.

In England the proportionality principle has only more recently arisen in case law and its relation with irrationality has been reviewed. There the principle of reasonableness may still leave more room for the administration to use its discretion (which was also the intention of the legislator). The reason for this is that initially judicial review was merely a review of competence. Later it was extended to the broader concept of lawfulness. In the Netherlands one sees that the proportionality principle and therefore a less marginal test by the court is applied, especially where administrative discretion is related to sanctions (especially financial ones) that have a punitive character. Moreover the court in these cases has to set the fine itself. In other cases it seems that the principle of reasonableness still gives rise to a marginal test of the court. By the way, often the administration has made policy-rules to flesh out its discretion, and although the test is marginal the courts are always required to do research into the individual circumstances of the case.

Germany is an example where the judge places him/herself in the shoes of the administration. A decision must be necessary in a broad sense but also in the narrow sense (means- end relation). The strong position of the German courts (towards the legislator and administration) is reflected in the Constitution. France where the division between the administration and the administrative court is not a principal issue is also an illustration of a system where the court acts as a kind of substitute for the administration.

Some final remarks here. Of course the plaintiff, possibly interested third parties and the administration form the parties in the proceedings. Sometimes you see that some kind of representation of the State is institutionalized either as a part of (some of) the courts and giving advice to the court, such as the *commissaire du gouvernement* in France and the *Oberbundesanwalt* in Germany, and sometimes really representing the State (*Vertreter des öffentlichen Interesses* in Germany). In the lower courts as a general rule plaintiffs don't need legal representation but in higher instances professional legal aid is often required. Although in most if not all systems fees to start court actions are not necessary or low other costs for court proceedings can especially be high in the case of (loosing) the application for judicial review in England. Sometimes courts seem to have much discretion in dealing with costs (France), sometimes it is (extensively) regulated (Germany). Also when an appeal is well founded the' winning' party cannot always claim all costs. For instance, for legal aid the amount of money that may be reimbursed in this respect is maximized (Netherlands). In the USA the principle 'everybody has to pay its own costs' is still strong but is moving.

The Ombudsman

In all States addressed here, there is an ombudsman of one kind or another. In the Netherlands, the ombudsman may only bring relief in matters for which one cannot avail oneself of the (administrative) courts. In France and the United Kingdom, there are also rules that deal with restricting access to the ombudsman when cases can be, or have been, submitted to the courts. For some States, the (exact) relation to the competences of the courts is somewhat unclear (Germany, European Union, United States).

Many states started off with an ombudsman at the national level, competent to deal with claims of maladministration/injustice of central government departments. Also at the EU level, complaints concerning maladministration of EU institutions/bodies can be made to an ombudsman. The European Ombudsman is appointed by the European Parliament. This ombudsman, and the same applies to the (national) ombudsman in some of the States addressed, can also conduct inquiries on his/her own initiative.

In the United Kingdom and France, complaints to the national ombudsman (the Parliamentary Commissioner respectively the *Médiateur*) can only be made through a Member of Parliament. In the United States at the federal level, there is not an ombudsman designated as such but there are several measures/bodies that serve much the same purpose, for instance, the Government Accountability Office. This Office works for Congress and deals with how well the executive branch agencies do their job/perform their tasks. Also in several federal programmes, ombudsmen have been introduced to hear complaints from affected citizens. In Germany, some states have a kind of ombudsman (*Bürgerbeauftragte*).

One can see that, more recently, ombudsmen at a state level lower than the national/federalized level have been appointed by representative bodies (the Netherlands and the United Kingdom).

The more political (as opposed to judicial) nature of ombudsmen is reflected in the possible outcome of complaints: in the Netherlands, the outcome will be whether or not the administration acted with propriety/due care; in Germany and France, the *Bürgerbeauftragte* and the *Médiateur* respectively, try to find acceptable solutions (mediation); in the United Kingdom, compensation can be recommended. This form of non-binding redress of grievances can be very effective, also in the broader perspective of public participation and a more open government. One has to be careful that this way of non-judicial accountability is not formalized too much in complicated rules, dealing with, for instance, the division of competences between national and local ombudsmen, the relation to the access to courts, the necessity of internal complaints to the administration before addressing complaints to the ombudsman etc.

2.6. ENFORCEMENT BY THE ADMINISTRATION

In most States it is often a specific statute that authorizes a specific authority, either the authority that took the decision that has to be enforced or another authority, to enforce in a specific way. There is no general set of administrative law enforcement instruments available in the States addressed here. Sometimes general rules exist about how certain instruments are used in relation to one another (for instance, the order to act in default with cost recovery versus the order under penalty, in the Netherlands) or about one specific instrument (penalty payments, in Germany). Sometimes administrative sanctions are rather recent and more linked to independent authorities (not the traditional local authorities), for instance, financial sanctions (in France). Before the actual enforcement order is taken usually a kind of warning notice from the administration is required, giving the person in question the possibility within the set time to restore the illegal situation.

In addition to administrative sanctions (orders with cost recovery, orders under penalty, fines, withdrawal of decisions), also criminal enforcement instruments may be applicable (mostly fines) and seem to be effective (United States). Sometimes there is something in between administrative law and criminal law enforcement (Germany, *Ordnungswidrigkeiten*). Also in the United States statutes provide for a range of potential penalties (by the agency or the courts) but in some areas these are part of enforcement 'agreements' (in other words, a form of individualized regulation).

In some States the administration can start criminal proceedings (United Kingdom, France) but often it is up to the public prosecutor (the Netherlands). In France, at least, criminal judges are allowed to check the legality of the administrative acts.

When it concerns the enforcement of EU legislation by the Member States, these in principle, have enforcement autonomy and may choose to use administrative or criminal law. Enforcement at the European level itself towards individuals is restricted to competition law (financial fines/penalties). Apart from instrumental standards, it is interesting to mention that the European Court of Justice considers general principles, such as proportionality and rights of the defence, to be of great importance here. Should what is applicable for the enforcement of EU-law also be applicable for the enforcement of national law?

While in some States the administration acting under private law is not possible because the use of existing administrative law instruments has comparable effect (the Netherlands) or agencies are not allowed to sue in tort to achieve regulatory compliance (USA), in other states (UK) local authorities on occasion may seek private law injunctions to prevent the infringement of the rights of the public.

One can write a lot on enforcement instruments under administrative law, criminal law and private law and the authors of the various contributions have done so, one with more elaboration than the other. In this area especially, it would be worthwhile to know not only how administrative authorities can enforce the violation of administrative legislation but if they actually do it. Is there discretion or not? In some States there is a lot of discretion (on the basis of most statutes) to initiate enforcement (USA), while in other States (the Netherlands) there is in principle a duty to enforce and citizens, with an interest, can go to court to have the (non)decision tested.

2.7. FINANCIAL LIABILITY OF THE ADMINISTRATION

When it comes to financial liability due to an unlawful act(ion) or omission of the administration – most often in practice a new decision by the administration suffices replacing an annulled decision by the court – in all the States addressed here legal ways exist to compensate the occurred damages. Although this topic especially is addressed differently and not always in an elaborated way by the various authors, a few comparative remarks can be made here.

As to the competent courts one can see that in some States only the ordinary courts have jurisdiction in actions based on tort law against public authorities to provide for loss and damage suffered by citizens. In some States (such as the Netherlands) citizens are obliged to go to the administrative court to get the decision annulled before starting a civil procedure. However, in some cases they can also choose to ask for compensation (when decisions and not factual actions are at stake) in a procedure before the administrative court. In the Netherlands in 2013 legislation changed (in some way) the relation between the administrative and ordinary courts in this respect. In the United Kingdom claims for damages could be included in judicial review proceedings but are often transferred out of the administrative court. In specific cases, for instance, under the Human Rights Act, monetary 'just satisfaction' is possible.

Although the competent court – ordinary or administrative – in compensation matters may differ, the applicable law can be the same: often the rules of general tort law apply. In France one can see that the administrative courts apply a separate set of rules regarding administrative (tort) liability, certainly in cases of factual acting (as opposed to legal decisions). In the United States also one can see exceptions to the general acceptance of the private law of torts to impose liability on the government for actions of the officials, for instance, where there is discretion.

In some States (recent) legislation provides for the possibility to ask for a fine (at the administrative court) for non-performance of the administration. In the Netherlands this is paid to the petitioner but this is not necessarily the case (compare the citizen suits in the United States).

Apart from the liability for unlawful actions in all States specific statutes exist that require the administration to pay compensation where no breach of law has been committed. Obvious is of course the field of expropriation (regulatory takings), where this is often based on the national Constitution. But less frequently occurring are obligations that are founded in general principles, such as in the Netherlands. Also at the EU-level, signs of that perspective can be seen, such as the principle of disproportionality.

All in all, it is surprising to see that, in all States the law of State liability especially for unlawful actions is not codified, or not codified comprehensively!

2.8. DEVELOPMENTS AND CONCLUSION

I think that this book succeeded in giving an introduction into general administrative law in the various systems: Germany, France, the Netherlands, the United Kingdom, at the level of the European Union and in the United States of America. The framework given to the authors certainly gave rise to comparable contributions. Also the editorial comments to the draft updates helped in this perspective. Sometimes it is better to see and discuss national law through the eyes of foreigners. But of course not all the contributions to this book are similar in every aspect. Some contributions are more detailed and refer to recent court cases (Netherlands). Other contributions are more basic (France). Also more practical items are not the focus but could be included in a next edition. For instance, I think that it would be worthwhile to address in more depth how the individual courts function in practice. One could also focus on what the qualification requirements for their judges are, whether or not courts are supervised and by whom, how many cases they have to deal with, whether provisional procedures form an important part of the entire work of the judges how claimants 'appreciate' their experiences with the administration, their day in court etc.

This is in my opinion the micro level of administrative law that is often far more an eye-opener than the macro level of general administrative law on which this book is focussed. I hope that for a following edition there is time to address one or more of these items. For this fourth edition I at least succeeded in letting the authors deal in more detail with the fees and costs of court proceedings and the possibilities to claim damages. Although general administrative law is something that could be defined as 'in operation' in all specific areas of administrative law, it would also be interesting to find out more about why and how in specific areas of administrative law exceptions are made to the general part (also in light of the fact that general administrative law does not seem to be an area that is frequently changing unlike certain specific branches of administrative law). In my opinion, since the third edition of this book, no major changes in the various States in the field of general administrative law have occurred. The Netherlands may be an exception in the sense that again (especially in 2013) many changes to the General Administrative Law Act saw the light or are on the fringe of coming about, mostly of a more procedural nature. The new cases approach by the Dutch courts is something new and aimed at efficiently ending the administrative law disputes at hand. Also in other states than the Netherlands developments have taken place or are in progress that have to do with more efficient decision-making, such as making procedures shorter and giving administrative competencies to agencies, to make legal protection procedures more uniform and to restrict these and court actions to interested parties. Administrative courts (whether or not as part of ordinary courts, and whether more or less 'independent' from the administration) have strengthened their positions.

There are always (some) cases of the European Court of Justice and the European Court of Human Rights 'that keep us awake'. The European dimension (Strasbourg and Brussels/Luxembourg) has not lost its importance for the action of the administration and how the administrative courts 'test' this action, in fact the contrary is true. Especially for the EU level: should there be a codification of general administrative law: for the EU administrative bodies or even for all national authorities dealing with the application of EU law?

Maybe in the next edition there is more to say about that. I think further codification of general administrative law seems to be the consequence but one can see that some countries stay behind while others go on further in this direction.

The contributions represented in this book illustrate formal differences as to the organization of the administration, the organization of the courts and the available remedies and competencies of judges to decide administrative disputes. But maybe the substantive differences in the application of administrative law and the outcome of administrative disputes may be less great. The Rule of Law is common to all the systems addressed in this book and implies that there is, in the end, an independent court (administrative or ordinary), that is fairly easy to access for persons with an interest (as to costs, legal aid, etc.) and that controls the lawfulness of actions of the administration or may provide for financial compensation in case of unlawful administrative action. Sometimes these courts are guided by codifications of administrative law, sometimes they aren't. But even in the former case these codifications are often and for a large part the result of case law. Of course where constitutional courts are in place even more special guarantees may exist.

For the European States addressed here, certainly the EU and ECHR rights will influence their administrative law systems and may illustrate the presence of or the direction towards a *Ius Commune.* In some way or another this is also the case in the United States where federal and State administrative law are also interacting in such a way. How the position of the UK will be in the coming years, due to the Brexit, has to be seen and the same applies to the United States, where also the current time illustrates that political changes can influence administrative action and how courts deal with this.

LIST OF AUTHORS

France

Prof. dr. Jean-Bernard Auby, Professor of Public Law (*emeritus* 2017), Sciences Po Paris (jeanbernard.auby@sciences-po.org)

Dr. Lucie Cluzel-Metayer, Professor at Lorraine University, IRENEE, CERSA-CNRS (lucie.cluzel-metayer@univ-lorraine.fr)

Dr. Lamprini Xenou, Associate Professor of Public Law, Université Paris-Est Créteil, Paris (lamprinixenou@yahoo.fr)

Germany

Prof. dr. Hermann Pünder, LL.M. (Iowa), Chair for Public Law, Administrative Sciences and Comparative Law, Bucerius Law School, Hamburg (hermann.puender@law-school.de)

Dr. Anika Klafki, Senior Research Assistant at the Chair for Public Law, Administrative Sciences and Comparative Law of Prof. Dr. Hermann Pünder, LL.M. (Iowa), Bucerius Law School, Hamburg (anika.klafki@law-school.de)

Netherlands

Dr. René Seerden, Associate Professor of (Comparative) Administrative and Environmental Law, Maastricht University; Administrative Judge at the District Court of Limburg (rene.seerden@maastrichtuniversity.nl)

Dr. Daniëlle Wenders, Coordinating Laywer, Department for Legislation and Legal Affairs, Ministry for Economic Affairs and Climate Policy and Ministry for Agriculture, Nature and Food Quality

United Kingdom

Dr. Katharine Thompson, Senior Lecturer, De Montfort Law School, De Montfort University, Leicester (kht@dmu.ac.uk)

European Union

Dr. Rolf Ortlep, Associate Professor of Constitutional and Administrative Law, Utrecht University School of Law (R.Ortlep@uu.nl)

Prof. dr. Rob Widdershoven, Professor of European Administrative Law at Utrecht University and Advocate-General of Administrative Law (r.widdershoven@uu.nl)

United States

Prof. Jeffrey S. Lubbers, Professor of Practice in Administrative Law, Washington College of Law, American University (JSL26@aol.com)